DO THEY HEAR YOU
WHEN YOU CRY

D1099370

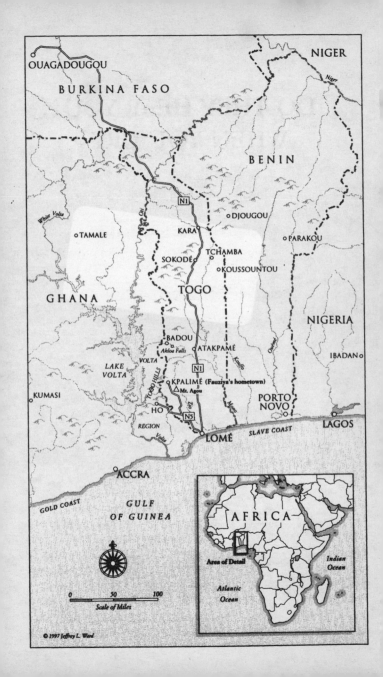

DO THEY HEAR YOU WHEN YOU CRY

Fauziya Kassindja
and
Layli Miller Bashir

BANTAM BOOKS
LONDON · NEW YORK · TORONTO · SYDNEY · AUCKLAND

DO THEY HEAR YOU WHEN YOU CRY
A BANTAM BOOK : 0553 50563 7

Originally published in Great Britain by Bantam Press,
a division of Transworld Publishers

PRINTING HISTORY
Bantam Press edition published 1998
Bantam Books edition published 1999

9 10

Set in 10/12 pt Garamond ITC by
County Typesetters, Margate, Kent.

Bantam Books are published by Transworld Publishers,
61–63 Uxbridge Road, London W5 5SA,
a division of The Random House Group Ltd,
in Australia by Random House Australia (Pty) Ltd,
20 Alfred Street, Milsons Point, Sydney, NSW 2061, Australia,
in New Zealand by Random House New Zealand Ltd,
18 Poland Road, Glenfield, Auckland 10, New Zealand
and in South Africa by Random House (Pty) Ltd,
Endulini, 5a Jubilee Road, Parktown 2193, South Africa.

Printed and bound in Great Britain
by Cox & Wyman Ltd, Reading, Berkshire.

Sûrah I

AL-FATIHAH, 'THE OPENING'
Revealed at Mecca

In the name of Allah, the Beneficent, the Merciful.

Praise be to Allah, Lord of the Worlds,
The Beneficent, the Merciful.
Owner of the Day of Judgment,
Thee (alone) we worship; Thee (alone) we ask for
help.
Show us the straight path,
The path of those whom Thou has favoured;
Not (the path) of those who earn Thine anger nor of
those who go astray.

BAHÁ'Í PRAYER

Glory be to Thee, O Lord my God!
. . . I beg of Thee to guard this handmaiden who hath
fled for refuge to Thee,
and hath sought shelter of Him in Whom Thou
Thyself art manifest,
and hath put her whole trust and confidence in
Thee . . .

CONTENTS

1

Prison

I returned to my cell after lunch. It was time for the Salat adh-Dhuhr.

I removed my shoes and washed my face, arms, feet and hands at the small sink. Then I carefully spread the bedsheet I used as a prayer rug on the cold concrete floor. I wrapped my head and neck in the veil we call a *mayahfi*, stepped on the sheet that faced East and began to pray. While I was kneeling on the sheet, clutching the ninety-nine beads of the *tasbih* . . .

'Kasinga!' My neck jerked upward when I heard the sound of my name come crackling out through the prison intercom system.

'Kasinga! Attorney visit!'

So they were here. But I wanted to finish my prayers.

Allau Akbar, Allau Akbar, Allau Akbar—

'Kasinga! Kasinga!'

I stood up, unwrapped my *mayahfi*, slowly laced my sneakers, and stepped onto the ramp outside my cell. Upper tier in B pod, maximum security, York County Correctional Facility in Pennsylvania – this was where I lived.

Down below me I could see the dayroom, a small, barren space with metal tables and stools bolted to the floor. Inmates in blue uniforms passed their time

11

aimlessly, watching TV, playing cards, talking, and staring into space. I slowly made my way along the ramp to the stairway and down the stairs. The guard in the booth tried to hurry me along by shouting my name repeatedly over the loudspeaker, but I wouldn't be rushed. I was still reciting my prayers. I had learned that prayer was what kept me going, enabling me to see beyond the grim gray walls of this place I was forced to call home.

By the time I reached the door to the hall, it had been opened from the control booth. A guard stood waiting in the doorway. She waved me through. 'Let's go, let's go!' We turned right and walked a few paces to a doorway. 'In here,' she said, motioning me into a small meeting room with four metal chairs and a metal table against the far wall. 'Wait here,' she said, closing the door behind her. I walked to the chair nearest the table, sat down, and waited for my visitors.

It was Saturday afternoon, February 10, 1996, my fourteenth month in prison, six weeks after my nineteenth birthday.

Back home in Togo, when my father was still alive and our family was still together in my father's house, my mother would fast on my birthday. She fasted on all her children's birthdays to thank Allah for keeping us well. Where was my mother now? Had she remembered to fast on my birthday this year? I hadn't seen her in almost three years, since my father's sister, Hajia Mamoud, evicted her from our house, four months and ten days after my father's death.

It was because of Hajia Mamoud and my father's brother, Malam Mouhamadou, that I was now thousands of miles away from everything and everyone I loved. When my father died, Malam Mouhamadou became my legal guardian. He and Hajia Mamoud sold

12

me into marriage to a man almost thirty years my senior who already had three wives. This man wanted my woman parts cut off before taking me as his wife. It is a traditional practice in my tribe, which we call *kakia*. Most people call it female circumcision. But that doesn't really describe what *kakia* is. Since I've been in this country, I've heard people refer to *kakia* as female genital mutilation. Mutilation. Yes, that's the right name.

Traditional though my father was, he had opposed this practice, so my older sisters were spared. But I was the youngest of the five girls, and after my father's death there was no-one to protect me. When my aunt told me she had arranged my marriage and that I was to be cut, I was terrified because I had known girls who had died from having it done. My mother's own sister had died from it, and I'd heard my parents speak of this event with horror. But my 'husband,' like most men in our tribe, wanted me to be cut so that I would be 'clean' for him. So my aunt had arranged for the women who do it to come to our house.

I've heard that during the procedure, four women spread your legs wide apart and hold you down so that you can't move. And then, the eldest woman takes a knife that is used to cut hair and scrapes your woman parts off. There are no painkillers, no anesthesia. The knife isn't sterilized. Afterward, the women wrap your legs from your hips to your knees and you have to stay in bed for forty days so the wound can close. After the forty days, you are 'reborn' for your husband, and delivered to his house to begin your new life as his wife.

This would have happened to me had I stayed in Togo. It happens every day to girls all over the world. But with the help of my oldest sister and money from my mother, I ran away, far from my home, my family, and my country. Eventually I made it to America where I thought I'd be taken in, where I thought I would be safe. But instead of finding safety, I'd found a jail cell – or actually a series of cells. I was now in my fourth prison. I had been beaten, teargassed, kept in isolation until I nearly lost my mind, trussed up in chains like a dangerous animal, strip-searched repeatedly, and forced to live with criminals, even murderers.

Why? I had committed no crime and was a danger to no-one. I was only a nineteen-year-old girl from Togo who desperately needed help. I was a refugee seeking aslyum, not a convicted criminal. I kept asking myself, why is this happening to me? My teachers in Africa said that America was a great country. It was the land of freedom, where people were supposed to find justice. But I was delivered to a dark corner of America where there was no justice. There was only cruelty, danger, and indifference.

And now I was ill. Even as I sat waiting for my visitors that day, my chest was burning. Each time I took a breath, it felt like someone was stabbing me with a knife. I was weak because I hadn't eaten much of anything for days. Swallowing food hurt too much. I didn't know what was wrong with me. I had asked to see a doctor several times but was never called to see one. I was afraid. Was I dying? Would I die alone in this place?

The meeting I was about to have was with members of my legal team, three people who were fighting for my release from prison: Layli Miller Bashir, Karen Musalo, and David Shaffer. Karen and David were relatively new to my case, Karen having gotten involved only last September, and David at the end of December. I had never met either of them before. But

14

Layli — Layli I felt I knew well. She was the young law student who had represented me at my asylum hearing back in August. After we lost that first hearing, she promised she would never leave me. She said she would keep fighting for me until I was free. She was like an angel, someone who had come to rescue me from the living hell I had endured since coming to the United States. Although she is a white American, and I am a black African, we had become sisters.

So I should have been happy to see Layli again, for I hadn't seen her in more than four months. As much as I loved her, however, I was hoping never to have to see her again. I wanted to leave her a note, thanking her and my entire legal team and telling them why I had decided not to wait for them to get me out. Now I would have to explain my decision face-to-face.

But how could I explain it? How could I explain to Layli, or to anyone who has never experienced them, the daily indignities and humiliations of prison life? How could I explain what it is like to live with only the barest essentials: a prison uniform, a cell, a bunk, a bedsheet, two towels, a washcloth, toilet paper, and tiny bars of harsh soap? How could I explain what it is like to have no privacy to shower or to use the toilet? How could I explain what it feels like to be counted like cattle every day, to eat when you were told to eat, sleep when you were told to sleep? How could I explain the mind-numbing, soul-deadening feeling of doing nothing but watching TV, day after day, week after week, month after month?

No, I could never fully explain what it is like to live in prison, which was why I'd stopped trying to communicate with anyone on the outside. I'd lost interest in writing letters and making phone calls. There was no more reason to talk to people, really. What could they say that I hadn't already heard? It was always the same old story: 'Hang in there, keep your spirits up, we're working hard, everything will be fine, just hold on a little while longer.' And then they'd always say, 'Oh, Fauziya, you are so strong, so brave.' But I wasn't, and I didn't want to hear it anymore. They meant well, I knew. But they couldn't possibly understand how I felt. I'd held on for as long as I could. Now I had to get out before I went crazy or died. My legal team had been working incredibly hard on my case and I would always be grateful to them. But in spite of all their work, I was still in prison. Nothing had changed.

Except me. I was changing. I looked down at myself, sitting slouched in the chair with the shirt of my blue uniform half unbuttoned and hanging out of my pants. Back home, I would have never dressed so sloppily, but after fourteen months in American prisons, I didn't feel like myself anymore. I didn't recognize the person I was becoming.

I prayed to Allah five times a day, every day, but for reasons I could not understand, He would not hear my cries. He had chosen not to deliver me from my ordeal. Now I was convinced that as long as I remained in America I would never be free. I was sick and getting sicker all the time. I thought I might be dying. If that was Allah's will, so be it. But I didn't want my fellow prisoners' faces to be the last ones I saw. I wanted to see my family again. I wanted to die surrounded by the people I loved.

Twice in my life already I had taken my fate into my own hands. Ten days earlier, I'd done it again. I'd sent a note to the prison counselor, telling her I wanted to speak with her. When I didn't hear from the counselor, I wrote another note, telling her why I wanted to speak with her: tell the INS to send me back to

Togo. My legal team would be upset when they heard about what I'd done, but I had to listen to my own heart.

I knew they'd try to talk me out of it. 'You'll be out soon,' they'd tell me again. They would try to convince me to stay for other people's sake. 'Fauziya, your case is going to help so many other women.' They might also say, 'You know what will happen if you go back to Togo, don't you?'

Yes, I do know what will happen to me. But I cannot stay in prison any longer. I must go home. Now.

2

Home

I needed to go home before I forgot my home, forgot where I came from, who I was, who my people were. My mother and father had disappeared, my father into the realm beyond life, my mother I knew not where. Oh, I had to go home, before everything disappeared, before I lost everything and everybody I had ever cared about. I had to go home before I lost myself, too.

Home was in the town of Kpalimé, a small city ringed by mountains, in the southwestern plateau region of Togo, in Africa. You won't find Kpalimé on most maps of Africa. You'll have to look close even to find Togo. It's a tiny country just above the equator, on the south coast of West Africa, between Ghana and Benin. Long and skinny, Togo is only about thirty-five miles wide at the coast, from which it extends three hundred sixty miles north, until it meets the border of Burkina Faso.

The capital of Togo, Lomé, is the only big city in our country, though it's not really very big. It's located on the coast, near the western border with Ghana, in a flat landscape of marshes and lagoons, of beautiful beaches where people go to picnic under the papaw trees, and swim in a sometimes treacherous ocean. The city itself is crowded, noisy, and busy, with a market to end all markets, the Grand Marché. Now that's something to see – a big three-story building just a couple of blocks from the water, where people from all over West Africa, Ghana, Benin, Nigeria, Senegal, and the Ivory Coast, come to buy and trade. Anything you want, you can find there, and the prices are low. And even though it might seem kind of backward to a westerner – you can't use credit cards or checks and you have to bargain for everything – it's a wonderful place to shop. Everything is beautifully displayed, from the oranges stacked in pretty pyramids to the shoes arranged in neat tiers and the jewelry in glittering glass showcases. Some say the Grand Marché is one of the five best markets in Africa. Lots of money changes hands, too – so much that we call the women who are cloth merchants Nana Benz, because they all seem to own Mercedes-Benz cars.

But you have to be on guard at the market, as you do everywhere in Lomé, if you don't want your purse snatched or your pocket picked – or worse. So I didn't go to Lomé very often, except to visit my oldest sister, Ayisha, who moved there after she married. I was always happy to see her, but I never stayed long. Soon I'd want to leave Lomé to go home, where things were more peaceful and no-one bothered you unless you needed help.

Going from Lomé to Kpalimé you head north, away from the coast, leaving the hot, humid climate of the lowlands and climbing up to the plateau region. Where I lived, the climate is more temperate, cool at night even when it gets hot during the day. We have our heavy rainy season from late April through July. Kpalimé is near the border with Ghana, in a lush green land of forests, mountains, and farms. Just to the south of it is Mount Ago, Togo's tallest mountain,

3,234 feet high, and a few hours directly to the north is Akloa Falls, a beautiful waterfall that I visited once on a school trip. It has steps carved into the rock so you can climb to the top.

As you head farther north of Kpalimé, on the main road that extends through the center of the country all the way up from the coast, the landscape becomes more dramatic. The road winds its way along sheer cliffs, and when the leaves are out, you can barely see the houses nestled in the foliage of the mountainsides. Soon you'll reach the town of Sokodé, near Tchamba, where my father's family comes from, and then Kara, where the president of Togo comes from. Approaching the northern border, you'll descend again, into the savannah, where the climate is much harsher, with greater extremes of heat and cold and a longer rainy season, lasting from April through October. People stay in during the rains, which can sometimes go on for three days without ever stopping. And when the dry season begins, usually in early November, the harmattan winds come, the sky gets hazy with grit, the leaves on the trees turn brown and shrivel up, and fires sometimes start in the bush.

We have many tribes in Togo. I don't know how many, but I've heard anywhere from twelve to seventy-five. Some tribes get along well with each other, some don't. One of the largest tribes is the Ewe, who live mostly in the south. Most of them practice *voudou*. You'd see *voudou* makers, the ones from the fetish house, on the streets all the time – men, women, and children, walking barefoot and bare-chested, all covered in beads with these strange scarring patterns all over their bodies. They looked more like fetish dolls than real people. Sometimes they'd ask for money, and if you didn't give them any, they'd mutter a curse. I don't believe in taking chances with *voudou* makers, so I always gave a few coins.

The other big tribe in Togo is the Kabye, who live mostly in the northern part of Togo. They practice Christianity. There's also the Kotokoli, Bassari, Mina, and many many more. My father's tribes, the Tchamba and the Koussountu, are small, and they are among the few tribes in Togo who practice the Muslim religion.

Although we are all from Togo and that makes us Togolese, most people in Togo don't think of themselves as Togolese, or at least not in the same way as they think of themselves as belonging to their tribe. The tribes, after all, existed long before Togo became a country. In the late nineteenth century, the Germans created what they called Togoland and became the country's first colonial masters. The French and British took Togoland away from Germany during World War I and divided it up, with the British taking the western part and adding it to Ghana, and the French taking the eastern part, which became Togo. That's how French became the official language in Togo. But outside of the capital, Lomé, where the main government and business offices are, most people speak their tribal tongues, not French, which is why I don't know much of the language.

Imagine what it was like for people of my father's generation to wake up one day in the same place their family had been living for generations and find themselves living in a country that didn't exist the day before. Or think what it must have been like to discover that that area just to the west of you, where some of your relatives live, is a different country now. The land didn't change, the people didn't change, but the country and its government did.

In general, people in my community don't have anything to do with the government. It has very little bearing on how they live their lives. The people of Kpalimé don't read newspapers very much – in fact many people in my community can't read at all – they don't follow current events, they don't travel. Their lives are centered around their families, their work, and their religion. If there is any kind of dispute or conflict, they don't go to the police, or to a lawyer. They're afraid of the police, and don't trust lawyers. In *madrasah* (an Arabic religious school), our teachers always said that lawyers lie to defend their clients, and judges find the innocent guilty and the guilty innocent. So in times of trouble people consult the heads of their families, their tribal elders, or the chiefs of their tribes. In the end, it's tribal law and custom we follow, more than national law.

I love my country and I am proud to be Togolese, but not in the same bone-deep, blood-thick way I am proud of being Tchamba-Koussountu and Muslim, and the daughter of Muhammad Kassindja from Kpalimé. That's how I identify myself: tribe, religion, family, community.

There's a train that runs between Lomé and Kpalimé, left over from when the Germans were there, but when I went to Lomé I usually traveled in one of my father's cars. Most people traveling between Lomé and Kpalimé go by passenger minivan, a three-hour ride. That is, it's three hours if the van doesn't break down, if there's no trouble at the police checkpoints, and if the driver doesn't have to stop too often to pick up and drop off passengers or pull over to let someone pee by the side of the road.

Once you get to Kpalimé, the van drops you off at the station, the *gare routière,* in the center of town.

There you'll see a train station, a gas station, a soccer stadium – everybody in Togo loves soccer – a big Catholic church, a hospital, a few banks, a building with a post office and a police station, and some shops, hotels, and restaurants, all of them fairly close to each other. The people you see in town are dressed in all kinds of clothes. There are young men in American jeans and T-shirts, others in round-necked, short-sleeved danshikis with matching trousers made of African cloth; boys and girls heading off to school in very proper-looking khaki uniforms, others running around shirtless and barefoot, playing with sticks and empty tin cans. Muslim men like my father typically shave their heads and wear small round white hats. They dress in sandals and loose, long-sleeved ankle-length caftans we call *agwada* or *patakari*. Men who are religious leaders – imams like my uncle Malam Mouhamadou – wear veils that cover their heads.

In Islam, it is a sin for women to dress in a way that arouses a man's lust. So Muslim women dress quite modestly, usually in long dresses made from three pieces of cloth – one for the floor-length skirt, one for the top, and one wrapped around the midriff. The women keep their arms covered at least to the elbow, except when they're working on the farm. Although a married woman might wear trousers if she's working on her husband's farm, she would never wear shorts. It just isn't done. My family was very religious but not as strict as some others, so my sisters and I wore short skirts – not real short, but up to the knee – and some of the old people disapproved. They called us modern children. 'Oh these modern children, what's happening to the young people today? They walk around naked.' My parents didn't feel that way, however, not about our skirts or about veils. When they were

23

children, all females, young and old, married and un-married, were required to wear veils covering their head. These days most young girls don't have to, but all women wear them after they marry. Very religious older women, like my mother, wear the long veil that we call *mayahfi*, a sheer, jewel-colored embroidered scarf that covers the head and crosses under the neck, with the ends thrown over the shoulders. Younger married women, like my sisters, prefer shorter veils that cover just the head and neck, so that people can see their fine clothes.

We have two markets in Kpalimé, one in a building, the other open-air. The open-air market is on the out-skirts of town, and since Kpalimé is located in farm country, its specialty is produce – cassava, yams, sugar-cane, corn, bananas, plantains, coffee, cocoa, cola nut, oranges, mangoes, papayas, and so forth. On Tuesdays and Saturdays you can see the people walking into town bringing food from the farms early in the morn-ing. The women carry the food in baskets they balance on their heads, using one arm to prop up the basket and swinging the other in rhythm with their steps. Some walk barefoot, others wear backless bathroom slippers on their feet. Market days are our main enter-tainment, so when visitors come, that's where we take them. Everybody enjoys the bargaining. It's a chance to see and be seen.

Beyond the market is the forest which is filled with giant trees. It's always cool and dark there even when the weather is hot and sunny outside, and it's so deep you could walk in it all day among the beautiful flowering shrubs and fragrant fruit trees, the birds and the butterflies. But I don't know why anyone would want to, because there are snakes in that forest.

Up the hill from the center of town is the place

where I lived. We were surrounded by farm country, where everything is very rural and natural and quiet. You can hear birds singing and roosters crowing. At night you can even hear the sound of the frogs croaking down below us.

My house is close enough to where the van drops you off that you could walk there if you wanted to. It would only take about forty-five minutes, unless you were a hometown person returning after a long absence; then it would take longer because you'd meet friends along the way and they'd want to catch up with all your news and tell you theirs. Or if you were a white person, it might take longer, too, because you would be such a rarity that you'd attract a lot of attention. When I was a child, we almost never saw white people in Kpalimé, and it was really uncommon to see them walking. My friends and I would run behind any white person we did see, calling out to everybody along the way, 'Come look, come look.' Sometimes we tried to touch him, because we thought if we touched a white person we would turn white too. Or we'd pretend to speak English: *'Arisha-arisha kotombray'* and other such nonsense words that to us sounded just like English.

If you did decide to walk to my house, you'd go up a gentle hill, on unpaved roads, asking directions of anyone you met if you weren't sure how to go, and although it would be an easy walk, you'd probably feel kind of dirty by the time you arrived because of all the sand and red dust you'd been kicking up. So you might decide to go to my house by car, instead. Then you'd hire a taxi at the *gare routière* in town and tell the driver, 'Take me to Zongo.'

'Which part?' he'd want to know.

'Al-Hamdu.'

'Where in Al-Hamdu?'

'I'm going to Tchambakomé.'

After the taxi dropped you off at the mosque, you'd just tell anybody you met on the street where you wanted to go. Anyone could help you, because even if the person didn't actually know me, he would know my family and what house my family lived in.

My father's house was one of the finest in Kpalimé. It was a cream-colored house with lots of windows that flooded the inside with light. In front of the house was my mother's stall. My mother sold foodstuffs like coffee, tea, bread, sometimes butter and ice cream, and household goods like needles, buttons, and threads. Her store was actually built into the front wall of my father's compound.

The house was surrounded on three sides by a cement wall that adjoined other compounds, but the front of the house faced the road, and was lined with flowers. On the right, there was a double metal gate that opened wide enough to let a car through. Inside the gate was a big open space, with a garage to the left, connected by a side door to the long porch that lined the right-hand wall of the house. The front of the porch was also bordered with flowers, and the back wall was shaded by trees, beneath which still more flowers grew. We had flowers everywhere, red and yellow and violet and pink, which were tended by our housegirl, Adjovi, a young woman from the Ewe tribe. Adjovi lived with us and did most of the marketing, cooking, and housework while my mother tended her stall. We also had a houseboy named Ahmed. He did all the heavy work around the house and helped wash my father's passenger vans. I'm not sure what tribe he was from, but he lived with us, too, and was sent to school by my father.

Our house had eight bedrooms in all – my mother's, my father's, my oldest brother Alpha's, the bedroom that all the rest of us children shared, and one that was used to store foodstuffs – which were all in the main part of the house; three others were located in a separate structure in the front left corner of the compound, near the water well. Although we called it the boys' quarters, that building was where Ahmed and Adjovi had their rooms, and where we put our guests. There was a small bath in the boys' quarters, and two bigger bathrooms in the main house, one of which was reserved for my father. Everyone wanted to shower in that one because it was the most modern, but my father didn't allow anyone else to use it except me, his favorite.

All the bathrooms were tiled in white, the halls in terrazzo. We had indoor plumbing, electricity, a radio, a television, a VCR, and a stereo with a cassette player. Although we didn't have air-conditioning, we did have a big fan in the main living room, which kept us comfortable, and my father had a tabletop fan in his bedroom. Besides the bedrooms and bathrooms and porch areas, we had a dining room and two living rooms, a small one off one side of the porch, and a bigger one off the other side. The bigger one was where we spent a lot of time together – when we weren't lounging in the cool, shady passageway between the main house and the boys' quarters – watching TV or just sitting and talking. A simple room with a linoleum floor, it contained a couch, a coffee table, a cabinet for the TV and stereo, and a table in the corner where my father kept a framed photo of his mother and himself, taken when he was a baby. On the walls were a couple of large framed paintings, one of a zebra, one of a tiger, and we also had some wood carvings of other animals, because my father was a big animal-lover.

It wasn't a fancy house by American standards. The rooms were small, the furnishings modest, and we didn't have a telephone. But it seemed like a palace to us. Africans would call it a rich man's house, and most people in Togo would have been proud to live there. Anyone seeing it would have said, 'Oh, this man is doing very well.'

Within the walls of my father's compound, life was comfortable, safe, even pampered. But once you walked out the gates, the stark contrast between our lives and those of our neighbors became painfully clear. Sometimes I used to walk down the road with my paper and pencils, find a bench or chair to sit on, and spend my time observing and sketching the life around me: an old woman sweeping inside the open doorway of her one-room house; a girl in a worn dress feeding a few scrawny chickens; a man in a tattered shirt, walking from house to house carrying a bundle of branches he'd collected from the bush, trying to sell them as firewood. But I didn't draw the worst of the poverty I saw. It made me too sad.

Our house was near the mosque compound that included the *madrasah*, the Arabic religious school where I studied the Qur'an. I loved living close to the mosque because I could always hear the call to prayer. Being Muslims, we worship five times a day. We call it *salat*. When it's time for *salat*, the call is broadcast in Arabic from a loudspeaker atop the minaret of the mosque. It's a beautiful sound, like a prayer to heaven wafting through the air. At night and at dawn, when everything was quiet, we could hear it really well. It was a wonderful way to wake up in the morning, with the call to prayer lifting me from sleep into a new day.

Although there aren't many Muslims in Togo, and most of the people who are Muslim live in the north, Kpalimé has a sizable Muslim community, big enough to support more than one mosque. The mosque near our house was the biggest, but there were also several small mosques in our area, including the one my father's brother, Malam Mouhamadou, the imam, had in his house.

Inside the mosque the women pray in a separate area in the back, behind a curtain, where they can neither see nor be seen by the men. Only after the service, when people gather outside the mosque to greet their friends and neighbors, do the women ever actually see the imam.

The brief interlude after services is always a nice break in the day, with everyone happy to have a few minutes to be together. After a little while everybody disperses, and you can watch the men walking home in their caftans and sandals, their *tasbihs* slung over their necks or arms, reciting their prayers.

My family was very religious, and in many ways very traditional, but not traditional enough to suit some, including my father's own brother and sister, who both lived in Kpalimé too. My uncle Malam Mouhamadou lived about a ten-minute walk away from us. I had a lot of other family in the area, mainly from my father's side, but also from my mother's. Her brother, Alhaji Djabarou, lived about ten minutes farther down the road past Malam Mouhamadou, near the clinic where my parents took us when we injured ourselves or got sick. And farther along from there was my father's older sister, the oldest of the three siblings, my aunt Hajia Mamoud.

All my family lived pretty comfortably, but I didn't think any of them had a house as nice as ours. Actually, few people do. Most of the people in Kpalimé live in really small houses, sometimes just one or two rooms, and most are lit by kerosene lamps, not electricity. Beside the house itself, there may also be a storage hut where farm tools and food that has just been harvested are kept, and maybe a bicycle, too, if the people who live there can afford one for transportation to their farm. If not, they walk, even though the farms are a fair distance away.

The better houses, like ours, have cement walls around them, but if there's not enough money for a cement wall, people usually build plywood walls or plant trees to shield them from passersby. Still, there are some homes that don't even have that much of a barrier to provide privacy. You can walk past them and see their inhabitants going about their business, especially if the homes, like many, don't have kitchens or indoor plumbing. Then you can see people cooking on a coalpot in front of the house.

Like our house, almost all the houses have stalls or tables and benches in front where people ply their trades or sell things. One person might be doing carpentry work, and you would go to him if you needed a new table or chair. Someone else will be hammering metal – *gung, gung, gung* – to make cooking pots or knives. Or maybe you want to buy some firewood, or charcoal, or soap – you could find those items in one of the little stalls. Lots of people sell food that they make, like *kenkey,* which is corn cooked with fried fish and hot pepper, mixed with fresh tomatoes and onions; or *agidi,* another dish made of corn, which is often sold along with turkey, which we call *chofé* in Togo; or *aboiboi,* beans with fried plantain and yams, seasoned with palm oil.

Anything you want to eat, really, you can buy on the

street, especially at night, and especially after a rain. Because people don't go to the market as much when it rains, everyone comes out to buy food from the food sellers. 'Oh, my friend! Come and buy from me!' you hear as you walk down the street. 'Come and taste my rice and beans' – or fried yams, or whatever.

It's very beautiful on those nights after a rain, when the moon is out and everything is bright and shining. We Muslims pay particular attention to the moon, because we follow a lunar calendar. When I was little, my sisters and I would lie on our back gazing up at the full moon and say, 'Oh look! I see Nana Zara and her husband the prophet. There's her hair, and there's her smile.' Of course, it's pretty at night when there's no moon, too. Prettier in some ways. The night is black then. The only light comes from the tables where the food sellers put their lamps, which are tin cans filled with kerosene, with a hole punched in the lid and a rag pulled through it to be lit like a wick. If you walk down the street then, all you can see are these flickering lights lining the road, one here, one there, and out of the darkness you hear the voices of the food sellers, inviting you to taste, to enjoy, to buy.

So perhaps you can see why I missed my home. My childhood was easy and tranquil. I wanted for nothing. My family was different from many of the other families around us. I would become acutely aware of those differences later, when I got older, but I wasn't conscious of them as a child. Then, I was happy in my world, a world that was stable, predictable. Of course, everything is different now. Not for the other people who live in Kpalimé. Their lives go on much as before. But for me and for my family, everything has changed, because my father is dead.

3

Yaya and Amariya

I dreamt once that my father came to visit me in prison. I was in a different prison then, where immigrants were confined in locked dormitories instead of cells. In the dream I was standing at the window of my dorm, looking out into the hallway, and suddenly there he was, walking toward me with that distinctive gait of his, right foot turned out. He filled the hall in my dream the way he'd filled a room when he was alive – not just physically but with his energy and spirit, too.

As he came closer I could see that he was wearing a beautiful light pink caftan made of *shadda*, a shiny type of fabric made from silk and cotton. I was especially fond of that particular caftan because he'd had a matching dress made for me out of the same cloth. Whenever he wore the caftan, he'd tell me to go put on my dress. He liked it when we dressed alike.

In the dream he walked up to my window and sat down on the floor in the hallway outside. I was surprised to see him. Not because he was dead. In the dream, he wasn't dead. In my dreams and in my heart, he isn't. No, I was surprised because he was in an area where visitors weren't allowed.

'Yaya, how did you get in here? Visitors aren't allowed back here.'

'Oh, you know how we are, Fauziya. No-one can prevent me from coming to you.'

'Yaya, the floor isn't clean. You'll get your caftan dirty.' My father kept himself meticulously clean and well groomed. He would never have sat on a dirty floor. But this time the dirt didn't seem to concern him.

Next I noticed that his feet were bare. 'Yaya, you're not wearing shoes. Why aren't you wearing shoes?' Yaya never went barefoot, or allowed us to either. He didn't want our feet to get dry and calloused like the ice-cream sellers'. In fact that's what he'd say if he ever caught us without shoes: 'Do you want to look like an ice-cream seller?'

But this time he seemed to have more important things on his mind.

'I was in a hurry,' he explained. 'I didn't take time to put them on. I had to see you right away. I came to tell you not to worry, Fauziya. Everything's going to be fine. So don't worry, OK?' He looked so calm, so confident, so certain, sitting there looking up at me. Of course I believed him.

'OK, Yaya. I won't worry.'

'Good. I have to go now. But I'll be back. I'll come to see you again, OK?'

'OK, Yaya.'

I woke up in my bunk in the same prison dorm where I'd been in my dream. For a moment there was no difference, no clear separation, between dream and reality. And then I remembered where I was. I remembered that I would never again see my father in this lifetime. My heart broke all over again, and I cried so hard and so long, I woke one of my dorm mates. She tried to comfort me, but she couldn't. Yaya was gone forever. He had died without my ever having had

33

a chance to tell him one last time how much I loved him. He had died without my ever having said goodbye.

My father's name was Muhammad Kassindja. He was formally addressed as 'Alhaji,' a title given to Muslim men who've made the pilgrimage, or hajj, to Mecca. His brother and sister, my aunt Hajia Mamoud and uncle Malam Mouhamadou, called him Boni, Tchamba for 'last born.' My mother and brothers and sisters and I called him Yaya, which means 'big brother' in Hausa. I don't know who gave him the nickname – perhaps it was my oldest sister, Ayisha – but that's what we all called him. Everyone who loved him called him Yaya except Adjovi, who had her own affectionate nickname for him. She called him Efo, Ewe for 'big man.'

Yaya was a big man, well over six feet tall and solidly built. He had light skin, a round face, pointed nose, dark eyes and dark hair – lots of hair. He shaved his head, but his eyebrows were bushy and his body was hairy.

There's a lot I don't know about my father's early life, and I never thought to ask. In Togo children don't ask grown-ups a lot of questions. Parents tell kids certain facts they think kids need to know, and pass on other kinds of information through stories. That's how I know most of what I do know about my parents, by listening to their stories.

I know my father was born on a Sunday. My father and mother and I were all born on Sunday. But I don't know my father's exact birth date. I did ask my mother once if she knew. She didn't, which isn't too surprising, because in her day people didn't put a lot of emphasis on remembering birthdays. A lot of people in Togo still don't. Counting back from how old my oldest sister was when my father died and how old my mother thought he was when they met and married, I'd say he died at around age fifty-eight, which would mean he was born in 1935. But that's just a guess.

I know my father's parents' names, but I'm not sure it's proper to say them without their children's permission, so I won't. My paternal grandfather died too early for me to have any memories of him, but my grandmother I knew well, because she came to Kpalimé occasionally to see her children. She was about five feet four inches tall, fair-skinned and fat, and she had tribal marks, three thin vertical scars on each check. She always arrived carrying her things in a brown plastic bucket that had a lid on top. That was her luggage. Whatever didn't fit in the bucket she tied up in a scarf bundle she carried in her other hand. When she visited us she refused to sleep on a mattress, because she thought mattresses were too soft and would make her sick. So she slept on a mat on the floor. She fussed over us children endlessly, hugging us, playing with our noses or ears, and always trying to do for us. But she wouldn't let us do anything for her. If we saw her coming back from the market with her brown bucket on her head, filled with all her purchases, we'd run to help her – children in Togo don't let old people carry things – but she wouldn't let us. 'No, no,' she'd say. 'It's too heavy for you.'

One thing that would upset her was hearing any of us speaking Hausa. She spoke only Tchamba and Koussountu, our tribal languages, and thought we should speak only Tchamba and Koussountu as well. But Hausa, which nearly all West African Muslims speak, was the only language my parents had in common when they met, and it was the language we spoke most often at home. My father would let his mother rant on about how terrible it was that we spoke so much Hausa. 'Yes, Mother. Yes, Mother.' Then he'd turn to one of us and, just to goad her, casually ask us in Hausa to please close the door. That was his way. My father loved to tease. But he loved his mother and she loved him.

Of her three children, she loved my father the most. When she came to Kpalimé for a visit, she spent most of her time at our house. In fact she died in our house. When I was about thirteen, she became very ill with asthma, and Yaya brought her down to Kpalimé so he could look after her. He wept when she died, which was the first time I ever heard him cry.

My father's mother was Tchamba, his father was Koussountu. According to our custom, that made my father Koussountu, since both tribes believe that children belong to the father. But my father rejected that custom, along with many others. When people asked him his tribe, he always said, 'I'm Tchamba and I'm Koussountu.' He told us it takes two people to make a baby, so he would always honor both tribes.

My father's father was a respected imam who put a lot of emphasis on education, especially religious education. He sent all his sons to elementary school, and all his sons as well as his daughters to *madrasah*, whether they wanted to go or not. My father's mother came from religious royalty. In fact she herself was apparently a queen or a chief, according to what I was told as a child. Her grandparents – my father's great-grandparents, my great-great-grandparents – introduced Islam to the Tchamba people, and are considered the founders of Islam in the tribe.

My father didn't grow up in Tchamba. He grew up in Koussountu, where his father's people lived. Though I've never been to Koussountu, I've been to

Tchamba a few times, which is nearby and very similar, so I have a sense of how my father grew up – and what a distance he traveled from home. It's a six- or seven-hour trip from Koussountu to Kpalimé, much of it over rough road, but the journey I'm talking about can't really be measured in hours or miles. Traveling from my father's home to Kpalimé is like traveling between two different worlds. The people up north are mainly farmers, but the soil isn't as rich there as in the plateau region, so most people can only grow just enough to eat, not to sell. They mainly live in small, thatched-roof clay houses that are little more than huts, many of them without windows, and most without electricity or running water. The rooms are tiny, but there will always be one room with a hole dug in the ground. That's the room that's used for birthing. When it's time for a woman to have her baby, she just squats over the hole.

Most of the people in Koussountu and Tchamba are poor, but my father's father wasn't. He wasn't rich, but his farm did fairly well. Still, it always amazed me that my father accomplished what he did and became who he became, given what I knew about his beginnings. I'm not speaking just about his success in business, either. My father came from a very traditional tribal background. But in many ways my father was not a traditional man. In Islam, a man is allowed to have up to four wives. According to my mother, my father's father had three, by whom he had a total of eleven children, three of them with Yaya's mother. My father, too, could have taken several wives, but he had decided early on that when he married he would take only one wife. I don't know when or why he made that decision. Perhaps he made it when he was still a boy, living in Koussountu, which is when he began questioning another tradition – that of *kakia*. Girls in our tribe traditionally undergo the procedure at around age fifteen, so he would still have been a young boy when the procedure was performed on his older sister, my aunt Hajia Mamoud. I seem to remember he said he watched the actual procedure, but it could be that what he saw was all the blood and all the suffering his sister went through afterward. Whatever it was he saw, it horrified him. That's when he started hating *kakia*. He began asking 'Why? Why do they do that?' The only answer he got was 'It's tradition. That's what our ancestors did. That's what we do.' Which wasn't a good enough reason for him.

It was also while he was still a boy that my father decided what kind of work he wanted to do as a man. He loved cars. They were his passion. Because his father insisted upon it Yaya went to both *madrasah* and elementary school, but he had no interest in continuing his education beyond that. He got his first job with a Nigerian man from the Yoruba tribe, who lived in Togo and owned and drove a passenger van. My father was hired to stand at the door of the passenger van, collect the fares, and call out their stops as the van approached them. In this way my father began seeing the world beyond his village.

His boss paid him a small salary, and sometimes he got tips too. In the evening, he'd go back to his boss's house and help him wash the van or do any other work that needed doing. He worked hard to please his boss because he wanted his boss to teach him to drive, which eventually the man did. Soon his boss put my father behind the wheel on days when he himself didn't feel like working. My father was always glad to do the driving, both because he enjoyed it and because he could earn extra money that way. And the more money he earned, the more he could save, and the sooner he could buy his own car.

Little by little my father did finally save up enough money to buy a car. He drove that car himself and immediately began saving to buy another one for someone else to drive. That's how he built his business – step by step. First he bought passenger cars and buses. Then later, around the time I was born, he heard there were good profits in transporting goods and livestock, so he branched out into trucking. He was always watching for new opportunities, always setting new and more ambitious goals for himself. My father didn't do anything halfway. By the time I was a little girl, he owned three buses, three trucks, and a pickup truck, and had bought and sold several different cars: a cream-colored Renault, an ugly green Volkswagen, a beautiful brown car that was either a Honda or a Toyota – I forget which – and a white Mercedes, which he taught my mother to drive. *That* raised a lot of eyebrows in our community. But then, so did many of my father's beliefs and practices, as both a husband and the father of five girls.

My father met my mother when he was in his late twenties. My mother was sixteen or seventeen at the time. They met at a car station near Djougou in Benin, where my mother grew up. Djougou was on the route my father was then driving between Togo and Benin. My mother had a table at the car station selling cigarettes, thread and needles, and other small items. He noticed her. She noticed him.

My father loved the way my mother walked – slow and stately, hips undulating, arms and hands making music at her sides. She'd walk through a room where my father was sitting and he'd stop what he was doing just to watch her. I used to watch him watching her and see him smile. 'Gorgeous,' he'd say, loud enough for her to hear. 'Look at the way that woman walks. Isn't she beautiful?' She'd wave a hand behind her back to shush him, but she'd be smiling too.

My mother is beautiful. She's taller than I am and light-skinned. She used to be slender, but she's heavier now. She has a round face, dark eyes, thick eyebrows, and dark hair, which she wore very long to please my father, because the Prophet said that a woman's beauty is in her hair and that she should let it grow long to look beautiful for her husband. My father liked her to look as gorgeous as she could at all times, but she wasn't one for fussing. She always made sure to pumice her feet and put cocoa butter lotion on them, because my father was a real stickler about our not letting our feet get callused and ugly (like the ice-cream sellers' feet). And that was about it.

My mother is soft-spoken and sweet-natured, always thinking about other people. If she heard that someone had died, she'd cry, even if she didn't know the person. As a parent she was easy going, but she demanded respect and made sure that she got it. If I ignored her calls to come help her with something one time too often, she'd come up behind me and give me a good hard knock on the head.

'Yeeeooww!'

'When I call you, you come.'

Once she'd made her point, her anger always passed quickly. Mine does too – that's one of the traits I got from her. Unlike me, however, she doesn't talk a lot, and I used to wear her out with all my talking. 'Please,' she'd say, after listening to an endless stream of chatter from me. 'I'm tired. Can I go to sleep now?'

Although she's not very outgoing, my mother smiles a lot – or at least she used to – and likes to laugh.

When she laughs, you can see her two upper front teeth flash gold, one gold tooth for each of her two trips to Mecca. This is a thing some Muslim women do to let people know they've been on hajj and should be addressed as 'Hajia.' It's a status symbol, a sign of wealth, because going to Mecca costs a lot of money. Some people who haven't been to Mecca will have a tooth capped in gold anyway, so people will think they're rich. My father used to tease my mother about hers. She'd be cleaning her teeth with a stick, looking at herself in a hand mirror, and he'd say, 'Oh! I can see myself in your teeth!' I'd start to laugh, but my mother would quickly silence me with a stern look. 'You can laugh at your sisters,' she'd say. 'But you don't do that with me.'

My mother's name is Zuwera. But nobody called her that except my father. And he called her Zuwera only when he had something serious or important to say. Usually he called her Amariya, a Hausa word that means 'bride.' So everyone else called her Amariya too. From the time she married my father and came to live with him in Kpalimé, she's been Amariya. Some people who know her well don't even know her real name.

Her mother was Fulani, her father Dendi. My mother calls herself Dendi because her tribes also believe children belong to the father. Her father, Malam Salifu, is an imam – like my father's father – which means I come from religious lineage on both sides of my family. My maternal grandfather is still alive, but he's very old now, the only one of his generation still living. Grandfather didn't visit very often; usually mothers visit their children more than the fathers.

My mother's mother, Hajia Maimouna, was one of

several wives, I'm not sure how many. She used to come to visit during religious festivals. She's dead now, but I still think of her often because I really loved her. She called me 'my friend.' I called her 'my sister.'

'My friend, do you want to read some Qur'an for me?'

'Sure, my sister, I'll read for you, if you give me an *alfa*.' I always asked for a bribe. She'd laugh and give me an *alfa*, and I would read for her. Then I'd run off with my *alfa* to buy roasted peanuts. She was sweet and easygoing like my mother, and she liked to laugh and joke. I'd run to her when my sister Narhila and I were fighting.

'Narhila knocked me!'

'Oh, she shouldn't do that to my friend. Go and call her. I will beat her for you.'

I'd call Narhila. She'd come and stand by my grandmother. She knew my grandmother was playing. My grandmother would tell me, 'OK. Spit in my hand.' I'd spit in her hand and she'd pretend to hit Narhila. Then she'd tell Narhila, 'OK, cry,' and Narhila would pretend to cry. My grandmother would say, 'There, I beat her for you,' and I'd be happy again.

My grandmother's business was selling beads. Every time she came to visit, she'd bring me new beads. It's a custom in my country for girls to wear strands of tiny beads around their waist. Mothers put them on daughters when they're babies. I've heard that in Ghana mothers do it so their daughters will have hips when they grow up, but that's not why we do it in Togo. It's just a fashion, although no-one ever sees them since they're worn against the skin, under clothing. Some girls don't like the beads and stop wearing them when they get older. Not me. I've worn beads ever since I was a baby. The strands are loose enough to slip down over the hips, but I never take mine off. I keep them on even in the shower. They're a part of me. I wear different colors at different times – black, white, gold. Sometimes I wear three strands, sometimes as many as five or six. Every time my grandmother came to visit, she'd check them: 'Fauziya, let me see your beads.' If she saw they were getting old or the strand was getting frayed or tight, she'd give me new ones. That's probably why they meant so much to me, because I got them from her.

My mother's parents sent her and all of her sisters and brothers, nine in all, to the Arabic school. But Amariya didn't attend any other school, which is too bad because she is really clever. Even now she can recite several *surahs* from the Qur'an from memory. Although nobody forced her to, she studied hard because she loved *madrasah*, unlike her siblings, who went only because they had to. She was a very good student and she was also the lead dancer at school. Whenever the girls performed, my mother was always put in the front, because she was so graceful and beautiful. 'People liked to look at me,' she told me once, and she remembered that with pride. Even after bearing seven children she still carried herself like a dancer, proud and elegant – the exact opposite of my father, who couldn't dance at all. It used to amuse us kids that he was so clumsy while our mother was so graceful. Sometimes music would be playing in the room and he'd sit there in his chair, moving his arms and upper body, doing everything wrong. We couldn't help but laugh at how awkward he was. He'd laugh too.

My father wasn't a dancer, but he was a handsome man. That was how he first attracted my mother's attention, back when she used to see him at the car

43

station where she had her table. Sometimes he'd buy cigarettes from her, but he was too shy to speak to her, and it wasn't proper for her to speak to him. For a while, then, they just watched each other. Finally one day my father asked one of my mother's girlfriends to deliver a message from him. He told the friend to tell my mother he loved her. My mother wanted to make sure she understood his intentions, and sent a message back through the same friend. 'Tell him I really like him, too,' she said, 'but I don't want to be his girlfriend. If he's serious, he should go see my parents to arrange the marriage.'

So that's what my father did. He didn't go himself, of course, because that's not the way things are done. The man sends someone from his family to speak for him. My mother's father said, 'Well, I can't say anything until I speak with my daughter.' Most parents in those days arranged a daughter's marriage without consulting her, but my mother's parents weren't like that.

Once Amariya had assured her father of her own feelings, and her parents had made inquiries about the suitability of the prospective groom and his family, the marriage plans began. My father sent his relatives to meet with her parents to decide on the *mahr,* the gifts the groom gives the bride's family as a bride price, and ten months after my parents first met, they were married.

I saw their wedding picture once. It was easy to see why my father had fallen in love with her. She was so beautiful in the photograph. She was dressed all in white, not for her marriage but because she was baptized in the Qur'an the same day. Her parents were so proud, she said, because it was a very unusual thing in her day for girls to be baptized in the Qur'an. It still is unusual – most girls don't want to put in the time it takes to study, nor do most of their parents want them to. Better to start trading early, in order to save up enough money to buy all the clothing and cooking utensils and other supplies a girl is expected to bring to her husband's home when she gets married. My mother did that, too, but whenever she wasn't selling at the market near the car station, she continued to study her Qur'an.

Within my mother's family there was no talk of *kakia* before the marriage. Her mother's tribe, the Fulani, don't practice it. Her father's tribe, the Dendi, do, but her parents didn't because they opposed it. My father also opposed it, so it was never discussed. There were no discussions about the fact that my father was from a different tribe and country, either. My mother's family didn't care about that. My father was a good Muslim from a good Muslim family and my mother was crazy in love with him. That was all that mattered to them.

Things were different with my father's family. Although my mother was also a good Muslim from a good Muslim family and my father was crazy in love with her, she wasn't good enough for them. When my father told them who he was taking as a wife, they tried to talk him out of the marriage. They opposed it from the beginning. They didn't even know my mother, but they didn't have to know her to dislike her. The fact that she was from a different tribe made her unacceptable.

'You should marry someone from your own tribes,' they said.

'But she's the woman I want,' he replied.

They argued with him, but he wouldn't listen. He married my mother anyway and brought her to

Kpalimé to live with him in his rented room. Perhaps he thought his family would accept her once they got to know her, but although his mother did eventually seem to accept her, his siblings didn't. My uncle was cold. My aunt was cruel. 'Divorce her,' my aunt told my father when he first brought his wife home. 'Leave her. Marry someone from your own tribes.'

'No. She is my wife. I love her.'

'Divorce her. She wasn't even a virgin.'

'I know my wife. I know who she is.'

'She's a prostitute.'

'A prostitute! How can you say that?'

'Look at the way she walks. She's a prostitute.'

I don't know why my aunt said these things. Maybe she was jealous of my mother. It wasn't because of any rudeness or unkindness on my mother's part. In all the years my mother put up with such insults, she never spoke back to my aunt, because my aunt was her husband's sister and she didn't want to be disrespectful to her husband's family. But she did tell my father how much the insults hurt her. My father told her to ignore my aunt. 'The important thing is that we are happy,' he said. As happy as they were, my aunt never stopped trying to come between them.

A year passed and Ayisha was born.

'Divorce her.'

Another year passed, and another. My parents were still living in their tiny room. My father bought a plot of land and was slowly building a house. One child, one room. A second child, a second room. A third child, a third room.

'Divorce her.'

My mother had three children by the time she and my father moved into our house. It wasn't finished yet. But it was finished enough to live in.

'Divorce her.'

'I won't divorce her. I love her.'

My father put finishing the house on hold for a while to focus again on his other goal: saving enough money to buy his own car. After he bought his own car, and then another, and then a truck, he had enough money to add another room to the house. Another child, another room. And then more children and more rooms. Still my aunt never gave up.

'If you won't divorce her, then at least take another wife.'

'I don't want another wife. She's the only woman I want. She makes me happy.'

'She's putting something in your food. She's working some strong magic on you. She has you under a spell.'

My aunt was right in a way. My father was under a spell. But it wasn't *voudou*. It was something much stronger. It had gripped my father and mother the first time they looked at each other, and in all the years of their marriage it never let them go.

I didn't understand until I myself was grown how remarkable my parents' marriage was. The love between them was just a constant, something my sisters and brothers and I took for granted. It was there in the way they looked at each other, the way they teased each other and joked with each other, the way my mother reached out and gave my father's hand a quick, hard squeeze when he made her laugh. It was there in the way she deferred to him as undisputed head of the household, the way he never returned from a business trip without a gift for her. It was there in the way she applauded his every achievement and the way he came rushing to tell her of every achievement, as if it didn't become real or meaningful to him until he had shared it with her. We didn't see our parents touching a lot. I never saw them kiss. I never heard them tell each other they loved each other. However, I didn't have to hear them say it to know how much they did.

My parents had separate bedrooms, but they didn't always sleep in separate bedrooms. I discovered that early, by accident, because I didn't like my own sleeping arrangements. My four sisters and I shared one bedroom. They slept two to a bed, but there was no room for me. Being the youngest – this was before my brother Babs came along – I got only a rubber mat on the floor. I would never have thought of asking to share my father's or older brother's bed, of course. But I knew my mother had a bed she wasn't sharing with anybody. So why should I have to sleep on a mat on the floor? She tried to keep me out – not always successfully – but there were times when I peeked my head through the door and she wasn't there. Early on I figured out that she must be with my father. 'Oh good, she's in Yaya's room,' I'd say to myself as I climbed into her bed, pulled up her light blanket, and settled in for a luxurious sleep, congratulating myself on my good fortune.

I was too young to know or care what my mother and father might be doing in his bedroom besides sleeping. All I cared about was that I had a whole bed to myself. Now, of course, I know what they were doing. We call it *anfani*, a Hausa word that means 'making important use of your wife.' Boys and girls are both instructed in *madrasah* about the importance of *anfani*. Girls are taught that a good Muslim wife is always available to her husband. She doesn't refuse him. Boys are taught that a good Muslim husband is gentle and considerate with his wife. He doesn't make

48

inappropriate demands, and he thinks of her pleasure as well as his own. My mother and father both went to *madrasah,* where they would have heard these lessons, and they were both good Muslims. The size of our family attested to that.

4

Daily Life

'Good morning! Good morning! Time to get up! It's time to get up and pray!'

My mother was always the first one up in our household. I woke every morning to the sound of her voice. It would be five A.M. and still dark out, because Muslims rise to pray before dawn. She'd come into our bedroom and switch on the light. I'd pull the cover up over my head and lie still for a little while longer. I'd listen to my sisters shifting and groaning above me, the birds starting to chatter outside, and the call to prayer wafting through the air. I'd lie there, letting it wash over and through me, drifting, floating. But there would be no sleeping through first prayers. My mother saw to that.

'Get up now! Time to get up! Hear the birds singing? Even the birds are awake and thanking Allah for this day. Are you not as good as the animals? Get up now! Time for prayers!'

We'd drag ourselves out of bed and head for the bathroom to wash. Muslims always perform an ablution called *wudu* before prayer, washing face, hands, and feet in a specific order a specific number of times while reciting specific words.

Once my mother knew all of the children were finally moving, she'd go to wake up my father. She always woke him last, both because she wanted to let him sleep a little longer and because he was always the hardest one to rouse. He worked hard and was away a lot. When he was home, he really enjoyed the comforts of his own bed. On days when he was particularly sleepy, she'd place a stool in his bedroom doorway, sit down on it, and begin reciting *surahs* from the Qur'an. Loudly. My mother recites in an exquisitely clear, strong voice. It's like music, beautiful to listen to and impossible to sleep through.

'Amariya, don't.'

She'd keep reading.

'Amariya, don't do that.'

She'd keep reading.

This would go on for a while, until finally he'd push back his blanket and sit up in bed. 'OK OK, you can stop now. I'm up.' He'd be annoyed, but only briefly. He didn't want to miss first prayers, either, and would have forced himself to get up on his own if he'd had to. Like us, however, he knew he could count on Amariya to get him up in the morning, so he let her do the job. My father was the undisputed head of the household, but my mother was the religious heart.

Not including my father, there were seven of us that my mother woke for prayers every morning. Americans would call seven children a large family, but we didn't. Women are expected to have lots of children where I come from. A woman without children is pitied. Women achieve status through their children, especially their boy children.

Ayisha's the oldest child in our family, about fourteen years older than I am. She's tall and plump and light-skinned, with a really lovely face. Ayisha is quite shy and hates to draw attention to herself. She is a very loving person, very thoughtful and considerate, always doing things for others. Whenever Ayisha would see Adjovi in the kitchen, she'd take over the cooking, because she thought Adjovi needed help. Sometimes she'd do Adjovi's housework, too – if my father didn't catch her at it – washing clothes, sweeping floors, changing the beds. A lot of people underestimate her strength because she's so kind and self-effacing. But Ayisha was always strong, always determined to do what she thought right, whatever other people thought.

One of Ayisha's projects was getting me to school each day. She watched over all her brothers and sisters, but she was especially motherly with me because I was the youngest girl. Each day she'd help me shower and dress, make sure I ate breakfast, iron my school uniform, pack my lunch and my books and anything else I needed, and then walk me to school across the border in Ghana, about half a mile away, because I was too little to go alone. Then, after school, she'd come get me and walk me home. I was a lot of trouble for Ayisha but she always took care of me. Always.

Narhila's next in line in our family. She's about eight or nine years older than me, and the exact opposite of Ayisha in personality. She never lifted a finger around the house. I didn't either, unless I was asked to, and then I'd always ask for money. But Narhila didn't even work for bribes. In fact the only time I ever saw Narhila work was when she was getting ready to go out for some special occasion. Then she'd wash and iron her own clothes to make sure they'd be perfect, because she was very vain. Narhila is tall and slender and athletic, the prettiest girl in the family and, especially when she was younger, very much in love with herself. My mother called her the queen of *kwalisa*, of showing off. She was always posing in front of a mirror wearing nothing but her underwear or a towel, admiring herself. 'Oh, look at my arms. Aren't they pretty? Oh, look at my legs. I really like my legs.' It used to drive me crazy, so I'd tell her she was too skinny. She'd go right on admiring herself. 'Excuse me?' she'd say. 'Are you talking to me, Balloon?' She called me Balloon because at that stage of my life I was fat. I'd get back at her, though. I'd walk into a room after she had just ironed one of her dresses and put my dirty hands all over it. 'Oh! Is this the dress you were going to wear tonight?'

She'd scream, 'What have you done! I'll kill you dead!' Then she'd chase me and if she caught me, she'd hit me – boom! – hard on the back. I'd hit her back and she'd hit me back and we'd keep at it until our parents made us stop. When we weren't fighting, sometimes we'd practice speaking English with each other. Narhila's smart; I have to say that for her. She was always good at languages, and is fluent in both French and English.

Shawana is the third child, about five or six years older than I am. Shawana and I both really loved studying and learning. It was one of our strongest bonds. Shawana also speaks a number of different languages, as do I. I speak Tchamba, Koussountu, Dendi, Hausa, English, and Twi, and I can understand Arabic. Shawana doesn't speak Twi since it's a Ghanaian language that I picked up only because I went to school in Ghana. But she speaks some other tribal languages that I don't know, and really perfect French.

Shawana loved to teach me things before the teacher discussed the subject in class. When I'd run home from school to tell her how I was the only person who raised my hand to answer some question she'd prepared me for, it always made her very proud. She was my champion. Even though both my parents cared about education, it was to Shawana I most often turned for support and encouragement in my studies, because my father was away a lot, and my mother took it so much for granted that I would do well that she was blasé about my achievements.

Shawana was kind of a recluse when she was young. Although none of us girls went out often, Shawana didn't even visit other girls at their houses or run occasional errands, the way the rest of us did. Maybe her sensitivity had something to do with her reclusiveness. She was excruciatingly sensitive to people's suffering. If she saw an old woman selling food in the street, she'd come home in tears. 'Oh, Amariya, I saw this poor old woman today and she didn't even have anything to sell, just this little bowl of spinach leaves from the farm. Nothing anyone would pay much money for. Oh, Amariya, I wish I had enough money to give her so she could go home to her family and never have to sell again.' And she'd start crying. Most people just accepted the poverty in Kpalimé. But Shawana never could.

Asmahu is the fourth child, about four or five years older than me. Of all us sisters, she was probably the most outgoing and the least academically inclined. As far as she was concerned, the only thing school was good for was to see her friends. At home she was a terror, always on the lookout for an insult, always ready to start a fight. My mother said that once when I was just a baby, she laid me down asleep on a bed and left the room. All of a sudden I started wailing, and when she ran back to check on me, she saw Asmahu bending over me. 'Asmahu! What happened! What did you do to her!'

'I pinched her.'

'You pinched her! Why?'

'She eyed me!' Eyeing is a way of insulting a person by rolling your eyes up and away when the person is speaking to you. That was Asmahu, just waiting for someone to laugh at her or look at her the wrong way, even a baby.

Next comes Alpha, the fifth child and first boy. Finally my father had a son. He's about three years older than I am. My father always loved the new baby best of all his children, but he was especially excited to have a boy at last. He's a handsome boy, a really hand-some boy. He's tall and dark with thick eyebrows and lots of hair like my father. Alpha loved all his sisters, but he especially doted on me because I was the only little sister he had. I adored him, too, almost as much as I loved my father. And he was always there to pro-tect me when I did something bad.

Dancing was Alpha's real passion. He lived to dance. From the time he was a little boy, he was always dancing. He danced when he was getting dressed, he danced on his way to school, he danced on roller skates. He knew all the dance steps from the Michael Jackson *Thriller* video and would dance in front of the television whenever that video was on. Later, when Alpha got a little older, he became the top dancer in our area. Shy as he was in every other context, he entered all the local dance competitions, and he always won. He was still dancing at clubs and parties the last time I saw him, though he wasn't dancing in competitions anymore.

Alpha partly followed in my father's footsteps and partly didn't. The traveling aspect of my father's busi-ness didn't interest him, as he discovered when they went out on a few trips together, but the big trucks themselves did, so he went into the repair end of the business. Now Alpha lives with his boss's family on the outskirts of Kpalimé, working as a mechanic for a big grocery store, where he repairs the trucks used for shipping produce.

After Alpha came me, and then, about three years later, the last child, my younger brother, Babs, whom we also called Baba. Baba was only thirteen the last time I saw him, but he was already almost my height, and still growing. He's tall like my father, with my father's hair and my father's hands and fingers and feet. He even walked like my father with his right foot turned out.

Alpha and I were very, very close, but Baba and I were always fighting. He was my punishment for every nasty thing I ever did to torture my sisters. Everything I did to them, he did to me. He'd grab my bookbag and dump the contents on the ground, run off with my purse, use my soap and towels, try to steal money from my piggy bank, hide my clothes. Every time I caught him, I beat him, but it didn't have any more effect on him than the beatings I got from my sisters had on me.

The two of us were always causing trouble for each other. He'd go to Yaya's room to ask him something in private. But instead of finding him alone, he'd find me there too, because I used to follow Yaya around all the time. Once he went to Yaya to ask for money for a new soccer ball. Or so he said. I knew better.

'Don't give it to him, Yaya. He wants the money to rent a bicycle.' Baba loved to ride bicycles, but Yaya didn't want any of us riding bicycles because it was very hilly and dangerous where we lived. A lot of children fell off their bicycles and got hurt.

'Is that what you want the money for?' Yaya asked.

There was a long silence.

'Then you don't get the money.'

While I giggled mercilessly, Baba was overcome with embarrassment and anger. I was almost always in his way when he wanted to spend time with Yaya. That was the real reason Baba and I fought – because we were rivals for our father's attention. Baba was jealous of me, and I don't blame him. He had reason to be. My father loved Baba. He loved all his children. But we all knew that my father loved me best. By all accounts, I was Yaya's favorite.

5

Favorite

My mother always said I brought my father luck. Just around the time she became pregnant with me, he decided to buy a truck because he'd heard that good money could be made moving salt from Burkina Faso to the Ivory Coast. He made a down payment on a Toyota truck, and worked out an agreement with the owner to pay the rest of the money in installments. But when my father returned with the rest of the money, the man who owned the truck wouldn't give it to him. Other men had come to the man in the meantime wanting to buy the truck and they were offering more money. My father was upset. They'd made a bargain. Wasn't a bargain a bargain? The man didn't say yes, he didn't say no. He wanted to think about it.

My father waited a few weeks and went to visit him again. He still hadn't made up his mind. He wanted more time. This went on for months. Finally my father stopped going to visit the man and waited for him to send his money back.

I was born on Sunday, January 1, 1977. The next day, my father finally received a message from the man: 'OK, you can come get your truck.'

He was so excited! 'This is a whole new beginning,' he told my mother. 'My business is going to take off, I just know it. This girl has brought me luck. What should we name her? We have to pick a good name.'

Someone suggested Fauziya – Supreme Success – which my father thought was perfect. My mother did too. But she drew the line when my father wanted to paint my name on the truck. 'Do you want everyone to know your daughter's name?' They kept my name secret, according to custom, until it was announced by the imam at the close of the child-naming ceremony.

My mother said she knew there was something special about me from the beginning. I started dancing early and I started talking early. In fact, my first word was the word for the part of my body I'd started dancing with even before I could walk: *duwawu*. Everything was *duwawu*. My mother never understood where I got that. But she remembers my first 'dance.' She and Ahmed were pounding *fufu* in the cool, shaded passageway behind our house. She was sitting, turning the pieces of cassava in a big wooden bowl while Ahmed stood beside her, pounding them with a big wooden pestle. *Poom. Poom. Poom.* The pounding made a rhythm like a drumbeat. I was a baby just able to crawl, but suddenly I started swinging my little *duwawu* back and forth, under the skirt of my dress, in time with the music. How I made them laugh, she said.

Once I started talking, I didn't stop. By the time I was two, I repeated everything anyone said in my presence. I was cheerful, talkative, quick, and very friendly. I loved everybody and everybody loved me. Yaya loved me best initially because I was the new baby. When he came home from a business trip, he would call for the youngest child first. After I came along, he called for me. And even after Baba came along, it was still me he called for. 'Where's my girl? Where's my little one?'

'Yaya!'

'There she is!'

I'd run to him and he'd lift me high in his arms. I was happy in anyone's arms, but I was always happiest in his. I'd wrap my little arms around his neck, and he'd carry me around while we talked.

'Hello, my little one.'

'Hello. Welcome home. How are you?'

'I am fine, thank you. How are you?'

'I am fine.'

'Were you a good girl while I was gone?' I'd nod emphatically.

'Did you have any fights today?'

'Just two!'

He'd laugh.

Then he'd have me recite the alphabet, or spell my name, or recite my times tables, or draw a picture for him. It was part of our welcome-home ritual. He always wanted to know what I'd learned in his absence, and I could never wait to show him.

Then we'd do our news update. 'What happened while I was gone?' he'd ask me. 'Did anyone come to see me?' He and my mother would sit and talk later, but I always liked to be the first to give him the news. And he always liked to get it from me first because my memory was sometimes better than my mother's. I remembered almost all his friends' names.

Soon we got to my favorite part, the domestic update – all the stuff I'd been saving up to tell him about when he got home, especially the tattletale reports about the bathroom. My father didn't like anyone using his bathroom. He let my mother use it when the other one was occupied, but only then. I was the exception to the rule, however. We had a secret code. He'd say, 'Fauziya, would you clean my bathroom for me? And while you're in there, take a shower.' I'd go

60

in and pretend to clean for a few minutes, then take a luxurious shower. I loved showering in his bathroom. It was all new, modern and mirrored. But I didn't use it when he wasn't home. None of us were supposed to. I guarded it during his absence and I took my job seriously. Though I didn't snitch on my mother, because I felt she had parental privileges, I always snitched on everybody else. It became a test of wits. One of my sisters would hang a dress belonging to my mother on the bathroom door so I'd think it was she who was showering. But that didn't fool me.

'Narhila? Is that you? Shawana? Asmahu? Who's in there?'

They wouldn't answer. My mother never spoke in the shower. She believes Islam forbids it. So when my sisters used the shower, they kept quiet too. I still wasn't fooled. I'd search the house for my mother. Aha! Amariya was in the kitchen. I knew it. The rest was a simple process of elimination.

'Amariya, where's Ayisha?'

'I sent her to market.'

That left three. I'd look for the others, maybe find Asmahu in the courtyard, Shawana in the passageway behind the house. So it was Narhila! I'd scurry back into the house, take up my post outside the bathroom door, and wait in silence until it opened.

'Aha! I caught you, Narhila! I caught you! I'm telling! Oooh, you're in trouble now!'

I always told, too. I never forgot. 'Narhila took two showers in your bathroom!'

'Did she?' That was as much reaction as my bathroom reports ever got. I wanted my father to get angry at the transgressor. It puzzled and disappointed me that he didn't. But I went right on filing my reports.

'And Shawana and Alpha had a fight.' I reported all

sibling arguments that had taken place during his absence. I took that as my duty too. My father didn't like us to fight. He said, 'There are seven of you. You should be friends. Friends don't fight.' He felt very deeply about this – that we must always stand by each other and love one another. So these reports got a stronger reaction, especially because I always made the fights sound worse than they were. But my father could never stay angry long. Soon he and my sisters would be laughing at my melodramatics, and that would be the end of that. I'd try to stay angry, but laughing was more fun, and soon I'd join in too.

I was a greedy little girl, especially about food. And I was always worried that someone else was getting more or better food than I was, or that someone might take a bite of mine. Usually we didn't sit down together at a table for regular meals. We ate separately, whenever we were hungry. When we did eat together, the older kids would share one bowl, the younger kids would share another, and my mother and father would each have their own. The proper etiquette when sharing a bowl is to eat the food directly in front of you. But I hated sharing and was never satisfied with the food in front of me. 'You're eating too fast!' I'd complain to my sisters. 'You're eating all the meat! There won't be any for me! Amariya, they're eating too fast!' I'd start crying and keep crying until my mother called me over to eat with her. Or, instead of eating the food on my side of the bowl, I'd reach over and take food from someone else's part of the bowl.

'Fauziya! What are you doing?'

'You have all the meat!'

'You want to eat from this side? Fine. Just say so.' My sisters would turn the bowl. I'd look again and decide

62

the best meat was still in front of someone else. I'd reach over there.

'Fauziya!'

'But you have better meat!'

They'd turn the bowl again, and again and again.

My complaints and tantrums were such a regular part of shared meals that it took my mother time to adjust when they started tapering off as I got older. The first few times my sisters and I ate together in peace my mother called to them. 'Ayisha? Shawana? Where's Fauziya? Isn't she eating?'

'Yes, Amariya, she's eating. She's right here.'

'She's there?' My mother would come to look for herself, and laugh in surprise. 'Can that be my Fauziya?'

I could be a handful, all right. I had a curious, restless nature, and had to keep busy all the time. A lot of things around the house ended up broken as a result of my antics. My mother, Ayisha, Shawana, and Alpha had a high tolerance for my destructive mischief. Narhila and Asmahu were another story. They came after me when I broke something of theirs the same way I went after Baba when he broke something of mine. If my father was home I ran directly to him. It didn't matter what I'd done. I knew he'd protect me. Nobody could touch me when Yaya was home.

The love my father and I shared was very special, very strong.

My mother knew how special it was. I asked her once why she thought it was so deep. 'Because you were so sweet to him,' she said. 'You always had time for him.' It's true. When I knew he was coming home, I came back from wherever I was, with no dawdling on the way. I eventually outgrew being lifted in his arms, but I never outgrew wanting to be the first to run and greet him. 'Yaya! Welcome home!' If he returned while I was out, he'd ask my mother, 'Where is she?'

My mother always knew who 'she' was. She'd laugh and say, 'Oh, she'll be here soon, don't worry.' Two seconds later, I'd burst through the door. My father would be sitting in a chair, talking with my mother, tired from his journey.

'Yaya!'

He'd look up, smile and open his arms. 'There she is. There's my girl.' That's what my father always called me. I was always his girl.

When my father was home, I left the house only when I had to and only for as long as I had to. I'd go to school and *madrasah* and come straight back. No lingering after class to talk with a favorite teacher. No strolling and chatting with friends. No stopping to buy roasted peanuts. I had no time for friends or anything else when my father was home. When Yaya was home, I wanted to be with him. And he wanted to be with me. If he was sitting on the couch watching TV, I'd be sitting beside him. If he was doing something in his room, I'd be sprawled out on his bed. If he got hungry and wanted to eat, he'd call me to eat with him, and I'd eat again even if I'd just eaten and was still full.

One of our favorite rituals was his asking me to pick out his clothes. I'd open his wardrobe closet and consider the choices. 'Let's see. Yesterday you wore yellow. Day before that you wore green. Today, I think I prefer blue.'

'Blue it is. And which sandals should I wear today?'

My father had an array of fine leather sandals. I'd examine them, select a pair.

'I think these.'

'Excellent choice.'

If Yaya bought himself new clothes during his travels, we'd stage a fashion show, with a twist. Instead of my father modeling his new clothes for me, he'd have me model them for him. I'd put on his new *patakari* or *danshiki* over my clothing, slip my feet into his new pair of sandals, and shuffle back and forth across the room, parading around while my father assessed his purchases with a critical eye. I was just a little girl, and he was a big man, so of course nothing fit. The neckhole would be the width of my shoulders, the sleeves would hang down to the floor, the fabric would be bunched at my feet, the heels of his sandals would extend a good way behind my own. But because we had similar facial features and skin tone, he used me as the test. If he thought the color and design flattered me, then he'd assume they'd do the same for him. 'Oh, I like that! That looks good! Yes, I can wear that.' If he didn't like the effect, he'd say, 'Hmmm. No, I don't think so.' He'd put the reject aside and tell my mother to dash it – to give it away. If he didn't think it looked good on me, it didn't get worn.

My father was always going on about the resemblance between us. When I was little, he'd sit me on his lap and say, 'Oh, this is my daughter. Look at her face. Who does she look like? Look at her nose. Just like me. Look at her ears. Just like me. We even have the same teeth!'

My mother used to tease him. 'No, she looks more like me.'

'How can you say that? Look at her face. Look at my face. Do you see any difference?'

'I think she looks like me.'

'You need glasses, woman.'

He even seemed to take satisfaction from the fact

that I had asthma. His mother had asthma. He had asthma. I did too. He wasn't glad I had it, but he wasn't above mentioning it as further evidence of how alike we were. It was also another reason he pampered and favored me the way he did.

My asthma was mild compared to his, mostly just a temporary struggling for breath and a whistle to my breathing when I exerted myself, like when I chased after Baba. His was really serious. Yaya had suffered from asthma all his life and had quit smoking because of it. Cigarette smoke, dust, perfume, the smell of cooking oil – all kinds of things bothered his asthma. He had different medicines for it, and he never went anywhere without his inhaler. It got especially bad during the dry season, from around November through April. He'd sometimes have attacks then, which usually lasted about three days. They'd come on slow and get worse and worse until he was completely debilitated, unable to leave his bed, unable to sit or sleep or breathe. He suffered horribly during these attacks. When things were at their worst, he'd call everybody to his bedside and say, 'Oh, I'm going to die, I'm going to die. Fauziya, say a prayer for me.'

And then he'd start distributing his worldly goods. 'Amariya, you take the house. Give my clothes to charity.'

If a friend came to visit, he'd say, 'Jimmy, is that you? Jimmy, I want you to have my car.'

We all thought it was funny. We'd laugh and re-assure him. 'Oh, Yaya, you're not going to die.'

'Oh, you don't know. Nobody knows how much I'm suffering.'

'You're not going to die.'

By the third day the worst would be past. He'd start feeling better, and before you knew it, he'd be completely recovered as if he'd never been sick at all.

Once, during the worst part of an attack, he handed me a huge sum of money when no-one was looking, something like 100,000 CFA in cash, over $1,600.

'Take this,' he said. 'Don't tell anyone I gave it to you. It's yours. I want you to have it. When I die, I want you to use it to finish your education, OK?'

I took the money and hid it.

Two days later, when he was feeling better, he called me to his bedside again. 'Fauziya, you can give me back the money now.'

'Give it back! But you gave it to me! You said I should keep it.'

'Yes, yes, I know I gave it to you, but that was because I thought I was going to die. I didn't die, so you can give it back now.'

I complained to my mother. 'Yaya gave me all this money and now he's making me give it back.'

She laughed. 'You see? That's what you get for being selfish. If you'd given the money to me, I'd have been able to keep it for you.'

'Give it to you? No way! He gave it to me!'

I got sick from asthma, too, sometimes, more often from other things. There are a lot of diseases and not much access to good medical care where I come from. My father worried about all his children when they were ill. But, because of my asthma and because I was his favorite, he worried especially about me. If a fever or headache or stomachache was making me miserable at night, he'd come sit with me, rest my head in his lap, and gently massage my back until I fell asleep. And even then he wouldn't sleep. When I was sick, my mother said, he'd be up all night, checking on me every few minutes to make sure I was OK.

Because my health sometimes bordered on fragile,

my father didn't like to see me exerting myself. If he thought I was doing any kind of housework, he'd get upset. Once, when I was little, I was with my mother in the passageway behind our house, watching her pound *fufu*. Ahmed usually did the pounding, but sometimes when he was out and no-one else was around to help, she'd do it herself, turning the pieces with one hand and pounding with the other. Pounding *fufu* is very hard work. I was watching, eager for her to finish so I could eat. My father was sitting on his porch. He heard the pounding, knew I was back there with my mother, and became very angry. 'Amariya! Don't let her do that! You know she shouldn't do that!'

'She's not!'

Even when my father came over to check on me and saw I wasn't working, he still wasn't satisfied.

'Fauziya, come away from there.'

My mother gave him an exasperated look. 'Really, Yaya. You don't want her to do anything. You forget she's going to get married someday and she's going to need to know how to cook.'

'She's not ready to get married yet. She has a lot of years of schooling ahead of her before she's even ready to think about marriage. She can learn all that later. Come on, Fauziya. Let's go.'

I loved to hear them competing over me, even if it was only in fun.

My father was a stubborn, willful man. I was definitely his daughter when it came to those personality traits. Like him, I wanted what I wanted and usually found a way to get it. These aren't considered appealing qualities in girls where I come from. A lot of fathers try to extinguish any sign of independent thinking in their daughters, but not my father. In fact he reinforced it, not in words but by the way he responded whenever I did assert myself. He was always interested in my opinion, whether it was on which clothes he would wear that day or which car he should buy. And he taught me early that I had the power and right to express myself, to make my own choices.

Another way in which my father prepared me, and all my siblings, for an adult life of independence and achievement was through education. Like many Muslim girls, my sisters and I were all sent to *madrasah* beginning around age six, to receive training in our religion. The *madrasah* in Kpalimé used to be a small, one-room schoolhouse, but when I was about a year old, someone – the Saudi Arabians, I think – donated money to build a bigger school, and the curriculum was also expanded, so that by the time I started it included a few secular subjects like French. Before the new school was built, parents who didn't have money could pay for their children's studies with food or farm produce. But after the new school opened, they had to pay in currency because the school needed money to buy books and pay teachers. Even though the monthly charge was minuscule, many people couldn't afford to pay it, and tuition is never waived, because we believe knowledge is valuable and isn't to be had for free.

If they could afford only a secular education for some of their children, parents would send their sons, not their daughters, to school, partly because they figured the boys needed the education more, so that they would be able to support their own families when the time came, and partly because many people didn't believe in educating girls. It was actually frowned upon, considered dangerous. There was no telling what kinds of ideas a girl might be exposed to in secondary school, what kinds of people she might be thrown in with, what kinds of behaviors and habits she might pick up. She could end up going astray, destroying her reputation, and bringing shame on her family.

These were not trivial concerns in my community. They were very serious ones, which my parents, being as straitlaced and traditional as any when it came to the moral rectitude they demanded of their children, fully shared. My father understood there was genuine risk in exposing his children, both his sons and his daughters but especially his daughters, to people whose ideas and values might not jibe with our own. My parents, however, were strong believers in educating all their children, in both *madrasah* and secular school. My father saw education as consistent with being a good Muslim because Islam emphasizes the importance of attaining knowledge. Yaya knew that keeping us uneducated wouldn't prevent us from going astray. And I think he trusted us. I know he did. He and my mother didn't believe in monitoring or trying to control us. They simply made clear their expectations and felt confident we would live up to them.

So, while most of my girl cousins had only a year or two in primary school, if that, my sisters and I all received a secular as well as a religious education. My sisters went to primary school for all six years, and then attended vocational school to learn skills like dressmaking and secretarial work. My own education would go much further – and would have gone further still if my father hadn't died. I started school at age five. My father's business was flourishing by then and he was always looking for ways to improve it. That's how I ended up going to school in Ghana. My father spoke many languages but understood English only when it was spoken to him. He couldn't really speak English, and he couldn't read or write it at all. As his business grew, his lack of English started to become a liability. My father needed someone to help him with English. I was the obvious candidate. I was smart, and about to start school, so why not send me to school in English-speaking Ghana? We lived within walking distance of a good school just across the border, which had both a primary school curriculum for the first six years and a middle school curriculum for the next four. Since he was intending to send me to both primary and secondary school it might as well be there, he decided.

He was very eager for me to learn English, and I was very eager to learn it for him. I studied hard. I always wanted to be able to show off my progress when he returned from a trip. 'There's my girl! Can you recite the alphabet for me?'

'H! I! J! K!'

'Good! Good!'

As soon as I was able to read sentences, he began giving me letters to read aloud to him.

'I can read it, Yaya,' I'd tell him, 'but I can't say it in our language.'

'Don't worry,' he'd say. 'I can understand when I hear it.' When I got older, he'd sometimes ask me to write letters to his English-speaking friends. Simple letters. Test letters, I realized later. My father was a practical man. He was always pleased when I came home with good scores on my exams, but he knew from experience that good scores and grades didn't necessarily translate into viable skills. He'd show the letters I wrote to his English-speaking friends and ask

71

them to comment, then report back to me.

'You know that letter I asked you to write for me, Fauziya?'

'Yes, Yaya.'

'Well, my friend was very impressed with it. He said it was really good.'

I'd be so happy!

'You're doing well, Fauziya. You should be proud. But remember you can do better.' My father always praised me when I did well, and he always told me I could do better. He taught me to live by the same code he lived by. Just as he took pride in his accomplishments but never rested on them for long, so he kept pushing me to improve myself. Rather than feeling pressured, I felt proud that he believed in me enough to think I was always capable of more. And I lived to make him proud.

6

Muslim Family Life

My brothers, Alpha and Babs, used to run around and you never knew where they were. They'd disappear early in the morning and not come back until late in the evening. My mother would say, 'Did you eat?' My father would say, 'Take a shower.' But nobody questioned them about where they'd been or what they'd been doing. They were boys and running around was what boys did.

My sisters and I stayed mainly at home, because that's what girls did. But we didn't stay home to do housework. None of us worked around the house except Ayisha, and she worked only because she wanted to. About the most any of us ever did was go on an occasional errand. If my mother needed something special for a dish she was preparing, she might send Narhila or me to buy it. But even that didn't happen often because we rarely ran out of anything. Our house was the hub of my father's business. His trucks and vans traveled to major markets throughout West Africa and usually returned laden with foodstuffs, so our food-storage room was well stocked. We always had rice, corn, yams, plantains, sugar, and other staples in storage, and milk and meat in the refrigerator. We did sometimes run out of Milo, because Asmahu loved that chocolate drink so much that it was hard to keep enough on hand, but for the most part we never had to do much food shopping.

We didn't shop very often for clothes either. If my mother and I happened to be at the market on a day when a new shipment of secondhand clothes arrived from France, I'd pester her to take me over and let me look through them. That was always a big event, when the *ofus* came in, packed in big burlap bags that the merchants quickly cut open. Some of the clothes were old and worn, others looked brand-new. If I saw something I liked – a silk blouse maybe – I'd ask my mother to buy it for me and she would because everything was so cheap. But that was about the extent of our clothes shopping, because my father always shopped for us. He never returned from a trip without a gift of cloth or new clothing for my mother, and he almost always picked up something for one or more of us kids too.

There was nothing my sisters and brothers could think to want that my father didn't or wouldn't provide. And no matter how much he had accomplished, he never stopped trying to do better, be better, so he could provide a better life for his family. By family I don't mean just his wife and children, but our extended family as well, many of whom benefited from his generosity. Family is everything in our culture. That and religion are what keeps people in my community together.

When I was growing up, religion permeated everything. I began praying before I knew what prayer was, mimicking my parents' and older siblings' movements and postures as they prayed. I was reciting passages from the Qur'an before I could read or write or had any understanding of what the sounds meant. All I knew was that the sounds were beautiful and soothing when my mother recited them and that I wanted to be able to say them, too. So she taught me. She was a good teacher, endlessly gentle and encouraging and patient. I was a good student, avid and quick. We were soon reciting simple passages together the way other mothers and children recite nursery rhymes together. Reciting the Qur'an together was something very special that only the two of us shared.

Amariya. To be with her again, to see my family again, to be home in Kpalimé again, especially during Ramadan. Sometimes it's all I can think of.

Ramadan is a month of prayer and fasting from predawn to dark. You wouldn't think people would look forward to that, but we did.

We Muslims believe that during Ramadan, God sends His angels to earth to remove all evil and cleanse all sin. We believe that during Ramadan, all the wild animals retreat deep into the bush and even poisonous snakes won't bite, that it's safe to walk anywhere even in the middle of the night because God's angels are protecting you from harm. We believe that people who die while observing Ramadan go straight to heaven because they die sinless. Ramadan is our holy month, a very blessed holy month, a time to renew and demonstrate devotion to God. The whole community came together during Ramadan. Everyone felt renewed, reconnected, reborn.

As Ramadan was approaching, we'd all wait through the last nights of the dark moon for the announcement to come on the radio that the new moon of the ninth Muslim month had been spotted somewhere in the west and it was time to begin fasting. The evening of the day the announcement was made people would gather at the mosque for the fourth prayer, the Salat al Magrib.

Afterward, everyone went home and had dinner,

but returned to the mosque for the fifth prayer, the Salat al 'Isha, and then an extra sixth prayer, the Salat Taraweeh, which we said only during Ramadan. That first night we'd welcome Ramadan and ask God to forgive and remove all our sins, both the ones we know to ask forgiveness for and the ones we don't. One of the teachings of Islam is that we don't know, can't know, all the sins we've committed against God and other human beings. All we can do is ask God to forgive them and help us not to commit them again.

Before we went to bed that night, my mother would store the food left over from dinner in special double-lined plastic containers to keep it warm. It didn't have to stay warm very long, because we'd get up the next morning at around three-thirty or four to have something to eat and drink before saying first prayers. Although normally we said our morning prayers at home, during Ramadan we often went to the mosque for the five A.M. prayer to join the other Muslims in our community. Then we came home again and slept for another few hours, after which we got up again and went about our day, taking no more food or water until we broke our fast after sunset. We repeated this routine for all twenty-nine or thirty days of Ramadan. But even though we were fasting and getting less sleep than usual, none of us stopped working or going to school or doing housework or whatever we usually did. We all just went on with normal daily life. For someone like me, who loved to eat so much, the fasting wasn't easy. But I always kept the fast because I loved Ramadan more.

Each day's fast would end after the fourth prayer. Then we'd go home to eat, often getting special treats. If my father had been in Lomé that day, he'd sometimes bring home a certain kind of chicken you could get only during Ramadan. The chicken was spicy and roasted and came with this wonderful soft, fresh-baked bread. Just the smell of it made my mouth water and my stomach growl. I'd think, 'Oh boy, I can't wait until it gets dark and I can stuff myself with that chicken.' But then I'd be able to eat only a few mouthfuls, because fasting had made my stomach too small. I'd be so frustrated because I loved that chicken and couldn't eat it.

Two or three nights into Ramadan, we'd see the first slender crescent of new moon. We'd watch as little by little it waxed into a full moon, then waned. When it disappeared entirely we'd still be fasting, but our anticipation would begin to mount because we knew Ramadan was almost over. We'd start listening to the radio intently, waiting for the official announcement to come: 'The new moon has been spotted in the west. Ramadan is over. Time to break the fast.'

Yaaaaaaaaayyyyy!

Sometimes the announcement would come while I was at school and I wouldn't hear it. I'd come home and see Shawana or Asmahu eating.

'What are you doing!'

'Didn't you hear? Ramadan is over. They announced it this morning.'

'This morning!' And I'd been starving myself all day! But I never wanted to risk breaking the fast too early.

The first full day after the announcement is 'Eid al-Fitr, the festival of fast-breaking. What a day that is! It begins with special prayers in the open field behind the *madrasah*. The mosque isn't big enough to hold all the people who come, because everybody comes, men, women, children, young people, old people, everybody. We'd all pray together in the field, saying goodbye to Ramadan, thanking God for forgiving our sins and asking Him to bless us, guide us, and keep us strong in the faith. And then we'd celebrate! The rest of the day was a holiday. My mother would prepare a huge feast, and we'd invite neighbors to share the food. People went from house to house visiting friends and relatives and exchanging good wishes and small presents. It was a time of renewing and strengthening ties, of forgiving and forgetting grudges and grievances against each other, of feeling our unity in God. It was also a time for family visits, and my mother's mother often came to celebrate the holiday with us.

'Eid al-Fitr is one of the two main festivals in the Muslim year. The other, which comes about two months later, is 'Eid al-Adha, the festival of sacrifice marking the end of the hajj period. That's when my father would slaughter a cow and a sheep. The beef we would exchange with other Muslim families. The mutton was fried up into a special seasoned meat that we ate as occasional little treats – that is, if Asmahu didn't get to all of it before we could get any.

After 'Eid al-Adha comes Moulid, the celebration of the Prophet's birthday. It's a quieter celebration, but I liked it, too. I was baptized during the month of Moulid, which is when baptisms are traditionally announced and celebrated in my community. Not everybody gets baptized. In fact, most people don't, because you can be baptized only when you've finished reading the Qur'an, and to get to that point is a long journey. Before you can be baptized, before you can even start to read the Qur'an, you have to learn the Arabic alphabet, how to read it, write it and pronounce it. I had a head start on my classmates because by the time I began studying at *madrasah* I was already reciting the Qur'an at home with Amariya, but the teacher still made me wait to begin my formal training in the Qur'an until he felt I was ready for serious study. I remember the day he announced my name along with those of four or five of my classmates.

'Fauziya, tell your mother to give alms and bless you and give you money for the Qur'an. You're ready to begin.'

I flew home.

'Amariya! Amariya! Malam says I'm ready to enter the Qur'an!'

'Oh, Fauziya! Oh, my daughter! That's so wonderful! I'm so happy!' She hugged me and kissed me and started crying and praising God.

I was the first kid at *madrasah* the next day. I couldn't wait to begin! When the teacher arrived, I was already there with my money in hand. My groupmates and I started with the first *surah*, Al Fatihah, 'The Opening,' which is the Muslim equivalent of the Lord's Prayer. It's the first prayer Muslims learn. All Muslims know it. I knew it already and was impatient to move on. But the teacher kept all of us working at the same pace for a while. We'd recite in unison until it sounded to him like we were all reciting correctly, and then he'd have each of us read individually to see who was doing well and who was having problems. I was always one of the three best readers. My friend Aziz was the only one who was consistently better than I was.

The *surahs* get longer and more difficult as you go deeper into the Qur'an. There's a natural sorting process that begins to occur at a certain point. The people who have been struggling all along start finding it harder and harder, and the ones who are doing well get impatient to move ahead. Our teacher didn't want to lose any of us, out of either boredom or frustration, so he broke us into two groups and worked with each group at its own pace. That's when Aziz and I really surged ahead. I was very competitive, and I loved having someone as smart as he was to compete with. It kept me working hard.

When I was ten or eleven, Aziz and I won an Arabic reading competition, and were awarded scholarships to study in Libya. My teachers, who thought I had a gift for Arabic studies, wanted me to go. Although my father was incredibly proud that I had won the competition, he wouldn't allow me to leave for Libya. He felt that I was too young to be so far away from home. I didn't want to leave Yaya anyway. Aziz did decide to go, however, and I missed him a lot. We'd been close friends as well as studymates and competitors.

Aziz was still in Libya when I was baptized. That was the only thing I would have changed about that day. It would have been nice to be baptized with someone I felt so close to, because baptism is a very big event in the life of a young Muslim and his or her family. For my parents it was particularly meaningful, as both of them had been baptized, and I was the first and only one of their seven children to be baptized too.

The day of my baptism was a very, very proud day for me and my parents. I was between twelve and thirteen. I'd finished reading the Qur'an about two years earlier, but you don't just finish reading it once and then immediately get baptized. It isn't that easy. The *malam*, the teacher at *madrasah*, is the one who decides when you're ready to be baptized. I'd already won the Arabic competition, which was a test of memorization, recitation, and mastery: 'In which *surah* does the Prophet say this?' 'In which verse of which *surah* does the Prophet say that?' (A *surah* is like a chapter.) Even that wasn't good enough for my teacher, however. He was very serious about reading the Qur'an and taught us to be equally serious about it. We believe that the Qur'an is the word of God and that reciting the Qur'an is a way of sending our prayers to Him. As the teacher told us, 'When you read the Qur'an, God is listening.'

The Moulid celebration in honor of the new baptisms at our *madrasah* is always held in the open field behind the school, and it always attracts a large gathering. Those who are being baptized dress all in white. I wore a beautiful white dress and a beautiful white *mayahfi*. My sisters helped me get dressed and fix my hair that morning. Then our family walked over to the field, all nine of us together. The celebration began with prayer and preaching. Our *malam* sat on a mat, reading from the Qur'an, and we students, who were all kneeling on mats behind him, repeated the passages together after him. After the program was finished, the *malam* said, 'This year, we're proud to announce that five people have finished reading the Qur'an and are being baptized today. Their names are . . .'

When my name was announced, 'Fauziya Kassindja,' my mother put her hands to her face and began to cry. I looked up at my father. He looked down at me, smiled, touched my cheek, and lowered his hand to my shoulder. The pride in his smile, and the love that shone in his eyes said more to me than words ever could. I will hold that moment in my heart forever.

And then everyone around me was hugging me and kissing me and congratulating me. Even people I didn't know seemed excited, because their faith makes them happy when anyone loves the Qur'an enough to make the long journey to baptism. And for a girl to do it! Women especially kept blessing me, for my achievement brought joy to their hearts. After the ceremony ended, there was food and drink for everybody.

Our teacher gave each of us a beautiful copy of the Qur'an that day as a baptism gift. 'Now, remember, Fauziya,' he said as he handed me mine. 'Don't go home and put it on a shelf and forget about it. You musn't think, "Oh, I'm done with the Qur'an now." You must read it every day. If you leave the Qur'an for one day, the Qur'an will leave you for ten.'

'Yes, Malam.' I had no intention of forgetting the Qur'an. I love reading the Qur'an. Maybe not quite as passionately as my mother does. I've never met anyone who loves the Qur'an the way she does. But almost.

The *malam* congratulated my parents, and then we all walked home. Every step of the way back to our house, people kept stopping us to give us their good wishes. You get a lot of respect when you're baptized. Everyone knows that you're a good Muslim girl. I was a good Muslim girl. So were my sisters. We were all good Muslim girls.

7

Muslim Girl

My father was a modern man in a traditional culture who neither repudiated that culture nor let himself be bound by it. He embraced some parts of it, rejected others, and never stopped reevaluating his beliefs about good and bad, right and wrong. He also never deviated from his Muslim faith. We, his daughters, were the same – part modern, part traditional, and Muslim throughout.

We were definitely modern girls when it came to the clothes we wore at home – shorts, T-shirts, whatever we wanted. But if we went out of the house, or if my parents had visitors, we always dressed modestly: nothing sleeveless or low-cut, no skirts above the knee, no pants or shorts ever. Although we didn't veil, which some of the more conservative members of the community (like my uncle) still expected even young girls to do, we didn't flaunt ourselves either. If we had, any adult in our community would have felt free to give us a good tongue-lashing and a knock on the head.

Most of the Muslim teachings we were expected to follow were about behavior, of course, not appearance. My sisters and I didn't smoke or drink because our religion forbids it. We didn't lie, cheat, steal, or swear (except occasionally at each other), and we didn't brag about ourselves or gossip. Well, sometimes we gossiped, even though our father abhorred gossip and said it was only for small-minded people, but we always asked Allah to forgive us afterward because we knew it was a sin.

My sisters and I never fooled around with boys. Our parents didn't forbid it, since that wasn't their style, but they let us know we were expected to use our good judgment. They'd say something like, 'You know what's good for you. So if you want to go off somewhere alone with a boy, that's your business. You wouldn't do it if you didn't think you could handle it. Just be sure you know what you're doing.' About menstruation and sex and topics like that, they never said anything at all. They didn't have to, because the *malams* gave us the instruction we needed in *madrasah*.

The teaching is called *phikihm*. It's part sex education, part religious instruction. The *malam* started teaching us when we were about twelve, boys and girls together. He explained that all of us would soon start growing hair under our arms, and after that the girls would start menstruating. With these physical signs of adulthood, we would no longer be children in God's eyes. He said we had to be careful then, because that's when God would start using His pen to record our good deeds and transgressions. What we call the *alkalimi,* or 'pen of God,' would keep track of all the bad things we did – lying and cheating and fighting and stealing and so forth – transgressions that are forgiven in children but are sins in adults. As adults we would be expected to obey all God's laws. As adults we would also have to fast during Ramadan, he said, and if we hadn't yet tried, we should do so now, even though it wasn't required, because it was good to have practice beforehand.

I'd already had lots of practice in fasting and praying, so I didn't have to worry about that. I was so skilled in prayer that the *malam* would often say he wished I were a boy, so that I could become a highly respected imam like my uncle. But women can't be religious leaders.

Part of the *malam*'s sex education consisted of teaching us girls about the special restrictions we'd have to observe when we entered womanhood. Women aren't allowed to pray at all when we're menstruating because we are considered unclean then. We don't pray, we don't touch the Qur'an, and we don't go to the mosque. If we start menstruating while wearing the clothes we wear during prayer, we have to wash them before wearing them for prayer again because they're no longer clean. Even if no menstrual blood touches them, we have to wash them. If we start menstruating during Ramadan, we don't fast. But we have to keep track of any days of fasting we miss so that we can make them up after we've stopped menstruating.

Before we can resume praying, however, we have to take a special ritual bath called *ghusl*. First we take a normal bath or shower to clean ourselves in preparation; then we take the ritual bath, which consists of washing our entire bodies in a prescribed way in clean flowing water while reciting specific prayers. Some women use something called a *buta*, which is like a giant teapot. They fill it with clean water and set it aside to be used after taking their first bath, then pour that water over themselves for the *ghusl*. They have to be careful not to put their hands in the *buta* water before finishing their first bath, though, because if they do, it's no longer clean and they have to dump it out and get more.

In Islam we have all kinds of special washing and bathing requirements. We wash before prayers, we wash in a special way for Salat al-Jum'ah, the Friday prayer. We perform a special bath in preparation for praying for the dead. Women perform one kind of bath after menstruation, another before marrying, another after childbirth, and men and women both take a special bath after having sex.

The *malam* had a lot to say about sex, both its sinful and its sacred aspects. Having sex outside marriage is *zina* in our religion, meaning the gravest kind of sin. The *malam* said it's like killing seven angels. Abortion and having a baby out of wedlock are also *zina*. So there's a great deal of emphasis placed on chastity and fidelity. We girls especially were told to guard our virginity. The *malam* said, 'If your husband finds that you're still a virgin when you marry, he will always love and respect you. Your parents will be proud and happy, and God will praise you and be pleased.'

Sex within marriage is as holy as sex outside of marriage is sinful. We were taught that a good Muslim wife always respects and obeys her husband and never refuses him when he wants sex. He said if a man wants sex in the middle of the night and his wife refuses him, the angels will curse her until daybreak. A good wife doesn't deny her husband or make him force her. In America, a woman can charge her husband with rape. Where I come from, people would laugh if a woman did that. They'd say, 'How can he rape you? He's your husband! He wouldn't have had to force you if you hadn't refused him. That's what you get for saying no.' But our religion also teaches that a good husband is considerate of his wife. The *malam* told the boys, 'You don't just come home, hang up your *patakari*, and jump on your wife. She's not a horse. You have to

86

show respect. If she's tired from working, you should let her rest. Don't think you can just have her anytime you want. She's not your slave. If she's not in the mood, you should try to put her in the mood. Play music, dance, hold her, make jokes, make her laugh. You have to play with her.' We'd all get really embarrassed when the *malam* said things like 'Play with her.' The *malam* never spoke about *kakia*. If it were a requirement of the Islam faith, the *malam* would have told us as much. But he never even mentioned the word.

He did talk about polygamy, though. He said, 'You know, we men are like devils. We have a beautiful wife at home, but we're never satisfied. We go walking down the street and we see another beautiful woman and we think, "Oh, I like her better than my wife." We start desiring her and then we start thinking, "Maybe I can have her as a girlfriend." But what are we really talking about? We're talking about having illicit sex. You know that's not permitted. So if you can't overcome the desire to have sex with her, then do it the right way. Take her home. Let your wife know about her. Marry her and make her your second wife. If you have the means and think you can treat them all equally, you can take as many as four. But think carefully before you do it. Just because you're allowed to take four wives doesn't mean that's what you should do. You have to consider their needs as well as your own. You have to think about whether you can be a good husband to your wives, whether you can support them all and treat them all equally.'

That's the part that never made sense to me. How can a man love different women equally? I think it must be impossible. Anybody who lives in a place where many of the households are polygamous has seen the resentments and bitterness that can result.

My own most vivid glimpse into such a household occurred when I was about ten. Several of my friends and I heard a terrible shrieking that sounded like someone being killed at a house nearby. We all ran over to see what was going on and saw two women having a terrible fight. They were hitting each other and pulling at each other's clothes and hair. After what seemed like for ever some adults rushed over and pulled them apart. It turned out the two women were both the wives of the man whose house it was, and the fight had begun when one woman took something that belonged to the other, and the other retaliated by coming up behind her and throwing boiling water on her back. Even after the grown-ups shooed us kids away and we left the scene, we could still hear the women screaming at each other. 'And those two women still have to live together in the same house' was all I could think of. I wanted no part of a polygamous domestic life.

Being still a child, I wanted nothing to do with any of it – boyfriends, marriage, sex. I thought it was all disgusting. I had a friend in *madrasah* whom I used to talk with after *phikihm*. 'Don't you think it's revolting?' I'd ask her. 'How could anybody ever do that? I'm never going to fall in love or be with a man.' But she always disagreed with me. And only a few years later she ended up marrying one of the young *malams*. Probably she had already begun her young womanhood and fallen in love while I was still just a little girl, horrified by the thought of sex. After I heard she was getting married, it made me laugh to realize how worlds apart we must have been when we were having those conversations. She became a wife and then a mother before I ever even kissed a boy – or wanted to.

Aziz, my friend from *madrasah,* could perhaps have been my first real love. But he left to study in Libya before anything could come of the closeness between us. If he had remained at home another couple of years, I might have been able to understand what my friend was hinting at when she told me, no, she didn't find the idea of marrying and having sex completely revolting. I might have understood because I might have been feeling some amorous yearnings myself. But as it was, I had no stirrings of love to pull me forward into womanhood. And so I remained a child, happy in my parents' love, indifferent to any other kind.

I couldn't imagine being in love or having sex. That whole world was just too remote from my personal experience.

Weddings, however, were quite a different matter. I loooved weddings! Weddings were the best.

8

Weddings

Ayisha was the first of us girls to marry. She was to marry a man from Lomé named Abass. What a celebration that was!

Weddings can last one to four days, depending on what the family customs are. Weddings in my family traditionally lasted the whole four days, from Thursday to Sunday. The wedding preparations often begin well in advance, practically the day the prospective groom's family visits the prospective bride's family to ask permission for the couple to marry, which usually follows fairly quickly after the two have met. We don't date in our culture. Muslims don't anyway. Couples fall in love and decide to marry in the same fashion that my parents did – that is, if they come from families that allow them to choose their own partners. Some marriages are completely arranged by the parents.

It's more customary these days, however, for a young man to select his bride. As happened with my father, he'll see a woman who captures his fancy and start watching her. Maybe he'll make a point of going to the market on the days he knows she's likely to be there. She may or may not realize she's being watched, may or may not be watching back. Eventually, the young man will approach the young woman and say some version of what my father said to my mother through her friend: 'I've been watching you. I really like you. I'd like to marry you.' If she doesn't share his feelings, she'll say, 'I'll think about it.' She won't say, 'Well, I don't want to marry you.' She'll be polite. Each time he approaches her, she'll say the same thing – 'I'll think about it' – until he gets the message that she's not interested in him. If he wants her anyway and thinks her parents would give their consent even without hers, which many parents in my community would do, he'll go around her directly to her parents. But most young men don't do that. They only want a woman who wants them. If she's clearly not interested, they back off.

If the woman indicates she is interested, the prospective groom will go home and tell his family he's found the woman he wants to wed. If they don't know her or her family, his parents will do some investigating to find out if she's a good Muslim girl from a good Muslim home. Once they are satisfied with her suitability, the young man's parents will send one of his brothers or sisters to the bride's family to request a meeting. Although the emissary does not specify the reason for the meeting, if the parents have one or more daughters of marriageable age, they will know immediately what is at stake. The father will then go to his daughter or daughters: 'Does anyone here know why this young man's family would want to come calling?'

'Yes, Daddy,' one of the girls will say. 'I told him to have his parents send someone to come talk to you' – a clear indication of her interest.

In families like mine the parents may do a little prodding to make sure of their daughters' feelings. With each of my sisters my father would tease her, asking: 'Is this really the man you want? Do you really love him?'

My sisters, being shy, were embarrassed that my father would ask such a personal question, but he was serious as well.

'You can say no, sweetheart. You don't have to marry anyone you don't love.'

Only when he was convinced that the match was her choice would he start looking into the suitability of the prospective groom and his family, doing the same kind of investigation that the young man's parents had presumably done on ours.

Many parents won't be so considerate of their daughter's feelings. If the young man and his family are acceptable to them, they'll issue an invitation to the parents to come negotiate the bride price – the *mahr* – and arrange the marriage without ever consulting the bride-to-be.

I don't know how Ayisha or any of my other sisters met their husbands. I didn't ask. At the time I didn't care, for love and marriage were of no interest to me then. Weddings, however, interested me very much. They were my favorite celebrations of all.

I knew that a wedding was coming soon when a sister's husband-to-be began visiting our house. That doesn't happen until after the wedding date has been set. Once it's set, the young man is permitted to come calling on his bride-to-be. They can sit and talk and laugh together, maybe share food from the same bowl. But they're not allowed to go anywhere together, even with a chaperon. The man can go anywhere and do anything with any of his intended's siblings – invite them out for ice cream, take them to a party. And the young woman can, in turn, keep company with his siblings outside the house. But the two lovers can see each other only when he comes to visit her.

This courtship period usually lasts a number of months, giving the couple a chance to get to know each other while the wedding itself is arranged. It takes time to arrange a wedding celebration of the size Ayisha and my other sisters had. Word has to go out to friends and relatives living in different countries, to allow plenty of time for travel. Food has to be bought and prepared. Music and entertainment and accommodations have to be arranged. It's a lot of work and expense. Sometimes the groom's family contributes something in addition to the *mahr* to help the bride's family cover the costs, sometimes not, depending on what his family can afford. It's traditional, however, for the groom to provide the paraphernalia for the ritual bridal bath: bucket, calabash, sponge, soap, candles, towel, bathroom slippers. Anything beyond that is optional.

My mother's three surviving sisters were always the first to arrive after a marriage announcement went out. They came about two weeks before Ayisha's wedding, from Benin and Nigeria, to help with the cooking and preparations. Ayisha worked, too, as usual, because she wanted to. Even my sisters and I pitched in. It was fun to be part of a houseful of women all running around cooking and cleaning and talking and laughing and getting more and more excited as the wedding approached. Although it was a lot of work, it felt more like a long party – an all-women's party. During this time my father and brothers made themselves scarce. Weddings are women's business.

The days of preparation passed happily, and then came Thursday, when the festivities really got started. My mother would do no work for the next four days, not even so much as getting up to answer the door. Neither would Ayisha. Until the end of the final day of the festivities, they were in *kara*, a period when no work was to be done. A tent had been set up in the courtyard for the evening's entertainment. The drummers, singers, and musicians arrived after seven, and by eight the celebrating was under way. There was drink, music, and dancing. The women drank, and clapped along to the music and danced. Two by two they entered a circle of friends, neighbors, and relatives and danced for Ayisha, dancing their happiness and love for the new bride.

As is traditional, when the sun set, Ayisha hid herself in the house and all the women in the family began looking for her. When we finally found her, we threw a porridgelike mixture of *laylay* and water at her, getting it all over her face, hair, and clothes. She was such a mess! Then she showered and got dressed while the house and the tent filled with more and more women.

Once the dancing in the courtyard outside had reached a certain peak, one person would announce, 'It's time for the *amariya* to come and dance' for Ayisha was still in the house. All eyes fixed on the doorway, until finally Ayisha appeared. A great cry went out as the bride, my beautiful sister, came out of the house and entered the circle, with her maid of honor.

And then Ayisha danced. My sister, who was usually too shy to dance in front of anyone, danced that night before all. As everyone began whooping and whistling and clapping, I watched transfixed. She was liquid. She was velvet. She was music itself. She was everything she was feeling at that moment, all her hopes and dreams for the life she was embracing and all her love for the life she was leaving behind. The moment she started to dance people began entering the circle to shower her with money, while her best friend and maid of honor hovered nearby, catching the money in a bowl as it fell. Ayisha looked so happy! And I was so happy for her, I thought my heart would burst. When the music ended, everyone broke into wild applause and Ayisha laughed and covered her face, suddenly shy again. Then she took her place of honor in the audience to enjoy the rest of the night's dancing.

Friday night's celebrations passed in much the same way. The groom doesn't attend any of these festivities. His family may hold a separate, smaller celebration if they can afford it, but the groom is a mere phantom presence at the bride's parties. Bride and groom don't see each other until Sunday night, after they're officially married, when she's delivered to his house.

On Saturday morning the *nachane* arrived. She's the old woman in our community who does all the ritual bathing of brides and new babies.

'Good morning! Good morning! Where is the beautiful bride?' she called out as she entered the house. After greeting Ayisha, the *nachane* led her to our food-storage room, where any accidental spills that occurred while she was applying the *laylay* dye wouldn't matter. First the *nachane* mixed the *laylay* with water in a plastic bowl to make a porridgelike mixture. Then she put the *laylay* mixture on Ayisha's hands and feet, and then wrapped them in plastic, like gloves and booties. Ayisha had to sit quietly for an hour or so, waiting for the dye to set. When the *nachane* decided it was time and removed the plastic, Ayisha's hands and feet had been dyed solid red. As the dye dried, they turned dark black. A few years later, when Shawana and Asmahu had their weddings, a new *laylay* technique, a kind of stenciling, had become fashionable in Togo, and the *nachane* brought a young woman with her who knew how to do it. The woman cut thin slivers of adhesive bandaging and applied them in intricate designs to the hands and feet before the immersion in the dye. It took her forever, but the results were really elegant, Asmahu's especially. When the strips were removed and the *laylay* had dried, it looked like someone had used a tiny brush to paint an intricate pattern of lilies all over Asmahu's hands and feet. But since that art hadn't come to Togo when Ayisha and Narhila got married, they both got solid black.

That night, Saturday night, there was more dancing, more eating. But Sunday's celebration would be the most spectacular of them all. Nobody had to wake me up that morning. My eyes popped open well before dawn. This was it! The *nachane* returned to the house to give the bride her ritual bath. 'Come with me, my beautiful girl,' she said, taking Ayisha by the hand. 'Come along now, don't be shy.' Ayisha was so shy! I followed them to the bathroom, but I wasn't allowed to go in. The bath was private, just the two of them. Listening by the door, I could hear the *nachane* crooning to Ayisha and praising her beauty, '*Traore! Traore!*' And then the water started running and I couldn't hear anything else. When Ayisha finally emerged, her hair was wrapped in a scarf.

'Ayisha! You're wearing a scarf!' I teased. Ayisha smiled an embarrassed smile.

The *nachane*, protective of her beautiful bride's feelings, gave me a disapproving frown that was half playful, half serious. 'Look at this girl!' she said, meaning me. 'What did you think, that a married woman would show herself bareheaded? Shame on you! Of course she's wearing a scarf! Your sister is almost a married woman now.' She wagged a finger at me. 'And don't you worry,' she said as she took Ayisha by the hand and led her away. 'You'll be a married woman, too, before you know it.'

'Oh no I won't! I'm never getting married!'

The *nachane* laughed. 'You say that now. But you'll change your mind.'

'No I won't,' I insisted, but the *nachane* and Ayisha just laughed at me.

The next step in the bridal ritual was the dressing and makeup. Some of Ayisha's girlfriends and a few of our female cousins came to help my sisters and aunts with this part of the ritual. I could barely fit in the bedroom, it was filled with so many women, all there to make a fuss over the bride, help her dress, wrap her hair in an intricately tied turban to emphasize her beautiful face, and adorn her with jewelry and makeup. When the work of art was finally complete and everyone stood back to admire the effect, I got my first full view of my beloved sister Ayisha as a bride. I was struck dumb. I just stood there, staring and staring. Ayisha? Could this dazzling creature be my sister? I wouldn't have believed it was possible for Ayisha to look more beautiful on Sunday than she had on the previous three days, but she did.

Something had happened in that room while the women were dressing Ayisha, some magic. This woman standing before me, smiling back at me, wasn't just my sister Ayisha anymore. Always beautiful, she had been transformed into the most radiantly exquisite woman I had ever seen.

'Ayisha?' My voice was a whisper.

She turned to me, smiling her sweet, loving smile.

'Fauzy?' The vision spoke! She'd spoken to me!

97

'Fauzy, would you mind bringing me a glass of water from the kitchen?'

Mind?! I was giddy with joy. Of all the people she could have asked, she'd chosen me!

Later that morning we all dressed up in our very best clothing, my mother, my father, my sisters and brothers, and me. The rest of the day was given over to an enormous party that spilled out of our compound and onto the street. The whole community was invited. There was food and drink and the guests exchanged soaps and packets of matches and other little gifts they brought with them to the party. Friends and relatives arrived from distant parts. Everyone who'd missed out on the previous three days of celebrating showed up on Sunday, as well as everyone who'd taken part in the previous celebrations. Sunday was also the big gift-giving day. My mother sat in her bedroom, looking as gorgeous as my father could ever desire, greeting a steady stream of friends, neighbors, and relatives, and accepting their gifts and good wishes on behalf of the bride. Meanwhile, the official religious marriage ceremony was being performed in the mosque, attended only by men.

As evening fell, the partying and celebrating went on and on. The stars came out. The moon rose. The music continued. And then came the sad part, for me: Ayisha's departure. On Sunday night, after all the guests had gone home, Ayisha said goodbye to her family and left our house to go to her new home and family, Abass's home and family. Ayisha, my Ayisha, was leaving. I cried. She hugged me and tried to console me.

'Don't cry, Fauziya. You should be happy for me.'

I was, but I was miserable for myself.

'Come on now,' she said. 'I'm not leaving forever. We'll still see each other. You know that.'

'But you won't be here! Who'll take care of me? You always took care of me.'

She laughed. 'I'm not abandoning you, Fauzy! You know I'll always be there for you. But you're getting to be a big girl now. You don't need me the way you used to. You can take care of yourself.'

But I still wouldn't stop crying.

'Fauziya, Fauziya. Come on now. Do you want to make me sad on my wedding day?'

I pulled myself together and tried to be strong, for her. It was tradition, I knew. It was what had to happen. On Sunday night, the bride leaves her home and goes to be presented to the female head of her new husband's family – his mother or aunt, or the first wife if she's marrying into a polygamous household – before being delivered to the groom. She goes with nothing other than the clothes she is wearing, to symbolize that she is leaving everything from her old life behind. Her gifts, her clothes, and all the other things she needs are delivered the following Thursday or Friday, the day she formally begins her new life as a wife.

And so Ayisha left. I'd seen how happy she was, and wondered if the *nachane* could have been right about me: Was it possible that someday I, too, would feel what Ayisha was feeling that night? I couldn't imagine it. But, watching her, I knew that she had found with Abass what my parents had found with each other.

In the years that followed all of my sisters married, one by one. Narhila would marry Sadque, who was from the Bassari tribe. Shawana married Mabruk, who is Kotokoli. Asmahu also married a man from the Kotokoli tribe, Awal. Each of my sisters was in love with the man she married, and each was joyous on her wedding day.

Maybe someday I'd find love, too, I would think as I watched my sisters go off with their new husbands. If that happened, then I, too, would marry. But if not, I wouldn't marry at all. So I believed.

9

Strife

It's hard to explain to someone from a different culture what family means in my culture – how broadly we define it and how seriously we take it. Where I come from, nothing matters more than family ties. Family is all and everyone is family. Well, not quite everyone, but just about. My immediate family is family. My extended family is family. Anyone related to me by blood, tribe, or marriage is family, no matter how distant or convoluted the connection. Say my mother introduces me to a girl I've never met before. 'Fauziya, this is my half brother's wife's sister's daughter.' I won't think, How is she related to me? I'll call her my sister. Anywhere I go, anyone I meet who's even a tiny part Fulani or Dendi or Tchamba or Koussountu I will also call sister or brother because those are my tribes. If my cousin marries someone from a different tribe, that person is also my cousin. If I meet his father, I will call him my uncle and I'll mean it. He and I are related now, and the relationship will be tight.

Friends are also family. I'll call a friend aunt or sister or mother in the same way that my grandmother Hajia Maimouna called me 'my friend.' We call people by the term that expresses how we feel about them. It doesn't matter if a person is or isn't my blood sister. If I love her like a sister, she is my sister.

Of course, people are not always so willing to establish such ties, not always so eager to welcome new family connections. I wish they were, but they're not. My father's siblings' refusal to accept my mother was painful proof of that.

My father's brother and sister both lived nearby, and both were very involved in our lives. But there were deep differences between my father and his siblings. While my parents tried to respect those differences, my aunt and uncle couldn't seem to do that. So there was constant conflict among the households.

My aunt, Hajia Mamoud, is the oldest of the three siblings. She's a big, dark-skinned, deep-voiced, physically imposing woman with big hands, thick fingers, and big feet like my father had. Her husband died when I was about nine, and she, the first of his wives, continued to live in her husband's house with his two other wives. All of her nine or ten children were pretty much grown by then. Her husband had done fairly well working the family farm, and had provided a comfortable life for his family.

My uncle, Malam Mouhamadou, is the middle child. He's about my height, both of us being the shortest in our tall families, and he has medium dark skin, and a gap between his upper front teeth. He shaves his head like my father did, but he wears a scraggly moustache and beard. He's a high-level imam and the headmaster of the *madrasah* – a very highly respected religious leader in our community. For a number of years he studied and taught in Saudi Arabia, where he earned a master's degree. He's had six or seven wives, counting the ones he's divorced, three of whom lived in Kpalimé when I was growing up and one in Lomé, where he also had one of his offices, so he was always traveling back and forth. There were somewhere between ten and fifteen children born to his various wives, so many, it was hard even for him to keep track of their number.

My father was the baby in the family. He was also the renegade, the independent thinker. While my aunt and uncle hewed to tradition, my father didn't, and they were never able to accept that.

Nor did they ever accept my mother. They had to accept us children, because we were blood family. But as far as they were concerned, a woman from another tribe could never be accepted as family.

When my father was away, my aunt would say cruel things to Amariya. 'Get out of this house! You don't belong here!' She didn't even care if we kids were standing there listening. 'Who are you to make the rules of the house!' I always thought she said these things because she couldn't accept that my father had chosen on his own to deviate from so many traditions, couldn't understand that one of the reasons my parents got along so well was because they were of one mind on these issues. I think she genuinely believed that my mother was controlling my father's mind.

Once when my father had left the house on an errand my aunt came over to see him. 'Where's my brother?' she demanded, walking into the kitchen where my mother was cooking. When my mother told her he'd be back soon, my aunt went to sit on the porch to wait. I happened to walk out to the porch just as a vulture flew by the house, very low. My aunt went berserk. She pointed at the bird and began shouting, 'I see you! I see you!' then jumped up and ran into the house, with me close behind her. When she got to the kitchen, she grabbed a spoon and a pot lid and began banging them together, right in my mother's face. My mother fell back, terrified. 'I've seen you!' my aunt yelled. 'You're a witch!' Where I come from, people believe *voudou* makers have the power to take animal form, and that loud noises frighten evil spirits away. My aunt kept banging those things in my mother's face, shouting at her that she was a witch, and that she should leave. 'Go away! Go away from this house.'

My mother didn't move or respond. Out of love and deference to her husband, she never said anything during these attacks. It was her role to show nothing but respect for his family. She took that role seriously. She just stood there in silence, her eyes filling with tears, until my aunt finished banging and yelling and left.

When my father returned home, she told him what had happened. She broke down crying as she told him. He became very upset. He loved my mother and hated to see her cry. 'Just ignore her,' he said. 'She can't do anything. I brought you into this house. Nobody can send you away.' Scenes like these were very hard on my father, because he loved his wife but he also loved his brother and sister.

They were hard on us kids too. Seeing our mother in so much pain. But like our mother, we never spoke back to them, for they were our elders, my father's family, and we were obliged to be courteous to them. My mother herself would never have countenanced our treating them with anything less than respect.

Unlike my aunt, my uncle managed to be civil to my mother when my father was home, but on the rare occasions when he came around in my father's absence he, too, could be very cruel. 'You don't belong in this family,' he'd tell her. 'You'll never be a part of this family.' One time when my father was ill and my uncle had come to visit, he spoke to my mother after he had left my father's bedside. Holding his *tasbih* in front of her face, he said: 'I swear by these beads, your husband will die and you won't get a pin from his property. He will die, and you won't have a place to live or enough money for a room to rent.'

My mother bowed her head. 'Only God knows what will happen,' she said softly.

When I found my mother crying, I felt as if a knife had been plunged through my heart. He could make good on his threat if it came to that. He knew it. My mother knew it. We all knew it. Under tribal law, everything my father owned belonged to his family. They could do with it as they wished. It was shocking enough for my uncle to make that threat. But to predict death for his own brother! How could he say such a horrible thing?

I could never understand how two such different men could come from the same mother and father. My uncle disapproved of just about everything my father did, beginning with marrying outside the tribe and taking only one wife. He disapproved of our living so luxuriously too. We were trying to act like white people, he said. He even seemed to disapprove of my father's financial success, despite the fact that my father was very generous with him, sending him to Mecca once, and doing many other things to help the family. In fact, he appeared to resent my father's generosity. 'He thinks he owns me because he sent me to Mecca,' he said one day, gesturing toward my father in the midst of an argument they were having.

Like my aunt, my uncle disapproved of my father sending his daughters to school, because he believed girls didn't need education and it would only encourage us to stray from our religion. He disapproved of our not being required to wear veils, disapproved of my father's encouraging his daughters to pick their own husbands. He even disapproved of the affection my father showed his children, especially me. He'd say, 'You play with her too much. You're spoiling her. You shouldn't do that. She won't respect you.'

And yet for all the hurt my aunt and uncle inflicted on my mother, and for all the differences in their values, our three families did manage most of the time to live in peace. My father would get angry at his sister and brother sometimes. 'Leave my wife alone! She's never done anything to hurt you! If you hate her so much, stay away!' But the storms would blow over and the families would come together again. There was never any serious breach. And then, one day, there was.

The two brothers became estranged over an incident involving female circumcision – *kakia* – which both my parents abhorred and both my father's siblings believed in and had had done to their own daughters. When Ayisha's first baby died shortly after birth, people said the baby had died because Ayisha wasn't circumcised. When my other sisters had difficulty getting pregnant right after they were married, people said it was because they were 'unclean.'

As a child I knew nothing about the procedure. However, I do remember hearing my mother and father talking in the kitchen one night. My father was holding my mother's hand, and my mother was crying. She was crying over one of her younger sisters, my aunt Amina, who had recently died from the procedure – although I didn't know that then. I knew she had died, but I didn't know from what. My mother,

106

who never liked to talk about sad things, didn't tell me what had happened until I was much older. Aunt Amina's husband had died, leaving her with two children and no money. It's very hard for a woman to support children alone in my culture. She needed to get married again. When she met a man from the Dendi tribe who wanted to marry her, she agreed to undergo the procedure because he made that a condition of their being married. Unfortunately, she developed tetanus afterward and died. My mother couldn't get over the fact that her sister had been so foolish. Whenever she talked about it, she'd end up saying the same thing over and over again. 'Why did she do that? Why did she agree?' But she didn't talk about her sister's death very often, and she never answered any of my questions about *kakia*.

To this day I'm not exactly sure of all the details of how it's done in my tribe, because it's something that isn't talked about. When I asked girls who'd been through it to tell me what it was like, they'd say, 'If you're so eager to know, you should go through it yourself.' I think they shared my father's family's feeling, that you couldn't be a real woman until you'd had it done, until you yourself had endured the pain. But I certainly wasn't going to satisfy my curiosity about *kakia* that way. From the bits and pieces of information I was able to piece together, it sounded horrendous. As I've been told, four women hold the girl down with her legs spread, while the *nachane* scrapes off her woman parts – I'm not sure how much of them with a razor or knife. Then she applies some herbs or something to stop the bleeding, and binds the girl's legs together from hips to knees for forty days to give the wound time to heal. During that time the girl remains in bed and is not allowed to see anyone except her immediate family and the *nachane*, who comes every day to help her urinate and check how the wound is healing.

It's my impression that the procedure is usually performed on girls in our tribe when they're about fifteen, though some families have it done when the girls are younger, some when they're older. I knew several girls who died because of *kakia*. A Tchamba-Koussountu girl died of a tetanus infection after being cut, just like my aunt Amina did. Another Tchamba girl and a Kotokoli girl bled to death after they were cut in preparation for marriage. People who believe in the procedure explain these deaths differently, of course. They believe terrible things can happen if a girl isn't cut, but would never admit that girls do in fact die from the procedure itself. It was her time to die, is all they would say.

Although my parents and my aunt and uncle had deep differences about *kakia*, they did not try to change each other's minds, for both sides knew it would be futile. It was an uneasy truce they had, but it held until my uncle violated it in a way my father never got over.

My father and his siblings have a number of half siblings by way of their father's other wives. When I was around thirteen or fourteen, one of their half sisters' daughters, a bright, pretty little girl named Asana, came down from the north country to live with us for a while. She was around nine or ten at the time. My father was thrilled to have her. We all were. I had just started boarding school, and I worried that my father would be lonely without me. I loved Asana, and I was glad she was there to keep him company when he was home. He made it quite clear that she was welcome to stay forever. He wanted to raise her, educate her, make sure she found a good husband, pay for her wedding, love and protect and provide for her like one of his own. Her parents were traditional like my aunt and uncle. Although they were a little nervous about letting their daughter live with us because they knew my father's values, they went along with it, hoping she'd soon decide to come home on her own.

Asana lived with us, but she came and went freely between our house and my uncle's house. She was technically as much his charge as my father's, and was always welcome to visit. One day, while my father was off on a business trip and my mother was out of the house, Asana went to visit my uncle. The *nachane* was there waiting. My uncle had arranged everything in advance. Asana didn't know, my mother didn't know, and my father certainly didn't know.

Word travels fast in our community. My mother heard what my uncle had done before she even got back to our house. When she heard, she began crying, but there was nothing she could do. It was too late to try to rescue Asana, and it wasn't my mother's place to go to my uncle's house and berate him. She couldn't even go to check on Asana's welfare. Tradition forbids it. There was nothing she could do but wait for my father to return home. When my father did return and learned what his brother had done, he became enraged. He went straight to my uncle's house. My mother prayed. She said she had never, ever, seen my father that angry.

He told her what happened when he returned. The first thing he had done after storming into my uncle's house was to demand to see Asana, because she was his primary concern. He took her directly to the hospital for an examination and tetanus shot. Then he took her back to my uncle's house to finish recuperating, and the two brothers had it out. Whatever was said between them, it was serious enough for the tribal elders to get involved afterward. They did their best to try to heal the breach, but my father was adamant. He would not forgive his brother. He had forgiven a lot, he said, but this he would not forgive. And he never did.

10

Tragedy

By the time Asana had come to live with my family, Babs was the only child left in the house. I was attending boarding school in Ho, Ghana, almost two hours away by car – farther away from my father than I'd ever been in my life.

It had been my choice to go. After six years of primary school, I took the common entrance exam to attend secondary school. When I found out I had passed, my father and I agreed that I should continue my education in Ghana. I'd come this far in an English-speaking school, and it made no sense to switch to a French-speaking secondary school in Togo. But all the secondary schools in Ghana in which I was interested were so far away that I'd have to go to boarding school.

I didn't mind that, or didn't think I did. I'd heard the older sisters of some of my friends in primary and middle school talking about boarding school, and they made it sound like fun. What I imagined was a bunch of girls living together in a kind of boardinghouse, no parents around, nobody telling them what to do.

I started secondary school at St Prosper's College in September 1991. I was wildly excited. I had my trunk packed days in advance. My father drove me to school on a Sunday, just the two of us. We arrived around midday, and I started having second thoughts as soon as we got there. I'd pictured a big, homey boarding-house. The school I saw was an impersonal-looking institution with three separate buildings, a boys' dorm, a girls' dorm, and the school proper. I'd imagined the school in the center of town, near lots of people and cars and activity. Instead it was on the outskirts of town in a very quiet rural area with nothing else around. Since most of the students hadn't arrived yet, the campus, too, was very quiet. It looked lonely, deserted.

'Uh, I think I made a mistake, Yaya. I don't think I want to stay here.'

He laughed and patted my hand. 'You'll be fine.'

We got out of the car and went to the office, where he filled out a bunch of forms and paid my fees. While he was doing that, I was told to go over to the girls' dormitory, where someone would help me carry my things to the dorm. When I saw the dorm my spirits sank even lower. It was a big room with two rows of bunk beds facing each other. Three or four beds were already made up. The rest were bare. I was assigned to one of the lower bunks, then shown to my storage locker, which was in a separate room. We were supposed to keep everything in our lockers except for a few personal items like soap and bathroom slippers. I almost fainted when I saw the bathroom. The showers were communal. No walls, no doors, no privacy – just a big tiled room with a row of shower heads along the wall. Shower naked? In front of other girls? I'd never shown myself naked to anyone in my life.

I was very, very depressed by the time I came back out to meet my father.

'I don't know, Yaya. I don't think I can do this.'

'You'll be fine. You'll see. It's just all new and strange now.'

'Do you really think I'm going to be OK in this place?'

'Yes, Fauziya, I do. I wouldn't have let you go to boarding school if I didn't have confidence in you.'

'But I don't know anybody here.'

'You'll make friends, Fauziya. Don't worry.'

'What if I hate it?'

'Give it some time. If you really hate it, we'll talk about it.'

'Will you come see me?'

He laughed. 'Of course I'll come see you. I'm going to visit you a lot. You think I wouldn't come see my girl?'

That first year was rough. I studied fourteen different subjects, including history, English, math, office practice, accounting, commerce and economics. I had a good head for numbers and was interested in business. My father and I both liked the idea of my becoming an accountant. The courses were tough, but I worked hard, as I'd promised my father I would. I studied late into the night and got up early in the morning to study some more. I was working such long hours, it started to affect my health. The higher my grades went up, the lower my weight dropped. My father noticed both changes. 'Fauziya,' he said, 'it's good to study hard, but it's OK to eat and sleep too.' I eased up a bit after that, but not too much. I never stopped working hard. And my father never stopped keeping a close eye on my grades.

The social adjustment was at least as difficult as the academic one. After my father drove off that first day, I returned to my dormitory room to find several other girls who'd come in while I was gone. None of us even spoke to each other that day because we were all feeling so lonely and scared. Or at least I was. That night I cried so much I never slept. At five A.M. I got up and prayed and then rushed off to the communal shower room to bathe before any of the other girls got up. That became my strategy to avoid disrobing in front of anybody else – to shower early or, if I slept too late, to shower late in the afternoon when everybody else was in the library or in class.

My father was right, though. It took a while, but eventually I adjusted and made friends, two in particular. I met my first good friend, my dorm mate Lisa, who was from Ghana, when she came up to me in our dorm one day and invited me to do my homework with her. We eventually became so close that I was even comfortable showering in front of her, although I was never able to do it with anyone else. I met my second friend, Okasha, in one of my second-year classes when the teacher made us deskmates. Ghanaian on his mother's side and Lebanese on his father's side, Okasha was tall and skinny and very white, the first white person I ever got to know. Until I got to know him, I had thought that white people were different from me somehow. He said, 'No, Fauziya. My skin is a different color, but that's the only difference between us. Other than that, we're both the same.' He taught me that it doesn't matter what a person's color is. We're all human beings. We all have the same heart.

My father was pleased with how well I was doing. And he kept his word and came to visit me often, usually every two to three weeks. Generally he came alone, because my mother didn't like to leave her stall, but sometimes Alpha or Asmahu came with him. Often he brought food my mother had sent from home.

I got to go home at least three times a year; there was a two-week break from just before Christmas to early January, a week during April, and a long summer vacation beginning in midsummer. Though we also had term breaks to divide up the three twelve-week terms, I didn't usually go home for them, because they were just long weekends.

During my summer break I went to *madrasah*. My first summer home I had thought about trying to get a part-time office job so that I could start practicing what I was learning at school, but my father talked me out of it. He wanted us to be able to spend time together. So did I.

I also wanted to spend a lot of time with Amariya, whose own mother, my grandmother Hajia Maimouna, had just died. She had gone to Mecca that summer, where my parents had sent her on hajj. My father had sent his mother a few years earlier, and then decided to send his mother-in-law, too, because she had never been. We were all so excited for her. My parents gave her extra money to do some shopping while she was there, and she asked each of us to tell her what we wanted her to bring back. I told her I wanted a *choka* – a short chain necklace – and she promised to bring me a nice one.

When it was time for her to return, we all went to meet her plane in Lomé. We saw a woman we knew getting off the plane, but we didn't see my grandmother. When we asked this woman, who was a distant relative of ours, if she had seen Hajia Maimouna, she said, 'Oh, she's on the next plane.' Where I come from people don't like telling other people things they know will trouble or grieve them. But the truth finally came out because when her husband heard what had happened, he said she had to tell us. As she then explained to us, my grandmother had one brief dizzy spell in Mecca but was well and active all the rest of the time, going on the various pilgrimages, shopping, enjoying herself. As they were waiting to board the plane to return, however, she told this woman, 'I'm going to rest for a while. Wake me when they start checking us in.' She stretched out on a mat on the floor, put her handbag under her head to use as a pillow, and fell asleep. But when it was time to wake her, she was gone. Gone to heaven. That was my mother's only consolation in her terrible grief, because we believe that any good Muslim who dies during hajj goes straight to God. The day was June 22, 1992.

My mother never saw her mother again. My grandmother was buried in Mecca that same day, for our religion requires that burial take place on the day of death. So the gifts she had bought us in Mecca turned out to be her farewell to us. I received a beautiful, delicate chain necklace and matching earrings made of Arabian copper and set with pretty red stones. I cried when I got them, because they were so beautiful and because they were from her. Now I had this necklace as well as the last strands of beads she had given me. Before, I'd always thrown my old beads away when they wore out or the strand broke, because I knew my grandmother would give me more. These I would have to take very good care of and save forever.

My mother was still grieving when I went back to boarding school that September, but she's a strong person, and assured me she'd be OK. She must have felt awfully lonely that fall, however, because a few months after her forced circumcision Asana left to go back home to her family in the north, and my brother Babs, the last of my parents' children who'd still been at home, came to Ho with me. He was starting at a school of design that was just a short walk away from St Prosper's College. It was a perfect school for him because he's always been good with his hands, always had a natural talent, passion, and flair for designing and building.

That period marked the beginning of a real change in my relationship with Babs. Because we were both homesick, we visited each other fairly often. Instead of fighting, we actually started to enjoy each other. I guess we were both growing up.

Our father couldn't come pick us up for Christmas break that year, so he sent one of his drivers to bring us home. What did we do during those two weeks? I can't remember. Nothing special. I turned sixteen that January 1. My mother fasted on my birthday, as usual. My father didn't give me a present that year. He'd given me a beautiful gold wristwatch with tiny diamond chips set in its face for my fifteenth birthday. 'Because you're becoming a beautiful young woman now,' he had said, 'and should have beautiful things.' I wore that wristwatch all the time. There was a long wrap-skirt I'd admired in a shop window, which I asked him to buy for me for my sixteenth birthday. Ayisha had one in that same style, and I always wanted what Ayisha had. My father said he would get it, but he hadn't gotten around to it by the time he drove Babs and me back to school at the end of our vacation. I reminded him about it after he dropped us off.

'Don't forget about my skirt, Yaya,' I said as he was leaving.

'I won't. I'll bring it with me in a couple of weeks on my next visit.'

'Promise?'

'Promise.'

That was Sunday, January 10, 1993. I was sitting in class a week later, on Monday morning, January 18, when someone came into the room and said something quietly to the teacher. The teacher nodded, then called my name.

'Fauziya?'

'Yes, sir?'

'You're wanted in the principal's office. Would you go there right now, please?'

Why would the principal want to see me? I couldn't imagine. When I arrived at his office, he was sitting behind his desk, holding a piece of paper.

'Fauziya, please sit down. I've just gotten a telegram. You're wanted at home immediately. You have to leave now.'

Go home? Why? Why would I – Something's happened. Something bad has happened.

'Please, sir, can you tell me why?'

The principal became uncomfortable, and started repeating himself. 'You're wanted at home, Fauziya. You should leave right now.'

It was bad. It was something very bad. 'Please, sir. Please, tell me. What happened? Why do I have to go home?'

Finally the words came out: 'I'm very sorry to have to tell you this, Fauziya, but your father has died.'

No. No. That was impossible. He must have made a mistake.

'No. That's not true.'

'Fauziya, you have to go home right away.'

I ran out of his office crying. Back in my dorm I stopped only long enough to grab my purse before running the several blocks to Babs's school. Still crying, I ran into his principal's office. 'Please, sir. Can you call my brother? We have to go home.'

'Why?'

I didn't want to say it. Maybe if I didn't say it, it wouldn't be true.

'What happened?'

I had to say it. 'Our father just died.'

He sent someone to fetch my brother, and then the next thing I knew the two of us were racing to the bus station to board the next bus for Kpalimé. That was the longest bus ride I've ever been on, my mind busy the whole time with fantasies that this was all a mistake. We'd get home and Yaya would be there and he'd be so surprised to see us and then we'd all have a good laugh.

We were the first off the bus when it finally arrived in Kpalimé. We half ran, half walked the rest of the way home. When we walked in the door, we saw that the house was filled with people. My mother was sitting in a chair across the room. My sisters and brother Alpha were gathered around her. She looked up at me. Her face told me everything.

I felt myself falling. Someone caught me and carried me sobbing to my mother's side. I collapsed in front of her and buried my face in her lap. 'No, no. Oh, Amariya, no.'

She stroked my hair. 'Oh, my poor baby. I'm so sorry.' She called Babs over and held both of us while she explained what had happened.

My father had died sometime around two or three A.M. on Saturday, January 16. My mother had sent a telegram later that morning, telling us to come home immediately so we could see him before he was buried. But the school office was closed on weekends. Nobody had seen the telegram until Monday. He'd already been in the ground for two days by the time we reached home. I would never see his face again.

Yaya was gone, and I never even got to say goodbye.

My mother told us everything. Yaya had started having problems late Friday evening, just as they were going to bed. He began coughing and wheezing and asked for his inhaler. But this time it didn't help. My mother wasn't worried, though. He'd had bad attacks before, during the January dry season and she thought this one, too, would pass. He went to bed, but he couldn't sleep. He kept getting up, using the inhaler, going back to bed, then getting up again. 'Oh, Zuwera, it's really getting bad.' My mother still wasn't worried. She gave him stronger medicines to try. When medicine after medicine didn't help, and his breathing became more and more labored, my mother started feeling very uneasy. It was time for him to start distributing his worldly goods the way he always did when things got bad during an attack. But he didn't do that this time. He lifted an arm and gestured for her to come lie down beside him.

That's when she knew.

My mother lay down beside her husband. He put his arms around her and held her close. He could barely breathe now. He spoke to her softly between rattling breaths. 'I bless you, Zuwera. You have been a good wife to me. God bless you and the children. May God be with you always. Take care of the children. Stay strong for them. Keep heart. Remember we are one. I'll always love you, and I'll always be with you.'

A little later his breathing stopped. Amariya closed his eyes, and then lay down beside him again to spend one last night alone with her husband.

At five A.M., she rose and prayed for him, then sent word out that Alhaji had died. While Amariya did the ritual bathing of my father and dressed him for burial, Alpha with the help of other men in the community dug his grave, for that is the duty of the oldest son. They buried him later that day.

Babs and I stayed home from school for almost two weeks. People came and went all that first week, consoling us, bringing us food. The house was constantly filled with people, and yet it felt empty, so strangely, achingly empty. It used to be that when my father went away for weeks at a time on business, his spirit still filled the house. Now his spirit was gone, and the house felt hollow and cold, no matter how many people were there.

I don't know how Amariya endured. She'd lost her mother in June, and six months later she lost her husband. But as tenderhearted as my mother is, she's strong. Her faith gives her strength. She'd cry, but when she heard us crying she'd try to console us. Soon she'd have us reminiscing, talking about all the happy times we remembered, the funny things he'd done, the way he teased us, and then we'd find ourselves laughing, not crying. Soon enough we'd be crying again, of course, but the laughter helped carry us through.

A second, larger funeral service was held the following Saturday. It's customary to hold a second funeral a week or two after a person has died, to allow time for news of the death to spread. That way people who don't live nearby will also be able to mourn him. The mosque was filled to capacity for my father's second funeral service. People came from all over to mourn his passing. It made my mother and all of us children feel very proud to see how many people had loved him. Everyone came back to the house afterward to offer condolences. Some people brought food. Some gave Babs and me gifts of money because they felt especially sorry for us as the youngest, the only ones who weren't yet fully grown when our father died. Everyone tried to comfort us by talking about what a good man my father had been. 'Try not to cry. Remember Allah loves you, and Allah loved your father. He always takes those he loves most.'

Later that afternoon my uncle called my sisters and brothers and me to his house, where he and some of the other elders in our family had gathered in the small room he had set aside as a mosque. It's customary when a man dies for the family elders to gather the children together to offer them counseling and advice. We didn't want to go, but we had to. My uncle was the head of our family, and he was also now the legal guardian for Babs and me because we were not yet adults. We walked in and sat on mats on the floor. I sat next to Babs and held his hand. Ayisha was crying. All our other relatives spoke first. They all had kind words for us. 'Don't be sad. Try to be strong. Remember how much your father loved you. We all have to go through this together. You're not alone. Everything will be OK.'

Then it was my uncle's turn to speak. 'These are my words to you,' he said. 'Your father is dead. He's dead, and he spoiled all of you. Especially you, Fauziya. He spoiled you the worst. He treated you like some fancy ornament he couldn't stop admiring. Well, that stops now. There'll be no more of it. I don't have time for that.'

I felt as if my heart were being ripped out of my chest. How could he speak to us like that? How could he be so cruel? Did he feel no sympathy for us at all? No love for his own brother? I wanted to get up and run out of the room, but I couldn't. My brothers and sisters and I had to show respect. For our father's sake and my mother's sake, we had to sit there and listen. I buried my face in my hands and sobbed. My sisters were all crying too. Alpha and Babs were stoic.

'What are you crying about?' my uncle said. 'I don't see why what I've said should make you cry. Are you crying because your father is dead? Well, he's dead. And there will be no more spoiling.'

That was it. Those were the words of counsel and advice my uncle chose to give us in our time of grief. He seemed very proud of them. The room was now silent except for the sobbing sounds coming from my sisters and me. Our other relatives didn't say a word. I don't know what they thought of what my uncle had just said to us. Perhaps they were shocked, but they wouldn't have said anything to him even if they were. He was the head of our family. He could speak to us any way he liked.

Ayisha stood up and walked silently out of the room. The rest of us followed, one by one.

That was the beginning of the end.

11

Nightmare

Babs and I went back to school two days after the second funeral. One of my father's drivers took us. I hadn't wanted to go because I was reluctant to leave Amariya, but we all knew how highly Yaya valued education and how important it was to him that we do well in school. My sisters were there to watch over our mother, and Amariya's sisters had come to stay with her for a while, too, so I felt a little less bad about leaving her.

I went to classes; I studied as best I could. But it was a very, very hard time for me. I felt dazed, numb. I tried to pay attention in class, but my mind would not stay put. It kept floating off to some other place – a place where my father was still alive. My father had dropped me off here, at school, how long ago? Just about a month ago. I'd often gone longer than that without seeing him. He was just off on a trip somewhere. He'd be back. I'd see him soon. This weekend probably. And he'd bring me that new skirt, like he promised. Ha! And he'd tell me all about the new clothes he bought for himself while he was away. 'Oh, Fauziya, wait until you see them. They're so beautiful you won't believe it.' Oh, Yaya. You're so funny.

But no matter how hard I fought it, I could never completely block out the truth. No, Fauziya. Your father will not be coming to see you this weekend. Or the next weekend. Or the one after that. He's dead, Fauziya. You have to accept it. He's gone.

Everyone at school knew, of course. Everyone said, 'I'm sorry. I'm so sorry.' But mainly people just let me be, which was what I wanted. My friend Okasha was kind. I could tell that he really felt bad for me, but he didn't try to make me talk. I was grateful. My friend Lisa would sit with me in the dorm. She didn't try to make me talk either. But if she heard me crying in the middle of the night, she'd come to me and hold me.

I saw Babs as often as I could. He was my only real comfort. He was my baby brother, but he watched over me like a big brother. We watched over each other. We had to, because there wasn't anyone else at school who could really understand.

We returned home in April. One of my father's drivers, the same one who'd brought us back to school, came to pick us up. It was good to see my mother again. I'd been worried about her. Nobody wrote to us while we were at school, so I didn't know how she was doing. When we last saw her, she was still grieving deeply. She cried sometimes, but mostly she was just quiet, quieter than ever.

The whole house was quiet. Quiet and empty. Ahmed and Adjovi had both left. There wasn't any work for them anymore. Sweet little Asana had returned to her family. All my sisters were married. Alpha was long out of the house, having moved in with his boss's family to be near his job on the out-skirts of town. And now even Babs was in Ho, at boarding school, with me.

My greatest desire as a kid was to have a whole bed to myself. Now I had a whole bedroom to myself, and all I wanted was for things to be the way they used to

125

be, with the house filled with family and me sleeping on a mat on the floor.

At least my aunt stayed away. I didn't see her at all during that break. That was a blessing. I saw my uncle when I went to *madrasah,* but he kept his distance too. We greeted each other politely. Beyond that we didn't speak, which was fine with me. All we'd ever asked of my aunt and uncle was that they leave us alone. It was beginning to look like maybe now they finally would.

When our school break ended, I said a worried farewell to my mother. As Babs and I got into the car that would take us back to Ho, she reassured us that she would be fine. She told us that no matter what happened to her from then on, she would be happy because her husband had blessed her before he died. As the car drove away, I turned and waved to her, but I don't think she saw me. Her head was down.

My grades had suffered badly the previous term, but spring term I did a little better. I was able to concentrate more. I measured my progress in how long I could pay attention in class without floating away, how many paragraphs I could read in a book without drifting off, and how many hours I went without crying. Sometimes I could go the whole day without breaking down, but I always cried at night. Though I still kept pretty much to myself when I wasn't with Babs, the wound in my heart was beginning to close, at least a little. And yet, there were still moments, when I least expected them, when it could rip open again. I'd be walking to my dorm or my class and I'd see someone wearing an especially nice shirt or driving a handsome nice car, and I'd think, 'Oh, Yaya would really like—' And then I'd catch myself and start to cry.

One of our relatives came to pick us up when school let out for the summer. I was eager to get home. No-one had written or come to visit us that term either, and I was anxious to see my mother. We arrived back early in the afternoon. I was sad to see that her stall was still closed, for I'd hoped that by now she would be feeling well enough to go back to work again. But the stall was empty. I got out of the car and ran into the house.

'Amariya! We're home!'

My aunt, Hajia Mamoud, walked into the room. Oh, God, what was she doing here? I greeted her politely and headed for the kitchen to look for my mother.

'She's not here,' my aunt said.

'Excuse me?'

'Your mother. She's not here.'

'Oh. Where'd she go?' Maybe she was at the market.

'She left.'

'Left? Left for where?'

'She went to be with her family in Benin. I'm staying here while she's gone.'

I felt like I'd just been punched in the stomach. Everything tilted and spun. My mother was gone? How could she just leave without even telling us? Couldn't she have waited until we got home? How could she just leave us here with our aunt! I felt a wail rising up inside me. My aunt stood watching my reaction. No! She would not see me crumble. I turned and walked woodenly out of the room, went to my bedroom, collapsed on my bed, and cried for a long while.

I stopped crying eventually and lay on my bed, trying to make sense of things. I was still angry. But I tried to see my mother's side. She'd been through so much loss, so much pain. Alpha and my sisters came to see her when they could, but they had their own lives now. Babs and I were gone too. Maybe things had just gotten too lonely for her, and she really did need to spend time with her family. Maybe she had wanted to wait until Babs and I got back, but then someone had offered her a ride and she decided to take advantage of the opportunity. Or maybe she thought she'd be back before we got home but had somehow gotten delayed. There was no knowing, no point in speculating, and no reason to take my anger and disappointment out on my aunt. There was nothing to do but make the best of things until Amariya returned.

So I did. I was polite to my aunt. I showed respect. I even kept silent when she moved into my mother's bedroom, which really upset me. I went to *madrasah*. I was polite to my uncle. I read. I watched TV. I kept myself busy. But I was still angry. Whenever I went to visit my sisters or Alpha came by to visit me, I couldn't help grumbling.

'I wish she hadn't done that. She could at least have waited until we got home.'

My sisters and Alpha made excuses for her. 'We know how you feel, Fauziya. We miss her too. We all miss her. But she really needed to see her family. Try not to be too upset. You just have to be strong and try to get along with Awaye, OK?' ('Awaye' means aunt, and that's how we referred to her.)

Easy for them to say. They weren't living with her. I decided to get away from the situation by going to see Ayisha. I'd been spending a week with her in Lomé during every long school break since she got married, so there was nothing unusual about this, and my aunt had no objections.

I went down by passenger van a few weeks later – but not one of my father's. My father's drivers were no

128

longer around to take me. They'd all drifted off in search of new jobs.

Ayisha and her husband, Abass, and their beautiful son, Ayatollah, lived in a rented room in a *n'gwa* called Agoi. Cramped as the accommodations were, I was so glad to see Ayisha. We greeted each other warmly and I teased her because her head was uncovered. 'Ayisha! Where's your scarf!' She laughed. I always teased her about that. She didn't hold to the custom of keeping her head covered at home. She went bareheaded even when company came over. Our mother knew, but it didn't bother her. 'She's a grown woman,' Amariya would say. 'What she does at home is between her and her husband.'

My mother's respect for other people's beliefs was one of the things that made my mother so special. But I was still angry at her.

I asked Ayisha, 'How could she just leave us with Awaye like that?' I started crying. 'Couldn't she at least have waited until we got home?'

Ayisha sat down across from me, looking very serious.

'Fauziya, I have to tell you something.'

'What?' I said belligerently. I was tired of the speeches all my siblings were giving me about how my mother had needed to see her family and I was going to have to be strong and try to get along with my aunt. Didn't anybody care about my feelings, my needs?

'Fauziya, look at me.'

I wouldn't look at her.

'Fauziya, please.'

I looked up. She was gazing at me tenderly. Her eyes looked tired, troubled, sad.

'Fauzy. Amariya didn't want to go. She had to go.'

'Why? Why didn't she wait until we got home?'

'Because she couldn't.'

'But why couldn't she?'

Ayisha sighed wearily. 'Because they made her leave, Fauziya. They sent her away.'

That's how I learned the truth. My sisters and Alpha hadn't told me because it was too hard for them. Besides, it wasn't their place. It was Ayisha's place, as the eldest, to tell me what had happened. My aunt wasn't just staying in our house for a while. She was living there. My aunt and uncle had done what they'd always wanted to do and now had the power to do – gotten rid of my mother.

Under tribal law, everything my father had owned now belonged to them, his house, his vans, his money, everything. Even Babs and I, the only two children left in the house, were now theirs. They'd allowed my mother to remain in the house for four months and ten days in accordance with tribal law. Then they'd given her a share of his money – the widow is supposed to get one third – and they'd told her to go. My mother hadn't gone off to visit her family for a while. She was never coming back. She'd been evicted from her home. I'd lost my father. And now I'd lost my mother too.

I went hysterical with rage and grief. Ayisha held me and cried with me. How could my aunt and uncle have done this? My mother never hurt them. She'd never hurt anyone. But they'd sent her away and broken up what was left of our family.

'Where is she?' I asked Ayisha. 'Where did she go?'

Ayisha wasn't sure. Benin, she thought, where most of Amariya's family lived. Or maybe Nigeria, where one of her sisters lived. When Amariya had gone to see Ayisha before she left home, she had told her she was going to stay with her family, but she hadn't said where. It depended on who had room to take her in. But she would almost certainly be leaving Togo because, like Ayisha, all my other sisters lived with their husbands in small rented rooms, and Alpha lived in his boss's house. None of them could afford their own homes yet, so they had no room for my mother. Besides, my sisters' husbands wouldn't have liked it. My mother knew that and wouldn't have stayed with my sisters even if they'd wanted her to. She was very traditional when it came to honoring the husband as head of the household, and would never have allowed herself to be a burden or irritation. She told Ayisha she'd send a message when she settled someplace, but so far there'd been no word. It isn't easy for people to communicate long-distance where I come from, because most people don't have telephones.

'How did she seem?'

'Calm. Strong. She said we shouldn't worry. She said to tell you she was sorry she had to leave but that you should be good and respect Awaye. She said Yaya would want that.'

My aunt. My aunt had lied! She'd let Babs and me believe that our mother had just gone off and left us, when in fact she knew the real reason Amariya left. I never wanted to see my aunt again. But I had no choice. I had nowhere else to go. I had to go back and live in my father's house with her until I returned to school.

I didn't say anything to Awaye when I came home from visiting Ayisha. I wanted to, but I kept all my thoughts and feelings to myself. When she greeted me upon my return, she could see that I now knew the truth, and I was sure she knew how I felt about it, because as soon as her eyes met mine she looked away.

131

I told Babs what I'd learned when he returned home from visiting with friends later that evening. He couldn't believe that our aunt had been so underhanded. 'All this time she let us blame Amariya for deserting us,' he said. But he took the news much more calmly than I had. No tears, no hysterics – at fifteen he was almost a man, after all. He was angry but rational, reassuring me that we would have to endure our aunt's presence only until we went back to school in September. Of course, since Babs spent most of his time with his friends, away from the house, this was going to be much less of a problem for him than for me.

I got through the rest of the summer as best I could. I was polite but distant. Before I'd gone to visit Ayisha I used to eat with Awaye. I didn't do that anymore. Nor did I ever voluntarily sit in the same room with her, not to read or watch television or anything. I came when called, did as told, and then retreated to my room.

I saw my uncle when I went to *madrasah*.

'Hello, Fauziya, how are you?'

My father had just died. My aunt had sent my mother away and was now living in our house. He knew that. It could only have happened because he had said it should. How did he think I was?

'Fine,' I replied.

I spent as much time as I could with my sisters. I'd go visit them, help them cook, eat with them. But I couldn't stay with them. There wasn't any room. In the evening, I had to come home.

I prayed. I read the Qur'an. I went to *madrasah*. I studied. I watched TV when my aunt wasn't watching it. I wrote to my friends Lisa and Okasha in Ghana and Aziz in Libya. I counted the days until school resumed.

Finally September came and Babs and I boarded the bus back to Ho. I'd have walked all the way if I had to, I was so desperate to get away from my aunt.

I was a lot happier when I got back to school. Not really happy, but happier than I'd been at home. I had my friends and my schoolwork. I had Babs just down the road, and I had Mr Bawa, my favorite teacher, who'd taken a special interest in me my first year at school and now seemed to go out of his way to keep my mind occupied with interesting and challenging work.

When Babs and I went home for Christmas break, nothing had changed. And all was still the same in April, when we went home again. Ayisha had heard from my mother by then. Amariya was in Nigeria with her sister. She wasn't sure how long she'd be there, but that's where she was for now and she had said that we shouldn't worry about her, she was fine. I cried in relief. I still didn't know when or if I'd ever see her again and I missed her terribly. But I thanked Allah that she was OK.

When I went back to school after spring break I worked harder than ever. School was all I had now. I had finished three years of secondary school, and had four more years before I finished. I wanted to go on to university after that. Nobody in my family had ever even gone to secondary school, much less university. My father and I had talked about my going. That's one of the reasons he had kept such a close eye on my scores and grades. If Yaya had lived, he would gladly have paid the costs. My aunt and uncle were a different story. I knew how they felt about educating girls, and since they controlled the family finances now I'd have to figure out some other way to go. Maybe I could get a scholarship. If not, I'd have to get a job.

But I'd worry about that later. At that point, I had to focus on my studies.

My father's passenger vans were gone when Babs and I came home from school at the end of that school year. I didn't ask my aunt what had happened to them and she didn't tell me. My sisters and brothers didn't know either.

'She must have sold them,' Babs said when we discussed it.

'Then Amariya should get a third of the money, shouldn't she?'

'Yeah, I think so.'

'You think she got any?'

Babs shrugged. We couldn't ask. That's just not done. We'd never know.

I resumed my old summer routine, going to *madrasah*, studying, spending whatever time I could with Alpha and my sisters. I still hadn't forgiven my aunt for sending my mother away, but now that I knew my mother was all right, I relaxed a little. I went back to eating with my aunt, and watching TV with her. I tried to stay on good terms with her, but it wasn't easy. She'd begun complaining about all the money my parents had wasted sending my sisters to school.

'For what?' she'd say. 'Look at them. They're all married now.'

Yes, I thought to myself, and except for Asmahu, who has a stall in front of her house, they all have jobs they wouldn't have if they hadn't gone to school. Narhila is a secretary, Shawana is doing catering work at a local restaurant, and Ayisha is a dressmaker. But I didn't say anything. It wasn't my place and it wouldn't have served any purpose.

'It's a waste of money,' she said one evening as we

were sitting and watching TV. 'You know how to read and write. That's enough.'

Oh, so now we were talking about me. I ignored her. I didn't care what she thought. She could complain all she wanted as long as she kept paying my school fees.

'Think about it, Fauziya,' she said a few days later as we were eating together in the kitchen. 'You're just going to end up married and spending the rest of your life in the kitchen. You don't need any more schooling. You've had enough.'

My stomach got queasy. She couldn't be serious. She wouldn't take that away from me too. She couldn't. It was all I had.

I stayed calm. Maybe she was just testing the idea out on me to see how I'd react.

'Of course I have to go to school.'

'I don't think so. I think you've had enough.'

'No, I have to finish. I have to go to school.'

She let the subject drop.

It was around this time that my aunt began talking about Ibrahim Ishaq, who seemed to be a new person in her life. 'He's a very respected man,' my aunt would say as we sat watching TV together. 'A very powerful and respected man. Very wealthy, you know.'

'No, I didn't know that.' I'd never heard of him.

'Oh, yes. He's the leader of Fiakomé.'

'Really.' That was a different *n'gwa*. Maybe that's why I'd never heard of him.

'Oh, yes. Anytime anyone wants anything done, they go to him. He fixes the roads, he helps build schools. He donates a lot of money to the *madrasah*, you know.'

'Really?'

'Oh, he's very well known for his charity. He gives

135

money to the mosque, he helps the poor. I hope you'll have a chance to meet him soon.'

'Yes, I hope so too.'

It sounded to me like my aunt was in love. It sounded like she might be getting married again soon. God, I hoped so. If she married this Ibrahim Ishaq and went to live with him in his *n'gwa,* maybe she'd let my mother come back home. I didn't catch the name of his tribe but I figured he must have been Tchamba-Koussountu, because I couldn't see my aunt marrying someone from a different tribe. My aunt told me that Ibrahim was forty-five years old, which would make him a good ten years younger than my aunt, but that didn't seem to bother her. I could only hope he felt the same way.

I was sitting on the porch reading one day a few weeks later when a tall, thin, pleasant-looking man approached.

'Hello, Fauziya,' he said.

I started a little. I'd never seen this man before. How did he know my name?

'I'm Ibrahim,' he said, smiling. 'Your aunt has told me a lot about you. Could you tell her I'm here, please?'

I went inside to get my aunt, then returned to the porch until my aunt came out. I wanted to be courteous to her suitor. When my aunt came out, I excused myself politely and went into the house.

'She's really beautiful,' I heard her friend say.

An hour or so later my aunt called to me. 'Fauziya! Could you come here, please? Ibrahim is leaving. He'd like to say goodbye.'

Did my aunt say please? She must be really trying to impress him.

I came out to say goodbye, and as we exchanged

pleasantries he handed me some money. Gee, maybe he really was rich. He was nothing like the impressive-looking figure I'd imagined from the way my aunt had described him, but he seemed to have money, and he was pleasant enough. I thanked him and went back into the house to let them say goodbye to each other in private.

My aunt came to find me as soon as he'd left. 'Well? What do you think of him?'

I couldn't believe it. She sounded just like the girls at school when they had a crush on some boy. What difference did it make what I thought?

'He seems like a very nice person,' I said. He did. He seemed perfectly nice.

My aunt was pleased. 'Oh he is,' she said. 'He's a very nice man.'

He came to visit about once a week after that. I was always polite. He'd ask me to bring him a glass of water and I'd bring it, and he'd praise me to my aunt. 'She's such a respectful girl.' He was always friendly. 'How are you today? How was *madrasah*?' I'd answer politely, then excuse myself until my aunt called me out to say goodbye.

'Well, what do you think?' my aunt asked after every visit. And I always answered favorably, because I wanted to do everything I could to encourage her feelings and speed this romance along. I kept hoping that if nothing else, it would distract her from the subject of my schooling, but it didn't. When she wasn't complimenting Ibrahim, she was complaining about the cost of sending me to school. Soon we were arguing every day about my returning to school, and the arguments were becoming more and more heated. Instead of softening her heart, her new romance seemed to be hardening it.

We were sitting at the table eating one afternoon in early July. Ibrahim had visited earlier that day.

'I told him you're not going back to school,' my aunt said.

Why had she told him? What business was it of his?

I began to panic. 'But why! Why can't I go back! I have to finish!'

'No, that's behind you now.'

'Behind me? What are you talking about?'

'You know how you're always saying what a nice man Ibrahim is?'

Why did she keep mentioning him? I just looked at her, puzzled.

'Well, he likes you too. He wants to marry you.'

'Marry me!' I exclaimed, shocked.

My aunt got angry.

'I'm not joking. I'm quite serious.'

'But I don't want to marry anybody! And I certainly don't want to marry him!'

'Stop it. You don't mean that and you know it. You like him. You've said so many times yourself. You're always saying what a nice man he is.'

'Yes! Because I thought you wanted to marry him!'

My aunt was taken aback. 'Me!'

'Yes! I thought he was going to marry you.' It would have been funny if it wasn't so horrific.

My aunt was silent for a moment. 'Well. He's a nice man, and he'll take good care of you, so there's nothing to be afraid of. You already like him. You'll learn to love him in time.'

This was some kind of bad dream. 'I won't do it! I'm not getting married.'

My aunt was steel. 'You will marry him, Fauziya. He is forty-five and can take care of you. It won't be so bad. He already has three other wives.'

My eyes opened wide. 'Three wives! He has three wives?'

She ignored me and continued. 'And once you are circumcised, you will learn to love him.'

My alarm grew. 'What? No! I don't want to be circumcised. Awaye, my parents would never do something like this to me. Why are you doing this?' I pleaded.

'Your mother was here and I told her all about it.'

I was stunned. 'Amariya was here? You saw Amariya?' Surely she was lying, just as she'd lied before.

'I don't care if you believe me or not. The fact remains that you're marrying Ibrahim, and your mother knows all about it.'

A few days later I went to visit Ayisha. Would she tell me the same thing my aunt had?

She did and she didn't. My aunt had been telling the truth. But she'd left some things out, Ayisha explained when I went to see her. Ayisha told me that while Babs and I had still been at school, my aunt had sent Amariya a message telling her to come to Kpalimé. My mother, who was by this time back in Benin, came as requested. She could only come when called or invited, and she could only stay as long as permitted. My aunt had summoned her to tell her that a man wanted to marry me. Ayisha told me that my mother pleaded with my aunt to let me finish school and kept saying that I was just a kid. But my aunt told my mother that she didn't need her permission or approval. In fact, my uncle, as my legal guardian, was the only person who could give or withhold approval. I believe my aunt told my mother of her plans for me mostly to see her suffer.

According to Ayisha, Amariya cried and begged my

aunt to reconsider. My aunt was unmoved.

Amariya went straight to Ayisha to tell her what my aunt had said. But there was nothing they could do for me. My mother had no home of her own now, and my brother and sisters couldn't hide me. My aunt and uncle would find me and claim me. I was their property now. They could do with me as they liked. That was tribal law.

I had to resist. That was my only recourse. I figured if I resisted hard enough, my aunt would get tired and relent and send me back to school just to be rid of me. My only hope was to try to wear her down.

Now when Ibrahim came to visit, I avoided him. I stayed in my room until he left. If my aunt called to me while he was there, I didn't respond. If I came home from *madrasah* and saw him sitting on the porch with my aunt, I'd turn and walk the other way. I wanted her to know my feelings. And I wanted him to know them too.

August came. It was time for my aunt to start buying the things Babs and I needed for the next school year – our shoes and uniforms and supplies. My aunt bought them for Babs, not for me. She meant it. She really meant it. I wasn't going back to school.

'Please! Please! I have to go back to school! I have to!'

We were sitting in the kitchen.

'No, Fauziya. You're not going to school. You're getting married.'

'No! No!' I was yelling at her now, screaming, out of control. 'I'm not getting married! I won't!'

I'd never yelled at my aunt before. She was enraged. She kicked hard at the edge of the seat I was sitting in and sent it tumbling over backward, with me in it. The back of my head struck the floor with a loud *thwack*.

'Don't you ever, ever, raise your voice to me!'

I got up off the floor and ran to my room, holding my head and crying. I threw myself on my bed and sobbed.

Awaye began training me, making me cook and clean and do laundry. I wasn't very good at any of it. I did it, but badly, which made her furious. I didn't care. I became less respectful and responsive. Before, I'd always come when she called me. Now I often didn't. The more I ignored her, the more furious she got. Soon we were at war. Babs got caught in the crossfire. My aunt was yelling at me all the time now, and she began yelling at Babs too. He didn't speak back, but whenever she raised her voice to him, he'd glare at her just long enough to make her feel uncomfortable, and then turn and walk out of the house. He could do that. He was a boy. Not even so much of a boy anymore – almost a man.

I thought I could wear my aunt down, but I was wrong. She would wear me down. I couldn't fight her. She was too powerful. My will to fight would slip away.

September came. Babs left for school. I walked him to the bus station. I was numb. He hugged me before he got on the bus. I gave him a limp hug back. He looked at me with concern. My eyes filled with tears.

'Are you going to be all right, Fauziya?'

I shrugged.

'Try to be strong.'

I started crying as Babs turned away from me to board. As the bus pulled out onto the road I walked beside it, still crying, eyes glued to Babs's face in the window, until there was nothing to be seen in the distance except a puff of dust where the bus had been.

And then there was nothing for me to do but turn back and go home.

Ibrahim didn't come around anymore, but that didn't seem to mean anything. My aunt was still talking about my marriage. She hadn't changed her mind. Just her tone.

'You'll be happy, Fauziya. You'll see.'

'I'm not getting married!'

'Don't worry. You'll feel differently after you're circumcised. It'll really help calm you down. Then when you start living with your husband you'll start to love him and you won't even remember there was a time when you didn't want to marry him, because you'll love him so much. You'll really feel attracted to him, and you'll want to respect him and obey him. You won't want anybody else but him.'

Wanting somebody else was not the problem. 'I don't want to get married! I'm too young!'

'Lots of girls younger than you get married, Fauziya.'

'But I want to go to school!'

These arguments would go on until I'd run out of the room, holding my ears. How could she do it? How could she force me to marry a man I didn't love? A man I barely knew? A man almost thirty years my senior who already had three wives?

'Please, please,' I'd beg my aunt. 'Don't do this to me. Let me just finish two more years of school. Please.'

But she never wavered from her plans.

September passed. I continued going to Arabic school. It was all I had now. I kept praying and reading the Qur'an. I spent as much time as I could with my brother and sisters. And I kept resisting. No matter how many times my aunt brought up the subject of my marriage, I kept saying no. It was the only thing I could do, the only way I could fight her.

She kept saying, 'You're getting married.' But she never said, 'You're getting married a month from now,' or 'You're getting married in two weeks.' I thought she was waiting for me to finally surrender and say, 'OK.' But I'd never say it. Never! I'd keep saying 'No!' forever. She won't force me, I thought. As long as I keep saying no, she'll wait. I clung to that hope. I honestly believed it, until the morning I woke up and saw the dresses and jewelry laid out on the bed.

12

Marriage

On Monday, October 17, 1994, I woke up as usual around five-thirty A.M. to do my ritual ablution and pray. Afterward, I went back to bed, slept a few hours, got up, got dressed, and left my room. Then I heard my aunt calling me from her bedroom. My mother's bedroom. My aunt had repainted and redecorated it. It was her room now.

'Fauziya! Come here!'

I ignored her.

'Fauziya!'

I knew she'd just keep calling louder and louder until I came, so I went. The door to the bedroom was open. My aunt was up and dressed, standing beside the bed with her hands clasped in front of her and a pleased expression on her face.

'Look!' she said, gesturing toward the bed.

Laid out on the bed, all neatly arranged, was a handsome display of women's clothing and accessories: two elegant dresses made of very fine cloth, one, yellow satin, the other, blue cotton with gold lace; a matching headscarf for each; two handbags and two pairs of shoes; two new sets of undergarments, bra and panties; and a collection of expensive- and delicate-looking gold jewelry, bracelets, necklace, ring, earrings. Everything was exquisite. There was also a candle, a fancy veil, and bathroom slippers.

'Aren't they beautiful?' my aunt said, beaming. 'And they're all yours.'

'What?'

'It's all yours! It's from your husband!'

'I don't have a husband!'

'You will soon, Fauziya. Today's the day.'

'What!'

'You're getting married today.'

'But how could I be? It's Monday!'

Weddings aren't held on Monday. They start on Thursday or Friday or Saturday or Sunday, but they are not held on Monday!

'Yes, I know,' my aunt said cheerfully. 'But your husband wants the ceremony performed today. So it's today.'

'No! No!' It couldn't be! She'd given me no sign, no warning. We'd fought again only yesterday.

'When you get married . . .' she said, and I exploded. We'd been having these fights every day for months now. But she'd given me no sign that the 'when' was to be the next day. She'd tricked me.

I began sobbing hysterically. 'Please! Don't do this! Don't do this to me!'

'Now, now,' she said lightly, waving a hand. 'There's nothing to get upset about. You're going to be fine, Fauziya. You'll see. Don't worry about the circumcision. We won't do that today. We'll wait until Wednesday for that. Today and tomorrow are going to be busy days.' She clasped her hands to her breast again and gazed down at the bed. 'Just look at all these beautiful things, Fauziya. You're going to look so pretty!'

This wasn't happening. It couldn't be happening! I ran to my room howling, slammed the door behind me, threw myself on the bed, clutched a pillow to my chest, and curled into a tight little ball.

My aunt rapped on the door. 'Fauziya.'

'Go away!'

She opened the door and walked in. 'Fauziya, someone's here to see you,' she said brightly.

The *nachane* walked in behind her, the same *nachane* who'd bathed my sisters for their marriages.

'Where's my bride? Where's my bride? Oh, there she is! Isn't she beautiful!'

I started to whimper. She came to my bedside, smiling and crooning. 'Oh, my baby. My sweetheart. Don't cry. You should be happy on your wedding day!' She went to take my hand. 'Come on now. You know the ritual.'

I clung to my pillow. 'No! No!'

'Fauziya, stop it!' my aunt said, irritated. 'She's just here to bathe you!'

The *nachane* caught my aunt's meaning. She clucked at me gently. 'There, there. Don't worry. There's nothing to be afraid of. We're not going to do that today. Today's your wedding day! You'll need time to rest.' She took my hand again and pulled it gently but firmly. 'Come on, now. I'm not going to hurt you.'

At that moment I left. No-one knew it. No-one saw it. I was still there, but I wasn't there anymore. The part of me that couldn't escape was still there. The part that could, ran away to some other place, and watched unseen, untouched, as the *nachane* pulled me upright, helped me to my feet, and led me unresisting down the hallway to the food-storage room. Inside, the younger woman who'd done the intricate stenciling on Shawana's and Asmahu's hands and feet was already preparing the *laylay*. When my sisters had gotten married, there'd hardly been space in the room

146

for a chair. To watch I'd had to sit on a bag of rice, surrounded by all the food and supplies we always had in storage. Now, like my mother's bedroom, this room was completely changed. Where once it had been full to overflowing, it was just a small, barren room with a tiny window, mostly empty shelves, a concrete floor, and some buckets, mops, brooms, and other cleaning supplies in one corner. Empty, empty – everything was empty now.

The *nachane* chattered and cooed over me as the younger woman worked on my hands and feet. I said nothing. I was a rag doll. I let them do what they wanted.

Afterward, I had to sit and wait for the *laylay* to dry. The *nachane* and the *laylay* artist sat with me for a while, trying to engage me in cheerful wedding-day banter. When I didn't respond, they fell silent. 'Maybe you'd like a few minutes alone,' the younger woman said. Still I didn't respond. They left the room. I looked at my hands and feet. I was a married woman now. The religious ceremony hadn't happened yet as far as I knew, but according to tribal custom, I was now somebody's wife. The *laylay* designs are like a branding. Once they're applied, a woman is considered married.

My aunt had won. I let my hands fall limp in my lap, leaned back against the concrete wall, and stared at the ceiling, trying to grasp this reality. I would never go back to school. That part of my life was over, just as my aunt had said. This was my life now. I had to accept it. Lots of girls married men they didn't love. They managed somehow and I'd have to manage too. No! I couldn't think like that! I had to fight this! They were going to cut me. It would hurt terribly. Maybe I would even die. My mind raced with thoughts of death. Some moments I feared it, others I longed for it, seeing it as my only escape.

An hour passed that way, two hours, three hours. Or maybe it was only ten minutes. I lost all track. People had begun arriving at the house. Women came back to the storage room to look in on me. My aunt's friends. I didn't know them. 'Oh, there she is! Oh, look at her! Isn't she beautiful? Oh, and look at her beautiful designs! Oh, I wish they'd been doing these designs when I got married. Aren't they lovely? Oh, I'm so happy for you!' I stared at them vacant-eyed. They went away.

The *nachane* reappeared. 'OK, my friend,' she said cheerfully. 'We have to take a shower now.' She led me into the family bathroom and closed the door behind us. Buckets, calabash, towel, bathroom slippers, soap, sponge, and all the other traditional accessories for the ritual bathing of the bride were arranged and ready. She'd turned a bucket upside down over the shower drain for me to sit on. She patted it. 'Here we go, my sweetheart. You sit here. Take off your clothes.'

I shrank back. Take off my clothes? I'd showered naked in front of my friend Lisa at school, but no-one else. The *nachane* prodded me gently, chattering and reassuring me to ease my discomfort. 'Oh, my sweetheart. I know, I know. Children are always shy. I was shy, too, on my wedding day. Come on, now. Don't worry. I've been doing this for years. Don't be shy.'

I took off my clothes, sat down on the bucket, and bent my chest to my knees to cover myself. 'There, now, you see? That wasn't so hard, was it? Oh, and look how beautiful you are. Your husband is going to be so happy! Look at my lovely bride.' She began praising me. *'Traore. Traore.'* Then she dipped a calabash into the water and began performing the ritual bath,

148

praying and speaking to God as she poured the water, calabash by calabash, over my head, hands, feet, and other body parts. 'Oh, God, we are cleaning this girl to be a good woman and wife. We're washing her to be a good mother . . .' I didn't hear most of it. My mind kept floating away. When she'd finished washing me she announced: 'You're no longer a girl now. You're somebody's wife. When you were a girl, you talked and laughed and played with your friends. But you're a married woman now. You have to respect and obey your husband . . .' She went on like that for a while. I saw her lips move, but her words kept fading in and out.

She left me there to take a second shower while she went to bring me a change of clothing. When she came back she had a long skirt and long-sleeved blouse she'd taken from my closet, and the long veil I'd seen on my aunt's bed, and she helped me dress and cover myself with the veil so that no skin was exposed except for my face and hands. I covered myself like that five times a day when I prayed. I'd veiled myself countless times. Why did this feel so different? I lifted my arm, testing the weight of the fabric. It was light, just like the veil I wore while praying, yet it felt like the weight of the world had just been draped over me.

The *nachane* took my hand and led me out of the bathroom into my aunt's room, where the *laylay* woman was waiting. They removed the veil, sat me in a chair, and talked happy bride talk as the younger woman did my hair and makeup and wrapped and pinned my turban. Then the two of them helped me into the beautiful yellow dress. 'OK, stand up now.' I stood up. 'Lift your leg.' I lifted my leg. 'Lift your arms.' I lifted my arms. They were playing dress-up with a doll that responded to commands. 'Oh, look at her. Oh, isn't she gorgeous?' Chattering away, they adorned me with bracelets, necklace, ring, and earrings, and guided my feet into a pair of shoes. 'Look how well the shoes fit her feet. Oh, this man really knows his bride.' 'Look how good she looks in that dress. It's exactly her color. Oh, her husband really knows her tastes.' 'Look at this jewelry. Oh, this man really wants her. My goodness! Look at all these fine things.'

They were fine things, the clothing, the shoes, and the jewelry. Everything was very beautiful and expensive-looking, finer than anything my sisters had received from their husbands. It was very unusual for a man to give his bride anything beyond the ritual bath items, and perhaps a dress or two a month before the wedding.

My aunt came to the bedroom to check on me at some point during this process. 'How's everything going in here?' she called cheerfully from the doorway. I lifted my eyes and looked into hers as she was about to step into the room. She stopped, stepped back. I held her gaze, watched her expression harden, saw fear come into her eyes. That's right. Look closely. Look well. Behold your brother's daughter on her wedding day. Feel what I'm feeling right now. Toward my husband. My marriage. You. Do you feel it yet? Yes, you're beginning to. I can see it in your eyes. Feel it more, my aunt. Feel it the way I feel it, if you can stand it.

She couldn't. She turned and walked away. The doorway was empty again, and I was empty again. Empty, hollow and numb. The *nachane* and her assistant took me back to my room, where I would remain for the rest of the day. Snatches of women's conversation drifted in from the living room as more of my

150

aunt's friends arrived to congratulate her.

Except for a congratulatory visit by a girl from the neighborhood, whom I barely knew, I continued to sit alone. Because I'd gone to school in Ghana, I had no friends in my own town. Besides, what friend who truly loved me would have wanted to congratulate me on such a terrible day? Had my sisters heard the news, I wondered.

Then, without warning, I had several new visitors: Ibrahim's three wives trooped into the bedroom. They came in order of seniority, first wife, second wife, third wife. The first and second looked a lot older than me, the third looked closer to my age.

'Oh, look at my baby,' the first wife said as they entered. 'Isn't she beautiful.' Strange. She sounded like a mother praising a daughter. But I wasn't her daughter. I was her husband's new wife. She came in and sat on the other side of the bed with her back to me, facing the wall. The second wife sat down in front of me on one of the mats my aunt had spread on the floor for visitors. The third sat down on the bed to my right, put her arm around my shoulders, and started talking immediately.

'Look at us! We're almost the same age! And we even look alike. Why, we could be sisters! Oh, I'm so glad our husband picked you! This is going to be wonderful. We're going to be so happy together. You'll see.'

The second wife sat smiling up at me. 'Welcome to the family, Fauziya. You're going to be our new sister. You're going to love living in our house. Our husband is so wonderful and caring. If you respect him, he will love you.'

'All you have to do is obey our husband and do what he asks,' said the third wife, 'and everything will be fine. And look at you! You're so beautiful! He's going to love you so much! Why, I bet he'll give you anything you ask for.' She nudged me playfully. 'And then whenever I want something, I'll ask you to ask him, and you can get it for me!' She and the second wife laughed gleefully. They went on like that for a while.

I just stared at them. They sounded so happy, as if they really got along and liked each other. And they seemed so thrilled that their husband had decided to marry me. Were they for real? I was the new wife! Their husband was going to sleep with me. He was going to prefer me for a while at least, because I was the newest and youngest. They knew it, I knew it, and yet they didn't seem jealous at all. Was such a thing possible? Or was this some kind of act they were putting on for my benefit? The only thing I could figure was that they were happy because they both had someone new to boss around now. As the new wife, I'd have to answer to and do for everybody, my husband and all three senior wives. Maybe that's why the third wife seemed so particularly happy about having me in the family. Finally she wouldn't be at the bottom of the hierarchy.

The first wife didn't join in any of the joking and giggling. She let the other two wives carry on for a while as she sat silent behind me on the bed. When she finally did speak, the other two wives immediately fell silent. There was no doubt about who was queen of this household.

'Well, Fauziya, I'm not here to joke with you or play with you,' she said slowly in a low, grave voice, still sitting and facing the wall. 'I'm happy to welcome you to our household, but you must know your responsibilities. You're no longer a child. You're a married woman. You're starting a new life. The life you lived in your parents' house is over.'

I felt a stab when she said that. Yes, it was over. It had ended twenty-one months ago almost to the day, the day my father died.

'From this day on, you must treat your husband with the same respect and obedience you showed your father,' she said. 'And you must treat your husband's other wives with the same respect you showed your mother. You must honor us and obey us as you did her. You must trust me and respect me most of all. If you do that, there's nothing to be afraid of. You'll have to work, of course. You'll cook, clean, go to market, wash dishes. You will have your own room, as we all do, which you'll be responsible for keeping clean, and you'll clean your husband's room, but the work won't be too hard. You won't ever have to do more work than you're able. We're all going to be living together, and we all need to help each other. If anything is troubling or bothering you, you must come and talk to me. You must never be afraid to come talk to me just because I'm older. If you remember these things, we will all be happy together.'

I didn't speak a word after this speech. Eventually a few of my aunt's friends drifted in and chatted with the wives. Women's talk swirled around me. When someone came in with a camera, the first wife came to sit at the foot of the bed, still facing away from me, for the picture. More time went by. And then, at a signal from her, as quickly as the three had come, they were gone.

An hour passed, two hours. More. Less. I had no idea how long it was between their departure and the arrival of three more women, this time women I desperately wanted to see: my sisters Narhila, Shawana, and Asmahu. As soon as I saw them in the doorway I started to cry. They surrounded me, held me, cried with me. How had they heard? The question washed into my mind and then out again, carried away in a flood of grief.

'Oh Fauziya, we're so sorry,' Shawana said, crying and holding me. 'I wish we could help you! But there's nothing we can do!'

I knew that, but it was such a comfort to have them near me that I could only thank Allah for this kindness. They would have to leave me before day was done. But they were here now. That was all I would think about.

We sat and talked. We even laughed a little. My sisters couldn't help commenting on the clothes and jewelry I was wearing. As a child I always tried to make them jealous. Now I really did have better things. Their wedding clothes hadn't been nearly as fine. But my sisters had all been so happy on their wedding days. They would have been happy wearing rags. I was dressed like a princess and all I wanted to do was die. The life I'd wanted for myself was over. I wasn't dressed for a wedding. I was dressed for a funeral. My own.

As my sisters kept apologizing over and over for not being able to help me, I couldn't help thinking how strange it was that, in a family as large as ours, there had only been one person out of nine who had any power. And now that that one person was dead, all of the rest of us combined counted as nothing in the face of the person to whom that power had passed when he died – my uncle. That was how things worked in our culture. My father had questioned and rejected a number of tribal customs and traditions, but he'd never questioned or rejected that one – the power of the patriarchy. Nor had I, until now. Maybe he would have, eventually, if he'd lived longer. He'd never stopped reevaluating his own beliefs about good and bad, wrong and right. But he was dead now. And I was living with the consequences.

My sisters stayed as long as they could. But they had to go home, finally, to cook dinner for their husbands.

'Oh, Fauziya, be strong,' Asmahu said, hugging me and crying. 'You've always been a fighter. Don't quit on us now.'

'I'll be praying for you,' Shawana said, her eyes glistening with tears.

'We'll all pray for you,' Narhila said. 'You'll come through this, and we'll stick by you through everything. We'll always have each other.'

As we all hugged one last time, none of us could stop crying. And then they were gone, and I was alone, and the numbness settled in again, and I felt nothing.

I sat for a long time watching the dusk fall. As my aunt's friends also began leaving, the voices from the living room faded out, until the whole house grew quiet. The silence was broken when my aunt strode briskly into the bedroom, holding a piece of paper in her hand. She'd armored herself this time. I saw it in her eyes. They were steel. She came and stood over me where I was sitting on the bed and thrust the paper at me.

'Write your name here,' she said. 'It's your marriage paper.'

'My what!'

'Your marriage paper. Your husband has written his name. The imam has written his name. Everyone has written their names. Here's where you write yours.' She thrust it at me again. 'Do it.'

I jerked back away from it. I didn't speak. I didn't move.

She threw the paper at me. It arced in the air and

155

drifted to the floor. 'Put your name on that paper, Fauziya! When I come back, I want it done.'

With that she turned and walked out of the room. As soon as she was gone, I broke down in tears. They'd done the ceremony at the mosque! I wasn't just married according to tribal tradition now. I was married according to religious law. I could be delivered to my husband that very night if he desired it. I wouldn't be because I hadn't been cut yet. That was the only thing left.

I did not love my husband. I did not want to be his wife. I would never sign that certificate. Never. That was one thing they couldn't make me do. I wouldn't even touch it. I left it on the floor where my aunt had thrown it.

A minute or an eternity had passed, I didn't know, when I heard a knock on the door. A soft knock, not my aunt's. Whose?

'Fauziya? Are you awake?'

Ayisha! I was in her arms before she was fully inside the room. I collapsed into her embrace, buried my face against her neck, and cried and cried and cried. She held me and stroked me and rocked me.

'Oh, Fauziya, I'm sorry, sweetheart. I'm sorry I'm so late. I came as soon as I heard.'

'Who told you?'

She'd heard the news through the Tchamba grapevine just that day. The Tchamba tribe is small. Everybody knows everybody and most everything about everybody. Someone had come up to her in Lomé earlier that day.

'Ayisha! What are you doing here? Why aren't you in Kpalimé?'

'Why should I be in Kpalimé?'

'Aren't you going to the wedding?'

156

'What wedding?'

'What wedding? Fauziya's wedding!'

Ayisha was taken totally by surprise. Nobody had told her. Nobody in the family had told my other sisters either, apparently. They'd all just 'heard.' My aunt had kept her plans very quiet.

'Stop crying now and tell me what happened today,' Ayisha said. 'Come on. Stop crying. That's not going to help. Tell me everything that happened.'

She looked very serious as she said these words, so I forced myself to do as she said. 'I woke up and Awaye showed me the clothes on the bed.'

'And then?'

'And then the *nachane* came and bathed me. She said she wasn't going to cut me until Wednesday.'

'Day after tomorrow. That's what she said?'

'Yes. That's what Awaye said too.'

'OK. Go on.'

I ran through the rest of the day, up to the moment when my aunt came in with the marriage certificate and demanded I sign it.

'Did you?'

'No.'

Ayisha went to pick it up from the floor, where it was still lying. She looked it over. 'No, you didn't. Good. That's good, Fauziya.' She folded it up and put it in her purse.

'Oh, Ayisha. What am I going to do?'

She came and sat down next to me and took my hands in hers. 'Stop crying, Fauziya, and listen to me. Do you hear me?'

I looked up at her, and saw strength. I grew calm.

'That's better. Now tell me again. Awaye said the circumcision wouldn't be until Wednesday?'

I nodded.

157

'OK. Don't worry. Nobody's going to cut you. I'm going to get you out of here before then.'

I laughed bitterly. 'And where are you going to take me? To your house? Ayisha, I'm married now! It's too late! You can't hide me anywhere. They'll just come and find me. You know that.'

'Fauziya, trust me. You're just going to have to trust me. I promise you. Nobody's going to hurt you. We're not going to let them.'

'Who's we?'

'Amariya and me.'

'Amariya! Is she here?'

'No, Fauzy, she's not. But we've been in touch. She's OK. She's fine. Now listen to me.'

I'd started crying again when she mentioned Amariya. I wanted my mother so much.

'Fauziya, stop it. Stop it. Listen to me now. Amariya can't come to you, you know that. But she's not going to let them do this to you. We're not going to let them hurt you. Do you understand?'

I nodded. I didn't understand anything. But I did know that Ayisha wouldn't lie to me. She'd never lied to me, and she'd always taken care of me. If she said she was going to help me, she would.

'OK, now listen carefully,' she said. 'Are you listening?'

'Yes.'

'OK. I'm not going back to Lomé tonight. I'm staying in Kpalimé. I'll come back tomorrow. I want you to stay calm and strong for me, OK?'

'OK.'

'Don't say anything. Don't do anything. When I leave, you just go to sleep. When you get up tomorrow, do whatever Awaye says. Can you do that for me?'

'Yes.'

'Good. Now, when I come back, you're going to have to help me. I'm going to need you to be strong and do just what I say, no questions and no arguments. Do you understand?'

'Yes.'

'All right. I'm going to go say goodbye to Away now. I'm going to ask her to let you walk me out to the gate. I want you to walk me to the gate and then come back and say good night to her and go to sleep. OK?'

'OK.'

Ayisha came back for me a few minutes later. I walked her outside to the gate of our compound. I wasn't allowed to go beyond it now. I wasn't to be seen in public until after I'd been delivered to my husband and started my new life as his wife. When we got to the gate, Ayisha hugged me.

'I'll be back tomorrow,' she said. 'Be ready. Stay strong.'

With that she left, and I turned and walked back into the house. Nothing about my situation had really changed. But now, I had hope.

13

Flight

My aunt was nice to me the next day. She spoke to me and treated me with a kindness, a tenderness, a warmth and concern she'd never shown me before. It makes me cry to remember it.

That morning, Tuesday, October 18, I came back to my room after my shower and found the second dress, headscarf, shoes, and set of underwear given to me by the man who was now my official husband all neatly laid out on the bed. This dress was blue, made of fine, light cloth, with gold threading and lace inserts throughout. I dressed myself, wrapped my hair, put on my wedding jewelry, and sat down on my bed. My aunt came to my room a few minutes later.

'Good morning, Fauziya,' she said softly. My aunt never said good morning to me. 'I thought you were still in the shower. How are you this morning?' My aunt never asked how I was. 'Are you OK?' Her voice, her eyes, her expression, her whole manner, conveyed genuine concern.

'I'm fine.'

'Are you hungry? Would you like some breakfast? Can I fix you something?'

'No thank you.'

'You need to eat something, Fauziya. How about some hot porridge? Can I fix you some porridge?'

'OK.'

'OK, I'll be right back.'

When she returned with the porridge, I accepted it politely, and waited for her to leave. She stood for a moment, hesitating, then sighed and sat down beside me on the bed. Neither of us spoke for a while. We just sat in silence. A sad silence. I could tell she was sad too.

'You're going to be fine, Fauziya,' she said gently. 'Really you are. You'll see.'

She was reaching out. And I felt myself responding, even against my will. Was she sorry for what she'd done? Now, when it was too late to undo it? Did she want me to forgive her? Say it was OK? I couldn't. I didn't speak. She sat awhile longer as the silence between us grew, and finally got up and left the room, quietly, as she had come.

We had no visitors that morning. My aunt stayed in her room. I stayed in mine, waiting for Ayisha. She hadn't said when she'd come. She might come at any minute. Or she might not come for hours. She'd just said, 'Be ready.'

Noon came and went. My aunt returned with some fried yams a friend had brought. 'I thought you might be hungry, Fauziya. You didn't eat your porridge this morning. You really do need to eat.'

'Thank you.'

'I brought you some water too.'

She stood looking at me for a moment again.

'Thank you.'

'You have to eat, Fauziya,' she said again, softly.

I kept my eyes lowered, and said nothing.

She sighed. 'Call me if you need anything, OK?'

'OK.'

She left, closing the door quietly behind her.

I love fried yams. I was starving. But I couldn't eat. I was too tense. Where was Ayisha?

One o'clock came. Two o'clock. I kept myself busy reading through old schoolbooks. I loved my books. Maybe Ayisha could bring them to me wherever it was she planned to hide me. Maybe I could even go back to school. No. School was expensive. Ayisha didn't have that kind of money. I looked around the room at my schoolbooks and notebooks and bookbag. I might never see them again after today. My aunt would probably just throw them away after I left. Wherever it was I was going.

Where was Ayisha?

My aunt looked in on me again at a few minutes before three. I was lying on my bed, still reading my books. The bedroom door was closed. She knocked softly, opened the door just a crack, and stuck her head into the room. 'Fauziya, it's almost three,' she said gently.

'Are you going to pray?'

'Yes, thank you.'

'OK. Just thought I'd remind you.'

She closed the door. Tears filled my eyes. My aunt knew how important prayer was to me.

I prayed. 'God, You know all things and You determine all things. Help me to be strong.' Ayisha had said I'd have to be strong. Where was Ayisha?

Four o'clock came. Five o'clock. Some women came to visit my aunt. I heard them talking in her room when I went to the bathroom.

Still no Ayisha.

Five-thirty. Six o'clock. Dusk began falling.

She wasn't coming. Something had happened. Something had gone wrong.

Six-thirty: My aunt came to my room, opened the

door, stuck her head in. I was on my bed. A school-book lay open and unread on my lap.

'Fauziya, someone's here to see you.'

Ayisha!

As I was about to bolt out of bed I remembered Ayisha telling me that I would have to appear calm at all times. I settled back again, unresponsive. It was my turn to give my aunt no clue that anything was about to happen. If anything was about to happen. Was it?

My aunt returned to her visitors. Ayisha came into the room and closed the door.

'Where were you!'

'Keep your voice down!'

I lowered my voice. 'Where were you? I thought you weren't coming!'

'I was waiting. We can't leave until it gets dark. I didn't want to come too early.'

'Oh God, Ayisha. What are we going to do?'

'We're going to stay calm, Fauziya. We don't know for sure, and she won't do anything while I'm here. So we're just going to sit here and talk until it gets dark.'

'Then what?'

'Then we're leaving.'

'Where are you taking me?'

'Somewhere they won't find you. That's all I can tell you right now, Fauziya. You'll just have to trust me and not ask questions. Can you do that?'

I nodded.

We sat and talked, waiting for darkness to fall. Ayisha talked mostly. She said she had money with her, the money my aunt and uncle had given Amariya before they'd evicted her. Amariya had asked her to keep the money until she found a place to settle for good, but when Amariya had come to see her after learning of my aunt's plans for me, she had told Ayisha

163

to do whatever she could to help me, and to give me the money if I needed it to go away.

Ayisha said her husband, Abass, was angry with her. When she'd told him the day before that she'd heard I was getting married and that she was coming to Kpalimé to see me, he'd told her not to. 'Leave it alone, Ayisha. It's a family matter. Don't get involved.'

She'd come anyway. She'd disobeyed her husband. It's a very serious thing in our culture for a wife to disobey her husband. Abass would not forgive her easily, if at all. She knew it. I knew it.

'What do you think he'll do?' I asked, worried for her.

She sighed. 'I'm not sure.' She gave my hand a squeeze. 'Let's not talk about that. Don't worry about me, Fauziya. I'll be fine. Besides, I had to come. Amariya and I couldn't just sit back and let this happen to you. We'd never forgive ourselves if we did, and you'd never forgive us either. We had to do something. I'm not sure this will work, Fauziya. It's in God's hands now. But whatever happens, you'll know we tried to help you. Remember that, Fauziya. At least we tried.'

Her eyes brimmed with tears. I was crying, too, now. I threw my arms around her neck.

My aunt knocked on the door just then. We dried our tears quickly. She opened the door and poked her head in.

'How're you two doing in here? Everything OK?'

'Yes, we're fine,' Ayisha said.

'Are you hungry? Can I bring you some food?'

'No, we're fine,' Ayisha said, smiling. 'Thank you for asking.'

'OK. Let me know if you need anything.' She closed the door and left. It was almost dark out now. I looked questioningly at Ayisha.

'Soon,' she said.

I looked around my room. 'Should I take anything?'

'No, you can't.'

We sat in silence for a few minutes, waiting for the darkness to become complete. My heart began to pound. Ayisha sat with her hands folded in her lap. Then she unfolded her hands and rose.

'OK,' she said. 'I'm going to go say goodbye to Awaye now. Then I'm coming back for you, so be ready. We're going to leave the house quietly. When we get outside, we're going to walk out the gate and down the street at a normal pace, a nice, easy, normal pace. Do you understand?'

I nodded. My voice was gone.

'You can't act scared, Fauziya. That's very important. You musn't do anything to attract attention. You have to walk normally. No looking behind you, no nothing. Can you do that?'

I nodded again.

She left the room, leaving the door half open behind her. I looked around the room frantically, my heart racing. My I.D. cards. I never went anywhere without my student and Togo I.D. cards. The dress I was wearing had no pockets, so I tucked them into the folds of my headwrap. What else? The necklace and earrings my grandmother had bought for me in Mecca, and an earring set, this one from Ayisha, a gift in happier times – I couldn't leave these things. I grabbed them and stuffed them into the folds of my headwrap too. Through my open bedroom door, I could hear Ayisha saying goodbye to my aunt.

Then she was back. 'OK, now. Let's go.'

I stood frozen in place.

'Fauziya, come on! We have to go!'

I couldn't move.

She came behind me, grasped my shoulders hard and shoved me forward to get my feet moving. 'Let's go, Fauziya. We have to go. Now!'

We slipped quickly and quietly past my aunt's room and out of the house, then slowed our pace and walked to the gate. Even if Awaye happened to see us, she might not think anything of it, since I'd walked Ayisha to the gate yesterday and returned without incident. We made it to the gate, walked on through it, turned left, and strolled slowly down the road, shrouded in darkness. I matched my pace to Ayisha's, fighting the impulse to run, braced for the sound of my aunt's voice.

She didn't call. We walked on, past one house, another house, turned a corner. A car was waiting.

'Get in,' Ayisha said.

The driver, whose identity I will never reveal and who will be in my prayers always, took us to the border. We got out of the car a short distance from the official crossing point, at a spot where people cross illegally through the forest. We could have crossed legally. But Ayisha was thinking ahead. She knew my aunt and uncle would search for me when they realized I was missing, and she didn't want any guard to remember seeing us. We walked through the trees to the Ghanaian side of the border. It was a scary walk. I never walk in the forest at night. But this time I had to. We emerged onto a road and walked back toward the official crossing point, looking for a car to take. Near crossing points there are always a lot of passenger cars dropping off and picking up customers, but because drivers charge by the passenger, most of them carry as many passengers as they can. Ayisha wanted an empty car. She strolled down the road, peering into cars. I followed behind her. One by one the cars filled up and drove away. It was getting darker and darker. I was becoming more and more frightened. The area was becoming deserted. What if we didn't find a car? Finally, an empty car came along and stopped in front of us. Ayisha strolled up to the driver's open window, leaned down, rested her crossed forearms casually atop the window, and talked to him for a while with her back to me. Then she waved me over. 'Let's go!'

We climbed into the backseat and the driver took off.

'Where are we going?'

'To Accra.'

Accra! Accra is the capital of Ghana. We had family there. Was that where I was going to live? With our relatives? When I asked Ayisha, she said no.

No, of course not. That wouldn't work. I couldn't stay with family, not even distant relatives. My aunt and uncle would know where to look for me, and whoever had taken me in would be in trouble. I was someone's wife now. You didn't help a wife run away from her husband.

So where were we going? Again Ayisha told me to trust her and not ask questions. I held my tongue. It was a long drive, in the darkness. When we approached the outskirts of the city, Ayisha leaned forward to talk to the driver.

'Take us to the airport.'

The airport!

'Ayisha! Where am I going!'

'I'm not sure yet, Fauziya, but you have to be brave. I'm getting you out of the country. They'll find you if you stay.'

My heart lurched. She didn't say 'You have to leave Togo.' That wasn't her meaning, and I knew it. I couldn't stay in Togo. I couldn't go to Benin. I couldn't stay in Ghana. People and information flowed easily through all three countries, as easily as we had crossed into Ghana through the bush. There was no place I could hide within the boundaries of this larger combined country where my aunt, uncle, or husband wouldn't eventually find me. I was going somewhere much farther away. Where?

I'd never been on a plane. The thought of flying terrified me. Whenever I saw a plane in the sky, I'd think, How does that thing stay up there? And I'd seen news reports about plane crashes. I didn't understand why anyone would do something so risky.

We arrived at the airport around eleven that night. When we got out of the car, Ayisha took my hand. It was trembling. 'Come on, Fauziya. Let's go.' She led me into the airport terminal. It was crowded and noisy and busy like the market in Lomé, but it didn't feel warm and friendly like the market. Ayisha turned to me. 'Wait here,' she said. 'Don't go anywhere. Just stand here until I get back.'

I stood frozen and watched her walk away. She approached someone – a man, a woman, I'd rather not say – gestured toward me, had a brief conversation, then returned. She explained to me that we would be put in touch with someone else, someone who might be able to help us. By this time my whole body was shaking with fear. I'd never traveled except to visit family and go to school. I'd never gone anywhere alone.

'Ayisha, I'm scared.'

'I know, Fauzy. But you have to be brave. You can't stay here. You have to go. You know that, don't you?'

I nodded. 'Yes, I know.' I did know. 'But I'm scared.'

'You have to be strong, Fauziya. We all have to be strong now. We have to have faith in God. That's what

Amariya said. She said, "Tell Fauziya to trust in Allah. He will protect her." She said to tell you she loves you and that she'll be praying for you.'

I started crying. Amariya. I hadn't seen my mother in a year and a half. I might never see her again. Or Ayisha. How could I face losing them, after losing my father?

Ayisha held me. She turned my face toward hers: 'Look at me, Fauzy. We can go back if you want. It's your decision. But you have to decide now. Stop crying and tell me what you want to do.'

I knew what awaited me if we went back. I couldn't go back. Amariya was right. I had to put my trust in God and go forward. Into the unknown.

'I want to leave.'

'You're sure?'

'Yes. I'm sure.' I stopped crying.

'OK. Then let's pray that this person can help us.'

We held hands and waited. The airport emptied out and quieted down. Finally, a man beckoned Ayisha over with a finger. She squeezed my hand. 'Wait here.' She got up and walked over to him, and the two talked for a long time.

When she came back, she said, 'It's all set, Fauziya. That man I was talking to helps people get out of the country. He told me he's taking other people out tonight, and he can take you too. I gave him some money, which he'll use to take care of your passport and ticket. There's a plane to Germany,' Ayisha said. 'That's where he's taking you.'

'Germany!'

'You'll be fine, Fauziya. He said he'll take care of you, but he told me to give you some instructions. He said you have to watch him and do whatever he tells you, but don't go up and talk to him. When he needs to talk to you, he'll come to you. Otherwise, you're to act like you don't know him. Do you understand?'

'Yes, I think so.'

'OK. He said he'll be on the plane but he won't sit with you. You'll be on your own. When you get off, he'll get you and the other people he's helping through customs, and then he'll take you wherever you want to go. He said he's been doing this for a long time so there shouldn't be any problem. But if there is a problem, Fauziya, if for any reason you don't get through, he won't come to help you.'

'What does that mean?'

'It means if you're stopped at customs, you cannot say that you paid him to help you.'

'What happens if I am stopped?'

'He said they'll put you on a plane and send you back. It's a risk we have to take, Fauziya. He said it hasn't happened yet, but you had to know that, OK?'

'OK.'

Germany! I didn't know anything about Germany! I forgot all about my fear of airplanes now. My mind buzzed with questions about what I'd do when I got *off* the plane. What would Germany be like? What would the people be like? Who would I meet there? How would I talk to people? What language would I speak? I didn't speak German. Where would I live? How would I live? Would I be able to go to school?

Ayisha opened her purse and took out a thick wad of bills. She held it out to me. 'This is from Amariya, Fauziya. It's three thousand dollars. It's everything that's left of the money she got when Yaya died.'

I started to cry. 'No! I don't want it. It's her money. She needs it.'

Ayisha took my right hand, laid it in her lap, opened my fingers, put the money in my palm, closed my fingers around it and held them that way. 'Take it, Fauziya. You'll need it, and Amariya wants you to have it. She said, "Ask Fauziya to please do this for me. Tell her it will make me happy. Tell her it's the only thing I can give her besides my love."'

'I'll pay it back. Tell her I'll pay it back.'

'She doesn't want it back, Fauzy. She just wants you safe. And she wants you to have this too,' Ayisha said as she opened her purse to reveal one of my mother's most treasured possessions, the *tasbih* she had brought back from her second trip to Mecca. I was so moved I couldn't speak. How many times had I watched her passing each of its 99 beads through her fingers. To touch those beautiful, hand-painted ivory beads was to be able to touch Amariya herself – a priceless gift.

An announcement came over the loudspeaker that a Ghana Airways flight was now boarding.

'That's your plane, Fauziya,' Ayisha said softly. 'You have to go now.'

No! Not yet! I looked around for the man, saw him standing off at a distance. He caught my eye, nodded, and turned away. I couldn't move.

Ayisha stood up, took my hands and pulled me to my feet. 'Come on, Fauzy. It's time to go.'

People were beginning to line up to walk through what looked like a freestanding door frame. The man began moving slowly in that direction. He'd told Ayisha to tell me to stay in front of him. She put an arm around my waist and walked me toward the line. When we were almost there, she stopped, turned me toward her, cupped my face in her hands, and looked long and tenderly into my eyes. Tears were streaming down both our faces. We wrapped our arms around each other and held each other close and hard.

'Be strong, Fauziya,' she whispered. 'Promise me you'll be strong.'

'I promise,' I whispered.

We held each other a moment longer. I didn't want to let go. I never wanted to let go.

'You have to go now, Fauzy. I'll stand right here and watch you until you're gone, OK?'

I withdrew my hands from hers. It was the hardest thing I'd ever done in my life. I joined the line. The man joined it two people behind me. I shuffled forward, my eyes on Ayisha until it was my turn to walk through the door frame. I didn't know what I was supposed to do. A guard stood beside it. I thought I was supposed to show some I.D. I stopped and reached up to my headwrap to take out my I.D. cards.

'Hey, keep it moving up there!' a voice boomed from behind me. The man's voice, I realized immediately. He was letting me know what to do. I was just supposed to walk through. As I did, I turned and looked back at Ayisha one last time. And then I walked through the doorway into a seating area, and Ayisha was gone.

The seating area was a long, narrow room with rows of chairs and a glass door that opened onto the tarmac. I sat down and waited. The man drifted over to stand beside me for a moment. He didn't speak to me. He just handed me a ticket and then drifted away again. The glass door opened and people began walking through it toward a plane outside, then up a ramp of metal stairs and into the plane. I stood and followed, making sure the man was behind me. A man and woman dressed in uniforms stood just inside the entrance to the plane on either side of the doorway. I saw the people in front of me showing them their tickets, so when I got to the entrance I held out mine.

'That's the first aisle to your right,' the woman said. And next thing I knew, I was on an airplane!

I walked down the aisle and found my row. I had a window seat, but I didn't think I could bring myself to look out when we were flying. I could barely look out while the plane was on the ground.

There were various announcements, someone helped me on with my seat belt, and soon the plane began to move. A few minutes later I felt my stomach drop as the plane gathered speed and rose into the air. Oh, my goodness! I was flying in an airplane!

When the plane stopped climbing and leveled off, men and women in uniforms came down the aisles with pushcarts, serving a meal. I couldn't remember the last time I'd eaten, but I was too nervous to eat now. Exhausted, I noticed a woman seated a few rows in front of me move to a line of empty seats in the middle section of the plane, lift up the armrests, and lie down across the seats as if they were a bed. There were other empty rows in the middle, so I decided to do the same thing. The next thing I knew, there was an announcement coming over the loudspeaker that the plane would soon be landing in Italy.

Italy! I thought. Wow! I'm not even in Africa anymore! I'm abroad! Then I started getting scared again. That meant we'd be in Germany soon. Germany was all white people. How would they treat me?

'Get up and fasten your seat belt,' a male voice said curtly. I looked up. It was the man. I sat up, and he sat down next to me.

'Do you know who I am?' he asked.

'Yes. You're the person who's going to take care of me.'

'OK, good. I'm going to talk to you now, and then I'm not going to talk to you again, so listen carefully. I

173

want you to do everything exactly as I say so there won't be any problems. When the plane lands in Germany, I want you to take your time getting off the plane. Let everybody else get off ahead of you. Keep an eye on me and make sure I'm behind you, you got that?'

'Yes.'

'There'll be six other girls besides you. You'll all be in front of me. Make sure I'm directly behind you. If you let yourself get separated from me, you're on your own.'

'OK.'

'We'll go through as a school group. I have the passports. When we get to the desk, I don't want you to talk. Don't do anything. Just stand there quietly. I'll take care of everything, OK?'

'OK.'

'Once we're in the country, you have to find your own way.'

'I do?'

'Yes, you do. Didn't your sister tell you that?'

'No. She said you'd take care of me.'

'Yes, I'll take care of getting you into the country, but I don't take care of you after that.'

'But I don't know what to do then.'

'Well, I'm sorry about that. You'll just have to figure it out. We're landing in Italy now. Stay on the plane. We'll be in Germany soon. Then do everything the way I told you.'

He got up and left.

I was going to be on my own! What would I do? How would I survive?

'Be strong,' Ayisha had said when we'd held each other for the last time. 'Promise me you'll be strong.' I had promised. But I was terrified.

The plane landed in Italy. People got off. Other people got on. The plane took off again.

'Trust in Allah,' my mother had said. 'God will protect you.' I prayed. And then the announcement came over the loudspeaker, in German, French, and English.

We were landing in Düsseldorf. I had arrived.

14

Germany

The plane landed in Düsseldorf at around nine A.M. on Wednesday, October 19, 1994. I did as the man had said and waited in my seat until everyone around and behind me had filed past, then got up and moved toward the exit. As I walked by his seat, he got up and followed me to the door. Five or six other girls fell into a loose group around me as we deplaned.

How did he clear us all through immigration? Did he move to the head of our group when we got in line? I can't recall. I do remember that he was standing at the counter when my turn came to approach the immigration officer. There was a stack of passports on the counter, blue ones and green ones, presumably including the one that was supposed to be mine. But I never actually saw it. The man spoke to the officer in a language that sounded like random noise to my ears. And then the officer addressed me in strangely accented English.

'Are you a student?'

I glanced at the man. He gave me a slight nod.

'Yes.'

'Here on vacation?'

Another nod.

'Yes.'

'Do you have money?'

Another nod.

'Yes.' I handed the officer the roll of bills. He counted it out: twenty $100 bills and ten $50 bills in American currency.

The officer's eyebrows went up as he counted. He looked at me curiously. 'Plan to do some shopping while you're here?'

Another nod.

'Yes.'

The officer took a corner of the outside bill between thumb and forefinger and glanced up at me again, eyes twinkling. 'Can I take one?'

I smiled shyly. 'Oh noooo.'

He smiled and handed the money back. 'You better put that money away somewhere safe, young lady. OK, have a nice stay.'

The man and I walked through. I was in Germany. Now what? Some of the other girls in the group walked over to where people were pulling luggage off a moving ramp and stood watching the ramp, looking for their own bags. The man walked in their direction. I followed, not knowing what else to do.

'Well, that's it,' he said without looking at me. 'You're on your own now. Good luck.' He walked away.

I stood alone, trying to figure out what to do next. I watched the man. He stood off a distance, waiting until all the girls had collected their bags, then herded them toward the lines of people in front of the baggage inspection counters. I joined one of the lines. The man and the other girls all passed through ahead of me. After all their bags had been inspected, he fell behind them again and they were swallowed up in a crowd of people passing through a big door.

'No bags?' the customs inspector said when it was my turn at the counter.

'No.'

Did he ask to see something? Did I show him something? Did he stamp something, give me something? I can't remember. I was in a daze. I joined the mob of people filing through the doorway into a concourse area. Directly in front of me, another group of people stood pressed up against a horizontal bar, scanning the crowd as we walked into the concourse. People were waving, shouting, calling to each other, hugging, kissing, laughing. I saw mostly white faces, a few black faces, no familiar faces of course. Nobody waved or called to me. Nobody even looked at me, really. I was invisible.

Where to go? What to do?

The concourse was vast, modern, clean, crowded. I'd never seen anything like it. People were rushing around in every direction, pushing carts filled with luggage, talking a language that didn't sound anything like any of the languages I knew or had ever even heard. Everyone was dressed in heavy clothing: sweaters, jackets, pants, skirts, socks, shoes, boots. I was wearing a thin, short-sleeved cotton dress and low-heeled shoes that were open at the sides. My arms, legs, and feet were bare. I was cold.

As far as the eye could see, the concourse was lined with stores. Bookstores, candy stores, toy stores, clothing stores, souvenir stores, and so on. Not knowing what else to do, I wandered along, looking in the shop windows, watching all the people rushing past me, hoping to see someone who looked African or hear someone who spoke English. But all I saw was a sea of white faces and all I heard was German. Eventually I walked into a shop that sold books and greeting cards and began looking at the cards, just to be doing something. A few of the cards were in

English. I picked one up and opened it and it played music! A singing card! I couldn't believe it. The lady shopkeeper came up to me.

'*Kann ich Ihnen helfen?*' I think she was asking if she could help me.

'I'm sorry, I don't understand. I don't speak German.'

She frowned and walked away. It was clear she didn't want me there, so I left. Next I wandered over to a shop that sold different cheeses and breads. I'd tried to eat a sandwich during the flight from Italy to Germany, but it had made me nauseous and I'd gone to the lavatory and thrown it up. I was starving, but all the food looked strange. I couldn't ask questions about it because I didn't speak the language, and all I had were American dollars, so I couldn't have bought anything anyway. I wandered on, from shop to shop to shop, until I came to the end of the concourse, then crossed to the shops on the opposite side and wandered back. When I'd completed my tour of the shops, I sat down across from one that sold china figurines. A man and woman who were chatting with one another in the shop happened to glance my way as I was looking at them, and the woman smiled in my direction. I looked over my shoulder to see who she was smiling at. There was nobody there. Oh. Me. But when I looked back, she'd returned to her conversation. I wished I had someone to talk to. I watched them a little longer, then got up and began wandering again.

Half an hour later or so, as I continued my wanderings, I saw the woman from the china shop standing in front of another shop, talking to someone else. Again she glanced up at me and gave me a little smile, then returned to her conversation. I kept walking for a long time, still hoping to hear someone who spoke English or appeared African. And then once again I caught the eye of the same woman, who was now seated alone at a table in a food concession area, drinking a cup of coffee. She was a short, solidly built woman with long, curly medium-brown hair, who looked to be in her thirties. She had a nice face, a friendly face, and she smiled at me before returning to the magazine she was reading. A lot of people had looked at me. Nobody had spoken to me. She was the only person who'd smiled at me. She'd smiled at me three times now. I had to try to talk to someone. Maybe she could help me find some African people I could stay with. I walked up to her.

'Excuse me,' I said in English.

She looked up and smiled again.

'Hello. My name is Fauziya. I was wondering if you could help me find some African people.'

Her face lit up. 'African! Oh, hallo! *Herzlich willkommen in Deutschland! Nett, Sie kennen . . .*'

'Wait! Please. I'm sorry. I don't speak German.'

'Oh. English? OK. Hello. How are you? I am fine.'

'Hello. Do you know where I could find some African people?'

'Oh, African goot! African goot!'

'Thank you. Could you help me find someone . . .'

'Yes! Yes! I help you.' She patted the empty chair next to hers. I sat down. 'You have address?'

'No, no address.'

'You have phone number?'

'No, no phone number.'

She looked confused. 'You have family? You have address, I take you.'

'No, no family, no address, no phone.'

She sat back in her chair and frowned at me. But

her frown didn't say 'Go away' like the frown the lady in the card store had given me. Hers was more puzzled. 'No family, no address, no phone,' she repeated. 'Why come Germany?'

It was hard enough to explain to someone who spoke the same language, which she didn't really. But she asked. She seemed genuinely interested. I had to try. It was an exhausting process for both of us. We made it through 'here alone, from Africa, family problem, no place to stay, no address, no phone.' I was trying for 'find African to stay with' when she waved a hand. She'd heard enough.

'You come my house,' she said.

I was startled. I wasn't sure I had understood correctly. 'You?' I pointed to her. 'Me?' I pointed to me. 'Your house?' I pointed to her.

'Yes! Goot! Goot!'

Stay with a white person? The thought had never occurred to me. And I didn't even know this person. She seemed nice, but she was a complete stranger. How could I possibly go home with her?

But what alternative did I have? I had nowhere else to go. I didn't know anyone in Germany. I was going to have to take a chance on trusting someone. If I passed up this chance, who knew when or if I'd be offered another? She'd been kind enough to talk to me, patient in trying to understand me. She liked Africans, she'd made that clear.

'OK,' I said. 'Yes.'

'OK, goot,' she said. 'We go.'

Her name was Rudina. She was a gift from Allah. She stood up and gestured for me to follow her. I had to hurry to keep up, as she walked through concourse after concourse at a rapid pace. Rudina walked briskly ahead, turning around every so often to call to me and hurry me along. 'We go! We go!' People stared at me. I knew I looked strange. Everyone else was wearing warm winter clothing, and there I was, scurrying along in my blue cotton dress with its gold threads and lace inserts, my headwrap and wedding jewelry, with Rudina calling after me. I felt like a circus animal following behind its handler.

At last we came to a descending escalator – something I'd never seen before – which took us out of the airport, down to an underground platform crowded with people. A train pulled in, the doors opened and people got off and on. Rudina gestured no. 'We wait.' I stared at the train in amazement. It was sleek and streamlined and modern – nothing like the trains in Togo. What a wondrous place Germany was! Trains, moving staircases, fancy shops, huge crowds, everything and everybody moving along so fast. I was dazzled.

As another train pulled into the station, Rudina took my hand and pulled me aboard. 'We go my car,' she said. 'Drive home.' She mimed holding a steering wheel. A man dressed in what looked to me like a policeman's uniform entered the car and walked toward us. I was terror-stricken. They'd found me! He was coming to get me! The man came and stood in front of us. I went rigid. Rudina opened her purse, took out a card, showed it to him and said something in German. He gave me a quick, cold glance, unsure what to make of me, handed the card back to Rudina, and walked away. A fare collector, a ticket taker. That's all he was. Yet my heart couldn't stop hammering for several minutes after he left.

As my terror subsided, cold set in. The train had emerged from underground, where we had been insulated from the weather outdoors, and was now running alongside a highway. I was freezing. As I rubbed my bare arms trying to keep warm, I noticed the *laylay* designs on my hands and feet. I'd forgotten all about them. No wonder the conductor had looked at me oddly.

After perhaps half an hour, we reached the place where Rudina had parked her car. When we got off the train and stepped outside, I thought I would die. It was bitterly cold and windy. I'd never experienced such cold. Rudina hurried me along, all but running through the immense parking lot. I wanted to run, but I couldn't. The open-sided shoes I was wearing were slightly too big and barely stayed on as I stumbled forward on my numbed feet. It seemed like an eternity before we finally reached her car. '*Mein auto!*' she announced as she rushed ahead of me to unlock the doors. When we got on the highway, she switched on the heat and sensation began to return to my frozen body parts. For the first time since I'd boarded the plane in Ghana, I remembered what it was to feel warm.

We drove about an hour north to the city of Bochum, where Rudina lived. I'd never seen such a place, so filled with people and cars and buildings and shops, everything so expensive-looking. Even the taxi cabs were fancy. They were Mercedes. I couldn't believe it. In Togo, only wealthy people, like my father, owned Mercedes. And then I saw the most amazing sight of all, a train running down the middle of the street. It pulled up next to us at a stoplight. '*Strassenbahn,*' Rudina explained when I pointed at it. 'Small train.' I was in awe. It was sleek and shiny and quiet. It didn't seem to make any noise at all. I felt like I was in heaven, except for the cold.

We drove on past the city to a quiet area of narrow

streets and two- and three-story buildings. Soon we pulled into a parking space near Rudina's home, which turned out to be a small second-story apartment as neat and clean and modern as everything else I'd seen so far. In the living room there was a beautiful rose-colored sofa that curved along two walls, a glass coffee table, television, stereo, VCR, and an exercise bike in a corner. There was also a cupboard filled with figurines, beads, and other pretty things, and lots of framed pictures of Rudina with people I assumed were family members. And she had an African wood carving of an animal-head mask on the wall! She saw me looking at it. 'Boyfriend African,' she said, patting her chest. 'Nigerian. No more boyfriend.' She shrugged. 'African goot.' So that's why she liked Africans.

She showed me her bedroom. She showed me the kitchen. All the rooms were tiny. When we got to the bathroom, she indicated I could take a shower. I was aching for a shower. It was midafternoon by then, and I hadn't bathed since the previous morning. I went into the bathroom, took off my wedding clothes, and climbed into the shower. The hot water felt wonderful. I checked my beads to see how they were holding up. I was still wearing the last strands my grandmother had given me, trying to take good care of them and make them last. I scrubbed away at the *laylay* designs and got most of them off. As I was washing, Rudina knocked on the door, opened it a little, reached in and put a pile of clothing on the toilet seat. 'Fauziya, this for you,' she said. After I had toweled off, I put on the clothes she'd given me: a pair of tight, stretchy exercise shorts to use as underwear, black socks, a pair of jeans, and two sweaters, one thin and one thick. The jeans fit in the waist and hips but were too short. I didn't care. Anything was better than wearing my wedding dress.

Rudina was sitting in the living room watching television when I finally emerged from the bathroom. Was I hungry she wanted to know, which she got across in sign language, pinching her fingers together and bringing them to her open mouth.

'Yes,' I said, imitating her sign language and nodding. 'Very hungry.'

She got up and went into her tiny kitchen to cook. When it was ready, she called me into the kitchen and set a plate of food in front of me: a clump of flat white noodles all stuck together with some kind of cream or cheese. I didn't especially like it, but I was so hungry I wolfed it down. My stomach rebelled. I ran to the bathroom and threw up. When I came out, Rudina helped me to the couch. She felt so bad! 'Oh, Fauziya! Sorry. Sorry.' She offered me various medicines, including milk of magnesia, but nothing helped. Then she picked up the phone, dialed a number, and began speaking in rapid German. After she'd hung up, she mixed some salt and sugar in a glass of warm water and handed it to me. How did she know?

'Good,' I said, smiling weakly as I drank. 'Thank you.' I patted my stomach to indicate I was feeling better. My stomach was anyway. It began settling immediately. The mixture Rudina had given me was the same remedy my mother had always used when my stomach was upset. It always worked. As the nausea subsided, waves of homesickness washed over me. I was so far from home, from everyone I loved.

Once my stomach settled, my appetite returned, but I didn't dare try to eat any more noodles. Rudina looked at me, concerned. 'What eat?' she asked.

'Rice,' I said.

'Chicken?' she asked.

'Oh, yes.'

'Chicken. OK. You stay. I go.' She put some rice on to cook, then grabbed her jacket and left the apartment. She returned ten minutes later with hot roast chicken she'd bought at a place near her house. It smelled so good! When the rice was ready, she called me back into the kitchen, sat me down, and served me a plate of roast chicken, rice with butter on top, and some french fries with mayonnaise. I'd never had french fries before, or mayonnaise either. Everything was incredibly delicious. It was the first real food I'd eaten in days. Rudina smiled with satisfaction as she watched me eat.

Now we talked again. She asked me questions and I answered them, both of us working hard to express ourselves and understand each other in a mix of sign language and rudimentary English. We began with my age.

'How old?' she asked.

'Seventeen.'

Her eyebrows shot up in surprise. 'Young!' she said. 'Where from in Africa?'

'Togo,' I said.

She nodded. She seemed to know of my country.

'Family in Togo?'

I nodded again. 'Yes. Brothers and sisters.'

'Father?'

'No.'

'No father?'

I shook my head, put my hands together as if praying, lifted my face to heaven, pointed up, folded my hands again and looked down. Oh, Yaya.

'Ohhhh,' she said softly. She looked sad. 'Mama?'

she asked gently. *'Mutter?'* She mimed rocking a baby in her arms.

'Mother?'

'Yes! Mother. *Mutti.* You have mama?'

'Yes,' I said. 'In Togo.' That wasn't exactly true, but it would have to do.

She looked puzzled. 'Why here? School?'

I shook my head. 'No. No school.'

'Why?'

We worked through it together step by step. 'Father die. Father's sister tell mother, "Go away."' I made a shooing motion with my hand. 'Father's sister make me get married.' I drew an imaginary wedding ring on my left ring finger with my right forefinger.

'No!' Rudina said. 'You too young!'

'Yes,' I said. Gradually we worked through 'Didn't want to marry. Didn't like man. Three other wives. Sister helped me run away. Came Germany. Here I am.' I didn't even try to explain *kakia*.

'Ach!' she said angrily, throwing up her hands and slapping them down on her thighs. *'Mein Gott!'* She looked at me, her face a mixture of anger and sympathy. 'OK,' she said. 'You stay with me. Don't worry I'm white, you're black. White, black, all good people. You stay, live here. Don't have to pay. When you have place to go, you go. Until then, you stay. No problem.' She smiled warmly.

'OK?'

I couldn't speak. I stared at her, at this good, kind woman sitting across from me, smiling at me, waiting for my answer. Tears filled my eyes. I sent up a silent prayer of thanks to Allah the Merciful, Allah my protector. I nodded. 'Yes,' I said, my voice a hoarse whisper. 'Yes, I'd like that.'

Rudina beamed. 'OK. Goot!'

And so my life with Rudina began. That night I slept on her couch, which became my bed, and the next day she began helping me get settled. She went through her drawers and closets and pulled out items of clothing. 'For you. You keep.' She gave me shirts, jeans, sweaters, socks, and exercise tights to use as underwear, as well as an old suitcase to use as a makeshift bureau. She showed me where the laundry was and how to work the machines. She showed me all the food in her cabinets and refrigerator and made clear I was to help myself to anything, anything at all, whenever I felt hungry. I liked that. That's how we did things where I came from too. She taught me the rules of the house, which mainly concerned housekeeping. She was extremely neat and got very annoyed when I was not, so I tried to do everything exactly as she did it.

When Rudina left the house in the mornings before I was awake – for work, I assume – she would set the table for breakfast and put some money for me next to the plate. Money for what? Where would I buy anything? I had no idea how to go anywhere or where anything was. After fixing myself breakfast and washing the dishes, I would go to the living room and watch television for a while. But everything was in German. Eventually I discovered something familiar – MTV! I knew MTV. There was a program from noon to one P.M. that I watched every day. But I kept the television on even when I wasn't watching it, just to keep me company. I tried to stay busy by washing the dishes, dusting, vacuuming, scouring the bathroom, and doing whatever else I could think of, but the apartment was too tiny and too clean to need much.

That was my life for the first few weeks. I woke up, showered, ate breakfast, cleaned the apartment, and watched television. I ate lunch, did the dishes, did laundry or whatever else I could find to do, then sat down and watched television again until Rudina came home. And I wrote one letter home, to Ayisha, telling her I'd arrived safely and explaining that I was staying with a very kind woman I'd met at the airport. As soon as I'd finished the letter I started to cry, thinking about my family and how much I missed them, wondering what they were doing as I sat watching MTV in a stranger's apartment in Germany.

During those first weeks I never left the apartment at all except with Rudina.

She was worried about me sitting alone in the apartment all the time. She wanted me to start venturing out. I still hadn't gone anywhere on my own. I went out with her – to the supermarket, to the shopping mall, to her aerobics class a couple of times – but never by myself.

I kept myself as busy as I could while she was away. I cleaned. I did laundry. I cooked rice and stew for dinner sometimes. She kept telling me I didn't have to do housework. 'No, Fauziya. Don't do. I do.' But I wanted to do something to repay her hospitality, and besides, it kept me busy. Housework and television – that was all I had to fill my time. And prayer. I couldn't live without prayer. When I first arrived I'd been too disoriented and depressed to pray. But now I'd begun praying again, using a big shirt Rudina had given me as a *mayahfi*.

So that was my life. Rudina had begun pushing me to expand it. She'd given me a key to the apartment so I could come and go freely while she was away, but I hadn't used it. Every night when she returned home, she'd ask what I had done that day, and frown at how little I had to report. 'Fauziya, you need go out,' she kept telling me. She told me how to ride on the bus and *Strassenbahn* to the shopping center. 'You go shop,' she said. 'No problem.'

I was scared. What if I couldn't find my way back?

'Ach,' she said, waving a hand. 'You smart. No problem.'

'No. I'll get lost.'

'Take phone number,' she said. 'You call. I come.'

I delayed for another week. She pushed for another week. 'Fauziya, you need go out.'

She was right. 'OK,' I said. 'Tomorrow, I go.'

She beamed and patted my hand vigorously. 'Goot! Goot! You go!'

The next day I watched MTV from noon to one, prayed, then got all dressed up in my new warm clothes, took a deep breath, and, for the first time, left the house alone. I was so scared! But I made it! I made it all the way to the shopping center, where I passed a couple of hours browsing through the stores before returning to the apartment. When Rudina came home that evening, she asked me, as always, what I had done, and I told her about my cleaning and TV watching and praying. Then she asked, as always, *'Und?'* And this time I had something to add.

'Und I went to the shopping center.'

She clapped her hands. 'Oh, Fauziya!' She squeezed my hand hard. 'Goot for you! Goot for you!'

I was so proud. I had somewhere to go now, a reason to leave the house. Not much of a reason, but it was something. I needed something to do besides sitting in front of the television, crying and missing my family. I needed a distraction, an occupation. Going to the shopping center became my occupation. I went every day after that. Each day I forced myself to go farther and farther away from the stores near the entrance, which was where I'd stayed that first day on my own, until I felt I could find my way anywhere within that mall.

My daily trips to the shopping center got me out of the house for a few hours, and took my mind off my worries: How long could I stay with Rudina? What if she got tired of having me there and asked me to leave? What kind of life was this even if she didn't? How long could I go on sleeping on someone's couch, watching TV, not going to school? I had to do something. But what? Why hadn't I heard from Ayisha? Didn't she get my letter? Had something happened to her? Had my family forgotten about me?

Going to the shopping center didn't solve any of my problems. But it helped me forget them for a few hours. I went every day, every single day, riding the *Strassenbahn* there and back.

That's how I met Charlie.

15

Charlie

I was on my way to the shopping center as usual. The *Strassenbahn* was crowded that day, so I had to stand. The man sitting in the seat in front of me tapped my arm and said something in German.

'I'm sorry,' I said. 'I don't speak German.'

'Would you like to sit down?' he asked in English. He stood up and gestured for me to sit. I sat down, thanking him as I did and feeling amazed that someone would be so kind to me.

He was tall, skinny, and black, a nice-looking man who appeared to be somewhere in his late twenties. He wasn't the first black person I'd seen since arriving in Germany – there were black people at the shopping center, and occasional black faces on the *Strassenbahn*, too – but he was the first black person I'd spoken to. And no black person had ever approached or spoken to me. The man stood beside me holding the back of my seat. I sat looking out the window.

Maybe I should try to talk to him, I thought. He was black. He spoke English. But he was a stranger. And he was a man. It's considered extremely improper where I come from for a girl to initiate conversation with a strange man. I'd never done it. I didn't know how.

'My name's Charlie,' he said, as though he'd

guessed my thoughts. He had a deep voice.

I looked up, still not sure he was speaking to me. He smiled. I smiled back. 'My name is Fauziya.'

'Fauziya,' he said. 'That's a pretty name.'

'Thank you.'

'Where are you from, Fauziya?'

'Togo.'

'Togo,' he said, smiling. 'That's great. We're almost neighbors. I'm from Nigeria.' He had a nice smile, nice even white teeth. 'Ever been to Nigeria?'

'Yes,' I said. 'I have an aunt there.'

'Really?' he said. 'Where?'

'In Ediaraba.'

'Oh, yeah. I know that area. A lot of Hausa people live there. Are you Hausa?'

'No. Tchamba.'

'I'm from the Bandar State. Ever been there?'

'No. Is that Ibo?'

'Yeah. That's my tribe.' He smiled. 'You look like you could be Ibo.'

'I hear that a lot. People in Nigeria are always telling me I look Ibo.'

I was talking to an African person! Oh God, it felt so good to be talking to an African. A couple of stops later, the woman sitting next to me got up and Charlie sat down. We talked and talked and talked. We talked about Nigeria. We talked about Togo. He asked me how long I had been in Germany and why I had come.

'It's kind of a long story.'

'Don't want to tell me?'

'Not really.'

'OK. No problem. So where do you live, Fauziya?'

'Here, in Bochum.'

'Staying with relatives?'

'No, a friend.'

193

'African friend?'

'No, German.' He was so full of questions! 'You ask a lot of questions,' I said.

He laughed. 'Yeah, I guess I do. I'm sorry. I'm just happy to be talking to an African sister.'

We rode along like that, talking and laughing. It felt so good to laugh again. I hadn't laughed in a long, long time.

'So where are you going, Fauziya?' he asked after a while.

'To the shopping center.'

'Would you like some company?'

Company? I didn't know how to respond. 'Aren't you going somewhere?'

'No, not really. I was just coming back from visiting a friend. How about it? I don't have anything else to do and it's fun talking to you.'

It was fun talking to him too.

'Well . . . OK.'

So that's what we did. He accompanied me to the shopping center and we walked around, looking in shops and talking. The time passed quickly. After two hours, however, I told him I was tired and hungry and wanted to go home.

'Don't go yet,' he said. 'We'll get something to eat.' He took me to a small restaurant. I'd never eaten in a restaurant. I'd bought myself juice or a Coke while wandering the mall, but I'd never sat down and eaten a meal. 'What would you like?' he asked.

'Chicken if they have it.' The menu was in German, so I couldn't read it.

He ordered me chicken and fries with mayonnaise, the same meal Rudina had brought me my first night in Germany. As we ate, we talked some more. He asked again why I was in Germany.

'There was a problem at home,' I said. 'I'd rather not talk about it.'

He asked who I was living with.

'A white woman,' I said. 'Her name is Rudina.'

'A white woman? Hunh. Wouldn't you rather live with an African? You could come live with me.'

I laughed.

'I'm serious,' he said, smiling.

'No, I can't live with you!'

'Why not?'

I laughed again. 'I don't even know you! And, anyway, you're a man.'

'So? It'd be nice. We'd be like brother and sister.'

'It's nice where I am,' I said. 'It's like sister and sister.'

'OK,' he said, smiling. 'Just asking.'

When the waiter brought the bill, Charlie insisted on paying for me, which I thought was very nice, and then he offered to walk me to the train station.

As we waited for my train we talked some more, and he asked if we could meet again. Was that a good idea, I wondered. The train was coming. I had to decide.

'Well? What do you say?'

I'd really enjoyed talking with him. He seemed very nice. He'd even bought me a meal.

'OK. I'll be here tomorrow around two-thirty.'

'Great,' he said, smiling. 'I'll be here.'

When Rudina came home that evening, I had something new to tell her.

'*Und* I went to the shopping center. *Und* I met a nice African man on the train. His name is Charlie. He's from Nigeria.'

She was so happy! 'Oh, Fauziya, you make friend!' She clapped her hands. 'Goot for you.'

When I got off the *Strassenbahn* at the shopping center the next day, Charlie was already there, waiting for me. We met regularly after that, not every day, but a lot. Charlie seemed to have a romantic interest in me, but I made it clear to him that I didn't like him in that way.

I didn't know where he lived or what he did for a living or even what his last name was. He didn't volunteer the information, and I didn't ask. People don't ask each other a lot of direct questions where I come from. It's considered rude. Besides, he was older than me, and a man. Young girls are not to question their elders, especially if they're men. So I didn't question Charlie. He, on the other hand, asked a lot of questions, but one thing he never asked me was my last name. I was glad. Since he was from Nigeria and he'd been to Togo, he knew people in my country. I was more comfortable with his not knowing my last name. It made it less risky for me to confide in him, easier for us to be friends.

I didn't tell him much about myself at first. I let him talk. He told me he'd been living in Germany for about seven years. His father was still in Nigeria, he said, his mother had died in an automobile accident. I felt bad for him when he told me that. I knew what it was like to lose a parent, I told him; I'd lost both of mine. He said he'd lived in Switzerland and Holland before coming to Germany and had visited a lot of other European cities. He seemed well traveled and sophisticated. I was impressed. He had one sister who was married and living in England. And he had another sister who used to live with him, but she'd gotten married recently and moved to France with her husband. He said that's why he'd asked if I wanted to live with him. He was alone now and lonely. I knew how it felt to be alone and lonely too. We had a lot in common.

'And what about you?' he kept asking me. 'I'm tired of talking about myself. Tell me about you. Why are you here?'

'Oh, it's a long story,' I always said, putting him off. Until one day I decided to trust him.

'You really want to hear it?' I asked. We'd been meeting for a couple of weeks at that point.

'Yes, I do,' he said.

So I told him. I told him everything. I even told him the part about the circumcision. He listened without interrupting. When I finished talking, he shook his head.

'That's really awful, Fauziya. I'm really sorry. You've been through a lot.'

'Yeah.'

We walked along in silence for a while. I appreciated the silence. I needed time to collect myself. I was glad I'd told him. It helped to talk, but it hurt too. It hurt horribly. It reawakened all the grief I was carrying inside me.

'Did you ask for asylum?' Charlie said.

'Did I what?'

'Ask for asylum. You should ask for asylum.'

'Asylum!' He thought I was crazy! I was devastated. 'Look,' I said, 'if you don't want to believe me, don't. But I'm not crazy. That's really what happened to me.' My eyes began stinging with tears. 'I want to go home now.'

He looked confused. 'Fauziya, what . . . Oh. Oh oh oh.' He started laughing.

Now he was laughing at me! I turned to walk away. He took hold of my arm.

'Fauziya, wait. I'm sorry. That's not what I meant. Really. I wasn't insulting you. You misunderstood me.

I didn't say you should live in an asylum. I said you should apply for asylum. It's a completely different thing.'

'What's that?'

'It's when you ask a country to take you in and protect you. It's called asking for asylum. That's what people do when they have to leave their own countries the way you did. You go to an office and talk to the people there. You tell them you came in without papers and then you explain why. You tell them your story just like you told it to me and ask them to let you stay. If they say yes, they give you papers and you get to live here permanently.'

'And if they say no?'

'Then they send you home. But I don't think they'd say no, Fauziya. They might, but I don't think so. And if they say yes, then they take care of you. They give you a place to live, money for food. You could go back to school and finish your education.'

'How could I go to school? I don't speak German.'

'You could learn German. I did.'

'Can you read it?'

'Some.'

'Could you read a schoolbook? Could you write an exam paper?'

'Well . . . OK. I see your point. It'd take a while.'

'It'd take years.'

'Well, what about Britain then?'

'What about it?'

'They speak English there. You should go there.'

'How can I go there? I don't have any papers, remember? Besides, I don't know anybody there.'

'You didn't know anyone when you came here either. You'd meet people. You should go to Britain, really.'

'No, Charlie. I don't know anything about Britain. I don't even know where it is.'

He thought for a moment.

'Well, what about America?' he said.

I'd just been thinking the same thing. I knew people in America. I had an uncle there. Well, he wasn't really my uncle, but I thought of him that way because our families were quite close. He'd moved to America when I was about twelve, and his wife and two of their children followed a few years later, but our families kept in touch. They were living in New Jersey now, wherever that was.

I had a half cousin in America, too, one of my mom's half sisters' sons, my cousin Rahuf. I didn't know him as well. He was older than me, closer to Ayisha's age, maybe older. He used to come around a lot when I was little. He and my dad used to talk about cars. He lived in a small town midway between Kpalimé and Tchamba, so I didn't see him much, but he was always friendly and kind to me when he did come around. He left for America when I was around eight or nine. He was married and had two daughters by then. His wife visited us a lot after he left. She used to call him collect every few weeks. I'd go with her to the post office and help her make the call because she couldn't speak English. I'd tell the American operator what number we wanted and who to say was calling. I'd recited the phone number so often, I knew it by heart. I didn't know where he lived in America. I only knew his phone number. He was family, but he was more distant family, and he was family on my mother's side, not my father's side, so the ties were looser. Still, counting Rahuf I had three relatives in America.

'I know people in America,' I told Charlie. 'I have family there. If I could go somewhere, I'd go there.'

'Then that's what you should do, Fauziya,' he said excitedly. 'You should go to America.'

'But I don't have any papers.'

'You don't need any. I told you. You just go there and ask for asylum.'

'But how can I do that? I can't leave Germany. I came in illegally. If I try to leave, won't they catch me and send me back to Togo?'

He smiled a satisfied-looking smile. 'Don't worry about that, Fauziya,' he said. 'I can help you with that.'

'How can you help me?'

'I have a passport you can use.'

'Whose passport?'

'My sister's. The one who went to England. You can use it to travel to America.'

'No I can't. It's not mine.'

'Yes you can, Fauziya. When you get there, you just give it to the customs officer and say it's not yours and explain what happened to you and ask for asylum.'

'I don't know, Charlie. I don't think so.'

'Fauziya, it'll be easy. Really. You just go there and tell them your story and they'll let you in. Tell them you have relatives there, and they'll call your relatives to come and get you.'

'You really think so?'

'Fauziya, trust me. You'll be fine.'

Maybe he was right. Maybe I should go to America. It was a good country from what I knew. I'd seen a lot of news reports at school about how America was always helping the needy, feeding hungry children, sending aid to refugees. I didn't know any Americans personally but they seemed like generous, kind-hearted people. My teachers at school had said it was a great country. They said people believed in justice in America. If I went there and I told them what had happened to me, surely they'd sympathize. Charlie sat watching me, waiting for my answer. Should I do it? Should I accept his offer? I was scared. I was tempted to say no. But I'd been scared and tempted to say no when Rudina offered to let me stay with her too. I hadn't had much choice then and I didn't now. Saying no would mean staying in Germany, where I knew I had no future. I sent up a prayer to Allah and took my fate in my hands.

'You'd do that, Charlie? You'd really give me your sister's passport?'

'Does that mean you want to go?'

I hesitated a long time.

'Fauziya, just think about it. Don't make up your mind right now. Think about it over the weekend,' he said. 'I can meet you on Monday if you want. We can talk about it again then, OK?'

That was good. Today was Friday. I'd have a couple of days to think things over. 'OK,' I said, and agreed to meet him again Monday afternoon.

My mind buzzed as I rode home. What a conversation! When Rudina returned that evening and asked me *Und?* I told her only that I'd met my Nigerian friend again. She was happy for me, and even more so when I told her I had plans to see him again the following week.

Charlie was there waiting for me, as usual, when I arrived at the shopping center on Monday. He smiled and greeted me warmly. I waited for him to raise the subject of the passport. I'd done a lot of thinking since Friday. I did want the passport, but I had decided I wanted to pay him for it, so I wouldn't owe him any favors, especially of the boyfriend–girlfriend kind, which he had been hinting at recently. Although he seemed hurt at first when I suggested paying him,

201

he eventually named a figure of $600. If we could meet again on Wednesday, he said, he would use the time before then to look into flights I could take.

I came back on Wednesday, with all my money in my purse. Charlie was there waiting.

'There's a plane to the United States every Saturday. I can try to get you a ticket for this Saturday if you want, or we can wait until next Saturday. It's up to you. How much time do you need?' he said.

I almost laughed. Time for what? Watching television? Wandering around shopping centers? Sitting alone in an apartment, aching for my family and crying over everything I'd lost?

'This Saturday,' I said.

'OK.'

He told me the price of the ticket in Deutsche Marks. It came to about $720 American. I had only hundred- and fifty-dollar bills. I gave him $750. Along with the $600 for the passport, which he hadn't brought with him that day, he now had $1,350 of my money, and I still didn't even know his last name or his address or phone number. Was I crazy to trust him? Looking back on it, I know I was. But I was desperate, and he was offering me the only hope I had.

'OK, I'll try for this Saturday,' he said. 'If I can't get you a ticket for this Saturday, I'll get one for next Saturday. I'll let you know tomorrow which it is.' He walked me to the train again. 'See you tomorrow, Fauziya.'

Would he? Would he be there when I returned? Or would I never see him or my money again?

'There's my beautiful sister!' he said when I got to our meeting place the next day. 'Good news, Fauziya. You leave this Saturday. You're on the plane.'

'You got the ticket?'

'Yep.'

'Oh my God, Charlie. That's wonderful! Did you bring it?'

'No. I'll bring it and the passport Saturday when we go to the airport.'

'You're coming with me?'

'Of course I am.' He put his arm around my shoulder and gave me a hug. 'You're my beautiful African sister, Fauziya,' he said. 'I have to take care of you.'

As we walked that day we talked arrangements. Charlie would meet me at the *Strassenbahn* station at ten A.M. to go out to the airport with me, he said. He'd have the ticket and passport with him. I'd be flying Lufthansa into Frankfurt on a flight that left around one P.M., and changing planes there for a flight to Newark. I had no idea where Newark was, but the word sounded like New Jersey, where my uncle lived. Maybe it was close by.

'Are you scared, Fauziya?' he asked.

I thought about it. Was I? I was nervous. I was excited. But I didn't feel frightened the way I'd felt when I left Togo. I didn't know what lay ahead, but at least in America I had family, people I knew who'd help me, and I'd be able to speak the language. And this time I was leaving of my own free will. I was heading into the unknown again, but I'd chosen this unknown. It made all the difference in the world.

'No, Charlie, I'm not scared,' I said finally. 'I'm really not.'

When Rudina came home that evening and we got to the *'Und?'* part of our daily conversation, I had a lot to tell her.

'Und I'm leaving, Rudina. I go Saturday morning.'

'Oh?' She looked concerned. 'Where you go? You have place?'

We went to work again, communicating in our usual mix of rudimentary English and sign language plus the sprinkling of German she'd taught me during my two-month stay. She was worried that I was leaving because I no longer felt welcome.

'Don't have to go, Fauziya,' she said. 'Want to go, fine. Goot. Be happy. But don't have to go. Can stay. OK.'

'I know, Rudina. Thank you. Yes, I have place to go.'

'But where . . .' She gave me a sly look and smiled. 'Oooh,' she said. 'Nigerian boyfriend.'

I wanted to say no, but Charlie had advised me not to tell her where I was going. He said it would only cause her worry. 'Tell her you'll let her know where you are when you get where you're going,' he'd said. Of course when I did, that only made her all the more convinced I was moving in with Charlie. And since that seemed to make her happy, I let her think it.

The next day she helped me pack my things in the suitcase she'd given me to keep my things in. There wasn't much to pack: a pair of jeans, a few shirts and sweaters, most of them Rudina's castoffs, underwear, socks, skin lotion, lipstick, hair rollers, my wedding jewelry, the necklace and earrings my grandmother had bought for me in Mecca, and the *tasbih* my mother had given to Ayisha to give to me before I'd left home. Each time its beads passed through my fingers I could feel her love surrounding me, her faith protecting me. Amariya. Where was she? How was she? What would she think about the step I was about to take? Would I ever see her again?

I woke up at five-thirty A.M. on Saturday, December 17, 1994, washed, prayed, showered, and dressed in a pair of jeans and a peach-colored sweater Rudina had given me. Then Rudina and I sat down for our last breakfast together. After I helped her clean up, I decided it was time to go. Charlie had said to meet him at ten. I wanted to allow plenty of time to get to the station in case I got lost. I put on the brown boots I'd bought with the first dollars I'd changed and slipped on the jacket Rudina had given me when I arrived. My suitcase was sitting by the door. Rudina walked me to the door and hugged me. I started crying.

'Oh, Fauziya, no!' she said. 'Be happy!' But there were tears in her eyes too.

I tried to thank her. But how could I? She'd taken me in when I had nowhere to go. How do you thank someone for saving your life?

'Thank you, Rudina. Thank you for everything. God bless you.'

'Gott bless you, Fauziya. Need place, you call, OK?'

'OK.'

'Go now.' She opened the door and shooed me out, smiling. 'Go. Be happy.'

I hugged her again, then turned and walked down the stairs, out of the building and out of her life.

'Ready to go to America?' Charlie asked, smiling, when I met him at the train station.

'Ready.'

'OK. Let's go,' he said, picking up my suitcase.

We got on the train and settled in for the long ride to the airport. Charlie pulled the ticket and passport out of an inner jacket pocket and handed them to me. I opened the passport to a photo of a woman who didn't look anything like me. Her hair was shorter than mine, her skin was darker. Her nose, eyes and chin were different. All her facial features were different. The information on the passport said she was five feet four tall and twenty-five years old. I was five feet six and would turn eighteen in about two weeks. But I was so excited about going to America I didn't stop to worry about whether anyone would notice that I wasn't the person in the photo.

We got to the airport well ahead of time and wandered around for a while looking in shops. It was so strange. I was doing everything I'd done the day I arrived, but this time in reverse. Charlie bought me an English-language paperback book to read on the plane. 'It's a long flight,' he said, smiling.

We joined a long line of people at the check-in counter. Because I couldn't speak German, Charlie handled everything. He walked me to the departure gate and sat with me until the flight boarded. He wrote his address on a piece of paper and handed it to me. 'Write to me when you get there, OK?'

Since my address book was in my suitcase, which was checked, I stuck the piece of paper in a jeans pocket. As people started lining up to board the flight, Charlie handed me the passport and ticket. This was it. Charlie and I stood up and joined the line.

'Now don't worry,' he said. 'Just do what I told you and everything will be fine. When you get to America, give them the passport and—'

'I know Charlie. I know what to do.'

He smiled. 'Good. They'll call your family to come and get you and you'll be on your way.' He gave me a hug. 'I'll miss you, Fauziya.'

'I'll miss you, too, Charlie. Thanks for everything.'

Just before boarding the plane I looked back at Charlie one last time. He smiled and waved. He really did have a great smile.

It was a short flight to Frankfurt, and soon I was boarding another plane, a much bigger plane, to America. The flight was crowded. All these people going to America, I thought. And I was going with them. I was going to America too.

The plane started moving, backward, then forward, slowly at first, then with gathering speed. Faster and faster and faster. And then we were in the air.

I'd made it! I was on my way! I sent a prayer of thanks to Allah as the plane climbed up and up. I was heading into the unknown again. I prayed some more. 'Allah, I put my faith in You. You know all things and You determine all things. Please guide me and protect me in my new life.'

16

Sister's Keepers

I was going to America. It was Allah's will. All the loss, heartache, chance, and luck that had led to my boarding the plane had been His work. I didn't get sick during this flight as I had while flying to Germany. I didn't feel frightened this time. I felt eager and hopeful. I thought the worst of my suffering was behind me. I thought I'd be with family in a day's time. I was wrong. I had no idea how wrong. This, too, was God's will. I believe God determines everything and has His reasons for everything, reasons we don't always understand. I believe He put me on that plane for a reason and drew Layli Miller Bashir and Karen Musalo and me together for a reason. We hadn't met yet, but our lives had already begun to converge. I wouldn't know for a long while how well God had prepared them before delivering my fate into their hands. I know now, and I am awed.

I need to introduce these two women now, for they are a big part of the rest of my story. Layli first, because she was there first. Layli means 'the beloved one' in Persian. That's what she is to me. She was born on March 24, 1972, making her five years older than me. She was only fourteen years old, a scrawny, gawky, frizzy-haired kid living with her family in Atlanta, Georgia, when she settled on the life path that would eventually converge with mine. From a very early age Layli was the same serious, earnest, intense person I would come to know nearly ten years later.

I believe much of Layli's seriousness of purpose has to do with her family's religion – the Bahá'í faith. The Bahá'ís are very committed to a global vision of peace and justice for all, and they work hard for what they believe in. They have a saying: 'You have to walk the spiritual path with practical feet.' The Bahá'ís believe that God speaks to humankind through many divine messengers in order to help us evolve and grow spiritually. In some ways their religion bears particularly close resemblance to Islam, but in other ways it is totally different. Although they recognize the Qur'an as a holy book ·and Muhammad as one of God's prophets, the Bahá'ís follow the teachings not of Muhammad but of Bahá'u'lláh, who lived and preached in Persia in the mid-nineteenth century. As with Muslims, prayer is an essential part of their faith and they fast once a year. They also go on pilgrimage, but to Haifa, Israel, not Mecca. Like us, they don't drink alcohol, and they believe in chastity before marriage. There isn't a lot of ritual in their faith, which is a big difference from ours. They don't go to mosque the way we do, and they don't have clergy either. They elect people to local and national decision-making bodies called Spiritual Assemblies, and to an international decision-making body called the Universal House of Justice. All decisions are made through a process of consultation, which involves talking things out until everyone agrees, a process that Layli says usually turns decision making into a very drawn-out affair but results in a valued sense of unity. The harmony between all races is very important to the Bahá'ís, as is the equality of the sexes. In fact, both are

209

considered prerequisites to society's being able to evolve to its next stage of development. But the equality between the sexes is particularly important. Like Muslims, the Bahá'ís believe parents are obligated to educate all their children, but if parents must choose between educating a son and educating a daughter because there is a lack of money, they educate the girl first: they feel that since girls grow up to become mothers and mothers are the first educators of children, their education is particularly important to the well-being of both family and community.

The Bahá'ís have been horribly persecuted in Iran because of their beliefs. When Islamic fundamentalists took power in 1979, they banned the Bahá'í faith, declared their marriages illegal and their children bastards, desecrated their holy places, and made killing a Bahá'í a legal act. Tens of thousands of Bahá'ís were murdered and tortured. Many thousands were forced to flee. The Bahá'ís know firsthand about persecution and suffering and exile. That's what I mean when I say I think being Bahá'í contributed to Layli's earnestness. She was thinking about all these issues when she was still a child.

Layli remembers the exact moment she first felt called to devote her life to good works. An African-American woman named Wilma Ellis, who was then Secretary General of the Bahá'í International Community Office at the United Nations, was giving a talk in Layli's family's living room about all the horrible injustice in the world and the importance of working to bring about equality and world peace. A wave washed over Layli as she listened to this woman speak, and she began thinking to herself that it was time to get serious about what she wanted to do with her life. At age fourteen! She spent the next summer working with a socioeconomic development project in south Georgia and organizing a Bahá'í youth project. That's how she met her future husband, Roshan Bashir. He was a twenty-two-year-old first-year medical student who was a singer and keyboardist with a popular Bahá'í band in Washington, D.C. When she called to invite the band to perform at a youth event, she and Roshan ended up talking on the phone for a long time. She sounded serious, mature, older than her years. In the weeks that followed, Roshan kept calling her, just to talk, and nearly fell over when he met her in person and realized her true age. But he bided his time. Impatiently.

Layli was oblivious, thinking of Roshan as just a friend. During her next summer vacation she spent the first part interning with the Bahá'í office at the U.N., and the second part traveling to the Soviet Union with a youth program. She wanted to see and improve the world. She was sixteen then. I was eleven. I could have gone traveling that year, too, if I'd accepted the scholarship to study in Libya. But my father didn't want me that far away from him, and I didn't want to go that far either. The next summer Layli interned with the Human Rights Department of the Jimmy Carter Center in Atlanta, Georgia. By then Roshan had declared his love. Layli was equally smitten. In 1989, he proposed and she accepted. After getting consent from her parents, as is required by the Bahá'í faith, they became engaged. But Layli, who was then only a senior in high school, wasn't ready to get married quite yet. He'd have to wait another year, she told him. There were two big things she wanted to do after graduating from high school, one being to live on a college campus for one semester, the other being to visit Africa. Layli wasn't sure why, but she'd always

211

wanted to visit Africa. Roshan suggested that she visit his older sister, Sherry, a dentist who lived with her husband in The Gambia, a tiny West African country even smaller than Togo.

Layli spent three weeks there, traveling part of the time from village to village with two Gambian co-ordinators of a Bahá'í agricultural development project, helping to plant banana trees. She adapted easily to the foreign ways of this impoverished country. She learned not to mind the heat. She learned how to pee in the bush at night. She learned to say 'Thank you' instead of 'No, I couldn't possibly' when a family welcomed her into their home, this white stranger, and offered her the only egg or piece of fruit they had to eat. The generosity she encountered everywhere, in a country where people had nothing, overwhelmed her. People weren't like that in America, and Americans had so much! But Layli didn't romanticize village life. She wasn't a tourist passing through in an air-conditioned van for a quick glimpse through sealed windows at how the 'natives' lived. She was living and working there. She saw the poverty, she saw the hunger. She saw how women were often abused and exploited in a typically patriarchal African culture. She saw firsthand, as I did as a child, the kind of jealousy and animosity women begin feeling toward each other when forced to share a household and husband. She saw a lot of things that pained her. But they didn't make her love the country or the people any less.

During that summer, she also heard about female circumcision. Some of the women in the market were talking about it, but they didn't discuss the anatomical details. Whatever it was, and Layli understood enough to know it was some kind of genital cutting, they talked about it so matter-of-factly that she accepted it matter-of-factly. The celebration surrounding the ritual seemed to be the main thing. The women became very animated when they talked about the parties and the gifts, so she was happy for them.

Layli cried when it came time to return home. She didn't want to leave The Gambia. Even though the country was poor and people had none of the material comforts Americans take for granted, they had a different kind of wealth – a warmth, a loving-ness, a generosity of spirit she'd never experienced before.

Allah is wise and merciful. I thank Him for that great gift, for bringing Layli to my world and preparing her heart in that way. One day, six years in the future, she would meet a young woman from Togo who would tell her she'd never wanted to leave Togo, would never have come to the United States if she hadn't feared for her life. Layli would remember how she herself had wept when she'd left The Gambia, and she would know this girl was telling the truth.

In January 1990, Layli started her classes at Agnes Scott College in Atlanta and six months later married Roshan. They lived in Atlanta, where he was beginning his residency at Emory University Medical School. Layli asked him about this practice, of circumcising girls that she'd heard a little about during her visit to The Gambia. Roshan had never heard of it but told her that if he saw any medical writings on the practice, he'd bring them home. Then one day he saw an article on female genital mutilation, or FGM, as the practice is often called in America, and realized this must be what Layli had asked him about.

'Look at this article!' he exclaimed, handing it to Layli when he got home that night.

213

She doesn't remember who wrote that first paper she read on the subject, but she does remember the descriptions and diagrams of the different types of procedures: cutting off the clitoris; cutting off the clitoris and labia minora; cutting off the clitoris, labia minora, and some portion of the labia majora and stitching the lips together, leaving a small opening near the anus for the passage of urine and blood. She read that FGM is commonly performed under the most unsanitary conditions, with no anesthesia or antiseptics. The cutting is often done with knives, razor blades, and pieces of broken glass. Oh my God! Layli thought.

Roshan kept passing her articles as he came across them. They both were appalled by what they were learning. He saw the practice as a public health problem: FGM poses serious medical risks, which include death, bleeding, pain, shock, psychological trauma, infection, disfigurement, scarring, loss of sexual sensation, all kinds of subsequent health complications. Layli saw it as a human rights violation. In the twenty-eight countries of sub-Saharan Africa where it is most commonly practiced, it is usually performed on girls sixteen or younger, often much younger, sometimes even in infancy.

'This is wrong,' she said. 'Wrong.'

I was fourteen, just starting boarding school, when Layli was reading these articles. I thought FGM was wrong too. Wrong for me, that is. What other people did was their business as long as it didn't affect me. Layli had a whole different attitude. She was thinking about others and learning to walk her spiritual path with practical feet. Throughout college, she kept up with her Bahá'í activities, interned at the Jimmy Carter Center again, and worked as a volunteer for the Martin

Luther King, Jr Center for Nonviolent Social Change. She had decided to pursue a career in international relations, and began to realize that having a law degree might be useful. But Layli had always harbored a deep distrust of lawyers, who too often seemed to her to cause conflict and discord rather than trying to ameliorate them. Weren't they part of the problem, not the solution? Not always, Roshan kept reminding her. They can protect people. They can help people. They can defend and fight for human rights. They can use their training and the respect a law degree commands to work for justice.

It was Roshan who finally talked Layli into applying to law school, but she decided she would apply only to schools that offered joint degree programs so she could study for a master's in international relations at the same time. Roshan was about to begin a medical fellowship at Georgetown University School of Medicine, in Washington, D.C., so Layli applied to American University, which is also in D.C. Even after she was accepted by American's Washington College of Law and the School of International Service in the summer of 1993, Layli was still debating whether or not she should study law. Maybe I'll just forget about law school and just pursue the master's, she thought.

I passed the summer of 1993 in Kpalimé, in the house that was no longer my home. My father was dead, my mother had been evicted, my aunt had moved into my mother's bedroom. I was counting the days until I could return to school.

Two weeks before her classes were to begin, Layli was still vacillating about law school, still saying she didn't want to go.

'Just give it a try,' Roshan said. 'Go to a few classes.

215

Take your first test. See how you do. You can always quit if you don't like it.'

'Well, OK,' she said. As I was going back to boarding school for what would turn out to be my last semester there, Layli was going to her first law school classes. She liked them. She did well. She was hooked. By the end of her first year, she had been appointed to the law school's *Journal of Gender and the Law,* an academic distinction granted after a writing competition. Everyone selected must write an original journal article. The articles are reviewed by the students and the best ones get published in the journal. Layli spent the summer of 1994 interning at the United Nations Information Centre in Washington, D.C., and pondering what subject to write about. Roshan was still passing her the medical literature on FGM, and everything she learned about the practice appalled her. Girls were being mutilated, thousands of them, every day. And why? To keep them pure, supposedly, to reduce their sexual feelings and desire, to keep them under men's control, to please men. It was wrong. Someone needed to sound an alarm about what was being done to these girls and infants. Hmmm. Maybe she'd write about that.

That was the same summer my aunt told me I wouldn't be returning to school. That was the summer she told me I was going to marry Ibrahim Ishaq and be cut.

In her second year of law school Layli took a course in criminal law. The students had to write a paper, on a subject of their own choosing. She knew exactly what she wanted to write about. She'd been thinking about FGM all summer. There should be laws against it. Were there? She'd do a paper on whether any countries defined FGM as a crime. She went to work

216

reading everything she could find about the legal status of FGM around the world, but there wasn't a lot written on the subject at the time, fewer than seventy papers. She read them all. She learned that Britain and Sweden had outlawed the practice, France was then considering passing a law, and a number of African countries had laws against it, some dating back to colonial times, most passed more recently. The majority of countries, however, had not banned it; and most of those that had, seemed to be putting no effort into enforcing their laws.

While Layli was working on her paper on FGM, my aunt was telling me how much calmer I'd be and how much I'd come to love my husband after I was cut. She married me off on Monday, October 17, and the following night I escaped on a plane to Germany, where I would spend the next two months. On the same December day I gave Charlie $600 for a passport that would take me to America, Layli wrote a note to herself on her calendar: 'Work hard on female circumcision.' Her criminal law paper was due that week. She turned it in on Friday, December 16, the last day of classes. The next day, I boarded a plane to Newark.

And Karen? As I was flying across the ocean and Layli was enjoying her first day of semester break, Karen Musalo, a well-known refugee-advocate lawyer, was considering whether to come teach at American University the next fall. Karen had been working on behalf of refugees since 1983, and was highly respected as a scholar and teacher in the field of refugee law. The job she'd been offered was a one-year appointment as director of American University's International Human Rights Clinic. One of the best law clinics in the country, it offers students a chance to get hands-on experience by working on real refugee cases. Professor Richard Wilson, the full-time director, was taking a sabbatical, and needed someone with exactly the kinds of expertise Karen possessed to fill the job. However, it would mean moving clear across the country, and Karen wasn't sure she wanted to do that.

'You're coming, right?' Rick Wilson asked her.

'I don't know, Rick. I haven't decided.'

Layli hadn't been sure she wanted to go to American either. But Allah had wanted her there, so there she was. He wanted Karen there too. She'd come. She didn't know it yet, but she would.

Karen was almost as young as Layli had been when she started down the life path that would eventually converge with mine. She, too, had an early awareness of the suffering and injustice of the world. She opposed the Vietnam War, and at age fifteen, when her brother was drafted to serve, she fully supported his decision to be a conscientious objector. Later she began to read various writings on nonviolence and social change, being profoundly touched by the autobiography of Mohandas Gandhi. After graduation from Brooklyn College, where she had been involved in antiwar activities, she moved to the West Coast, where she worked as an editor and journalist for a small community newspaper, focusing on environmental and animal rights issues. In 1978 she began law school with the idea of specializing in environmental law. After graduating from the University of California School of Law, Boalt Hall, in Berkeley, she took a one-year fellowship in environmental law with the Massachusetts Public Interest Research Group, a Ralph Nader organization in Boston. But Karen didn't like living on the East Coast, and when the fellowship ended she returned to California.

While she was getting settled back in on the West Coast, Karen began to do free legal work for worthy causes – pro bono work. That's how she got into refugee law. At that time, the early 1980s, there were tens of thousands of refugees fleeing the political violence and civil wars in Central America. Many of them arrived in California with little more than the shirts on their backs. One of the legal organizations that came into existence to represent them in their pleas for asylum was the San Francisco Lawyers' Committee for Civil Rights. The Lawyers' Committee interviewed newly-arriving asylum seekers, evaluated their cases, and attempted to provide representation for indigent clients with worthy claims. One day the Committee contacted Karen about the case of a young Salvadoran refugee who had been detained in the Oakland jail. The Salvadoran death squads had killed his nephew, his cousin, and two of his brothers, and then came looking for him. He'd eluded them by hiding in a closet and later fleeing to America. The government wanted to send him back. Could she help him? Karen didn't speak Spanish. She'd never taken a course in immigration or refugee law. How could she help him? But how could she say no?

It was an incredibly difficult case, but Karen hung in there. She never gave up, and in the end, her client was granted asylum. This first asylum case changed Karen's life. She had found what she wanted to do. From then on, in different capacities, as both a lawyer in the trenches and a faculty member at various law schools, Karen would focus all her energies on refugee and human rights issues. She also became an activist in an area of asylum and refugee law that was just beginning to attract serious attention in the

1980s: how to recognize and respond to the many kinds of persecution that are specific to women and girls, including rape, sexual slavery, forced abortion and sterilization, domestic violence, female genital mutilation – the list goes on. She joined the growing movement to get crimes against women recognized as human rights abuses and as valid grounds for seeking asylum, even if the crimes didn't appear to be politically motivated – or weren't *considered* 'political.' For example, for many years rape was not considered a 'political' act. But as a member of a human rights delegation that went to the former Yugoslavia in 1993 and that published a report on the Serbs' widespread policy of the rape of Muslim women, Karen helped to prove that rape can indeed be a political act. The report made a powerful case for recognizing rape as a war crime, and giving protection to women refugees fleeing such crimes. Canada would become the first country to issue formal guidelines recognizing certain gender-specific forms of persecution as grounds for asylum. That happened in 1993, the same year my father died, my mother was evicted, and my life fell apart.

By the time I first met Karen, she was uniquely qualified to handle my case. Not only was she a seasoned, savvy, sophisticated lawyer who had been arguing asylum cases for years, she was a crusader in the battle to get the law to acknowledge that women suffer differently from men, and that their sufferings constitute persecution. I see the hand of Allah at work both in the specific events that led to her coming to American University, and in the forging of a lawyer whose areas of expertise so completely matched my needs. Karen wouldn't put it that way. She doesn't talk about God the way I do. She talks about 'being put in a position where you have an opportunity to do some good.' But either way, there is no question that by December 1994 we were on converging paths. Mine took me across an ocean. Karen's was going to take her across a continent.

17

America

It was a long flight to America, all over water. I tried
not to think about that. It made me nervous. I read a
little, slept a little, and made a few unsuccessful
attempts to chat with the men seated on either side of
me, neither of whom spoke any English. Time passed
very slowly.

I had fallen into a light doze, halfway between
waking and sleeping, when at last I heard a stewardess
announce over the speaker system that the plane
would be landing in forty-five minutes. We were
almost there! I checked the time on my watch: 10:15
P.M., German time. My watch. The beautiful watch my
father had given me for my fifteenth birthday. 'Because
you're a beautiful young woman now,' he had said,
'and you should have beautiful things.' I had my
beads, too, the last four strands my grandmother had
given me. I was also wearing one piece of my wedding
jewelry, a butterfly ring, and a necklace and earrings
Ayisha had given me. I touched my earlobes, my neck,
feeling for the long copper earrings made up of little
columns of *x*'s and *o*'s, and the thick copper cross on
a black cord, gifts from Ayisha for no special occasion
but just because she loved me. Ayisha. Please, Allah, let
her be safe and well. I'd written to her from Germany,
but she hadn't written back. Had she received my

letter? I'd write to her again, first thing, as soon as I got to my uncle's house. She was probably worrying about me right now, wondering if I was all right.

Ping. I looked up. The *Fasten Seat Belts* sign had come on. The stewardess came back on the speaker system. 'We are now beginning our descent to Newark International Airport. Local time is four o'clock.' This was wonderful! If all went well, I might be with my aunt and uncle in time for dinner.

The plane began dropping, down, down, down. Another drop, a surge, a drop, and then, bumpety-bump, we were down. This was it. I closed my eyes. 'Allah, You know all things and You determine all things. I trust in You. My fate is in Your hands.'

I followed the other passengers off the plane, through a set of doors into a big, open room with a long row of immigration counters along the far wall. Someone in a uniform who was controlling passenger flow directed me into a line of people headed toward a counter with a woman officer behind it. Allah was with me, I thought. I'd much rather tell my story to a woman than to the man who was at the other booth where noncitizens were being directed. A woman would sympathize. She'd understand.

My turn. I approached the booth, heart pounding, and handed the officer the passport. 'Hello,' she greeted me. She was a white woman with short brownish hair, not friendly, not unfriendly.

'Have you been to this country before?' she asked.

'No, please.' I wanted to be as courteous as possible.

'You haven't been here?'

'No, please.'

'Well, the person this passport belongs to has been here.'

223

'Oh, excuse me, please. That's not my passport.'

'It's not your passport?'

'No.'

'Can you explain what you're doing with this passport?' the officer asked calmly.

'Oh, yes, please. I want political asylum.' That's what Charlie had said to say, so that's what I said.

'You want asylum.'

'Yes, please.'

She studied me for a moment. I wasn't sure what to do. Did I tell my story now? Did I wait until she asked me to tell it? Or maybe I wouldn't have to tell my story. Maybe she'd know just by looking at me that I wouldn't have come if I hadn't had to come. Maybe she'd say, 'OK, go ahead, welcome to America,' and wave me through. She didn't. She shook her head slightly, pulled out a form and picked up a pen, to take down my story I thought. It was around four-thirty P.M., December 17, 1994. I thought my time of worst trials and suffering was about to end. It had just begun.

'Do you have a return ticket?' she asked.

I gave her my ticket receipt.

'No, a return ticket.'

'You mean to Germany?'

'Yes.'

'No.' Why would I have that?

'Do you have any money with you?'

'Yes.'

'Could you tell me how much?'

'I'm not sure.'

'Could you count it for me, please?'

I took my money out of my purse, counted it, and told her the total: $595.

'May I have it, please?' She held out a hand, palm up, as she wrote something on the form.

Oohhh! She was teasing me! Like the customs officer in Germany had before he'd waved me through.

She looked up from her form, her hand still out. 'May I have it, please?' She wasn't smiling. She wasn't teasing. 'Don't worry,' she said. 'You'll get it back. I've marked the amount right here.' I handed her my money. She picked up the form, the passport, and the ticket. 'Have a seat there,' she said, pointing to a waiting area with several rows of benches. 'I'll be with you as soon as I can.'

'Yes, please.' I sat down. I was the only passenger there. I guessed I'd have to tell my story after all. She probably needed to write it on the form. That made sense. I looked around for a telephone. I didn't see one. There were a couple of doors along the wall I was facing and a small hallway to the right. I'd ask the lady where the phones were when she got back to me. I didn't have my uncle's telephone number. Maybe she'd help me find it and call him.

I saw the lady officer talking to another officer, a man, who came over to me afterward. 'Would you follow me please? We need to take your picture and your fingerprints,' he said. 'It'll only take a minute.' He stood me in front of a wall, held up a camera and took my picture. Then he led me to a table and held my hand, guiding my thumbs from inkpad to paper. 'OK, that's it,' he said. He gave me a tissue to wipe off the ink. 'You can sit down now.' Wow! I was impressed. They were making me a passport right there! I'd never heard of using fingerprints on a passport, but what else could the picture be for? This was so wonderful! I'd tell the lady my story, they'd give me the passport, she'd help me call my uncle, he'd come get me, and I'd be on my way. What a great country America was!

About an hour later the lady had finished with the

line of people who had been behind me. She opened one of the doors along the wall I sat facing and showed me into a tiny room with a table and two chairs. As we sat down across from one another, she took out a pen and some sheets of paper.

'OK, now, let's talk,' she said. 'I want you to tell me why you came here and what you want from the United States. I want you to tell me everything and I want you to tell me the truth, OK?'

'Yes, please.' Gladly.

We began with my name: Fauziya Kassindja.

'Fauziya. Could you spell that?'

I spelled it.

She didn't ask me to spell my last name. Although I saw her write 'Kasinga,' I wasn't sure if it was proper to correct her, so I didn't. She asked me my birth date. I told her. She asked where I was born. I told her. She wrote 'Kpalome' instead of 'Kpalimé.' I didn't correct that either. She asked my citizenship. I told her. She asked why I'd come to America.

I told her my father had died on January 16, 1993. I told her that after my father had died, my aunt had evicted my mother, pulled me out of school, and forced me to marry a man old enough to be my father who already had three wives. I told her my oldest sister had helped me escape to Germany, where I'd met Charlie and bought the passport from him for $600. I told her I wanted to be allowed to live in a country where I had family and spoke the language. I wanted to live with my uncle and go back to school. I wanted to build some kind of new life for myself now that the life I'd known and loved had been taken from me. I wanted political asylum.

I didn't tell her about *kakia*. She was a woman, but she was a white woman and she was American. How could I explain *kakia* to someone who'd probably never heard of it? She might think I was lying, making it up. And it was such a horrible, personal, intimate thing. I couldn't bring myself to speak of it. It was too shameful. I'd told her enough, I thought. More than enough. Any person with a caring heart would sympathize with my situation. She'd welcome me to her country, and I'd be free to go.

'That's it?' she asked when I'd finished telling my story. 'That's everything?'

'Yes.'

She gave me the sheet of paper to read and sign. She hadn't written much: name, date and place of birth, citizenship, that I'd bought the passport from Charlie, and that I'd come to the United States because 'my aunt wants me to marry someone I don't like.' It wasn't the whole story, but it was true as far as it went. Maybe that was all she needed for her records. I signed the paper and handed it back. At this point she opened the door and called in another officer, who seemed to be a supervisor of some kind. He looked over the paper I'd just signed and then turned to me with a frown.

'This is no reason to grant you asylum,' he said to me.

'Excuse me?' I'd misheard him. I must have misheard him.

'Do you want to go back to Germany?'

'No, I don't want to go back to Germany. I want political asylum.'

'Do you want to go to Britain?'

'No. I don't know anyone there.'

'Do you want to go back to Togo?'

'Togo! No! I can't go back to Togo! I want to stay here! I want political asylum!'

'Well, I'm sorry, but there's no reason here for us to give you asylum. I suggest you go back to Germany. If you stay here, you'll go to prison. Do you want that?'

Prison! What was he talking about? He couldn't mean that. He was trying to scare me. Why was he trying to scare me? I didn't understand. My head spun. I was starting to lose my bearings.

Now there was another woman in the room, a woman dressed in a dark suit. Had someone left the room to call her? I don't remember. She was just suddenly there with my suitcase. The woman in the suit was holding what looked like a little black radio in her hand. I think the supervisor said she was the captain of the plane I'd flown in on, but I could be wrong. I was so frightened, I couldn't think straight by then. 'She'll take you back on the plane to Germany,' he said. 'The plane leaves in a few hours.'

The lady in the suit smiled. 'Why don't you come with me,' she said. 'I'll see that you get back safely.'

'But I don't want to go back to Germany! I want political asylum!' I couldn't go back to Germany. They'd stop me at the airport. They'd send me back to Togo.

'You can't stay here,' the male supervisor said. 'If you stay here, we'll have to send you to prison. Is that what you want?'

'No! I want political asylum!' I kept repeating it over and over. Maybe they were just testing me. Maybe if I kept repeating it long enough, they'd finally say 'OK' and let me go. And then a horrifying thought suddenly flashed through my mind. Oh God. That's what I'd thought about my aunt – if I just kept repeating over and over that I didn't want to get married, I wanted to go to school, she'd finally relent. But she hadn't.

That's why I was here. I had to think of something else to say. My uncle! Maybe I hadn't made it clear that I had relatives here. 'I have an uncle in New Jersey,' I told the male supervisor. 'Can I call him? He'll come get me.'

'No, you can't call him. You're not allowed to call anyone.'

What was he saying? Was this some kind of joke?

'You can still change your mind and go back to Germany. Otherwise you go to prison,' he said.

'No! No! I don't want to go back to Germany! I want political asylum!' I started to cry.

The lady in the suit shrugged and left. The lady officer gave the male supervisor a reproving glance and spoke to me calmly. 'Look, we can't grant you asylum,' she said. 'Only a judge can do that. We're not judges. You have to go before a judge.'

'Then I want to see a judge! Can I see him now?'

'No, you can't. You have to wait.'

'How long?'

'I can't tell you that.'

'You'll have to go to prison first,' the male supervisor said.

'But I don't want to go to prison! I've never been in a prison in my life!' I started crying again.

The lady officer gave the supervisor another look. He shook his head and left. 'Don't worry,' she said to me. 'It's not a bad prison. You'll meet other Africans there.'

What was she talking about? I asked myself. Just because a person was African didn't mean I'd want to be their friend. Did she think all Africans were alike? I felt insulted, but I said nothing.

'And you won't be there for long,' she continued. 'Just till Monday. You'll see a counselor from your country, and then you can call your relatives and go home to your family.'

'Why can't I call my uncle now?'

'Because you can't,' she said. 'It's not allowed.'

Another male officer came into the room. He seemed to be a supervisor too.

'She says she's from Togo?' he asked the lady officer, jerking his head in my direction. She nodded. He turned to me. 'You're from Togo?' His tone was rude.

'Yes,' I said.

'Parlez-vous français?'

I knew enough to know what he was asking me, but not much more. I told him no, I didn't speak French.

'And you say you're from Togo?'

'Yes.' But I'd gone to school in Ghana. I'd told that to the lady officer. I was scared, confused. It didn't occur to me to explain it again.

He put a piece of paper in front of me and handed me a pen. 'Can you draw the flag for me?' he said. I took the pen. My hand was shaking. I drew the flag: five horizontal stripes with a star in a box in the upper right corner. No, the left corner. I was always confusing that. I knew my flag, but I knew Ghana's flag better.

'That's not Togo's flag,' he pronounced accusingly.

'I made a mistake. The star goes in the other corner.'

'You don't know your own flag?'

'Yes, I know my flag!'

'Tell me the colors.'

'The stripes are green and yellow. The star is white and the box is red.'

'Those aren't the colors.'

'Yes they are! Those are the colors!' I may have put the star on the wrong side, but I did know the colors of my own flag!

'You don't speak French, you don't know your own flag.' He snorted. 'She's not from Togo,' he said to the lady officer. 'She's lying. She's probably from Nigeria.'

I exploded in rage. 'I am not lying!' I yelled. 'I know what country I'm from! I'm from Togo!'

He shrugged. 'Suit yourself. Take a seat outside.' I stood up, walked out into the waiting room, and sat down. I was numb. This wasn't happening. It was too crazy. They weren't really going to send me to prison. They couldn't! I hadn't done anything wrong!

As I sat there the two officers wrote their report on me. I wouldn't see that piece of paper for a long, long time. This is some of what they wrote:

Subject claims to be born in Togo. Subject has no knowledge of Togo (geography, language). Subject does not speak French. Subject wants asylum so that she can stay here and study. Subject does not know what the flag of Togo looks like or what the national colors are. She has elected to go before the Immigration Judge rather than return to Frankfurt. Appears excludable . . .

I sat alone in the waiting room for about another half hour. Waiting for what? I didn't know. What were they going to do with me? They couldn't possibly be serious about sending me to prison. Why would anybody want to send me to prison?

Other immigration officers walked in and out of the room, and looked at me. One even asked me where I was from. When I told her, she sucked her teeth. 'I don't know why these people can't stay in their own countries.' I couldn't believe she said that to me. A chill went through my body. Things weren't supposed to be like this.

231

After a while a short, heavy black woman dressed in a light blue shirt and black pants entered the waiting room and walked toward me. The immigration officers all wore white shirts, I'd noticed. So she wasn't an immigration officer. She was something else.

'OK, let's go,' she said.

'Where are we going?'

'To the holding room.'

'The what?'

'Come on, come on, let's go.'

'Do I take my suitcase?'

'No.' I left the suitcase, with the strap of my purse wrapped around the handle, and followed her down a short hallway into another room. It was larger than the interview room, but it didn't have any table or chairs in it – just a metal bench along one wall. There was a bathroom at the back of the room. It was so foul, it made the whole room smell like a toilet. The guard followed me into the room, closed the door behind her, and told me to put my jacket down on the bench. I did.

'Are you wearing a belt?' she asked.

'Yes.' What a strange question.

'Take it off, please.'

'Take off my belt?'

She gave me a cold look. 'Don't make me repeat myself,' she said.

I took off my belt.

'On top of your jacket.'

I put it on top of my jacket.

'Shoes.'

'Shoes! Why—'

'I said shoes!'

I took off my boots.

'Jewelry.'

I took off my earrings, necklace, watch, and ring.

'Now your jeans.'

My jeans! I began to panic. Was this the prison? In Togo, I had heard they made men strip to their underwear when they put them in prison. Was this where they were going to keep me? In this stinky room?

'I said jeans!'

I took off my jeans.

'Socks.'

I took off my socks.

'Sweater.'

I took off my sweater.

'Undershirt.'

I took off my undershirt.

'Bra.'

'My bra! No! Please!'

'Take it off!'

I took it off and instinctively crossed my arms over my chest to cover myself.

'Hands at your sides.'

I dropped my hands and hung my head, my face burning with shame.

'Underpants.'

'No! No! Please! Not my underpants! Please! I'm menstruating! I'm using a pad!'

'Off!'

'I can't. Please. Don't make me.'

'I said off!'

I took off my underpants and stood in front of her completely naked, soiled pad exposed, shamed beyond words.

'OK, now, squat and cough.'

I had no idea what was going on, why she was making me do this. I dropped down quickly, coughed, bounced up.

'Not like that. Do it slowly. Squat, stay down, cough three times, then stand up.' I did as told. 'Now turn around. Do it again, backside to me.' I turned around and did it again. It didn't matter. It wasn't happening to me. I wasn't there anymore. I had gone someplace far away.

'OK, get dressed. Everything but your belt, shoes and jacket.'

I got dressed. She took my belt, boots, and jacket, walked out of the room, and closed and locked the door behind her. I sat down on the metal bench.

Cold set in. I hugged myself and rubbed my feet together, trying to keep warm. I was freezing. I was hungry. I had to use the bathroom, but I couldn't stand the thought of going near that putrid-smelling toilet. When was the guard coming back? They wouldn't just leave me here like this all night. What if they did? What if they kept me here like this until Monday? What if they kept me here forever? They could. Nobody knew where I was. Nobody would ever find me. No! I couldn't think like that. They wouldn't do that. But what if they did? Oh God, I was losing my mind.

I sat there alone like that for about four hours, unable to think straight. It was after ten P.M., when the same guard who'd made me strip walked in carrying my boots, belt, and jacket. She put them on the bench.

'Put these on.' She didn't have to tell me twice. I was freezing. 'OK, let's go,' she said, holding the door open. 'Out.' As I left the room I saw another guard outside, a tall, fat black man who had my suitcase at his side, the purse strap still tied around its handle.

The female guard reached into her back pocket and pulled out a pair of handcuffs. She took hold of my right wrist. 'Please!' I began crying hysterically. 'No! Don't put those on me! Please! Don't take me to prison! I don't want to go to prison!'

She snapped the handcuffs around my right wrist and took hold of my left wrist.

'Please! Please don't!' I sobbed.

'I'm just doing my job.' She snapped the handcuffs around my other wrist and squeezed them tight.

'They hurt! They're too tight!'

She loosened them. 'That better?'

I nodded, sobbing, tears streaming down my face. As the male guard continued to stand by silently, looking at the floor, the female guard put a heavy metal chain around my waist. Next she put two more chains on me, one around my right ankle, one around my left, and attached them to the chain around my waist. Finally she put a chain between my ankles. I was completely trussed in chains. Like a criminal. Like a murderer.

'Pick up your suitcase,' she said.

I bent down, took the handle in both hands and lifted, holding the suitcase flat against my legs. It was the only way I could carry it. She and the male guard took up positions on either side of and slightly behind me and began leading me down a long hallway, each one holding the back of an arm. With my ankles trussed closely together in heavy, clanking chains, I couldn't walk very well. The suitcase was heavy and bounced against my knees with each step I took. It kept sliding off to my left or right side. I had to stop every few steps and haul it back in front of me. Neither guard offered to carry it for me. They let me struggle with it myself. We finally emerged into a dark night where a waiting van was parked at the curb. The woman guard slid the side passenger door open. 'Get in,' she said. I tried to lift my suitcase into the van. I couldn't do it. I was exhausted. It was eleven P.M. local time, five A.M. German time. I'd been awake for nearly twenty-four hours. I tried again, lost my balance, and almost fell. Finally the male guard caught my arm to steady me, took the suitcase from me and lifted it easily into the van, then half lifted me in beside it and shut the door. In another minute we were on our way, the male guard at the wheel, the female guard seated next to him in front. I couldn't see much through the tinted windows, the dark shapes of cars going by, some lights. We seemed to be on a highway. I didn't know where they were taking me. They didn't tell me. I was going to prison. That's all I knew.

After a short ride, ten or fifteen minutes at most, the driver left the highway, made a number of turns, drove on a few minutes more, and then stopped in front of a huge metal gate. He talked into a black hand-held radio: 'Open G-Five.' The gate rattled up. He was speaking into a walkie-talkie, telling someone in a control booth to push a button and open the gate. I know that now. I didn't then. I'd never seen a walkie-talkie. I couldn't believe what I thought I was seeing: a gate that understood human commands! He drove the van into a dark, enclosed space and down an incline. The gate rattled shut behind us, sealing us inside.

The female guard climbed out of the van and opened my door. 'OK, come on, let's go.' I wasn't sure I could manage to climb down without falling, trussed up like that in all my chains. As I hesitated, the male guard came around and helped me down and took my suitcase. We were in some kind of garage area where a number of other vans had also been parked. The female guard took hold of the back of my right arm and led me up some steps to a metal door. The male guard followed, carrying my suitcase. The female guard pulled out her own walkie-talkie and spoke into it. 'Open Seventeen.' With a loud metal *clang* the door slid open to admit us, then clanged shut behind us. Another door was in front of us. 'Open Eighteen.' *Clang.* 'Open Nineteen.' *Clang. Clang, clang, clang, clang,* door after door, hallway after hallway we walked, through a brightly lit, white, silent, deserted space. There were cameras mounted everywhere on the walls. No people. No sounds other than the rattle of my chains as we walked. It was eerie, like something out of a nightmare. Then I realized that it was a nightmare— mine.

'OK, stop here,' the female guard said. The next thing I knew, the male guard had left and the female guard was removing my chains and handcuffs and ushering me through yet another big metal door. Now I was in another cold, stinking, barren room, this one much bigger than the one at the airport, with a metal bench running along three walls, a metal toilet-and-sink unit sitting out in the open on the far side of the room, and one narrow vertical window cut into the upper portion of the door.

'Take off your jacket.'

Oh God, no! Please not again!

'I said take off your jacket! Come on, hurry up. It's late. I'm tired. I want to go home.'

I took off my jacket.

'And your boots.'

I took off my boots.

'And your socks.'

I took off my socks. I took off my jeans, my sweater, my undershirt, my bra, my watch, necklace, and earrings until I was naked again except for my underpants and beads.

237

'And your underpants.'

'Please! Not my underpants! Please! I'm menstruating! I need the pad!'

'Off! Don't make me angry. Don't make me tell you again.'

I stepped out of my underpants.

'On the bench.'

I put them on the bench with my other clothing, trying unsuccessfully to hide the soiled napkin without soiling something else. I felt utterly shamed, humiliated, degraded. I put my hands to my face and began to cry.

'Move away from the bench.'

As I stood naked and barefoot in the middle of the cold concrete floor, she walked to the bench, gathered up my belongings, and left the room, letting the door slam behind her with a wall-shakingly loud bang! Again I was alone. And freezing. And faint with exhaustion. I had to sit down. But there was no toilet paper, or anything else I could use as a pad, and I didn't want to soil the bench with my menstrual blood. So I'd have to sit on the toilet. Lowering myself to the cold metal seat of the dirty toilet, I crossed my arms over my chest and bent my chest to my knees, to try to cover myself, to keep warm. As I sat rocking back and forth, shivering, my mind began slipping, sliding, flying away, until I was no longer there.

A rap on the door. I looked up. A man's face was at the narrow window, looking in on me as I sat naked on a toilet seat. Oh, God. This wasn't happening. I lowered my head and covered my face with my hands. My body was no longer my own. Anyone could look at it. I had been stripped naked and put on display like an animal in a zoo. I covered my face. It was the only thing I could hide.

He knocked again and called through the door. 'Excuse me, ma'am! Have you had anything to eat?'

I kept my head down, my face covered. 'No!'

'Are you hungry? Would you like some food?'

Food. I'd forgotten all about food until the man mentioned it. Terror had chased out hunger. Now it returned. I hadn't eaten since breakfast with Rudina in Germany that morning. That morning. Had it been only that morning? It seemed such a distant memory now. I'd been too excited to eat during the flight. Excited. Had that been me? That innocent, modest, naive young girl? Or was this me? This shivering, tired, frightened, soiled, hungry, naked creature crouching on a toilet seat in a prison cell.

'Yes!' I forced myself to reply.

The man returned about ten minutes later. He knocked again. 'Here you go, ma'am.' He opened the door a crack, reached an arm in and deposited a small brown paper bag on the floor. Then he closed the door and left. He didn't look in through the window at me this time. Maybe he hadn't known the first time he looked that I'd been left sitting naked. Maybe he did. It didn't matter. Nothing mattered. Nothing was real.

The bag contained a sandwich wrapped in plastic and two small cartons of milk. I unwrapped the sandwich: two pieces of thin, spongy white bread, a slice of some kind of cheese and a slice of some kind of strong-smelling red meat. Pork? I couldn't tell. I don't eat pork. I couldn't eat this strange meat anyway. I put the sandwich aside, opened the milk and drank it. The taste of it shocked me. This was milk? We drank condensed, sweetened canned milk at home. This milk was thin and watery. But I'd had nothing to drink for more than seven hours, so I drank it anyway, gulping it down to get past the taste. That was a mistake. As soon as it hit my stomach it churned back up. I ran to the toilet, knelt naked on the floor, and vomited into the pee-encrusted bowl. I vomited again and again. Everything came out. I kept retching, my body seized in spasms, my face drenched in sweat, until there was nothing left inside me, nothing but terror trying to throw itself up. The spasms subsided. I spat into the bowl, over and over, trying to clear the taste from my mouth. There was no water in the sink unit, no towel, nothing with which to clean myself. I wiped my mouth with my hand, lifted myself off the floor, and sat back down, limp, weak, and shivering, on the toilet seat. Sharp pains shot through my stomach. I wrapped my arms around myself and prayed. 'Give me strength. Oh, Allah, let me survive this. Let this be over soon.'

Another rap on the door. It opened and a female guard stepped into the room. A different one, not the one who'd left me here. A walkie-talkie and a big bunch of keys hung from her belt. She stood for a moment with a hand on one big hip, just looking at me. Her expression was hard, mean.

'Stand up.'

I stood up, stooped and shivering, arms crossed over my breasts. She looked me up and down coldly. 'What's your name?'

'Fauziya.' It came out a tiny, quivering whisper.

'What!' she boomed. 'Speak up!'

I started crying. 'Fauziya. My name is Fauziya.'

She handed me a bag containing the clothes I'd been wearing and told me to get dressed. Next she walked over to the door, keys jangling, her huge buttocks shifting from side to side, and waved me through disgustedly. 'Let's go. Into the shower. Move,' she said, pointing across the hall. We entered a large beige-tiled room with a line of shower stalls along one wall. When I had undressed again, I asked the guard if there was a waste can where I could put my soiled sanitary napkin. She ignored me.

'Please,' I asked again, my voice shaking. 'Can you tell me where I could put my pad?'

'I don't know. Why don't you eat it?'

No. She couldn't have said that. 'Excuse me?'

'I said you can eat it!'

I reeled. How could anyone talk like that? How could a woman say such a disgusting thing to another woman?

'In the shower! Let's go!'

Ice-cold water shot out of the shower head when I turned it on. I screamed and ran out.

'Back in the shower!'

Reluctantly, I walked back to the stall and eased my way, body part by body part, under the ice-cold spray, trying as much as possible to keep my back to the guard. She never stopped staring at me the whole time. When I was finished she handed me a worn, stained white towel. I took the towel and sniffed it. It smelled used. 'Come on, come on, I don't have all night.' I stepped out of the wet stall, turned my back to her, and began drying myself, when suddenly I felt a slight tug on my beads. I looked down. She was fingering one of the strands. I wanted to slap her hand away, to jerk myself away from her reach. But I couldn't. If I did, the strand would break and my precious beads, the last strands my beloved grandmother had given me, would go scattering all over the floor. I willed myself to remain still.

'What the hell are these?' she asked.

'They're my beads,' I said quietly. 'It's my custom.'

She let them go. 'Whatever.'

She let me keep them. I would learn later that this was unusual. She could have taken them away from me, but she didn't. Later, much later, I would remember that as a kindness. Her only real kindness.

I finished drying and reached for my clothes to begin dressing. 'No, not those,' she said. 'These.' One by one she began handing me items from a pile of clothing I hadn't noticed, holding each article between the tips of two fingers, as if she didn't want to touch them. I could see why. The underpants she held out to me were dark green with a yellow-stained crotch. I couldn't bear the thought of them touching my body.

'Please,' I said. 'Can I wear my own underwear?'

'No you cannot wear your own underwear,' she said in a mocking, whining, singsong voice. 'Put those on.'

'But they're too big. Can I have a smaller pair?'

'Put 'em on!'

I hesitated. 'Please, I need a pad. I'm menstruating.'

'I don't handle that. The officer you see in the morning will give you a pad.' There was nothing in the shower room I could use to line the underpants, no toilet paper or paper towels. I put on the underpants. They were so huge I had to roll the waistband around my beads to keep them from falling off.

She handed me a worn-out, yellowing bra, also way too big. The back hook was broken off.

'It's broken,' I said. 'I can't wear it.'

'Don't. I don't give a damn.'

I put it on the bench.

Next came a light blue V-necked polyester shirt, short-sleeved, also far too large. I slipped it on with no comment. The matching pants with an elastic waistband were too small and, when I pulled them on, uncomfortably tight from waist to knees. The worn

242

white socks were also too small, and there was a big hole in the toe of the right sock through which my big toe protruded. Worst of all were the brown plastic sandals she gave me, both for the right foot, both too big, and both impossible to keep on my feet because their buckles as well as the straps across the insteps were broken. As I put them on, a sweet memory flashed, of my tiny little-girl feet in my father's huge sandals when I'd modeled his new clothes for him as a child. What do you think, Yaya? How do I look? Do you like me in these clothes? Look at your little girl now.

'OK, let's go. I gotta book you in.' I shuffled down the hallway in front of her, until at last we reached a counter. There was an upright scale, which she motioned me onto. I took a step and almost fell over. My feet came right out of the shoes. I stepped back into them and shuffled toward her. 'Let's go! Let's go!' I stepped out of the shoes and onto the scale. She measured my height and weight and wrote it on the clipboard: 5'6", 163 pounds.

She walked to the other side of the counter we'd come to and pulled my jacket and boots from a bag.

'These yours?'

'Yes.'

'That your suitcase?'

I peered around the counter. 'Yes.'

She wrote out a tag and attached it to the suitcase. Then she wrote out another tag and attached it to a net bag into which she dumped the contents of my bag of clothing, which also included my watch and other jewelry.

Next she wrote my name and the number 100761 on a strip of plastic, which she wrapped around my left wrist and attempted to fasten with a pair of metal

243

pliers. But the pliers missed the plastic and grabbed my skin instead. I screamed and yanked my arm away.

No reaction, no apology, nothing – she just grabbed for my arm and held it flat on the counter. A huge blister was forming where she'd caught my flesh. 'Let's try that again. Hold still.' I did. She fastened the bracelet very tightly and released my arm. Now she began stacking on the counter the items I would be using for daily life – blanket, sheet, pillowcase, towel, all of them worn, frayed, discolored – plus a plastic cup, spoon, and fork. 'Take your stuff. Let's go.' She gave me a shove in the back, pushing me before her down more silent hallways, through more metal doors that clicked open at the commands she issued from her walkie-talkie, until finally she waved me through one more door – 'Open Kilo' – into a darkened room. She followed me in and let the door slam behind her. Bang!

I heard soft groans and saw movement to my right. It was coming from a row of beds lined up against the wall. The noise of the door slamming must have awakened some of the sleepers in those beds. 'Bed two!' she boomed, pointing to the second bed against the wall. I looked where she'd pointed. As my eyes adjusted to the darkness I saw that the bed was empty. Stripped and empty. 'That's your new home since you guys can't stay in your own country,' she boomed. She spoke loudly into her walkie-talkie. 'Control. Open Kilo.' The door clicked unlocked. She opened it, walked out, and let the door slam again. Bang!

More soft groans. Bodies shifted in beds. I stood frozen in terror, holding my pile of things. I was locked in a dark room with . . . Who? Men? Women? Murderers? Prostitutes? Who were these people? I was near collapse, faint from hunger and exhaustion. I had to sit down before I fell down. I shuffled over to the bed as quietly as possible. The mattress was thin and hard, with a plastic cover that crackled when I sat down, and a small, thin pillow also covered in plastic. I didn't make my bed. I didn't lie down. I did the only thing I could manage. I slipped out of my shoes, slid back against the wall, pulled my knees up to my chest, bent my head, covered my face with my hands to muffle my sobbing.

'What's your name?'

I was hallucinating, hearing things, imagining a woman's soft voice.

'What's your name?'

I looked up and saw a face. A woman's face. A kind face. A black face. African, I guessed. I wiped my eyes and looked again. A sturdily built woman who looked to be somewhere in her twenties stood in front of me, wearing a strange kind of nightgown. She smiled at me.

'What's your name?' she asked again.

'Fau, Fau, Fauziya.'

'Fauziya,' she repeated softly. 'That's a beautiful name.' She sat down beside me. 'When did you arrive?'

'Today. This afternoon.'

'Where are you from?'

'Togo.'

'Togo! We're neighbors, then. I'm from Ghana.'

'You are?'

'Uh-huh.' She smiled.

'I went to school in Ghana,' I said.

'Is that where you learned English?'

'Yes.'

'Well, you speak it very well.'

'Thank you . . .'

'Mary.'

'Mary,' I repeated.

'How old are you?'

'Seventeen. Almost eighteen.'

'Oh, you poor thing. And they brought you to this place. They should be ashamed. Do you have relatives here?'

'Yes. An uncle. And a cousin.'

'Were you able to call them?'

'No, they wouldn't let me.'

'Well, don't worry. We'll call them in the morning. I'll help you.'

'Is there a phone we can use?'

'Yes. It's right over there.'

'Where?'

'Shhhhhh. People are sleeping.'

'Oh, I'm sorry.'

'That's OK. It's right over there. See?' I squinted and saw a phone on the opposite wall. A phone!

'Can I call now?'

'No, they shut it off at night. We have to wait until morning. Right now you need to sleep. Come on, get up. I'll make your bed.'

Who was this kind lady? Her kindness brought me back to myself. My mind cleared a little. 'Where am I?' I asked softly as she put the sheet on my mattress.

'You're in Esmor. It's a detention center.'

Esmor. So that's what that word was. It was written on every article of clothing I was wearing.

'What's it like here?'

'Oh, it's bad,' she said as she tucked in my sheet. 'The food is awful. They keep us locked up in these rooms. You never get to go outside.' She finished with the sheet and picked up the pillow and pillowcase. 'They don't treat us like human beings. They're just making money off us. They never release anybody. They keep us locked up here until they're ready to send us home.' She finished with the pillow and reached for the blanket.

'What do you mean, they never release anybody?'

'Well, not never. But hardly ever.' She finished with the blanket. 'There. All made.'

'But the officer at the airport said I'd be out on Monday. She said I'd talk to a counselor and then they'd let me go.'

'They told you that too?' She shook her head. 'They say that to everyone. They told me the same thing and I've been here four months.'

I half sat, half collapsed on the bed. 'Four months!'

'Four months. And I haven't even seen a judge yet.' She sat down next to me again and laughed softly. 'I got tired of waiting. That's why I'm here.'

'Here in Esmor?'

'No, here in this dorm. This is K. I was in N before with a lot of other women from Ghana. They moved me out as part of my punishment.'

'Punishment for what?'

She laughed again. 'I tried to escape.'

'Escape! Why? How? When?'

'Shhhhh. I'll tell you tomorrow. Now I want to go back to sleep. You should sleep too. Don't worry. Nothing's going to happen to you.' She pointed to the bed next to mine nearest the door and big window. 'I'm in bed one. I'm right next to you, OK?'

'OK.'

'The toilet's back there if you need to use it.' She pointed to the back of the room. 'There's a sink and shower back there, too, behind that half wall.'

'Are there any sanitary pads back there?'

'No. Why? Do you need one?'

'Yeah. I asked the guard for one, but she said I had to wait until morning.'

'The guard who brought you in here?'

'Yeah.'

'That's Kim. Watch out for her.' She laughed. 'She's bad.'

'She was real mean to me.'

'She's mean to everyone, but they're not all like her. Some of them are nice. Hold on. I'll get you a pad.' She went to her bed, pulled a plastic box out from under it, felt around inside it and came back with a pad. 'Here you go. We'll get you another one in the morning. I'm going back to bed now. Try to get some sleep. We'll talk tomorrow, OK?'

'OK. Thank you, Mary.'

'You're welcome. Try to sleep.'

She went back to bed. After going to the toilet area to put my pad in place, I returned to my bed and lay down in my clothing. The pillow crackled. The mattress crackled. The room was cold. I wrapped myself in the thin woolen blanket to try to get warm. It made my skin itch. I lay there, exhausted, numb, staring at the ceiling, my mind spinning.

Mary was wrong. She had to be wrong. Maybe she didn't have family here. Maybe that's why they were keeping her in this place. I'd call my uncle in the morning and they'd let me out. They would. They had to.

18

Esmor

My mother came into the bedroom to wake us. 'Good morning! Good morning, ladies!' Her voice sounded strange. 'Come on, ladies! Time to get up!' Amariya, I wondered, why are you yelling? 'Out of bed, ladies!' A blaze of light. A rattling of metal. 'Come on, ladies! Who cleans today!' I opened my eyes. The lights were so bright! When did they get so bright? What were those huge pipes doing in the ceiling? Why was I sleeping in my clothes? Where was I?

And then it all came back and I remembered where I was. Amariya, where are you now?

'Come on, ladies! Time to get up!'

I sat up. The mattress crackled. My back hurt. I was cold. I rubbed my arms and tried to look around. Any way I turned when I lifted my head, I got hit in the eye with a beam of high-intensity light from one of the lamps mounted at ceiling height in the four corners of the room. They weren't regular lamps. They were the kind of lights people back home rent for weddings and festivals, the kind that turn night into day. The light was blinding, painful. I had to keep my head down.

A television came on at top volume, blasting at us from high up on the wall opposite me. A thin black female guard stood in front of it with her back to me, adjusting it. The sound went down a little. 'Come on, ladies!' she called out. 'Who cleans today!'

'OK, OK, I'm coming.' Mary was sitting up in bed. She saw I was awake and smiled at me. 'Good morning, Fauziya.'

'Good morning, Mary.' It wasn't a good morning. But it was good to see her sweet face. I thanked Allah for that mercy.

The guard left the room. Mary stood up, rubbed her back, walked to the door, picked up a broom that was leaning against the wall next to a mop and bucket and some other cleaning supplies, and began sweeping. I shielded my eyes again and took my first real look around at where I was. There were four more beds along the wall to my right. Women were sleeping in them, or trying to. They groaned and shifted. How could anyone sleep with all these bright lights and all this noise? How could people sleep on these hard, crackly mattresses? How could they sleep in this cold?

I looked around the room. It was a long, narrow room with a concrete floor. The walls, floor, and ceiling were all painted off-white. A maze of giant pipes ran across the ceiling. Somewhere in their midst there was a small skylight cut into the ceiling, and a huge, thrumming air-conditioning unit. No wonder the room was so cold. A big interior-facing window, the only window, looked into the hall, and an oblong metal table and six metal stools, all of them bolted to the floor, stood in front of the window. The shower, sink, and toilet were opposite the window along the back wall. A low half-wall ran in front of them, shielding them from the view of people in the hall but leaving them exposed to people in the dorm. The telephone was on the wall to the left.

The telephone! Finally I could call my uncle. I headed toward the phone.

'Not yet, Fauziya,' Mary said, seeing where I was going. 'They don't turn it on until eight o'clock.'

'What time is it now?'

'A little after six. Wake-up is at six.'

Two hours! What was I going to do for two hours?

'Why don't you go back to sleep? Breakfast isn't until seven. I'll wake you up.'

'No, I can't sleep.'

Still wearing her nightgown, Mary was already at work. I watched her sweeping the floor with quick, hard strokes. There was an energy, an efficiency to her movements that I liked. She was short, wide, and solidly built, strong-looking, heavy but not fat. She had a smooth, round, beautiful face with pretty features. Her skin was very black.

'Why are you sweeping?'

'It's my turn to clean. We rotate.'

'Can I help?'

'No, Fauziya, you should sleep. You didn't get much rest last night.'

'No, I can't sleep. Let me help.'

She stopped sweeping. 'You sure?'

'Please. What can I do?'

She smiled. There was a space between her upper front teeth. 'OK. See the spray bottle and rag over there by the door? You can clean the table and window if you want.'

After I did that, she showed me how to use the mop-squeezer attached to the bucket and I mopped the floor while she scrubbed the shower, toilet, and sink. When we finished cleaning, we put the supplies back by the door, and she rapped on the window. The same female guard I'd seen before appeared on the

251

other side. 'OK!' Mary called through the glass. The guard nodded, opened the door, and took everything away.

'Someone does this every morning?' I asked Mary after the guard had left.

'Every morning,' she said. 'And guess whose turn it is tomorrow?'

'Mine?'

She laughed. 'That's right. But don't worry. I'll help you.'

Tomorrow. Tomorrow was Monday. I'd be leaving tomorrow. One day. That's all I had to get through. One day and one more night.

The other women in the room were still in their beds. Mary made her bed, pulled the box out from under it, and took out a towel and some clothing. I looked under my bed. There was a box there, too. My towel, cup, fork, and spoon were in it. Mary must have put them there the night before. She gathered up her towel and clothing and headed to the back of the room toward the shower.

'What time is it now?' I asked.

'Six-forty.' Only six-forty! How could the time be passing this slowly?

I sat on my bed while she showered, to give her some privacy. She kept her back to the window. The half wall concealed the lower half of her body but the upper half was exposed, and she was short! The wall would cover even less of me. She was standing under the spray. That meant the water wasn't cold. That was good. I yearned for a hot shower. But not here, where everybody could see me. I'd wait until tomorrow, when I got to my uncle's house.

Mary finished showering and came back to her bed dressed in blue pants like mine and a yellow T-shirt. It was a lot nicer than the blue shirt I was wearing. The cotton looked softer. I asked her where she got it.

'You don't have a T-shirt?'

'No. Should I?'

'Yes. You're supposed to get two. We have to wear the blue shirt only when we go out into the hall. When we're in the dorm, we're allowed to wear T-shirts. Kim didn't give you any?'

'No.'

She shook her head, pulled the box out from under her bed, and handed me her other T-shirt. 'Here, Fauziya. Use one of mine. It's more comfortable. We'll get you your own when Miss Jones comes in to-morrow.'

'Who's Miss Jones?'

'She's one of the officers.'

'Does she give out the nightgowns too?'

Mary laughed. She had a lovely musical laugh. 'No, Fauziya, they don't give us nightgowns here. We sleep in our T-shirts.'

'But you have a nightgown.'

She laughed again. 'No, that's not a nightgown. It's a hospital gown.'

'A hospital gown.' I was confused. 'Where'd you get a hospital gown?'

'Where do you think, silly?'

'From a hospital?'

'Smart girl!'

'You were in a hospital? What for?'

'For my ulcer.' She wasn't laughing now.

'You have an ulcer? Oh, Mary, I'm sorry!'

'Thanks, Fauziya.'

'Does it hurt a lot?'

She shrugged. She didn't say yes, she didn't say no. I knew what that meant. Where she and I come from, people didn't burden others with their problems. Mary hadn't said she was hurting, but she hadn't denied it either. I know that meant she was suffering.

'Well, you looked pretty in the gown anyway,' I said.

That's the polite thing to do in our culture. People get embarrassed when a conversation turns to their problems, so we try to change the subject, make a joke, lighten the conversation somehow.

I heard a rumbling in the hallway and then someone rapped hard on the door.

'Breakfast!' Mary called loudly. The women in the other beds groaned and began sitting up. The door opened and the female guard reappeared, this time to hand in food trays two at a time to Mary, who put them on the metal table. When the door closed again, I could see the guard passing in front of the window pushing a big metal cart, which was the source of the rumbling I'd heard.

'We eat in here?' I asked Mary.

'Breakfast, lunch, and dinner.'

'There's no dining room?'

She laughed. 'No, no dining room.'

'Do we stay in here all the time? In this room?'

'Pretty much.'

'You're kidding!'

'No, I'm not.'

A whole day locked up in that freezing cold room with its blinding lights and blasting TV? A whole day with no fresh air, without even being able to look outside? I wasn't sure I could take it, not even for a single day.

Mary sat down on one of the metal stools and patted the table. 'Come on, get your fork and spoon and come eat while it's still warm. It may be the only half-decent food you get today.'

I wasn't hungry. But I went to the table and sat down across from Mary, more for the company than anything else. I examined the food. The trays were divided into sections. The food was served right on the tray, no plates or bowls. Five trays had the same food: a small scoop of gray oatmeal; a small, limp slice of dry French toast; a couple of spoonfuls of honey in an indentation in the tray; four packets of sugar; a little clear plastic cup of pale orange juice; a small apple or orange; a small carton of milk. Mary's tray had different food: a small slice of dry white toast; a small glob of something yellow that I learned later was scrambled powdered egg; a small box of cereal; a tea bag.

'Why is your food different?'

'Because of my ulcer,' she said as she put some of the yellow stuff into her mouth.

I tasted the oatmeal, then pushed my tray away.

'Aren't you going to eat?'

'No.'

'Fauziya, you have to eat.'

But I couldn't. The food was too disgusting. I was here, alone, in this awful place, and I was starving for something decent to eat. I started to cry.

Mary came around the table and sat down next to me. She took one of my hands in hers. 'Come on, don't cry. It's not going to help.' Oh, God. Now she sounded like Ayisha. I began crying harder. The other women in the dorm had wandered over to the table by then and were scooping their oatmeal into their cups to store in the boxes under their beds with their cartons of milk and fruit, saving it until a little later when they felt like eating, a trick I'd eventually pick up too. I would come to know and like them later. Lola was from Cuba, Jasmine from Honduras, Maria from

Brazil, and Rosa from Guatemala. They made sympathetic noises as I sat crying. But I couldn't respond. I just sat there, not looking at them, continuing to cry. Mary tried to comfort me. When that failed, she tried joking with me. 'Come on, Fauziya. If you don't stop crying, I'll have to start singing to you, and, believe me, you don't want to hear me sing.' I forced a smile. She was so sweet, and she was trying so hard. 'That's better,' she said. 'Come on, now. Try to eat something.' She reached across the table and took the toast from her plate. 'Here, have a piece of toast at least. Come on, take a bite or I'll start singing.' I took a bite. It was dry, cold, tasteless. It stuck in my throat. She handed me the cup of orange juice. 'Take a sip.' I sipped. It tasted like orange-flavored water. Another bite, another sip, another bite, another sip.

'What time is it now?'

She looked at her watch. 'Seven-twenty.'

Oh, God. Wouldn't it ever be eight o'clock?

'You should take a shower,' Mary said. 'It'll make you feel better.'

'No, I can't,' I said. 'Everyone will see me. And I don't have any clean clothes. I don't even have a fresh pad.'

'I'll take care of things for you,' she said. She knocked on the window. The same guard came. 'We need a pad!' Mary called. The guard brought a pad.

'That's Miss White,' Mary said, handing me the pad. 'She's one of the nicer ones. Some of the other guards . . .' She shook her head. You had to knock on the window and call a guard when you needed something, she explained, but some of them wouldn't bring it. No matter how many times you asked, they'd ignore you. Miss White didn't do that, Mary said. She was nice and usually responded.

Mary got me into the shower by promising to stand in front of the half-wall to shield my nakedness as I bathed. I didn't have a toothbrush, so I couldn't brush my teeth. I rinsed them with water and checked my reflection in the mirror above the sink. It wasn't a real mirror, just a sheet of metal, wavy, dull, and tarnished. I couldn't really see myself in it. It was just as well. I didn't want to see myself in prison clothing. I didn't want to believe I was there. The shower did make me feel better, though.

Seven-forty. I tried the phone. Dead. No dial tone. Mary and I sat at the table to talk. We switched from English to Twi, a Ghanaian language I'd picked up at school. She'd also fled to escape a harsh tribal tradition, and she'd come to the United States because she had a sister here.

'You have family here and they're keeping you in this place anyway?'

'Yes. Why?' Her expression turned tender. 'Oh, you thought . . .' She smiled sadly. 'No, Fauziya. Yes, I have family here too.'

No! That couldn't be! It couldn't! I rushed to the phone. Still no dial tone. 'What time is it? When can I call?'

'Just three more minutes,' Mary answered tenderly.

I hung up the phone, keeping my grip on the receiver, my mind racing and spinning. Mary had a sister here. Maybe that was the problem. Maybe women didn't have any power in America. Maybe it was like in Togo, where men make all the decisions. That had to be it. But I had an uncle here. He'd be able to get me out. I picked up the phone twice more. Nothing. And then, finally, I got it – a dial tone!

'It's on! Mary! Quick! I have to call my uncle! What do I do?'

257

She came to the phone and took the receiver. It wasn't a regular phone. It was a prison phone. You had to go through a complicated procedure to place a call, listening to recordings and pressing buttons and talking to operators and doing all kinds of things I didn't know how to do. You could only call collect, and you had to tell an operator what number you were calling. Mary asked for my uncle's number. I didn't know it.

'But I know he's in New Jersey,' I said. 'Ask the operator to find it.'

'No, they don't do that here. You have to know the number.'

'But I have to find him! I have to call him! What will I do?' I started to panic.

'Fauziya, calm down. Is there someone else you can call?'

'No! I have to call my uncle!' Oh, God! What if I couldn't reach him? 'Wait! Yes! My cousin! I have a cousin!' I'd forgotten about him. I knew his number. I could call him! Sometimes when I'd helped his wife call him from Togo, he'd passed along news about my uncle and aunt. That meant he spoke to them, and he'd know their number.

I told Mary my cousin's number. She placed the call. I waited. I prayed. Oh, God, please let that still be his number. Please let him be there. Let him be home. Somebody answered! Mary handed the phone to me.

'Rahuf!'

'He's not here,' a male voice said. 'Who's calling?'

'Fauziya!'

'Fauziya? Well, he's not here, Fauziya. He's still at work.'

'When will he be home?'

'In a couple of hours. Do you want to leave a number?'

'Mary! What's the number here!'

'He can't call you, tell him you'll call back.'

'I'll call back! Could you tell him I called? Could you ask him to please not go anywhere until I call? It's important.'

'OK, Fauziya. I'll tell him.'

I hung up the phone. Thank God! It was still his number. He'd be home soon.

I waited exactly two hours and called again. He answered the phone and accepted the call even though he didn't remember me at first. I'd helped his wife call him dozens of times, but I'd never spoken to him myself. I didn't know it then, but I was the last thing he needed at that time in his life. Rahuf was living and working in the Washington, D.C. area, sharing an apartment with roommates and working two or three low-wage jobs in order to save money to send home to his family in Togo. I showed up out of the blue, a half cousin on his mother's side whom he hardly remembered, calling collect to tell him I was here, I was in trouble, and I needed help. He responded. He put everything on the line for me when others whom I'd thought I could count on to help, and who could have helped a lot more easily, turned their backs on me. He's a good man, my cousin Rahuf. *Good* doesn't begin to describe him.

'Rahuf!'

'Yes.'

'It's Fauziya! Yaya's little girl!'

'Oh! Fauziya! Where are you?'

'I'm here! I'm in America!'

'In America! Where?'

'Mary, where am I!'

'K dorm at Esmor Detention Center in Elizabeth, New Jersey.'

I repeated it. 'Rahuf, I'm in prison! You have to help me! You have to get me out!' I burst into tears.

'Fauziya! Calm down and tell me what happened.'

But I couldn't calm down. I couldn't stop crying.

Finally Rahuf broke in: 'Fauziya! Put the other woman on the phone.'

I handed the phone to Mary, still crying. She listened for a while. 'No, you can't,' she said. 'She has to go before a judge. You have to hire a lawyer.' A lawyer! I didn't hear what else she said. I was crying too hard. She spoke for a few more minutes then handed the phone back to me. 'Fauziya, he wants to talk to you. Calm down and talk to him. The phone's going to cut off soon.' Prison phones cut off automatically after certain set periods of time, which vary from prison to prison. The phones at Esmor cut off after fifteen minutes. If you wanted to talk longer, you had to redial. But if someone else was waiting to use the phone, you couldn't redial.

I took the phone back, still crying.

'Fauziya, stop crying. I'll help you. But you have to calm down and tell me what happened. How'd you get here? Who'd you come with?'

I forced myself to stop crying and told him the whole story quickly. He knew the background. He knew about the tensions between my father and his siblings. He knew my aunt and uncle had never accepted my mother. He knew my father had died. I filled him in from there. 'And now I'm in prison! Oh, Rahuf, you have to help me!'

'I will, Fauziya, but you're going to have to be strong.' He'd asked Mary if he could come bail me out. No he couldn't, she'd told him. I had to see a judge, and I'd need a lawyer to present my case. The judge would decide whether to free me or deport me. I wouldn't see a judge the next day. I might not see one for a long time, Mary had told him. I probably wouldn't be getting out on Monday. I'd have to stay there for a while.

'Oh God! No! No! No!' I started crying again.

'Fauziya, calm down! Have you called your uncle?'

'No! I don't have his number! Do you have it?'

Yes, he did have it, and fortunately for me, he said, my uncle lived in Newark, very close to where I was being held.

'Newark! That's the name of the airport I flew into! That's right here!' I could hear the planes roaring low overhead from inside the dorm.

'Call him and tell him you spoke to me,' Rahuf said. 'Tell him you need a lawyer. He should know a good one. Tell him I'll help pay. Call me back after you talk to him and tell me what he said, OK?'

'OK. Thanks.'

'You're welcome, Fauziya. Now don't cry anymore. It's not going to help. You have to stay strong. Don't worry, I'll help you. Your uncle and I will both help you.'

Mary helped me call my uncle, but for some reason we couldn't get the call to go through and I had to call Rahuf again to ask him to get in touch with my uncle for me. He agreed and told me to check back with him in half an hour.

I called Rahuf again. Great news! Unbelievably great news! He'd spoken with my uncle. My uncle had a good lawyer. He couldn't call the lawyer that day because it was Sunday, but he'd call first thing the next day. He'd tell the lawyer to come and get me out of there right away. Rahuf said my uncle had agreed to sign a paper saying I could come live with him. He'd take care of me. I'd be out tomorrow after all!

I hung up the phone, grabbed Mary, and hugged her. 'Oh, Mary! I'm going to get out! My uncle's going to sponsor me! He's going to send his lawyer to come get me tomorrow!'

She accepted my hug more than she returned it. 'I hope so, Fauziya,' she said softly. 'I hope so.'

I was too excited to pay attention to the doubt in her tone. 'You need a lawyer, Mary!' I said happily. 'You should tell your sister to get you a lawyer so you can get out of here too!'

She sat down at the table again and looked at me like she wasn't sure how to tell me what she was about to say. She sighed. 'I do have a lawyer, Fauziya.'

'You do?'

'Yes, I do. Everybody here has a lawyer.'

No. That couldn't be. My stomach twisted a little. 'But . . . Why are you here, then? Why are these other women here?'

She sighed again. 'It's not up to the lawyers, Fauziya. It's up to the judge. The lawyer presents your case to the judge, but the judge is the one who decides. You don't get out of here unless the judge says so. You have to wait to see the judge.'

'But you've been waiting four months!'

'Yes, I have. And some of the other women have been waiting even longer.'

I called Rahuf again in a panic. 'Rahuf! Mary says everyone here has a lawyer! She says I won't get out! She says I'll have to stay here until I see a judge!'

Again Rahuf told me to calm down. He said I shouldn't let Mary frighten me. Maybe she and the other women didn't have good lawyers. My uncle had said he had a very good lawyer. My uncle had said he'd get me out. He'd sounded very sure. Why would he say that if it wasn't true?

'You're right. I'm sorry. I got scared.'

'Try to stay calm, OK?'

'OK.'

'OK. I have to go out now, but I'll be back later. Call me tonight so I know you're all right.'

That had been my third long-distance collect call to him that day. Collect calls cost money. Rahuf didn't have much money. I didn't know that then. He didn't mention it. Call again tonight, he'd said, so I know you're OK. That was all he'd said.

I felt better again when I got off the phone.

I spent the rest of the day with Mary, talking, learning to play dominoes, watching TV. Lunch came at eleven-thirty: sliced potatoes, tomato sauce and cabbage. The potatoes were cold and mushy, the tomato sauce was watery, the cabbage was overcooked and tasteless. I pushed the tray away. Mary pushed it back. 'You have to eat, Fauziya,' she said. 'You'll starve if you wait for decent food.' I ate, to please her. After lunch we watched a movie on TV. But I couldn't watch it for too long. The high-intensity lights beaming down from every corner of the room hurt my eyes.

'Isn't there anything else to do here but watch TV?' I asked Mary.

'Not much,' she said. 'There's a recreation area with some exercise equipment in it. But it's not finished yet, so they don't let us in there much.'

'Do they ever let you outside?'

'No.'

'Not ever?'

'Not ever. They let you visit other dorms. I can't do that anymore because I'm being punished, but you can. The only other thing there is to do, really, is work in the laundry. I used to do that. I can't do that either anymore, but you should do it. The man who runs it is really nice, and it gives you something to occupy your time. You should tell Miss Jones you want to do that.' She smiled. 'If you stay here I mean. But you probably won't. You'll probably be gone tomorrow.' She didn't really believe that, I could tell. She was just being nice to me.

'Tell me how you tried to escape,' I said, to change the subject. She sighed, laughed, and told me. She'd paid a guard some money to help her escape during one of the regular visits she made to the hospital to have her ulcer treated. But she'd gotten caught when the getaway driver panicked and refused to take her. When the guards who'd taken her to the hospital discovered she was missing, they ran out and found her, still sitting in the car, screaming at the driver. They'd brought her back in her hospital gown, the gown I'd mistaken for a nightgown, and put her in segregation for thirty days. When they let her out, they'd moved her out of her old dorm into this dorm to separate her from the other Ghanaian women. She smiled. 'So here I am.' She said her lawyer had told her sister she'd never get asylum now, she might as well forget it and go back to Ghana. The lawyer wouldn't take her calls anymore. 'She won't take my sister's calls either,' she said. 'My sister has paid her a lot of money, too, more than four thousand dollars. And now she won't even talk to us.'

Rahuf was right, I thought. She has a bad lawyer. My uncle had a good lawyer. I'd get out.

'What are you going to do?' I asked Mary.

She sighed. 'I can't stay here forever, I know that,' she said. 'Not in this place. That's why I tried to escape.' She shrugged. 'I guess I'll have to go back.'

264

'Back to Ghana?' I asked.

She paused. 'I'll figure something out. You've got your own problems to worry about. Don't worry about me. I'll be fine.'

Mary told me who was in the other dorms. Chinese women, Albanian women, Yugoslavian women, women from Ghana, Nigeria, Ivory Coast, Zaire, Uganda, Somalia, women from Guatemala, El Salvador, Honduras, Haiti, all kinds of different countries.

'Are any of them Muslim?' I asked.

'A few, I think. Why? Are you Muslim?'

'Yes.'

'I think there are more Muslim men here than women,' she said.

'There are men here, too?'

'Oh, yeah. A lot of men.'

'So there must be a lot of people here.'

'Oh, yeah, a lot.'

'How many do you think? Twenty? Thirty?'

She laughed again. 'Oh, no, a lot more than that. Something like three hundred.'

Good God! There'd only been about a hundred and fifty students in my whole boarding school and I'd thought that was big! This place was huge! I wondered what the building looked like from the outside. I hadn't been able to see anything when they'd brought me in. I'd see it tomorrow, when I left.

Dinner was at four-thirty, and it was just as bad as the other meals, maybe worse, but this time I was more interested when the other women in the dorm tried to talk to me. They smiled. 'Hi.' 'How are you?' Mary showed off her Spanish. *'Buenos días.'* The other women laughed.

'Sister?' one of the women asked her, pointing to me.

Mary put an arm around me. 'Daughter,' she said, smiling.

'Pretty,' the woman said, smiling at me.

I called Rahuf again at around seven, as he'd told me to do, and he said to call him again the next morning, after ten. By then he'd be back from his night job and would have had a chance to talk to my uncle to find out when the lawyer was coming.

Mary warned me just before lights-out: 'Kim's on duty tonight. She's going to come in late to do count. She'll make a lot of noise and grab your wrist or leg.'

'Why do they have to count us?'

'To make sure we're all still here.'

'Where else would we be?'

She laughed. 'People try to escape, remember?'

'Oh, yeah . . . Do they only do count at night?'

'No, they do it a lot. Remember when Miss White came and stood looking in the window for a while?'

'Yeah.'

'She was doing count. Most of the guards don't bother you. But Kim . . .' She shook her head. 'She's bad. She'll pull your blankets off, grab your wrist, maybe hit you on the bottom of the foot.'

'Does she do that to everyone?'

'Everyone. Every night she's on duty. She won't really hurt you. But she might scare you.'

Sure enough, when Kim came in that night, doors banging open and shut at her entrance and walkie-talkie blaring, she walked to Mary's bed, flung the blanket off her, grabbed her wrist and jerked her arm up. When she got to me, she grabbed my ankle. Then she moved on to the next bed. She hit the woman next to me on the bottom of a foot with her fist. *Whap!* The woman yelped. And so on down the line. When she was done, she left the room, letting the door slam behind her again. Bang!

I lay in bed seething with anger. They didn't treat people like human beings here. They treated people like animals. No wonder Mary had tried to escape. Thank God I wouldn't have to stay here after tomorrow . . .

The next thing I knew it was six A.M. again, and the television was blasting, the lights were glaring. 'Let's go! Let's go!' I bolted upright in bed. A female officer stood at the metal table, banging it with a baton. It wasn't Miss White. It was someone else, a thin, short, fair-skinned older woman with dark, intelligent-looking eyes.

I looked at Mary, who was also sitting upright in bed. 'Where are we going?' I asked, confused.

'Nowhere,' she said, waving a hand. 'That's just the way she talks.'

'Let's go! Let's go!' she said, her voice keeping time with the baton. 'Who cleans today!'

As I would soon learn, this was Miss Jones. She terrified me with her banging and yelling. She was loud, strict, and very tough. Nobody messed with Miss Jones.

'Let's go! Let's go! Who cleans today!'

'I do,' I said. My voice was shaking with fright.

She walked over, stood in front of me with her hands on her hips, and looked down at me. 'A newcomer,' she said.

'Yes, please,' I said softly.

'Up! Up!' She gestured for me to stand. I stood up and stepped aside as she bent, pulled the box out from under my bed, took out my towel and handed it to me. 'Did you get two towels?'

'Yes, please.' I was too scared to say anything else.

'No, she didn't,' Mary said. 'She only got one.'

'Did you get two T-shirts?'

'Yes, please.'

'No!' Mary said.

'Did you get two pairs of underwear?'

'Yes, please.'

'No!' Mary said. She laughed. 'You have to tell her, Fauziya, so she can bring you what you need.' I couldn't get the words out, so Mary told her. 'She needs another towel, a washcloth and another sheet. She only got one of each.'

'OK. What else?'

'T-shirts. She didn't get any. Another pair of underwear and another uniform. She only got one.' Miss Jones stood directly in front of me, literally under my nose, with her head turned toward Mary as Mary recited the list. I could smell her perfume. It was light and fresh-smelling. I breathed it in, wishing I had some to wear. The air in the room was so stale.

'A bra, too,' Mary said. 'The one she got was broken. And another pair of socks. And some sanitary pads. She needs some pads.'

Miss Jones nodded and turned back to me. 'OK. Into the shower. Go on, go! I'll get your stuff.' She left the room without slamming the door. I headed for the shower. I had no choice. I hated that shower. The half-wall in front of it didn't even cover my butt. But I did as told and I did it quickly. When Miss Jones told you to do something, you did it. I could tell that right away. My other dorm mates were still in bed, thank goodness. They seemed like nice women, but I felt shy about their seeing me naked. I stripped and turned on the water. At least it was hot. Miss Jones came back while I was showering and stood watching me for a few moments before going away again. I didn't like that. But I was losing count of how many people had seen me naked now.

Mary brought me a change of clothing from the pile Miss Jones had left on my bed. The bra and underpants were still big, the T-shirt was worn and frayed, the pants were a little snug, but these clothes did fit better than the ones I'd been given before. Miss Jones must have been looking at me in the shower in order to figure out what size clothing I wore.

Mary and I cleaned together that morning, which helped fill a little of the long wait to ten o'clock when I was supposed to call Rahuf again. He'd spoken to my uncle, he said when I reached him. My uncle had said he'd talked to his lawyer. Everything was being arranged.

Thank God! 'When is the lawyer coming? Did he say?'

My uncle had said he didn't know yet. Rahuf would have to call him back.

'But he's coming today, right?'

'That's what he said. Call me back in an hour. I should know then.'

I waited an hour, one of the longest hours of my life. When I called Rahuf again, he said my uncle still didn't know when the lawyer would be coming. He'd told Rahuf to call in another hour.

And so it went, hour by hour, phone call by phone call, for the entire day. Mary sat at the table watching me with a soft, sad look on her face. I didn't want to see that look. I was getting out today. I knew I was.

I didn't realize it then, but Rahuf was giving up a day of work to help me. He couldn't afford to do that, but he did it anyway.

After lunch that day, I heard a loud rumbling in the

hall. 'Man in the area!' someone shouted. The lawyer! He was here! He'd come!

No. 'Laundry day,' Mary said. She'd told me. I'd forgotten. It was the rumbling of the laundry cart I was hearing. 'Come on, Fauziya, get your dirty towels and clothes. I'll strip your bed.'

'No, that's OK.' I stayed at the table. I didn't need clean stuff. I was getting out today. I was.

My dorm mates stripped their beds and rolled up their dirty towels and clothing in the sheets. When Mary finished rolling up her things, she gathered and rolled up mine. The laundry cart appeared in front of our window. A man was pushing it, a tall, heavy, solidly built black man with a round, smooth, handsome, friendly face. He looked like he was maybe in his late thirties or early forties. I couldn't tell for sure. He had a nice face. He looked kind. He smiled at me so I smiled back. The door clicked unlocked, Mary handed out the six rolls of dirty sheets and clothing and received six clean rolls in exchange.

'That's Mr Williams,' Mary said as the laundry truck continued on down the hall. 'He runs the laundry.'

'He has a nice face,' I said.

'Oh, he's a very nice man. I really miss working with him.' She sighed, shrugged. 'But there's nothing I can do about that now.' She squeezed my hand. 'Really, Fauziya, you should tell Miss Jones you want to work in the laundry.' I noticed she didn't say 'if you stay' this time.

An hour or two later, the door clicked open and Miss Jones came in holding some sheets of paper. The lawyer was here! She'd come to take me to him! Those must be my release papers.

No. She walked into the room and put the sheets of paper on the table. 'Here you go, ladies. I'll be back for them later.' She left the room and the locks clicked closed again. Mary sat down beside me with a pencil in her hand. 'It's the commissary list,' she said. I looked at the paper. There were all kinds of things listed on it with prices printed next to them: shampoos, soaps, skin lotions, candies and cookies, writing paper, stamps, envelopes, pens. Mary was examining the list, checking off items. 'These biscuits are good,' she said, pointing to an item on my list. 'See? You check off what you want here and they deduct the money from your account. It's kind of expensive and they don't always bring what you order right away, but it's that or nothing. They don't let anybody bring you anything from outside.' She went back to her list. I put mine aside. 'Want anything, Fauziya? How about some hot chocolate?'

'No.' I was leaving today. I was.

I called Rahuf again. He'd spoken with my uncle. My uncle had told him the lawyer couldn't make it today. He'd come tomorrow.

Tomorrow! I hung up the phone and cried. Oh, God. Another night in this place! Another night!

The rest of the day passed in a fog. I went to bed that night praying to God. Please, God. Let the lawyer come tomorrow. Please, please, please . . .

I was just dropping off to sleep when the door banged open and the lights blazed on.

'Out! Out! Dorm search! Everybody out! In the gym!'

I bolted upright. Two guards stood in the doorway, shouting orders at us. Mary and my other dorm mates threw their covers off and jumped out bed. Mary held out her hand to me. 'Come on, Fauziya. Let's go.'

I took her hand and followed her barefoot out the

door past the guards. The hall was filled with women. There were guards everywhere. Male guards, female guards, all shouting and yelling. The guards herded us through the hallways to a walled-in, concrete-floored recreation area. There was a Ping-Pong table and a couple of exercise machines in the room.

'What's going on?' I asked Mary.

'Dorm search,' she said. 'They like to surprise us. This is the first time they've done it at night, though.'

'What're they going to do?'

'Search the rooms for stuff we're not supposed to have.'

'Like what?'

'Food. Extra towels, clothes. Whatever they find.'

'What happens if they find something?'

'They take it away.'

The gym was crowded now. I looked around at the other women. So many beautiful, interesting faces! Some of the women leaned against the wall with their eyes closed. Others squatted or sat on the floor, talking softly with their friends. We were all in our nightclothes. A bunch of guards stood inside the door, watching us.

'How long are they going to keep us here?' I asked Mary.

She laughed. 'Until they're done. There's no telling.'

Some of the women fell asleep while waiting, but I was too cold to sleep. After a long, long time the male guards left the area and the women guards started barking more orders. 'Up! Up! On your feet! Everybody line up!' We formed ourselves into a long line that snaked around the room.

'What are they going to do now?' I asked Mary.

'Body search,' she said.

Oh God! Not again? In front of all of these people! Why were they doing this?

The guards started with the women nearest the door, three guards, three women. 'Drop your pants! Lift your shirt!' The women did as told. The guards patted them all over their bodies. 'Turn!' The women turned and the guards patted them all over again. 'OK, out.' Another guard opened the door for them and the women filed out. The three guards doing the searching moved on to the next three women in front of them, then the next three, and so on until it was my turn. By the time Jasmine, Mary, and I filed out of the gym it was twelve forty-five A.M. They had held us for more than two hours. Our dorm had been ransacked. Sheets and blankets had been pulled off the beds and left where they'd fallen. All the boxes had been pulled out from under the beds and emptied. Everything was scattered all over the floor. Mary simply sighed, walked to her bed, and began putting her things back in her box. I burst into tears. Please God. Let the lawyer come tomorrow. I can't stay in this place.

I called Rahuf the next morning sobbing. 'I have to get out of here! When is the lawyer coming?'

Rahuf still didn't know. He'd spoken to my uncle. My uncle had said today for sure, but he didn't know when yet. He'd told Rahuf to call back.

I kept calling Rahuf. Rahuf kept calling my uncle. My uncle kept telling him to call back. The lawyer didn't come that day. Or the next. Or the next. Or the next. My uncle put me through five days of this torture before finally telling Rahuf on Friday afternoon, the day before Christmas Eve, that he wasn't going to send his lawyer. According to Rahuf, my uncle said that he wasn't going to help me at all. He told Rahuf to let the immigration people send me back to Togo.

Rahuf was furious. But he said nothing to my uncle of his feelings, because we don't speak disrespectfully to our elders where we come from. Instead, he'd put his energy into engaging a lawyer for me himself – something he was trying, unsuccessfully, to explain to me. I couldn't hear him because I'd started to cry hysterically. I couldn't believe that the man who had known me since childhood, whom I thought of as an uncle, had refused to help me when I needed him the most.

'Fauziya! Calm down! Stop crying! I am going to help you! I said I would and I will. I've hired a lawyer.'

'Oh, God! You have!'

'Yes. Get a pencil and paper and I'll give you the information you need.'

The lawyer specialized in helping immigrants, Rahuf said. He had an office in the Washington, D.C. area where Rahuf lived. I would learn later that he was Rahuf's lawyer. He'd already talked to this lawyer, he said, and the lawyer had agreed to take my case. His name was Eric Bowman. Rahuf gave me his phone number and had me repeat it to make sure I'd gotten it right. It was past five o'clock then, too late to call that day. Rahuf told me to call Monday morning, the day after Christmas. My first Christmas in America I was going to spend in prison.

While I was getting through those first terrible days at Esmor, Layli was in Washington, D.C., using her Christmas break to do more reading and research for her law journal article on female genital mutilation – a term I hadn't yet heard. Karen was in California on break from teaching at Santa Clara University, still weighing Rick Wilson's invitation to come to American University the following fall.

I hadn't met either of these women yet, nor had

they met each other. None of us knew it, but we all came one step closer together that Friday afternoon, the day before Christmas Eve. My uncle had abandoned me to my fate. Eric Bowman was part of my fate. It was through him that I would eventually meet Layli, and through Layli, I would meet Karen. Eric was the link.

19

Bowman

I called Eric Bowman on Monday morning, the day after Christmas. My voice was shaking, unable to rise above a whisper. I'd never talked to a lawyer before. A deep male voice came on the phone after I'd identified myself to the secretary.

'Hello, Fauziya,' it said. 'It's good to hear from you. I've been expecting your call. Did you get through the weekend all right?' He sounded warm, friendly, kind. I relaxed a little.

He chatted with me for a few minutes to put me at ease, and then it was down to business. Time to tell my story. 'I'm going to ask you some questions, and I want you to answer them as fully and honestly as you can, OK?'

'OK.'

'Try to speak loudly and slowly so I can hear you, OK?'

'OK.'

'If the phone cuts off, just hang up and call me back, OK?' Obviously he knew about prison phones, which meant he must have a lot of experience helping people get out of prison. That reassured me.

We started with how I'd gotten the passport, from whom, how much I had paid, and what I'd said to the immigration officers when I arrived at Newark Airport.

He said he needed to know everything exactly the way it happened. I told him what I remembered. I told him how they tried to send me back to Germany, how they thought I was lying about being from Togo. Then we went over why I'd come to America and why I was asking for asylum. I broke down crying several times as we talked. He was very patient. He'd wait until I regained my composure and then ask me to continue. We talked nearly half an hour, with recorded announcements interrupting us frequently, and one cutoff after the first fifteen minutes. I told him everything. I even told him about *kakia*.

'OK,' he said after we'd gone over my story. 'The first thing I need to do now is get a copy of your INS file.'

'What's that?'

'The people who interviewed you at the airport wrote out some forms, right?'

'Yes. And they took my picture and fingerprints.'

'Well, all of that goes into a file. That's your INS file. INS stands for Immigration and Naturalization Service. That's the branch of government that handles immigrant and refugee affairs. That's who the immigration inspectors work for. They write up a report – what you said, whether they think you were telling the truth . . .'

'I did tell the truth!'

'I'm sure you did, Fauziya. But I need to see what they wrote. That's what the INS is going to look at when we ask them to let you out of prison, and that's what the judge is going to look at when we ask him to let you stay in this country. I need to know what the report says so I can decide the best way to present your case at your hearing. But the hearing won't be for a while. I want to try to get you paroled before then.'

'Do you think you can?'

'I don't know, Fauziya. I can't promise. But I'll do everything I can.'

'When will you know?'

'I can't say for sure. A week, a few weeks.'

A few weeks! Oh God! How could I survive that long in prison?

A recording interrupted again, telling us that our second fifteen minutes were almost up.

'I have to get out of here,' I said, my throat so constricted I could barely speak. 'Please help me.'

'I'm going to do my best. I'll stay in touch through Rahuf,' he said. 'You talk to him regularly, right?'

'Yes.'

'OK. He'll keep you posted on how things are progressing. I'll want to talk to you again. I'll tell Rahuf when I want you to call, OK?'

'OK,' I whispered, struggling not to break down. A few weeks!

'I'm sorry, Fauziya. I'll do everything I can to get you out, but it's going to take time. You're going to have to hang in there for a while. Can you do that?'

'I guess so . . .'

I hung up the phone, pressed my forehead against the wall, and sobbed. I felt a hand on my shoulder.

'Oh, Fauziya.' Mary put an arm around my waist and led me to my bed. She sat with me and held me while I cried. I cried and cried until my sobs faded into sighs. I wiped my eyes and sat limp, empty, staring at the floor. I was going to stay in prison. I was going to be here for a few weeks at least. Maybe more. Mr Bowman had been very clear about that.

I called Rahuf at ten and told him about my conversation with Bowman.

'I like him,' I said. 'He was very nice. And he was honest with me. He didn't lie.'

'He's a good man,' Rahuf said.

I didn't know it then, but Bowman had agreed to handle my case for much less than he'd normally charge. Even so, it was more than Rahuf could afford to pay. But he'd agreed to pay it. Some of his friends who'd also come to America from Togo helped him raise the first five hundred dollars. They didn't have much money either, but they gave what they had.

Bowman told Rahuf we needed to 'document' my story – produce letters, papers, and anything else we could get that showed I was telling the truth. Rahuf said he'd already spoken to some of his relatives back home and told them to get a message to Ayisha.

Ayisha! 'Oh, Rahuf, find out how she is. I haven't heard from her since I left. I wrote to her from Germany but she didn't write back.' I started to cry. 'But don't tell her I'm in prison, Rahuf. Please! Don't! You didn't tell your relatives I'm in prison, did you?' I was desperate for my family not to know, not to have to worry about me.

'No. All I said was that you're here and I'm helping you get your papers straightened out and I need to talk to her.'

Papers . . .

'Rahuf! Ask Ayisha if she still has the marriage certificate!'

'What marriage certificate?'

'They drew up a marriage certificate! Everybody signed it except me. Ayisha took it away with her. She might still have it.'

'OK. I'll ask her. Can you think of anything else?'

What else? I went back over that horrible day in my mind. What happened that day? I got up, Awaye showed me the clothes, the *nachane* bathed me, she and her girl who did the *laylay* designs dressed me, Ibrahim's three wives came, someone took a photograph.

'There's a picture,' I said.

'What kind of picture?'

'Of when the other wives were there. Someone came in with a camera and took a picture of all of us sitting on the bed, but I don't know who it was. I can't remember.'

'Do you think Ayisha could get it?'

'I don't know.'

'I'll ask her. I'm going to ask her to get in touch with Amariya too. Bowman says we need to try to document everything that happened to you and to her, how you escaped, where you got the money . . .'

'But what can Amariya do?'

'Maybe she can write a letter saying she gave you the money.'

'But she doesn't know English.'

'I don't think she has to actually write it. She can dictate it and someone else can write it. She just has to sign it, I think. Does Ayisha know English?'

'Not enough to write. Alpha and Babs can, but I don't know if they can get to Amariya. They may not even know where she is.'

'Don't worry, Fauziya. We'll figure something out.'

Don't worry! I hadn't seen my mother in a year and eight months. I didn't know where she was. I didn't know how she was. She'd sacrificed so much of her inheritance to help me escape, to help me flee. And where had I ended up? It would break her heart if she knew.

After I hung up the phone I went and sat on my bed. I couldn't cry anymore. I was out of tears. I sat there dazed, numb, mute, trying to adjust to the fact that I was going to have to get through several more weeks in prison.

When Miss Jones brought in the commissary lists later that morning, I asked Mary for a pencil. Such a trivial thing, asking for a pencil, but my eyes welled with tears as I did it. It was an excruciatingly painful moment for me – a moment of truth. By filling out the commissary list, I was admitting that I was going to stay in prison. Mary handed me the pencil and said nothing. But she understood. She sat down beside me.

'You bought the biscuits last week,' I said. 'I'll buy them this week.'

'I'll buy the hot chocolate,' she said.

When I heard the laundry cart come rumbling down the hall later that day, I stripped my bed and rolled up my dirty laundry myself. Mary handed the dirty rolls to Mr Williams.

'This is Fauziya,' Mary said as she took the clean rolls he gave her in exchange. 'Fauziya, this is Mr Williams.'

He nodded politely. 'Hello, Fauziya. How're you doing today?' He put the emphasis on *you* – how're *you* doing today. I liked that.

'I'm fine,' I said shyly.

'You taking care of her, Mary?'

'Oh, yes.' Mary smiled at me. 'She's my daughter. Aren't you, Fauziya?'

Mr Williams nodded. 'That's good,' he said seriously. 'This is no place for someone as young as her.'

Had he really said that? None of the other guards or officers had commented on my youth. None of them seemed even to notice it.

'What a nice man,' I said to Mary as he left.

'He is,' she said. 'He's very nice. Really, Fauziya, you should tell Miss Jones you want to work in the laundry. It's hard work, but it'll give you something to do besides sit in this room all day, and Mr Williams is a good man to work for. You get paid, too.'

'Really? They pay you?'

'Not much. Just a dollar a day.' She grinned. 'But it'll help keep us in biscuits.'

When Miss Jones came by later to collect the commissary lists, Mary told her I wanted to work in the laundry. I did, but I was too scared of her to say so myself.

'No,' she said brusquely. 'Mr Williams doesn't need any new workers right now. And she's only been here a week. Nobody works in the laundry until they've been here three weeks.'

'You should have waited,' I said to Mary after Miss Jones left. 'Now she's mad.'

'No she's not. That's just her way. You have to start early and just keep bugging her. Otherwise she'll forget and pick someone else when there is an opening.'

'I don't think so, Mary. I don't think I can do that. She scares me.'

Mary laughed. 'You'll get used to her. She's not so bad.'

I would eventually come to like Miss Jones. Although she was cold and brusque with new arrivals and yelled at everyone, she was also kind, fair, and caring. You had to earn her respect and trust, but once you did she became your friend. She became my friend, anyway. She was a good person with a good heart.

Since I had stopped menstruating, I could resume my prayers. But, I didn't have a *mayahfi*. I didn't have

282

a prayer rug. I didn't have a Qur'an. Amariya's *tasbih* was in my suitcase, where I couldn't get to it. I wasn't sure which direction was east. But I'd have to make do. I spread newspaper on the floor by my bed as a prayer rug, washed, wrapped one of my clean towels around my head, stepped barefoot onto the newspaper, facing away from the window in the direction I hoped was east, and asked Allah to forgive my lapses and accept the devotions I was about to offer Him. My dorm mates sat still and quiet on their beds as a gesture of respect. I asked Allah to keep me strong, strong in spirit, strong in faith. I asked Him to guide and protect me and keep me near Him. I prayed for mercy, for deliverance. I asked Him to help me accept His will. 'Oh, Allah, You know all things and You determine all things. I don't know why You've chosen for me to suffer this way. Help me understand. Help me find peace. You have brought me here to this place and only You can free me from it. It's in Your hands. Your will be done.'

I had begun the process of settling in to prison life. I'd just have to get through this a day at a time, I'd decided, for however long it lasted.

I wrote to Ayisha to let my family know I was OK. I said I was in America. I said Rahuf was helping me get my papers straightened out. I said I was staying for a while in a place called Esmor, which I described as being like a boardinghouse. I said I was sharing a room with five women who were all very nice and that I'd become very close friends with one of them, a woman named Mary from Ghana. *Isn't that great? My best friend is from Ghana, just like at school.* I made it sound nice because I didn't want them to worry. I wrote out my address and asked them please to write and to send pictures of everyone. *I'll kiss them every*

283

*night before I go to sleep until God grants that we can
all be together again.*

I didn't cry so much during the day anymore.
Mainly I just sat with Mary. Day after day after day. She
couldn't leave the dorm. Not knowing anybody in any
of the other dorms, I had no reason to leave it. We
talked, we played dominoes, we watched TV. The talk
shows were shocking. Sex, sex, sex. In America, it
seemed like everybody had sex and then went on TV
to talk about it. One program I loved, however, was
Video Music Box. I lived for that program – sixty minutes of music and people dancing. *Video Music Box*
came on at four-thirty, which was also when our dinner was served. Since the food was disgusting, I
danced instead of eating. While my dorm mates sat
down to dinner, I danced by myself. They laughed.
Guards stood in front of our dorm window and
watched. I didn't care. For one short hour every day,
Monday through Friday, I let the music fill me, lift me,
carry me, out of prison, out of myself.

I kept in close touch with Rahuf those first days,
calling him two or three times a day for a while, sometimes more.

Any news?

Nothing yet. 'Are you all right, Fauziya?' he would
ask. 'How are you holding up?'

My back hurt from the hard mattress. My eyes were
beginning to burn and water from the harsh lights.
The room was freezing. I'd asked Miss Jones for a
second blanket. She'd said no. The room was windowless, airless. I could hardly hear Rahuf for all the noise.
The food was revolting. I was developing an itchy red
rash all over my body.

'I'm fine.'

'I wish I could come visit you, Fauziya,' he said one

day, 'but it's hard with you that far away and me working two jobs.'

'That's OK. You're doing so much for me already. Don't worry. I'm fine. Really. How are you?'

'Oh, you know, working, paying the bills. You'd be surprised how fast money goes in America. Food bills, rent bills, telephone bills. There's always some bill to pay.'

When I caught this first casual mention of telephone bills, I felt ashamed of myself. I'd been so wrapped up in my own problems that I'd never stopped to think what my calls were costing Rahuf. He was talking code, letting me know that my calls were costing him a lot, more than he could afford. He'd never say that. Nor would I ever say to him, 'I didn't call because I know the calls are costing you too much.' But from then on I did try to call only when I really needed to. Anyway, there wasn't much point in telling Rahuf about problems he couldn't fix.

In fact, it was beginning to feel like nobody could do anything to help me. I was becoming more and more depressed. One unending day of prison life after another had made me so miserable that I started to lose track of time. Already it felt like I'd been in prison forever. I was lying in bed one night, shivering and scratching as usual, when I heard what sounded like a lot of people counting backward real loud.

'Ten! Nine! Eight! Seven!'

'Six! Five! Four!'

What was that?

'Three! Two! One! Happee New Yeeaaarr!!!'

No. It couldn't be.

'Happy New Year!' People were cheering, whistling, clapping.

It was Sunday, January 1, 1995. My eighteenth

birthday. Happy New Year. Happy birthday to me. I had to laugh. Happy birthday, Fauziya. How do you like your birthday so far?

The only comfort I found in my misery those days was prayer. But sometime around then I realized that the newspapers I had used to improvise a prayer rug were not acceptable. Newspapers have pictures in them and Islam prohibits gazing at images of any kind while praying.

'What am I going to do?' I said to Mary.

'What if you had an extra sheet?' she said. 'You could use the sheet as a prayer shawl and stand on your extra towel.'

'But I don't have an extra sheet.'

'Well, we'll just have to get you one.'

'Miss Jones isn't going to give me an extra sheet, Mary. She said no when I asked for an extra blanket, remember?'

'I didn't say we were going to ask for one. I said we'll have to get you one.'

She did. A friend of hers named Elsie from N dorm worked in the laundry and sometimes pushed the laundry cart and handed out the clean rolls. Mary told her I needed an extra sheet. She smuggled one in to me in a roll of clean laundry. It was found and confiscated during a dorm search. No problem. Mary passed the word to Elsie, who smuggled me another one. More than four months at Esmor, Mary was seasoned, resourceful, wise in the ways of bending and getting around rules. She was my first instructor in prison survival.

One thing she wasn't able to help me with was the prison medical system. It was around then that I made my first visit to a prison doctor, hoping he would give me something to relieve my rash. When the doctor asked me what my problem was, I showed him my arms, which were covered with tiny, itchy red bumps.

'Hmmmm,' he said, gently turning my arms this way and that. 'Is it just on your arms?'

'No, all over. It itches like crazy.'

'Does it itch all the time?'

'Yeah. Especially after I take a shower. It seems to get worse then.'

'How often do you shower?'

'Once a day.'

He nodded. 'Shower once a week,' he said. 'See if that helps.'

Do what? 'Excuse me?' I said.

'It gets worse after you shower, right?'

'Yes.'

'So don't shower so much. Cut back to once a week. That's the only thing I can suggest, since medicine would be expensive, and I can't just give it out to everyone who asks.'

I thought he was joking. 'But I need something,' I said. 'It itches. What am I supposed to do?'

'If showering less doesn't help,' he said, 'read your Bible when the itching gets bad.'

'I'm Muslim,' I said coldly. 'I don't read the Bible.'

'Then read the Qur'an. Concentrate on that until the itching stops.'

It didn't seem worth mentioning that even if I had wanted to use the Qur'an in such a disrespectful way, I didn't have one. I stood up and walked out into the waiting room, where a guard was waiting to escort me back to my dorm. I couldn't believe I'd gone to a doctor who had advised me to either be dirty or be itchy.

It was such a crazy place, Esmor. Some people were mean, some were nice, some were mean one minute

287

and nice the next. You never knew what to expect. Sometime that same week, a guard came into the dorm and noticed me scratching.

'How long have you had that rash?' she asked.

I told her.

'Does it bother you all the time?'

'Yeah, especially after I shower.'

'What kind of soap are you using?'

I told her. It was one of the brands on sale at the commissary.

'Well, that's probably what's doing it.' She'd asked such a simple, obvious question. Why hadn't the doctor thought to ask about the soaps that I came into contact with? She looked at my arms. 'Your skin's all dried out. You should use lotion. Do you have any?'

'I bought some from the commissary but it isn't helping,' I said, scratching again. 'It seems to make it worse. I can't get the kind I like.'

'What kind do you use?'

I told her. 'I have some in my luggage but they don't have it in the commissary.' We weren't allowed to get anything out of our luggage.

'Come with me,' she said. She took me to book-in. 'Wait here,' she said as she disappeared into the back room. I waited. She reappeared with my suitcase and put it down in front of me. 'Get your lotion,' she said.

'Really?'

She was breaking the rules, and she and I both knew she'd be in trouble if anyone found out. She did it anyway. I looked at her. She held my gaze for a moment then looked away, trying to hide her heart. 'Come on. Hurry up.' But I'd seen it. I'd seen her heart. I wasn't just a prisoner to her. I was a person.

I opened my suitcase and took out the lotion, hesitated over a small tube of skin cream.

'You want to take that?' she asked.

'Can I?'

She nodded.

She let me take my skin cream, my comb, my deodorant. She let me take my little pocket-size address book and my kohl, which I used as eyeliner in Togo. She also let me take my watch and my mother's *tasbih*. Such small things. Such insignificant things. But they were the most precious things in the world to me. Everything I was, everyone I loved, came back to me when I saw them. The guard had given me an invaluable gift. But I can't give her credit for it by naming her because it could get her in trouble.

Sometime during that week I called Rahuf again. 'Bowman wants you to call him,' he said.

'Oh my God! Am I getting paroled?'

'I don't think so, Fauziya. Don't get all excited now. He didn't say that. He just said to have you call him.'

Don't get excited, I told myself as I placed the call to Bowman, but I was excited. I couldn't help it. Maybe he wanted to tell me himself before he told Rahuf.

'Good news, Fauziya!'

My heart leapt at these words. But what followed didn't live up to them. It wasn't bad news, it wasn't good news. It was no news as far as I was concerned, because it wasn't news about my getting out. I only half listened to what Bowman said once I realized it wasn't about getting paroled. He'd be coming to see me the following Monday, when we'd go to something called my 'calendar hearing,' he said. It wasn't my real hearing, just a preliminary appearance before a judge at the Esmor courthouse. The real hearing would be later, but he didn't know when.

'How much later?'

'I don't know yet, Fauziya. It's scheduled after the calendar hearing. What we'll do on Monday is tell the judge you're seeking asylum, then listen while an INS attorney presents the charges against you—'

'Charges! What charges?'

'That you tried to enter the country with a fraudulent passport.'

'What does *fraudulent* mean?'

'It means you tried to pretend the passport was yours.'

'But I didn't!'

'I know, Fauziya. That's what we'll tell the judge at the calendar hearing. The INS presents its charges, we respond to the charges, we say you're asking for asylum, and then they schedule the hearing.'

Now I had another weekend to get through, somehow. And then I'd still only be at the preliminary hearing stage. I spent part of that weekend writing a letter to Rudina, wishing her a belated Happy Christmas and Happy New Year. She'd be able to read those words in English. She'd probably have to find someone to help her translate the rest. I kept my letter short and simple. I told her I was in America now, staying at a place called Esmor. I didn't tell her I was in prison, either. It was too humiliating. I asked her to do me a favor. In the excitement of packing my things the day before leaving Germany, I said, I'd left my Togo and student I.D. cards behind. Could she please send them to me? Bowman had said we needed documents to prove I was telling the truth. The I.D. cards would at least prove that I was from Togo.

Monday morning at seven-thirty Miss Jones showed up at our door, yelling 'Seven Six One!' I glanced around at my dorm mates to see what to do, but they just went on with what they'd been doing. So I ignored her too. She came into the room and stood with her hands on her hips, angry now. 'Seven Six One! Seven Six One!' she bellowed.

'Fauziya,' Mary called to me from the table where she was sitting. I looked at her. She held up her left wrist and pointed to her I.D. bracelet. 'Check your number.' I looked at the number on my I.D. bracelet: 761. Miss Jones was calling me. By my number. I didn't have a name anymore. I wasn't Fauziya Kassindja anymore. I wasn't even Fauziya Kasinga. I was Seven Six One.

'I'm sorry, Miss Jones, that's me,' I said, scrambling to my feet.

She walked over and stood in front of me, glowering. She was furious. 'Who do you think you are?' she bellowed. 'An African princess?' She waved a hand. 'Let's go! You have a visitor.'

A visitor. Me? Did she have the right number? Was today Sunday, one of the regular visitors' days? I thought it was Monday. I kept losing track of the days. And then I remembered. Yes. Monday. Bowman had said he'd be coming today. I'd forgotten. To protect myself, I think. I'd spent my first week at Esmor waiting for a lawyer my uncle had said would be coming. He'd never come. Maybe my luck was changing now. Bowman had said he'd come today and he'd come.

'Let's go! Let's go!'

A guard was waiting outside the door to escort me to the tiny room where I would be meeting Bowman. She left me there alone, seated at a small table, looking out the window at the male guard posted in the hall outside. I was nervous. I'd never met a lawyer before. After a few minutes a man walked in carrying a briefcase. He smiled and held out his hand. 'Hello, Fauziya,' he said. 'I'm Eric Bowman.'

I took his hand. I was speechless. This was my lawyer? He was very tall, very handsome, impeccably groomed, dressed in a well-tailored dark suit. He was black. I'd expected a white man. My lawyer was black! I was overjoyed. He sat down across from me and smiled. I couldn't stop staring. I felt shy, happy, nervous, scared, thrilled, all at the same time. It must have shown.

'There's no need to be nervous, Fauziya,' he said gently. 'I'm here to help you. We can just sit quietly until you feel more comfortable if you like. We have plenty of time.'

'No, that's OK.'

'Do you have any questions you'd like to ask me before we get started?'

I nodded. Yes. One. Only one. The same question I'd never stop asking: 'When am I getting out?'

We started with that, bad news first. Not yet. He'd received the final, official word on Friday from the INS that my request for parole had been denied.

I felt like I'd been punched in the stomach. I couldn't breathe. My head spun. 'Denied! Why?'

As I later learned, under the law, at the time I was detained, a person whose continued detention is deemed not to be in the public interest may be paroled at the INS district director's discretion. I'm not sure how the public interest was served by my incarceration. All I know is that when I arrived at Newark Airport, there was a bed available at Esmor. Esmor is a private corporation that the INS was paying a huge amount of money – more than nine million dollars a year – to run the detention center at Elizabeth, New Jersey. Nine million dollars and they fed us inedible meals and gave us used, stained, tattered clothing to wear. Nine million dollars and I wasn't allowed to have a second blanket. Nine million dollars and the doctor wouldn't give me any medicine for my rash.

I started crying. 'I can't stay here! I can't! You have to get me out!'

'I'm trying, Fauziya,' Bowman said gently. 'We're not giving up. I'm going to try to get your case transferred to Baltimore where they have a more lenient parole policy. If I can get you transferred to a prison down there, I think we'll have a better chance of getting you out.'

'When will that happen?'

'I can't say. I'm not even sure I'll be able to do it. The Newark district director has to approve the transfer and there are all kinds of requirements. It's complicated. I'm not promising anything, but I'm going to try.'

'When will you know?'

'I can't tell you that either. I'll do everything I can. That's all I can promise.'

'So I have to stay here?'

He nodded. His eyes were sad. 'For a while. Yes.'

I put my head down on my arms and cried.

He put a gentle hand on my arm and let me cry.

'I'm sorry,' I said when I'd cried myself out.

'No, don't apologize,' he said gently. 'It's OK to cry.'

People don't say that where I come from. They say what Rahuf and Ayisha always said when I cried: 'Don't cry. Crying isn't going to solve anything.' But Americans say what Bowman said that day: 'It's OK to cry.' I would hear that a million more times during the period of trials and suffering that lay ahead of me. No matter how many times I heard it, however, it never stopped sounding strange to me.

'No,' I said, smiling and wiping my eyes. 'Crying won't solve anything.'

'Well, do you feel up to answering some questions?'

'Yes.'

'OK.' He lifted his briefcase onto the table, opened it, and took out a tape recorder, a bunch of papers, and a notebook and pen. 'I'm going to tape our conversation so I can use the information to work on your case. And we're going to go over everything again in detail. I'm going to ask you a lot of questions. I want you to relax and take your time in answering. You don't have to hurry. Just tell me everything exactly as you remember it, OK?'

And so we talked. I told him everything I'd told him before, but in much more detail. My face burned with shame and my voice faded to a whisper as I talked about *kakia*. He had to keep reminding me gently to speak louder. But he was kind and patient, and I trusted him.

When we'd finished going over my story, he asked me about alternatives to staying in America. 'What if you went to Benin? Would you be safe there?'

'No, they'd find me in Benin.'

'What about Ghana?'

'No, they'd find me there too. Why? Do you think they're going to send me back?'

'I'm not saying that.'

'They can't send me back. We have family all over West Africa. My aunt and uncle would find me wherever I went. I have to stay here. They have to give me asylum! They have to!'

'I wish that were true, Fauziya, but it's not,' he said. 'You have to understand that. It's up to the judge. He can say yes or no. You have to be prepared for that.'

The male guard who'd been patrolling back and

forth in front of the window came into the room as we talked. He was carrying a length of heavy metal chain in one hand. I thought he was going to tell us our time was up. Instead he came to my side of the table, squatted, grabbed one of my ankles, wrapped the chain around it, and attached it to the table leg. I was being chained up like some kind of dangerous criminal in front of my lawyer.

Bowman was enraged. 'What are you doing?' he demanded. The guard was impassive. 'Just doing my job, sir.'

'But this is outrageous! I'm her lawyer! This is an attorney visit!'

'Sorry, sir. It's the rules.'

The guard left. Bowman fumed. I cried from the humiliation of it.

'This is preposterous,' he said again, sounding angry at the guard and sorry for me at the same time. Then he bent down to examine my chains. 'I don't believe it,' he said as he straightened up. 'Look at this, Fauziya.' He took hold of the table and pulled. It moved. 'The table isn't even bolted down. I could lift it up and slip the chain right off.' We looked at each other and started laughing at the sheer absurdity of it. We laughed and laughed. It felt good, a lot better than crying.

Since I spoke English so well, Bowman asked me if I could write in English. When I told him yes, he gave me a seven-page form. It was the asylum application. He told me to look over the form now to see if there was anything I needed explained to me while he was here to do it. There wasn't, so he gave me a self-addressed stamped envelope and told me to mail the form back to him. 'Fill out as much as you can,' he said. 'If you have questions later, call me and we'll discuss it on the phone.' The form looked daunting, but I promised to fill it out and get it in the mail that same day.

We talked a little longer, then Bowman checked his watch. It was going on eight-thirty. 'The hearing is at nine,' he said. 'Do you want some time to get ready?'

'Yes. I haven't showered yet.'

'OK.' He knocked on the window. The guard appeared. Bowman waved him into the room. 'We're through now.' The guard nodded and squatted to remove my chains. Bowman and I exchanged smiles over the top of his head and almost started laughing again.

The calendar hearing lasted about ten minutes. The judge asked me my name, whether Mr Bowman was my attorney, whether he was authorized to speak for me. Bowman told the judge we were seeking asylum. She asked how we pleaded to the allegations against me. There were three. The first was that I had obtained 'a visa or other documentation by fraud.' Bowman denied that one. The second was that I didn't have a valid visa. Bowman admitted that one. The third was that I had tried to pass myself off as the person whose passport I had presented to the immigration inspector. Bowman denied that one as well. 'OK,' the judge said. 'I'll give you until January nineteenth to submit an application for political asylum.' And that was it.

January 19! That was only ten days away! I was ecstatic. I was going to have my hearing in ten days! Oh, my God! This was too wonderful! What a lawyer I had! What a great lawyer! I was giddy with joy.

When the hearing was over, Bowman left to go back to D.C. and I returned to my dorm, where Mary was waiting to hear my news.

'Mary, slap me!'

She knew that expression, knew it meant I was about to tell her something that would amaze her. She laughed. 'What! Tell me!'

'You won't believe it! Guess when my hearing is?'

'When?'

'In ten days! I only have to wait ten days!'

Her eyes went wide. 'You're joking.'

'No! It's on January nineteenth! Can you believe it! Isn't that incredible! Just think! I'll be out in ten days, and then you can tell your sister to call Bowman and he'll get you out too!'

'Ten days,' she said softly. 'That's amazing. How'd he do that?'

'He's just a really good lawyer. You've got to use him when he's through with me. Really, Mary. He's the best.'

I sat down at the table and got right to work filling out the asylum application form. I couldn't understand a lot of it, but I filled out what I could, concentrating on two questions on a page Bowman had called particular attention to. The one at the top of the page read: 'Why are you seeking asylum? (*Explain fully what is the basis – attach additional sheets as needed.*)' I could read the question. But I couldn't read the sentence that came after it. I thought my answer had to fit in the top half of the page. *The reason I am seeking asylum,* I wrote, in my limited written English, *is that I am a young girl of 18 years and when my father who was my legal gaurdian past away I was sold into an arranged marraige without my consent, and against my will. This man which I am being forced to marry is old enough to be my father, has many wives, and has requested that I be circumcized.* The second question read: 'What do you think would happen to you if you returned to the country from which you are claiming persecution? (*Explain fully – attach additional sheets as needed.*)' I wrote simply: *I will be forced to marry an old man, and be circumsized.* What more would anyone need to know? I put the form in the envelope, sealed it, and gave it to a guard to put in the mail for me that same day. Next I called Rahuf, timing my call to catch him after he came home from his day job and before he left for his night job. I couldn't wait to tell him the great news.

'Eric Bowman is so great!' I gushed. 'He's such a nice man!'

'How did it go?'

'You won't believe it! My hearing is on January nineteenth! That's only ten days! I'll probably be out in ten days!'

Rahuf was thrilled for me. He laughed and whooped with joy.

When I called him again a few days later, however, he sounded very serious. He'd spoken to Bowman, he said. 'Your hearing isn't on the nineteenth, Fauziya.'

'Yes it is.'

'No it's not, Fauziya.'

'Yes it is! The judge said so!'

'No, Fauziya. I talked to Eric. You misunderstood the judge. She said you have until the nineteenth to file your application for asylum.'

'You mean the one I filled out? But I sent that off right away.'

'I know.'

'So if they have the application, why can't we have the hearing on the nineteenth?'

'Because it doesn't work that way. They have to assign a hearing date.'

'Have they assigned one?'

Silence.

'Are you there?'

'Yes, I'm here.'

'So have they assigned one? Do we have a date?'

'Yes, Fauziya.'

'So when is it?'

It sounded like he said January 22.

'The twenty-second?'

'Yes.'

'Oh, well, that's not so bad. That's only three more days.'

'No, Fauziya. Not January twenty-second. June twenty-second. Your hearing isn't until June.'

'No! It can't be! It can't be!'

'I'm sorry, Fauziya, but it is. It's not until June.'

June! But this was only January! June was, June was . . . I recited and counted. January, February, March, April, May . . .

And then all went black. I didn't pass out. I didn't faint. I just saw nothing but blackness. It was the black of my future, a long, dark, endless suffocating tunnel from which I could see no escape. This was the end for me. A death sentence.

20

Prison Life

For a while after I got the news about my hearing date I just went away, somewhere out of myself, someplace far away from Esmor. It was nice there. Peaceful. I didn't have to hang in and be strong there. I stayed there for a while, not even knowing I'd gone anywhere, and then one day I came back. Somehow in the midst of my blackout I'd realized I had to get down to the business of surviving.

I began by resuming my prayers. I rose every morning at five A.M., spread a towel on the floor, washed, wrapped myself in the spare sheet Elsie had smuggled in to me, put my mother's *tasbih* on the towel, stepped barefoot onto the towel, and began to pray. 'Trust in God,' my mother always said. 'God will protect you.' I put my trust in God. If it was His desire that I endure and survive, I'd endure and survive. If not, I wouldn't.

I endured. I survived.

I soon realized that if I was going to be there five months, I was going to have to find something to do with myself. The only thing there was to do was work in the laundry. But Miss Jones had said no to that request once already and I was too frightened to ask again. But I'm a hard worker by nature and that would be my route to her favor, I decided. Miss Jones liked people who worked hard.

She was a hard worker herself. She worked six A.M. to two P.M., Monday through Friday, and was often still there working long after her shift ended. One of the things she did was to serve breakfast and lunch. So one day I volunteered to hand out and collect the food trays. She accepted my offer. It worked out well for both of us. I got out of the dorm for a little while, she didn't have to work so hard.

'Thank you, Seven Six One.'

'You're welcome, Miss Jones.'

'Would you like to help again tomorrow?'

'Yes, please.'

I didn't have a name yet, but I had a job.

A week or so later, something went wrong in the laundry and a huge amount of washing, drying, and folding had to be done in a day. It was much more work than the women on laundry duty could finish in that time so Mr Williams came around with Miss Jones, pushing a cart full of clean, unfolded laundry, asking women if they'd be willing to do some folding. When they got to our dorm, Mr Williams asked Mary if she'd help, since she knew how to do it, having worked with him before, but she said no, she was too tired. Tired from doing nothing. I was beginning to feel that same kind of tiredness creeping into me. It felt like a sickness trying to take hold. I was determined to fight it.

'I'll help,' I said, getting up off my bed.

'Thank you, Seven Six One,' Miss Jones said.

She plopped a big pile of men's clothes on the table and I started folding. Mary kept watching TV, but my other dorm mates came to help too. We finished in no time. I knocked on the window for Miss Jones to collect the laundry.

She was impressed. 'That was quick. Would you be willing to do more?'

'Sure!'

Mr Williams brought us another pile.

'Are you going to pay us?' I asked, smiling shyly. I was teasing, sort of.

He returned my smile. 'Sure,' he said. 'If you come work in the laundry, I'll pay you a dollar a day.'

'Can I?'

'Not right now. I don't need anyone right now. But I might soon. You never know.'

He was right about that – righter than he knew. On the day we spoke he had a full crew of workers – Mary's friend Elsie and five other women from N dorm. Then suddenly he had none.

It was all because of something that happened about a week after that conversation. One minute we were having one of our typical dull, routine, endless days, the next minute the place was swarming with officers in uniforms who stormed in with big dogs on leashes.

'Move! Against the wall! Everybody up against the wall!' they shouted. My dorm mates and I jumped off our beds and huddled against the wall under the television, terrified, while the dogs ran all over the room, sniffing. Whatever it was they were looking for, wasn't in our dorm, or, so far as I know, in any other dorm. But N dorm got into trouble that day. While the women in N were standing huddled against the wall, waiting for the raid to end, one male officer had said to another, 'Let's strip-search 'em. What'dya say?' The other had laughed. 'You wanna?' They assumed nobody knew enough English to understand their lewd joke, but Elsie did. She translated what they had said for her dorm mates, and she and a few of her laundry co-workers decided to retaliate. At a signal from her, they dropped their pants and lifted their shirts, exposing their bras and underpants. The male officers were embarrassed at being found out and left.

I couldn't believe Elsie had done such an outrageous thing, but I kind of admired her for it. I thought the guards had gotten what they deserved. When Miss Jones found out about it the next morning, however, she was furious and fired the entire laundry crew on the spot. Mr Williams suddenly needed a whole new crew. Miss Jones came around asking who wanted to work.

'Seven Six One, do you want to work in the laundry?'

I leapt off my bed. 'Yes!'

That's how I started working in the laundry.

The new crew consisted of me, Lola, Jasmine, Maria, and Rosa, plus two Chinese women from J dorm, Siu Sing and Wang. Poor Mr Williams. He had to train us all from scratch, and there was a lot to learn about doing laundry for such a large institution. There were nine men's dorms at Esmor, A through I, and five much smaller women's dorms, J through N, housing about 300 INS detainees, about 54 of whom were women. Since I was the only member of the crew who spoke English, and I was the one who caught on fastest and worked hardest, I became Mr Williams's deputy in charge. He knew he could rely on me. We became friends. He started calling me 'Fauz.' I started calling him 'Frank.'

It was a real education, working in the laundry. It was pitiful, the clothes people were given to wear in that place. Since there wasn't enough women's underwear for all the women, a lot of their rolls had to be made up with men's underwear. Not surprisingly, some of the women broke the rule that said you were supposed to turn in your underwear with the rest of your dirty laundry. Once they got their hands on a semi-decent pair of underwear, they held on to it and washed it themselves. I felt especially bad for the men. Their uniforms were even more tattered and stained and in even shorter supply than the women's clothing, and their underwear was especially disgusting. Frank said he'd told his bosses about the situation time after time, but they never did anything about it.

I was very glad to have my work in the laundry. It passed the time, and it took my mind off things. But even when I was hard at work I never knew when grief would overwhelm me. Sometimes I'd be in the middle of doing something and I'd see my father's face or think of Amariya and suddenly break down sobbing. At those moments Frank would come over and put a gentle arm around my shoulder. He was so kind, so unfailingly kind. He'd let me bury my head against his chest, my tears soaking his shirt, as I cried and cried. 'It's OK,' he'd say gently. 'Go ahead and cry.' Frank cared for me like the father I'd lost.

My co-workers and I all knew how lucky we were to have our laundry jobs. We worked hard. We wanted to hold on to this good thing we'd found.

'Hey, Fauz! I need ten rolls!'

'OK-la.'

That's what my Chinese co-workers, Siu Sing and Wang, always said. 'OK-la.' I started saying it too. They taught me Chinese. I taught them English. But their pronunciation always made me laugh. 'Fonsinya' they called me. If I did something they thought was funny, they'd tell me I was 'clasy.'

Frank tried to make things as pleasant as he could for us. He brought in a tape player so we could listen to music while we worked. I couldn't get enough of Whitney Houston singing 'I Will Always Love You' from the soundtrack of *The Bodyguard*. What a song! What a voice! Sometimes, when there was no work to do, the other women and I would turn up the volume and dance. Frank would sit and watch, laughing and clapping.

'Go, Fauz! Oh, Fauz, can you dance!'

Miss Jones sometimes came in when we were dancing or playing cards. It was OK with her. As long as we got our work done, she didn't mind if we enjoyed ourselves too.

Actually, she seemed to want to make things more bearable for us. Once she came into my dorm with a bottle of perfume. She had noticed that one of the women in the dorm didn't shower as often as the rest of us would have liked – it was hard not to notice, since the dorms weren't ventilated – and she walked around the room spraying whiffs of perfume in the air. It was the same light, fresh scent I'd smelled on her my first Monday at Esmor. She winked at me as she left. I wished I could capture the scent, preserve it, make it last. But of course it didn't last. It lingered for a couple of days and then it died. That's what life was like at Esmor. An occasional whiff of perfume, an hour of dancing to *Video Music Box*, a few hours each weekday working in the laundry, and then it was always back to the same cold, stinky, airless, windowless, noisy, harshly lit room, back to the same inedible food and hard, crackly mattresses, back to nothing to do but watch TV or lie on my bed thinking, thinking and crying, hour after hour, day after endless day.

But there came a time when that dorm would seem like heaven to me. Mary had warned me I didn't ever want to find out what segregation was like. Soon I would understand what she meant. After I'd been at

305

Esmor a few weeks, we were all told we couldn't take showers before six A.M. wake-up. I didn't shower early, but I did rise every morning at five to wash and pray first prayers. Kim, the same guard who was so mean to us when she did count at night, was often still on duty at five. I was just finishing my washing one morning when she came banging into the room.

'Turn the water off!' she yelled. 'No showering before six!'

'I'm not showering,' I said. 'I'm washing for prayer.' I was standing at the sink, fully dressed. She could see I wasn't showering. I kept washing and silently reciting the words Muslims use as we wash different parts of our body in preparation for prayer. She walked over to the sink, turned off the water, and walked away. I hadn't finished yet. I still had to wash my legs. I turned it back on.

'I said turn it *off*!' she bellowed. I was finished now. I turned off the water. She left, letting the door bang shut behind her even though people were still trying to sleep, and I performed my morning prayers.

She was on duty again the next morning. It was almost like she was waiting to catch me. The moment I turned on the water, she came banging into the room.

'Turn it off!'

'But I have to wash for prayers,' I said calmly.

'No showering before six!'

'I'm not showering,' I said calmly. 'I'm washing for prayers.'

'No washing before six!'

That wasn't the rule. The rule was no showering. 'I'm sorry, I have to wash,' I said calmly. 'It's part of what I have to do to pray.'

'Are you getting smart with me?'

306

'Excuse me?' I'd never heard that expression. I didn't know what it meant.

'I said, are you arguing with me?'

'No, I'm trying to explain. I have to—'

'That's it!' She grabbed my right wrist hard in her left hand, took her handcuffs off her belt with the other hand and snapped them around my wrist. Snap!

I was stunned. 'What are you doing!'

She snapped the handcuffs around my left wrist, grabbed my upper right arm hard, and yanked me forward. 'You're going to seg.'

'No!' I turned toward the shout. It came from Mary, who was sitting up in bed, her hands clasped over her mouth. Her eyes looked terror-stricken, grief-stricken. Her eyes were the last thing I saw as Kim half dragged me out of the dorm.

Kim took me down a maze of white hallways, stopped in front of a metal door, took off my handcuffs, opened the door, shoved me through it, and locked it behind me. I found myself in a tiny concrete cell. There was nothing in it but a metal bed, toilet, and sink. The narrow glass window in the middle of the door was so small that I couldn't even see down the hallway. I sat down on the bed in a state of shock. The mattress was the same as the one in my dorm: thin, hard, and covered in the same crackly plastic. There was a thin pillow on the bed, also covered in plastic, a thin blanket, and one sheet. The cell was cold and harshly lit. I shivered. I was locked in a box! I was locked up all alone in a cold concrete box! No, this wasn't really happening. Kim wouldn't leave me here. She was just trying to scare me. She'd leave me here for a few hours and then she'd let me out. She would. She had to.

She didn't. She left me there. I had no television, no

watch, no way of telling the time, nothing, no reference points, nothing at all to pass the time with, just blank walls. Blank walls, a bed, a toilet, and a sink. Sometime during that first day a guard led me handcuffed to the shower room, the same room where I'd taken my ice-cold shower the night I arrived. The cuffs were taken off and I was allowed to shower (this time I was able to use the shower knob to turn on the hot water). Then I was handcuffed and taken back to my cell. Three times that first day the cell door opened and a guard brought me a meal on a Styrofoam tray. Sometime at the end of the day, the lights went out. Sometime, a minute or eternity later, they went back on. Lights out, lights on. One day down – and how many to go? I had no idea. Lights out, lights on. Two days. I cried. Nobody heard me. What if they kept me here forever? What if they never let me out? No! They had to let me out! They couldn't keep me here forever! I hadn't done anything! Lights out, lights on. Three days. I was freezing, terrified. Oh, God, what if they kept me here a month? That's how long they'd kept Mary when she had tried to escape. I'd lose my mind. I'd go crazy! What if I couldn't work in the laundry anymore when I got out? What if I was confined to the dorm the way Mary was? Lights out, lights on. Four days. I cried until I couldn't cry anymore. I went numb. My mind shut down. Lights out, lights on. Five days.

On the fifth day, I was led handcuffed to a male officer who sat behind a desk. I was charged, judged, and sentenced. 'You broke the rules and fought with an officer,' he said. I'd done neither, but I said nothing. What was the point? Truth didn't matter in this place. Justice didn't exist in this place. I was in prison, where people in uniforms had absolute power to do whatever they wanted to do with me. 'You're sentenced to five days in segregation,' the officer said. 'You've served your sentence. You can return to your dorm.' The guard took me back to my dorm, removed my handcuffs, opened the door, and waved me in. Mary was sitting on her bed when I walked in. She let out a cry when she saw me, rushed over and threw her arms around me. She was crying. I didn't cry. I didn't hug her back. I walked to my bed, sat down, drew my knees up, and stared at the television. Television. I could watch television. I didn't have to think. I didn't have to feel. I could just watch TV. That's what I did.

Kim was on duty that night. That meant she'd still be there the next morning. I rose at five A.M. to wash for prayers. I went to the sink and turned the faucet little by little until water dribbled out the spigot into my right hand, then turned it off while I washed. I turned it on again little by little and washed my left hand. I washed as quietly as I could, running as little water as possible, hoping Kim wouldn't hear it. She either didn't hear it or ignored it. I thanked God. That's how I washed from then on. I never stopped washing or praying. Nothing and no-one was going to stop me from praying. I didn't want to go back to segregation ever again in my life, but if that was the price I had to pay for worshiping God properly, I would pay it. Fortunately, I didn't have to.

I was also allowed to go back to the laundry, and I wasn't confined to the dorm. I thanked Allah for those great kindnesses. I thanked Frank and Miss Jones too. Not in words. In my heart. Had they tried to help me when I was in segregation? Did they get me out sooner than I'd have gotten out otherwise? Was it because of them that I was able to return to the laundry? I didn't know, but I thought so, hoped so. Anyway, it was over now, and I didn't want to talk about it. Not to them, not to anyone. All I wanted to do was forget.

The hurt passed. And then something wonderful happened. I got a letter from Ayisha. I ripped it open and unfolded two thin sheets of paper. They were folded around two photographs. One was of my mother, my beautiful Amariya. The other was a snapshot of me and my sisters, which had been taken when I was about nine, during the festival of 'Eid al-Fitr. I thought my heart would burst from looking at it. There we were, the five of us, all dressed up and looking so happy. My sisters. 'We'll always have each other,' Narhila had said the last time I'd seen them. I didn't have them anymore. But I had this picture now. I could look at their sweet faces again. I wiped away my tears and sat looking at them, one by one. Ayisha. My beautiful Ayisha. Narhila, queen of *kwalisa*. Shy Shawana. Bubbly Asmahu. And me. Was that me? That lovely, well-dressed, proud-looking, confident-looking girl? Or did that only used to be me? I hadn't seen my own face clearly since I'd arrived in America. I didn't know what I looked like anymore, but I knew how I felt. I didn't feel proud, dignified, or confident. When had I changed? I stared at my face in the photograph. Is that how my sisters remembered me? Would they even recognize me now?

I kissed both photographs, pressed them to my heart, put them down beside me on the bed, and picked up the two thin sheets of paper. Two letters, one from Ayisha and one from my mother. My mother! I hadn't seen or heard from her in almost two years. It was written in Hausa. I read it hungrily for the first of a hundred times, a thousand times. I read that letter so often during my time at Esmor that I memorized it. And lucky for me I did, because there would come a time when that letter, like so much else, would be taken from me, never to be returned.

My beloved daughter, my mother had written. *I am so happy to hear you are in America. I thank God you are safe. You must stay there, where nobody can hurt you. Do not come back. You can't come back and let them do this horrible thing to you. You must stay there. Your father would wish it. I am proud of you, my daughter. Your father would also be proud. Remember that. It will give you strength. I love you and miss you. You are in my prayers always. May God bless and protect you. Your loving mother, Amariya.*

My mother didn't say where she was. She didn't even say how she was. But she was alive. She loved me and missed me. She was proud of me and prayed for me. That would have to be enough for now.

Next I read Ayisha's letter, which was written in English. She said nothing about whether her husband had forgiven her for disobeying his orders not to help me. But his prediction that helping me would cause trouble for them had proved true. She wrote that my uncle had gone to the police and filed a missing-person report after my aunt discovered I'd fled. The police had come to Ayisha's home and workplace looking for me. She told them she didn't know where I was. But they kept coming back and threatening her. They said she'd stolen someone's wife and she'd have to go to jail if she didn't produce me. But she held firm. She didn't have me, she told the police, and she didn't know where I was. Finally they stopped bothering her and left her alone. She was OK, she wrote. I wasn't to worry. She was only telling me this because she'd sent a copy of the police report to Rahuf. She'd also sent him two letters dictated and signed by my

311

mother, and the marriage certificate, she said. And now she was working on getting a copy of the wedding photograph. She'd send it as soon as she got it. Oh, Ayisha! I laughed out loud. She'd get the photograph! I knew she would.

My wonderful, brave, clever Ayisha. I picked up the photograph and gazed at her sweet face again. How it fooled people! They saw the sweetness. They didn't see the strength. It didn't show in her face, but it was there. It had always been there. Ayisha had always been strong. I looked at me again as well, that proud, dignified, confident-looking young woman I hadn't recognized before. I remembered her now. I felt like her now. Yes. That was me.

I got another letter a few days later. This one came to me by mistake. Some of the male and female detainees wrote to each other. The nicer guards delivered letters back and forth. One of the male detainees had written a note to someone else and it was accidentally delivered to me. I sent it back with a polite note saying it had been delivered to the wrong person. He wrote back, telling me a little about himself, including the fact that he was Muslim, and asking politely if I'd be his pen pal. I was thrilled to have a chance to write to someone of my faith. It was clear from his letter that he himself was very strong in faith and very proud of his religion. I wrote back saying I was Muslim, too, and would be honored to be his pen pal. I asked if he knew when Ramadan started. He wrote back that it was coming up soon, in just a few days, on February 1, and he sent me a Muslim calendar.

I was deeply touched. I sat down at the table to write a thank-you note. I meant to write a short note, but the letter got longer and longer and longer.

Everything poured out in that letter, all my grief, all my heartbreak, all my sweet memories of everything I'd lost. I described what Ramadan was like back home in Togo. I told him about the delicious treats that my mother and Adjovi would prepare for us to eat when we broke fast. I told him about the boys who went from house to house calling the community awake at that same early hour, singing and reciting passages from the Qur'an. The *tashey* children we called them – the 'wake-up' children. I told him how we'd walk to the mosque for first prayers in the predawn darkness, all of us together, the whole family. I told him what a special time evenings were during Ramadan, how happy and friendly people were, talking and laughing and greeting friends and neighbors. I told him how we'd all watch the moon as it waxed and waned and finally disappeared, and how we'd begin listening to the radio then, waiting for the announcement: 'The new moon has been sighted! Ramadan is over!' I told him how we celebrated, the whole community together, everyone praying and celebrating together, everyone feeling renewed, reconnected, reborn.

As I wrote that letter it all became real again. I was home, my father was alive, our family was together. I didn't ever want to stop writing. Finally, I folded the letter, went to my bed, and put the letter in the box underneath. I'd write another thank-you note tomorrow. I wouldn't send this one. I'd keep it. I was in prison now. It was all I had now. I lay down on my bed and closed my eyes. Tears ran down my cheeks and I wept. Yaya must have heard my cries, because that was the night I dreamt about his visiting me in prison. I was so happy when I was dreaming that dream, but when I woke up and realized he was gone forever, it was as though I'd lost him all over again.

Mary went back to Ghana soon afterward. I was brokenhearted. My very first day at Esmor she'd told me she was thinking of going back. It hadn't mattered to me then. Whether she stayed or left had been her business. The more I'd come to know her and love her, the more it had become my business too. Who would I talk to if she was gone, who would take care of me?

'Please don't go, Mary. Please stay. Stay here with me.'

'I can't, Fauziya. I can't take any more.'

She'd written letters to her lawyer, to her sister, to the INS, telling them all she wanted to go back. She was desperate for the INS to come get her.

'What are they waiting for!' I heard her tell her sister over the phone one day. She sounded angry. She was sounding angry more and more lately, losing control of her temper. 'Well, call again! Yes, today! No, I don't have to be patient! Don't tell me to calm down! I've been here six months! They won't let me see a judge for my hearing! They won't let me out of my room! Now they won't let me leave? What kind of craziness is this? Call again!'

She'd begun crying softly at night. She'd never cried before. I'd go to her and hold her.

'I'm sorry, Fauziya,' she'd say, crying uncontrollably. 'I don't want to leave you. You know I don't. But I'm cracking up.'

'I know,' I'd say softly as I held her. 'It's OK. I know.'

She was cracking up, it was true. She'd been at Esmor a little less than six months. I'd arrived in December. My hearing wasn't until June. Six months. She'd cracked in less than six months. Would I?

When the INS finally came to get her, I broke down sobbing. We hugged and kissed and held each other. I didn't want to let go. I couldn't bear to lose her. 'What's going to happen to you?' I asked, sobbing. 'Where will you go? What will you do?'

'I don't know,' she said softly into my shoulder as I clung to her. 'But whatever happens, it can't be worse than staying here.' She eased out of my embrace, reached up and laid a warm hand on my left cheek. She smiled, her eyes shining with love. 'Don't worry about me,' she said softly. 'I'll be fine. I'll write and let you know where I am.'

'Do you promise?' I was still crying.

'I promise, but you have to make me a promise too.'

'What?'

'You have to promise me you'll stay strong.'

'Oh, Mary!' I covered my face with my hands, heaving with sobs.

She pulled my hands down gently but firmly, grasped my chin, and made me look her in the eye. 'I mean it, Fauziya,' she said, still holding my chin in her hand. 'You have a good case. You have to hang in. Don't give up and don't go back, no matter how long it takes. Stay strong.'

We had one last embrace. And then a guard led her from the dorm. I never saw Mary again.

Ramadan ended on March 1. The next day was 'Eid al-Fitr, the festival of fast-breaking. Back home the whole community would be gathering together for prayers, to mark the beginning of a week of celebrating and visiting friends and neighbors. The holidays just aren't the same when they have to be observed and celebrated alone. Communal observance, prayer and celebration, are part of what makes them so special. So another Muslim woman and I, a Somalian who'd come to work in the laundry, requested permission for the Muslim women to gather for holiday prayers in the women's gym. Eight or nine of us gathered in the gym that day. Until then I hadn't realized how many of us there were. Although I wasn't the oldest present, it was decided that I would lead the prayers, because the others had heard I was good at it. I did it gladly, pleased and honored to have been asked. I thanked Allah for allowing us to come together to praise His name and for allowing us to experience some of the joy and comfort that comes of praising Him in communal worship. I closed with a prayer for all of us. 'May Allah grant that we will all be somewhere else next year, in a better place, where we can celebrate with joy in our hearts.'

'*Insha-Allah*' (by the will of God).

We all cried and hugged and held one another then, a small community of Muslim women refugees, strangers, sisters, united in sorrows, connected in our love of God. And then we parted and returned to our separate dorms. As it turned out, we would all be somewhere else next Ramadan. Everyone at Esmor would. Perhaps some of them landed in better places, as I had prayed to Allah would happen, but not me. I'd be someplace far worse.

Days passed. Weeks passed. Day after endless, identical day, week after endless, identical week. Weekends were hardest. The laundry was closed on weekends, and there was nothing else to distract me from my problems. A lot of the other detainees had visitors – I'd see them pass by my dorm all visibly excited for their company – but no-one came to see me. Rahuf lived too far away and worked weekends. And, of course, my uncle who lived in Newark never came.

I called Frank at home sometimes on weekends. He'd given me his number and told me to call anytime

I needed to talk. I didn't call a lot, because I didn't want to run up his phone bill, but it meant the world to me to know I could. It made me feel cared for, watched over, protected, a little less lonely. The calls really made me feel like I was part of a family. Frank is Catholic, a good Christian man in the truest sense of the word. He reminded me of Ayisha. He had the same gentleness, the same goodness, and the same inner strength. As Ayisha was a second mother to me, Frank was a second father to me. I lived for Mondays when I could go back to the laundry and see him.

Shortly after Mary left, two more of my dorm mates were deported. People were always getting deported and new people were always coming in to fill their beds. Fortunately, this time the two new people were my two Chinese co-workers from the laundry, Siu Sing and Wang, who moved from J dorm into my dorm, K dorm. Another of my dorm mates, an African woman from Cameroon named Laura, who had moved in not long ago, was chosen to join the rest of us in the laundry service.

Frank still needed one more worker. Miss Jones selected a young woman named Esther. She'd recently arrived from Ghana, so they'd put her in N dorm with the other Ghanaians. I'll never forget the first time I saw her. There were a lot of lovely women at Esmor, but Esther was stunning. She was twenty-five, about my height, slender but shapely, with smooth dark skin, delicate features, and long, shiny black hair. She had a femininity that I lacked entirely and a queenly bearing that reminded me a little of Narhila. She had a slight touch of vanity that also reminded me of Narhila. I would tease her about it when I got to know her better. She was like a princess, a sweet, modest, gentle, beautiful princess. I learned later that her father was a king and she really was a princess. At home she would have been dressed in jewel-colored silks, satins, and velvets, but at Esmor she wore the same tattered clothing all of us wore. But unlike us, she looked beautiful in it. There were certain similarities between her story and mine, but the exact details of why she had to flee I wouldn't feel comfortable sharing.

At first I was too awed by her beauty to even speak to her. But she was so sweet, warm, and unpretentious that we soon became friends. She came to visit me one afternoon in K dorm. 'Euugh,' she said. 'I don't like this dorm. It's too small. It feels like a cell.'

I laughed. 'Not to me it doesn't.'

'Well, it does to me. Come visit me next time.'

I visited her often after that. There was a window in N dorm, too narrow to see much out of; but sometimes I could catch sight of a plane if it was flying low, and I could hear the noise of its engines. I stared and stared at the little I could see. There was a different world out there, right there on the other side of the window. I wondered what the outside world was like.

I missed the outdoors so much – the air, the sights, and the natural light too. The harsh prison lighting made my eyes burn and water horribly, especially whenever I tried to read or watch TV. The problem had gotten so bad that I'd filed another request to see the prison doctor. I was hoping to get a different doctor, but it was the same one. I told him my problem. He told me not to read so much. It was the same kind of advice he'd given me last time. 'You itch when you shower? Don't shower.' 'Your eyes burn when you read? Don't read.'

My health just seemed to be giving out. Besides the fact that my eyes were bothering me more and more, I was being troubled again by boils for the first time in

318

years, and my back hurt much of the time. None of this was hard to understand. The prison lights were harsh, the mattress I slept on, hard and thin. I was getting no exercise, no fresh air. The food was inedible. I was living mainly on starch and the occasional piece of fruit. Kim was still playing her nasty night games. I was desperately homesick, and filled with anxiety about the future.

I knew I had to be strong, and I tried to be, but my body wasn't cooperating. Allah took mercy. He'd heard my cries when I'd lain in bed on my stomach one night, whimpering in pain from a boil on the back side of my leg, calling out for my mother. He didn't send me my mother. But he did send Sylvie in her place. Esther and Sylvie – God sent me both at the same time, a wonderful friend and a loving second mother.

Sylvie was from Liberia. We met when she started coming to visit a friend of hers who had moved into my dorm. Sometimes I would see her there, sometimes I would see her when I went to visit Esther in N dorm, because that's where she lived too. She was a short, heavy, dark-skinned woman of thirty-eight. She had long black hair, twinkly eyes, and a wonderful smile. She was always smiling, at me anyway. She took a special liking to me the first time we met. 'Oh, and who is this?' she said, beaming at me. 'Look at this beautiful girl!' She came and sat down next to me on my bed. 'What's your name, my precious?' I told her. 'Fauziya,' she said, smiling and stroking my hair. 'What a beautiful name. A beautiful name for a beautiful girl. I have a daughter just around your age. Do you like Milky Ways?' I nodded shyly, a little overwhelmed by her outpouring of affection. 'Good! I have some in my box. I'll bring you one tomorrow,

OK?' It was mother love at first sight.

She brought me treats and candies every time she visited my dorm from then on. And every time I visited Esther and Sylvie in N dorm, Sylvie would insist that I help myself to a treat from her box. She began calling me 'Baby.' I began calling her 'Mom.' Sylvie wore multiple strands of beautiful colored beads around both her ankles. I commented one day on how pretty they were and told her I was wearing beads, too, around my waist. So was she, she said. She asked to see my beads and she showed me hers. They were really beautiful, like the ones she was wearing around her ankles.

'Would you like some?' she asked me.

They were exquisite, as precious and meaningful to her as mine were to me, as intimate a part of her as mine were of me. 'Oh, no, I couldn't take your beads.'

She sat down on her bed. 'Sit,' she said, patting the mattress beside her. I sat. She reached down and cut a length of the beautiful beads off her left ankle. 'Give me your foot,' she said. I put my left foot on the bed. She lifted it onto her lap, tied the beads around my ankle, and gave my foot an affectionate squeeze. She looked up at me and smiled tenderly, her eyes filled with affection. We just sat there for a moment smiling at each other, my foot still in her lap. The relationship had been sealed. She was my mom for sure now.

My dorm mate Lola was transferred to Miami with her husband, who was living in the men's section. After several other roommate shuffles, Sylvie came to K dorm. I had my mom in the same dorm with me now, day and night. Soon another woman who would become important to me moved in too – Oche from Nigeria. She was a tall, solidly built, light-skinned woman of twenty-eight. She was very educated. She'd graduated from university before fleeing Nigeria. She had left because her family was involved in politics and got into trouble. I admired her because she was educated and spoke English beautifully, but I didn't like her at first. She seemed a little too full of herself, too convinced that her opinions and viewpoints were right. We were both stubborn, both strong-willed, both proud, sometimes a little too proud. We clashed at first but we soon came to like and respect each other. We became fast friends.

Sylvie and another of my dorm mates, a Chinese woman, joined the laundry crew. Five of the six women in K dorm now worked in the laundry – everyone but Oche. We were the working dorm, Frank's special clique and Miss Jones's special pets. As measured by prison standards, we had it pretty good. We had first pick of T-shirts, socks, underwear. We had extras of everything: underwear, uniforms, towels, sheets, blankets. We made up our beds with white sheets atop the blankets so the beds matched the white walls – the closest we could come to a decorator touch. We were hardworking, well behaved, respectful. We kept our dorm spotless. We were the model dorm, the showcase dorm. When official visitors toured Esmor, Miss Jones showed them our dorm. Sometimes she showed it when we were in the laundry and the room was quiet and empty. On another occasion we came back to our dorm to find two guards standing at the open door, barring our entrance. Miss Jones was inside with two visitors, a man and a woman, and four women inmates from other dorms. I knew those women. They were among the most soft-spoken, timid, well-behaved women in the place. They were sitting at the table playing a game of checkers, pretending they were in their own dorm, while the man videotaped them and the woman asked questions.

'How's the food here?' the interviewer asked, with Miss Jones standing right there.

'It's all right.'

'How do they treat you here?'

'They treat us OK.'

'Do you have any complaints?'

'No.'

It made me sick. Tell them the truth! I screamed silently. Tell them what the food's really like! Tell them how they really treat us! Tell them what they don't even know to ask! Tell them about our torn, stained underwear. Tell them about the exposed showers. Tell them we never go outside. Tell them about the dorm search in the middle of the night. Tell them about segregation. Tell them about the so-called doctor. Tell them about being chained to a table when you're talking to your lawyer. Tell them about waiting months to see a judge. Tell them about Kim! Tell them this isn't even your dorm!

But, of course, the women couldn't do that. As furious as I was, I kept my mouth shut too. That's what we all did. We kept our mouths shut. We were refugee women from countries where women are taught to be docile and submissive. And since we were in jail we were frightened and powerless in addition to being docile and submissive. We didn't complain. We didn't speak out.

Somebody was talking, though. I didn't know it then, but complaints were getting out about Esmor. Looking back later, it would occur to me that this may have been why those visitors were there. The truth was starting to get out about how detainees were treated at this detention center. The inmates had begun complaining to lawyers. Lawyers and refugee-advocate groups were starting to press the INS and the people who ran Esmor to look into and respond to these complaints. Pressure was being applied from outside for changes and improvements in the way the place was run.

A different kind of pressure was building up inside. My pen pal told me in one of his letters that conditions were really bad in the men's dorms. 'You wouldn't believe the way they treat us,' he wrote. 'Some of the men are really getting fed up and angry. I pray to Allah that we'll both get out of here before something bad happens.'

Ironically, I would later look back on this time as the best of my bad times in prison. In fact, there was a period when things got better for a while, almost bearable, before everything became a million times worse. A new man, Willard Stovall, came in as the chief administrator. Small changes and improvements started happening around then, not enough to relieve the pressure that was building in the men's dorms, but some. The women got some new underwear and T-shirts. I finally got a better pair of shoes to wear. I'd been wearing my broken brown plastic sandals, both for the right foot, all that time. We were allowed to receive a limited number of items from outside after Mr Stovall came in: soap, skin lotion, sanitary pads, and other necessities. Best of all, the men's gym area was now made available to us for the first time. At first women could use it only during the morning hours, which was when I was working in the laundry, but later it was open in the afternoons, too, when I was free to use it. It was bigger than the other two exercise rooms and the roof was made like a gate, so you could get fresh air. It was almost like being outside. Exercise!

Basketball! Volleyball! I loved running around and getting sweaty. It felt great to use my muscles again. I especially loved volleyball.

Another thing that happened around this time was that Miss Jones and Miss White, one of the nicest of the guards, came up with the idea of offering an aerobics class for the women. They seemed genuinely concerned that we women didn't have anything to do except sit around all day every day watching TV and thinking about our problems. A number of women, including Sylvie, Oche, Esther, and me, signed up immediately. It sounded like fun to us.

It was. We exercised for thirty minutes every other morning in the women's exercise room across from the L and M dorms before going to the laundry. Miss White led the class. She brought in a tape player so we could exercise to music. After the class was over, we moved out into the hall and danced! Miss White would put a dance tape in the tape player and we'd line up on both sides of the hall, everybody clapping, and take turns dancing in the middle two by two, just like back home. It was so much fun! Miss Jones always danced with me. We were partners. Frank would come to take us to the laundry and see Miss Jones and me dancing and laugh. He'd start clapping and chanting in time to the beat. 'Go, Fauz! Go, Fauz! Go!' Then we'd head for the laundry.

Those were the good times, the best of my prison times. They were to last less than six weeks, from the end of April until around midnight, Saturday, June 17. Things were looking up, I thought. Just a few more weeks until my hearing on June 22. I had actually just about made it to the day I had been waiting for six months. I only had to hang in, hold on, be strong for a little while longer.

My spirits really improved during those weeks. I began to see that not everybody got deported, that maybe there was hope. A woman named Susan from N dorm was granted asylum and released around the beginning of May. My pen pal, who'd appealed his ruling, won on appeal and was released around that time too. Allah had granted his prayer! He told me the good news in a letter. He sent me his Qur'an with that letter. *It has given me strength,* he wrote. *I want you to have it. You can return it when you're released.* It was a beautiful Qur'an. I cried when I received it. I'd been without one all that time.

Somewhere around the third week in May, Miss Jones came to our dorm asking if we'd be interested in participating in a fashion show.

'A fashion show!' I blurted out. 'You mean with real clothes and everything?'

She laughed. 'Real clothes and everything.' She and Miss White would provide the clothes, she said. Miss White would rehearse us. She'd teach us how to walk, pose, turn. If enough women were interested, of course. We were definitely interested.

A fashion show! What a great way to fill the time before I got out. I couldn't wait to write Ayisha about it. I'd received another letter from her with pictures of Babs and Alpha. I'd write and tell her about the fashion show and tell her not to write to me again until I could give her my new address. Rahuf's address. The mails were slow. It took weeks for her letters to reach me. Why should she write me here when there were just a few more weeks until my hearing, and then the judge would grant me asylum and release me? Better to write her from Rahuf's with the good news. Oh, I got so excited just thinking about it!

21

Layli

I didn't know it then, and neither did Layli, but with each day God was bringing us closer together. While I was at Esmor counting the days until my hearing, Layli was preparing for my hearing, too, though she wasn't aware of it. Later, much later, when she filled me in on what she had been learning, writing, working on, and thinking about during my days at Esmor, we would be amazed by the incredible coincidences.

Christmas break between the first and second semester of her second year in law school was a long break, almost a month. She and Roshan were both exhausted, she from her studies, he from the final months of his medical fellowship. But much as she would have liked to use the time for a long vacation, there was something else she felt she had to do. Having decided to write her law journal article on FGM, she wanted to make as much headway as she could in her research on the subject before classes resumed in January. She saw the article as a chance to call attention to a form of human suffering, a human rights violation.

Her original idea, she told me later, was simply to build on the paper she'd done for her course on criminal law. She planned to use the information she'd gathered on what other countries were – or weren't

– doing to eradicate the practice, as a springboard for discussing what her own government was doing to eliminate it in the United States. FGM had begun taking hold in America, too, and was now being performed in immigrant communities among people who'd brought the custom with them from their own countries. Layli was concerned, and had learned that some other people were as well, including Congresswoman Patricia Schroeder of Colorado, who introduced a bill in Congress in 1993 to prohibit the practice and educate against it.

Layli was thinking only about the criminal law side in the beginning. But the more she read about FGM, the more she began thinking about the asylum side of the issue too. Her research turned up articles by people like Deborah Anker and Nancy Kelly of Harvard University, who criticized the INS for failing to recognize that the kinds of crimes committed only against women – rape, forced marriage, sexual slavery, domestic violence, FGM – are forms of persecution from which women deserve protection. They argued that these kinds of crimes should also be considered valid grounds for asylum. The articles Layli read didn't cite specific examples of how American immigration judges had ruled on requests for asylum from FGM. So far as Layli could find out, there didn't seem to have been any such cases yet.

I found out on the second Friday in January that my asylum hearing wouldn't be until June 22. The following Monday, Layli returned to school and started her course in asylum law. Her professor was a well-known refugee advocate named William Van Wyke. Layli had heard from other people at the law school that he was 'a good guy, a real human rights guy,' who'd done a lot of work with refugees from El Salvador and

Guatemala. The first day of class, Van Wyke asked the students to introduce themselves and tell a little about any work they'd done with refugees. Layli talked about the summer she'd worked as an unpaid intern with the Bahá'í Office of External Affairs in Washington, D.C., helping to get a resolution passed in Congress condemning the ongoing persecution in Iran. Other students had their own stories to tell. Layli listened with interest. Almost every one of them had done or was then doing something to try to help refugees. One student, Cindy Lewis, talked about her work in the office of an immigration attorney who specialized in helping refugees from Africa. Cindy said she loved the job. Layli could see why. A chance to do real hands-on legal work, to help refugees, and specifically refugees from Africa, which was where FGM was most prevalent – Layli was intrigued.

Van Wyke told the students that they'd have to write two papers for the course, one short, one long. When he handed out a list of suggested subjects, Layli looked them over, but she didn't see her subject on the list. She told Van Wyke that she'd already decided she wanted to write about FGM. The subject was fairly new, he told her, and very complex. It had just begun to emerge as an asylum issue, and judges and lawyers were just starting to deal with it. The courts hadn't issued any clear rulings on it. No-one was quite sure how to handle it. 'Are you sure there aren't other topics on the list that you'd rather write about?'

'No,' Layli said politely. 'I really want to write about FGM.'

The short paper was due first. Layli had been read-ing about some of the arguments being put forth by people who opposed offering asylum to women on the basis of gender-based persecution. One of the main arguments was that such grants of asylum would open the 'floodgates.' The gist of this argument was that America couldn't afford to offer asylum to women subjected to these forms of persecution, because they're too widespread. Every year millions of women and girls are forced into marriage, raped, sold into sexual slavery, and beaten and killed by their husbands. Female genital mutilation is inflicted on at least two million girls each year. That's six thousand girls per day, or five girls every minute. America can't offer asylum to every female who wants to escape this kind of suffering.

In her paper, Layli disputed the floodgates argument as it applied specifically to FGM. First, she pointed out that of the one million people who come to America in any given year, only around one-tenth are refugees seeking asylum, and less than a third of those refugees are women. She also pointed out that in countries that practice FGM, the procedure is usually performed on girls age fifteen or younger, often much younger. Most of these girls live in poor African countries with high female illiteracy rates. They have no money, no resources, no skills. They couldn't run away even if they wanted to, and most don't want to because it would mean leaving all that is familiar to them. Besides, in countries that practice FGM, the vast majority of women and girls embrace the custom. As further evidence that the dreaded hordes would not materialize, Layli noted that France and Canada had recently recognized FGM as grounds for asylum and neither country had been inundated with women seeking protection from it. No flood. Hardly even a trickle. For America to deny asylum to the rare female who did oppose the practice and did manage to flee it – out of a baseless fear that millions of women would follow behind her – would be a terrible injustice, Layli concluded.

I was that rare female. Layli and I hadn't met yet, but she was already fighting for me. Doing a good job of it, too – Van Wyke gave her an A on that paper.

For her second and longer paper, Layli decided to focus on whether a woman fleeing FGM could theoretically qualify for asylum under the standards and requirements of existing American asylum law. As Layli explained it to me later, in much simpler terms, to qualify for asylum any woman refugee (like any man) has to prove a number of things. First, she has to show that she has a 'well-founded fear of persecution.' Then she has to show that the persecution will be inflicted either by the government or by someone whom the government can't or won't control. Finally, she has to show that the persecution is aimed at her because of her race, religion, nationality, political opinions, or membership in a particular social group – the so-called five grounds criteria. This last was the most difficult criterion for a refugee woman to meet. Women aren't a race, a religion, or a nationality, and being a woman is not a political opinion. Building on the work of several scholars, Layli argued, however, that a woman's being vulnerable to persecution does constitute her membership in a particular social group.

Before Layli ever got the chance to show her paper to Van Wyke, he left his job at American University to accept an appointment as an immigration judge. Layli was sad to see him go, but she knew that the appointment was very good news for people in the refugee-advocate community. Friends of hers who had worked on immigration cases at the law school's Human Rights Clinic had told her how frustrating it was to work with immigration judges, because most of them had been appointed after years of service with the INS and didn't seem to have any empathy for the refugees and detainees who went through the system. As INS attorneys, they had learned to take an adversarial stance toward us. The more judges there were like Van Wyke, people with a human rights background and an understanding of the plight of refugees, the better.

When it came time for my hearing, I'd get someone who'd been appointed a judge after nineteen years of service with the INS. I'd be asking someone who'd spent nineteen years playing the role of prosecutor in asylum hearings to listen to my story, sympathize with my situation, and award me what's formally called a 'discretionary grant of asylum.' Discretionary – meaning it would be up to him. I'd be asking this man to grant me asylum from a kind of gender-based persecution that hadn't even been clearly established as a valid ground for seeking asylum. Layli would be asking, that is.

After Van Wyke left, Layli got a new teacher, Owen 'Bo' Cooper, the associate general counsel and director of the Asylum and Refugee Law Division of the INS, who was an adjunct professor at the law school. By day Bo Cooper worked at the INS, at night he taught the asylum law class. He was organized, animated, very enthusiastic about his subject. It was obvious to Layli that he really loved his work. But he worked for the INS! The INS were all bad guys. Weren't they?

Bo wasn't. He told Layli almost immediately that he thought her subject was both interesting and important. He discussed it with her at length. He suggested other sources of information, including a July 1994 report on FGM issued by the INS Resource

Information Center as part of a series of papers it offers to asylum and immigration officers to keep them abreast of human rights conditions and issues on the global scene. One particularly valuable piece of information Layli picked up from this report was that the 1993 Canadian guidelines on 'gender-related persecution' explicitly state that women vulnerable to persecution can constitute a social group. The very fact that the INS had begun paying attention to FGM was news to her.

Layli was pleased with the way her second paper turned out. So was Bo Cooper. This encouraged her to expand the scope of her law journal article, which she had formerly envisioned as focusing strictly on the legal efforts to criminalize FGM. By incorporating material from the paper she'd just completed, she could do further work on the asylum side of the FGM issue.

Could a woman fleeing FGM qualify for a 'discretionary grant of asylum'? In the arguments she set forth in her asylum law course paper and at greater length in her law journal article, Layli made the case that the woman's attorney could demonstrate that the client's fear of being persecuted if returned to her country was 'well-founded,' by presenting affidavits by expert witnesses and authoritative studies and reports documenting the social pressures placed on girls to undergo the ritual and showing how many females in her country, tribe or ethnic group are mutilated. In some countries, like Somalia, Layli noted, studies show that the most severe form of FGM, everything cut off and sewn shut, is performed on close to one hundred percent of the women. In others, the countrywide statistic might be lower, but the statistics on how many females in that woman's particular tribe or ethnic group could still be high. To establish that the persecution constituted 'a serious threat to life or freedom,' the woman's lawyer could submit medical studies and reports documenting some of the immediate and long-term consequences of the procedure: pain, hemorrhaging, shock, death, infection, tetanus, gangrene, painful intercourse, and so forth. The lawyer could also cite any number of U.N. resolutions and international covenants condemning FGM as 'a serious human rights violation' that deprives women of 'the equal enjoyment, exercise and knowledge of human rights and fundamental freedoms,' such as the freedom to experience sexual desire and enjoy sexual intercourse. To show that the persecution faced by the asylum seeker is being committed either by the government or by groups of people that the government can't or won't control, the lawyer could submit studies and papers like the ones Layli had gathered while researching her paper entitled 'The International Criminalization of FGM,' which made it clear that countries weren't doing much to eradicate the practice. Layli quoted from the INS's own report, the one that Bo Cooper had suggested she look at, which stated that 'women have little legal recourse and may face threats to their freedom, or social ostracization for refusing to undergo this harmful traditional practice or for attempting to protect their female children.'

As for demonstrating that the feared persecution is on account of 'race, religion, nationality, political opinions or membership in a particular social group,' Layli cited a growing consensus of opinion, within the United States and globally as well, that women often suffer persecution because of their membership in a particular social group. With the guidelines it had issued in 1993, Canada's Immigration and Refugee Board had already taken the groundbreaking step of accepting this new gender-based concept of persecution, she noted. America had not.

However, there were two definitions of 'social group' in U.S. law that Layli believed *would* apply to women fleeing FGM. One had been established in a decision by the Board of Immigration Appeals, or BIA, a sort of Supreme Court of immigration courts. In a case called 'Matter of Acosta' the BIA had ruled that a 'social group' could be defined as 'a group of persons all of whom share a common immutable characteristic [that they] either cannot change or should not be required to change because it is fundamental to their individual identities or consciences.' Layli argued that a woman who wished to escape FGM but who belonged to a tribe or ethnic group that forces FGM on all its members would meet this definition. The woman's ethnic group or tribe is an immutable characteristic. She can't change that. Her intact genitalia and sex drive are also immutable characteristics, and she should not be required to change those.

The second legally accepted definition of a 'social group' had been established by the Federal Ninth Circuit Court of Appeals in a case called *Sanchez-Trujillo* v. *INS*. In this case, the court defined 'social group' as 'a collection of people' who associate with each other voluntarily and are 'closely affiliated' because of 'some common impulse or interest.' Layli argued that a woman fleeing FGM could meet this test, too, because by rejecting the mores of her community, this woman was 'voluntarily associating' with others in her community who are considered immoral, heretics, betrayers of community standards. She was also 'voluntarily associating' with other women in her tribe or community who reject the practice out of a 'common belief' that it is harmful and shouldn't be done. 'Based on the court decisions noted,' she wrote, 'a woman who can demonstrate that she has been mutilated, or will be, on account of her gender and nationality . . . or her gender and other characteristics, such as tribal group, religion, or other common belief . . . may qualify for a discretionary grant of asylum under United States asylum law.' Going beyond these existing rulings, she argued that 'the recognition of FGM as grounds for asylum based on a social group defined by gender would be an important development in United States asylum law, reflecting the United States maturing understanding of the global oppression and subjugation of women, the severity of which rises to the level of persecution.'

Layli submitted the article to her fellow student editors at *The American University Journal of Gender and the Law* around the end of April 1995, two weeks before the end of her second year in law school. It was reviewed and judged one of a select number of articles worthy of publication.

When she first wrote that article, there was no known case that tested her theory. Layli thought it would be interesting to find a case in which a woman requested asylum on the grounds that she was facing persecution in the form of FGM. She'd soon be totally immersed in working on that case. The perfect test case. Mine.

After turning in her law journal article, Layli's next project was to find a summer job. A paying job. She'd loved all the internships and volunteer work she'd done during summers past, but she needed to make money now. She and Roshan were living month to month on his medical fellowship salary and it wasn't enough. She needed to contribute. She was trying to figure out what kind of summer job she would apply for when she remembered Cindy Lewis, the woman whose description of her work in an immigration attorney's office had so intrigued Layli on the first day of class in her asylum law course. Maybe she should ask Cindy if there were any jobs available in her office.

Layli was walking down the hall at school a day or two later when she saw Cindy Lewis walking toward her. This was her chance. Cindy turned out to be very receptive to Layli's questions about her work, pleased that Layli found it so interesting. They talked for a while. A summer job? Layli might be in luck. The lawyer Cindy worked for had said something about wanting to hire another law clerk for the summer.

'I don't know if he's hired anybody yet,' Cindy said. 'I don't think so. Would you like me to give him your resumé?' Layli gave Cindy a copy of her resumé the next day in class.

'Great,' Cindy said. 'I'll give it to Eric today.'

That's who Cindy worked for – Eric Bowman.

Bowman was impressed with Layli's resumé, which mentioned her article on FGM, and he called her in for an interview. He told me later that they talked during that interview about the research and writing she'd done on FGM. He said that really jumped out at him when he saw her resumé, and it was one of the reasons he was interested in hiring her. My hearing was approaching. He'd hit nothing but dead ends in his attempts to get my case transferred. He could use someone with Layli's expertise. Later that week he offered her the job – either she could work full time as an unpaid intern and receive credit, or he would pay her and she would receive no credit. The salary Bowman was offering Layli struck her as the equivalent of twenty hours of pay, not forty.

Layli went home and discussed it with Roshan. She wanted the job, she wanted the experience, Eric Bowman seemed like a nice man. But the pay was so low, and they needed money. Maybe she should say no and look for a better-paying job.

'But you want this job.'

'Yeah, I do. I really do.'

'Then take it.' God was working through Roshan too.

Layli went back to Bowman with a counteroffer. Twenty hours a week of work for twenty hours' worth of pay and twenty hours a week to count as school credit. Full-time work for the same pay and school credit too. Fine with him, he said. She'd still be working full time at the salary he was able to offer. If the school had no objections, neither did he.

Because internships for school credit have to be supervised by a faculty member, Layli approached Professor Lauren Gilbert, the director of the Women in International Law program, who agreed to be her supervisor. Everything was in place now. Layli started working for Bowman on Tuesday, May 30, 1995, four days after the INS finally followed Canada's lead and issued its own guidelines on gender-based persecution, in the form of an official memorandum entitled 'Considerations for Asylum Officers Adjudicating Asylum Claims from Women.' Layli and Karen told me later that the people in the human rights, women's rights and refugee-advocate communities were jubilant. All the hard work Nancy Kelly, Deborah Anker, and others from those communities had done to prod the INS into taking that step had finally paid off. The guidelines educate asylum officers not only about all the terrible kinds of suffering inflicted on women simply because they're women, but also about how hard it is for female refugees to speak of their suffering to a stranger. Especially if it's unspeakably traumatic or of an intimate, sexual nature. Especially in front of a male stranger. Especially in front of a uniform-wearing male stranger. If the people I'd encountered after landing at Newark had been sensitized by reading the INS memorandum, perhaps my own experience would have been very different, but the memo was distributed to asylum officers, not immigration officers or judges.

Bowman was on vacation the week Layli started working for him, but returned to the office the following Monday. Sometime Tuesday afternoon, June 6, 1995, he came out of his office and walked over to Layli's desk carrying a file in his hand.

'See what you can do with this,' he said, handing her the file as he headed back to his office. 'The hearing's in a couple of weeks.'

Layli held the file in her hand. It was thin, light. She turned it sideways to read the name on it. 'Kasinga, Fauziya.' She put it down on the desk and opened it. There wasn't much in it. A copy of my seven-page asylum application form. Typed. Bowman must have had someone retype it, with the answers to the questions on why I was seeking asylum and what would happen if I returned to Togo exactly as I'd written it. Layli read through it. She was confused. It was poorly written, and the spelling was so bad. She wasn't familiar with all the rules and regulations of asylum forms and procedures. Maybe they're supposed to be submitted exactly as the refugee wrote them, she thought. There was a copy of the police report my uncle had filed, forwarded by Ayisha. The report was written in French and hadn't been translated. The marriage certificate was also in the file. It was written in French and Arabic. An English translation was attached. And there were two letters from my mother addressed to Rahuf, written in English and signed by my mother in Arabic. Although I heard about those letters, I didn't see them for a long time. The first was dated December 27, 1994, less than two weeks after I'd arrived in America. Since we follow the Muslim calendar back home, it's possible the letter was misdated, but I don't know. *Hi*, the letter read. *[T]here is something happening in the house which is very serious. Fauziya's father's family want to circumsice her and then marry her to an old man. Which Fauziya and I don't like. So I gave her money to leave. Since the time she left I did not know where she is. And later her Father's sister told me. She has reach America.* My mother must have meant Ayisha, my sister, told her. I don't think my aunt knew where I was, but perhaps word had somehow leaked out through Rahuf's relatives. News travels fast in Togo once it does get out. That's why I'd had to leave. That's why I couldn't go back. *I was very happy when I hed that,* the letter continued. *She even told me she had posted her identity card and marrage setificate.* Ayisha would have told her about the marriage certificate. *So good luck to her*, the letter concludes, *bye! Fauziya's Mother.*

Bye! Such a cheerful *bye!* But my mother probably had been feeling cheerful when she'd dictated that letter. She thought I was in a kind of boardinghouse. She thought I was happy and safe. She didn't know I was in prison.

The second letter was dated December 30, 1994. *It was on 20th October when they get to know she has run*, the letter read, *and they reported it on 21st to 22nd October, so the police are seaching for her and*

*so far as she has reach America I know they will not
get her. What hert me so much is the circumistion
before the marrage and he is even an old man. I wish
you all the marry ex'mas bye. Fauziya's Mother.*

That was it for my file – my asylum application, an
untranslated police report, a translated copy of my
marriage certificate, and two letters from my mother.
No clear written summary of all the facts and details of
my case. And, so far as Layli can recall, no transcription of my lengthy taped interview with Bowman the
day of my calendar hearing. But it was enough for
Layli. More than enough. Her heart started pounding,
because, in that instant, everything made absolute
sense to her. Her inexplicable obsession with FGM.
Her insistence on finding out more. The research and
reading she'd done. The papers she'd written. Layli
hadn't known the reason for it, but now she did. God
had been preparing her. To help me. She was determined to do her best.

She went into Bowman's office after reading the file
and they discussed the case. He told her to write a
brief, which is the formal written document that
reviews the facts of a case and the laws pertaining to
it.

'I need to talk to Fauziya,' she told Bowman. 'I need
to get more facts on her case.' She had no experience,
but she knew there wasn't enough information on me
in the file to build a brief around.

'That's a problem,' Bowman said. I was in prison.
Unfortunately, nobody could call me. 'We have to wait
until she calls us.'

'But what if she doesn't call?' Layli said. 'I really
need to talk to her. Isn't there some way we can reach
her?'

'Well, she keeps in touch with her cousin. I'll tell

Rahuf to tell her to call the next time he hears from her. But don't wait for that. Go ahead and start working. The deadline for submitting the brief is coming up fast.' Bowman consulted his desk calendar. 'Monday the twelfth.'

Monday the twelfth! It was already June 6 and the day was almost gone! Wednesday-Thursday-Friday-Saturday-Sunday – Monday! She had less than six days! Layli went to work immediately. She worked late into the night, then got up early the next morning to put in a few more hours before going to Bowman's office. She didn't have much time, and she didn't have much information about me. But she did have a lot of background on the subject and she had her journal article, which she could use as the basis for the arguments she wanted to make in the brief. This was all well and good, but it wasn't enough. She needed to build the brief around the specific facts of my case. Now if only she could talk to me.

And then I called, just when she needed me to. It must have been because Rahuf told me to, but I don't remember. When I asked for Bowman, Layli came on the line instead.

'Hellooo, Fauziya?' a sweet, soft, high-pitched girlish voice asked. And so Layli and I met for the first time. By phone.

Layli would remember feeling nervous, excited. My call had caught her unprepared. She didn't have all of her questions together yet. She remembers being struck by all the noise coming through from my end of the phone. She remembers the annoying recorded announcements constantly interrupting our conversation. She remembers how softly I spoke, how difficult it was for her to hear me and understand me. My accent was fairly thick. She had to ask me again and again to please speak up. I remember that she sounded nice – warm, kind, friendly. I liked her voice and gentle manner. She told me she was a law student and that she was going to help me. She needed to ask me some questions so she could write a brief. I didn't know then what a brief was, but I understood she was going to help me.

'I know about female genital mutilation,' she said.

I'd never heard the term before. I had to ask her what it was.

'It's the same thing as female circumcision,' she said.

'Oh.'

'It's performed in different ways in different places,' she went on. That was news to me. I didn't know other people did it too. 'I need to know how it's performed in your tribe,' she said. 'Can you tell me?' She wanted to know as many details as possible because she thought it might help her make the argument that FGM qualified as persecution.

I couldn't tell her much. 'I don't really know,' I said. 'I've never seen it performed. I know an old woman performs it. I think she uses a knife. And then they bind you from the waist to the knees for forty days to give the wound time to heal. I know that.' Layli would tell me later that what I described sounded to her like it might be infibulation, the most severe form of FGM, everything cut off and sewn shut. But she couldn't be sure. She asked me different questions about it. 'I don't understand,' I said in answer to many of her questions. I said that a lot. We'd both remember that. She asked me the name of my tribe. Tribes, I told her. Tchamba-Koussountu. She asked me to spell that. I tried. She had trouble hearing me. She asked me what part of Togo they're from. As she explained later, she wanted to see if she could do research on how they practice FGM.

What else did we talk about during that first phone call? Neither of us would remember later, but at the end of the conversation, Layli asked me to call again the next day so she could talk to me some more. During our next phone call, I told her about how my uncle had gone to the police when he and my aunt realized I was missing. I told her about how the police had come bothering Ayisha. I told her how Ayisha had helped me escape. I told her my mother had given me the money.

'Where'd you get the passport?' she asked.

'I bought it from a boy named Charlie,' I said.

'Who's Charlie?'

'Someone I met in Germany.'

'Germany? You were in Germany?'

She told me later that she was thrown by that and knew immediately that it could present a problem. If an asylum seeker has passed through another country on the way to America, the judge could say, 'She didn't have to come here. She could have gotten asylum there.'

'Did you apply for asylum in Germany?' Layli asked.

'No.'

'Why not?'

'Because I didn't know anyone there and I couldn't speak the language there. I want to go to school. I want to finish my education.'

We talked again the next day. My hearing was less than two weeks away then. Less than two weeks! Layli told me she'd be writing the brief that weekend. It had to be submitted on Monday. She wished me luck at my hearing. She wouldn't be there. For all we knew then, we would never meet face-to-face.

'I'm praying for you, Fauziya.'

She was. I knew it. I could tell by the way she said it.

'Thank you, Layli. I'll pray for you too.'

Layli worked feverishly on my brief all through the weekend, following the form of a sample brief that Cindy had given her. The brief explained that I had been placed in exclusion proceedings, which meant that because I'd been stopped at the airport, I'd never officially 'entered' the United States. I'd been 'excluded.' The distinction made no sense to me. I was being held in a prison in America, but according to the law, I'd never entered America and therefore wasn't entitled to the same legal rights and protections as an immigrant discovered living illegally in the United States – much less the rights of a U.S. citizen. The brief continued with a statement of the facts of my case, then the argument, which was basically the same argument Layli had made to support a claim of asylum in the papers she'd been writing for school and for the law journal.

Layli gave the brief to Bowman on Monday morning, June 12. After he looked it over, he brought it back to her with a few suggested corrections and changes, but overall he thought it was an excellent piece of work. She made the corrections and gave it back to him for one final review before they sent it in – just in time for the deadline. Done, Layli thought. That's it. I've done everything I can. All I can do now is pray. But Bowman had another assignment for her: to put together the list of questions he would use to elicit the facts of my story in court – the direct examination.

On Wednesday, June 14, Layli packed a bag. She was leaving the next morning to fly down to Atlanta, Georgia, to attend an Immigration Lawyers

Association conference and spend time with her family while she was there. She was looking forward to the conference. It would give her a chance to meet refugee-advocate attorneys who were prominent in the field and talk to them about my case. She told me later that she talked to a lot of good people there, people who had information that was useful to her. She ran into her former teacher Bo Cooper and told him about my case. He thought it was great that she was getting an opportunity to work on a case that dealt with issues she was so committed to. She met Deborah Anker, one of the two Harvard women who'd been mainly responsible for getting the INS to issue its new guidelines. Anker was very interested in my case. She organized an informal discussion group on gender-based asylum claims, where Layli met and talked to some of the other people involved in these issues. Layli was grateful. She knew that a lot of requests for asylum were denied and that most such decisions were automatically appealed. She was praying that I'd be granted asylum. But she wanted to be prepared to help with the appeal if I wasn't. She wanted to learn as much as she could, know everything there was to know. She was thinking ahead.

That Thursday was fashion show day for me. It was my best day at Esmor, my best day in prison. We'd spent the last two weeks practicing. Esther had taken me under her wing and spent hours trying to teach me to walk like a model – or at least like a woman. I walked too much like a man, she kept saying. 'This is how it's supposed to look,' she'd say. And then she'd float across the room with such elegance that I no longer even saw the blue prison uniform she was wearing. In my eyes she was dressed in silks and rubies like the princess she had been in her former

345

life. Now all of us could put aside our prison uniforms for this one brief moment and dress up in the clothes Miss Jones and Miss White had brought in for us to model.

When we looked at the hallway we would be using as our runway that day, we saw that it had been decorated with flowers and balloons. Miss White had brought in her tape player so we'd have music. She and the other guards set out about twenty chairs along both sides of the hall for the audience – some of the other detainees, and the other female guards. That's who we'd been told the audience was going to be, just the people we saw every day. Miss Jones brought in makeup and mirrors for us to use. She put it all in N dorm, which we used as our dressing room. It was so much fun! It was almost like being in a dorm in a boardinghouse, a dorm full of women getting all dressed up for a fancy party. We did one another's hair and makeup. We helped one another dress. What a transformation. We stared wide-eyed, amazed, as if we'd never seen each other before. We hadn't. Not as women. We'd never seen one another in anything but our ugly blue prison uniforms.

When Miss Jones came in to check on how we were doing, she made an announcement: If we wanted to, she said, we could keep the clothes we were modeling after the fashion show.

'Keep them?'

'Yes. They'll be put in the property room for you with your checked luggage if you like.' She was standing next to me. She gave me a wink. 'What do you say, Fauzy? Would you like to keep yours?'

Would I? I loved my outfits! I'd chosen a fancy evening suit with a short black lace skirt and pink jacket with gold buttons and black lace sleeves, and another evening outfit with a long gray stretchy skirt and gray top with a beaded flower design on the front. I could just see myself walking around in my new life wearing my two beautiful outfits.

Miss Jones had another announcement. If there was time after the show, she was going to bring in chicken and rice from outside for those of us who'd participated. I loved chicken and rice! Oh, this was too wonderful. This was like a dream! 'What do you say, ladies? Would you like that?'

Like it? Would we like it? We answered in a resounding chorus. 'Yes!'

She laughed. 'OK, hurry up and get ready now. It's time for the show.'

When Miss Jones went out into the hallway, I noticed that the chairs were filling up with men and women whose faces I didn't recognize. But I was too excited even to wonder who they were. And then the music sounded and Miss Jones said a few words of welcome to the audience. With that the fashion show began. 'And here comes . . .'

The first two women walked out into the hall. People clapped as the two walked down the 'runway,' kept clapping as they came to a halt and went through the poses we'd been taught, and didn't stop clapping until the women had turned and come back, laughing, their faces flushed with excitement. Oh God, I was so nervous waiting for my turn. Esther was next. She was wearing loose, flowing black pants and a strapless red top, and she looked absolutely gorgeous. I was glad I wasn't partnered with her. I don't think anyone so much as glanced at her partner. Not with Esther to look at. People applauded, they whistled, they went wild. Esther floated back in smiling. People were still applauding in the hall.

My turn was coming up. Suddenly I felt half naked in my short black lace skirt. It was one thing to practice my walk in front of a few friends. It was another to do it in front of all these people. When Esther told me she'd just seen Frank in the audience, I lost my nerve entirely.

'I can't do it!' I wailed to Esther. 'I can't go out there wearing this in front of Frank.'

She laughed. 'Yes you can. Don't worry. You'll be fine. Just remember, slow and graceful. No stomping, no walking on your heels. Remember what I taught you, OK?'

I'm afraid I didn't do justice to all the hard work Esther had put into me. But I did my turns and received my applause and had my fun, laughing all the way. Oh, it was so much fun.

And then it was over. It was time to take off my beautiful clothes and put on my blue prison uniform again. The other models and I began changing. Slowly. Reluctantly. None of us wanted to put our uniforms back on. But we had to. I heard a few of the Ghanaian women who'd been modeling grumbling among themselves. They were upset about something. I didn't know what. I found out when Miss Jones came to see us in the dorm after the guests had left. She was in a very good mood, really pleased that we'd all done so well. 'That was great!' she said. 'You were all wonderful! Did you enjoy it? Did you have fun?'

A chorus of enthusiastic yeses, mine among them. And then an angry 'no' from one of the Ghanaian women.

I was startled. So was Miss Jones.

'No?' she said. 'Why not?'

'Who were those people in the audience? They don't work here. You said it was only going to be us and some of the guards. Who'd you invite? Who were they?'

The warm, friendly, cheerful, laughing Miss Jones disappeared. Poof! Just like that she was gone, replaced in an instant by the tough Miss Jones, the cold Miss Jones, Miss Jones the prison officer. 'I didn't invite them,' she said stiffly. 'I didn't know they were coming.'

'Then who did? Who were they?' The Ghanaian woman was pressing her luck and ruining the good mood for the rest of us. But I saw her point. I thought of the day my laundry co-workers and I had returned to our dorm to find Miss Jones in there with those women from the other dorms and those two interviewers. I was quite sure the people in the audience didn't work here. We'd never seen them before. They must have been from the outside. INS officials? Whoever they were, they'd seen a good show. If the Ghanaian woman's suspicions were right, we'd been tricked. We'd shown those visitors how happy we women were here at Esmor, how much fun we had, how pleasant life was. That's what they'd seen. It was a lie. Today had been fun. One day out of six months had been fun, happy, pleasant. Every other day had been and would be the same miserable prison life. The visitors didn't know that and probably never would know it. 'Who were they?' the Ghanaian woman asked again.

Miss Jones didn't answer. She didn't have to. She was Miss Jones. 'No rice and chicken,' she said curtly.

We did get rice and chicken later that day. It had already been ordered, and she didn't send it back. But the mood was spoiled.

The next day, Saturday, dragged. The fashion show was behind us now. Practicing for it had given us something to do for a couple of weeks. Now it was back to the same boring, endless, mind-numbing prison routine.

But that was OK. This was my last weekend. I lay in bed that night thinking about that marvelous, unbelievable fact. Now there were only five more days to my hearing. Then the judge would grant me asylum and I'd be free. Bowman would take me back to Washington with him, to Rahuf's apartment, and Rahuf would take me out to celebrate. I could wear one of the new outfits from my fashion show. The black lace one. With high-heeled shoes this time. And stockings.

Washington . . . I wondered what it looked like. I wondered what America looked like. There was a whole country outside this prison, a whole world I hadn't seen. I'd see it soon. It was almost over now, almost over. It was all going to be all right, just like Yaya said. I closed my eyes, drifting into sleep. Maybe I'd dream of him again tonight. Maybe he'd come visit me one more time in prison. One last time before I was free.

22

Riot!

Kim made her usual rounds later that night, banging in and out of dorm after dorm, going from bed to bed, snatching off blankets and yanking at wrists and ankles. When she finished count and left the J dorm, the last on her route, quiet descended. Blessed quiet. Darkness. Stillness. I was settling into sleep, comforted by the idea that my ordeal was almost over now. Almost over. Only five more days . . .

Suddenly I was jolted awake by what sounded like a loud explosion, like a bomb going off. I lay still in the darkness, listening – listening to nothing. Silence. I must have dreamt it. I closed my eyes, quieted my nerves, and began drifting back to sleep.

Again – a loud crash.

I bolted upright in bed. 'Sylvie! What was—'

And then the night, the darkness, the stillness exploded into terrifying sounds of chaos: glass shattering, metal slamming against metal, men shouting, the fire alarm ringing, women screaming.

'Sylvie! What is it! What's happening?'

'It's a riot!' she screamed. There was terror in her voice.

The next thing I knew, there were men outside the door to the women's wing, hammering away with heavy metal objects, trying to break in. And then the hall was swarming with men. Men were everywhere, running around in the darkness, shouting and yelling, smashing at everything.

'Oh my God. They're going to rape us. Oh my God,' Sylvie cried.

Suddenly there were men at our dorm window. 'Get back!' they yelled. 'Cover your eyes!' They began slamming at the window with long pieces of metal. The window shattered, spraying flying glass half the length of the room.

The men yelled at us to come out. 'Out! Everybody out of here!'

I started to shake uncontrollably. My three Chinese dorm mates clung to each other, crying hysterically. We were all crying, except Oche who stood like stone, frozen. I closed my eyes and sent my last prayers to God. 'Please, Allah, bless my family. I die as a true believer. Show mercy, Allah. Let my death be swift.' As I prayed I could hear the voices of my dorm mates calling out the names of their families.

'Come out! Now!' the men ordered us.

Glass was being shattered. Women in the other dorms were screaming. I didn't know how we managed to comprehend anything through all the noise and darkness and terror and chaos, but somehow the men eventually got us to understand that they weren't going to hurt us. They wanted to move us into the men's gym, where we'd be safer. We came away from our corner and moved toward the window, which was now just a gaping jigsaw of shards. Someone put folded blankets over the jagged pieces of glass in the bottom of the window frame, and we climbed out one by one as the men steadied us, easing us through the window and helping us jump down into the hall. The floor was wet with water that was running down the walls.

Everything was so dark that we could barely see what was going on, but we could hear the fire alarm wailing and the sound of things being smashed against the walls and windows. We were surrounded on all sides by a mob of angry, shouting men, pushing and shoving. The men who had come to our dorm were clearing a path through the chaos, leading groups of crying, terrified women in the direction of the gym. Sylvie, Oche, my three Chinese dorm mates, and I fell in with one of the groups. I grabbed hold of Sylvie's hand to keep her close. The whole time I was crying, shaking. Oh God, help us! The fire alarm. Some part of the building must be on fire! We'll never make it! We'll never make it through alive.

As we stumbled along through the darkness I saw tables and chairs stacked against one of the doors leading to the main entrance. 'Sylvie!' I shouted. 'Sylvie!' She couldn't hear me, so I tugged on her hand. She turned around. 'Look over there! Why is everything stacked up like that?'

'Oh my God!' she wailed. 'They've built a barricade. We're trapped. We're trapped in a riot!'

I began crying hysterically and wouldn't let go of Sylvie.

Panting with terror herself, she tried to reassure me as she pulled me forward through the darkness. 'Everything is going to be OK, sweetheart,' she gasped. Surrounded on all sides by a mob of angry, shouting men, we held on to each other, a ragtag line of women, until at last we found ourselves in the men's gym, a large wire-roofed enclosure, open to the sky. Women were sitting on the floor in clusters with their backs against the wall. One very tall man was guarding the door holding a baton, letting the women in, keeping the other men out. I don't know where he got the baton from. And then I saw James, sweet shy James, a kitchen worker whom I had always liked to tease because he was so short. He was also standing by the door as a guard. Short as he was, when a couple of much bigger men tried to push into the gym behind us, James stepped in front of them, blocking their way. 'No men in here!' he shouted. 'Women only!' He said it with enough ferocity that the men retreated in the face of his command.

Sylvie and I spotted Oche and our three Chinese dorm mates and joined them in a huddle on the floor. We hugged each other and wept and prayed. Meanwhile the rioting went on and on and on. I don't know how long the rampage lasted. It seemed to go on forever.

And then the sirens stopped. The sound of things smashing tapered off. We could still hear shouting in the background, and the whoosh of the water escaping from broken pipes, but little by little things quieted down enough for us to be able to hear the sounds of our own wails and prayers. The men's fury seemed spent.

'Oh God,' Sylvie moaned. 'We're going to pay for this. They don't know what they've done! They don't know what a real prison is like! I know! I've been there! The police will be here soon and that's where they'll send us.'

This spread among the women, language to language, and triggered a renewed chorus of crying and wailing. Where *would* we go? What *would* they do with us? We sat anxiously and waited for whatever would happen next.

James came over to us to ask if we were OK.

'Why did you do this,' I asked him angrily. 'Why?'

'*I* didn't do this,' he said. 'Me and a lot of the other men, we wanted nothing to do with it.'

After a while some of the men began asking the women if they wanted to get anything from their dorms. If they didn't get it now, chances were they wouldn't be able to later. We were all cold and hungry. Everyone wanted to salvage what little they could from the shambles – clothes, food, personal items – so a lot of women took the men up on their offer, including Sylvie and Oche. Since I didn't want to be separated from Sylvie for a moment, I decided to go with them. We asked James to accompany us, because we knew we could trust him.

He led us back down the dark, wet, debris-strewn hallways to our dorm, back through the shattered window. Sylvie and Oche got busy right away, gathering up their own possessions. I could hardly think what to take, I was so beside myself, but I forced myself to focus. I put on two T-shirts, two pairs of socks, and my extra prison uniform over what I was already wearing. I found my watch, and put that on too. I collected my *tasbih* and my Qur'an and put them in a pillowcase, and then threw in a few food items. What else? I put my little address book, my I.D. cards, letters I'd received from Rudina and Mary, and, most precious of all, the letters and photographs from Ayisha and Amariya in a small brown envelope. I stuck the envelope in my bra.

James helped us climb back out the dorm window and we started making our way back to the gym. Someone shouted out that one of the telephones in the officers' room in the women's section was still working. Sylvie and Oche went on, to the gym, but I was desperate to get word to Rahuf. If something happened to me, if I disappeared, Rahuf would at least have some warning. James and I headed to the officers' room.

When we got there, we found that the room had been ransacked. Desks were overturned and there were papers all over the floor. A lot of people were already in there, trying to call friends and family. When my turn at the phone finally came, I started talking as soon as Rahuf's voice came on the line. With so many people still waiting to call their own families, I had to tell my story fast.

'Fauziya! What's happened!' He sounded sleepy.

'There's been a riot!' I repeated.

'A riot? Are you OK?'

'I'm fine. The men are breaking things and we don't know what's going to happen. I just want you to know, in case . . . in case you d-d-don't hear from me.' The truth was, I wanted him to know what had happened in case I died, which I truly believed might happen.

'I'll call Bowman!' Rahuf said. 'Fauziya, be careful! Please!'

Rahuf tried to ask me more questions, but there was no time. I hurried off the phone.

James and I made our way back to the gym, and I sat with Sylvie and Oche. Esther and the rest of the laundry gang were also there now. We cried, we prayed, we waited to find out what would happen to us.

When dawn started to break I saw that there were three men in dark uniforms standing atop the high walls of the wire-roofed enclosure, looking down at us. They were carrying guns! I started crying hysterically. Other women spotted them and began screaming and crying as well. Sylvie shook me. 'Calm down! Calm down! They're not going to shoot us without hearing what happened. They'd be shooting already if they wanted to do that.' She was right, of course. They just stood there looking at us for about fifteen or twenty minutes and then they went away.

A group of male detainees appeared at the door, saying they wanted to speak to us. 'Listen up,' they said. Somehow we had to get out of here, and they had a plan. Everyone would walk out together, but the men wanted the women to walk out first. 'We'll be right behind you. If you go first, they won't hurt you,' they said.

The women first? No way! Were they crazy? 'We didn't do this!' women were yelling. 'You did it! You go out! You talk to the police!'

The men tried to reason with us. A lot of the men hadn't been involved either, they said, but the police weren't going to care about that. If the men went out first, the police would just start beating them. If the women were in front, they wouldn't do anything violent because they'd know the women hadn't had anything to do with it and weren't dangerous. The men were asking us to help them. If we went out first, fewer people were likely to get hurt. But we refused. We were just as frightened of the police as they were. And no-one could be sure that the police would not beat us as well. So it was decided we'd all go out together, but through the emergency exit in the N dorm, not the main entrance. We were thinking maybe that way we would be able to avoid the police.

Women began standing up and crowding through the gym door, heading back to N dorm with the men. We were on the move again, toward God only knew what. All we thought about was getting out as quickly as possible.

In order to get into the N dorm, we all had to pass

through the officers' room and then climb through the broken window. The N dorm was soon packed with people – a huge jostling crowd of terrified men and women. After everybody had crowded in, we waited for the signal to leave. My heart was pounding because I knew there were policemen outside the building. What would they do to us? We were strangers to this country and we had busted up their prison. Well, not all of us, but we didn't know if the police would give us a chance to explain. I sent up a prayer to Allah. 'Please, God. Don't let them hurt me. Please.'

'Here we go!' one of the men at the door shouted. They opened the door. This was it.

The people at the front surged through the exit, but were instantly met by a blast from a water hose so huge and powerful that at first the men were unable to close the door against the pressure of the spray. Pandemonium erupted. Everyone started screaming, yelling, running and scrambling to get away from the door. 'Back to the gym!' someone shouted. 'Get back to the gym!'

I joined the panicked crowd of people pushing and shoving their way through the narrow spaces to get back to the gym. I had just reached the hallway when I heard two earsplitting gunshots ring out somewhere in front of me. Everyone screamed in terror. The police were in the building! They were shooting. I dove into the commissary, which was the room nearest me. The floor was strewn with biscuits, candy, and all the other things that were sold in the commissary. I stumbled over people who'd run into the room before me, while other panic-stricken people pushed in from behind. 'They're coming!' someone yelled. 'They're coming down the hall!' I scrambled into a space against a wall, trying to make myself invisible.

One of the men who worked in the kitchen came and sat in front of me. 'Are you OK, Fauziya?' I nodded my head.

'Everybody stay down!' one of the men in the room shouted. 'Stay down. Don't move!' I heard two or three women crying, but there were mostly men in the room. I put my forehead on my knees, covered my face with my hands, and prayed. 'Please, God. Don't let me die like this. Don't let me die without seeing my family again.'

Suddenly the door to the commissary was filled with the shapes of two big policemen looming over us. They were carrying heavy batons and wearing helmets and rubber masks with big plastic eyes and animal-like snouts strapped over their faces. 'Everybody stay where you are!' one of the policemen yelled. The next thing I knew there was the sound of gas hissing and the policemen went running out of the room, shutting the door behind them. I couldn't breathe. My eyes were on fire. Everyone around me was screaming. 'Oh God!' 'My eyes! My eyes are burning me!' We were all choking, coughing, crying. The policemen left us there, sealed in that room, blinded by our own tears, gasping for breath.

After a few minutes, the doors opened again and one of the policemen entered the room swinging his baton at random. I heard people shout 'Oh, my head!' 'My back' 'Oh, my shoulders!' Bam! Bam! Bam! There was so much noise from their wailing that I couldn't hear my own screams. I scrunched down even lower, put my head between my knees, and threw my arms up over my head to try to shield myself from the blows I knew were coming. My friend sitting in front of me pushed back against me to cover even more of me. The policeman worked his way around the room striking one person after another with his baton. Then he was pounding my friend who was protecting me. He howled in pain as the blows came raining down on him. One savage blow struck at my left wrist, which was one of the few parts of me that were still exposed, because my arms were covering my head. Despite the searing pain, I didn't move my arms, figuring it was my wrist or my head. But the policeman had finished with me, anyway. His baton came down on the man next to me – Bam! Bam! – then on the man next to him. Everyone got hit, once, twice, three times. I was lucky, lucky and grateful to the good, brave man in front of me. May Allah bless him. He took my blows. I got hit only once.

Through eyes streaming with tears I could dimly make out people being shoved and clubbed forward, toward the door. Men, women – it didn't seem to matter – the blows were falling on everyone. Then it was my turn. 'You! Out!' one of the policeman shouted at me. I got to my feet and stumbled blindly toward the door, cradling my left wrist in my right hand, coughing, choking, crying. Unable to see where I was going, I tripped and fell. The policeman kicked me hard on my lower back as I tried to get up. I fell forward onto my hands and knees and crawled out the door.

The other policeman was waiting in the hallway. 'On the floor!' he shouted through his mask. 'On your stomach! Spread your legs! Hands behind your back!' The floor was filthy, covered with rubble. He kicked my legs apart, stood astride me, wrenched my arms up hard behind my back, yanked my wrists together, fastened them with some kind of plastic handcuffs. He pulled the handcuffs so tight, it felt like they were slicing into my skin. I screamed.

'Shit, another woman' was his response. He called for a woman officer to come get me. 'On your feet!' With my wrists handcuffed behind my back I couldn't get up. He jerked me up to a standing position and handed me over to a woman officer who was coming down the hall. 'Here, take her out,' he said. The female officer grabbed my left arm and pulled me forward. As I stumbled along beside her, my eyes still streaming with tears, she guided me down the hall to the main entrance and outside into a new June day. It was Sunday morning, June 18, 1995.

'Sit!' she snapped after we'd walked a ways, pushing my shoulders down so that I fell hard on concrete. All I could see through my burning eyes were the vague shapes of a group of women sitting in a long, straight row, with their hands cuffed behind their backs, like mine. I was in intense pain, as many of them must have been, too, judging from the crying and moaning I could hear all around me. But I was alive. Merciful God, I was alive.

'Seven Six One! What happened! What happened!'

I looked up, squinting. Alison Johnson, one of the nicest of our guards, one of our favorites, was crouching in front of me, crying. I asked her to wipe my eyes.

'What happened?' she asked as she gently wiped my eyes with a handkerchief.

'Tear gas,' I sobbed. Oh, God, her handkerchief felt so good.

'There,' she said. 'Is that better?' I nodded feebly.

'What happened?' she asked again. 'I came to work this morning and I see . . . this! They said there'd been a riot! What happened?'

'I don't know!' I sobbed. 'I don't know! The innocent ones are suffering. The men did it and now we

361

are suffering. Do you know what they are going to do with us?'

'I'm sorry, Seven Six One. I wish I knew,' Alison said softly, 'but I have no idea.' She went off then, walking toward some of the other officers.

Now that my eyes weren't tearing so much, I could see a little more clearly. We seemed to be in some sort of industrial park – warehouses, fences, and concrete in all directions. There were police cars, ambulances, and fire trucks everywhere, all kinds of trucks, cars, buses, and vans. There must have been at least a hundred policemen and all kinds of officers and guards, most of them wearing black uniforms. People were shouting and yelling, radios and walkie-talkies were crackling and blaring. I'd never seen anything like it. I saw a group of male Esmor guards standing off to the side with their hands on their hips, shaking their heads and talking. I saw male police officers leading handcuffed male detainees out of the building, one by one, and people with cameras filming the men as they left the prison. Nobody seemed to be paying any attention to us women.

It was a sunny day, my first time outdoors in six months and a day. This was how I finally made it outside. But where was I going? All I could think about was whether they were going to send us all back to our countries.

Oche! Another female police officer was leading Oche toward my group. She saw me and walked over to where I was sitting. We saw Esther come out a little while later, all bent over, her shoulders and back heaving with sobs. Then Sylvie came out, too, her eyes filled with tears. They were led to another group of women.

We sat there like that for a long time, an hour, two

362

hours maybe. Then three men – I don't know who they were because they weren't wearing any uniforms – came over and started taking names, asking us our age, native country, and date of arrival in the United States. I was sure this meant we were going to be sent back. One of the three, a big, burly man in dark sunglasses, strode over and began counting a group of us off. 'One! Two! Three! Four! On your feet!' he said, continuing to count until he'd collected twelve women. 'Over by that van!' We struggled to our feet and a number of female police officers escorted us to the van he had pointed to. Oche was with me.

'Where are they taking us?' I asked a female officer who was standing by our van.

'I don't know' was all she would say. I watched as Sylvie and Esther were counted off into a group that was being herded toward a large bus. As they walked away I mouthed a silent prayer: Please God, let them take me someplace safe.

'OK, listen up!' shouted the female officer I'd spoken to. 'Anybody carrying any personal belongings, turn them over before getting in the van!' In all the confusion I'd lost my pillowcase sometime during the night, but tucked inside my bra I still had the envelope containing my address book, I.D. cards, letters, and family pictures. As the line began moving forward and it came my turn to board, I foolishly answered yes when the officer asked me if I had any personal belongings. I didn't want her to frisk me as she was doing to the others.

'I have an envelope in my bra,' I said. 'I can't get to it.'

'OK.' The officer reached into my shirt and pulled the envelope out of my bra.

'What are you going to do with it?' I asked.

363

'Don't worry,' she said. 'You'll get it back.' She asked me my number and wrote the number on the envelope before tossing it on top of a small pile of things on the ground near her feet.

'You didn't write my name on it,' I said.

'Don't worry, we'll take care of it,' she said. 'In the van.'

Another officer steadied my arm as I climbed into the van through the open side door. I didn't know it then, but I was never going to see my envelope again. The letters from Ayisha and my mother, the pictures, my address book, my I.D. cards – lost for ever.

As the van started to move I asked the driver where we were going. He didn't answer. Maybe he hadn't heard me. I started to ask him again. 'Excuse me, can you tell us—'

'You fucking people,' he exploded. Not everybody on the van spoke English, but you didn't have to know the language to understand his hatred. It hit us like a hard slap. 'I'll tell you where you're going!' he bellowed. 'You're going back to your fucking countries!'

I believed him and I was terrified. There would come a time when I'd look back and wish that driver really had taken me to the airport and put me on a plane to Togo. Instead, he was about to deliver us to a place called Hudson County Correctional Center in Kearny-Hackensack, New Jersey. I would learn later that Hudson, or Kearny-Hackensack as it's frequently called, was a prison that had been built by court order to relieve overcrowding at the old Hudson County Jail. Hudson opened on June 4, 1990, with an official capacity of around 1,500 inmates. When I arrived, on Sunday, June 18, 1995, it was already over capacity, with a mix of county and state prisoners.

The words Sylvie had spoken as we'd sat together in

364

the gym while the men were rioting would turn out to be prophetic. 'The idiots!' she'd said. 'They don't know how bad a real prison can be.' I didn't either. My education was about to begin.

Once we got to Hudson, a journey of only about twenty minutes or so, the twelve of us – Oche and I plus two women from Pakistan, two from Cuba, two from other Latin American countries, and four from China – went through the standard prison ritual of being processed and booked. The details vary from prison to prison, but the essentials are the same. We were taken to a back room, where female officers removed our plastic handcuffs. I yelped in pain as the officer lifted my arms behind me to remove them. My arms hurt from being wrenched back when the policeman had put the handcuffs on me. My back and shoulder throbbed where the other policeman had kicked me. I brought my wrist around in front of me and examined it. It was the first chance I'd had to look at it since I'd been beaten. It was swelling and turning purple.

'Strip,' one of the female officers ordered. The order came like another blow. All of us? All of us together? 'Strip!' she repeated. Until that moment I wouldn't have believed my mind or body capable of registering any more degradation and trauma than I'd already endured, than we'd all endured, during the riot and its aftermath. But this was even worse – twelve women being forced to strip, squat, cough, turn, squat, and cough in front of each other, and under the eyes of a strange prison officer. But what choice did we have? The twelve of us did as we were told. We didn't look at one another. We kept our heads down, our eyes, filled with tears, cast down.

After we put our clothes back on, we were weighed,

measured, photographed, fingerprinted, and issued new I.D. – not bracelets, as at Esmor, but photo I.D. cards that hooked onto our uniforms. 'Please,' I said to the officer when my turn came, extending my left wrist toward him.

'Please,' I whispered pitifully. 'It hurts. Can I see a doctor?' Tears spilled out of my eyes. He examined my wrist. 'That looks mean,' he said. 'You can't see one now, but I'll make a note that you need to get that examined.'

After we'd all been processed, we were marched single file into a large room. We sat on metal benches, numb and silent. We still didn't know what prison, or where it was. I covered my face with my hands, bent my chest to my knees, and sobbed.

We sat there for I don't know how long. Eventually we were served dinner in the bullpen. The food looked like the food at Esmor – a scrawny, uncooked chicken leg with something unrecognizable beside it. I don't know if it tasted as bad as it looked, because I was too upset to eat.

Finally, two female prison guards came in and led us to the laundry room, where we traded in our Esmor uniforms for different ones. We were each issued two dark green uniforms, which, although they weren't brand-new, were better fitting and in better condition than the ones we'd worn at Esmor. The style was the same as the Esmor uniform: short-sleeved, V-neck shirt, and a pair of pants with an elastic waistband. We were given three sets of new underwear – really new, to give credit where it is due, not the stained, torn underwear we'd had to wear at Esmor. We were also given the standard prison issue supplies: one thin blanket, two sheets, one pillowcase, two towels, a washcloth, a toothbrush, a small tube of toothpaste, and plastic eating and drinking utensils. We kept our shoes and socks.

The inmate who worked in the laundry room told us that we had to give him everything that didn't belong to Hudson prison. As I took off my watch I noticed that the time was wrong. I held it to my ear. It wasn't ticking. I tried to wind it. The wind stem was jammed in and bent sideways. Huh? How did . . . ? Suddenly I realized that when the policeman had hit me on the wrist with the baton, my watch must have taken much of the force of impact. It was Yaya, still protecting me.

Next we were led by guards back to book-in, and from there through a maze of wide beige-painted hallways, through a series of double sets of sliding, clanging metal doors, to a bank of elevators and up to the third floor. Eventually we found ourselves in a large, light yellow, high-ceilinged, roughly triangular-shaped room, with a staircase leading up to a landing that ran along two of its walls. This was what they called the dayroom. Above and below the landing the walls were interrupted by narrow metal cell doors, sixteen on top, sixteen below, each with a vertical slit of window, and a number stenciled above the window in black. I could see women's cheeks, noses, and eyes pressed against some of the windows in the cell doors, and could hear the muted sounds of their voices, shouting and yelling inside their cells.

In the dayroom a number of women in prison uniforms seemed to be on some kind of clean-up detail, talking loud among themselves. Other women were sitting on the beds that were lined up on the walls between the cell doors. Three or four more women sat on beds lined up against the third wall, which extended from the dark-tinted window of an elevated guard's booth located just outside the dayroom, to a wall-mounted television set, and from there to six wall-mounted telephones. Some of the women were sitting quietly. Others were shouting and yelling and screaming. One woman was sitting on a bed directly beneath the phones, a skinny black woman with a half-bald shaved head who was screaming and gesticulating and acting insane. The guards escorting us didn't even seem to notice her. But one of the guards had warned us before we came in that some of the inmates were crazy. Oh, God! Was this where I was going to sleep? On one of these beds in this big room? With crazy people?

Then it hit me: the smoke. People smoked in here. I can't be around smoke. It aggravates my asthma and makes me physically ill. The room was freezing cold. Cold and smelly. Stinky with cigarette smoke and other odors I couldn't and didn't want to identify. At the far end of the room, seven large, shiny metal octagonal-shaped tables were bolted to the floor in rows, three in one row, four in another. The tables had pale-green pedestals that branched treelike into four round, shiny metal seats.

I didn't know it yet but I was seeing this room at its best. We'd entered during 'lockdown,' when inmates from the cells that lined the walls on either side of the dayroom are locked in their cells, and inmates assigned to beds in the dayroom are confined to their beds. I was frightened to tears by my first hints and imaginings of what life was going to be like here. The reality was going to be even worse, as I would soon find out.

Fortunately, those of us from Esmor weren't assigned to beds in the dayroom or put into cells with the other female inmates. The officers led us up the stairs to the upper deck and broke us into pairs. 'You and you. You and you.' I was paired with a Chinese woman and led to cell 607 along the left wall. Oche was paired with a Pakistani woman and led to cell 610 along the other wall.

The female officer escorting my partner and me walked us to our cell door, unlocked the door, and waved us inside. 'Someone will come by later to make sure you have everything,' she said as she closed the door behind us. The bolt locked with a loud bang. We were standing in a tiny cell, a tiny shoebox of a cell even smaller than the one I'd been locked up in when I was put in segregation at Esmor. It was about seven feet wide and ten feet long, with beige cinderblock walls and a low ceiling. A small metal toilet-and-sink unit was located just inside the door with a metal mirror above it, and there was also a metal table and stool, a light fixture above the table, and two narrow metal bunks, one atop the other, across the back wall. The bunks were furnished with a thin plastic-covered mattress and one pillow each. There was a narrow vertical slit of window in the back wall behind the top bunk and another narrow vertical slit of window in the door. Like the dayroom the cell was cold and smelled of cigarette smoke. The toilet stank. My roommate and I couldn't move without bumping into each other. It was a box, a tiny, freezing, stinky, cinder block and metal box hardly big enough for two people to stand in much less live in. We both broke down crying. I gestured feebly for my roommate to choose whichever bunk she preferred. She gestured back for me to choose first. I put my things down on the bottom bunk and sat down on the hard mattress. She put her things on the top bunk and sat down beside me. We sobbed loudly, but I doubt anyone heard us.

A female guard came in an hour or so later to take me to the medical unit to have my wrist checked. She led me back out to the elevator, down one level, and then left down the hall to one of the prison's 'satellite' medical units, where a doctor examined my wrist. 'It's not broken,' he said. 'Just badly bruised. You'll be all right.'

When the doctor dismissed me, the officer took me back to my cell pod. I walked through the door and into hell. The cell doors had been unlocked during my absence. There were some sixty shouting, screaming, smoking, hollering, shoving, pushing women now at loose in the dayroom. The television on the wall to my right was on now. Some of the women stood or sat directly beneath it on brown molded plastic chairs. I could tell the TV was on because I saw images on the screen, but I couldn't hear any sound above the screaming and yelling. It was like a madhouse!

There'd been about sixty women in all of Esmor, the same number as were now in this one room. The women at Esmor had all been INS detainees. These women – I didn't know who or what they were. The women at Esmor had all come to America to escape trouble. These women were all here because they'd made or gotten into trouble of some kind. I'd been frightened of them for that reason before I'd even encountered them. What I saw now frightened me even more. There were no guards in the room trying to control the bedlam. They were all safely behind dark-tinted glass in the guard's booth outside. Oh God, help me! Help me! I kept my eyes down and started walking rapidly to the stairwell.

'Hey! You one of them refugees?' a tall black woman standing near me shouted as I passed.

I kept my head down. 'Yes.'

'Wachuu doin' here!' She sounded angry.

I backed away a step, shook my head. 'I don't know.'

'Damn!' she said, slamming the knuckles of her fists hard on her hips. 'Well, you tell'em ta getchall outta here! Ya hear me!' She shook a fist at me. 'Tell'em y'all dohn belong here!' I nodded, backing away. I was terrified of her, but it meant a lot to me that she said that. She was right. We didn't belong here.

As I hurried up the stairs I saw Oche standing on the deck in front of her cell. I ran to her and we went and hid in her cell, which was pretty much exactly like mine. Her roommate wasn't there. Oche said she'd gone to find the other Pakistani woman.

'Oh, God, Oche! What are we going to do!' I said through my tears.

She sat like stone. 'I don't know,' she whispered. 'I don't know.'

'Hey, Esmor! Esmor!' we heard women shout from the dayroom.

Oche and I looked at each other. 'You go,' she said.

I walked out on the deck. Three women, including the black woman who'd spoken to me before, were standing below Oche's cell, calling and waving frantically toward the television. 'Esmor! They're talking about the riot!'

I ran back into the cell. 'Oche! They're talking about the riot on TV!'

We ran down to the dayroom, where some of the women in our group were already standing under the TV. Others came down the stairs after us.

The news footage showed the men being led out of the prison in handcuffs. Some looked frightened. Most looked sullen, stoic. There was no footage of the women being taken out. Why didn't they show us?

Why didn't they show us as we were led out, a bunch of innocent, terrified women stumbling into the daylight coughing, choking, weeping, sobbing? Why didn't they show what the riot and the police had done to us? Some of the inmates shouted and hooted at us as we watched the TV coverage. 'Hey! That your prison? Why'd you bust it up?'

We hadn't busted it up. The men had. As for why, I found out later that the INS was asking the same question. They investigated and did a report – 'The Elizabeth, New Jersey, Contract Detention Facility Operated by ESMOR Inc. *Interim Report*' – which was published just over a month after the riot.

According to the report, pro bono refugee-advocate attorneys, relatives of detainees, and even some unidentified Esmor guards had been complaining about conditions at Esmor for some time before the riot occurred. On May 30, 1995, two weeks before the riot, INS Commissioner Doris Meissner had ordered an INS assessment team to look into conditions at Esmor in response to these complaints. May 30 was just around the time Miss Jones came by asking us if we'd like to participate in a fashion show. Coincidence? The assessment team conducted their review of Esmor on June 7 through 10. I never saw any signs of any review, but that's what the report says. Is that who some of the strangers were at our fashion show on June 15 – members of the assessment team? I don't know.

The report says that during the review, prior to the 'disturbance,' the assessment team interviewed some twenty-four detainees, as well as various guards and other Esmor and INS personnel. I don't know who the detainees were. I never heard about anybody being interviewed – unless you counted the women I'd heard being videotaped that day in my dorm while Miss Jones listened to every word they said. Most people, like those women, like me, would have been too afraid to speak honestly even if they had been interviewed. But somebody talked – a lot of people, it seems – because the report contains a huge long list of problems and complaints, most of which I knew about firsthand or had heard about from other refugees. In fact, virtually every horror I had experienced there was described accurately in that report.

The report also criticized the Esmor management as well as the INS for having provided the guards and officers with no training in how to handle a 'disturbance.' Nobody anticipated one, apparently, until it happened. So when a riot did break out, the guards didn't know what to do. Even though they had access to riot helmets, shields, and batons, they panicked and abandoned the building.

The convict inmates laughed when the TV report ended. 'Whooee! You really busted that place up!' I walked away crying. I never would have believed, during the six months I spent there, that a day would come when I'd actually wish I could go back to Esmor. But that day had arrived. I would have given anything to be back at Esmor just then. I wanted to be back there with my friends. I wanted to be back there with Frank and Miss Jones.

Frank! I could call him! I knew his number by heart! I hurried to the phones. I had to call Frank! He'd be worried about me. When I dialed, however, a recording told me his number couldn't be called on that phone. What? I tried again. It had to be a mistake. Same message. I tried again. Same message. Just then I heard a series of loud clicking sounds. A guard in the control booth was opening and closing the cell doors.

I saw that everybody was returning to their cells, so I hung up the phone and joined the turbulent stream of women climbing the stairs, jostling and shoving and hitting each other. When I made it back to my cell, my roommate was already there, lying on her upper bunk, crying softly. I closed the door and lay down on my lower bunk. Soon the metal lockbolts in all the metal doors began slamming locked. They didn't all lock at once, but in rapid sequence, like bombs exploding in a deafeningly loud chain reaction: Bang! Bang! Bang! Bang! Bang! Bang! Bang! We were locked in for the night.

Layli's trip to Atlanta was coming to an end that same day. After she got home, she turned on the TV and heard the news about the Esmor riot from a CNN report. She told me later that it was while watching that report that she realized she knew absolutely nothing about 'detention.' Until then it had never occurred to her that a detention center might be anything like a jail – a jail so bad that it would push its inmates – who were detainees, not hardened criminals – to the point of rioting.

The next morning she rushed to work and went straight into Bowman's office to find out if he had any more information about the riot, but he hadn't even heard the news yet. The two of them began trying frantically to find out what had happened to me. Where was I? How was I? And was my hearing still on for Friday? Bowman tried to call Esmor. No answer. He called again and again and again. No answer. He called some other office, where someone told him to call some other office, where someone told him to call yet another office. 'Where's my client?' Nobody knew. Nobody knew anything. Nobody could help him. I'd just . . . disappeared.

Meanwhile, my first full day at Hudson had started about five hours earlier, around four in the morning, with what sounded like a thousand heavy metal bolts being thrown open. Women began pouring out of their cells, but my roommate and I, like the other Esmor women, stayed put. We didn't know what was happening, until a guard came and explained that we had to go down to the dayroom for breakfast. I opened the door to my box and walked out onto the deck. Below me, women were lining up in the dayroom in front of the huge food cart that delivered our meals. As my roommate and I moved toward the stairs that would take us down to the food line, Oche called to me from in front of her cell, asking me to bring her a tray. She didn't want to go down there, and I didn't blame her. At four-thirty A.M. the place was already a zoo, and the air was already thick with cigarette smoke. Women were shouting, yelling, banging trays and cups, flinging food and utensils at each other, shoving, pushing, hitting. I kept my eyes down on the floor, shuffling forward in line, took two yellow trays, and made my way back up to Oche's cell. I was desperate to get away from there, not just because of the convicts, who terrified me, but because the smoke was making me wheeze and cough.

We hid there, in Oche's cell, with the door open. Having the door open made it a little less claustrophobic. But having the door open scared us too. What if some of those crazy women came in and tried to hurt us? There were no guards in the cell area. They were all outside in their guard's booth, behind a thick wall of glass.

We ate breakfast, or what we could of it. After breakfast, I went to look out the big window in the dayroom. There were warehouses in the near distance, hills beyond a fenced-in asphalt area with a basketball hoop immediately below us. Suddenly one of the inmates was yelling at me: 'Don't let the guards see you crossing that line!' I didn't know what she was talking about. But then I noticed there was a red line painted on the floor in front of the window. Oh. So we weren't even allowed to look out the window.

Soon it was 'Quiet time!' when we had to go back to our own cells. I climbed onto the top bunk so that I could look through the tiny slit of window at the rear of our cell. I saw blue sky. I wanted to disappear into that sky. I wanted to go away and never come back. I wanted to be with Yaya. I wanted to die.

When the doors unlocked again, I steeled myself and ran to the dayroom to make a phone call. I had to get out of there. Bowman had to help me! But all the phones were already in use. I waited my turn, listening to the women on the phones screaming to make themselves heard above the bedlam. The same crazy woman I'd seen the first time I walked into the dayroom was shouting and yelling again. Finally one of the Latin American women from my group hung up a phone in tears. I grabbed it and tried to call Bowman. A recording told me I couldn't call that number from this phone. Panicked, I tried Rahuf. That call went through. And he was there!

'You've got to get me out of here!' I yelled into the phone. I was babbling, crying hysterically.

'Fauziya! Where are you!'

'It's crazy here! Get me out of here!'

'Fauziya, where are you? Tell me where you are!'

'I don't know! You have to help me!' I heard a crash, a scream. A few feet away from me, the crazy woman was hitting another woman over the head with a bucket! The other woman screamed and flailed out at her. They started punching each other, ripping at each other's clothes and hair. Other inmates flocked to the scene, shouting, jeering, yelling. I screamed in terror, slammed down the phone and ran back to my cell.

I found out later that Rahuf immediately called Bowman to tell him he'd heard from me, but I'd been hysterical on the phone and couldn't tell him where I was. So Bowman still had no idea how to find me. And no matter how many calls he made, nobody else seemed to either. I was lost in the system.

On Wednesday, after three days of calling around, Bowman got through to someone at INS, who told him the courtroom at Esmor had been demolished, my hearing 'would definitely not be held as sched-uled, all hearings were canceled until further notice, and all detainees had been shipped out. The person Bowman spoke to didn't know where I was. The detainees had been scattered to different prisons, but nobody seemed to know who'd been sent where.

After I called Rahuf on Monday, I didn't call again. I didn't call Bowman either. I was afraid to go near the phones. I didn't go down to the dayroom again except to retrieve meal trays for Oche and me. I lived upstairs entirely – ate, slept, showered, and prayed there. Once when I'd glanced down, I'd seen two women battering each other with brown plastic chairs while other inmates stood in a circle around them shouting and jeering. The female guards in the booth called for male guards as backup. One of the women fighting fell to the floor and the other jumped on top of her and started slugging her. The male guards finally arrived and broke up the fight. They hauled the women who were fighting off somewhere. Segregation, probably.

Sometime Wednesday, the day Layli and Bowman

found out my hearing had been canceled, I returned to my cell from Oche's cell to wash for prayers and saw that one of the two apples I'd saved from an otherwise inedible meal was missing from the metal table where I'd left them. Stolen. I took the other one off the table, carried it one step to my bunk and bent over, tucking it into the crevice between the wall and my mattress to hide it.

'Hey! Where's the other apple!'

I started and hit my head on the metal underside of the top bunk.

'I said, where's the apple!'

I turned, rubbing my head, expecting to see a guard. An inmate was standing in my cell, an ugly, mean-looking black woman. Her hair was half braided, half unbraided.

'Where's the other apple!'

'What apple?' I said. I knew now where the first one had gone.

'It was on this table. Give it to me. I want it.'

'No, it's mine.'

She took a menacing step toward me, backing me up against my bunk.

'Give me the apple,' she growled. She was standing so close, I could smell her foul breath. She narrowed her eyes, looked me up and down. 'You either give me the apple or you sleep with me. Which is it?'

Sleep with her? What was she talking about? Sleep in her cell? Sleep in her – And then it clicked. Sleep with her. She meant have sex. I'd heard that expression on TV at Esmor. I'd heard it applied to women at Esmor too. Once some of the Ghanaian women in N dorm were gossiping about one of the female guards 'sleeping with' one of the female refugees. I hadn't heard of such a thing. I'd heard of men being with men, but I'd never heard of women being with women. Ever.

'Well?' the inmate standing in front of me growled. 'What's it gonna be?'

I gave her my apple.

She snatched it out my hand and leaned her face closer to mine. 'You keep your mouth shut,' she said. 'You hear me? Don't you go talking about me to the guards 'cause if you do I'm gonna be all over you, y'understand what I'm saying?'

I didn't exactly. I'd never heard the phrase *all over you* before. But I caught her drift. I nodded. She left the room. I ran to Oche's cell, terrified, hysterical. She held me and rocked me as I wept.

We were allowed outside later that day for a half hour of fresh air and exercise in the asphalt area I'd glimpsed through the big window in the dayroom. I stood with Oche against a wall, just breathing the fresh air. I was grateful for the fresh air. The smoke in our cell pod was making me ill. I was coughing, wheezing, feeling dizzy and nauseous. My asthma was getting worse and worse. As the sun sank toward the hills in the distance, I watched it, thinking about the passage of time. It was Wednesday afternoon. Tomorrow was Thursday, June 22, 1995. The day I'd been waiting for, praying for, for six long, miserable, horrible months. The day of my hearing. I closed my eyes and prayed for the miracle my instincts told me wasn't going to happen. 'Please God, let someone come for me tomorrow. Let my hearing be tomorrow. Let this all end tomorrow.'

Nobody came for me the next day. I waited all day, alternately crying and praying. But nobody came. At day's end I was still in prison.

Layli told me later that she, too, prayed that day. It

was my hearing day and she and Bowman still didn't even know where I was. I'd been lost, misplaced, like luggage gone astray. Layli was distraught and appalled. This was how her government treated detainees? This was its level of caring and concern? Good God! It was an outrage! She couldn't put me out of her mind, couldn't stop worrying about me. Roshan kept counseling her to detach a little, not get so emotionally involved. For my sake as well as her own, he said – because she wouldn't be able to function well professionally if she didn't. But Layli was already emotionally involved and there was nothing she could do about it.

Friday, June 23. A guard came to my cell sometime before four A.M. 'Pack up your stuff,' she ordered my roommate and me. 'Let's go! Let's go!'

Go? 'Where are we going?' I asked.

'Atlanta.'

'Is that near Washington, D.C.?'

'Yes,' she said as she walked out of the cell.

Leaving! My roommate and I threw our arms around each other and jumped up and down. We were getting out! Oh, great merciful God! We were getting out! And we were going to someplace close to Washington, where my lawyer was!

We stripped our beds, collected and folded up our bedding, clothing, and other prison-issue supplies. When the guard opened the door again and led us out, I could see the rest of our group coming out of their cells too. We were taken back to the laundry room, where we were given our Esmor uniforms again, as well as any personal possessions we'd had. I got my watch back then. From there we were taken back to the processing area and separated into tiny, narrow rooms, so small I felt like I was in a cage.

We were given breakfast in the bullpen. I didn't touch mine. I was too anxious about what was going to happen next. What kind of place were they going to take us? I prayed to Allah. 'Oh God, please, let it be someplace better than here. Let it be a place only for refugees. No more convicts.'

After breakfast some uniformed INS officers appeared at the door to the bullpen. They were carrying heavy chains. Oh God, no! Not chains again! I knew what those chains meant.

Once again I found myself being chained up like a dangerous criminal. Once again there were chains at my ankles and my waist, this time with another chain joining me and Oche at our wrists. And soon I was once again riding in an INS transport vehicle, being delivered to yet another prison, without any idea of where I was going. The guard who had told me we were going to Atlanta was wrong. Or else she was lying. We were going to a prison in Pennsylvania. God had not listened to my prayers. This prison we were going to wasn't someplace better.

23

York

The place we were going that Friday in late June, 1995 was York County Prison in rural York, Pennsylvania. I don't think Hudson ever housed INS detainees before we were sent there because of the riot, and I don't think it ever has since. York, however, is one of the prisons the INS routinely uses to hold its detainees.

The INS pays York something like $50 a day for each detainee, even though the cost of housing a detainee is only about $24 a day. Housing INS detainees is such good business for York that there were plans to expand the prison so it could hold five hundred more detainees. It was like Esmor all over again. All that money. And the prison didn't treat refugees any better than it treated convicts. If anything, it treated us worse.

A large bus drove us through the predawn darkness to York, several hours away. Once there, we were taken into another drab processing room where our chains were removed. Next we were herded into the medical room where we were strip-searched, right in front of the American inmates who worked there, then ordered into showers that had no curtains or doors, while a guard stood watching us. When we came out of the shower, she sprayed our hair, underarms, and private parts with some type of disinfectant that stung.

'To kill bugs,' she said matter-of-factly. After our shower, we were given uniforms to wear – blue again, like Esmor's – and issued the usual supplies. This was my third prison. I was getting to know the drill.

Our dinner was given to us in a gym. As I sat there with yet another inedible prison meal in front of me, I glanced out the gym window into the hallway and saw several refugees from Esmor walking past. There was Sylvie! And Esther! I hurried over to one of the guards who was supervising us.

'Excuse me, can you tell me where those women are going?' I asked, pointing to the window.

'Back to their dorms,' he said.

Their dorms! Allah had answered one part of my prayers. We were in a prison that had dormitories. That wouldn't help me, however, because it turned out that the dorms were only in minimum security. For some reason – or more likely no reason – the group I arrived with that day was sent to maximum security. We were split up and assigned to one of four cell pods, A, B, C, and D, where female inmates were housed in two-person cells, not dorms. Unfortunately, Oche was sent to B pod, while I was sent to C with three other detainees.

The guard delivered us to the door of the C pod, and left us there. I wasn't really sure where I should go, so I walked into the dayroom and stood for a few minutes, looking around. The air in the C-pod dayroom was thick with smoke – Oh God, no, not again – and the room was only slightly less noisy than the dayroom at Hudson. But nobody was fighting. I thanked God for that.

The dayroom had a wall of windows facing out into the hallway, and windows on either side facing into neighboring cell pods. A metal stairwell on the far left side of the room led to a deck that ran along the rear wall. There were eight cells upstairs, eight downstairs. Each cell door had a narrow vertical opening cut into it. The walls and cell doors were painted off-white, the floor was gray concrete. There were telephones against one wall.

Some thirty or so women in blue prison uniforms were sitting at metal tables in the dayroom, talking, shouting, playing cards, or watching the TV, which was mounted high up on one of the walls. I saw one woman braiding another woman's hair. Refugees! They had to be. When I looked closer, I saw they were women I knew from Esmor. There was Dulcie, who was Ghanaian, Wang, my Esmor dorm mate and co-worker on the laundry crew, a Haitian girl whose name I can't remember now, one woman from India, and another from Cuba. I thanked Allah for that. What a terrible thing, to be grateful to see other refugees thrown into this terrible place with me, but grateful I was. I was glad not to be the only refugee among all these convicts – women who were considered danger-ous enough to be held in maximum security.

As I stood taking it all in, Dulcie and the other detainees from Esmor noticed me and came over to greet me. We all hugged each other. Dulcie checked my bracelet for my cell number.

'Oh, no,' she said. 'You have the worst roommate in the pod.'

She pointed to my cell, which was in the corner. I went to check it out. It was about twice the size of the cell at Hudson, with the same kind of furnishings – metal toilet-and-sink unit, metal table and stool, metal bunk bed. The window, opposite the cell door, was also bigger than the cell window in Hudson and gave onto the outside, but all I could see through it was another part of the prison. The lower bunk was already made, so I proceeded to make the upper bunk. The cigarette smoke was even thicker in the cell than in the dayroom. An ashtray overflowing with cigarette butts was on the table. Oh God. A smoker!

'Hi.'

I turned around. A tall, skinny black woman was standing slouched against the doorway. She was missing one of her front teeth, her hair was pulled back into a tight ponytail, her features were hard, and her face was bony. She looked like she was maybe in her thirties. She was smoking a cigarette and looked really scary. I couldn't stay here with a convict. What if she was like the inmates in Hudson – always fighting, always shouting? They had to move me!

She came into the cell and stubbed out her cigarette in the ashtray. 'What's your name?' she said.

'Fauziya.'

'Fauziya, I'm Bernice. Don't worry, we're gonna get along fine, long as you don't touch my stuff. That's the only rule. No touchin' my stuff, OK?'

I looked around the cell. She had a newspaper spread neatly underneath the window, with food, toothpaste, and other things one could get from the commissary neatly arranged on it.

I nodded and quickly left the cell. I had to get out of here! Out of this cell! Out of this pod! I headed to the phone to call Bowman. It was the usual prison phone: Listen for the beeps, press the buttons, hope your call will go through, pray the person you're trying to reach is there because nobody can call you back. This time the call did go through, and Bowman was there.

'Fauziya! Oh, thank God. We've been trying to find you! Where are you! Are you OK?'

I started to sob hysterically. 'You have to get me out of here! You have to!'

'Fauziya, try to calm down. You have to pull yourself together and tell me where you are.'

'I don't know!'

'Fauziya, take a deep breath,' Bowman said, very slowly and quietly. 'Calm down.'

I took a deep breath, let it out.

'OK, now try to listen to me, OK? You've got to find out where you are. Is there someone there you can ask who knows?'

An American inmate was standing a few paces off with her back to me. I called to her. 'Excuse me?' She turned. 'Can you tell me where this prison is?'

'York County Prison, in York, Pennsylvania.'

I repeated what she said to Bowman. And then I started crying again. 'You have to get me out of here! They have me in with smokers!' I didn't say anything about my asthma. I wasn't thinking clearly enough to be that specific.

'I'm working on it, Fauziya,' Bowman said. 'I'm still trying to get your case transferred.'

'Does that mean I'll get out of prison?' I asked him.

'Maybe,' he said. 'I can't promise, Fauziya, but I'm hoping.'

'What about my hearing? I missed my hearing!'

'I know, Fauziya. I'm sorry. But the hearing was canceled. They were all canceled after the riot.'

'I still get one, don't I?'

'Yes, you still get one.'

'When?' Soon. It had to be soon. I'd already waited six months!

'I don't know, Fauziya.'

'What do you mean, you don't know? Didn't they give us a new date?'

386

'No. All the hearings were canceled until further notice.'

'You mean I have to wait here?'

'Yes, Fauziya. I'm sorry. But we're going to do everything we can for you.'

When I hung up the phone, I couldn't stop crying. For six months I'd been waiting to get out of prison, only to find myself in an even worse prison – two worse prisons, so far. Now I was in a real prison where I had to share a cell with a convict instead of being in a detention center where there were only refugees. And I didn't have a hearing date anymore. The light at the end of the long tunnel was extinguished. I wanted to go to sleep and never wake up again.

As far as Bowman and Layli were concerned, the phone call that plunged me back into despair was cause for rejoicing. Layli told me later that Bowman came rushing into her office as soon as he hung up the phone. 'Fauziya just called!' I was alive. I was OK. I was at York. And now that the hearing had been postponed, and they'd found me, they'd be able to do a much better job of preparing me for it when it was eventually rescheduled. That was their view. Not mine.

After I hung up from my conversation with Bowman, my head in a fog of misery, I was heading back to my cell when I heard a familiar voice.

'Fonsinya!'

Wang! Wang, seeing that I was in tears, had come over to comfort me. I was glad to see her, but too caught up in my own problems to notice that she was wearing a gauze bandage on her leg. Later I would learn that she had been hurt during the rioting. She'd been taken directly from Esmor to a hospital and then directly from the hospital here to York. But now she was 'OK-la,' as she would say. Wang started following me back to my cell but kept looking over her shoulder, saying 'Officer. Officer.' Oh. Finally I got it. We weren't allowed to go to anyone else's cell. Was that it? Yes. So I went with Wang to the dayroom instead, where we joined the group of detainees from Esmor. We sat together taking what comfort we could from the feeling of safety we had in one another's company. And we had a lot to talk about. Everyone had their own horror story about the riot. Everyone wanted to compare notes about where they had been taken afterward. I told them that the five days I'd spent in Hudson felt like five years. Dulcie told me that she'd been transported to the same place as Sylvie and Esther when everybody was shipped out of Esmor – a place called Varick in New York City, which she said was much better than York. She said in Varick they were treated like people instead of criminals. But they'd been transferred here on Tuesday. At first they'd all been put in maximum, but Sylvie, Esther, and most of the others in their group had been moved to minimum earlier that day. Dulcie and the two Haitian women had been left back here.

I thought to myself, Sylvie and Esther were moved! That meant I could get moved too! No, wait. Maybe it didn't. Dulcie hadn't been moved. The Haitian women hadn't been moved. But they had to move me! I couldn't stay here! The smoke would kill me! And I had to be with Sylvie and Esther!

Was there any way of getting moved to minimum? I wanted to know. Dulcie said the American inmates had told her it was up to the counselor, so she'd talked to the counselor. The counselor had told her she wasn't ready to move anybody yet, but she would put Dulcie's name on the list. And how do you get to talk to the counselor? Knock on the window, Dulcie said.

Ask the guard for a request form, fill it out, and the guard will put it in the counselor's box.

Please, I wrote, once I got the form. *I need to be moved. I have asthma. I can't be around smoke. It makes me sick.*

I asked Dulcie if there was any way I could see Sylvie and Esther while I was still in maximum. She explained that the prison didn't allow women in maximum and minimum to visit each other. 'But you can see them tomorrow,' she said. The women in maximum were allowed outside into a fenced-in enclosure for about an hour in the morning if the weather was good, and if a guard agreed to take them out. The women in minimum were allowed out into a larger enclosure anytime at all between eight in the morning and eight at night. 'If you want to see them, go outside tomorrow morning,' Dulcie said. 'If they're not out there, tell someone to go in and get them. You can see them that way.' Our conversation was interrupted by the crackling of the loudspeaker.

'Count time!'

Oh God, no! At Hudson, you had to be locked in your cell with your cellmate during count. I didn't want to be locked in with Bernice. But I walked back to my cell, trying to steel myself for lockdown. Bernice was standing outside the cell. She stopped me as I was about to enter. 'You don't have to go in,' she said. 'We just have to stand by the door.' Oh thank God. We stood on either side of the door, while a guard walked through the pod with a clipboard in hand, checking off each inmate. Another guard stood at the door to the pod, keeping an eye on everything. During count, when the guards were in the pod, the entire place was silent. The guards wouldn't allow any talking and even the television was turned off. As soon as they left, the place exploded in noise again.

I asked Bernice how often we got locked in. 'Just at night,' she said. Lockdown for the night was at eleven P.M., and the doors were unlocked at seven A.M. Once they opened, they stayed open all day. So I'd be locked in with her only at night. I didn't know how I was going to bear that, but at least I wouldn't be locked in with her for hours every day. That was something to be grateful for.

My first night at York I learned that Bernice snored. When she was asleep, her snoring kept me awake. When she was awake, the smoke from her cigarettes made me wheeze, cough, and gag. I lay in my bunk as she smoked, watching the smoke curl upward in the light coming in from the dayroom. Every half hour, a guard came by and shone a flashlight in the bunk, doing count. The cell was cold, my blanket was thin, my mattress and pillow were hard and crackly. The lights in the dayroom were kept on at night, which meant that light came streaming into the cell through the window in the door. What with the light, Bernice's snoring and smoking, and all the terrible thoughts running through my head, it was impossible to sleep.

By the time the doors unlocked again the next morning, I had a raging headache and my mouth tasted like cigarette smoke. I had to speak to Bernice. I screwed up my courage, then got the first words out.

'Please, Bernice. Can you do me a favor?'

She didn't look at me. She just sat perfectly still.

I forced myself to go on. 'I have asthma, and cigarette smoke really, really makes me sick. Can you try not to smoke in the cell at night?'

She frowned, pursed her lips, lifted her eyes and glowered at me. I didn't know what to expect. She was a convict, after all, and I assumed that she was in maximum security for something serious. So, asking her to give up the one thing that gave her pleasure and satisfaction in prison was very bold of me. How would she react? Would she explode in anger and shove me? I'd seen a lot of that kind of behavior at Hudson. That and worse. She could hurt me if she wanted to, because the guards were out in the hall. I stood still, waiting.

She sighed. 'OK,' she said. 'I'll try.'

'Thank you, Bernice.' Thank you, God. But I had one more issue to discuss with Bernice. I needed to pray, and I needed a clean place to pray. I couldn't pray in the dayroom because it wasn't private enough. And it was filthy. I had to pray in the cell, so I offered her a trade. If she would let me set aside a space for praying, I would clean the cell.

'Oh no you don't,' she said. 'No touching my stuff. You can clean your part. But don't touch my part.'

We worked out which part of the small space was hers and which was mine, which I could clean, which not to touch. I got my bunk, part of the table, and a small section of floor space along the right wall to use for praying. I asked her not to walk in shoes on the place I had designated for prayer, and she agreed.

'Prepare for breakfast! Prepare for breakfast!' I heard the call for breakfast come crackling over the loudspeaker, and went into the dayroom to join my friends. I didn't feel much like eating, but Dulcie told me I had better eat then, because it was usually the best meal of the day.

It wasn't great but it was edible – waffles, syrup, fruit, milk. Lunch and dinner, there was no telling – no telling whether you could stand to eat it, no telling what it was even when you were looking right at it. Muslims don't eat pork, and since I had no way of knowing what a lot of the meat-based dishes were made of, I usually left them alone. I'd eat the chicken if it wasn't too awful, fruit if we got it. But mainly I'd been living on starch – cereals, waffles, pancakes, bread, potatoes, rice. I would do the same at York, even though all the starch made me feel soft and fat and pasty.

After breakfast I waited to see if we would be allowed into the yard. According to Dulcie, the guards would let us out if it was good weather. I'd looked out the window in the cell first thing that morning and seen that it was a nice day. I was desperate to go. Outside, where I could breathe fresh air, outside where I could see Sylvie and Esther.

I sat with Dulcie and Wang in the dayroom, waiting, praying. Please, God, let the guard take us outside. At around nine-thirty she led us out of our pod, down the hall to a door at the far end, then waved us through.

Oh God, I was outside. Out in the fresh air and sunshine. Outside, standing on the earth. On real grass. It reminded me of Kpalimé, my lush, green, beautiful, lost home. I got down on my hands and knees and put my nose to the ground, inhaling, filling my lungs, my heart, my spirit with the sweet smell of earth. Wang laughed. 'Fonsinya! You clasy!' Dulcie tapped her arm. 'Let her be,' she said. She understood. I got up off my knees, ripped a handful of grass from the earth, crushed the blades between my fingers and smelled them. Home. It smelled like home.

Oche was there too. She'd come out with some of the other women from B pod. We walked over to the fence to look for Sylvie and Esther. I had imagined a single fence separating us from Sylvie and Esther, a fence we could put our fingers through to touch each other. But I was wrong. We were in one fenced-in enclosure, separated by several feet from the larger fenced-in enclosure for the women in minimum. We wouldn't be able to touch. We'd have to call out to each other.

A few women were out in the minimum enclosure, but not Sylvie and Esther. A couple of the women were dressed in regular clothes, the others were wearing uniforms. Later I found out that convicts in minimum could wear their own clothes, even though the refugees couldn't – one of many ways in which convicts got better treatment than we did at York. I shouted and waved to one of the women in a prison uniform whom I recognized from Esmor. 'Helloo! Helloo!' She looked up, came to the fence. 'Get Sylvie! Go get Sylvie! Tell her Fauziya is here!' She nodded, waved, went inside. I waited. And then there she was, my mom. Sylvie. Sylvie was running toward me, crying and running toward the fence. 'Oh my baby! My sweetheart!'

And then there was Esther, sauntering across the yard behind her, smiling and waving, looking beautiful, even in another ugly prison uniform. Looking like the beautiful princess she was.

We stood at our fences – Wang, Dulcie, Oche, and me at our fence, Sylvie and Esther at theirs – crying, laughing, shouting back and forth to each other. Sylvie and I did most of the shouting, as we caught up on what had happened to each of us after the riot, and what was going on with us now. When I told Sylvie that I was in a smoking pod, she said she'd speak to the counselor about getting me out.

'I'll tell her you're my daughter! You have to be with me!'

I laughed. 'OK, Mom! Tell her!'

She would too. I knew it. She'd fight to have me with her.

'Hey, Fauziya!' Esther shouted. 'I talked to Frank!'

Oh God, how I missed Frank. 'Is he OK? I tried to call from Hudson, but the call wouldn't go through!'

'Call him! He's worried about you!' She gave me his telephone number. It turned out that the number I'd been dialing for Frank was wrong. Somehow my memory had failed me and I'd reversed two of the digits.

'Who's there with you?' I wanted to know.

Sylvie shouted out names. So many of my friends from Esmor. They were all together in minimum! I wanted to be in minimum too! I wanted to be with my friends!

The male guard who was stationed in a box outside the fence blew a shrill whistle. 'Away from the fence. You can't touch the fence.' And soon a female guard came outside and ordered everyone from maximum back inside.

No! Not already! It felt as though we'd just come out.

'Let's go! Let's go!'

I turned away from the fence, walked back across the soft earth and green grass, lifted my face to the sun, took a few last breaths of fresh clean air, and went back inside.

As soon as I was back in the dayroom, I went to the phone and dialed Frank's number.

'Hey Fauz!' he said as soon as he heard my voice. Oh, I was so happy to be talking to Frank again. He told me his mother had called him the Sunday morning after the riot to tell him what had happened. He'd rushed right over, but he'd missed us. He'd been sick with worry when he hadn't heard from me for so long.

He said the guards and officers had been allowed back in after the riot, before the cleanup crews went in. 'My God, Fauz. The place was destroyed.'

'I know.'

'They didn't touch the laundry though. Isn't that something?'

'You're kidding.'

'No. I couldn't believe it. The whole place is trashed and then I walk into the laundry room and it's like nothing happened. I couldn't figure it out.'

'It's because you're such a good man, Frank, and everybody knew that. The men weren't angry at you, so they left the laundry alone.'

'Maybe,' he said. But that wasn't important. He had something else to tell me. He and Miss Jones had gone to K dorm when they'd been allowed back in. They'd looked around for things they thought maybe they should save for us before the cleanup crews came in. They'd found my Qur'an and my *tasbih*. 'I've got them, Fauz. I thought you'd want to know.'

My *tasbih*! My mother's beautiful *tasbih*! I put my face against the wall, held the receiver to my heart, and cried for joy. I cried in gratitude, to God, to Miss Jones, to Frank.

'You want me to mail them to you?'

'No!' What if they were lost again, or taken from me? They were safer there with him than in prison with me. 'No. Can you keep them for me? Until I'm out?'

'Sure, Fauz. I'll keep them until I can give them to you in person. How's that?'

Oh, please God, let that be soon! 'Thank you, Frank. God bless you.'

'You too, Fauz.'

'Thank Miss Jones for me?'

'I will. She's been worrying about you too, you know.'

Miss Jones. Oh God, how I missed her.

Our time was almost up.

'Call whenever you want to, don't disappear on me again, OK?'

'OK.'

Next I tried Rahuf.

'Fauziya! Are you all right?'

'I'm OK.' He said Bowman had called him on Friday to tell him he'd heard from me. He'd been so relieved. He'd been waiting to hear from me, worried about me. And now he had a surprise for me.

'A surprise? What?' I couldn't imagine.

'Fauziya, I'm coming to visit you soon.'

That should have been wonderful news. But I didn't hear it that way at first. All I could think of was that at York, the women in maximum weren't allowed what are called contact visits, where you can actually sit in the same room with your visitor. We had to sit in booths, and talk to visitors on phones. It didn't matter that we were detainees and not convicts. York made no special allowances for us. I wasn't sure I could stand to have Rahuf visit me that way – it seemed too humiliating – and I tried to talk him out of coming. It was too long a trip for him to make just to sit and talk to me over a phone, I said.

'No, I've made up my mind, Fauziya,' Rahuf said. 'I want to see you and I'm coming as soon as I can. After all, I haven't seen you since you were a little girl.'

'That's true,' I said, forcing a laugh. He was trying to cheer me up, I knew. It was only polite to try to respond. Besides, I didn't have the strength to argue anymore.

'I remember the last time I saw you at the house in Kpalimé.'

'Yeah, so do I.' It was a sweet memory. I couldn't have been more than eight or nine years old at the time. My father had just bought a beautiful brown car and Rahuf had come to see it. I'd stood beside my father in the courtyard as he showed it off. Rahuf had walked all around it, admiring it, looking at everything. 'It's a beauty, all right,' he'd said. My father had smiled and winked at me. 'Fauziya helped me pick it,' he'd said. 'Didn't you, Fauziya?' Oh, I'd felt so proud! So special, so loved, so happy. It seemed like a dream to me now. Had I ever really been that happy? Had I ever really been that happy, bright, loved, pampered little girl?

Our time was almost up. The phones cut off after ten minutes.

'Take care of yourself,' Rahuf said. 'Call me next week, OK?'

'OK.'

I hung up the phone and returned to my cell pod. The rest of the day was a noisy, smoky blur. I watched television. I lined up for meals. I lined up for count. I watched more television. I made it through the day. I made it through the night. I had learned how to survive.

We couldn't close the cell door ourselves because the doors were controlled from the guard's booth. So if I wanted privacy to use the toilet in my cell, I had to go down to the dayroom, knock on the window, and ask the guard on duty in the booth to close my cell door. Then when I was finished I had to holler through the door to get somebody to go tell the guard to open the cell door. Announcing my toilet needs to a guard, knowing the guard would then be waiting in her booth to hear when I was finished, was humiliating. But it was better than using the toilet with the door open, which is what a lot of the other women did.

I also had to tell the guard if I wanted to take a shower, because the shower stalls were visible from the hallway. If a man was walking through while you were taking a shower, the guard would make you get out, even if you were all covered with soap. It was bad enough that there were only two showers for thirty-two women in our pod – the one that was next to our cell, and one directly upstairs on the next landing – but we couldn't even count on being able to finish a shower when we finally got a chance to take one.

On Monday, after my first weekend at York, the prison loud-speaker blared my name. 'Kasinga. Report to Medical!' I walked across the hall for my health evaluation. I'd been through one at Esmor, but they'd skipped it at Hudson.

The doctor was a middle-aged white man. He took my blood, gave me a TB test, asked me a few questions.

'Are you taking any medications?'

'No.'

'Are you pregnant?'

'No!'

'Have you ever tried to kill yourself?'

'No!' I'd come here to try to save my life, not end it.

He checked off some boxes on a form.

'Please,' I said. 'I need to be moved. I'm in a smoking pod and I can't be around smoke. I have asthma. It makes me sick.'

'Sorry,' he said, checking off some more boxes on the form. 'This is a smoking facility.'

'The whole prison?' I asked him.

'Sorry,' he said.

He hadn't answered my question.

'The whole prison?' I asked again. 'The whole prison is smoking?'

'Sorry,' he said. 'OK, that's it. You can go.'

I returned to my pod, my stinky, smoke-filled pod. I was in total despair. Dulcie saw me come in. She was sitting at one of the tables watching TV. York, Hudson, Esmor. It was the same everywhere. Nothing to do but watch TV. Nothing to do but sit, think, worry, cry, and watch TV.

'Fauziya!' She waved me over, then saw the look on my face. 'What is it? What happened?'

I sat down next to her. 'Oh, God, Dulcie, what am I going to do? The doctor says the whole place is a smoking facility and I'll die if I have to live with smokers. I have to get out of here.'

'Don't listen to that doctor. It is not all a smoking facility. A pod is nonsmoking and I think the dorms are nonsmoking, one of them at least. You already put in a request to talk to the counselor, right? Well, when you see her, tell her the problem. She seems pretty nice. Tell her they at least have to move you into A pod. They can't keep you in a smoking pod if it's going to make you sick. They have to move you right away.'

That's what she thought. That's what I thought. We were wrong.

One good thing at York was the gym. We were allowed to go there for thirty minutes every morning. I was grateful for that, grateful for any chance to get out of that smoky dayroom. My first time there (except for the day of my arrival, when we'd all been fed dinner there) I went with Dulcie. Guards escorted us out the door and past the guard's booth, which looked out over all four of the adjoining cell pods, A, B, C, and D. When we got to our destination, I saw that the gym was a regular indoor space, somewhat larger than Esmor's open-roofed enclosure, with a basketball hoop, a volleyball net, some exercise equipment. I just sat, watching the other women run around, content to be breathing the smoke-free air. Dulcie joined me for a while.

'What are the guards like here?' I asked as we sat together. We spoke in Twi so nobody would understand us.

'Some are OK, some you have to watch out for. Like Jean Brown.'

'Which one is Brown?'

'She's big, white, and mean-looking. You know the one I mean? She's the worst.'

'Are there any nice ones here?' I asked Dulcie.

'Arlene,' she said. 'She's the nicest. Short white woman with short dark hair? She treats everybody like a human being. Some of the others . . .' She curled her lip.

'Who's the one who strip-searched us when we came in? Kind of skinny.'

'Oh, that's Geena. She's OK, but she talks too much. She's into everybody's business.'

I soon learned that this was true. Geena loved to gossip. But sometimes she had interesting information. One day she told me that there were at least one hundred of us detainees in York.

At least a hundred! 'All from Esmor?' I asked her.

'No, there's a whole bunch of Chinese guys here from somewhere,' she said. From the *Golden Venture*, I learned later, the freighter that had run aground on a sandbar just off a beach in Queens, New York, the night of June 6, 1993, with a smuggled cargo of 286 Chinese men and women and children, many of whom were fleeing China's practice of controlling population growth through forced sterilization and forced abortion. Some had since been sent back to China, some had been sent to other countries, and some had been released. But a lot were still in prison, some forty of the men right here at York. They'd been in prison two years by the time I arrived.

One day that first week I was called to the counselor's office. She was a short, heavyset white woman named Amy Jefferson.

'What can I do for you?' she said brightly.

'Please,' I said. 'I'm in a smoking pod. I have asthma. The smoke is making me sick. Please, can you move me? Can I go to minimum? I have friends in minimum. Please. I'd like to be with my friends.'

She was nice, friendly, cheerful. She told me the same thing she'd told Dulcie. 'I'm not ready to move anybody yet, but I'll put your name on the list.'

'But I have asthma,' I said, struggling not to cry. 'I can't breathe in there. Please. Can you at least move me to a nonsmoking pod?'

'I'm not ready to move anybody right now, but keep your fingers crossed. I'll put your name on the list.'

I waited all day. Nothing happened. She didn't move me. I waited all the next day and the next day and the next day. I went out in the mornings and cried to Sylvie, who was campaigning hard to get me transferred. So hard, in fact, that the counselor finally got annoyed and told her to stop bugging her about me.

They didn't move me. I stayed where I was. For the entire week.

Layli told me later that Bowman spent that week calling here, there, everywhere, trying to find out if hearings were being rescheduled yet, trying to get me a date. By the end of the week, around the same time it was becoming clear to me that I wasn't going to be moved anywhere anytime soon, it was becoming clear to Bowman that my hearing wasn't going to be happening anytime soon either. That was bad for me but good for Bowman and Layli. It gave them all the more time to prepare my case. Layli's focus now was on the 'exhibits' to be submitted in support of the brief she'd turned in earlier. Exhibits are the studies, articles, letters, affidavits, and other documents that a lawyer attaches to the brief as evidence that the refugee is telling the truth, that his or her request for asylum is based on valid grounds, and that the request should be granted. In the rush to get the brief written and submitted in time to meet the original deadline, Layli hadn't been able to pull together much in the way of exhibits. She and Bowman had attached the two letters from my mother, the marriage certificate plus English translation, and the untranslated police report my uncle had filled out when he and my aunt had discovered I was missing. That was it. That's all there had been time for. Now that she had so much more time, she could make use of some of the information she'd been able to get at the Immigration Lawyers conference she'd gone to in Atlanta a week earlier.

Thank goodness she'd made that trip, she thought. Several of the people she'd met there had been extremely helpful, and very interested in my case. Layli started working the phones, calling everyone she thought might be able to give her new ideas, new information. Soon fat packets of material concerning gender-based claims began arriving daily at Bowman's office, all of them addressed to Layli. Roshan helped her locate articles on FGM in medical journals, including one in the September 15, 1994, issue of *The New England Journal of Medicine* by Dr Nahid Toubia of

402

Columbia University's School of Public Health, which contained a full-color, detailed photograph of what remained of a seven-year-old Sudanese girl's genitals after she'd been infibulated. Layli wanted to reproduce the photograph in color. She wanted to make a strong statement. No more of this 'circumcision' nonsense, which made it sound so harmless, even healthy. She wanted the judge and the INS trial attorney to see what FGM really is. The color-copying would cost a lot of money because the exhibits apparently had to be submitted to a lot of different people. Layli talked to Bowman. He recognized Layli's passion and enthusiasm for my case, and didn't want to squelch it. He agreed that the photo made a powerful statement, and since he knew Rahuf couldn't afford the copying expense, he agreed to pay it himself.

Layli began searching for statistics on FGM in Togo. There weren't any statistics on FGM in Togo, really. There were estimates, guesses, but no surveys or studies of the kind that had been conducted in other countries.

She called universities, trying to find an expert who could testify in writing that what I was saying about the way things worked in my tribes and culture was true. My country is small. My tribes are small. It wasn't easy to find anyone who knew anything about them. But the phone trail finally led to an assistant professor of anthropology at Duke University named Charles Piot, who'd spent three years in northern Togo doing research on the Kabye tribe. Piot hadn't really studied FGM, or *kakia*, as we call it. He knew it was practiced, but he couldn't say how extensively. Based on his familiarity with the anthropological literature on the cultures of northern Togo, he was able to confirm that the Tchamba do expect their women to be circumcised and he thought it likely that a man would want his wife to be cut before marriage, but that was about as far as he could go in support of my story.

All Layli's hard work culminated in a thick packet of new exhibits, all organized in five categories: general information on FGM; INS response to FGM; United Nations response to FGM; U.S. Congress response to FGM; and medical community's response to FGM. She included Dr Toubia's *New England Journal of Medicine* article, a copy of a really thorough report on FGM called 'Female Genital Mutilation: A Call for Global Action,' also by Dr Toubia; a copy of the new INS guidelines on gender persecution; a copy of the INS's report on FGM that Bo Cooper had given her; a copy of a December 7, 1994, article reporting that the American Medical Association had come out in favor of legislation banning FGM. Layli also included the text of the bill that Congresswoman Pat Schroeder was still trying to get passed prohibiting FGM. Shroeder had introduced it again, for the third year in a row, on February 14, 1995.

Bowman watched as packages piled into the office for Layli. One day, as Layli was showing him all of the information she had put together so far, he said, 'How'd you like to argue the case?'

Layli didn't have to think twice. Although the huge responsibility was a bit daunting, she knew her answer. She felt so passionately about my case. The issues involved in it were ones that had concerned her for a long time. It was as though she was destined to be my advocate. Now she would be, and she looked forward to the challenge.

While Layli continued working on my case, I was spending my days in a smoking pod. During my second miserable week there, I started coughing. A persistent cough that was making my chest and throat sore. I again asked the counselor to please move me. Again she was friendly, cheerful. But this time she told me that she couldn't move anybody because the INS didn't allow the prison to move refugees without its consent. What? What was she saying? They moved people! I knew they moved people! Why was she telling me this? Why?

I saw a doctor again that week too – a different doctor from the one who'd done my initial health evaluation. I had developed another boil, which had gotten bigger and bigger, more and more painful, until finally it came to a head and started draining. It needed treatment. The doctor cleaned it, applied ointment and bandages, prescribed antibiotics. I asked that doctor, too, to please move me. 'Please,' I said. 'I have asthma.' Nothing happened. I saw a doctor or nurse almost every day that week to have the bandages changed. 'Please move me.' Nothing happened. Now when I coughed, there was blood in my mouth. I was coughing up blood.

I called Bowman again in desperation. 'You have to get me out of here!' I said, crying. 'I can't be with smokers!'

'I wish I could, Fauziya,' he said. 'But there isn't anything I can do.' We just had to hope my hearing wouldn't be too far off.

'Do we have a date yet?'

'No, we don't.'

'When will they give us one?'

'I don't know, Fauziya. They're not rescheduling hearings yet.'

Oh God! 'What about the transfer?'

He had news about that. He tried to make it sound

405

good. My case had been transferred, but not to Baltimore. It had been transferred to Philadelphia. That's where my hearing would be.

Philadelphia! I didn't know anything about Philadelphia but I'd heard things that frightened me about one of the judges who used to come to Esmor to do hearings. His name was Ferlise. He hadn't granted asylum to any of the refugees I knew. A number of the women who'd gotten him as their judge had come back from court in tears.

'Do we know who the judge will be?'

'No, Fauziya. We don't even have a court date. Stay in touch with Rahuf. I'll call him as soon as I know anything.'

I hung up the phone, shaking, crying, more frightened than I'd ever been before. I still didn't know when my hearing would be. And now, for the first time, I had reason to fear it. What if I got Ferlise? I went back to my pod, walked across the dayroom, went to my cell, climbed into my bunk, and got under my blanket. I curled up on my side, shivering, gripped by a coldness that seemed to be inside me, somewhere in the pit of my stomach. I prayed to God. 'Please God, make this feeling go away. Make it wrong. Don't let it be telling me what it seems to be telling me. Not Ferlise. Please God. Don't let me get him.'

As Layli got further into her work on my case, she continued to consult with Bowman. One thing she wanted from him was the opportunity to accompany him to an asylum hearing before arguing my case. He agreed that it would be a good idea for her at least to see one before she had to participate in one, and promised to let her know when his next case went to court.

Oh, and there was something else she needed to

talk to him about. When Layli had first started working for Bowman, she sat in while Cindy Lewis interviewed a client at length, going over and over the facts of his story. Cindy had then worked that information into an affidavit that presented the facts and chronology of his story in clear written form. After having the client review it to make sure it was accurate, she had him sign it, and then submitted it along with the legal papers filed on his case. Should Layli try to do one for me too? Bowman didn't think an affidavit was necessary, since Layli had already explained the facts of my case in the brief and since I was going to testify in court. Well, Layli thought to herself, one less thing I'll have to worry about. She could concentrate on everything else she had to do. She was just starting out. She didn't know. Bowman didn't know either. He didn't know who my judge would be. He was trusting in the way hearings generally work. He thought I would have ample opportunity to tell my story in court. He was giving advice based on past experience. Layli was trusting his advice.

When Layli went to Bowman's next asylum hearing, which was in Arlington, Virginia, she thought it seemed like very valuable preparation for what was to come. It was the first asylum hearing she had ever attended, so she took careful notes on everything. The judge was cordial, respectful, attentive. He gave Bowman all the time he needed to question his client thoroughly, gave the man all the time he needed to tell his story fully and make as strong a case for asylum as he could. The judge listened carefully, asked questions politely. He even put the INS trial attorney in his place for trying to intimidate the man. 'That's really not necessary,' the judge said calmly, in response to the attorney's aggressive tactics. Layli was impressed. Oh, so this is the way it works, she kept thinking. The judge then retired to his chambers to consider his decision. Bowman had done what he could with what he had to work with, but the man's case was thin. When the judge returned to the courtroom, he explained in detail how he'd reached his decision, and then issued his ruling: asylum denied. Layli felt bad for the man, but she felt that the decision was fair. The fairness of the decison made her feel encouraged about arguing my case, which she thought was much stronger than that of Bowman's client. With a judge as thoughtful and attentive as the one she'd just seen, she felt confident that she could convince him of the validity of my request for asylum. And there was no reason for her to expect that my judge would be any different.

All this work she was able to do without me. But she wished she could have easier access to me for the part of her job that required my participation. It's standard procedure for lawyers to prepare clients for hearings by reviewing the series of questions they'll be asking them in court as often as possible ahead of time, so that the clients will feel comfortable speaking up during the actual hearing. The answers to the questions tell the clients' story. Since I was in prison I wouldn't be able to come into the office for my run-through. She would prepare me by phone and hope for the best.

Layli kept talking to everybody she could think of about my case, anybody she thought might think of something she had overlooked or forgotten. One person she consulted with was a close friend named Denise Wolf, who was the editor-in-chief of the *Law Review,* the most prestigious of the law school's journals. 'Media attention,' Denise suggested to Layli.

'Newspaper coverage.' She should try to get a reporter interested in writing about my case. People needed to know about me, Denise said. Media attention could arouse public sympathy. Public sympathy could work in my favor. Denise told Layli to contact a friend of hers who was a reporter at a Philadelphia newspaper. 'She writes about women's issues,' Denise said. 'She might be able to help you. Tell her I told you to call.'

Should she? Layli discussed it with Bowman. Absolutely, he said. He agreed that media coverage might help.

Layli called the number Denise had given her and left a message on the woman's answering machine, but when the woman didn't call back, Layli decided to call a couple of other local newspaper reporters. Nobody returned those calls, either. Her first attempts at dealing with the media had failed. Well, I'll just have to keep trying, she decided.

Layli was doing all that work, for me. And I didn't even know it. While she was working on my case, doing everything she could to prepare for my hearing, I sat in prison, growing more and more depressed every day, feeling completely hopeless and alone. How could everybody just keep ignoring the fact that I had asthma? I felt the whole world had forgotten about me.

Why was God doing this to me? I asked God that question every time I prayed, every day, five times a day. I never stopped praying. I was in hell, but I still prayed to God. I prayed in my cell, standing barefoot on a towel on the little patch of floor Bernice had allotted me, my head and hair wrapped in a piece of bedsheet I'd talked one of the laundry workers into giving me. 'Please, God. Deliver me from my suffering.'

But God wasn't listening. God didn't hear my cries.

Then one Sunday morning, I was in the yard waiting to see Oche. I asked another refugee from Oche's pod to ask her to come outside.

'Oh, she was transferred,' the woman told me. 'This morning.'

Oh God! Oche! 'Where? Where'd she go?'

'To her hearing, but I don't know where.'

Oche was the first of my friends to be shipped out of York without warning. Afterward it seemed like two or three people disappeared every other day or so. We assumed they were all going to their hearings, but nobody told us anything and we were never really sure. I knew my hearing was coming up, but when? I didn't want to be taken by surprise that way. I wanted some warning. 'Any word on my court date yet?' I kept asking Rahuf. No, he said. No word. He'd checked in with Bowman, but there was no date yet.

I lived for the mornings, for the thirty minutes I could spend outside breathing clean air and holding shouted conversations with Sylvie, Esther, and my other friends in minimum. I lived for phone calls, counting the days until I could call Frank or Rahuf. 'Call anytime,' they both told me, those two good, kind, generous men. But they couldn't afford that, I knew. So I was careful not to call them too frequently.

That was my life, day after day. Day after endless, identical, unendurable day. One week. Two weeks. Three weeks. Four weeks . . .

'Prepare for breakfast!'

It was Wednesday morning, July 26, 1995, the fourth day of my fifth week in a maximum-security smoking pod. I got my cup and got in line. The line shuffled forward. One of the food servers, an

American inmate, handed me a tray, and delivered a message.

'Your mom is in the hallway. She's leaving. She said to tell you to go to the window and watch for her. She wants to say goodbye.'

Sylvie! My heart stopped. Sylvie was leaving. I dropped my tray on the nearest table, ran to the window and looked down the hall in the direction of the waiting room, or holding room, where inmates are held on their way into or out of the prison.

And there she was. A female officer was escorting her out of the holding room.

'Mom, where are you going?' I shouted as loudly as I could.

She heard me, turned, smiled, shouted back to me. 'I don't know. Bye, baby! I love you, baby! I love you, sweetheart! I'll write.' And with that the guards led her away.

Later that morning I went outside, walked numbly to the fence, and shouted across to someone in minimum to get Esther. She came out and shouted across to me that Sylvie had been taken to her hearing, too, but she didn't know where. That's how they did things at York – in all the prisons I'd been in, in fact. The guards had come for her that morning and told her to pack her things. That was the first time she knew she was going. Would I ever see Sylvie again? I had no idea.

'Kasinga! Kasinga!'

It was around four-thirty that same afternoon.

'Kasinga! Kasinga!'

Oh, God, what now? I climbed out of my bunk and walked out into the dayroom. A guard was standing in the hallway. She motioned me to the door, opened it.

'Pack your stuff,' she said. 'You're moving.'

God had finally taken mercy on me. At around four-thirty on Wednesday afternoon, the day Sylvie left, I was told I was being transferred to minimum. Dulcie was going too.

Oh God, Thank you! Thank you! I ran to my cell, grabbed my cup, toothbrush, and spare uniform. Then I ran back out to the dayroom, shouting and laughing. 'I'm going to minimum! I'm going to minimum!' Wang was sitting at a table. She jumped up and hugged me. 'Oh, Fonsinya! Gooda!' Wang. I wanted to take her with me. But I couldn't. I hugged her back quickly and ran to the door, where the guard was waiting to lead me to my new home.

It was a large dormitory, one of York's two minimum security dorms. The room had eight long rows of brown metal bunk beds, and behind the last of the rows, several decent-size windows giving on the outside. There were some two dozen or so women in the room, sitting and lying on beds, talking, reading, or just looking out the windows. Such a small thing. Such an incredible thing. To be able to sit on a bed and gaze out a real window. The women were another mix of convicts and refugees, mostly convicts. But since these convicts were in minimum, I wouldn't have to fear them as much, I hoped. One of the first refugees I recognized was Khadija. She was Muslim, from Somalia. We used to pray together in Esmor.

As soon as Khadija spotted me, she jumped up from the bunk where she'd been lying, ran over to me and hugged me. Then she took me on a tour of my new home. It was heaven, by prison standards. Absolute heaven. There were two tall rows of lockers on both sides of the room, one per person, where we could each store our things. We were even allowed to keep money in our locker if we had any. My money from Esmor had been transferred while I was in maximum. Now that I was in minimum, I would be able to keep it with me.

There was a separate bathroom, which connected the two minimum security dorms. The bathroom had four toilets, four sinks, and four showers. The showers had curtains and the toilets had doors. I'd been in prison more than six months, always in dorms or cells with a toilet right there in the same room. A separate bathroom seemed like an amazing luxury.

Women could go in and out of the dorm at will. The door was open. Khadija said it was closed and locked only at night. When we walked out the door and nobody stopped us, I just couldn't get over it. For the first time since I'd arrived in America, I had the freedom to walk through a door. The door led to a large common living area, shared by both dorms, which contained regular tables and chairs, two small sofas, a television, vending machines. Vending machines! My head spun. There were two telephones on one wall of the common area. You had to sign up for one ten-minute interval at a time, but if no-one else was waiting to use the phone, you were allowed to make extra calls. It was still a prison phone, though, and you would be interrupted three times in a ten-minute phone conversation with an announcement that the call was coming from the York Correctional. On one side of the common room was a kitchen area with a sink as well as a refrigerator. Women in maximum weren't allowed to save food, although many did anyway, but women in minimum were – fruit, milk, hot chocolate packets. Khadija said women could get second helpings on the food. You could save the extra helping in the refrigerator, heat it up on the stove

413

range, and eat it whenever you wanted. Whenever you wanted!

Connected to the big common area there was another smaller room, with a Ping-Pong table, television, and several books. This was where I was going to spend most of my time, when I wasn't in the dorm, because that's where the other detainees usually hung out and it was a no-smoking area. The dorm was a no-smoking area too. People could smoke only in the big common room.

I couldn't get over the freedoms! You could get packages from outside if you had anyone to send things to you – books, magazines, all kinds of stuff. There was a small separate laundry room with washers and dryers where you could do your own laundry! You could go outside whenever you wanted to, for as long as you wanted, anytime between eight in the morning and eight at night. You had to come in for meals and count and lockdown, but otherwise you had free access to the yard. All you had to do was sign out at the security desk. I could go outside! Anytime I wanted! Oh, God, I could just walk outside!

'And we're allowed contact visits too,' Khadija said. Unlike the women in maximum, the ones in minimum didn't have to sit in a booth talking by phone to friends or family members who were on the other side of a glass barrier. They could sit with their guests in the common area. They could touch, hug, kiss. My God, that would be the most freedom I'd experienced since arriving in America. I couldn't believe my luck, that I'd be in minimum when Rahuf came.

There was a big clock on the wall in the common area. Nine P.M. Rahuf would be home from work now. I went to the phone, waited my turn, and called Rahuf.

I was so excited that I was hyperventilating when he came on the line.

'Fauziya, what happened?' Poor Rahuf. He thought something terrible had happened. Again.

But this time something wonderful had happened. 'I'm in minimum! They finally moved me! Today!'

'Oh, Fauziya! That's great!'

'I'm in a nonsmoking dorm! I can go outside! And guess what? If you come visit me now, we won't have to talk on the phone!'

'Really?'

'Really! We'll be able to sit in a room and talk like regular people!'

He laughed. 'Well, guess what?'

'What?'

'I'm coming this Saturday. It's all arranged. A friend of mine has a car. He and another friend are driving me. I was waiting for you to call so I could tell you. I'll see you in three days.'

Saturday! This Saturday! Oh God, it was too much. Too incredibly, unbelievably wonderful! I was finally in minimum. And Rahuf was coming on Saturday!

I spent the next three days enjoying my new freedoms. I took showers without worrying about being called out of them. I played Ping-Pong. I visited Esther in her dorm, even though I wasn't supposed to. The women in the two dorms were allowed to socialize in the common area, but they weren't allowed to go to each other's dorm. I sat with other detainees, talking, gazing out the window. I made new friends. I braided women's hair. I asked the detainee I'd seen knitting to teach me how to make a belt and sweater. She gave me needles and yarn and began teaching me. I saved fruit and milk in the refrigerator and ate when I wanted to eat, not when the prison said I had to eat. I went outside when I wanted to. I came back in when I wanted to. It was almost like being in boarding school back home.

Back home. Rahuf was from home, and I was going to see him soon. Women in minimum had daily visiting hours. They were officially allowed a maximum of three half-hour visits a day, which was pretty liberal for a prison. But only thirty minutes per visit! Thirty minutes, no matter who the visitor was, no matter how far the visitor had traveled, no matter how long it had been since you'd last seen the visitor or how long it would be until you saw each other again. But the guards sometimes bent that rule and let visitors stay through two and sometimes all three thirty-minute time slots. I was hoping the guards would be in a rule-bending mood on Saturday. Rahuf was taking time off from work, from earning the money he so desperately needed to earn, to make the two-hour trip from Washington, D.C. to York, Pennsylvania, just to see me. My good, kind, wonderful cousin was going to spend four hours in a car to spend possibly no more than thirty minutes with me. Please, God, let the guards let him stay longer. Please.

'Kasinga! Visitation!'

Rahuf arrived around three in the afternoon on Saturday, July 29. I hurried to the common room. I was so excited! So nervous! I hadn't seen him in something like ten years. Had he changed? Would I recognize him? Would he recognize me?

I was standing against the wall with a couple of my refugee friends when he walked into the common area with his two friends. Rahuf. I recognized him immediately. He'd gained a little weight. And he seemed shorter, which he wasn't, of course. I was just taller. But otherwise he looked exactly the same. I watched

416

him scan the room, waited to see if he'd recognize me. He didn't. He looked right past me. I started to wave at him. Rahuf turned to his friend and said, 'Who is that girl? She thinks she knows me.' Then I started walking toward him.

His eyes came back to me, this stranger who was walking toward him. I was a lot taller than when he'd seen me last, and a lot heavier-looking too. I was wearing an ugly blue prison uniform, and my face was broken out in pimples. My months in prison had changed me. He stared at me for a moment, looking for the pretty, happy child he remembered in the female inmate who'd waved to him. He didn't find her. That happy child was gone.

'Fauziya?' he asked. 'Is that you?' I saw confusion, shock, and sadness in his eyes. I looked down at the floor, shy and ashamed.

'Yes, it's me.'

'Fauziya. Oh, Fauziya.' He took my hand and his eyes filled with tears. Rahuf. My cousin. My blood. All my grief, all my loss, all my heartache, all the pain and fear I'd been holding inside me for so long, broke loose and came rushing up and out. I broke down completely.

When I finally stopped crying, he led me to a table where we sat down together, still holding hands. I couldn't let go of his hand. He was my cousin, my family, my only living connection to everything I'd lost. He introduced me to both of his friends, one from Togo, the other from Ghana. We sat and talked, four people from Africa. Rahuf and I talked in Koussountu. Our language. What joy, what a relief, to sit in a room with a member of my own family, speaking my own language. We talked, and I began remembering. Everything started coming back to me. My memories.

They weren't just dreams. They were real! This man was my cousin. He knew. He remembered too. He knew who I was. I was Fauziya Kassindja. I was the youngest daughter of Alhaji Muhammad and Hajia Zuwera Kassindja. I was my father's beloved. I was Yaya's girl. I'd had a life, a family, a culture, a country, an identity before coming to America. Rahuf gave them back to me. Rahuf gave me back myself.

We talked and talked, with me never letting go of Rahuf's hand. What did we talk about? I don't remember. It didn't matter. Rahuf was there. That's all that mattered. Rahuf was there, my blood cousin, holding my hand.

'Are you OK?' he asked. 'Are you all right?'

'Yes, I'm fine.' I did tell Rahuf a little bit about the prison conditions I'd lived through, but when his eyes started to fill with tears, I stopped.

I gave Rahuf all the money that had finally been transferred from Esmor, around $450, to help him with the legal fees. He didn't want to take it, but he didn't have much money himself.

'Fauziya, you have to keep something for yourself.'

Rahuf fished in his pockets and pulled out a few crumpled dollar bills and a handful of coins – for the vending machines – and handed them to me.

I took it. 'Thanks, Rahuf.'

And then, suddenly, our time was up. Visiting hours were over. We stood together, awkwardly, neither of us knowing quite what to say. Rahuf looked at me tenderly. We were still holding hands.

'I'll try to come visit you again, Fauziya,' he said. 'But I don't know when it'll be. You know, with work and everything.'

'I know, Rahuf. It's OK. Really. You came today. That's all that matters. I can't tell you what it means to me. I don't know how to thank you. God bless you.'

'You, too, Fauziya. I'll pray for you. Are you going to be all right here?'

'Yes, I'll be fine now. Seeing you . . .' There were no words. I couldn't tell him. But he knew. I saw it in his eyes. I smiled. 'I'll be fine.'

He pulled me toward him and we hugged. And then he was gone.

I walked back to my dorm and lay down on my bed, happy. Everything was going to be all right, just like Yaya promised. I was feeling hopeful again, confident again. I was in minimum. Rahuf had come to visit me. My fortunes were changing. Allah had finally heard my prayers. He'd shown mercy. The worst was behind me now. I was sure of it.

So sure, so sure. . .

24

Lehigh

I'd been transferred to minimum on Wednesday afternoon, July 26. For the first time since coming to York
on June 23, for the first time since the riot, in fact, I
felt hopeful, happy. A week later that would change.

'Wake up.' A hand shook my shoulder. 'Come on,
get up.'

I opened my eyes. It was still dark. A guard was
standing over me.

'Come on, get up. Pack your things.'

Pack my things! 'Why?'

'You're leaving.'

'Where am I going?'

'All I know is I was told to ask you to pack.'

No, I thought. That's not right. She had the wrong
bunk. She had me confused with someone else. I
didn't have a hearing coming up. I'd just talked to
Rahuf. I didn't have a date yet.

'I'm sorry, there must be some mistake,' I said.

'No mistake. You're moving. Come on, get up.
Move. Let's go!'

'No, there has to be—'

'Don't argue! You're on the list, you're moving.
Let's go. Let's go.'

Leaving! I couldn't be leaving! I just got here! I
didn't have a hearing coming up! What was going on?

'Hurry up. They're waiting.'

I started to cry, but I did as I was told. I got up, washed quickly, dressed. Then I went to Dulcie's bunk and shook her awake.

She woke with a start, saw me standing over her crying, and sat up. 'Fauzy, what is it?'

'Oh, Dulcie! I'm leaving!' Now the other women started to wake up. Khadija helped me pack, and I gave her the coins I'd gotten from Rahuf for the vending machine. I went quickly to the next dorm and woke up Esther. I gave her Rahuf's telephone number and asked her to call him for me. When I returned to my dorm, Khadija hugged me and kissed me on the cheek. Everybody wished me luck.

'Let's go!' the guard called, and I hurried to the door.

The guard took me and another detainee from Esmor named Juliet to the holding room. Juliet was from Tanzania. She was a tall, pretty, dark-skinned woman with long, dark hair. She was only seventeen.

'Where are they taking us?' she asked me. Her voice was shaking.

'They must be taking us to our hearings,' I said, trying to reassure her.

'But I don't even have a lawyer,' she said.

We were served breakfast in the holding room. Neither of us ate much of anything. I had an apple, but I couldn't eat the pancakes or cereal. I was too anxious. I sat waiting, praying, my mind whirling. I didn't know what to think or feel. Today! What if my hearing was today! My God, I could be free today! It could all be over today! I could walk out of a courtroom today and never have to come back to prison again! I prayed to Allah. 'Please. Please let the judge grant me asylum. Please. Please.'

The door opened. 'OK, let's go.' The prison guard took us to the book-in area, where the INS officers put handcuffs on us before taking us out to the small van that was waiting to transport us. James, my friend from Esmor who helped us get through the riot, and another man were already in the van. I noticed that James had scars on his face, which he said he had gotten when he was beaten during the riot.

Soon we were on our way. It was Wednesday morning, August 2, 1995. I'd arrived in America on December 17, 1994. I'd been in America almost eight months, in prison the whole time. I was now on my way to my fourth prison in a little less than eight months.

We drove for two hours, three hours, I don't know how long. We drove and drove, and then the van stopped. We had arrived at Lehigh County Prison. We were processed and booked in the usual horrible way. Juliet and I were strip-searched, together. 'Strip, squat, cough.' We took showers. We were sprayed with disinfectant. We were issued clean uniforms, tan ones this time, sheets and towels. We were measured and weighed. I weighed one hundred and sixty pounds. We were fingerprinted and photographed. Our York I.D. bracelets were clipped off and replaced with new Lehigh bracelets with our pictures on them. And then we sat, waiting to be taken to our cells. There was a phone on the wall in the waiting room.

I called Bowman collect.

'Fauziya! Where are you?'

'I'm at Lehigh! They moved me! They said my hearing is today!'

'Yeah, they just told me.'

'You know! When did you find out? Why didn't somebody tell me?'

422

'Calm down, Fauziya. It's not going to be today.'

My head spun. It was today. It wasn't today. Which was it? 'I don't understand,' I said. 'Is it today or not?'

'No.' Bowman said he'd just been notified himself that it had been scheduled for that day. 'I told them they have to postpone it.' He had another hearing scheduled. 'They have to give us until next week,' he said.

'When next week?'

'I don't know yet. But they'll let me know.'

Oh God, no. No. Not again. Not another delay. I hung up the phone, walked back to the bench, and sat down next to Juliet in a stupor. I couldn't think. I couldn't feel. My body functioned, but everything else shut down in self-defense. I was numb.

A guard told Juliet and me to stand up. We were handed a pass and given directions to our new cell pod. When we got there the common area was absolutely silent, empty. It looked like we had entered during lockdown. There were cell doors running along two walls. The guard who let us in pointed out our cells to us. Mine was wedged in the corner, where the walls met, directly across from the guard's booth. Juliet's cell was next door. My stomach twisted when I saw mine. The cell door had a narrow, head-high opening covered by a grate, and a little metal door at the bottom. I knew what that door was for: sliding things into and out of the cell. It was a segregation cell. Why were they putting me in there?

It was a tiny, claustrophobic concrete box with a small window in the rear wall, just like the segregation cell at Esmor. There was a metal bunk just inside the door to my left and a metal shelf on the right wall. There was a metal table and stool on my right, and a metal toilet-and-sink unit in the far right corner. While

I was making my bed, a guard came over and explained that this whole pod was a segregation area.

'Please,' I said. 'I didn't do anything. Why do I have to be here?'

'Sorry,' she said. 'Rules. It's just for a coupla days, until you pass your medical screening. We have to screen you first. Can't have people spreading disease.'

After she left, I began looking around and noticed things I hadn't seen at first. There was an intercom on the wall. And the small window on the far wall faced onto a street, so I could see cars and buildings. I sat down on the bed, another thin, hard, crackly mattress. Through the wall I could hear the sound of a television coming from Juliet's cell. I called the guard over the intercom to ask if I could have one too. She said she would bring me one when one became available.

Well, maybe this wouldn't be so bad. At least there was a window. I was alone in a cell, but that was better than having a cellmate who smoked. And it was thankfully quiet in this pod.

As it turned out, Juliet and I were allowed to leave our cell to eat with the other inmates in the common area. Shortly after supper, the intercom speaker in my cell blared 'Miss Kasinga. You're going to Medical.' The lock in the door clicked and I pulled the door open. As I left my cell, Juliet emerged from hers, and the two of us went together to the medical unit. This would be my third medical screening since arriving in America, my second in little more than a month.

The nurse asked me some questions and filled out some forms. I told her about the asthma. But I can't remember if I mentioned that I'd been coughing and threw up blood a couple of times. The coughing and vomiting had subsided after I'd been moved to the nonsmoking dorm in minimum, so I'd stopped thinking about them so much. The nurse drew blood for yet another HIV test, then gave me another TB test, too, after which she put a large, square pinkish-colored adhesive bandage over the injection site on my upper arm. I wondered what would happen this time. When I had my first TB test, at Esmor, my arm swelled up afterward. But the nurse at Esmor had said not to worry, that happened sometimes. Some people just had bad reactions, but it didn't necessarily mean anything. I hadn't had any reaction at all to the TB test at York.

As I was leaving, the nurse told me not to remove the bandage she had just put on. 'We'll call you back Friday,' she said, dismissing me.

Juliet and I returned to our cells.

Thursday, August 3, my second day in segregation, was Layli's last day working for Bowman. He told her I'd been moved to Lehigh but he didn't have a new court date yet. It was back to calling and waiting and calling. Layli still wanted to represent me at my hearing, even though she wasn't working for Bowman anymore. Was that OK? 'Sure,' he said. She told him that she'd be home on vacation all the next week, then at school during the day starting Sunday, August 13, to attend meetings for the law journal and start her part-time job as a Dean's fellow. Classes began the following Monday, August 21. She'd be in town for a week of classes, then out of the country for the next two weeks attending the United Nation's Fourth World Conference on Women, in Beijing, China. She'd be leaving for Beijing on Sunday, August 27, and returning on Tuesday, September 12. She and her mother would both be attending the conference as members of a Bahá'í organization's delegation. It meant missing two weeks of classes, but she figured she'd make up the work somehow. How many chances was she going to get to attend a U.N. women's conference in Beijing?

Her only real worry was my hearing date. What if she was in China then? Bowman didn't have a date yet. He was still trying for a day next week, but it was beginning to look doubtful they'd get it. That left only two weeks before Layli left for China. Layli asked Bowman to let her know the minute he heard about the hearing date.

Friday, August 4, was Layli's first day of vacation. It was supposed to be my first day of relative liberty too. On Friday afternoon, the message came over the loud-speaker again: 'Miss Kasinga. Medical.' I collected my pass and Juliet and I were off again. We were so excited! No more segregation! Once we were through in Medical, they'd move us to regular cells. We sat down in the waiting room outside.

'Let's ask if we can be roommates,' I said to Juliet as we waited our turn.

'Oh, Fauziya, you think they'll let us?'

'No talking,' one of the guards said.

'We can ask,' I said.

'No talking!'

Juliet went into the office first, while I waited. She came out beaming. 'All clear!'

My turn. I went into the office. The nurse motioned for me to sit. I sat. She took the adhesive bandage off my arm.

'Hmmm,' she said.

Hmmm? I looked. My arm was swollen and green-ish-colored where I'd received the injection. Oh, God. Not again.

The nurse examined my arm closely. 'It might just be a bad reaction,' she said.

'I had one before,' I said.

'Swelling?'

'Yes. The first time, at Esmor. But it went away.'

'Well,' she said. 'It's probably nothing, but we'll have to do a chest X ray to make sure.'

'Now?'

'No, not now,' she said. They couldn't do the X ray until Monday and it would be another three days or so after that until they had the results. In the meantime, they couldn't take chances, she said. I couldn't be released into the prison population until they knew for sure. This meant five more days in segregation, and no more leaving my cell to eat meals with the others. I couldn't believe it. How would I survive?

When I got back to my pod, the guard at the door handed me a white paper face mask with long strings attached. 'Use this,' she said, before turning to go back to her booth. It was a mask like the ones I'd seen on television when the doctors are in surgery. But I'd never seen one in real life and I had no idea how to use it. As I held it in my hand, the guard, who had returned to her booth, yelled at me through the speaker: 'Cover your face!' Her scream hit me like a slap. Then bang! I was back inside my box. Because the gated window in my cell faced directly into the guard's booth, she could look straight at me. When she saw I still wasn't wearing my face mask, she yelled at me again. 'Put your mask on!'

'I don't know how.'

'Tie the strings behind your head,' she yelled. So there I sat, alone in my tiny box of a cell, breathing through a face mask. It was stifling. This was ridiculous! Why did I have to wear this thing? There was no one in here but me! I took it off. The guard came out of the booth. She peered in through the window. The mask was lying beside me on the bunk. I picked it up, stood up and took a step toward the door. 'Do I have to wear this in—'

'Get away!' she yelled. 'Stay away from the window!'

I stumbled back in shock. My God! She was frightened of me! Terrified of getting too close to me!

'No! You don't have to wear it in the cell!' she shouted. 'But put it on before you come near the door! We don't want anyone catching your disease!' She walked away.

I was speechless, stupefied. Disease! What disease? I didn't have any disease! I'd had a bad reaction to my TB test, that's all. Hadn't the nurse told her that? Why was she so afraid of me? Maybe there was something else. Oh, God. What if I was sick? What if I really was?

Lunchtime. The gate in the bottom of the door opened. A cardboard tray was pushed in. I didn't see any face. I didn't even see a hand. I went to the door and bent to speak to the person on the other side while the gate was still open.

'Excuse me—'

'Wait! Wait! Get back,' a woman's voice shouted. 'Get back until I close the gate!'

Get back! What was this? I took the tray of food and backed away from the door, and the guard slammed the gate shut. 'Just put it in the garbage when you're finished. Just throw everything away,' she yelled as she left.

They were treating me like some kind of wild animal in a cage! I went back to my bed, sat down, and started crying. Why were they doing this to me? Oh. Yes, of course. They wouldn't want to touch anything I'd touched. No, of course not. I forgot. I have a dangerous disease.

I cried until I had no more tears, then lay down on my bunk and stared at the ceiling. I closed my eyes, opened them again. The ceiling was still there. And the toilet, and the table, and the walls, and the television they'd brought me after the first day. Amazing. It all looked so real. But it wasn't, was it? Wasn't it just a bad dream I was having? One I would wake up from soon? Then why couldn't I wake up? I kept trying, but the nightmare wouldn't let go of me.

Monday, the nurse had said. They'd call me back for the X ray on Monday. Sunday came and went. Monday came and went. Tuesday came and went. I was taken out for ten-minute showers once a day. The rest of the time I stayed in my box. I was given no change of clothing. I ran out of toothpaste and soap, and no matter how many times I asked, nobody would bring me any. The guards would say they would, but they never did. After I got the TV set, sometimes I tried to watch it, to lose myself in it, to drive back the panic. The reception was fuzzy and there was only one channel. But I needed to hear voices, any voices. I couldn't stand the loneliness. I felt myself slipping, becoming more and more frightened. Why wasn't anybody coming for me? What was wrong with me? Were they going to leave me here forever?

Wednesday came. I pressed the button.

'Yeah?'

'Please! Somebody call Medical! I was supposed to have an X ray!'

'OK. In a minute.'

'No! Now! Please! Call now!' I was slipping, slipping, slipping.

'OK, OK. Hold on.'

Some time later the voice over the intercom in my cell announced: 'You have to go to Medical, you have to have an X ray.'

No kidding! 'I know!' I said. 'They were supposed to call me on Monday!'

'They said they did but you refused to go.'

This was a joke. It had to be a joke. 'What are you talking about? Refused how? How could I refuse to go? Look at me! I'm locked up in a cell! Nobody came for me!'

'Well, that's what they said.'

'Let me go now then. I'll go right now.'

All of a sudden a female guard just opened the door, let me out, wrote out a pass, and let me go. Wearing my mask, I went straight to the medical unit. A technician X-rayed my chest. I'd never had an X ray before. He had me hold a metal plate against my chest. It was cold. Then he stepped behind a partition. 'Stand still,' he said. 'Don't breathe.' I held my breath. 'OK, that's it.' That was it? 'We should have the results in three or four days,' he said. He said it so casually. Just three or four more days. Days when I would be locked up alone in a box! Please God, please God, let it be only three days, not four.

Thursday came and went. And Friday. And Saturday. And Sunday.

On Monday I pushed the intercom button.

'Yeah.'

'Please, I'd like a medical request form.'

The gate in my cell door opened. A hand reached through and dropped some forms on the floor.

'Wait, please!'

'Drop it through the window!'

I filled out a form: *Please. I want to know the results of my X ray.* I dropped the form through the window. I waited, and waited, and waited. Nothing happened. I stayed in my box.

On Tuesday I wrote out another medical request

form. I watched the gate in my cell door, waiting for it to open, ready to pounce. When it finally did, I ran to the window, thrust my nose between the bars, and began shouting. 'Please! Call Medical!'

'Get away from the window!' A female guard was on the other side of the door.

'Please! I want the results of my X ray! I have to get my results!'

'Get back!'

'Call Medical! Somebody has to call them for me! If I'm so sick, give me medicine!'

'OK! OK! Hold on!'

I couldn't hold on anymore. I'd been in segregation for almost two weeks. Two weeks with no contact with another human being except for my visits to the medical unit. Nobody came near my cell except to push food trays through the gate in the door. I had nobody to talk to, nobody but myself and the phantom people on my fuzzy black-and-white TV. I'd begun talking to those fuzzy phantom people on television. They were all I had now. I kept the television on twenty-four hours a day. I was hanging by a thread, and the thread was almost broken.

The guard returned. She was angry. 'Look, don't give me any crap.'

'I'm sorry,' I said. 'I don't understand.'

She'd called down to the medical unit, she said. There wasn't any X ray. They'd told her I'd never had one.

The thread snapped. I started yelling, shouting, crying. I was hysterical. 'They're lying! I had an X ray! I was there! Take me there! I'll show you the person who did it.'

The guard walked away.

I collapsed against the wall and slumped down to

the floor, howling and bawling. I couldn't stop. Wave after thunderous wave of rage, pain, and torment rose up inside me, broke down over me. My cries filled the universe, but nobody responded, nobody came.

Long stretches of the days and nights that followed are a complete blank. I remember shards, fragments. I remember standing at my metal toilet-and-sink unit, staring at my distorted reflection in the wavy metal mirror, talking to myself, flipping back and forth between torment and giddiness. I was delirious. I'd stand there watching myself sob, watching tears stream down my contorted face. Then I'd laugh hysterically. I was going crazy.

My hearing. Somewhere during that time I ricocheted into sanity just long enough to remember something about a hearing. I was supposed to have a hearing, wasn't I? When was it? Last week? This week? Next week? What day was this? What week was this? Oh God, I had to call Bowman! I pressed the intercom button.

'Yeah.'

'I have to make a phone call! I have to call my lawyer. I have to find out about my hearing!'

'OK, just a minute.'

A guard shouted through the intercom. 'Put on your mask.'

My mask. By this point I had several. I put one on. From her booth, the guard opened the door and let me out. There were a few women in the common room playing games at the tables. As I walked toward the phone, the guard's voice shouted through the prison loudspeaker: 'MOVE BACK! TB coming through! TB coming through!' What was she doing! She was making a freak out of me! I threw off my mask, ran back to my cell, crying and burning with

432

shame, slammed my door, and started hitting my head against the wall.

I cried for hours, days, years, I don't know how long. They were killing me! Oh, God, let them be done with it! Let it be over! Please, God, let me die!

God didn't let me die. He let me cry and wail and howl until there was no crying, no howling, left in me. He left me huddled on the floor of my cell, limp, spent, whimpering, quivering. He let me suffer, but He didn't let me die. He kept me alive. But I stopped being able to eat. The disposable meal trays sat untouched on the floor until I hurled them in the garbage. I couldn't bear to look at food anymore. The sight and smell of it revolted me. If God wanted me to live, God would have to keep me alive.

And then I heard a voice. A deep, tough woman's voice.

'Fonzie! Fonzie!'

That voice. Where was it coming from? I picked myself up off my stomach and squinted through the window in my cell door. There was a face on the other side of the window, a nose poking through the bars. I rubbed my swollen eyes, looked again. It was still there.

'Fonzie!'

I knew that voice! That face! That nose!

'Nadine!' It was Nadine. She was the Jamaican woman who'd been in my dorm at Esmor.

'Get away from the window!' a guard called from the booth.

The nose disappeared. 'Shaddup!' Nadine yelled back at the guard. The nose reappeared. I laughed. That was Nadine, all right! But how did she know I was here?

'Fonzie! Come here, baby. Come talk to me.'

'Get away from the window! You'll catch her disease!'

'Shaddup! She hasn't got any focken' disease!'

Nadine! That was definitely Nadine!

'Fonzie. Come here and talk to me, baby.'

'Put on your mask!' the guard ordered me from the booth. I started to put on my mask.

'Take that damn mask off your face!' Nadine ordered.

I took off my mask, laughing. Nadine!

'Get away from the window!' the guard ordered Nadine. Nadine ignored her. 'What're they doin' to you, baby?'

I told her what they'd done to me, what they were doing to me. I told her I didn't know what to think anymore. Maybe I was sick. Maybe I really was.

'They given you any medicine?'

'No.'

'You feel sick?'

'No.'

'Shhyiiit. You're not sick. They're focken' with you. I shared a dorm with you at Esmor. If you were sick, I'd be sick. I'm not sick. You're not sick. They're jerkin' you around. You should sue their focken' asses.' And then she started singing to me. Nadine knew how much I loved music and dancing, so she sang, just to cheer me up.

I laughed! Nadine! God bless Nadine! I'd always kind of kept away from her at Esmor, always found her too coarse and rough for my tastes. Nadine! I don't know how she found out I was there, but she did. And she came to me. Came to me in all her coarseness and roughness, blasting right through the vortex of insanity I was being sucked into. Nadine threw me a lifeline. May Allah bless her. She restored me to sanity just long enough for me to see the insanity of my situation for what it was. I wasn't sick! She was right! I'd know if I was sick.

Finally the guard ordered Nadine away from the window – 'Now!' – and she had to go.

And then I slipped away again into my madness, and came back again, and slipped away again, and came back again. And then it was another morning. The gate in my cell door opened. Another disposable tray was pushed through. This time I went berserk. I threw myself against the door, screaming, kicked the tray aside, grabbed the bars of the window and began banging my head against the door, screaming at the top of my lungs. 'Let me out of here! Let me ouuuuuuuuut!'

They did. It was Monday morning, August 21, 1995, the morning of my twentieth day in segregation. I'd spent the preceding nineteen days locked up alone in a tiny concrete and metal box, trying to get someone to talk to me, listen to me, find my X ray, check my X ray, tell me what was wrong with me, let me go if nothing was wrong with me. Nobody would talk to me, nobody would listen to me. For nineteen days they'd left me locked up in a box. On the morning of my twentieth day, when I went completely crazy, they let me out.

A guard unlocked the door from the booth and waved me out of the cell. 'You have to go to Medical,' she said. When I got to Medical, a nurse asked me why I was there.

'I don't know,' I said.

She checked some records and said something about a bad reaction to a TB test. She didn't say anything about any results of any X ray. She didn't say anything about my needing any X ray.

Nothing. She just said something about a bad skin reaction. 'Oh, it was just a bad skin reaction,' she said. 'That happens sometimes.'

'Step in here, please,' she said. I followed her into another room. 'On the scale, please.' I stepped on the scale. She fiddled with the sliding weights, wrote something on a clipboard. 'A hundred and thirty,' she said.

No. That couldn't be right. 'Excuse me,' I said. 'Is this the same kind of scale as the one in book-in?'

'Yes.'

'Could you check my weight again, please?'

She fiddled with the weights again.

'Yes, that's right,' she said. 'One thirty.'

One thirty. I'd weighed one hundred and sixty pounds when I'd been weighed during book-in on Wednesday, August 2. I'd lost thirty pounds in nineteen days in segregation.

But that was over now. I was given directions, told my cell number, and sent to another cell pod. I kept my head down as I walked into the dayroom of my new pod, trying to make myself invisible. I didn't want to be seen by anybody. I'd lost over thirty pounds. My eyes were swollen from crying. I was a skinny, disheveled, swollen-faced wreck.

'Fauziya!'

I looked to my right.

Oche! Oche was there, talking on the phone. She hung up immediately and ran over to me, hugging me.

'Oh, Fauziya!' Oche walked alongside of me as I headed toward my cell. 'Fauziya, what happened? What did they do to you?' When I looked at her, I saw she was crying.

'It's OK, Oche. I'm OK.'

I was OK. I was alive. I'd survived segregation – or

436

what they called the behavioral adjustment unit, or B.A.U., in Lehigh. I told Oche I'd come see her as soon as I'd gotten myself settled.

I went into a cell about the same size as the cells in B.A.U. and started making up the empty upper bunk. Soon my cellmate came in, a dark, heavyset woman who looked to be in her early forties. Thank God! It was Alma, a Haitian detainee I knew from Esmor. She greeted me warmly in her very limited English, and we tried to make a little conversation.

After I made the bed, I left the cell. I needed to find out when my hearing was. I'd last spoken to Bowman Wednesday morning, August 2. Next week, he'd said then. He was trying to get me a hearing date for next week. That had been almost three weeks ago. I'd been locked up in B.A.U. from then until now. Had he gotten me a date for that week? Had I missed my hearing again? Would I ever have a hearing? Or was this going to be my life, being bounced around from prison to prison, never knowing when or where or why, waiting for a hearing that would never happen, a day that would never come?

I decided to call Rahuf first. He would probably have been in touch with Bowman, and Bowman was often hard to reach. Rahuf was home. He took the call.

'Fauziya! Thank God! What happened! Why didn't you call!'

All I wanted was to put the last nineteen days behind me. 'I couldn't,' I said. 'I was in B.A.U.' I left it at that.

Rahuf didn't pursue it. 'Call Bowman,' he said. 'He's been waiting to hear from you.'

'Did I miss my hearing?'

'No. You've got a date, Fauziya.'

'I do! When?'

'I'm not sure, but I think it's soon. Call Bowman.'

I hung up the phone without even saying goodbye and called Bowman. Four days, he told me when I reached him. My hearing was going to be on Friday, four days from then.

'What do I have to do? Do I have to do anything?'

'Yes. Do you remember the lady you talked to on the phone when you were at Esmor?'

'Layli?'

'Yes.'

'Yes, I remember her.' I remembered her well.

'Well, she's the one who's going to be asking you questions in court, and she'd like to talk to you,' he said. 'She wants to take you through the questions ahead of time so you'll feel comfortable answering them in front of a judge.'

'OK.' That sounded like a good idea. 'Is she there?'

'No. Call back tomorrow at six o'clock. She'll be here then, OK?'

When I hung up the phone, I was in a daze. Oche was sitting at a table, watching me with concern. She took my hand. 'Are you OK, Fauziya?' I looked at her. My friend.

'Oh, Oche.' Her hearing was coming up, and mine was too! We might both be free soon, out of prison soon, if Allah willed it. I hugged my friend, laughing and crying, laughing and crying again at the same time. 'Oh, Oche! I have a hearing date! I have a date!'

I spent the rest of that day trying to recover from my ordeal and adjust to my new surroundings. I was in yet another prison, in yet another big, noisy, scary cell pod filled with a mix of inmates and immigrants, mainly inmates, in yet another concrete and metal cell. I was back to being locked up in a cell for hours at a time during lockdown, back to lining up for miserable meals with the food served right on a partitioned tray. But at least it wasn't like Hudson, where there were fights, and at least it wasn't a smoking pod. Besides, I felt lucky to be there after the hell I'd just left. That's what nineteen days in B.A.U. had done to me – I felt 'lucky' to be in a prison.

For the first time in almost three weeks, I could walk out of my cell when the doors were unlocked. When I was locked into my cell that day, I wasn't locked in alone. There was another human being locked in with me – Alma, a sweet, kind, motherly woman who didn't scare me. I thanked God for that. I thanked God for every shred of dignity and humanity I was allowed to reclaim now that I was out of B.A.U.

Soon after I arrived in my new pod, I took a shower and brushed my teeth and changed my uniform. And then I climbed up to my upper bunk, lay down on my clean sheets, and slept for hours. I slept and woke and slept through the rest of the day and into the night. Monday night. Tomorrow was Tuesday. I'd talk to Layli tomorrow.

Layli spent that same day and night in a controlled frenzy. Like me, she'd just found out about my hearing. Now she was down to a mere four days to prepare for it. She told me later that she thanked God she'd already written out the questions she wanted to ask me in court. Bowman had told her when she'd first started working on them to make sure they allowed me to tell my story fully and completely. She spent that day and evening polishing and revising her opening and closing statements, polishing and revising her list of questions, rereading her brief, refamiliarizing herself with all the material in the attachments, reviewing her arguments. That night she worked late, sitting at her computer long after Roshan had gone to bed, doing database searches to find out if there'd been any new case-rulings or any other developments in the last few weeks that might bear on my case.

Both of us spent the next day much as we had the one before. I was recovering, readjusting, resting. Layli was working madly on my case. For me the time passed slowly, like all days in prison. For her it went too quickly. Suddenly she saw that it was after five. She had to get to Bowman's office to take my call! She hopped in her car with plenty of time to spare, she thought. Layli drives fast. But you can't drive fast during rush hour, and she got caught in bumper-to-bumper traffic. Five-thirty. Five forty. Come on! Let's go! Five forty-five. Fifteen minutes. I was going to call in fifteen minutes! Five fifty. She was going to miss my call!

Six o'clock. I picked up the phone.

Six o'clock. Layli was still stuck in traffic. Dying of anxiety and frustration.

'She's not here yet,' Bowman told me. 'She should be here soon. Call back in a little while.'

I hung up the phone at 6:05. A little while. How long was a little while?

Layli came tearing into the office at 6:07. 'Did she call?'

'Yeah,' Bowman said. 'You just missed her.'

Layli was beside herself. She felt like she'd just missed the most important telephone call of her life! Please, God, Layli prayed, let her call back. She watched the clock, waiting and praying. Tick, tick, tick, tick. Time played the same cruel games with her as she waited for my call that it had played with me in B.A.U. Tick, tick, tick, tick. She waited eight minutes, eight eons. And then the waiting was over. We were on the line together, her musical girlish voice talking to my soft, heavily accented voice.

I called back five or six times before Layli was satisfied that we'd covered everything. We ran through all the questions she planned to ask me in court: my name, my age, where I was from, how much education I'd had, every detail about my family, about FGM, about what happened to me, and what would happen to me if I was sent back to Togo. We talked, the phone cut off, I called back. We talked some more, the phone cut off again, I called back again. The dayroom was noisy. It was hard for me to hear Layli and hard for Layli to hear me. She had to keep asking me to speak up or repeat what I'd just said. And we kept getting interrupted by recordings. But we stuck with it.

She made notes as we talked, writing down every new piece of relevant information that cropped up as I answered her questions. She didn't try to tell me what to say. The purpose of our conversation was to familiarize me with the questions she'd be asking and make me feel confident of my ability to answer them in court. The preparation helped, but I was extremely nervous. 'What do you think?' I asked her again and again. 'Am I doing OK?' Layli was endlessly encouraging, reassuring and supportive. 'Yes,' she said, 'you're doing fine.' She asked me to call again the next day, Wednesday, two days before my hearing, so we could have another session. She wanted a chance to review everything with Bowman, and then run through the questions with me again.

Wednesday was my third day out of B.A.U. The initial novelty of being 'free' had worn off by this time, so it was another endless, unendurable day in prison. I called Rahuf whom I hadn't spoken to since he'd told me to call Bowman about my hearing. He had a surprise for me: 'The photograph came, Fauziya.'

The photograph. 'What photograph?'

'Your wedding photograph. Ayisha sent it. I wanted to tell you on Monday but you hung up too fast.'

Ayisha! Oh, wonderful Ayisha!

The photograph arrived at Bowman's office that same day. Layli told me later that Bowman showed it to her when she arrived there early that afternoon for another review of her work on my case. While they were glad to have it, they weren't sure how much good it would do. It was another precious piece of evidence that I was telling the truth, but it had arrived too late to be submitted as an 'exhibit' ten days prior to court date as required. Some judges allowed additional evidence to be submitted and accepted into the official record during the actual hearing, some didn't. They'd just have to bring it with them to court and hope for the best.

After taking one last look at Layli's opening and closing statements, and her list of questions, Bowman was very supportive: 'Looks good,' he told her. 'Looks to me like you've made a great case for her.'

By the time I called Layli that day, she'd done further revisions on her questions for me. We went through everything all over again, and then again and again and again. This was the last time we'd talk before the day of my hearing, she told me. She'd be at school the next day working with a professor of hers, Lauren Gilbert, who had supervised her summer internship with Bowman. Gilbert was going to do another review of Layli's work on my case. 'But I'll see you before the hearing on Friday,' Layli said. My hearing was scheduled for one o'clock. Layli said she'd be coming down early so we could go over everything one last time in person before going to court. In person! I wondered what she looked like. I couldn't wait to meet her.

'OK,' she said finally. 'I think that's it, Fauziya. Do you have any questions?'

Only one: 'Do you think I'll win? Do you think the judge will grant me asylum?'

Layli wished she could say yes, knew how desperately I ached to hear her say yes. But she couldn't say yes. It would have been dishonest.

'I don't know, Fauziya,' she said. 'But I think you have a strong case, and I'm going to do everything I can to help you.'

It wasn't what I wanted to hear, but it was something. I had a strong case. She thought I had a strong case. I clung to that.

Layli spent all Thursday at school. She and Lauren Gilbert worked together for hours going over everything. Lauren read through Layli's brief, examined the 'exhibits,' made suggestions on how Layli should revise her opening and closing arguments, gave her a lot of constructive criticism and advice on how to revise and rephrase her questions. Being a novice, Layli hadn't mastered the subtleties and intricacies of how to question a client in court, so Lauren's help was invaluable.

Layli told me later that she also talked briefly that day with another of her faculty advisors, visiting professor Richard Boswell, a tall, slender, gentle-mannered, soft-spoken African American who also happens to be married to Karen Musalo. Professor Boswell, or Richard as we would both come to call him, was co-teaching the public interest law clinic that Layli was taking. The students in the clinic had each been assigned to one or another of the co-teachers.

Layli had been assigned to Richard. Clinics are designed and structured to give law students real hands-on working experience. Layli was about to go into her first real 'clinical' situation: my hearing. Since Richard was her supervisor, she thought maybe he could give her some pointers.

The most important thing to remember, Richard said that day, was 'to make a record.' The record includes all the evidence and exhibits submitted and accepted prior to or during a hearing; and everything said in court. Everything the lawyer says, everything the client says, everything the INS trial attorney says, everything the judge says – it's all tape-recorded and all becomes part of the record. Richard told Layli that it was crucial to make a full and complete record at this stage, to get all supporting evidence and documents on record, to make sure her questions pulled out all the facts and details of my story. If the judge ruled against me and we had to appeal, he said, the record would be all we had to stand on. That's what the Board of Immigration Appeals, or BIA, would review. Once the asylum hearing was adjourned, the record was closed.

Oh, God, Layli thought. Had she done that? She'd submitted a thick packet of evidence and exhibits. Was that part of the record full and complete enough? Had she missed anything?

Layli stayed at school working on the final details of my case all that day and evening. In class they hadn't yet gotten to the part about presenting evidence, so she read ahead in her evidence textbook, trying to prepare herself for what was to come. She also took another last-minute stab at trying to get some media coverage of my case. She aimed higher than the local Philadelphia papers this time. Why not? She had nothing to lose. She knew from her research and readings that a columnist named Judy Mann at *The Washington Post* and a columnist named A. M. Rosenthal at *The New York Times* had both written on FGM. Wouldn't it be something if she could get someone at one or both of those newspapers to write about my case? She called and left messages for them. When she got home from school that night at around eleven P.M., she spent another hour practicing her opening statement in front of Roshan. She wanted to get it down perfectly, the statement, her presentation, everything. She asked Roshan the same question I'd asked her when we'd practiced on the phone. 'What do you think? Am I doing OK?' He gave her the same answer she'd given me. 'You're doing fine. You're going to do fine.' Oh, God, she hoped so.

Layli told me later that she spoke to her mother, Carole, in Atlanta, that evening too. She'd talked to her mother a lot about my case, had told her often what a good strong case she thought it was, what a wonderful opportunity she thought it offered to make good law. If things went well, we might all walk out of the Philadelphia courtroom the next day with a clear ruling by an immigration judge that FGM qualified as a basis for asylum. If things went well, I might walk out of a Philadelphia courtroom the next day a free person and my eight months of horrible suffering in prison would finally end.

'And if you don't win?' her mother asked gently.

Layli didn't like thinking about that possibility, but she had to. 'It would be a tragedy,' Layli said. I'd been through so much loss and pain and suffering already, she said. If I lost, we'd have to appeal and I'd have to go back to prison until the BIA ruled on the appeal. It would be horrible.

But even if I did lose, some good could come of it, she said, thinking out loud. If I won tomorrow, she said, I would win my case, my freedom. If I lost, though, the case would be appealed to the BIA. Rulings by the BIA are often binding on all immigration judges in the United States, Layli told her mother. BIA rulings provide critical interpretations of the law, which immigration judges administer. If the BIA ruled that FGM constitutes a severe enough form of persecution to qualify as a basis for asylum, then that would be governing precedent. Immigration judges would no longer be free to have differing opinions about the subject. Women seeking asylum to avoid FGM would then have one less obstacle to overcome. That would be a major breakthrough, Layli said. That could help a lot of women, not just me. That would serve an even greater good, if it happened.

But Layli wasn't concerned about the greater good just then. She was passionately committed to helping one suffering human being. Me. She was fighting for me, praying for me. She wanted me to get out of prison. She was praying I'd win.

So was I. That's what I did Thursday while Layli worked on my case. I prayed. I prayed all day. I prayed all evening. I prayed all night. I lay in my bunk that night praying with every breath I took, every beat of my heart. Please, God. Don't let me get Ferlise. Let me get a different judge. Let the judge grant me asylum tomorrow. Let me get out of prison tomorrow. Let all my pain and suffering end tomorrow. Please. I beseech You. Let it all end tomorrow.

25

Hearing

'Wake up!'

I jolted awake in darkness, heart pounding, mind racing. What was happening? Where was I? Esmor? No. Hudson? No. York? No.

'Wake up! Let's go! Let's move!'

Lehigh. I was at Lehigh. It was Friday. My hearing was today!

There wasn't time to shower. I washed quickly in the dark cell, brushed my teeth and put on clean underwear, clean socks, and a clean uniform – a prison uniform. It made me so angry, so ashamed, I wanted to cry. I was going to court to ask permission to live in this country and I would be appearing before the judge dressed like a convict. I wanted to look good, show respect, make a positive impression. But I couldn't.

'Let's go.'

I was ready now. The guard who had awakened me gave me a pass and told me to go downstairs to the book-in area. My heart wouldn't stop pounding as I walked. I was finally going to my hearing. I was excited, nervous, and scared, all at the same time. I imagined a big courtroom like the ones I'd seen on TV, filled with lots of people sitting on rows of long benches, me in a box next to the judge's bench having to tell my story to a roomful of strangers. Oh, God. Would I be able to do that? I didn't know if I could. Would the judge believe me? Would he grant me asylum? Please, God.

I must have sat in the holding room for a while. I must have been served breakfast there. I don't remember. I know I wouldn't have eaten anything. Something had happened to my appetite during my time in segregation. I still hadn't recovered it, and I was far too nervous and scared to eat anything before going to court.

After a while a male officer in a green INS uniform came to get me, handcuffed me, and led me out the door into the warmth of a late August morning. Warmth – that was the first thing I always noticed when I went outside. All the prisons I'd been in had been air-conditioned, and I was always cold. The warmth of the sun always felt so good. I climbed into the back of the waiting INS car, where another officer was already in the driver's seat, ready to take off, and found myself sitting next to a huge dark-skinned man trussed up in the most horrible chains I'd ever seen. As the car began to move, I saw that there was a thick metal cuff around his neck, and a thick chain running from the neck cuff to the chains around his waist. His wrists were handcuffed tightly. I shifted against the door, trying to put as much space as possible between myself and the man sitting beside me. I was sealed in with him behind a plastic panel that separated the front and back seats, and I was terrified. He was sitting hunched over, muttering angrily to himself in a language I didn't understand. He glanced up and caught me staring. I looked away immediately.

'Africa?' he said in an angry tone of voice.

I nodded, too frightened to speak.

'Zaire,' he said. 'You?'

'Togo,' I said in a whisper.

He grunted. 'Africa good,' he said. His face contorted in disgust. 'America bad,' he said. 'America very bad. INS very bad.' He leaned forward in his seat. 'INS, you are cheat!' he shouted, spitting his words at the plastic panel separating us from the officers in the front seat. 'INS, you are cheat! You steal!' I don't know if the officers heard him. If they did, they ignored him. 'But I beat you,' he shouted at them. 'I beat all INS!' He growled, grunted, then turned his attention back to me. 'You go to airport too?'

'No,' I said. 'Hearing.'

He sneered. 'Go home,' he said. 'America bad. These people bad.'

I didn't want to hear this. Not now. But he insisted on telling me. In broken English he told me his whole miserable story, from the time he'd gotten to the United States right up to that very moment. He'd come from Zaire, he said. He didn't say why or when. He'd been at Esmor. He said officers had beaten him badly after the riot. He didn't say which officers or at which prison, but later I learned that twelve guards at Union County Prison in New Jersey had been indicted for doing horrible things to some of the Esmor men who'd been moved there after the riot. They beat some of the men, stomped on them, shoved their heads in toilet bowls, and made them kneel naked on a hard concrete floor for hours without moving. I didn't want to hear that that kind of thing happened in America. He'd been moved around to several different places before ending up at Lehigh, he said, and now he was being deported. He'd lost his hearing, I guess. The INS had taken him to the airport the previous morning and tried to put him on a plane without

449

his luggage, but he'd refused to leave without it. He said the officers had tried to force him onto the plane, but apparently he put up quite a fight. 'I beat all INS!' he crowed. From the size of him, I could believe that. After the plane left without him, he was subdued, trussed up in chains like he was now, and taken back to Lehigh for the night. Now he was on his way to the airport for the second time.

'Go home,' he told me. 'INS bad. America bad. These people very bad. They don't want anyone come America. America very bad.'

We drove and drove, for a long time, for what seemed like hours, with him talking to me the whole way, until finally we got to our destination. The officer in the front passenger seat got out, opened my door, and waved me out into a huge parking garage. The man from Zaire was led, in his heavy chains, to one elevator and I never saw him again. I was led in handcuffs to another.

Soon I was uncuffed and left in a small holding room, waiting for my hearing, listening to the pounding of my heart. Eight months I'd been waiting for this day, and now that it was here I was terrified.

Layli's heart was pounding, too, she told me later – much later, when it wouldn't bother me to find out how scared she had been. And she was also alone, on the hour and a half train ride from Washington, D.C. to Philadelphia. She had hoped Bowman would travel with her so that she could get some more feedback on her opening and closing statements and the direct-examination questions she would be asking me, but he had made other arrangements. He told her he'd meet her at the courthouse early so they could prepare me together. In the meantime, she tried to focus on a last-minute review of all the materials she was

450

going to be presenting for my case. She desperately wanted to do well in court, not for herself, but for me. She knew that her future would hold many opportunities to go before judges. For me there might be only this one chance.

When Layli arrived at Philadelphia Immigration Court around eight forty-five, she discovered that Bowman wasn't there yet. She waited impatiently for fifteen minutes, then decided it was time she went in to see me without him.

I sighed a huge wave of relief when a guard came to tell me he would be taking me to my lawyer. I'd been waiting in the holding room for at least an hour. It must be Layli! She said she would come early. The guard led me down a hall and into a room with a line of three glass-enclosed, partitioned visiting booths along one wall. I couldn't believe we would have to talk in one of these! The guard led me across the room to the farthest booth and deposited me there, then turned on his heel and let the door slam behind him. I looked for the phone, but there wasn't any phone, just a small round vent with horizontal slats in the middle of the glass partition. I was going to be meeting with my lawyer and I couldn't even talk to her over a phone. Why was I being treated this way? I wasn't a convict. Maybe the man from Zaire was right. Maybe the American people didn't want anyone else coming here. I sat hunched over on my side of the booth, feeling frightened and humiliated, my stomach muscles quivering, my heart pounding.

The door opened. A tall, slender young white woman walked in, smiling, a very beautiful woman with blue eyes, fair skin, and masses of long, light curly hair. This was Layli? I was amazed. Somehow I'd never thought that Layli might be white. Bowman was

African American, and I had just assumed Layli was too. My experience in prisons had led me to believe that the races didn't mix in America, didn't like each other. I couldn't imagine that a black man would hire a white woman. And I couldn't believe how elegant Layli was. I'd grown accustomed to prison uniforms, guards' uniforms, INS uniforms. Suddenly here was this beautifully dressed woman in a long-sleeved white jacket with black trim and a slim, well-cut black skirt – the best-dressed person I'd seen since coming to America. Clothes make a big impression on me. I am my father's daughter in that way. This wonderful-looking woman sat down on the other side of the partition. I couldn't get over the idea that this white woman was Layli, the person who was going to be representing me at my hearing. I became self-conscious. How would such a person be able to understand anything about me? My culture. My experience.

'Fauziya. Hiii. I'm Layli.' I knew that musical, girlish voice. It really was Layli. I learned later that she was as surprised by my appearance as I was by hers. She had seen only one photograph of me, my wedding photograph. She wasn't at all prepared for the frail, defeated-looking creature she saw on the other side of the partition, hugging herself and staring down at the floor. She thought I looked like a lost, frightened little girl.

'Fauziya! It's so good to meet you finally!' she said in as upbeat a manner as she could muster. I didn't respond at first. I was overwhelmed. 'Now don't worry,' she said, trying to reach out to me, to make the situation seem a little less overwhelming. 'There's no reason to be nervous. Everything's going to be fine.' She was as scared as I was, but she didn't want to scare me more by letting her own fear show. It didn't.

'Now, you know what a courtroom looks like, right?' she asked me as she began the process of getting me ready for my hearing.

'Yes. I've seen them on TV.'

'I'm sorry, Fauziya. It's hard to hear through the vent. Could you speak a little louder?'

I tried to speak up, but I was so nervous that it was hard to force the words out of my throat.

'Yes,' I said a little louder. 'I've seen them on TV. Is it going to be a big room like that?'

'No, it won't be like that,' Layli said reassuringly. 'It'll just be a small room, and there won't be a lot of people. Probably just you, me, Eric, the INS attorney, and the judge.'

The judge.

'Do you know who the judge is?' I asked Layli.

'No, I don't.'

'Could you find out? I really hope it's not Ferlise.'

'Why? What have you heard about Ferlise?'

'He's bad,' I said. 'He denies everyone.'

'How do you know that?'

'That's what all the women say.' Nobody wanted Ferlise. I told Layli that one woman I knew said he had told her he never granted asylum to anyone, so she should just go ahead and tell him whatever lies she wanted to tell him. Another woman who'd been in his courtroom said he had walked out in the middle of her hearing, because she broke down after her lawyer asked her to describe having been raped. As he left, Ferlise apparently told her lawyer to call him when she stopped crying. I can't say for sure whether the things I'd heard about Ferlise were true, but at the time, as I waited to start my hearing, I fully believed them to be.

Layli looked thoughtful as I told her all this. 'We'll just have to hope we don't get him. But I'll look into it when we're through preparing, OK?'

'OK.'

She explained what would happen in court. I'd sit in a witness box. She'd ask me questions – mainly the same ones she had been reviewing over the phone with me. The judge might also ask me questions while she was questioning me. And then the INS attorney would also have an opportunity to question me. At the end the judge would do one of two things: adjourn the hearing and issue a written decision sometime in the future, or make an oral ruling today, after retiring to his chambers to consider it.

'Do you think we'll win?' I asked in a whisper. I wanted her to say yes.

'I don't know, Fauziya,' she said as gently as she could. She could see how fragile I was, how close to breaking, and didn't want to risk putting me over the edge. But she had to be honest with me. She repeated what she'd said to me before when I had asked: 'I don't know for sure, but I think you have a strong case.'

I did have a strong case! I had to win. I would. All any judge had to do was listen to my story. That's all. I would tell my story and the judge would sympathize. How could he not?

'Now, if we lose,' Layli continued in a calm, neutral tone. Poor Layli. She told me later that she hated even mentioning the possibility of losing, but she knew she had to. If we lost, she said, we could appeal. It would be up to me if I wanted to. Some people choose not to, she said. Some decide to go home.

'No, I can't go home,' I said. 'I can't.'

Then if we lost, she explained, we'd appeal. The case would go to the Board of Immigration Appeals, or BIA. They could do one of two things: they could review the record and issue their own ruling, or they could send the case back to the judge, for him to reconsider his decision.

Layli was doing what a responsible lawyer does, giving me the facts. But I wasn't really listening. I couldn't bear to think about losing. I'd win. I had to win. I covered my face with my hands. Oh, God, please. Please let me win.

Layli's heart was breaking for me, she told me later, but she couldn't let that show. It wouldn't have been professional. She opened her briefcase and took out her list of questions. Where was Bowman? she kept wondering. He'd never actually heard her run me through the questions, hadn't listened in on any of our phone sessions. She'd been counting on his being here as we went over them this final time, had wanted him here to offer pointers, guidance, suggestions, encouragement, something. Where was he!

'Do you have any questions for me before we begin, Fauziya?' Layli asked, trying to move forward as best she could without Eric.

'No.'

'OK, then I'd like to go over the questions I'll be asking you in court one last time.'

'OK.'

'Now, try to remember to speak loudly and slowly, OK?'

Layli began asking me questions and I began answering them. But with my heart pounding and my stomach muscles shaking so uncontrollably, my voice could barely rise above a whisper. Again and again she had to remind me to speak up.

Oh, God. I wasn't doing well! What if I didn't do well in court?

Layli told me later that as we ran through the

questions she began worrying about that, too. I spoke so softly, she had trouble hearing me through the vent, and my accent was thick. She understood me when I spoke because she'd spent time in West Africa, but the judge might have difficulty understanding me. It was important that I speak loudly and slowly, but every time she asked me to speak up, it only made me more nervous. Over and over she had me answer her questions, louder, louder, going over everything repeatedly. And then we seemed to be at the end of her list of questions. Finished, I thought. At last.

No. There was one more thing. Layli opened a folder, glanced up at me, hesitated a moment, then: 'I have your wedding photograph here, Fauziya.'

The photograph! My eyes filled with tears.

'We'd like to try to enter it in evidence during the hearing if that's OK with you,' Layli said gently. 'Would you like to see it? Do you think you can look at it?'

I nodded, wiping tears from my eyes.

She held it up to the partition.

My wedding photograph. There I was, all dressed up in my wedding clothes, all dressed up and made up, my hair wrapped in a headscarf, my hands and feet covered with *laylay* designs, sitting on the bed in the bedroom I'd once shared with my sisters, surrounded by my so-called husband's other wives. I was looking down in the photograph, my gaze lowered. My expression was composed, resigned, withdrawn. I looked exactly the way I'd felt when that photograph had been taken. I looked like a beautiful young woman who was preparing herself to be ritually sacrificed. I looked like a young woman preparing to meet her death.

Layli pointed to that young woman. 'This is you?'

I nodded.

'And these other women?'

I identified them: my so-called husband's other wives; my aunt just edging in the frame.

'Would you be willing to identify this photo in court?' Layli asked gently.

'Will it help my case?'

'It could, Fauziya.'

I nodded. 'Yes.'

She nodded. 'OK.' She put the photograph back in the folder. That was everything. We were through. Layli had hoped Bowman would arrive before we were finished, but we had now been working for two hours and there seemed nothing more to say. We sat in silence, an awkward silence, still waiting, until Layli excused herself to go to the bathroom.

On her way back from the ladies' room, she stopped by the judge's chamber and asked the secretary who was conducting hearings that day. The secretary told her: Judge Donald V. Ferlise.

Layli's heart dropped. How was she going to tell me? She didn't want me going into my hearing feeling any more frightened than I already was. That wouldn't help at all.

When Layli came back into the room, she sat in front of me, searching for the right words to say in response to the question she knew would be coming.

And then I asked it: 'Did you find out who my judge is?'

She looked at me, hesitated.

I knew. I knew from the long silence before she answered. I knew from the look I saw in her expressive blue eyes.

'We have Ferlise, Fauziya,' she said as quietly and calmly as she could.

I burst into tears, folded my arms on the table, put

457

my head down on my arms and sobbed. She watched me for a while, not knowing what to say. I was overcome with fear and grief. She realized that for me what would happen today was a matter of life and death. This was not a law school clinical exercise. This was my life.

'Fauziya. Fauziya.' I couldn't stop crying. 'Fauziya, look at me. Listen to me.' I lifted my head, sobbing, and looked up into her eyes. She told me later that she knew full well that what she was about to say went against everything she'd been taught in law school, knew full well that once she spoke the words she was about to speak, there was no taking them back. Don't do it, her law-school training told her. Don't say it. It's not smart. It's not professional. Lawyers don't get paid for that. Don't cross that line. Her heart told her differently. Cross it, her heart said. Cross it and let God guide you. She listened to her heart.

'Fauziya, listen to me,' Layli said. 'Whatever happens in the courtroom today, I'll stay with you. I won't leave you. I'll keep fighting for you.'

Did she mean it? Did she know what she was saying? I searched her eyes.

'No matter what?' I asked her. I knew the answer. I saw it in her eyes. But I wanted to hear her say it.

'No matter what,' she said. 'If the judge denies us, then we'll appeal. We'll keep fighting. I won't leave you, Fauziya. We'll keep fighting until we win. I'll do whatever it takes.'

That was one of the most moving moments of my life. We joined hearts in that moment. We were sisters now. She knew it. I knew it. I wasn't alone anymore. I'd never be alone again.

But I had Ferlise! Oh God, I had Ferlise. 'If we have to appeal, do I have to stay in prison?' I asked.

'I'll try to get you out on parole,' Layli said. 'That will be my first priority.' Parole first, then asylum.

'How long will it take?' I asked. 'Because I've already been in prison eight months, and I'm not going to stay another eight months.' I was so adamant about that, as if it were really up to me. My words would come back to haunt me later.

She didn't know, she said, but here were some of the practical things she thought she could do for me if we lost the hearing. She told me about her upcoming trip to Beijing to attend the women's conference. She'd be leaving for China on Sunday, two days from now, and staying about two weeks. It was a big conference, she said. There'd be a lot of important people there from all over the world, people who cared about women's issues, people who were fighting to help women like me. If I lost, then she'd go to the conference and talk to everybody she met there about my case. She'd tell everyone about me. Every single person she met. She'd meet people there who'd want to help me and know how to help me. She was sure she would, she said. She wasn't sure really, but she wanted to give me hope.

We talked some more, and then sat in silence for a while, exhausted, depleted. The silence wasn't awkward this time. It was intimate, a sad sisterly silence.

'*Ni how,*' I said to Layli, breaking the silence.

'Excuse me?'

'*Ni how,*' I repeated. Layli looked baffled. 'Don't you speak Chinese?' I asked.

She laughed. 'No, I don't speak Chinese.'

'You're going to China and you don't speak Chinese?'

She laughed again, shaking her head no.

'Well then, I'll teach you. Say "*ni how*." That means "How are you?"'

Layli thought I was joking, trying to lighten the mood, but she soon realized that I was completely serious. She was going to China, where she was hoping to meet people who'd be able to help me. I thought she should be able to speak at least a little of the language, and I wanted to help her, using what Siu Sing and Wang had taught me.

'When did you learn to speak Chinese?' she asked.

'I picked some up in the prison from my Chinese dorm mates. I have a knack for languages.' I mentioned to Layli the other languages that I spoke back home. Layli was amazed, though she didn't show it at the time. Until then she had seen me only as a victim – someone God wanted her to help. She now realized that I was much more than a detainee behind bars. I was a person who had a past life in my native country, a life she knew nothing about. And I was clearly very smart and had wasted eight months in a prison. Because I insisted, Layli tried to learn a few of the phrases I was teaching her. Layli is terrible at speaking foreign languages, but we kept at it for a while. It passed the time, and it made me think I was helping *her* for a change.

Finally, Layli made motions to leave. She was tired and wanted to get some lunch before it was too late. 'Will you be OK by yourself until I see you in court?' she asked.

'No, please! Don't leave me!' I hadn't known I was going to say that. It just burst out. If she left, I'd have to go back to the holding room and be alone again. 'Please. I don't want to go back to that room. Just sit here with me, OK? Please?'

Layli told me later that she would always remember

460

that moment, the moment I first reached out to her. Our relationship completely changed in that moment. I wasn't reaching out to my student lawyer. I was reaching out to Layli because I needed a friend.

Layli heard me. Layli heard my cry. She stayed with me and we talked. Actually, Layli did most of the talking, because I was too scared to talk, too distracted and anxious. She kept the one-way conversation going as long as she could, telling me about anything she thought might interest me – her trip to The Gambia, Roshan's family and her work with a Bahá'í development project there, the Bahá'í religion and its similarities to the Muslim religion. And then at last Layli announced that she really did have to go. It was nearly noon, and my hearing was set for one o'clock. 'I must get some lunch, Fauziya. Is that OK with you?'

'Yes,' I said. 'I'll be all right now.' And I really did feel calmer by then.

Just as she was writing a note to leave for Bowman, he walked in.

He was here! Oh, thank God. Bowman came in smiling. He was the same tall, handsome, well-dressed, dignified-looking man I remembered, the same friendly, easygoing man. I was thrilled to see him. Later he would explain to Layli that he had been caught in traffic. When he greeted me warmly, I felt happy and shy at the same time. Layli quickly filled him in on what we'd done that morning. Bowman was confident, cheerful, reassuring. 'You're going to be fine,' he said to me. Layli had told me the same thing, but the words seemed to carry more weight coming from him. He was my lawyer and he was a man. I come from a country, a culture, where men are the power holders and decision makers. I was going to be fine. My lawyer had said so.

461

Layli and Bowman went off to have lunch and I was sent back to the holding room. I thought I would be there for only an hour or so. But as the wait grew longer and longer, my heart began pounding again. My stomach twisted inside me, and I shook with nervousness. This felt like much more than an hour. After a while I realized I could see a clock in an office across the way, which showed that the hour for my hearing had come and gone. What was happening? Why hadn't they come to get me? Was there a problem? What was going on?

Court was running late. That's what was going on.

When Layli and Bowman came back from lunch, they waited about a half hour wondering what was going on before being told that the case being heard before mine was in recess, still awaiting the judge's verdict. Bowman was annoyed. Not because court was running late – that happened a lot and was often unavoidable – but because the judge hadn't had the courtesy to notify them in advance and to give them some kind of rough estimate of how late it would run. He just kept them waiting. He kept all of us waiting, me in the holding room, Bowman and Layli on benches outside the courtroom.

As Bowman and Layli sat in the waiting area, Shirley Tang, the INS trial attorney assigned to my case, walked in. Tang was also the attorney for the preceding case, so she was waiting to be called back into the courtroom for Ferlise's decision. Layli said her hopes shot up when she saw that the INS attorney was a woman. A woman would be sympathetic, she thought. Layli and Bowman introduced themselves to Miss Tang. They were both eager to get a sense of her intentions, chat with her about my case. Had she read my brief? Looked over the attachments? What'd she think?

'What's the case about?' Miss Tang asked, in response to their introductions.

What's it about? Layli was confused. Wasn't the INS trial attorney supposed to be familiar with the file before a hearing?

'It's about a young woman from Togo who's fleeing FGM,' Layli offered.

'Oh, it's one of those gender-type asylum claims,' Miss Tang said dismissively.

Layli was stunned. Miss Tang's remark struck her as callous. 'Yes,' she said evenly. 'Yes. It's one of those. Do you have a copy of the brief with you?'

'Look, I just got assigned here. I caught a train in this morning.'

Layli had brought along extra copies of the brief and all the attachments. Now she pulled a full copy of my file out of her briefcase and handed it to Miss Tang, who took it and walked away, flipping pages.

Although Layli was amazed, Bowman wasn't. He knew that INS trial attorneys are often overworked, that it's not at all uncommon for them to come into a hearing without having done much more than glance through the case file. But he thought that could work in our favor. The less prepared the INS attorney, the better the chances that Layli's arguments would carry the day. This could be good, he thought. This could be good.

After about forty minutes the doors to the courtroom opened. The attorneys on the case that had caused a delay in mine came out with their client. Their expressions were somber. Clearly they'd lost. Layli's heart started pounding. Oh God, she thought. Here we go. Bowman and Layli picked up their briefcases, walked to the door of the courtroom, and poked their heads in. The judge was standing behind the bench. Bowman introduced himself and Layli as the client's representatives for the next case. Should they come in and start getting ready? 'No,' Ferlise said. 'I need a lunch break. Come back in forty-five minutes.'

Meanwhile, I was still waiting, with no word from anyone about the reason for the delay. I passed the time in mounting terror. Had my hearing been canceled again? Had something gone wrong? I sat. I waited. I prayed.

At last the door opened. A male officer in a green INS uniform walked in and handcuffed me.

'Let's go.'

I couldn't move, I couldn't stand. My heart was banging wildly. I was sweating, freezing, shaking uncontrollably. I felt dizzy, nauseous, faint. I wouldn't make it. I couldn't do this on my own. I closed my eyes and surrendered myself to God. I am Yours, Allah. Do with me as You will. Help me. Give me strength.

'Let's go!'

God gave me strength. I stood up. The officer led me out the door, down the hall to the courtroom where Bowman, Layli, and the INS attorney were seated. It was time for my hearing to begin.

After the lawyers all went in, I followed the officer into the courtroom. It was a small room, just as Layli had said it would be. The INS trial attorney was sitting at a table on one side of the room facing the judge's bench. Layli and Bowman were sitting at a table on the other side. I looked at Layli, focused on Layli. She smiled at me. I held on to the sight of her. She told me later that she'd never forget watching me walk into that courtroom as the officer led me to the witness box to the left of the judge's bench, still in handcuffs. It was her first full-length view of me. She said she

464

wanted to cry. I looked so frail, so exhausted, so frightened.

Next, Ferlise came sweeping into the room. He walked very fast to the judge's bench, his black robe billowing, and sat down. Ferlise. This was Judge Donald V. Ferlise. The man who held my fate in his hands. He was white, middle-aged, maybe in his fifties, with white hair. I studied his face – not his features, but his expression. He didn't look mean. There was nothing out of the ordinary in his face.

Layli told me later that she wasn't even sure she'd recognize him if she saw him again, partly because he *was* so ordinary-looking, and partly because she was so nervous, she never really saw his face clearly. She said she'd know his voice, though. She'll never forget his voice. She'll never forget the way he yelled at us. Neither will I.

He didn't start out yelling. There was a moment, at the very beginning, when I thought maybe the stories I'd heard were untrue, maybe he was actually a nice man, a sympathetic man. The INS officer sat me down in the witness box in my handcuffs and started to walk away. Layli was dumbstruck. The officer was leaving me handcuffed during my hearing! Wasn't I to be allowed any human dignity at all?

'Take those handcuffs off her,' Ferlise barked to the INS officer. The officer came back and removed them. Then Ferlise announced that we should move things along, since it was Friday afternoon and we were getting a late start. He switched on the tape recorder and spoke into it. 'Today is Friday August the twenty-fifth, 1995. This is Immigration Judge Donald Vincent Ferlise presiding in Philadelphia, Pennsylvania, in the matter of Fauziya Kasinga.' My hearing had officially begun.

The transcribed tape recording of the proceedings would become part of my official record. Ferlise would switch the tape recorder off at various points during the proceedings to speak 'off the record.' The quality of the recording was so poor that a lot of what was said on the record didn't come through either. The transcript was interrupted by frequent 'indiscernibles.' There were many errors in the transcription too. Written transcripts never fully capture the tone and tenor of the proceedings. Yet, however flawed and incomplete a transcript is, that's what the BIA relies on when a case goes to appeal.

Ferlise started out polite. He asked me my name. He called me 'ma'am.' He asked if I was comfortable having the hearing conducted in English. I said yes. He asked Bowman about the papers he'd filed to allow Layli to serve as co-counsel, and they had a brief discussion about that. Bowman said Layli was his law clerk and a full-time law student who'd been working on my case as part of an approved legal internship. Ferlise had no problem with allowing Layli to represent me.

Ferlise asked me if I understood that Layli was going to speak for me. I said yes. He didn't hear my answer. I was so terrified my voice was a whisper. 'Yes?' he asked.

'Yes,' I repeated. There was a microphone in front of me. He asked me to pull it toward me and speak into it, nice and loud.

Then there was some discussion about exhibits being accepted and 'marked' in evidence. Ferlise sat at his bench, thumbing through papers and assigning exhibit numbers to the different documents Layli had submitted – various reports, the letters from Togo, general information about FGM, INS response to FGM, and so forth. FGM.

Ferlise looked up at Layli. 'What is FGM?'

What is FGM! Eric and Layli told me later that they both had the exact same reaction at that moment. Their hearts sank. My God, he hasn't read the file, Layli thought. Bowman saw the competitive edge he'd thought the INS trial attorney's lack of preparedness gave us fly right out the door. Her lack of extensive familiarity with the issues could work in our favor, Bowman had thought, so long as the judge had read the file and was familiar with the issues. But it seemed that he hadn't, and he wasn't.

Layli explained to Ferlise that FGM stood for female genital mutilation. There was more discussion of exhibits and evidence. And then Ferlise turned to me. 'Ms Kasinga, will you stand and raise your right hand? Do you solemnly swear the testimony you give today will be the truth, so help you God?'

'Yes.'

Ferlise didn't hear my answer. 'Yes?' he asked.

'Yes,' I repeated. Yes. Help me, God.

'Ma'am, you speak very low,' Ferlise said. 'You must speak up loudly.' He was still being polite. 'Nice and loud now, OK?'

Ferlise indicated to Bowman and Layli to proceed.

'Your Honor, I'd like to make a brief opening statement,' Layli said. She launched into the opening statement she'd worked so hard to prepare and memorize. 'This case is about an eighteen-year-old girl who has courageously defied the social mores of her community by rejecting a ritual ingrained tribal practice known as female genital mutilation or female circumcision. Ms Kasinga was able to—'

'Objection, Judge, she's basically testifying on

behalf of the applicant,' Ms Tang interrupted.

Layli was confused. 'It's an opening statement,' she said.

'Is it lengthy?' Ferlise asked.

'Five to ten minutes,' Layli said.

'Go right into your direct exam,' Ferlise said brusquely.

Layli looked to Bowman for help. Bowman said nothing. I saw the distress and confusion on Layli's face. I was beginning to sense trouble.

Layli started asking me her questions – my name, my age, where I was from, how much education I'd had. I needed two more years of schooling to finish high school, I said, though I didn't say it clearly enough. My English wasn't that good. I wasn't speaking loudly enough either. Ferlise interrupted. 'I'm sorry?' I repeated my answer. Layli went on with her questions. Why hadn't I finished high school? 'Because my aunt stopped me,' I said. 'Your aunt stopped you?' Ferlise repeated. 'Yes,' I said. He reminded me again, still politely, to speak up. Oh, God. I wasn't doing well! I wasn't doing well!

'Why did your aunt stop you?' Layli asked. 'Because she wanted me to marry a man,' I said. 'But I didn't want to marry him. And I didn't want to be circumcised.' Was I speaking loudly enough? Expressing myself clearly? Had Ferlise heard me? Understood me? I was shaking uncontrollably, my teeth were chattering.

'How old is this man?' Layli asked.

'Forty-five,' I said.

'How many wives does he already have?'

'He—'

'Objection, leading,' Ms Tang said. Layli fumbled, asked the question again the same way. She wasn't far enough into her law school studies to understand the problem, and Bowman had given her the impression that the court proceedings would be much more informal than they were turning out to be. Ferlise stepped in and rephrased her question for her. 'Is this man, was this man previously married?' Yes. 'Does he have any other wives?' Yes, three. He turned the questioning back to Layli. She asked me the name of my tribes. I told her. Ferlise stepped in again. What was the name? And where were they from? Togo? What part of Togo? Northern Togo?

And so it went. It was becoming a nightmare, one that got worse and worse. Layli would ask a question. I'd try to answer. Ferlise would cut me off and ask a similar question. I'd try to answer his question. He wouldn't be able to hear me. I'd answer again. He'd ask me more questions, question after question, and we'd go through the same process. He pretty much took over the questioning from Layli during much of the hearing.

Still, despite all the interruptions from Ferlise, Layli kept struggling to ask her own questions, to get as much as possible of my story 'on the record,' as Professor Boswell had told her to do. My mother was from northern Benin. I didn't know where she was now because after my father died his family had driven her away from the house. 'Why did your aunt and family drive her away from the house?' Ferlise asked. I tried to explain that they had the right to do that under tribal law. A man's family has the right to send his widow away and take all the man's money and possessions. 'Was your father rich?' Ferlise asked. Yes, he was. 'How did he become wealthy?' He had trucks. 'Drugs?' Ferlise asked. No! 'Trucks! Big trucks!' Oh, God.

Layli got to ask me another couple of questions – when my father died, how many brothers and sisters I had – and then Ferlise took over again. My sisters lived where? What did they do? How many brothers did I have? What did they do? How old was my oldest sister, the seamstress? Was she married? Was she circumcised? No. And my second oldest sister, the caterer? Was she married? She wasn't circumcised either? No. And the third sister, the secretary? How old? Also married? And the fourth sister, the salesclerk? How old? And none of them had been circumcised? How had they all escaped being circumcised? Oh, because my father had stepped in. But all the women in the tribe are circumcised? Yes, it's part of our culture. But your sisters weren't circumcised? Because my father prevented it. How did he prevent it? I was beginning to panic. My thoughts and answers were getting jumbled as I tried to explain. My father had encouraged my sisters to marry men outside our tribe who didn't believe in circumcision. And they'd done that? Yes. That's permitted? Yes. So it was only men in my tribe who demanded women be circumcised? Yes. No. Oh, God. Oh, God, help me!

Layli made a valiant effort to take back the questioning.

'Is your mother circumcised?'

'She's not.'

'Why?'

'Because her big sister, her older sister, she died through circumcision.'

'How did she die?'

'Tetanus,' I said. 'Bleeding. After the circumcision, she just kept bleeding and bleeding.'

'Why did you come to the United States?'

'Because I knew the United States believes in justice

and I've got a lot of relatives in America.' America did believe in justice, didn't it? I was right in believing that, wasn't I?

'Can you describe what female circumcision is and how they do it?' Layli asked.

I could tell what I knew. I didn't know much. When a girl is fifteen years old, she is circumcised. But that hadn't happened to any of the women in my family? Ferlise asked. No. Yes. 'My auntie,' I said. 'The one who's trying to get me circumcised. She was circumcised.' 'And this happens once you turn fifteen?' Felise asked. Yes. 'And how old are you now?' Eighteen. 'Well, how did *you* avoid it?' he asked, emphasizing *you*. His tone sounded accusatory. Because when my father was alive he was able to prevent it, I said. 'Well, how would he prevent that?' He was wealthy, I said. He could do what he wanted. 'OK, so what's different now?'

What's different now? What's different now!

I knew then. Ferlise wasn't going to be sympathetic to my plight. I was lost.

'Now he's not alive,' I said softly. 'He's no longer living.' That's what was different now. Everything was different now.

No, no, that wasn't what Ferlise was getting at. If my father could say 'My daughters are not going to be circumcised,' why couldn't I? Why couldn't I just say 'I'm not going to be circumcised'?

'I can't say that, because I don't have the right to say that.' My father could, but I couldn't.

Ferlise wouldn't accept that. How long had my tribe been circumcising females? Fifty years? Hundreds of years? Thousands of years? A long time? So if that was the law in my tribe, how could my father prevent it? I had already answered that question! Because he was rich and powerful! Oh, God! Somebody help me! I answered the questions again in more detail. Ferlise finally seemed to understand. He turned the questioning back over to Layli.

Poor Layli. Poor brave, struggling, determined Layli. 'Make a record, make a record,' Richard Boswell had repeated over and over. This was it. This was her last chance to create a full and complete record. There were so many things she had to try to get on that record. She went straight to trying to establish that FGM qualified as persecution. That was crucial to her argument.

'How exactly do they perform the operation?' she asked me. 'What tools do they use?'

'They use knives,' I said.

Ferlise didn't want to hear it. 'Is that germane?' he asked.

Layli tried to explain. 'Yes, because it speaks to whether or not it's persecution.'

'What are the tools they use?' Ferlise asked. His tone of voice suggested he found this a ridiculous question.

Layli persisted. The question of tools was relevant to how severe and damaging the procedure is, she tried to explain.

Ferlise didn't seem to think it was important, however. He told Layli he was limiting that line of questioning.

Layli regrouped. Ferlise didn't want to hear about how it was done? OK. She'd come back at the same issue from a different angle. 'What kinds of effects happen to your body?' she asked me. 'What side effects does it produce?'

'Well, bleeding. I knew four girls who'd bled to death.'

Ferlise interrupted again. I knew four what? Four girls who bled to death? From circumcision? Yes. He asked me some rapid-fire questions I couldn't quite follow, something about who did it. I tried to answer, but I didn't quite understand what he was asking. He kept shooting questions at me. I learned later that Ferlise had been an INS trial attorney for nineteen years before he'd been appointed a judge. He was still a trial attorney. A trial attorney in a judge's robes.

Layli jumped in to try to rescue me and establish another critical point, that my fear of being subjected to this form of persecution was well founded. She tried, but she didn't get very far. One question. That's as far as she got. 'Is your father the only person who would be able to protect you from circumcision?' she asked. Yes, I said. Yes he was.

'And why is that, ma'am?' Ferlise asked. My mother couldn't protect me? Well, what about my sisters? I tried to explain that after my father's death my aunt became my legal guardian. She could do whatever she wanted to do with me. My sisters had no power to interfere.

And how old was I when my aunt pulled me out of school and told me I was going to get married and be circumcised? Seventeen? And she told my mother? My mother was in the house? No, no, she wasn't there. She'd been sent out of the house. So where was she living? I didn't know. I didn't know but my aunt knew? How did my aunt know? I didn't know. So my aunt got together with my mom and told my mother what her plans were for me? Why did she do that? I wanted to say: for the sheer pleasure of torturing my mother and watching her cry. But I couldn't. My English wasn't that good. Why had my aunt informed my mom? Did my mom have to give her permission? No, I said. No!

473

Just to let her know what they were going to do to me. Even though she'd been chased out of the house? Yes. Yes. Oh, please. Please God. Let this end.

Layli came back again. She muscled in a few questions, clarified a few points, got a few more things on record. We established that my father's siblings were staunch believers in circumcising girls, that they'd never accepted my mother because she was from a different tribe, that they'd evicted her after my father had died. And then we were back to the question of how I had escaped circumcision even though I was married. Ferlise was skeptical. Hadn't I said that no man in my tribe would marry an uncircumcised female? I tried to explain. He cut me off. 'That doesn't make any sense,' he said. So what was I saying? That a special exception had been made in my case? Yes. No. He didn't understand! I couldn't make him understand!

Layli tried to clarify the point. 'Have you ever slept with your husband?' she asked. No, I'd never slept with anyone. Why hadn't I slept with my husband? Because I hadn't been circumcised yet. Before being sent to him I would have to be circumcised. Layli got a few more things on record. My so-called husband's other wives had all been circumcised. Layli asked how I'd avoided being circumcised. My sister helped me escape, I said. She took me by car to the airport in Ghana. Ferlise took over again. What day had that been? October 19, 1994? And if I hadn't fled Togo, there would have been no way to avoid being circumcised? No. 'But you did, didn't you?' he said. 'I mean, you told them you didn't want it.' Yes, but they would have forced me, I said. 'Well, you stopped them.' Yes, when I left the country! No, no, he didn't mean that. I'd been married off. I hadn't been circumcised first. I'd been married uncircumcised. So I'd stopped them,

474

right? No! No! Hadn't he heard when I tried to clarify that? Why was he doing this to me? Why didn't he understand? At one point as I was struggling with a question from Layli, Eric tried to rephrase it so that I could understand it better. Ferlise silenced him. Layli was questioning me, not him, Ferlise said. Eric was stunned by Ferlise's action. Layli was a law student. He was the supervising attorney. It was his responsibility to step in when he felt it necessary for a client's sake. Other judges understood that. He couldn't believe Ferlise was making an issue of it.

Germany. Layli was asking me about Germany. 'Why did you fly to Germany?' Because it was the only available place to go, I said. Ferlise took over again. Who decided on Germany? My sister. Which one? The oldest? Yes. Layli asked me how I'd entered Germany. I didn't tell the whole story, may Allah forgive me. I said I'd shown my I.D. cards, the immigration officer had asked if I was on school vacation and whether I had any money, that I'd said yes, shown him my money, and that he'd let me pass. I didn't say anything about the man at the airport with the passports. I was too afraid. Afraid for Ayisha. 'How long did you stay in Germany?' Ferlise asked. Two months, I said. And how had I supported myself? I stayed with a German lady I met at the airport. Did I know her? No. I flew into Germany and met a complete stranger at the airport who let me stay with her for two months? Yes. How had that happened? I told him. So I'd just gone up to her and asked her if she knew where I could find people from Africa and she'd just invited me to come live with her? Yes! And what was her name? I told him. And then what? What happened after two months? Then I met Charlie, I said. Where? In a train. In a train? Yes. I met Charlie and told him my story, I said. 'He was the one who helped me to the United States,' I said, the one who'd sold me the passport. Ferlise questioned me through my arrival, all the details of my encounter with the immigration inspector. If the inspector had just said to me, 'All right, pass on through,' would I have entered the country? No, I said. Charlie had told me to ask for asylum. That had always been my intention.

Then Ferlise went back to the question of why I had had to leave the country to avoid circumcision. Had I ever thought of going to the government or the police for protection? They wouldn't have helped me, I said. But did I ask them? They couldn't have helped me, I repeated. But did I ask them? No.

Layli tried to get on record why I hadn't considered going to the police. 'What is your husband's relationship with the Togo police?'

'Objection. Leading.' Miss Tang. She was still there.

Layli tried again. 'Does your husband have a relationship with the Togo police?'

'Objection. Leading.'

Layli tried again. 'Why can't you return to Togo?'

'Because the police were looking for me,' I said. 'If I went back, they'd hand me over to my aunt and uncle, and they'd circumcise me and send me back to my so-called husband.'

'How do you know this?'

'My mom wrote to me. She told me the police want me.'

Ferlise pounced. How did my mom know where I was? I'd written to her through my sister, I said. So my sister knew where my mother was? Yes. Well, if my sister knew, how come I didn't know? I tried to explain. Because my aunt prevented me from having any contact with her – she thinks my mother can poison my mind. Clearly Ferlise didn't believe me. He raised his voice to me. 'No. Be responsive.' My aunt knew where my mother was, my sister knew, how come *I* didn't know? I tried again to explain. Ferlise searched through his papers. What about these letters from Togo? Had my mother written them? No, my mother couldn't write English, I said. My sister had written them, but, as I wanted to explain, my mother had dictated them and signed them. Ferlise wouldn't let me explain. He exploded at Layli.

'Were you aware of that, Counsel?' – that these letters that were signed by my mother were in fact written by my sister? Yes, Layli said. She tried to explain. He didn't want to hear her explanation either. He accused her of trying to deceive the court. 'You should have told me that these letters are not from the mother, they were not written by the mother. Tell me the way they came about to be transcribed or whatever.'

The letters had been in my file when Eric Bowman turned it over to Layli. She didn't know how they'd been obtained. 'You would have to ask the witness, exactly—'

'No, ma'am!' Ferlise bellowed.

'I'm not—'

'What I'm telling you is to be candid with the court!' He was shouting!

Bowman jumped in. He tried to explain. Ferlise yelled at him too. 'These are not letters written for her from her mother! These are letters written by her sister, purportedly from information derived from the mother!'

'Correct,' Bowman said.

'But that is not her mother's letters!'

'We would state that it is her mother's letters.'

'Well, I would state, sir, that it is not.'

Oh God! Ferlise was yelling at my lawyers! I wanted to run out of the courtroom! Layli persevered. She tried to go back to demonstrating my 'well-founded' fear. 'What would happen to you if you were forced to return to Togo?' I'd be handed over to the police, to my family, to my husband, I said. I'd be circumcised. 'Is there anyone who can protect you?' No!

Ferlise took over again. He went back to my not knowing where my mother was. How was that possible, he wanted to know. I tried to explain that my mother had moved to Benin for a while but was now trying to come back to Togo, but I didn't know if she had yet. My sister knew. But my sister hadn't told me? No. Had I ever asked her? No. And then he said the cruelest, most heartless thing of all: 'You're not interested?' His sarcasm flayed what was left of my torn and bleeding heart.

And then he turned to Layli. 'Anything further, Counsel?' he asked impatiently.

Layli soldiered on. Yes, she said. She'd like to ask me to identify the people in a photograph. My wedding photograph. Ferlise asked if the photo had been accepted into evidence. 'Yes,' Layli said. Bowman interceded. No, he explained. It had just arrived from Togo.

Ferlise asked me to identify the people in the photograph. I did. And what was the occasion? Why was everyone all dressed up? 'That's the day of the wedding,' I said. He agreed to accept the photo into evidence.

'Anything further, Counsel?' Layli made one last effort. She got on record that as a fourth wife, I'd be the one who had to do all the work, all the other wives' bidding. She asked again one last time. If I were returned to Togo, was there any way I knew of to avoid being circumcised and returned to my husband? No. No. No. She was through with her direct questions.

Now it was the INS counsel's turn to have at me. Miss Tang asked if I'd sought refugee status in Ghana. No, I said. When my aunt had told me she was marrying me off, why hadn't I just run back to Ghana? Was there an age at which a female who hasn't yet been circumcised need no longer worry about being circumcised? I didn't understand what she was asking. Ferlise asked if all the people in my tribe believe in the practice. Yes, most of them, I said. What about other tribes? Did they believe in it? Did I know which tribes? How many tribes? How many people in these tribes? I didn't know! 'A lot of people – a lot.' Ferlise passed me back to Miss Tang. Could I have run away to live with a different tribe? No. Did I know why my husband had his wives circumcised? No. Where had I stayed during the two days between my marriage and my escape? In my aunt's house, I said. My father's house, I meant, which had become my aunt's house. Why was I staying there? Why hadn't they circumcised me immediately after the wedding? I tried to explain that once I'd been married under Islamic law I'd become my husband's property. My aunt hadn't needed to rush to circumcise me after that. I'd been tied and bound by religious law as surely as if I'd been tied with rope. So why hadn't I tried to escape before the marriage? Because 'I didn't know when the marriage was going to be held. It was impromptu,' I said.

Ferlise jumped in again. All those fancy clothes and the fancy jewelry and the *laylay* designs on my legs? All that had been done on the spur of the moment? I tried to explain that I never believed my aunt would really make me get married, but I couldn't make him understand. When had my aunt started telling me I was getting married? In July? And the marriage hadn't happened until October? And I hadn't run away in all that time? Why not? I'd already explained that. I didn't know I was getting married on Monday until Monday! And I'd had time to get all my fancy clothes together and invite people? No, No. It wasn't like that . . .

Ferlise passed me back to Miss Tang again. During my two months in Germany, had I ever asked for refugee status there? No. I wanted to explain that I hadn't known what refugee status was. I'd never heard of it until I'd met Charlie. But I couldn't explain. I didn't even try. I was too tired. Had I asked Rudina to help me? No. That's all I said. No. Had I told her my problems? Yes. Was I in any other kind of trouble with the Togo police or authorities when I'd fled? No. With that Miss Tang had finished with me.

It was Layli's turn again. Why hadn't I sought asylum in Germany? she asked. Because I want to finish my education, I said. I couldn't do that there. I didn't speak the language. And I didn't have any relatives there, no family to help and support me.

She asked what happens to a woman who tries to leave her husband in Togo. I said the woman would be forced to return. She asked if the Togo police could reach me in Ghana. Easily, I said. Now Ferlise wanted to know if 'the Ghanaian police allow Togo police to come onto their territory and make arrests?' I didn't know anything about the police, I said. 'Well, that's what you just answered.' I knew nothing about what the Ghanaian police 'allowed,' is what I meant. I only knew about the way things really worked. Borders didn't stop the Togo police. Layli asked why the police were looking for me. Miss Tang objected to the question. 'Isn't her redirect limited to my cross?' Miss Tang hadn't asked anything about the police looking for me, so Layli wasn't supposed to ask about it, either, on redirect – something she probably wouldn't have done if she'd been more experienced. But Ferlise let her ask anyway, and it got put on record that the police were looking for me because I was a missing person. Layli asked permission to ask one more question about the police. It was a crucial question that went straight to the issue of 'well-founded' fear. Ferlise allowed it. 'What is your husband's relationship to the police?' He was a very good friend to them, I said.

'Thanks, Your Honor,' Layli said. She was through.

Ferlise was ready to recess to consider his ruling. Eric asked him to please wait. He had one other item: the letter from Charles Piot, assistant professor of anthropology at Duke University, attesting that the Tchamba tribe does expect women to be circumcised. The letter had come in too late to be submitted ten days prior to my hearing. Ferlise agreed to accept it because since we were in temporary quarters (due to the Esmor riot) he had decided to drop the ten-day requirement. It was Bowman's 'lucky day,' he said.

'One more thing,' Bowman said. 'We would like to make a brief closing in this case.' Layli's closing statement. Ferlise hadn't allowed Layli to make her opening statement. He agreed to let her make a closing one if she kept it very brief. 'Because we're quickly running out of time,' he said. 'Just don't rehash what's in the brief and please don't rehash what we've heard today. All right?'

Layli and Bowman were both floored. Don't rehash what's in the brief? Had he even read the brief?

Bowman asked Ferlise if he intended to issue an oral decision today or a written decision later.

481

'Oral, today,' Ferlise said.

Bowman politely expressed his concern that 'the Court' perhaps hadn't had sufficient opportunity to review the materials he and Layli had submitted.

'I've seen them,' Ferlise said.

Bowman tried again. 'We wanted to make sure the Court —'

Ferlise cut him off. 'How long is your closing statement?'

'It's between five and ten minutes,' Layli said. 'I can make it five.'

Do that, Ferlise basically said.

Layli gave it her best shot. 'Very quickly, Your Honor,' she said, 'female genital mutilation does rise to the level of persecution. The INS accepts as persecution something that is a serious threat to the life or freedom of an individual. As demonstrated by the medical evidence in our brief and in our exhibits, female genital mutilation is a severe threat to the life or freedom of an individual. A study in Kenya demonstrates that over eighty percent of all girls who undergo the practice suffer from at least one medical complication. Another study demonstrates that between fifteen and thirty percent of all women who undergo the practice die.'

Beep! Beep! Beep! Beep!

The tape recorder had started to make a high-pitched beeping noise in the middle of Layli's closing. She paused, waiting for Ferlise to change the tape or do something to stop the noise. But he simply waved her on to continue. Layli had to shout the rest of her closing statement to make herself heard over the beeping.

She called Ferlise's attention to a letter she'd submitted from a doctor at Morehouse University testifying that FGM is a serious threat to the life or freedom of an individual, 'which according to the INS manual, rises to the level of persecution.' She said the INS manual also states that 'serious violations of human rights' can constitute acts of persecution.

'What INS manual?' Ferlise asked.

'The INS Service Manual,' Layli said.

'It's a handbook for asylum officers,' Bowman said.

'I'm not bound by the manual,' Ferlise said.

'As guidance, Your Honor,' Layli said. 'It indicates—'

'No. I'm not guided by the manual, ma'am,' Ferlise said brusquely.

'OK,' she said. 'The international community has recognized female genital mutilation as a basic human rights violation.' What about that? Was Ferlise guided by that? She quickly mentioned some of the documents she'd submitted attesting to that fact, several of them documents she'd originally unearthed in the research she'd done on her law journal article the preceding April. She cited the BIA ruling in a case called 'Matter of Acosta' that persecution can be defined as any act that 'seeks to overcome a particular belief or characteristic of the individual.' She argued that the characteristic that FGM seeks to overcome is a woman's sexual drive or desire to enjoy sex. Therefore, FGM qualifies as persecution. She argued that the persecution I was fleeing met the necessary requirement of being 'at the hands of the state or by a force that the state cannot or will not control.' The 'force,' in my case, she said, was Muslim law. It would have been more accurate to say tribal law and family tradition, but I probably hadn't made that clear to her. The state in my case, she said, was the Togo police, who refused to protect girls from this practice. And lastly, she said, I met the necessary requirement of being persecuted on account of my membership in a 'particular social group' as the BIA had defined 'social group' in its ruling on 'Matter of Acosta.' That is, I was a member of a group of persons who shared a 'common immutable characteristic' that the members of the group either cannot or should not be required to change. My social group was the women of my tribe. The immutable characteristics were our gender, our resistance to female genital mutilation, our forced submission to it, our religion, and our tribe.

In sum, Layli said, 'we submit that Ms Kasinga has demonstrated that she deserves asylum based on her well-founded fear of persecution, or of female circumcision, based on her membership in a particular social group.' And one last thing. If I were sent back to Togo, I couldn't escape the persecution I was fleeing. 'The police are looking for her,' Layli said. 'And as indicated in the State Department Report that you have in your evidence, she has no right to divorce. Thank you.'

I hadn't understood the content of her argument, but I'd understood her passion, her fire, her spirit, her heart, her resolve, her will. She would keep her promise. I knew it with all my heart and soul. She would never leave me, no matter what. She would never stop fighting for me. She would fight until I was free.

Ferlise turned off the tape recorder. 'Give me twenty minutes,' he said. Twenty minutes. I'd waited in prison for more than eight months for my hearing and he was going to decide my fate in twenty minutes.

Both Ferlise and Miss Tang left the courtroom then. So did I, because the INS officer came in, handcuffed me, and led me out to the waiting area. But Layli and Bowman stayed at their table, silent and grim, staring into space. Layli was so rigid with tension as the minutes passed that her fingertips became numb.

When Ferlise returned to the courtroom, I was led back to the witness box, where the INS officer removed my handcuffs. Ferlise switched the tape recorder back on and rendered his oral decision.

He began with the facts of my arrival in America. I was an eighteen-year-old female, native and citizen of Togo, who'd arrived in the United States on December 17, 1994, and been placed in 'exclusion proceedings.' I'd arrived without a visa, carrying a false passport. I'd said I'd immediately told the immigration officer the passport wasn't mine and that I wanted political asylum. Ferlise believed that part of my story. 'I find that the applicant did not attempt to commit a fraudulent entry,' he said. Then he got down to business. A grant of asylum, Ferlise said, is 'discretionary.' He recounted what he understood to be the facts of my case.

In June 1994, after my father had died, I'd come home from school in Ghana, where I'd spent 'approximately twelve years,' and my aunt had told me I was going to be circumcised. My aunt had 'sought out' my mother, whom my aunt had 'previously chased out of her household,' Ferlise said, and had told my mother she was taking me out of school and marrying me off to a forty-five-year-old man. And then Ferlise plunged a dagger into my heart. 'Apparently,' he said, 'her mother showed no opposition to both of these wishes.' As Ferlise understood it, it seemed not only that I didn't care about my mother. It also seemed that she didn't care about me.

He went on and on, retelling my story as he'd heard it, making it sound totally implausible, before getting to the heart of the matter: 'The credibility of the applicant is of extreme importance in assessing the alien's claim,' he said. 'I have taken into account the lack of rationality, the lack of internal consistency and the lack of inherent persuasiveness in her testimony and have determined that this alien is not credible.'

He was accusing me of lying! How dare he! I had to sit there and listen to him call me a liar. I sat, burning and trembling with rage. I wanted to stand up and scream at him: 'Who are you to judge me? You know nothing! You aren't my judge. God is my judge! God knows I'm telling the truth!' I would have been even more outraged had I understood that Ferlise hadn't just dealt me a devastating personal blow; as I learned later, he'd dealt me a crippling legal blow as well. 'Not credible' is practically the worst thing a judge can say about an asylum seeker, according to Layli, because the BIA customarily relies on the judge's assessment. It is the judge, after all, who has seen the person, heard her testimony, observed her demeanor. Layli had been prepared for Ferlise to deny me asylum on legal grounds, because he didn't think FGM qualified as persecution or because he didn't accept Layli's social group definition. She'd been prepared to challenge those judgments on appeal, difficult as it would be to do. But how do you disprove a judge's finding that an asylum seeker is 'not credible'? How do you convince the BIA that the judge's impressions were wrong? It would make our appeal that much harder.

Ferlise went on to recite all the reasons he'd found me 'not credible.' I'd said my aunt had driven my mother out of our house. Then I'd said my aunt had arranged a 'rendezvous' with my mother to 'consult' my mother about her plans for me. 'The Court wonders why would an aunt who has just dispossessed an individual from the house seek such counsel of that individual,' he said. 'It just doesn't make sense.' Ferlise said I would 'have the Court believe' that female circumcision is an 'absolute rule' in my tribe, and yet my sisters and I had all avoided it because my father had objected to it. And I'd been married before being circumcised, 'contrary to tribal law . . . The Court wonders then how absolute can this tribal law be with so many exceptions being allowed for that rule.' Ferlise found my story of my 'fortuitous meeting' with Rudina to be 'beyond belief.' My story of my chance meeting with Charlie was 'incredible.'

As for demonstrating a credible fear of persecution, even if he believed my story, 'which I do not,' he said, he was unconvinced that I'd be persecuted if sent back to Togo. I hadn't demonstrated that I was being persecuted on account of my membership in a particular social group. Besides, Ferlise said, it appears that 'all tribal women from certain Northern tribes allow themselves to be circumcised.' This wasn't persecution – just part of tribal culture. I hadn't asked the government for help and there was 'no evidence' that the police couldn't or wouldn't have helped me if I had gone to them. I wasn't being 'singled out' for circumcision, he said. 'Apparently all members of her ethnic tribal group are being pressured into being circumcised.' The government of Togo had 'nothing to do with it,' he said. I could have left my tribe, he said. I could have gone to live with my mother, 'who is of a different tribe.' I could have sought asylum in Ghana or in Germany. 'She did none of this,' he said.

To qualify for asylum, he said, I had to establish a 'well-founded fear' of persecution. I had to convince him, in other words, that my fear was both subjectively and objectively reasonable. He was not convinced. Asylum denied.

It was 'ordered,' Ferlise said, that I be 'excluded and deported.' It was ordered that I be sent back to Togo.

Ferlise pronounced this judgment on me, passed this sentence on me, and then turned to me and asked, 'ma'am,' if I'd heard and understood his decision.

I didn't answer. I couldn't speak. I sat still and silent, eyes down.

'Hello?' he called to me sarcastically. 'Do you understand that I have denied your application for asylum?'

I didn't move, I didn't answer, I didn't speak.

'Hello?'

I lifted my eyes to Layli, saw my own agony reflected in her eyes.

'Say yes,' she mouthed. I had to answer.

'Yes,' I whispered.

'Yes?' Ferlise repeated.

'Yes.'

'OK.'

He turned to Layli and Bowman. 'Counsels, you've heard my decision. Do you wish to accept my decision as a final order or do you wish to reserve your right of appeal?'

'Yes, Your Honor, we will appeal,' Bowman answered. I'd never heard anyone sound so angry.

They wanted to appeal. I didn't. No, I thought. No appeal. This was supposed to have been my day in court. I'd tried to tell my story. Ferlise hadn't let me explain things clearly. He hadn't believed me. I couldn't go through this torture again. My story wasn't going to change. If he didn't believe me, who would? No. Let them send me back. I couldn't take any more time in jail.

'All right,' Ferlise said. 'There being nothing further, Counsels, we stand adjourned.'

The INS officers came in with their handcuffs and

started cuffing me right there in the courtroom while Bowman and Layli were trying to talk to me. They had to speak rapidly. The guards were in a hurry.

'It's going to be OK, Fauziya,' Layli said. 'We'll get you out. We will. Remember my promise.' There were tears in her eyes. Her voice was shaking. She was fighting hard not to cry. 'I leave for China on Sunday,' she said. 'I'll tell everyone about you while I'm there. I'll talk to everyone. I'll find people who can help us. We'll get you out. Just hold on for two weeks until I come back, OK? Can you do that?'

I nodded. I couldn't speak.

And then the officers were leading me away, out to the INS bus that was waiting to take me back to Lehigh. Back to prison.

As soon as I was out of the room, Ferlise removed his judge's robes and started making small talk. Now that my hearing was over, he wasn't in any hurry to go anywhere. All of a sudden, he had all the time in the world. As Layli remembers it, he at first tried to engage Bowman in 'good old boy' banter about various people from Baltimore they both knew, but Layli interrupted. She couldn't help herself.

'Excuse me,' she said stiffly, 'but I don't understand why you found our client not credible. What happened to her happens to a lot of people.'

Ferlise seemed unaffected by her anger. 'Oh, you know those people,' he said. 'You never know what the fate of asylum applicants will really be if they are forced to return. You know, they'll do anything to get here. All they're thinking is America, America, America.'

That wasn't true in my case. I'd left a home that I loved and come to America only because I had nowhere else to go.

'I can understand why everyone wants to come here,' he continued. 'I understand that living outside of the United States is a lot like camping. I'd want to live here too. But, hey, that's what keeps us in business.'

Business? Layli thought to herself. This is a man who adjudicates people's lives every day in this courtroom. How can he be so flip? 'This is not a business—' Layli began.

'No, no, you misunderstand me,' Ferlise cut in. 'I just mean that that's what keeps us busy. Anyway,' he said, speaking of me, 'she wouldn't have gotten asylum even if I had believed her. That area of the law is too unsettled.'

Layli took him on. She cited decisions by circuit court judges who'd ruled that persecution on account of gender can be a basis for asylum. Ferlise asked her what rulings she was talking about. She told him. 'They're in the brief,' she said. He should have known about them if he'd read the brief.

'And then there's the new INS guidelines,' Layli said.

'What guidelines?' Ferlise said.

The ones that had been issued that May, Layli said. The ones that state that FGM could be a basis for asylum.

It seemed to Layli that Ferlise had never heard of them, either.

'They're in the brief,' Layli said. 'They're one of the attachments.'

'Well, but those are for asylum officers, aren't they?' Ferlise said.

'Yes,' Layli said.

'Well, I'm not bound by those,' he said.

The discussion continued, with Layli and Ferlise

going back and forth about what constituted persecution, what qualified as a social group, and so forth. Ferlise seemed to enjoy the argument. He had rushed us through my hearing, but now that he was finished working for the day, now that my hearing was over, the tape recorder switched off, the record closed, and the asylum seeker herself dispensed with – now he was of a mind and mood to discuss all the theoretical issues and points of law raised by my case.

Both Layli and Bowman were furious, but Layli couldn't pass up the opportunity to try to reach Ferlise, talk to him, get him to look at some of these issues differently. She was thinking ahead to my appeal. The BIA could send my case back to him. She was also thinking about other women who might come before him in the future seeking asylum from FGM. Trying to reach him seemed hopeless, however. Ferlise seemed unpersuaded by any of her arguments, and her passion appeared to leave him unmoved. 'Look,' he said. 'Women are treated badly all over the world. We can't help everyone. Don't worry,' he added. 'She'll probably go back to Togo.'

Layli was outraged. Ferlise had made this callous remark to the wrong woman.

I'm going to prove Ferlise wrong, she thought. Fauziya will not be sent back to Togo. No, she won't. I'll make sure of it.

Layli had no idea what odds she was facing. Her own client – me – would be one of her obstacles, and not the least of them, either. I didn't want to stay and fight, I wanted to go home. But Layli was getting ready for the battle, my battle, before she'd even left Ferlise's courtroom.

It would turn out to be a very long siege.

26

Beijing

'Let's go!' Someone was shaking my shoulder. I opened my eyes. I must have fallen asleep during the bus ride to Lehigh. It was time to get off the bus and go back to book-in. There, a female guard patted me down, gave me a pass, and sent me to my cell pod. Oche was talking on one of the wall phones to the right of the entrance as I walked through the door. I desperately didn't want to have to talk to her right then, but I saw her eyes follow me to my cell. My roommate, Alma, was watching me, too, waiting for me in our cell.

'Well?' she said expectantly, as soon as I walked in.

'So what happened?' Oche's voice.

I turned around. Oche was standing just outside our cell. She wanted to know too.

'Well?' Alma asked again.

I was back in prison. That should have told them everything about what had happened, but they hadn't had their hearings yet. They didn't know. I didn't want to tell them. I didn't want to say it.

'So what happened?' Oche asked. 'The judge didn't decide?'

'No,' I said softly. 'He decided.'

Oche waited. I didn't say anything else. She lost her patience. 'Fauziya! So what did he say?'

I didn't want to put it in words. But I had to.

'Denied.'

Alma's eyes went soft with sadness. 'Oooh, Fauziya.' She wrapped her arms around me and hugged me gently. 'Oh, Fauziya, I'm so sorry.'

I broke down sobbing.

'Ooh, Fauziya.' Alma tried to hold me, comfort me.

I pushed her away. 'Go away! Both of you! Leave me alone!' I ran over to Alma's bunk and threw myself down on it.

I cried. I cried until I was exhausted, numb, empty of tears. I cried for what seemed like forever, and then I picked myself up off Alma's bed, stripped out of my clothes, put on a long T-shirt to cover myself and went to take a shower. All I wanted was to lie down and go to sleep, block it all out. But as I returned to my cell, I suddenly remembered that I had to call Rahuf. I was supposed to call him today. But not from here. I wasn't supposed to be calling from here. And then I was crying again, sobbing again. Not from here.

I left the cell and went to the phones. Rahuf was home. He accepted the call. Another collect call from Lehigh Prison. Again. He knew what that meant.

'Oh, Fauziya.' His voice was heavy with sadness. 'What happened?'

'The judge denied me,' I said, my voice cracking.

Rahuf was silent for a moment. 'What did Bowman say?' A recording interrupted, announcing that the call was coming from Lehigh Prison. I started crying.

'Fauziya, come on, calm down. What did Bowman say?'

I had to stop crying. I took a breath, let it out. It came out as a strangled sob. 'He said we'd appeal.' I choked back another sob. 'He said we'd keep fighting.'

'Well, that's good, Fauziya. Then there's still hope.'

Hope. There was no hope. 'No. I'm still in prison.'

'I know, Fauziya, but you have to be strong.'

I wanted to scream, 'Don't say that! I don't want to hear that!' Rahuf didn't know what I was going through! Nobody did. But there was no point in my telling anybody, because there was nothing anybody could do about it.

The only person who could do anything was me, and I had now decided to do it. I told Rahuf what I had decided.

'No, I'm not strong. I can't take any more of this. Tell Bowman to let them send me back.'

A long silence at Rahuf's end. Then: 'You don't want to appeal?'

'No. If I stay in here I'm going to die.'

'Fauziya, don't say that. You're not going to die.'

'Yes I am! Yes I am!' I started sobbing again.

'Fauziya, come on, stop it. Don't talk like that. What about Layli? What did she say?'

I told Rahuf what she'd said. She was going to China. She'd meet people who could help me. She was going to try to get me out.

'But that's good, Fauziya.'

Good. 'Yeah, that's good. But I'm still in prison.'

'But she's going to try to get you out.'

'But she doesn't know when. I've been in prison eight months. Eight months! I can't take it any longer. I can't. Let them send me back.'

Another silence. 'It's your decision, Fauziya. I'll help you do whatever you want to do.'

'Tell Bowman to let them send me back.'

Another silence. 'You don't want to think about it?'

'No.'

494

Another silence. 'Well, it's too late to call him now. I can't call him until Monday. Call me again on Monday. If you still feel the same way then, I'll tell Bowman that's what you want to do.'

'OK,' I said wearily.

'Call me Monday, OK?'

'OK.'

Rahuf. My wonderful cousin. He didn't have any money. He couldn't afford to pay whatever it would cost for me to appeal. He should have been encouraging me to go home. It would have made his own life so much easier. But he wasn't thinking about himself. That's not the kind of man he is. He was thinking about me.

I hung up the phone, walked over to the guard's table, and asked for a request slip. Right there and then I wrote out a request to see the counselor. Rahuf couldn't talk to Bowman until Monday and this was Friday. I didn't want to wait even that long. I wanted the INS send me home immediately.

Was I deceiving Layli? I couldn't think about that. She'd asked me to hold on until she got back from China. I'd nodded. But I hadn't meant yes. I'd nodded mechanically, numbly. I couldn't do anything about that now. She'd just have to understand and forgive me. I'd never forget what Layli had done for me. She'd be in my prayers always. I'd tell Rahuf to thank her for me if I left before she got back. But I had to get out as soon as possible, any way I could. I'd start the INS process here at Lehigh. If Layli got back and was able to get me out before the INS got to me, fine. Whoever got me out first, that was who I'd go with.

Where was Layli when I was writing out that request? Perhaps she'd gotten home by then, or maybe she was still on the train. Bowman had driven her to the station after the hearing. In the car neither one of them spoke for a long time.

'Well, that really sucked,' Bowman said finally, breaking the silence.

'Yes, it did,' Layli said softly. More silence.

'So you want to help with the appeal, right?'

'Yes, I do.'

More silence.

'Don't worry, Layli, we'll beat this,' Bowman said.

He was trying to boost her spirits. Layli appreciated that, but she couldn't respond. She was still too stunned and devastated to speak.

They arrived at the train station in silence.

'When do you get back from China?' Bowman asked.

'The twelfth,' Layli said.

Bowman nodded. 'OK. I'll file for the appeal while you're gone.' Ferlise had given us a deadline of September 5 to file and pay the $110 fee.

Layli tried to say thanks, but her facial muscles were frozen. She nodded mechanically, just as I had, and then said good night.

When Layli got home that evening, Roshan wasn't there, so she called her parents in Atlanta.

'Layli! Honey! How'd it go?'

Layli told them in full detail, her voice cracking with emotion. It had been awful. A disaster.

Carole and Larry consoled and sympathized. Their daughter was in pain. I was still in prison. They hurt for both of us. But Carole wouldn't let Layli surrender to tears and self-pity. Layli's religious faith is strong. Carole's is stronger. She talked to Layli about God, about keeping faith, about higher purpose.

'Everything happens for a reason, Layli,' she said gently.

Layli didn't want to hear it. 'You don't understand, Mom. Fauziya's already suffered so much, and now she's back in jail, and the credibility ruling is going to make the appeal so much harder.'

'I do understand, honey. It's a tragedy. When I think about what that poor child has been through. But there must be a reason, sweetheart. Everything happens for a reason. God must have a larger purpose.'

Layli told me later that, as unwilling as she was to see any of this in a positive light, as soon as she heard those words she had a flashback to the conversation she and Carole had had the day before. What if her mother was right? What if God wanted my case to go to the BIA? What if the purpose was to go to appeal and win a ruling that would help a lot of women, not just me? What if God wanted my case to become a landmark case, a celebrated case? What if—

Who was she kidding, she interrupted herself midthought. That wasn't going to happen. She was still just a law student, and besides, immigration cases never got that kind of attention. Get real, she thought. Forget it. It would take a miracle for that to happen.

Yes. It would.

'I don't know, Mom,' she said, her voice shaking.

'You have to have faith, Layli,' Carole said gently. 'You have to trust in God.'

It could have been Amariya talking. My mother would have said the same thing.

Layli couldn't talk any longer, not without crying, and she didn't want to listen to any more talk about faith and God's purpose. She said good night to her parents soon afterward. She hoped what her mother had said was true, but what she needed most was a good cry.

It was Roshan, who came home a little while later, who had to hold and comfort Layli as she wept out all the tears she'd been holding in. He tried to tell her she needed to back off, not get so emotionally involved, but he could see he wasn't getting through to her. That night, after she and Roshan finally went to bed, Layli had her first nightmare about the hearing – Ferlise yelling, my being led away in shackles and chains, the whole horrible scene repeating itself over and over. She woke up crying. She cried all the next day as she dragged herself around the apartment getting ready for her trip to China.

China. She'd been so excited about attending the women's conference. She wasn't excited anymore. She wanted to call her mother and say she wasn't going. But she couldn't do that. The trip was paid for. Her mother had cajoled her father into giving it to her as a twenty-third birthday present the previous March. It was a trip they had been looking forward to taking together. She couldn't back out on her mother. And she couldn't back out on her promise to me. She'd promised that if I lost my hearing, she'd go to China and tell everyone about me. She had to go. She had to find people who knew how to help me. She had to try to drum up some media attention.

And then she had to come back and help me find new legal representation. She'd started thinking about that this morning after she woke up from her nightmare. I was going to need help with my appeal, really top-notch legal help. Obviously she couldn't provide it. She was just a law student. She didn't feel Bowman had the resources to provide it. I needed the best. And I needed it to be free, pro bono, because neither Rahuf nor I had any money. She had some ideas about where she could get me that kind of help.

When she got back from China, she'd start working on that.

Layli and Carole left for China the next day, Sunday, August 27, to attend the United Nations Fourth World Conference on Women – two conferences, actually. There was the official United Nations conference in Beijing from September 4 through 15, and a non-governmental (NGO) world women's gathering that was convening earlier in a town called Huairou about an hour outside Beijing.

Carole told me later that she spent the entire flight to China and the first couple of days after their arrival tending and ministering to Layli, trying to lift her out of her deep, dark well of depression. She'd never seen her daughter so depressed, and was seriously concerned for her. She prayed to God to heal Layli, to give her the strength to keep fighting for me.

She and Layli didn't attend the NGO forum at all those first couple of days. Layli was too upset to be able to make that kind of effort. They went for long walks in the rain under leaden skies that seemed only to reflect and deepen Layli's dark mood. Layli told Carole what she had already told Roshan as she lay sobbing in his arms after my hearing: she was questioning whether she'd chosen the right profession; she was having serious doubts about whether practicing law offered any real opportunity to work for justice. Her experience in my hearing had only reinforced her initial doubts about the legal system. To her the whole system seemed unjust. Roshan's response had been practical: 'But you only have one year to go. Don't quit now.' Carole's response was related to 'spiritual purpose.' Layli had to have faith that justice would prevail, she said again and again. She had to believe there was a purpose to my suffering. Carole didn't know what it was. She didn't pretend to. Only God knew, she told Layli. But God did know. Of that she was sure.

Carole walked with Layli, talked with her, urged her to keep faith – and told her to stop feeling sorry for herself. As tenderhearted as Carole is, she doesn't believe in giving in to self-pity. For her part, Layli thought she was entitled to a long sulk. Carole's ceaseless optimism and faith wore her down. But she did recognize that she had to get hold of herself. She had come to China for a purpose – two purposes, actually, the one she'd known about when her parents had given her the trip as a birthday present, and the one God had revealed to her only in the last few days. She was there with her mother and other Bahá'ís to do what she could to help change the world, and she was also there to do everything she could to help me.

Would she be able to do either? What, after all, could be accomplished at a U.N. conference? Whatever documents come out of it, in whatever form – resolutions, covenants, treaties – are really little more than wish lists for the betterment of the world. Even if and when they are sent to the U.N. to be ratified by a vote of the General Assembly, and then signed by the U.N. delegates from individual countries, they are still little more than indications of good faith. And even if a country's federal lawmaking body then ratifies such a document and it becomes law, there is no guarantee that that country will actually abide by it. Some do. Some don't. Some ratify it just to gain status in the eyes of the world community, and then ignore it and go right on committing the kinds of crimes against humanity and the planet that they've just promised not to commit anymore. Other countries ratify the document because it reflects and affirms their policies and values. They're already doing or genuinely trying to do what the document urges them to do. They sign on more as a way of encouraging other countries to follow their lead.

And then there are countries that tend not to ratify these documents at all. According to Layli, America falls into this third category. America has yet to ratify a number of important U.N. treaties, resolutions, and covenants that were ratified by other countries ages ago. Included among these is a document called the Convention on the Elimination of All Forms of Discrimination Against Women, or CEDAW, which was ratified by the U.N. all the way back in 1979. CEDAW is a comprehensive document that not only prohibits discrimination against women but also requires countries to take specific steps to eradicate it.

And even in countries where such documents don't get ratified, they can have an effect. In the United States, for example, CEDAW and another document, the United Nations Declaration on the Elimination of Violence Against Women, which emerged from the June 1993 U.N. Conference on Human Rights in Vienna, both influenced the ongoing debate about whether the various forms of suffering inflicted solely on women and girls constitute human rights violations, and whether as such they could qualify as grounds for seeking asylum. Nobody was really asking that question before at the U.N. conferences, according to Layli. It used to be that persecution specific to females was uniformly dismissed as 'domestic problems' or 'traditional or cultural practices.' The documents produced by these conferences make it clear that these forms of suffering *are* violations of basic human rights. And in May 1995, the INS cited both documents in the guidelines it issued at that time on 'Adjudicating Asylum Claims from Women.' If it hadn't been for those documents, the INS might not have issued the guidelines at all.

That's why Layli was so excited about attending the conference in Beijing even before she met me. She saw it as an opportunity to work for social change by having some small voice in shaping the documents that came out of the conference. She also knew that these conferences have a way of generating more than treaties and documents. Sometimes events publicized in the course of an international conference can galvanize the conscience of the world. With respect to FGM, for example, that had happened during the U.N. Conference on Population and Development held in Cairo, Egypt, in September 1994, when Christiane Amanpour, a CNN reporter who was covering the conference, wandered off on her own and somehow convinced an Egyptian man to let her film the circumcision of his five-year-old daughter by two men in a barbershop. When CNN broadcast the footage, while the conference was still in session, it was seen not just in Egypt but all around the world. While it didn't depict the graphic details of the procedure, it did show this poor little girl being held down by two men and it did record her screams of agony.

The broadcast caused such a huge furor that it put a spotlight on the issue of FGM and made it impossible to ignore, even though it is one of those 'traditional or cultural practices' that the big conferences tend to shy away from in order to avoid offending the countries where they occur. Subsequently, the document that came out of the conference in Egypt contained a number of passages condemning FGM as a violation of reproductive health and rights. The ongoing uproar and sustained media attention to the issue also helped prompt countries around the world, including the United States, to start examining their own policies regarding FGM. That was the beginning of a flood of resolutions, reports, and articles on FGM – which I would later see reflected in the documentation Layli submitted in support of my request for asylum. Almost everything she included on FGM was from 1994 and later, because the number of articles published in that time period was dramatically higher than in earlier years.

It was the CNN broadcast that really shook people up and made them start paying attention. FGM had become a hot issue, all because CNN had had the guts to broadcast what Amanpour filmed. That's what can happen when something stirs people's hearts and minds, as Layli explained to me when she told me why she felt it was so important for her to attract media attention to my own case. That's what the media can do.

Now that she was in Beijing, she needed to figure out how to get that kind of attention for me, but she didn't know the first thing about how the press works. So far her attempts had been completely unsuccessful, both at the national level when she'd tried to contact reporters at *The Washington Post* and *The New York Times*, and at the local level when she'd called reporters in Philadelphia. One thing she did know, however: she wasn't going to get anywhere if she didn't start circulating, networking, putting my story out to everyone she could approach.

OK, OK, she told herself. She had to do it. She had to get out there and start talking to people. But she didn't feel ready to do it alone. Turning to her mother for support, she asked Carole to accompany her to one of the refugee law workshops. Although Carole's field is civil rights, not refugee issues, and she had her own work to do, her own workshops and panels to attend, she put her interests aside. She was in fact overjoyed to be able to do this for Layli. Her daughter was slowly coming back to life. Anything she could do to speed that process along, she would do.

During the days that followed, Layli chose the events she and her mother would attend, with the focus always being on me: which panels and workshops would bring her into contact with people who might be able to help me, which of them would give her information that might be relevant to my case. They went to sessions on asylum law, refugee law, refugee women, FGM. At the end of each event, Layli approached the speakers and presenters to tell them about me. She kept her promise. She spoke to everyone she could find. She met with all kinds of responses. Some people were too busy or thought themselves too important to talk. Other people's eyes wandered or glazed over as she spoke. Some gave her a few seconds of their time. She got good at spitting out the facts of my story straight and fast in a single breath: 'Young woman, Togo, eighteen, fleeing FGM, father protected her, died, sold into marriage, forty-five-year-old man, three wives, wanted her mutilated, escaped, came to America, asked for asylum, denied, in jail, filing for appeal.' Whenever there was even a flicker of interest, Layli took down names, addresses, and phone numbers so she could follow up when she was back in the States. It was an exhausting, frustrating, and discouraging process. She'd hoped that every person she met who might be in a position to help me would jump at the chance. Most didn't. But it wasn't necessarily that they didn't care. In most cases they did. But these were people who already had their hands full trying to help other women and girls, many of whom were suffering even more than I was. They sympathized. They wished Layli strength and luck. They gave what advice and encouragement they could. But a lot of them made clear they couldn't do more than that. They had their own causes to pursue, their own victims of persecution to try to protect.

This wasn't a time in her life when Layli felt up to facing discouragement of any kind. She was tempted to go back to sulking in her room. But Carole wouldn't let her.

She attended a panel at which Deborah Anker was one of the speakers – the same Deborah Anker who'd brought all those people together at the Immigration Lawyers Association conference in Atlanta in June where Layli picked their brains. After the panel she made her way over to Anker and gave her a quick report on the outcome of my hearing. Anker wasn't too busy to listen either. She listened, asked questions, expressed her sympathy and her dismay. Then she went further. She offered concrete help. When she heard we were filing an appeal, she offered to write an *amicus* brief. This is a document that sometimes gets submitted when a case involving complex or unsettled points of law comes before a court, and the attorney handling the case, or sometimes the court itself, asks an organization or individual in that area of law to clarify the legal issues at stake. The organization or individual who prepares the document is acting as a 'friend' – *amicus* – to the court, helping to educate the judge. Deborah Anker, of Harvard University, had offered to do that for me. Layli was thrilled.

By this time Carole had left Layli on her own, while she went into the mountains to the north to do some work with a Bahá'í organization she was involved in. Without her mother to urge her on, Layli was again beginning to succumb to exhaustion and depression. But because of her promise to me, she forced herself to stay in the public arena. So it happened that she met Surita Sandosham, executive director of Equality Now. It was a law school friend of Layli's, Monica Selter, who was the bridge. Layli ran into Monica at yet another of the events she'd dragged herself to on my account. Once again she found herself having to tell the sad facts of my hearing to someone who had heard all about the 'before,' but not the 'after.' As soon as Monica heard Layli's story, she told her she had to meet this woman named Surita, who was a director of something called Equality Now. She'd already told Surita about my case, Monica said, and Surita would definitely want to hear about the outcome. With that Layli found herself being pulled over to a small, slender olive-skinned woman with short, shiny black hair, fine features, and big, fiery black eyes. When Monica introduced Layli as the person who was handling the FGM case she'd been telling her about, Surita seemed instantly alert.

'What happened at the hearing?' she asked in what sounded to Layli like a vaguely British accent.

Monica answered for her. 'They lost,' she said. 'It didn't go well.'

'You're appealing, of course?' Surita asked.

Layli wasn't sure how to respond to Surita's intensity. Who was this woman? A woman of substance, clearly – direct, focused, serious, and no-nonsense. Layli couldn't quite place where she was from. She'd learn later that Surita Sandosham was originally from Singapore. Layli was impressed by her from the beginning. But why was she so interested in my case? Why had Monica even been talking to her about my case? What was Equality Now?

'I'm sorry,' Layli said to Surita. 'I don't know your organization. Equality Now, is it?'

Equality Now was founded in 1992, by Jessica Neuwirth, Navanethem Pillay, and Feryal Gharahi. Surita and Jessica were both lawyers, both human rights advocates who had worked for Amnesty International. This got Layli's attention. She knew Amnesty International as the highly respected international human rights organization that can give worldwide exposure to individual instances of human rights abuse. Things tend to happen when Amnesty International focuses on a case.

'Boy,' Layli said. 'If only Amnesty International would get behind Fauziya's case.'

That was the problem, Surita explained. Amnesty International does good work, but because its resources are limited, it can focus on only so many cases. I was just a young woman fleeing one of the countless kinds of suffering inflicted on millions of women and girls every day. Human rights organizations can't rally behind every case like mine, Surita said. They're too commonplace. That's why Jessica Neuwirth, Navanethem Pillay and Feryal Gharahi founded Equality Now. They'd decided the world's women needed an Amnesty International of their own.

Publicity and pressure – those were their main tactics, Surita went on. They would pick an individual case or target a specific women's rights issue, such as the practice of FGM in Egypt, and then put out a bulletin about it to their members, about three thousand people, in about seventy different countries. 'We call it "Women's Action,"' Surita said. 'It goes out in four languages, English, French, Spanish, and Arabic.'

It tells people what's going on and asks them to do something specific like write letters condemning FGM to the president of Egypt and the Egyptian minister of health. 'That's one of the issues we're targeting now,' Surita said. They were working closely with Congresswoman Pat Schroeder on that one.

'You know Pat Schroeder?'

'Yes, we do a lot of work together.'

Layli was getting more and more impressed. Pat Schroeder was the Democratic congresswoman from Colorado who'd been trying to get an anti-FGM bill passed.

Surita told Layli about some of the other work they'd done including the case of 'Nada,' the Saudi Arabian woman who'd been the first woman granted asylum in Canada from gender-based persecution. Equality Now had done a big action around her case. Jessica Neuwirth had written an article about it in *The Christian Science Monitor* that got a lot of attention from the Canadian parliament.

Surita was definitely interested in doing something with my case. 'Look, you need publicity,' she said. 'That's what we know how to do. We'd like to help.'

Layli nodded. She didn't know what to think. Could Equality Now really do anything for me? She'd never even heard of them before.

'Do you have anything with you? Any papers we could read?'

'No, I'm sorry,' Layli said. She'd brought a number of copies of my brief to the conference, but by now she'd given them all away to various people she'd met during the preceding days.

Surita gave Layli her card. 'Will you send us something when you get back home?'

508

'Yes, of course.' She looked at the card. Equality Now, New York, New York.

'We want to help,' Surita said again. 'We can help you.'

Soon after, an exhausted Layli left the party and stumbled back to her hotel room. She added Surita's name to her list of people to follow up with back in the States, and then fell into bed.

On Tuesday, September 5, 1995, eleven days after Ferlise denied me asylum, First Lady Hillary Rodham Clinton addressed the United Nations Fourth World Conference on Women in Beijing. Mrs Clinton said, among other things, that 'on the eve of a new millennium,' it was time for women to 'break our silence' and proclaim to the world that 'it is no longer acceptable to discuss women's rights as separate from human rights.' She then listed a number of the worst human rights violations committed against girls and women – including FGM. 'It is a violation of *human* rights when young girls are brutalized by the painful and degrading practice of genital mutilation,' she said. The First Lady of the United States had just announced to the world that FGM was a violation of human rights. And there I was, sitting in a prison in the United States because an immigration judge had denied me asylum, in part because he didn't think my fears of being cut amounted to persecution under the law.

Layli told me later that the conference was a life-changing experience for her – a humbling and sobering experience. The women gathered in Beijing were waging battles against injustices that Layli, as a white middle-class American woman, would never have to face. She was forced to reevaluate her feminist priorities. Yes, it is important for American women to break new ground in the workplace and in the political arena. But the world's women were in desperate circumstances, and their struggle to survive needed urgent attention. I'll support their fight for justice, she vowed. The Beijing conference helped reinforce Layli's original desires to use her skills as a lawyer to help women like me.

On the flight back from Beijing, Layli was so revived, so excited about the contacts she'd made and the hope they had given her, that she barely noticed she was on a plane. Her head was buried in the materials she'd collected, her mind busy making lists of things to do and people to follow up with. She was her old passionate self again.

God had answered her mother's prayers. God had healed Layli, renewed her strength, her spirit, her faith. Layli was ready now. God had prepared her for the next stage in the battle for my freedom.

27

In Position

I wasn't waiting for Layli to free me. I was trying to free myself. Let them cut me, kill me, send me back to my so-called husband, I didn't care anymore. I just had to get out of prison. That's why one of the first things I'd done after returning from my hearing was to write out a request to see the INS counselor, Natasha. All I wanted was for her to tell the INS to send me home.

That evening, after I gave the request slip to the guard, I went to my cell, climbed into my bunk, and lay there staring at the ceiling, seeing nothing, feeling nothing. Alma came in a while later, around lockdown time at ten P.M., and prepared for bed. I heard her lower herself onto the metal bunk beneath mine.

Lights out. Darkness. Silence.

Then: 'Fauziya?'

I didn't answer.

'Fauziya? Are you awake?'

'Yes, I'm awake.'

'Fauziya, I'm sorry.'

'It's OK,' I said. 'I'm going home.'

She was silent a moment. 'Home? How, Fauziya?'

I told her I'd put in a request to the INS counselor. I was going to tell her to tell the INS to send me home.

Another silence. And then a soft, sad sigh. 'Oh,' she said. 'Yes. Me too.'

What? I turned over on my stomach. 'What do you mean, you too?'

'Me too,' she said softly. 'I go home too.'

Alma hadn't even had her hearing yet, but she couldn't take any more either. She'd already seen the counselor to tell the INS to come get her. Now she was waiting for them to send her home.

Waiting? My stomach twisted. 'When, Alma? When did you see the counselor?'

'Oh, long time.'

Long time? 'How long, Alma? How long have you been waiting?'

Silence. Another sad sigh. 'Long,' she said softly. And then she started to cry. It tore at my heart. But soon both of us drifted off into sleep, our only escape.

We woke at seven A.M. when locks on the lower-tier cell doors were opened for breakfast. Alma rolled out of bed, took our cups and utensils out of the boxes under her bunk, put mine on the metal table across from the bunks, and walked out of the cell to give me room to climb down. I stepped down to the ground, using the metal stool in front of the table as my stepladder, took my cup and utensils, and followed her out into the dayroom, where the food cart had already arrived. Two female inmates were handing out breakfast trays to a fast-moving line of women, which Alma and I now joined. Meals were all rush-rush-rush at Lehigh, because there weren't enough metal tables in the dayroom for all eighty to ninety women who lived in the pod to eat at the same time. We ate in fifteen-minute shifts, lower-tier cells first, upper-tier second.

That morning I couldn't eat anything, but I sat next to Alma and drank my juice while she ate. She'd barely finished when the guards in the control booth in the hallway started throwing the metal locks in the bottom line of cell doors – the signal that it was time to gulp down the last bite. Sometimes the guards in the dayroom with us would start clapping and shouting and banging the metal tables if we weren't moving fast enough. So Alma and I quickly joined another fast-moving line of women, turned in our trays, and went back to our cell. We were locked down until nine A.M.

I sat on Alma's bunk while she got ready for the day. The first thing she always did after breakfast was take a T-shirt out of her box and poke it into the openings in the wire mesh in our cell window so that she couldn't be seen from the dayroom when she was using the toilet. I turned my face to the wall to give her some privacy and waited for her to finish. I just wanted to close my eyes and sleep all day. I wanted to go to sleep and never wake up, but I couldn't. I had to get up if I wanted to shower, because the water was always cold after nine-thirty.

I took my turn on the toilet, and then Alma took the T-shirt 'curtain' off the window in the cell door, put it back in her box, sat down on her bunk and patted the space next to her on her thin, hard mattress. I sat down beside her. Alma reached into her box and pulled out a deck of cards. 'Want to play?' she asked. Alma loved playing cards. I didn't feel like playing, but I knew it would please Alma, and help pass the time until the cell doors were unlocked again. 'Sure,' I said. Her beautiful face brightened. We sat on her hard metal bunk in our tiny concrete-and-metal cell, playing cards. Another day in prison.

Nine o'clock: all the upper and lower cell doors began sliding and banging open. 'Time we clean!' Alma said, gathering up the cards and putting them back in her box. I followed her out into the dayroom, where women were scurrying all over the place. Daily inspection was at nine-thirty. We had half an hour to polish, sweep, neaten, organize, scrub, and mop everything in our cells. I went to the supply room to get spray bottles, rags, and brooms, while Alma went to another supply room to get a mop and pail. Then we carted our cleaning supplies back to our tiny corner cell and got to work. I didn't mind cleaning. I liked having something to do and I liked keeping a clean cell. I was grateful for the daily cleanings and inspections. That was one thing I had to say for Lehigh. It was clean. That's what prison life came down to: being grateful for a clean cell and clean showers – even if there were only eight stalls for all eighty or ninety of us and never enough hot water.

Alma and I set to work, polishing and sweeping. When we finished, we returned our supplies and came back to the cell to finish getting ourselves ready for the day. Usually, I wore my T-shirt and the pants that came with the uniform. That morning I decided to put on my uniform top as well because you weren't allowed out of the pod unless you were wearing the entire uniform. If I got called to see the INS counselor today, I didn't want to waste time going back to my cell to put on the uniform top. I wanted to be ready.

The loudspeaker crackled. 'Inspection!'

We gave our bunk beds a last smoothing, looked around to make sure everything was neat and clean, then waited for the prison officer to arrive. Usually we left the cell and went into the dayroom while inspection was done. But that morning we happened to be in our cell to hear the verdict. The officer looked us up and down, nodded approvingly, walked into our cell, looked around, touched a few surfaces checking for dust, came out and wrote something on her clipboard.

514

'Very nice,' she said. 'Very clean.'

I felt good. I was pleased by her praise. Yaya had taught me to work hard and do my best at everything I did. I was still working hard, still doing my best. I was still his girl. See, Yaya? I did well. Are you proud of me, Yaya?

Yaya?

Oh, God. What was I thinking? What was I doing? Something internal shifted, slipped, floated up, and I was suddenly outside myself, looking down on myself, seeing myself as Yaya would have seen me then: a thin, dull-eyed, exhausted, defeated, broken girl dressed in an ugly tan prison uniform meekly awaiting the results of inspection. That was what had become of Yaya's girl. He wouldn't be proud of me. He would be ashamed. Eight months in prison had reduced me to this – to feeling proud that a prison officer had praised me for keeping a clean cell. I had to fight back my tears as the officer continued with inspection.

As soon as she finished and left, the dayroom exploded with noise and activity, women calling, laughing, shouting, swarming along the upper decks, down stairwells, out onto the dayroom floor. Free time. All the cell doors would stay open now for the next hour or so, until eleven A.M. Inmates could do what they wanted for one precious hour, not that there was much to do: watch TV, read, write letters, play games, talk, braid each other's hair. When I walked into the dayroom, I saw Oche, who looked at me questioningly.

'Why are you wearing your uniform top?'

'In case I get called.'

She looked puzzled. 'Called where?'

'To see the counselor.'

'What do you mean?'

515

I might as well tell her. She'd find out soon enough. 'Natasha,' I said.

Oche's no fool. She looked at me in stunned silence for a moment. 'Fauziya, you're not serious.'

I didn't answer.

She grabbed my arm. 'Fauziya, don't. You can't.'

'Leave me alone, Oche.'

'Fauziya, listen to me. Don't be stupid.'

'Stupid! It's stupid to stay here, in prison, trying to appeal when I know it's hopeless!'

'You can't go back,' she said.

'Yes I can,' I said. Around and around we went, yelling at each other at the top of our lungs, while poor Alma watched, helpless, horrified.

'Don't fight,' she kept pleading. 'Nooo.' We ignored her and continued our battle.

'Fauziya, think! You have to appeal.' Oche wouldn't quit. 'You can't give up! You can't! You're just doing it because Alma did.'

'That's not true, Oche. I didn't even know she'd done it until last night.'

'Fauziya, I won't allow you to do this. When they call you, just don't go. Say you changed your mind. Then the first thing you have to do is get a better lawyer. I'm telling you, Fauziya . . .'

'Oche, please.' I put my hand up to silence her. 'Don't start with that again, OK?' Ever since we'd been at Esmor, she'd been telling me my lawyer wasn't any good. He never came to visit. Hers came every other week. I had a bad lawyer. She had a good lawyer. My lawyer was stupid. Her lawyer was brilliant. She had the best lawyer on earth. It used to drive me nuts. Not anymore. There was no point in discussing it now. It was a dead issue. I'd lost my hearing. I wasn't going to appeal. I didn't need a lawyer.

'Fauziya . . .'

'Oche . . .'

The loudspeaker crackled. 'Lock up for chow!' It was eleven A.M. Time to go back to our cells and wait for lunch.

At eleven-thirty we were let out again. Then we did the hurry-up eating-by-shifts routine again, bottom tier first, top tier next. Afterward we stayed locked in until twelve-thirty, when the doors all slid open and most of us poured into the dayroom, where we could stay until another lockdown at two P.M.

When Alma and I walked out to the dayroom that afternoon, we went over to the area where the detainees gathered. We tended to stay to ourselves. There was a fair number of us there, from many different countries, but there were very few white-skinned women among us. I didn't really think about that at the time. I just figured most all the refugees who came to America were black. I found out later that that's not true. Every year thousands of Caucasian immigrants come to America without legitimate papers to do so, just like I did in December 1994. You just don't see a lot of them in prison. Later someone told me how this was all detailed in an article entitled 'Voices from Around the Country Call for INS Detention Reform,' which Joan Marushkin wrote for the magazine *Migrationworld News*. Marushkin took statistics from the INS's list of 'top 20' countries of origin for illegal aliens in 1993, and compared them with INS detention statistics for 1994, to show that the treatment of illegal immigrants reveals 'a decidedly racist pattern of detention.' She says, for example, that Poland ranked fifth on the 1993 list of top 20 countries. Some 91,000 illegal Polish immigrants came to America in 1993; but only 119 Polish immigrants

517

were detained in 1994. Ireland ranked seventeenth, with some 36,000 immigrants; but only 21 Irish immigrants were detained. By contrast, Haiti ranked seventh, with some 88,000 immigrants, and 2,269 Haitians were detained. The Dominican Republic ranked fifteenth, with some 40,000 immigrants, and 5,095 Dominicans were detained. And although China didn't even make the top 20 list in 1993, the INS detained 2,733 Chinese immigrants. According to Marushkin's article, 'the color factor in detention becomes obvious on realizing that . . . over 97 percent of the detained immigrants are people of color' – even though 5 of the top 20 countries of origin for illegal immigrants are Caucasian. In other words, it isn't that white-skinned illegal immigrants don't come to America, as I once thought. They come. They just don't get put in detention.

As Alma and I sat down at one of the metal tables with our fellow asylum seekers – yellow-skinned women, brown-skinned women, black-skinned women like me – some of the American inmates began assembling in small groups, waiting to go to their various afternoon classes and programs. They could go to Alcoholics Anonymous meetings, drug rehabilitation programs, life skills training classes, educational classes that led toward a high school degree. Lehigh had a lot of programs for convicts. But there weren't any programs or classes for us. The educational classes weren't open to us, and most of the immigrants couldn't speak enough English to make use of them anyway. We weren't drinkers or drug users, so even if we could have gone to those programs we wouldn't have.

A few jobs were open to us – not as many as were open to the American inmates, but some. We could serve meals or work on cleaning detail. Besides that, there was almost nothing. We could read if we knew how to read English, watch TV if we understood English, write letters, play cards and board games, talk, braid each other's hair, or sleep. Sleep was the great seducer. You could almost tell how long an immigrant had been in prison by how much she cried, how much she slept. New arrivals tended to cry a lot. I'd been one of them once, a new arrival. Then came reality time, the time when you realized this wasn't a nightmare. You were really here, really in prison. You were going to have to live through it somehow. Sleep was the answer, the escape, for a lot of us.

I wanted to sleep, too, but I couldn't. Now that I'd decided to go home, I was too tense, jumpy, and distracted, waiting to see the INS counselor to set the process in motion. I hadn't been called in the morning, but maybe it would happen that afternoon. Please, God. Please let them call me. They didn't.

I went to bed that night praying I would get called on Sunday. But I didn't. Sunday afternoon I was so agitated about not being called that I even blew up at Alma when she asked me to play cards. I felt myself losing my temper, spinning out of control, the same way Mary had during the months she had had to wait after asking the INS at Esmor to send her home. So that's how I spent my first weekend back at Lehigh – fighting with Oche, having a temper tantrum even with my beloved Alma, praying to see the INS counselor, and waiting, waiting, waiting. That same weekend, while I was praying to be sent back home, Layli, knowing nothing of what I had done, was flying to China, where she hoped she'd be able to find people who would somehow be able to help me with my appeal – the appeal I didn't want to make.

Monday. Another day in prison. I called Rahuf that morning and told him I hadn't changed my mind.

'Tell Bowman to let them send me back.'

He was silent for a long time. 'You're sure, Fauziya?'

'Yes.' I told him I'd already put in a request to see the INS counselor. I was going to tell her the same thing. Rahuf promised to tell Bowman.

I waited to see the officer. I waited all Monday. I waited all Tuesday. I waited all Wednesday, Thursday, and Friday. Still I didn't get called. I called Rahuf again Friday evening.

'Have you talked to Bowman? Did you tell him?'

'Yes, I told him.'

'Well, what did he say?'

'He said it's your decision, Fauziya.'

'Good.'

Rahuf wasn't telling me the whole story. He did tell Bowman I wanted to go back to Togo, but he also told him to go ahead and file the appeal in case I changed my mind. Bowman filed the form and paid the filing fee that same day. Another $110 out of Rahuf's pocket. I had told Rahuf to just let the INS send me back, but he couldn't do that. Why not? Because he knew Amariya and Ayisha were counting on him not to let that happen. He had promised Ayisha in a letter that he would take care of me. If I returned home, it would seem like he had failed to keep his promise. Rahuf didn't feel it was right to try to talk me out of my decision. It was my right to determine my own fate. By telling Bowman to file the form, he simply made sure I hadn't yet sealed it. He was keeping my options open for me.

Thanks to INS inefficiency and incompetence, time was on his side – his side, Amariya's and Ayisha's side, Layli's side. My side, too, but I didn't know that then.

After I said goodbye to Rahuf, I walked to the guard's table and wrote out a second request to see the INS. That night, I lay awake in my bunk wondering what would happen to me after they sent me back. I'd have to return to my so-called husband. Then I'd be cut, and maybe I'd die. And if I didn't? If I lived? No, that would be worse. Real death would be better than the living death my life would become if I survived. I'd rather die. But I wanted to see my family first. All of them. Just once. I wanted to see Ayisha, to kiss her sweet face and thank her for always taking care of me. I wanted to see Babs, my big baby brother. He'd been growing so fast when I'd left home, looking more like Yaya every day. How handsome he must be by now. I wanted to see Alfa dance one more time. I wanted to call Narhila 'queen of *kwaliza*' and tease her about having an ugly belly button. I wanted to teach Shawana to say 'hello' in Chinese, the way Wang had taught me. With her love of languages she'd like that. I wanted to embarrass Asmahu by telling stories about what a greedy girl she had been, drinking all our Milo, eating our special 'Eid al-Adha treats. No. I didn't want to tell the stories. I wanted to listen to Amariya tell them, to hear her tell stories about all of us, and about Yaya. Oh, God, I wanted to see my mother. I wanted to see her beautiful face one more time, hear her musical laugh one more time, listen to her read from the Qur'an one more time. Just once. And then. Well, what would be be would be . . .

Days passed, and soon another week had gone by. What happened that week? Nothing. Nothing but bad things. Alma, who often had terrible shooting pains in her chest, had a really bad attack and was taken to the hospital again. She was still in pain when they brought her back the next day. She started crying every night.

We both cried at night now. We were both cracking. I started getting pains in my chest, too, sharp, stabbing pains, like I was being stuck with needles. My eyes got worse and worse. I couldn't read or watch TV for more than a few minutes, my eyes burned and watered so badly. I put through a request to see the doctor. I wrote that my chest hurt and my eyes were bothering me. I didn't get called to see the doctor, but I did get called one morning when the nurse came to the cell pod to dispense medicines. She asked me what was wrong with my eyes. I told her. She said she'd give me drops for a couple of weeks and see if that helped. The next morning she came back and put the drops in my eyes. Oh, they burned and they watered even worse that day too. I took the eyedrops for a few more days, hoping they'd help eventually, but they didn't. My eyes just kept getting worse. Finally I told the nurse no more. And then I fell. I was climbing into my upper bunk a night or two later when my foot slipped off the metal stool I used as a stepladder. I tumbled sideways and landed hard on the concrete floor. Alma sprang out of bed to help me. I hadn't hit my head, thank God. Nothing was broken, but my stomach and side hurt for days. 'You should see the doctor,' Alma said, concerned. I told her I already had a request in. I'd tell him about the fall when I got called to have my chest examined. But I didn't get called.

I put through a third request to see Natasha. Still nothing happened. When Layli returned from China, on Tuesday, September 12, 1995, I was right where I was when she left – in prison. I hadn't expected to be. But I was. She told me later that she arrived home cross-eyed from exhaustion and jet lag. She fell into bed, woke up the next morning, Wednesday, September 13, still exhausted and jetlagged, and got right down to the business of trying to free me. She called Rahuf first thing to see how I was.

Rahuf mumbled something vague. I was . . . OK. Not great. He didn't tell her I'd decided to let the INS send me back. Rahuf knew how much Layli cared about me, how determined she was to help me. He knew how that little piece of news would affect her, so he just didn't mention it.

OK, here's the deal, she said. She'd done a lot of thinking while she was away. It was up to him and me, of course, but here's what she thought we needed to do. The appeal was going to be difficult, she said. Ferlise had seen to that. She was still convinced I could win, but not with my present level of legal representation. I was going to need better than she could provide, better than Bowman could provide. I was going to need the best. Now, best usually means most expensive, she said. But it doesn't have to. Her suggestion for how to get the best, at a price we could afford – in other words, virtually nothing – was to take my case to a university law clinic, because they do all their work pro bono. The cases are assigned to law students, who work under the supervision of clinic directors who are experts in their fields of law. Her first choice for where we should go would be American University's own International Human Rights Clinic, which ranked as one of the best in the country, and which offered the very big advantage of being right there at her own school. She herself wasn't a student in the Human Rights Clinic, unfortunately, but the clinic director might let her help out, serve as backup, keep a hand in, stay involved. Another option was that she could approach the Immigration and Refugee Clinic at Harvard, whose director, Deborah Anker, she had met several times, most recently in China. But because she was hoping to continue some level of involvement in my case herself she preferred to approach the American University clinic first. It was up to Rahuf and me, however. She'd do whatever he wanted, whatever I wanted. What did he think?

What did Rahuf think? He had me on one side saying I wanted to go back, Amariya and Ayisha on the other saying make sure I stayed where I was. He wanted to do right by all of us, but he hadn't felt justified in asking me to reconsider my decision unless he could offer me some real hope. That's what Layli seemed to be offering now. What did he think? Thank God is what he thought. God had sent us an angel in the form of Layli, is what he thought.

'Whatever you think best,' Rahuf replied. 'Whatever's best for Fauziya.'

'OK,' Layli said. She gave Rahuf her home phone number and asked him to give it to me the next time he heard from me. Did he know when that might be? No, he wasn't sure. I usually called on Friday or Saturday. It was Wednesday then, so he probably wouldn't hear from me for a couple of days at least. In the meantime, Layli said, she would look into whether the clinic could take my case, in the hope that if I agreed to go there, it would be all set up the minute I said yes.

'So tell her to call me right away, OK?'

'I will, Layli.' He would if I called, he meant. Would I? Would I even be there on Friday or Saturday? Or would the INS come to get me first? He had no way of knowing and no way of reaching me. But he didn't tell Layli that.

When Layli went back to school that day, she didn't go directly to the person God still needed her to meet.

She went to class first and talked to her public interest law clinic professor, Richard Boswell. They hadn't spoken since before my hearing, when she'd asked him for pointers and he'd hammered home one crucial piece of advice. 'Be sure to make a good record because that's what the BIA is going to look at if you have to appeal.' Richard welcomed her back. 'How was the women's conference?' he asked. She told him. Wonderful, exhausting, inspiring, humbling. 'How did the hearing go?' he asked. She told him. A total disaster. She didn't go into all the gory details, but she told him as much as she could bear to repeat about Ferlise's behavior, and then about her own determination to appeal, but with more high-powered representation this time. Richard responded sympathetically and gave her his next piece of good advice: 'You might want to talk to Professor Musalo then.'

Professor Musalo was Karen Musalo, acting director of the International Human Rights Clinic, the very clinic Layli was hoping would take my case. Until then Layli had never spoken to Karen, although she recognized her from having seen her around campus, and she was a bit nervous about bringing my case to the clinic because she knew that whatever steps she took now would help to determine my fate. Richard's words reassured her that she was doing the right thing. She would go see Karen that very day, she decided.

Layli didn't know it yet, but Karen was perhaps the best possible person from whom to seek help. During Karen's years 'in the trenches' as a refugee advocate, and later as a law professor, she developed certain innovative approaches that would prove invaluable when it came time to help me. She understood the importance of demonstrating credibility – the very issue Ferlise had raised in denying my request for asylum – and had been a leader in making use of expert witnesses to establish it. Testimony from psychologists, anthropologists, and other experts helped her explain to judges that what might appear as dishonesty on the part of a client was often the result of psychological trauma or cultural differences. Karen was one of the first refugee-advocate lawyers to start introducing the kinds of affidavits from experts that Layli had used in preparing my brief – statements from recognized authorities on a particular country, culture, tribe, or religion, who can testify that what a client is saying is true. Karen also had a great track record. Just as Layli had promised herself that she would not allow me to be sent back to Togo, Karen had made a similar vow about her clients – and kept to it. From the time Karen began practicing refugee-advocacy law to the day Layli went to see her for the first time, Karen had never once had a client deported. Although they weren't all granted asylum, and some had to find other countries to live in, no-one had ever been forced to return home. I would say that God had picked, and prepared Karen just as carefully as He had Layli. Karen would say that she was 'in a position to have an opportunity to do some good.'

Karen was walking out of her office when Layli went to see her that day, but she paused long enough for Layli to tell her that she wanted to discuss a case with her. 'Why don't you give me a brief description of it now,' Karen said, 'and then maybe we can schedule a time to talk at greater length later.' Layli launched into the one-breath spiel she had developed for use in Beijing: young woman, eighteen, from Togo, fleeing FGM, father died, sold into marriage, husband wanted her mutilated, escaped, came to America, in jail, asylum denied, appeal pending.

Layli stood ready to leave after making an appointment to come back at a better time – that afternoon, the next day, whenever was convenient for Karen. That's all she was hoping for, that Karen would be interested enough to want to talk more. But suddenly it seemed Karen wanted to talk now. 'Come in,' Karen said as she turned around and walked back into her office. She gestured toward the couch near her desk. 'Sit down.'

They talked only briefly that day, but long enough for Layli to explain to Karen why she was hoping the clinic might be willing to take my case, long enough for her to convey to Karen something of my experience during my time in America. Karen was disturbed by everything Layli told her, but she wasn't surprised by any of it. My incarceration, Ferlise's behavior, and his ignorance – it was all too familiar. More the norm than the exception, unfortunately.

Layli told Karen that day that she was hoping she could stay involved in my case if the clinic took it on. If it was OK with Karen, that is. She wasn't a student in the clinic. She understood that. But she'd been involved in the case from the beginning and knew a lot and had some ideas and . . . Karen asked about her other commitments. How much time would she realistically be able to devote to helping on a regular basis. 'Wellll,' Layli said. She had her law journal responsibilities, and her twenty-hour-a-week Dean's fellow job. And she was already in another clinic, of course, the Public Interest Law Clinic, where Richard Boswell was teaching. And she was studying for her law degree and her master's degree in international relations at the same time. And there were the two weeks of classes she'd missed while she was in China to make up. But, you know, everybody's busy in law school . . .

Karen didn't say yes to taking the case, she didn't say no. She told Layli she'd need time to think. She had a lot of factors to take into account. The clinic was already handling a number of cases. She would have to think about whether the clinic had the time and resources to take on another one. There was no point in saying yes if the students were already so over-burdened that they couldn't give my case the attention it required. Karen asked Layli to check back with her in a few days. 'I'll know then.'

Layli thanked Karen for her time and walked out the door. She was tremendously relieved. The meeting had gone well. Karen was obviously interested. Layli prayed. Please. Please let the clinic take the case. Please let Karen say yes.

I was praying too. As Layli sat talking to Karen, I sat in Lehigh Prison, waiting to be called to see the INS officer. Please. Please let them call me.

At some point that day I was sitting at a table with Oche and a few of the other immigrants when Oche got up, bored and restless, and wandered over to see what was on TV. I stayed put because my eyes had gotten so bad by then that I could barely watch TV anymore.

'Fauziya!' Oche shouted suddenly. 'Get over here quick! They're talking about you!'

What? What was she talking about?

She rushed back to the table, grabbed my hand, and dragged me over to the TV. 'They're talking about it on TV!' she said excitedly, dragging me along.

It? What it? What did she mean?

FGM. That's what she meant. It was being discussed

on the Oprah Winfrey show. I couldn't believe it. Actually, I could barely hear it. There was only one TV in the dayroom, mounted high on a pillar. The dayroom was always crowded and loud, filled with the noise of women talking, shouting, and laughing, chairs scraping, doors banging. I went and stood directly under the TV, concentrating, squinting up. Although I could hear only snatches of what was being said, it sounded like one of Oprah's guests was talking about the medical complications of the procedure. Oh, God. I didn't want to know. Another woman seemed to be talking about her own experience. I heard 'at age six.' I heard 'mother.' I heard something about 'happening in the United States.' I heard . . . And then it was lock-up time again, and I had to return to my cell. I turned away from the TV and walked back to my cell. I was stunned. They were talking about FGM, on TV, in America, as though it was something serious, something that shouldn't be happening, something that had to be stopped. But they certainly weren't doing anything to help me. What kind of crazy country had I come to? I felt trapped in a nightmare – a crazy, contradictory nightmare where nothing made any sense.

Layli says there's a saying in America: 'It's always darkest before the dawn.' That's what that time of waiting was for me – my darkest time yet. Dawn was coming, but I didn't know that then. I was waiting not for dawn, but for the chance to return home, to whatever new kind of nightmare I would face there.

The dawn broke the day I finally called Rahuf. There would be plenty of dark times afterward, darker even than the ones I'd lived through already, but this would be one of those brief periods of hope, of light.

'Fauziya! Thank God!'

'Thank God for what?' I said, angry. 'I'm still in prison!'

And then he told me the news. Layli was back from China and she had a plan.

A plan? 'What kind of plan?'

'She says she's going to find us a new lawyer. And listen to this, Fauziya. She says she's going to find someone who can help us for free.'

'For free!'

'That's what she says.'

'I didn't tell her anything, Fauziya,' Rahuf said slowly. 'About your wanting to go home, I mean.' He fell silent. He was asking me a question.

My mind raced. Layli was back. She'd made me a promise. The first thing she'd do was get me out. I had to get out, one way or another. I'd tried to get myself out when there'd seemed no other way. I was still here. Layli was back now. She had a plan. Maybe she could get me out.

And then it struck me – my God! – what I'd almost done! I hadn't been seeing clearly before. Thank God I hadn't been called to see the INS officer yet. I didn't have to go home. I didn't. Layli would get me out. She'd get me out. And then she'd get me asy—

Oh, God, what if it was too late?

'I want to appeal, Rahuf! I changed my mind. Is it too late? Can I still do that?'

'No, Fauziya—'

A recording broke in.

No! Oh, God, please.

Rahuf came back. 'No, Fauziya, it's not too late. Yes, you can still appeal.'

Rahuf. My wise, wonderful cousin. May Allah bless him forever. Because of him, I could still appeal.

'OK,' he said. 'If you're going to appeal, Layli needs

to talk to you. You have to call her right away. Here's her number . . .'

When I reached Layli, she explained everything to me, how she was trying to get the American University law school's Human Rights Clinic to take my case, but that she hadn't gotten an answer yet from the director. She told me to stay in touch with Rahuf because she'd call him the moment Karen gave her a decision.

Some days later, Layli stopped by Karen's office again. Karen's door was open and she was at her desk, hard at work. Layli knocked politely.

Karen looked up. 'Layli, come in.'

Layli stepped into Karen's office and stood nervously just inside the door. 'I was wondering if you'd reached a decision yet.' Layli held her breath.

'Yes,' Karen finally said. 'Yes, we can take the case.'

Layli squealed with joy. She was ecstatic. Karen's involvement could change everything for me, she was sure of it.

But this was no time to celebrate, Karen made clear: there was work to be done. Barely breaking stride, Karen switched instantly into work mode. Layli followed her lead, put aside her excitement and switched into work mode too. OK, Karen said. These were the things they needed to do immediately.

The clinic needed to get a copy of my file yesterday if not sooner. The first order of business was the request for parole. Karen understood in a way Layli didn't yet, couldn't yet, how imperative it was to get me out of detention. Parole would require approval of the INS district director in Philadelphia. Layli told Karen she'd met a woman named Surita Sandosham at the women's conference. Surita was part of an organization called Equality Now, and she'd said she wanted to help out. Layli was going to follow up with her, send her information on my case, in case her connection with Congresswoman Pat Schroeder might be helpful. And Layli knew another congresswoman, Cynthia McKinney, an African-American woman from Georgia who'd been a professor at Layli's college before becoming a congresswoman. She was thinking she should contact her too, maybe get her to write a letter supporting a request for parole. Yes, yes. Karen liked the idea of getting congressional support. I was young, had no criminal convictions, had family and lawyers in the area, and would be a good candidate for release. A parole request explaining these factors and accompanied by supporting letters from two congresswomen should be enough to sway any reasonable district director toward granting parole. *Reasonable.* That was the key word.

They talked about Ferlise's ruling and how to attack it on appeal. The 'adverse credibility' ruling was a bad blow, Karen agreed. But not a fatal one. It would be difficult to get it reversed but not impossible. It could be done. It had to be done. It was that simple. The BIA had to be convinced I was telling the truth about what had happened to me and what would happen to me if I were sent home. Then and only then would they consider the legal merits of my case, whether Ferlise had been right or wrong in denying me asylum. If the BIA didn't believe I was telling the truth, well, then, there'd be no reason for the BIA even to get into the legal arguments. I'd lose on the adverse credibility ruling alone.

Karen had decided to give the case to two students, Denise Thomasson and Nileema Pargaonker, she explained to Layli. They were already working on another gender-based asylum case involving a woman from India who was fleeing domestic violence, so they wouldn't be starting from scratch, they were already up to speed on some of the issues and arguments. Karen told Layli I needed to sign forms authorizing each of them – Karen, Denise, and Nileema – to act as my attorneys. Layli said she could take care of that. Good.

Layli said she'd start working on a written statement of the facts of my case. Good, Karen said. Denise and Nileema would find that useful to look at before they interviewed me for the affidavit that would accompany the appeals brief. Layli said she'd also write up a separate memorandum summarizing other background information she thought might be useful to pass along: people she'd been in touch with; ideas she'd had about how to argue the appeal; that kind of thing. If Karen thought that would be helpful, that is. Layli just wanted to do whatever she could to help. Yes, Karen said. That would be useful. OK, Layli said. She'd get to work on everything right away. Karen stood up. Layli stood up too. They shook hands. Karen and Layli. The first Fauziya Team handshake.

Layli went home that evening and celebrated with Roshan. She also called Rahuf and told him the great news. 'So tell Fauziya to call me right away!' When I did, she had more news to tell me: Roshan had a medical conference in Philadelphia the following weekend. She'd go with him on Friday, then drive from there to Lehigh on Saturday, while he was busy with his conference. How did that sound?

'You're coming to visit me? Really?'

Layli laughed. 'Yes, Fauziya. Really.'

A visitor. I'd been in prison more than nine months now. In all that time, I'd had three visits: one from Eric Bowman, one from two of Rahuf's friends who had come down from New York City while I'd been at

Esmor, and one from my wonderful cousin himself during my brief time in minimum at York. Now I was going to have another visitor – Layli.

It helped to have her visit to look forward to that week. It helped me get through another week in prison – another terrible week, during which Alma got sicker and sicker and, like me, never got called to see the INS officer. That was OK for me, now that I'd decided to go forward with my appeal. But Alma needed to go home.

Layli called Bowman early that same week. She needed to get my file from him, but she wasn't sure how he would react to the news that the clinic would be representing me. What if he was angry, or offended? But as soon as he heard about the clinic, Eric was supportive. He felt they had more resources to put into the case than he did as a solo attorney.

'No problem, Layli. Good luck. And give my best to Fauziya.'

After Layli got off the phone, she realized that she should have known Eric would respond the way he did. His supportiveness was completely in character – understanding, sympathetic, kind.

Layli was scared stiff as she drove from Philadelphia to Allentown to see me that Saturday. She'd never been to a prison in her life, and didn't know what to expect.

Soon after her arrival she found herself being led by a guard through a seemingly endless series of locked doors, the doors clanging open and shut with the ear-shattering bangs I heard every day of my life now. For Layli the experience was a shock. She couldn't believe the noise level; when she finally got to a room filled with people, she froze. Was this a visiting room? It looked like a big kindergarten room, like a kiddie playroom, only it was populated by big men in orange jumpsuits and full-grown women in regular street clothing who were sitting at tiny little tables on tiny little stools, while all around them little children were running and playing and fighting. When Layli walked in, the room was vibrating with noise – the noise of all those people talking and laughing and shouting, and all those kids screeching and hollering. But at the sight of Layli, everybody went silent. Dead silent. Everybody looked up at her. Everybody stared. Dressed up in a suit as she was, she looked like she'd come from another planet. And then some of the men started hooting and hollering and whistling. Whoooiieee! Hey baby baby baby! Oh, mama!

At first Layli thought with horror that this was where she was going to have to meet with me, but then the guard led her to an interview room, one of a series of small, windowed rooms off to one side of the large room she'd just been in. She settled down to wait, trying to steel her nerves for whatever was to come.

And then there I was, walking across the main visiting room toward her. She saw me approaching through the window. I was wearing a tan uniform. My hair was braided into a mop of thin, short African braids. I looked like I'd gained a little weight too. That was good. And no handcuffs. Oh, thank God, she thought. No handcuffs.

I entered the room.

'Fauziya,' Layli said warmly.

We were standing in a room together. No booth. No partition. No barrier between us. We were both awkward and shy. I saw her make a half move toward me, then check herself. She told me later that she felt an impulse to hug me, then stopped herself, realizing she didn't know if I wanted to be hugged or not. Did I? I couldn't have said. Yes. No. Maybe. Maybe not. Layli didn't know it, but she'd done me a great kindness in checking herself. It was sensitive of her. She was treating me with respect. I was grateful. I wasn't allowed much dignity or choice in prison. Freedom from uninvited physical contact was about all that had been left me.

'Fauziya,' Layli said again. 'It's so good to see you again.'

'It's good to see you too, Layli,' I said softly.

We sat down at the table, still shy and awkward with each other. 'I have some forms for you to sign, Fauziya, if you agree to have the clinic represent you,' Layli said. She fished them out of her briefcase and handed them to me – three identical forms, with a different name on each form: Karen Musalo; Denise Thomasson; Nileema Pargaonker. She explained what the forms were, who each of these people was.

'Now, it's your decision, Fauziya,' she said. 'So think carefully. I want you to take your time and make sure this is what you want to do. If you sign these forms, then that means your case will be transferred to the clinic. Karen will become your new lead attorney, and Denise and Nileema will be like the junior attorneys.'

'And you too, right?'

Layli hesitated ever so slightly. She smiled. 'Yes,' she said. 'Me too. I'll be helping as much as I can.' She told me later that she'd felt a twinge then. She was turning my case over to the clinic, for my sake, and she'd have to step back now. She smiled again. 'It's up to you, Fauziya. If you're not sure this is what you want to do, we don't do it. It's your decision.'

My decision. *My* decision. 'Really?' I asked Layli. 'It's really up to me?'

'Completely up to you,' Layli said.

536

It's hard to explain to someone who's never been in prison how rare and precious a thing it is for a prisoner to be able to decide something for herself. People don't get to make their own decisions in prison. 'It's your decision,' Layli said. Something stirred inside me when she said that. It was as if with those three simple words, she gave me back a lost part of myself. Yes. That was me. I remembered that now too. I was a person who could make decisions about my own life. My spirits lifted immediately. I felt some of my old strength and energy return.

I grinned. 'Well then, let me sign!' I spread the forms out on the table in front of me, stared at them, signed them. Three forms! Three lawyers! Four counting Layli. 'Wow,' I said. 'I've got lots of lawyers now!'

Layli laughed. I did, too, for the first time since . . . When? I couldn't remember. It felt good to laugh again – a little at least. A little was all I could manage.

We spent the rest of Layli's visit going over the detailed written case history she was preparing. She'd brought a copy with her. It covered a lot of material, from my family background to my forced marriage, my flight to Germany, my arrival in the States, my incarceration, right down to the details of my hearing. Layli read me everything, word by word, sentence by sentence, as I listened carefully.

I corrected. She made notes. I thought of other things to add, things we'd skipped or forgotten. She made more notes. She asked more questions. I answered them. Then we reviewed everything again. And again. And again. Until we got it all right.

Then we talked over some ideas she'd had about other evidence she wanted to try to gather to substantiate the facts of my story. She didn't know if we'd actually be able to use any of it or not, but she thought it might be worth gathering, just in case.

'I was thinking, for example, that it might help if we could get a letter from Rudina. What do you think?'

'OK,' I said. 'The only problem is I don't have her address anymore.' I'd had it written in my little address book, the one I'd lost during the Esmor riot. It had been in the envelope that had been taken from me before I climbed into the van to Hudson. My address book, my one letter from Rudina, my letter from Mary, my letters from my mother and Ayisha, my family photos – everything had been in that envelope. And now the envelope was gone.

'You don't remember Rudina's address?' Layli asked.

'No, not all of it. I remember part of it, I think.'

I told Layli the part I thought I remembered. She wrote it down.

Then Layli asked how I felt about publicity, having people write about me in the newspapers.

'Would it help me get out of prison?'

'It could, Fauziya, if we can get people interested in writing about you.'

'Would they have to use my picture?'

'That would be up to you.'

'No pictures. I don't mind my name being used. But no pictures. It would shame my family.'

'OK. No pictures.'

It was getting late now. We'd been talking for about three hours. The main visiting room was now empty. Layli looked tired. I was tired too. But I was always tired now. I was in prison. Layli had a long drive still ahead of her.

'You should go,' I said. 'It's late, you need to get back.'

'One more thing,' she said. She pulled out a piece

of paper, wrote on it, passed it to me. She'd written two phone numbers on it. She pointed to the first. 'This is my home number. You already have that.'

I nodded.

She pointed to the second. 'This is the clinic number. It's a 1-800 number. That means you don't have to call collect. Just dial all these numbers and you'll get through directly, OK?'

Then she stood up slowly, almost as though she didn't want to leave, and followed me out of the interview room, through the empty visiting room, toward the locked metal door – the door she could pass through and I could not. We walked together, side by side, our shoulders touching. We were exactly the same height. Look at that. We both seemed to notice at the same moment. We turned our heads toward each other, glanced down at our touching shoulders, looked up, gazed into each other's eyes, smiled. Sisters.

She sighed sadly, opened her mouth to speak, fell silent again. Then I said what we were both thinking: 'I wish I could go with you.'

Layli looked at me and smiled. 'I wish you could too.'

With that our time together was over. And then we were at the door, saying goodbye, and suddenly Layli was hugging me, and I was hugging her back. And I realized then how much I'd wanted her to hug me, all along.

After Layli left, I stood gazing at the door she'd disappeared through, imagining, pretending I'd walked through it with her. I pictured us walking together, the two of us, shoulder to shoulder, side by side, down a corridor, out the entrance, right out the door. Oh, God. Would it ever happen? I saw myself hugging Layli again, outside prison, hugging her and laughing, 'I'm free! I'm free!' It was such a sweet fantasy. Would it ever come true?

I turned away from the door and went back to my cell pod. Please God. Please. Let it come true. Soon.

28

Battles

Once I got back to my cell pod after Layli's visit, a guard stopped me at the door to the dayroom. 'Up against the wall, hands on the wall, legs apart.' If I'd been returning from a visit from relatives or friends, I'd have been strip-searched to make sure no-one had slipped me any drugs or other contraband. Because I'd been with my lawyer, I got off easy – just a quick body frisk. But it was a reminder that even though I had all these new lawyers now, I was still in prison.

After the guard finished patting me down, I went directly to my cell, to pray. I spread a towel on the floor, washed, wrapped my head and shoulders in the bedsheet I used as a *mayahfi*, stepped barefoot onto the towel, turned toward the east, toward Mecca, bowed, and began my devotions. I professed my faith, reaffirming my relationship to Him. I belonged to God. If it was His will that I stay in prison, then I'd stay in prison and worship Him in prison. Wherever He put me, whatever He did with me, I would praise His name. Then I broke down crying and began my supplications. My new lawyers were going to try to get me out. That was the first thing they were going to do. Would they succeed? Only if Allah willed it. I prayed with a humble, breaking heart. I asked God to take pity on one poor suffering believer. 'Please, God. Hear my prayers. Don't make me stay here. I beg You. Have mercy. Let them free me.'

The INS finally came for Alma around this time. I cried my heart out the day she left, heartbroken for myself and for her. She'd fled her country to escape suffering. Now she was going back to escape even worse suffering here. Prison had been killing her, literally killing her. She had to go home.

Once Alma was gone, I had a TV installed in my cell. Inmates were allowed to do that if they had money to pay for it, and Rahuf had sent me some when I'd decided to stay and appeal. It wasn't the same as having Alma to talk to. And I couldn't really watch for long periods of time because of my eyes. But I could listen. At least I had TV voices to keep me company in the cell.

I asked the guards if I could move to the bottom bunk after Alma left. I'd fallen out of the upper bunk once already and the bottom one was now empty. No. I had to stay in the top bunk. Why? Because that's the one I'd been assigned. You stayed where you were put. That was the rule. I didn't argue. You never, ever, argue with a guard. I just went ahead and moved myself to the bottom bunk. Nobody said anything – maybe because I was one of the immigrants. Some of the guards were willing to make little allowances for us every now and then.

One other good thing that happened around then was that I got a work assignment. Soon after I made the decision to appeal, I asked Fay Parker, the prison counselor, to find me work, because I knew I would need something to keep me busy during this time, keep my mind off things. After she got my request she called me in and told me she'd put me on a list. I'd been on a lot of lists by then and knew what that usually meant: 'Don't hold your breath.' But for once I didn't have to wait long. I started work that October on cleaning detail. I would get about five dollars a week for the work, and a few privileges, too, like being able to get out of my cell before the other inmates in the morning, which would mean I could go to the showers early, when there was still hot water.

But in general my life was still hell. The food was still inedible. The noise and cold were still constant. The waiting – for anything – was still endless. I did finally get called to see the INS officer. When did that happen? A month after my request? Six weeks later? Something like that. 'Thank you,' I told the guard, 'but I don't need to see her anymore.'

After Layli returned to D.C. she got right down to work polishing her summary of the facts of my case and writing a 'transfer memorandum' of other useful information for my new legal team, the Fauziya Team. She did her usual incredibly thorough job, reviewing not just the legal aspects of my case but my family situation, my relationship with Rahuf, further thoughts she'd had about how best to make an appeal, other cases she'd heard about recently that involved FGM, and even my emotional state – not good, partly because I was so distraught about not hearing from my mother and my sister. Then she began following up with the people she'd met in China. She sent all the people who had expressed interest in my case a personal cover letter reminding them of who she was and why she was writing; a very quick restatement of my case; and a copy of the more lengthy written summary she had just completed. The packets, one of them addressed to Surita Sandosham of Equality Now, went out early that same week.

Two days later, at around ten on a Friday evening, in

the midst of a Bahá'í gathering she and Roshan were hosting at their apartment, the telephone rang. Layli took the cordless into the bedroom to get away from the noise. The caller identified herself as Jessica Neuwirth, of Equality Now. 'We just got your package,' Jessica said, 'and we're very interested.'

She explained that she and Mimi Ramsey, an FGM activist visiting from California, had spent the day lobbying people about the FGM controversy, which had come to something of a head because of the ongoing battle against it in Egypt. When they returned that evening to Jessica's apartment, which is located one flight above Equality Now's New York office, Jessica had looked at the day's mail and discovered Layli's packet about me. She and Mimi both read it, and it made such an impact that Mimi decided they should visit me immediately. Jessica had called Surita for a quick phone conference, then called Layli. 'We're really eager to work with you on this case,' Jessica told Layli. 'We want to visit Fauziya this weekend. Can we do that?' After hearing something about the strategy they were proposing, Layli said she thought that would be fine and gave Jessica directions to Lehigh.

As soon as Layli hung up the phone, she raced to tell Roshan the news. 'Oh, Roshan! Do you realize what this could mean? Equality Now is like an Amnesty International for women! And they're going to get involved! They want to help with publicity!'

I was in my cell the next day, sleeping, when one of the guards in the day room called my name. 'Kasinga! Visitor!'

Visitor? Me? Were they sure? Yes, they were sure. But who'd be visiting me? Two women I didn't know, I discovered when I got to the visitors' room. One was a short, solidly built white woman in pants and shirt with short dark hair, dark, bespectacled eyes, and a squarish, friendly face; the other, a somewhat taller, older, brown-skinned woman in a dress with short dark hair, warm dark eyes, and pretty features – Jessica Neuwirth and Mimi Ramsey. Why had they come to see me? What did they want? I was nervous, confused, frightened – visibly shaking with terror, according to what Jessica told me later.

Jessica did most of the talking at first. She introduced herself and Mimi to me, though I didn't catch Mimi's name when I first heard it. She told me what Equality Now was, why they'd come, how Equality Now wanted to try to help get publicity for my case. The more she talked, the more I relaxed. Jessica is a very down-to-earth person, warm, funny, smart, unpretentious, easy to be with, easy to talk to, easy to like. Mimi had a more concerned and protective, motherly quality about her. She was more openly hurt for me, angry for me, more focused on offering me emotional comfort and support. I felt embraced by both these women, deeply, powerfully, quickly. They cared so much that as soon as they read Layli's packet, they'd made arrangements to come to see me. I had been right to trust, right to hope. Look! Already God had sent me these two wonderful women. My hopes lifted. My heart lifted. It was a sign.

I began to open up to them, reach out. I was even able to talk some. I mentioned the Oprah Winfrey show I'd seen. Did they know that Oprah Winfrey had done a whole show on FGM? A whole show! Jessica and Mimi exchanged glances. Mimi leaned forward and took my hand. 'You saw that show?' she asked gently. Yes, parts of it. Did I remember the woman named Mimi Ramsey? No, I hadn't been able to hear any of the women's names. Well, did I remember there was an Ethiopian woman who talked about being circumcised at age six and about the husband who beat her? Oh, yes. I remembered her. She'd talked about how painful the procedure was. Yes. I remembered that. The woman holding my hand smiled a sad smile. 'That was me,' she said. No! 'You? That was really you!' Yes, she said, that was really her. I felt so bad for her when I heard that, I broke down crying. 'Oh, I'm so sorry,' I said. 'I'm so sorry you had to go through that.' She started crying too. We sat there holding hands and crying together. 'Why did they do that to you?' I asked her. She'd been cut, severely, at age six. Her mother had asked her to 'please do it for me.' Now Mimi was fighting to protect other little girls from being forced to undergo it. I was so impressed, I could hardly speak.

'You're my hero,' I told her shyly.

She smiled, squeezed my hand. 'And you're mine.'

Me? Why? 'Because you ran,' she said. 'That took tremendous courage. You should be proud. You did the right thing.'

We talked some more. Jessica told me that Mimi and Surita Sandosham, the executive director of Equality Now, were going to be meeting with a congresswoman named Patricia Schroeder the very next week and would discuss my case with her. Jessica suggested I write a note to Schroeder, which she'd give to Surita to deliver on my behalf. Would I be willing to do that? Oh yes! She gave me pen and paper. I wrote the note in my imperfect English.

Congress Women Schroeder. Jessica had to tell me how to spell Schroeder. *Hi. I'm Fauziya from Africa. I'm 18 yrs old who asked for assylum in U.S.A. based on female genetal mutulation but the I.N.S. put me in exclusion of deportation. Please help me. I don't want to go back . . . Thanks Alot. F. Kasinga 10/7/95.*

Before they left that day, Jessica gave me Equality Now's phone number and told me to call anytime I wanted, even if it was just to talk. She wasn't there all the time herself, she said, because she was also working another job. But Surita was there a lot, and she was really looking forward to talking to me, so I shouldn't be shy about calling. Mimi gave me her phone number too. In California. I should call her, too, she said. OK? OK. Promise? Yes, I promised. Soon, Jessica said. I should call soon or else they'd worry about me.

I talked to Mimi once or twice a week after that, calling collect all the way to California. I placed my first collect call to Equality Now in New York City a few days later and met Surita Sandosham by phone. Surita, Sonia Nanda, Mandy Sullivan – I got to know everyone in that office. They were always there for me. At no time during any of my many collect calls did Mimi or anyone from Equality Now mention to me that they were struggling to do their work on almost no money.

Back at the clinic, the push was on to get me paroled. Denise and Nileema finally got my file from Eric Bowman in mid-October. They had to go to Bowman's office and ferret it out themselves in the end, but they got it. They found the paperwork Bowman had sent to the Newark district director requesting parole, but the request had been denied. They also found papers indicating Bowman had tried to get my case transferred. There was no transcript of any taped conversation with me, however. No tape, no transcript, nothing. Bowman told me later the tape had been transcribed and a copy of the transcription should have been in the file. Maybe it should have been. But it wasn't. Karen, who understood the horrors of detention, knew how urgent it was to try to get me out as soon as possible. So she asked Denise and Nileema to coordinate the process of getting letters from Congresswomen Schroeder and McKinney in support of my parole, while she wrote the formal letter of request.

On October 19, 1995, the parole request went out to Philadelphia district director J. Scott Blackman, who had sole authority to grant or deny me parole now that I was in a Pennsylvania prison. The letter argued that I had a good case and it was 'highly likely' I'd win on appeal. I hadn't tried to enter the country illegally, I wasn't a security risk, I hadn't committed any crime, and it was 'generally considered to be in the public interest to parole juveniles, or persons with serious medical conditions.' Although I was no longer technically a juvenile, since you must be seventeen or younger to be considered as such, at eighteen I was still very young. The letter also said that my health had suffered during my time in detention. I was 'extremely allergic to cigarette smoke,' and yet I'd been exposed to it and had begun coughing and spitting up blood. I'd been in isolation at Lehigh because the prison thought I had TB. And I had a place to live, with my cousin, who lived near my attorneys. I wasn't going to disappear anywhere. I was actively pursuing a claim for asylum. My continued detention constituted 'an unnecessary financial burden on taxpayers.' For all these reasons, my attorneys were requesting 'a favorable exercise of your discretion in this case.' The letter Surita and Mimi had gotten from Patricia Schroeder in support of my request for parole was attached. Let her go. The letter Layli had solicited from Congresswoman Cynthia McKinney followed a few days later. Let her go. Surita Sandosham wrote a third letter. Let her go.

Let me go, let me go, let me go. Please.

The next big push was going to be the appeals brief. But the Fauziya Team couldn't really start writing it until they got the transcript of my hearing, which hadn't arrived yet. Nor had they been given the deadline for submitting the brief. They wouldn't get that until they got the transcript. In the meantime, there was plenty to do. Karen told Denise and Nileema to get up to speed on all the facts and issues of my case. She instructed them to read through, organize, and summarize the contents of my file, and read Layli's hearing brief and all the attachments. She also had them research any asylum cases dealing with FGM. Karen also instructed them to find an expert who had studied my specific culture and tribes, someone with unassailable credentials. Once they prepared my affidavit, they could show it to the expert and ask him to submit a sworn affidavit verifying that everything I was saying about what had happened to me and what would happen to me if I were sent home was consistent with what he knew about how things worked in my culture and tribes. The purpose of preparing these two affidavits, mine and the expert's, was to demonstrate to the BIA that Ferlise had been wrong in finding me 'not credible.'

What did I do during those days? I waited. I prayed. I tried to keep my hopes up, but it wasn't easy. After nine months in prison, I felt very beaten down.

Oche finally had her hearing during this period. After endless delays and postponements, she had her day in court. She'd been so certain of winning. She had the best lawyer in the world. Her case was political. She was going to win. She was so sure she wouldn't be coming back to prison after her hearing that we said our goodbyes the evening before. I was happy for her. I'd be losing her, but she'd be free, and that's what really mattered. She promised to write and give me her new address as soon as she got out.

But she didn't get out. She came back just the way I had. Her lawyer hadn't even shown up. Her wonderful, sensitive, world's best lawyer hadn't bothered to attend her hearing. She'd sent some sort of assistant instead. Oche said the woman hardly asked her any questions. All Oche could do was sit in the witness box, terrified, while the judge asked her question after question.

Asylum denied. Oche cried and raged and cursed after she came back from her hearing. She cursed her lawyer. She cursed the judge. She cursed the INS. Then she did the same thing I'd done. She filled out a slip to see the INS counselor. She was fed up, disgusted. She wanted to quit, to go home.

'No, Oche, you can't,' I told her over and over. 'You have to appeal.' Our positions were now reversed, and she was as stubborn and willful as I had been. She waited to be called, just as Alma and I had waited. And during that time I worked on her, just as she had worked on me. Finally she came to her senses, as I had, and decided to appeal.

On October 26, Karen received notice from the INS District Counsel's Office in Philadelphia, which was the INS trial attorneys' office for my jurisdiction, that the INS wasn't going to bother filing an appeals brief in my case. As Karen later explained to me, when an asylum ruling is appealed to the BIA, both sides are given an opportunity to file a brief to try to persuade the BIA judges to their point of view. An asylum seeker like myself has to prove that she is entitled to protection as a refuge. Since the judge had already ruled against me in the most damaging way – finding that I wasn't even credible – the INS assumed it didn't need to expend much effort in fighting my case. It could sit back and ignore what it considered to be a hopeless or unimportant case, and issue a statement like the very minimal one the INS district counsel sent regarding my appeal, which simply said that the INS believed that 'the decision of the immigration judge correctly states the facts and the law of the case.' The clinic, of course, was intending to file a brief. As my attorneys, they had to bring forth all the evidence and arguments to convince the Board of Immigration Appeals to reverse Judge Ferlise's finding that I was not entitled to political asylum.

Meanwhile, as October slid by, day after day, day after endless, identical, miserable prison day, there continued to be no response to my request for parole. District Director Blackman was taking his time.

When the transcript of my hearing finally arrived, on October 30, along with a November 22 deadline for submitting my appeals brief – less than a month away! – everything kicked into very high gear. Karen read the transcript. It was even worse than she'd expected. There was, first of all, the dismal quality of the transcript itself. There were 160 places where words, passages, and whole sentences were transcribed as 'indiscernible,' most of them when I was speaking. My testimony was essentially lost. Nothing unusual about that, Karen told me later. Hearing transcripts were often bad, but that could be used to our advantage. The clinic could argue that the transcript had so many gaps in it that the BIA couldn't rely on it as any kind of evidence that I was not credible.

Then Karen looked at what had actually gone on during the hearing. What Karen felt, and what she hoped the BIA would conclude, was that there had

551

been problems with my legal representation: Eric Bowman had not properly mentored Layli in what to do in her first hearing; Layli was not experienced enough to get on the record everything that was necessary; and I myself had been under-prepared for the grueling experience of an asylum hearing.

After reading through the transcript, Karen immediately gave Denise and Nileema two new assignments. Assignment Number One: Get to work on preparing a sworn affidavit in which I told my entire story clearly and consistently. They would have to interview me – beginning with an in-person interview, and then following up either in person or by telephone. The interviews were essential. Karen wanted a totally exhaustive, absolutely accurate affidavit based on as many interviews as necessary to produce it. The affidavit would need to be reviewed, corrected, sworn to, and signed by me.

Assignment Number Two: Start researching how to submit new evidence to the BIA. It would be difficult but not impossible to get the BIA to agree to accept and review these affidavits. As Richard Boswell had explained to Layli, the BIA judges usually review only what's already on record and make their ruling based on that. But they have the jurisdictional authority to accept new evidence if they choose to do so. Karen wanted them to because the existing evidence was so inadequate. And she was hoping that if the BIA did accept the new evidence, the facts would speak so strongly for me that the BIA would not bother to send the case back to Ferlise for another hearing, but would decide it themselves. Although it was standard procedure to send the case back to the original judge, Karen didn't want that to happen, because if Blackman refused my request for parole, it would mean I would have to remain in detention while Ferlise reviewed the case. Karen felt that the wait would be devastating for me.

All of this was to be completed in just a few weeks, on top of all their other commitments. Denise was also working twenty hours a week as a Dean's fellow assistant to a professor, like Layli, and working at another job on top of that to pay her way through law school. Nileema was in a joint-degree program, like Layli, and was also then preparing for her wedding, a huge, elaborate affair to take place back in India over Christmas break. But neither protested. They were thrilled to be working on my case. They got down to work immediately, and they simply gave up sleeping in the weeks that followed. Karen, realizing how difficult it was going to be for everyone to do the work involved in preparing the appeals brief on time, put in a request for an extension. They were eventually granted the extension to December 7, but there was still a huge amount of work for everyone to do in a very short time.

Karen instructed Denise to start researching the possibility of arguing ineffective assistance of counsel. Denise called Rahuf the same day the transcript arrived, to introduce herself and do some poking around about Eric Bowman, too. She asked about his fees, and the payments. Rahuf reported that Bowman had told him to forget about paying the rest of what he still owed him for handling my case. Rahuf had paid enough, Bowman said, and now the case was in some-one else's hands. Very few lawyers would have done that, I think, and the gesture points to Eric Bowman's fundamental decency. Denise did as she was told and looked into whether they could make a case that there had been ineffective assistance of counsel. In the end my lawyers did not argue 'ineffectiveness of counsel,' but in her appeals brief Karen did point out what she considered to be Bowman's deficiencies. The brief asserted that Bowman had not given Layli enough training to conduct my hearing and he had not come to her aid effectively during the hearing. Also, the asylum application, which Bowman allowed to be submitted in my own imperfect English, did not provide sufficient information regarding my claim. He did not accompany my asylum application with an affidavit setting out in detail the facts of my case. Karen felt that it was important that she address these issues on appeal. That was going to hurt Bowman, and when I heard about it later I'd feel bad about it. But Karen felt that she had an ethical obligation to pursue this.

I spoke by phone with Denise for the first time within a day or two of the arrival of the hearing transcript. Layli arranged that first link-up by calling me care of the prison counselor, Fay Parker, who sometimes allowed prisoners to make and receive calls on the phone in her office, although the prison charged for the outgoing calls. When I called Layli back from the counselor's phone, she said a few words to me and then put Denise on the line. Layli later described this as her stepping-back moment. Ever since taking my case to the clinic, she had always known this moment would have to come. When it did, it was a hard one – harder even than she'd anticipated.

During that get-acquainted call with Denise, and a subsequent one with both Denise and Nileema, I was given their home phone numbers and told to call collect, any time I needed to talk. I called often, both because we needed the time to review everything for the affidavit they were working on and because I wanted the company.

One thing that happened during this period that really meant a lot to me was that I was finally given a prayer book. Layli had been trying to send me a Qur'an ever since I'd mentioned I didn't have one. She sent it twice and twice it came back to her. The third time it somehow got directed to the prison library. The prison chaplain told me I could borrow it if I wanted to – borrow my own Qur'an! The chaplain wasn't Muslim. He didn't seem to understand how important it was to me to have a Qur'an. But I found out through a refugee from Yugoslavia, who was the only other Muslim in my pod, that there was a Muslim counselor I could see. Even though he was really there just for the male inmates she'd been able to meet with him, and he'd given her a Qur'an. I put through a request to see him too. May Allah bless him, he responded to my request quickly. We met and talked in a small meeting room up on my floor. I told him I had no Qur'an, no *mayahfi*, no *tasbih*. Within a day or two, the chaplain came to see me with a package from the Muslim counselor. I cried when I saw what he'd sent. There was a prayer book for newcomers to Islam, a lovely *tasbih* made of pale green beads, and a *mayahfi* that was one of the prettiest I'd ever seen. I could pray properly now, show proper respect to Allah. I'd been using a towel and bedsheet for five months. I'd begged Allah's forgiveness every time I prayed. Had I offended Him by not worshiping properly? Was that why He hadn't heard my prayers? I could pray properly now. Maybe now He would answer my prayers.

Denise and Nileema came to visit me in early November so that we could work together, in person, on my affidavit. Although I was looking forward to meeting them, I was also depressed and apprehensive.

I was going to have to talk about everything all over again, all the pain, all the loss, and all kinds of very personal and intimate things having to do with the cutting of genitals. Again, again, again.

We met in the usual place, one of the small interview rooms off the big, crowded, noisy main visiting room. I arrived first. After a few minutes in came two young women – tall, blond, beautiful Denise, and smaller, darker, equally lovely Nileema – both clearly nervous at being in a prison for the first time. I was sitting curled in on myself hugging myself when they arrived. Nileema later said I looked like a lost little girl. 'Fauziya? Hi.' I broke down crying right away. I didn't mean to. I couldn't help it. I couldn't take any more. I had to get out.

That's why they were there, they reassured me. To try to get me out. We got down to work right away. It was up to them to produce an affidavit that clarified everything, addressed every single gap in my story, every single seeming contradiction or inconsistency in my testimony, every single point that had made no sense to Ferlise or that Ferlise had misheard or misinterpreted or misunderstood or simply not believed. I cried a lot as we worked, having to relive the painful facts of my family history and of what had happened to me since leaving home. We worked for hours until the loudspeaker system crackled 'Feeding time!' and the guard told them they'd have to leave. Denise and Nileema were shocked. Feeding time! That's what they called mealtime? Denise told me later that all she could think about during the long drive back from the prison was my parole request. I didn't belong in such a place. Surely Blackman would grant me parole.

He didn't. In a letter dated November 15, Philadelphia District Director J. Scott Blackman sent the clinic a letter saying 'Upon careful consideration, I have determined that Ms Kasinga will remain detained pending completion of exclusion proceedings in her case.' He cited codes stating that applicants for admission to the United States 'not clearly and beyond a doubt' entitled entry were required by law to be detained. He cited other codes stating that applicants who arrive 'with false documents or no documents' may be considered for parole only 'for emergent reasons' – that is to say, if I were very, very sick – or for 'reasons strictly in the public interest.' I didn't meet these requirements. Negative health consequences from exposure to smoke? He didn't buy it. 'INS is already aware of Ms Kasinga's sensitivity to smoke. As soon as that sensitivity became known to INS, Ms Kasinga was immediately transferred to Lehigh County Prison, a smoke-free facility.' What a misreading of the facts that was! After weeks of complaining about the smoke in my pod, I was transferred to Lehigh, but only because I was supposed to have a hearing that day, not because of my sensitivity to smoke. Blackman had further determined that though I might not present a security risk if paroled, not being a known dangerous criminal of any kind, '[s]he clearly presents a risk to abscond.' I'd lived in Germany for two months, purchased a false passport, used it to come to America. He found these facts to be 'evidence of both an inclination and ability to disregard lawful process.' He cited Ferlise's damning credibility finding. The parole request said if released, I would live with my cousin, but the letter had contained 'no evidence corroborating that relationship.' But even assuming 'the claimed relationship exists,' that was no guarantee I wouldn't split and run. I'd 'already abandoned other similar and stronger ties' in my 'journey to the United States.' As for my youth, whatever that might count for was 'outweighed by the adverse factors stated above,' including my 'protracted solo travels en route to the United States.' There was 'no information or argument in your letter upon which I could conclude that Ms Kasinga's continued detention is not in the public interest. The rule of law is mandatory detention. The exception is parole. The factors which you cite . . . are simply insufficient to support the exception over the rule.' Accordingly, 'your request for parole is denied.'

Nileema phoned me with the bad news. She tried to soften the blow. They were committed to getting me released, she said, and were not going to give up. But this was a blow that couldn't be softened. I started spiraling down, down, down into blackness. Again. I wrote a letter to my mother and sister. I let everything spill out. No more holding back anything. I was in America. Oh, yes. Did they want to know about my life in America? I was in prison! Prison! I'd been in prison since the day I landed! Four horrible, terrible prisons over the course of almost eleven months now. Did they want to know what prison was like? This is what prison was like: I'd been caught in a prison riot. I'd been locked up in a maximum-security smoking pod with an inmate who scared me for weeks! I'd been locked up alone in a cell for weeks! I'd lost thirty pounds! I'd been denied asylum after a hearing that turned out to be more of a nightmare. *This was my life in America!* I was in hell! I wouldn't wish this hell on anybody! Not even my worst enemy! Not even my aunt! And to make matters worse, I had not received a letter from anyone in my family since I was in Esmor. Didn't they care about me anymore? Had they completely forgotten about me? Why didn't they write to me? I was going to die!

The Fauziya Team fought on.

The deadline for the brief to the BIA was quickly approaching. Recognizing that Denise and Nileema were overwhelmed by the amount of work required in such a short time, Karen realized she would have to write the brief herself. Denise and Nileema continued to work on the attachments, including my affidavit. I was talking to Denise and Nileema just about every night during that period – talking so much, in fact, that Nileema ran up a $700 phone bill, which she paid herself.

After going down an incredible number of dead ends, Denise and Nileema found an expert on my culture. Merrick Posnansky was Professor Emeritus of History and Anthropology at the University of California, Los Angeles, and he'd done all kinds of work in Africa over the past thirty years. He'd lived in Ghana, right next door to Togo, from 1967 through 1976, and had first visited Togo in 1967. From 1979 on, his work and research focused mainly on Togo and Benin. He'd worked with the Togolese ministry of education, run exchange programs, chaired conferences in Togo, published a newsletter on Togo, was responsible for UCLA having one of the most extensive collections on Togo in the country. He'd visited Togo some sixteen times in the past five years, five times for a month or more, had done all kinds of studies on Togo, visited all parts of Togo including Tchamba and Kpalimé, met and interacted with people from all kinds of tribes, including the Tchamba-Koussountu people living both in northern Togo and in Kpalimé, written papers on Togo. He knew my country. He knew my culture. He knew my tribes. He knew my home. He knew I was telling the truth!

Karen worked virtually around the clock to finish

my brief. It was submitted on December 7, accompanied by the affidavits from both me and Merrick Posnansky. Posnansky's affidavit explained that FGM is 'a very common practice' among members of my ethnic group. It's a very painful procedure with 'very serious health related side-effects.' Young people in my culture are 'given very little liberty and do not have much say in what happens to them.' He could 'personally understand' my 'well-founded fear of female mutilation.' My father's wealth would have enabled him to defy tradition. His community and siblings probably would have resented this deeply. Polygamous marriages are very common in my ethnic group. Marriages are arranged. Mothers have little say. Young women have none. Even without the bride's consent, the marriage is legal. Tradition would allow my father's family to take over after he died. My story about my mother being evicted from our home 'conforms with Tchamba tradition.' It's also 'highly probable' that I'd been taught to show great deference to my father's family and would therefore refrain from questioning my aunt's authority. My mother would have been 'afraid to contact her daughter at the family house.' I couldn't have asked people of other tribes to help me. I probably had little contact with them and 'certainly could not receive help from them.' It's 'extremely difficult' in West Africa for a young woman to leave her ethnic group and very difficult for her to live on her own. Had I tried to live on my own in Ghana, I probably would have drifted into prostitution just to survive. My husband could easily locate me in Ghana. 'The border between Ghana and Togo is very porous.' No passport is needed to cross it. My husband could easily have found me anywhere in Togo, Ghana, or Benin because I am a member of a small ethnic group. Police can be bribed. He was 'certain' that the police in Togo would not protect me. If I were sent home, 'it is very unlikely that the present political structure would be able to protect Ms Kasinga from future persecution caused by female genital mutilation and a forced polygamous marriage.' In sum: 'As I have made clear, it is my opinion that Ms Fauziya Kasinga's assertions are both true and credible.'

The appeals brief itself presented a series of powerful arguments on my behalf. The brief would argue that I was being persecuted on account of my membership in 'a particular social group.' The courts are often reluctant to grant refugee status on the basis of social groups, fearing that their rulings will be interpreted to provide protection to large classes of people – in other words, they fear the floodgates. With this in mind, Karen wanted to define my social group in a way that was no broader than what was necessary to describe my situation. She defined it as 'young women of the Tchamba-Koussountu tribe who resist these practices, but have no protection against them.'

Karen then took on, one by one, every single point Ferlise either didn't understand or didn't believe about my story, including his skepticism about how I met Rudina and Charlie. Maybe my story 'does not comport with the judge's notion of how the world is, but one should be careful not to rely upon so-called "common sense" assumptions. Common sense is "culturally determined and thus not universal." . . . There are kind and generous people in all parts of the world.' In a country like Germany, 'two Africans on a train would certainly notice each other, and it would not be remarkable if they decided to chat.' In finding me not credible, Ferlise 'relied upon nonexistent inconsistencies, and made incorrect assumptions about cultural norms in Togo' – assumptions that Professor Posnansky's affidavit 'directly rebuts.'

Karen also attacked the quality of the hearing transcript, quoting some of the passages where key parts of my testimony are rendered as 'indiscernible.' She then reminded the board of some of its own past rulings emphasizing 'the importance of having an accurate and clear record when credibility is at issue,' and of a ruling by the United States Court of Appeals for the Second Circuit that when a record is as defective as mine was, 'the applicant's procedural and substantive rights have been violated.'

After attacking Ferlise's reasons for denying me asylum, Karen presented the arguments in favor. I had established the existence of 'a clear threat' to my 'life or freedom on account of my membership in a particular social group,' and the facts suggested that if I returned to Togo, there was a 'more than fifty percent probability' that I'd be subjected to this threat 'through the infliction of FGM, and the requirement of living in a forced [and polygamous] marriage' – the latter a deprivation of 'fundamental civil and human rights.'

Conclusion: Ferlise's decision was 'legally erroneous' and against the weight of evidence. The BIA should 'exercise de novo review,' consider the new evidence submitted with this brief, and 'grant the requested relief.' Karen also requested 'the opportunity to appear before the board to present oral argument.' Most attorneys request oral argument, but the board permits oral argument in only a limited number of cases. Karen felt it was particularly important that she be able to do so; the brief was strong, but in Karen's experience presenting arguments before BIA and federal court judges was very helpful to her clients because then she would be able to address the judges' specific doubts or questions.

Jessica and Surita received copies of the brief and the affidavits and used them to solicit media interest. It worked. On Sunday, December 10, 1995, my name appeared in print for the very first time in an article in *The New York Times*. The article, written by Barbara Crossette, one of Equality Now's media contacts, featured a picture of Mimi Ramsey and described the origins of her anti-FGM campaign. Two years earlier, she explained, she'd attended a birthday party where she'd seen a little girl, only a year and a half old, huddled in a corner, and found out from the girl's mother that the poor child had just been cut. In America! 'I was enraged!' Mimi said. The article also discussed various bills and laws to ban the procedure in the United States, and two recent rulings on whether FGM qualified as a basis for asylum, one of which said yes, the other, no. And there I was, right after the paragraph about the asylum rulings. 'Fauziya Kasinga, 18, who fled last year from an impending operation in Togo, is now in prison in Pennsylvania, appealing a deportation order after a judge ruled that her asylum request was not credible.' One sentence in *The New York Times*. The publicity campaign had begun.

The following Sunday, December 17, 1995, was the anniversary of my arrival in America. I'd been in prison now for one full year. I spent my one-year anniversary on cleaning detail, mopping hallways, scrubbing toilets in the guards' bathroom.

The next week was Christmas. I sent Christmas cards to various people who cared about me, including one to Merrick Posnansky thanking him for his affidavit, and I received a number of cards too. But I heard nothing from my mother or sister. I hadn't heard from them now in more than six months.

One day the guards came into my cell and took my TV. They told me that they had to remove it because I hadn't paid for it. Hadn't paid for it? But the money was supposed to have been taken from my account, which had enough to cover it! Well, some record or other said I hadn't paid for it – a clerical error. Too bad for me. No more TV. Not long after that, a guard walked up to me holding a Walkman radio she'd found in my cell. At Lehigh the guards could go into your cell and search through your things anytime they wanted. 'Where'd you get this?' she demanded. I told her a friend, Tina, had given it to me. She'd bought the Walkman from the commissary and left it behind for me as a gift when she was released. Unh-unh, the guard said. Passing along purchased items was against the rules. Inmates are allowed to possess and use only items they'd purchased themselves and it was Tina's ID number on the Walkman, not mine. I was fined forty-eight hours of unpaid cleaning work for having broken the rules. I began paying down my fine, hour by hour, day by day, washing walls in the cell pod, washing down the stairwell with a rag, on my hands and knees.

The next week was New Year's Day, my nineteenth birthday – my second birthday in prison. I received no birthday cards from anyone. There were none from my family, none from my legal team, not even one from Layli. I called Layli at home and cried and cried. You didn't send me a birthday card! You forgot my birthday! Layli felt so bad, she didn't know how to respond, but Roshan overheard what was going on and took over. 'Let me talk to her,' I heard him say in the background, and then he sang me the most beautiful Happy Birthday I had ever heard. Since Roshan used to be in a band, he can really sing. I was so moved, so touched. It was a wonderful birthday present he gave me.

When the new school semester started in early January 1996, I found out I had a new pair of lawyers at the clinic. Denise and Nileema never stopped supporting me emotionally, being there for me, talking to me, but the legal work they had been doing would now be handled by my new student lawyers, Sidney Lebowitz and David Shaffer. Since Karen had assigned my case to them just before Christmas break, they had spent their vacation reading through my file, familiarizing themselves with my case, getting up to speed on everything fast. No time to waste. They immediately started preparing the groundwork for filing the writ of habeas corpus. Karen had begun to consider filing an appeal with the federal district court, in the form of a writ of habeas corpus, arguing that Blackman had abused his discretionary powers in denying me parole ever since December. That's what a writ of habeas corpus is – a suit maintaining that someone is being held in prison illegally. Karen was going to get me out of prison one way or the other. But she was hoping she wouldn't have to file the writ. Parole decisions are discretionary, and it is always difficult to win an appeal from a decision that is discretionary. Karen was not altogether hopeful that the higher court would overturn Blackman's decision, so she wanted to find an alternative method for getting me out of prison.

Since November, Equality Now had been working with Pat Schroeder's office collecting signatures from members of Congress for a petition to Janet Reno asking that I be released on parole. Karen told David and Sidney to get involved with the petition. They could

565

use it as an attachment to the writ.

Meanwhile, Jessica and Surita continued to solicit media interest. They felt that I needed media exposure, and plenty of it. Perhaps the right kind of negative exposure might create enough of a problem for the higher-ups at the Justice Department and the INS, people like Janet Reno and Doris Meissner, that they'd be scrambling to release me.

Jessica came to visit me at Lehigh the following week. She brought a camera, took a few snapshots of me, and had me write notes to three newspaper reporters – Judy Mann of *The Washington Post*, A. M. Rosenthal of *The New York Times*, and Ellen Goodman of *The Boston Globe*. I didn't want to write the notes at first. I didn't want publicity, but Jessica reasoned with me. Yes, publicity was a total invasion of privacy, but I wanted to get out of prison, didn't I?

Yes, yes, yes, more than anything. Then I needed publicity, Jessica explained. People needed to know what the INS was doing to me. People paid attention to what these reporters wrote. If they wrote about me, it could help get me out of prison.

I wrote the notes.

On Friday, January 19, 1996, Judy Mann wrote a column about me entitled 'When Judges Fail.' She devoted her entire column to telling the facts of my story, drawing those facts from my appeals brief. She ended the column with this paragraph: 'A request for humanitarian release for Kasinga was denied on Nov. 15. She turned 19 on Jan. 1, having spent a year among criminals in a jail. At the very least, she should be released while her appeal is being considered. This is a plucky young woman who has shown a lot of courage. She's the kind of person we should want to protect, not further persecute.'

The phone started ringing at the clinic the same day Judy Mann's column appeared. That one column brought in more than one hundred telephone calls, many from reporters, many others from ordinary citizens who felt moved to call after reading about how the INS was treating me. Everyone at the clinic was ecstatic over the public response to Judy Mann's column. It showed that people really cared.

At that point, I did not know anything about the first outpouring of public interest in me. I was in prison, becoming more and more hopeless and depressed. Ramadan had started on Sunday, January 21, 1996 – my second Ramadan in prison. Back home in Togo, the whole community would be celebrating together, fasting together, praying together, breaking fast together, watching for the moon together. Oh how I missed my home.

I called Mimi collect, bawling on the phone. I can't take it anymore, I told her. I can't. I want to go home. No, she said. 'You can't, Fauziya. You have to be strong. You have to have patience. You're going to be a hero to African women.' Jessica had said something like that during her last visit. 'You're the first,' she said. 'It's hardest for you. But if you win, Fauziya, it's going to be easier on every woman who comes after you.' I didn't care. I didn't want to be a hero. I didn't care about helping other women. I just wanted to get out of prison. I wanted to go home.

And then one morning I thought my wish was going to come true. A guard came to my cell carrying big plastic bags. 'Pack your things,' she said. 'You're leaving.'

Leaving! Oh God! Thank You, God! Thank You! I laughed, I shouted, I whooped with excitement. I didn't know where I was going. I didn't care! I was so happy to be leaving Lehigh! Anyplace would be better than this place. Anyplace!

Once again I was wrong.

It turned out I wasn't the only one leaving. All the immigrants were being shipped out of Lehigh. Oche and I and six other female immigrants were taken down to book-in, handcuffed in pairs, and loaded into a prison van. We were going back to York, though we didn't know that. This was only two weeks before February 7, 1996, the day the petition went out to Janet Reno. Twenty-six members of the U.S. Congress, starting with Patricia Schroeder, who'd been in my corner from the beginning, would be interested enough in my case to sign a petition urging Reno to 'ensure' my release and 'take appropriate action' to brief immigration judges on 'the devastating practice of FGM and the circumstances that would justify a claim for political asylum.'

But on that late January day when I was told I was leaving, I was still just a piece of cargo, to be hauled from one place to another at the whim of the INS.

29

Desperation

I went back to York with seven other women, including Oche and Siu Sing. We were transported handcuffed in pairs. We were strip-searched again, told to shower, and then sprayed with disinfectant again. We were all put in maximum. Again.

Oche, another woman, and I were all put in A pod, a smoking pod. Once again I was in a maximum-security smoking pod with an inmate who smoked. I called Denise that same day. 'I'm in smoking! They put me back in smoking!' Blackman had written in his letter denying parole that the INS was fully aware of my sensitivity to smoke. And they'd put me where? Karen got on the phone right away, calling and calling – until they moved me. I was moved to B pod, another maximum-security pod but a nonsmoking pod, two days later. That same day three other women from my group, including Oche, were moved to minimum.

By then I'd found out from Officer Geena, who liked to gossip, that Sylvie had returned from her hearing, and she was back in minimum with Esther. Sylvie and Esther! I wanted to be with them so much! We hadn't been within touching distance, hadn't even been in the same room since we'd sat huddled together in the gym at Esmor the night of the riot. Please, I said in a written request to the counselor.

Please move me. When I saw her later in the hall, she smiled. She was nice. Guess what she said? I'll put you on the list.

I stayed where I was, assigned to an upper bunk in an upper-tier cell with a black American inmate who'd been convicted of murder. She told me she'd caught her boyfriend, the father of her children, with another woman and had shot the woman in a fit of jealousy, then felt so bad about it that she'd turned herself in. She told me this one night as we lay in our bunks. 'Men,' she said. 'Don't ever trust a man. Men are dogs.' Then she asked if she could tell me something else. Sure, I said. She fumbled for words, suddenly shy. Uh-oh, I thought. Here we go again. Yep. She told me she loved me and wanted to be my lover. It didn't shock me. I was getting used to it. I assessed the situation. She'd killed someone but she didn't have a gun in prison and she was smaller than me and not at all threatening. I was becoming prison-savvy. I could handle this.

'Look,' I said. 'I don't love women that way. I love you like a friend. We can be friends but that's all.'

She became very embarrassed and backtracked immediately. 'Oh, no! Me too! That's what I meant! You misunderstood me!' I hadn't misunderstood her. She'd been very specific. But I let her pretend. 'Me too!' she said. 'I love you like a friend.' Good, I said. Then we could be friends. That was that. She was shy with me after that, thank God. No hostility, no harassment. She was transferred out about a week later and I got a new roommate, a refugee this time – Sheila from Yugoslavia. Sheila was Muslim like me, but she didn't pray and she didn't observe Ramadan. I prayed and fasted alone.

There were other refugees in the pod. Ellen from Ghana was there. I'd known her at Esmor. Another woman named Sharon from Nigeria was there too. I hadn't met her before. She was shorter than me, incredibly strong, loud, boisterous, and very funny. We became friends right away. Thank Allah for these two women. They were both so kind to me. I was out of money again, couldn't even buy toothpaste. I didn't tell Rahuf. I just couldn't. He had already given me so much. I survived on Ellen's and Sharon's generosity. It was OK. It wouldn't be for long, I thought. Please, God. Not for long.

I had given up again. Rooming with a murderer, being assigned initially to a smoking pod again, stuck in maximum security again – it was more than I could bear. Soon after arriving at York, I'd written two notes to the prison counselor, telling her to have the INS to come and get me. I'd called Rahuf and told him to tell Bowman the same thing. But I didn't tell my new legal team. I knew how hard they were fighting to free me. I didn't want to hurt or insult them.

I began preparing to leave. I made a final round of calls. I called Mimi and told her I wanted to go home. No, don't do it, she said. Hold on. 'You haven't seen America. Prison isn't America. America is a good country. The American people are good people.' Bye, Mimi, I said silently. I called Frank. I hadn't been able to call him from Lehigh and he was so happy to hear from me. 'Hey, Fauz!' I tried to sound cheerful, for his sake. 'Hey, Frank!' 'I still have your Qur'an and your *tasbih*, Fauz,' he said. 'I'm taking good care of them until I can give them to you.' Goodbye, Frank. 'You stay in touch with me now, OK?' I promised I would. I would if I could. I didn't tell him I was leaving. I knew how much that would upset him. But I didn't want to leave without speaking to him again. I said goodbye, without saying goodbye.

I wrote a note to Sylvie in minimum, telling her what I'd decided to do. She wrote me a very angry note back. 'Are you crazy! Are you out of your mind! You can't go back!' The note hurt me. Sylvie had never been harsh with me before. I wrote again, asking her to please not be angry, please try to understand. No, she couldn't. She wouldn't. We wrote back and forth. But I was just too miserable to give in to Sylvie's attempts to make me stay. My chest was hurting again. The stabbing pains had returned worse than ever. I was starting to have terrible heartburn. My stomach hurt when I ate. I'd asked twice to see a doctor. I hadn't seen one yet.

I made a round of calls to some of the many wonderful people who were fighting to free me – Layli, Denise, Nileema, Surita. Layli told me that she and Karen and David, one of the two new law students assigned to my case, would be coming to visit me on February 10. Layli would later remember that I didn't sound very excited about this visit, which worried her. Was I losing hope? Losing faith? I was, but I didn't want her to know.

'Hang in there,' everyone kept telling me as I made these calls. 'Keep your spirits up. We're working hard, making progress. Everything's going to be fine.' I stopped calling people then. I didn't want to hear it anymore. I'd heard it long enough.

I'd been in prison eight months when Layli had first promised to stay with me and fight for me. I'd told her then that I wasn't going to stay in prison another eight months. That had been in August, the day of my hearing. It was February now, almost six months later, and almost five months since I'd signed the papers transferring my case to the clinic. *And I was still in prison!* I'd given up. I was going home.

I had wanted to be gone by the time of my legal team's visit. But I wasn't. I was praying in my cell that afternoon when I heard my name called over the loudspeaker.

They were here.

The guard led me out of my cell pod into a small, barren visiting room. The door slammed behind me. Layli was going to walk through that door any minute. I hadn't seen her since she'd come to visit me at Lehigh more than four months ago, but I had no pleasure in thinking about her visit, because I was going to have to tell her something she would hate hearing. Dread made the time pass slowly, slowly. As I sat there waiting I began to notice my own appearance – how the shirt of my blue uniform was half unbuttoned and hanging out of my pants, how I was slumped down in my seat. Once I had taken great pride in my appearance. Now I didn't care. Nothing mattered anymore.

When at last Layli arrived, there were two people behind her. But I didn't really see them. All I saw was Layli, and when I looked at her, I saw her expression change from happy anticipation to shock. Yes, Layli. Look at me, look at what's become of me. This is what four more months in prison have done to me. Look at me! No, don't look at me! Oh, God.

Layli came over and hugged me then, and I burst into tears. Karen and David disappeared. It must have been clear to everyone that I was falling apart, that I needed some time alone with Layli.

Through my sobs, I blurted out what I had to say. 'I'm sorry, Layli. I'm sorry. I know you're trying to help me. I know how hard everyone is working to help me.

573

But you've been working since September and nothing has changed, and I can't stay here anymore. I can't. I'll never forget you, Layli. When I go home, I'll tell everyone what you tried to do for me. But I want you to forget me. I want you to stop working. You can't free me. It isn't your fault. Nobody can free me. So I'm going home. I've already put a request through. I'm going to tell the INS to send me home.'

Layli did just what I knew she'd do. She tried to talk me out of it. Not right away. She let me cry first. I cried and ranted and raged. 'Look at me, Layli! Look at me! I don't even know who I am anymore!' I was becoming coarse and rough and unkempt. This wasn't me! I felt like I was turning into some kind of animal and I couldn't stop it from happening. I couldn't do anything except watch it happen! I had to get out before I went crazy or died.

Layli stayed strong. She had to. She let me cry and rant and rage until I was spent. Then she pulled up a chair and sat very close to me, facing me, knees touching, and started talking to me very softly.

'I understand, Fauziya,' she said.

I exploded again. 'No you don't! Nobody does! You don't know what I'm going through! You can't!'

Layli bowed her head. 'You're right,' she said softly. 'I don't know.' She looked up. 'But I know this. You haven't been broken, Fauziya. You've gotten stronger.'

'Stronger!' I almost laughed in her face. 'Are you crazy? Are you blind? Look at me!'

She stayed calm. 'I am looking at you, Fauziya. Look at yourself. Listen to yourself. You're angry.'

'Yes, I'm angry!'

'Yes, you are. You're very angry. That's what I mean. I've never seen you angry before. I've seen you cry, but I've never seen you get angry. That's a good sign,

Fauziya. Anger is a sign of strength. You haven't been broken. You've gotten stronger. God is making you stronger.'

I didn't want to hear it. 'No He isn't! He's making me suffer!'

She didn't argue. She couldn't. She pulled her chair even closer, spoke even more softly. 'Fauziya, do you know the story of my name?'

I groaned and rolled my eyes. I knew what was coming. Yes, I knew the story – the story of Layli and Manjun. I'd seen a movie version of it in Togo. In the story, Manjun loved Layli, loved her and lost her and began searching for her. He searched everywhere, but he couldn't find her. His heart was breaking but he didn't give up his search. Then some bad men started hunting him. He believed they wanted to kill him. He tried to hide from them but he couldn't. They spotted him and started chasing him. He tried to flee. They pursued him. He ran and ran until he came to a wall. They had him surrounded. They were going to kill him! He tried to climb the wall. It was very high and difficult to climb. He wasn't going to make it! They were closing in. He cried out to God. Why was God doing this to him! Why was God making him suffer this way! God had taken away his beloved. And now God was going to let these men kill him! With a last burst of strength, he heaved himself up and over the wall just as they were about to get him. He fell down the other side, into a garden. And there was Layli.

God's purpose. That's what the story was about. Manjun had thought God was punishing him but in fact God was leading him to his beloved. God was making me suffer, yes, Layli said. I didn't know why. She didn't know why. 'But there must be a reason,

Fauziya,' she said. 'We have to trust. We have to have faith.'

I argued. 'I do have faith, Layli. But you don't know for sure that God wants me to stay here. Nobody can know what God wants.' Maybe He wanted me to go back, I said, just like He'd wanted Manjun to go over that wall. 'Maybe that's what God wants.'

'Maybe,' she said. 'Or maybe not. We don't know. You're right. We can't know what God wants. But what about your father, Fauziya? Think about your father. What would he want?'

Yaya. That got me, more than anything else she'd said. Layli wasn't being fair. She knew what my father would want me to do. I didn't answer.

She asked again. 'What would he want, Fauziya? What would your father want?'

He wouldn't want me to go back. Going back was a betrayal of everything he'd believed in, everything my mother believed in, everything they'd taught me to believe in. I sighed. 'He'd want me to stay,' I admitted. 'He'd want me to fight.'

Layli nodded. She didn't say anything. She didn't have to. She knew. If anything could get me to change my mind, that was it. But it couldn't. Not even that. Not anymore. I shook my head no. 'I'm sorry, Layli,' I said. 'I can't. Five months! And nothing has happened.'

'That's not true, Fauziya,' she said softly. I was still in prison, yes. That was true, and that was awful. It was an outrage. 'But things are happening,' she said. 'They are.' She'd let Karen tell me, if I felt up to talking to Karen, that is. Karen and David were outside. How did I feel? Did I want to meet them?

I sighed again. I was feeling calmer now. They'd come all this way. It had been kind of them to come.

'Yes, it's OK,' I said. 'Yes, I want to meet them.'

'OK. I'll go get them. I'll be right back.'

Layli left the room. 'Fauziya's decided to go back,' she told Karen as soon as she got to her. 'She's already put through a request.' Karen was extremely concerned. The INS wasn't supposed to send an immigrant with an appeal pending back without clearance from the attorney. That put her mind to rest a little, but not completely. You couldn't be sure with the INS. The INS made mistakes sometimes. But that wasn't her main worry. Her main worry was for me.

Layli came back in the room with Karen and David. David is a white man, tall, very good-looking, with dark hair and dancing eyes and the nicest, friendliest manner. He was a third-year law student, like Layli. I found out later he'd quit his paying job when he'd been accepted into the clinic so he could devote more time to his clinic work, that's how dedicated he was. And Karen. So this was Karen Musalo. She wasn't at all what I'd expected. I'd heard so many times from everyone what a good teacher and lawyer she was, how committed, how smart. I'd expected somebody very hard and formal and strict, somebody dressed in a suit and carrying a briefcase. That's not Karen. She was dressed very casually, the way she always dresses when visiting clients. When she introduced herself there was such warmth in her voice. She just radiated warmth and energy and caring. I felt comfortable with her immediately. Everyone pulled up chairs. Layli sat next to me. Karen and David sat across from me.

Karen didn't start talking about my case right away. That could wait. She reached out to me first. She pulled her chair close, leaned forward, folded her hands in her lap, and gazed into my eyes. She didn't speak immediately. She let me search her eyes.

Then she spoke. 'I'm sorry we haven't been able to get you out yet. What's it like for you here?' she asked gently. 'What are you going through? Tell me.'

She meant it. I knew it. There was something in her eyes, something about the way she asked the question that told me I didn't have to be polite with her, didn't have to hold back with her the way I always did when I talked with everyone else – Denise, Nileema, Layli, Surita, Mimi. Everyone always asked how I was doing, but something always told me I couldn't really tell them. They asked, but they didn't really know what they were asking. I almost felt I had to protect them. But I didn't have to protect Karen. I could tell her the truth.

And I did. I don't remember much about what I told her, I just remember that I told her a lot, and the whole time she listened calmly, intently, completely focused on me. Her eyes never left mine. She took it all in. Then she asked me if I needed anything. Yes, I said. I needed everything. Toothpaste, underwear, soap, everything. But they couldn't send me anything because I was in maximum. People in maximum weren't allowed to receive packages. They had to get me out of maximum!

'OK,' Karen said. 'We'll get working on that immediately. What about the commissary? Does the prison have a commissary?'

'Yes.'

'Do you have money to buy things?' she asked me point-blank.

'Not much.'

Layli told me later that she felt ashamed then. She'd never even thought to ask me that. She didn't know enough about what prison was like to know to ask.

'OK,' Karen said. That was one thing they could do something about immediately. They'd put some money in my account before they left. 'What else?' she asked. 'What else can we do for you?'

'Find my luggage,' I said. It was supposed to have been transferred to York after the Esmor riot. That was eight months ago now. It hadn't shown up. Everything I'd brought with me from Togo and Germany was in my luggage. The necklace and earrings my grandmother had bought for me in Mecca, my wedding jewelry, my clothes, everything. Everything was lost.

'OK,' Karen said. 'We'll track it down. What else?'

'Get me out of maximum,' I said again.

'We will. What else?'

'Get me out of prison!'

'We're working on that, Fauziya.' She went on to tell me she'd been a refugee-advocate attorney for thirteen years and had never once had a client sent home. Never once. She wanted me to give them a little more time. Things were happening.

'But when am I getting out? And don't tell me soon. I hate that word. I don't want to hear "soon." I want to hear "now." Or when!'

I told her that I was going to ask the INS to send me back. So, we started bargaining. I forget where the bargaining began. I think Karen asked me to give them two months before I sent a request to the INS. No, I said. Two weeks. I'd give them two weeks. No, a month, she said. One month. One more month. They were really close to making things better for me.

'How close?' I asked. I was being a tough bargainer. Karen got into the spirit of it. She held up her right hand, folded the last three fingers into a fist, extended her thumb and forefinger and measured about an inch of vertical space between them.

'This close,' she said, smiling. 'One month, Fauziya, that's all I'm asking. Just give us one month and things will change.' If things didn't change, I could send INS a request to send me back home, and they wouldn't try to stop me. Karen was taking a risk, but it was a calculated risk. She really did feel hopeful, really did think there was a good chance I'd be out in a month. Things were happening, she said. They were working on getting me publicity. Oh, yes, that. I knew about that. And I didn't like it, not at all.

I'd seen my name in the article about Mimi by then. I'd seen Judy Mann's column too. A whole column about me! But I wasn't thrilled about seeing my name in the paper. Strangers knowing and talking about my personal business. Everything about it felt strange and wrong. People guard their privacy where I come from. Modesty is a virtue where I come from, in women especially, but in men too. My father had been a very modest man. Proud but modest. He'd never sought recognition. He'd never even liked it when people had come to our house to thank him for his charity. It had always embarrassed him, and he'd always hated being talked about. So do I. Being the center of attention goes against all the values my parents modeled and taught me. It goes against my nature, my religion, my culture. I didn't want to have anything to do with it.

But everyone on my legal team wanted me to. Publicity, or 'media exposure,' was the reason Karen was feeling so hopeful. After the Judy Mann column appeared, print and even television reporters began calling to ask about me. When Karen saw what kind of response they were getting on my case, she decided to see how much use she could get out of it, how much bargaining leverage it might give her with the INS, which would surely be eager to avoid the kind of public relations fiasco that was now brewing. She placed an exploratory call to a colleague and friend who was working in the INS General Counsel's Office.

'Did you see Judy Mann's column?' she asked. Yes, he said, he and several other lawyers in the General Counsel's Office had seen it and there was some concern. She explained that the clinic was planning to file a writ of habeas corpus to get me out of detention, but that they would prefer to avoid litigation if they could. Did he think David Martin, the general counsel of the INS, would be open to a conversation about my parole? Yes, he did think so.

That was Karen's cue to call Martin. If he was receptive, my chances of parole might be very good, because the General Counsel's Office works closely with the district directors. If the General Counsel's Office agreed that parole was in order, they could recommend to Blackman that he reconsider his original decision. Karen called and left a detailed message about why she wanted to speak to David Martin, and got a call back within a day or so from the associate general counsel in charge of refugee and asylum law, who was calling at the behest of the general counsel. During a long talk, Karen filled him in on all the facts of my case. FGM. Request for asylum. Asylum denied. Adverse credibility ruling. Appeal. Detention. Parole request. Parole denied. Writ of habeas corpus suit if necessary. Hoped it wouldn't be necessary. Calling to see if the General Counsel's Office would be willing to step in, weigh in on the issue, get the word to Blackman that the General Counsel's Office would look favorably on his reconsidering his refusal to grant parole.

The associate general counsel seemed concerned,

receptive, cooperative. Concerned about Ferlise's denial of asylum, concerned about his credibility ruling, concerned about Blackman's denial of parole, concerned about everything, Karen would maintain later. He asked her to send over a copy of her appeals brief to the BIA, and of the parole request and Blackman's denial. He'd take a look at them, get right back to her, see what could be done.

Great! As Karen then reported to the others on my legal team, she'd just had a very encouraging conversation with someone in the General Counsel's Office. A man named Bo Cooper.

'Bo!' Layli said. 'I know Bo!'

'Oh, really?' Karen said. What a coincidence.

Another thing had happened after the Judy Mann column appeared. On January 25, the BIA directed the INS to file a response to Karen's appeals brief. My case would now require special handling. First the INS asked for and received additional time to file a brief. Then when the INS brief was submitted, Karen would discover that David Martin, the general counsel himself, had been directly involved in writing it.

This fact, of course, was not yet known to me on that early February day when the Fauziya Team showed up to visit me, but Karen had plenty of other reasons for optimism. Even if the General Counsel's Office decided not to put pressure on Blackman, the congressional petition that had gone out to Attorney General Reno just a few days before, on top of all the press interest in me, might help persuade him. Karen was feeling very positive and confident indeed. Lots of things were happening. The signs were good. That's why she felt justified in asking me for another month.

A month. Another month in prison.

'Two weeks,' I said.

'A month,' she said. She needed a month, begged for a month. One month, that's all. Just a month.

'OK,' I said. 'One month.'

Deal. Karen held out her hand. 'In the United States, when we make a promise, we sometimes shake hands on it,' she said. 'Can I shake your hand?' It seemed to mean so much to her, and I liked it that she'd asked. I extended my hand and we shook. My handshake was soft, an African handshake. Hers was firm – an American handshake – and warm, like her. She reached out and took my other hand and held both hands firmly. 'A double handshake means a double commitment,' she said with a warm smile. I smiled too.

It was getting late. We'd been talking for hours. Karen, Layli and David had a long drive ahead of them back to D.C. It was time for them to leave. 'I'm coming back,' Karen said, still holding my hands. 'I'll be back in two weeks. From now on I'll try to visit every other week, OK?' I smiled, nodded. OK. We said our goodbyes. I shook David's hand shyly. Layli and I hugged. I held her close. 'One month,' Karen said again as they headed out the door. I nodded. One month. She smiled again. And then they were gone.

They stopped at the front desk on their way out, emptied their wallets, and left something like a hundred dollars to be deposited immediately into my prison account. Then they walked out the door, out of prison, got into Layli's car and started the long drive back to D.C. It was dark by then.

Layli told me later that they drove a good part of the way with the lights on inside the car, mapping out the new emergency Fauziya Plan. Not the legal plan – the emotional-rescue plan. Layli was deeply distressed. She was shocked and frightened by my condition. I'd reached my breaking point. That was painfully clear to everyone, Layli most of all. Clearly the first order of business was to do something to lift my spirits and restore my hope. They drove back talking, planning, discussing strategies. Karen took charge. David took notes. Layli talked and drove.

They mapped out a four-point plan. One: From now on, someone would call me every day. They dubbed that part of the strategy the 'call-a-day' plan. Layli and David would check with everyone, assign days. A guard at York had agreed that if my legal team needed to speak to me, they could call the prison's central control number and ask that I be brought to the phone for attorney-client communications. Two: They'd get me out of maximum. Sidney would take charge of that. Three: They'd track down my luggage. David would take charge of that. Four: Karen would come visit me every other week. Anyone else who wanted to commit to visiting was welcome to do so too.

A month I'd given them. That's what they thought. I hadn't really. I'd lied. I couldn't stay in prison another month. I couldn't. I sat in the visitors' room alone again for a few moments after they left, thinking over our meeting, crying. Forgive me, Layli. I'm sorry. I'd held her long and close when we'd parted. Saying goodbye without saying goodbye. Bye, Layli. God bless you. Then I walked down the long hallway toward the rear of the prison, toward maximum, away from the front desk, away from the entrance Karen, Layli and David had walked out a few minutes before. Out. Out of prison. Out into freedom. That's where I wanted to go too. Even if it meant returning to Togo. They'd stopped at the front desk on their way out. I made a stop on my way back to my cell pod too.

I stopped at the table in the hallway where the request forms were kept. I filled out another request to see the prison counselor. My third. 'Tell the INS to come get me. I want to go home now. NOW!'

30

Crisis

The call-a-day campaign was kicked off immediately. Layli called the very next day, Sunday. Karen, Denise, Nileema, David, even Sidney, whom I had not yet met – they all signed on to the campaign. So I talked with them, too, in the days that followed, in addition to Surita and Jessica. It did lift my spirits to get calls every day. But I knew what everyone was up to. They were trying to keep me busy, connected, distracted, so I wouldn't think about giving up and going back to Togo. I appreciated the effort, but the ploy didn't work. I remained determined to go home.

That first week I was allowed to take the calls on the hallway phone the prison officers used. But soon the guards started getting ornery because I was getting too many calls. They started to take a long time to call me to the phone. Then they refused to call me to the phone but agreed to take messages so that I could call back. But I had to use the regular prison phone in the cell pod, not the hallway phone. Eventually they 'forgot' to deliver my messages. This didn't all happen right away, but over time it became very difficult to communicate with my legal team. Sidney tried to find out exactly what the prison's official phone policy was. She spoke to all kinds of people, asking politely to see any written policy on phone calls, and got a different story, different response from everyone she talked to. I could have spared her all the effort. I could have told her what the phone policy was – not the official policy, but the real policy. It was whatever the prison decided it was on any given day for any given inmate or immigrant.

Sidney got the same run-around when she tried to find out how to get me transferred from maximum to minimum. She started making calls about that first thing Monday. She called the INS officer at York Prison first. He told her he had no say in where the prison put people. That's their decision. She called the prison counselor, Amy Jefferson, who transferred her to someone else, who said all kinds of contradictory things: there was no waiting list to move immigrants to minimum; people were moved to minimum on a space-available basis; no immigrants were ever put in minimum. I stayed in maximum.

I did two telephone interviews with reporters sometime around then. I didn't want to, but Karen and everyone else on my legal team kept urging me to. They said it could help me get out of prison. But in my mind there was only one way to get out of prison – and that was to go home. But I did the phone interviews anyway, mainly to make Karen and everyone else happy. Sidney arranged my first interview with Maimona Mills of *Voice of America*, which is broadcast all over the world, including Togo. Maimona asked me if I knew that. Yes, I said. We used to listen to *Voice of America* on our home radio. So I understood that people back home might hear this interview? Yes, I understood that. And I was still willing to talk to her? Yes, because FGM is wrong, I said. It has to stop. People have to know about it. If people don't know about it, they can't stop it. She thanked me for agreeing to talk to her. She said she'd pray for me. I appreciated that. She sounded like she really cared. The second interview was with a free-lance reporter named Linda Burstyn. She was so sympathetic and she seemed so angry for me. I was beginning to understand what Mimi had said. No, prison wasn't America. The American people were good people.

Meanwhile, Layli, Sidney, and David were all working on various aspects of a preliminary draft of the writ of habeas corpus suit, just in case the clinic decided to go that route. David began looking into arguments they could make that the INS was holding me illegally, that Blackman had 'abused his discretionary powers' in denying me parole, and that the INS and York were just generally abusing and mistreating me and violating my basic human rights. One angle he was pursuing had originally been raised by Bo Cooper, of all people. Much earlier in the case Bo had asked Layli whether I'd ever had something called an APSO program interview. APSO stands for asylum pre-screening officer. It turns out that the INS had instituted something called the Parole Project in 1992, mandating that aliens like me who arrive in America without proper papers be interviewed by one of these officers, in order to determine who really deserves to be held in detention and who qualifies for parole. The interviews were supposed to be conducted at several major ports of entry, including Newark International Airport, and at selected INS detention facilities – like Esmor. I, of course, had been at both. When Bo asked her about it, she hadn't known what an APSO program interview was, but now that the clinic was considering a suit, David wanted to find out whether I had had one. No, he discovered, I hadn't. They could make that an issue in the suit.

Sidney and Layli were also trying to hunt down a good psychologist or psychiatrist. In case it did come down to suing, Karen wanted to get an expert who could attest to the extreme mental stress I'd been under during my imprisonment.

Karen kept her promise and came back to see me again two weeks later, on February 24. I don't remember much about that visit. I was extremely depressed by then, and getting sicker by the day. Karen remembers that this was when I first talked to her about the stabbing pains in my chest.

To me it seemed that nobody was making any progress on anything. David still had not been able to track down my luggage. I suggested to him that maybe he should enquire about it under the name and number on the passport I'd been carrying when I arrived in America. He said he'd give that a try. Despite her repeated efforts, Sidney was still unable to get me transferred to minimum. Everyone was working so hard, and nothing was happening. The rest of the month of February passed with not a single good thing happening, as far as I could tell. Meanwhile, I kept getting sicker and sicker. I wrote out a request to see a doctor on Monday, February 26. *I have pain in my chest anytime I took a deep breath*, I wrote. *I feel it whenever I touch* – I meant 'cough' – *and my back ache real bad please I need to see the doctor. Thank you very much.* I didn't see a doctor, but I did see a nurse. She diagnosed me as suffering from 'anxiety' resulting from my environment. She told me to put through another request to see the doctor if the pains persisted. The pains did persist, so I put through another request the next day. *I have a very serious heartburn and my heart hurt like is being stuck by niddles. Please I want to be examine to know what's wrong with me. I need a doctor. Thanks a lot.* I saw the same nurse again. I told her I was having 'burning in my heart,' and that I was having trouble eating because of the pain and discomfort. She still didn't think there was anything really wrong with me, but she said she'd recommend that I see the doctor. I went back to my cell pod. Waiting. Waiting to see the doctor. Waiting to be called to see the INS officer. Waiting, waiting, waiting, as always.

And then finally God granted a blessing. Sidney's efforts finally paid off. I was transferred to minimum! I'd given up on that ever happening and resigned myself to staying in maximum until I went home, or died, whichever came first. I'd even begun worrying that maybe my lawyers' efforts to get me transferred would backfire. I had a lot of advocates fighting for me, pestering the prison about me. The prison didn't like it. That was becoming clearer and clearer. Surita told me that someone at the prison had told her that if I didn't like where I was and if everyone didn't basically get off the prison's back about transferring me, they'd send me back to Lehigh, how would I like that? That really scared me. They could do it. They could do anything they wanted with me, send me wherever they wanted. They'd proved that often enough. So when my name was called over the loudspeaker one day toward the end of February, I got frightened. They were going to send me back to Lehigh! But they didn't. They moved me to minimum! Oh, God, thank You! Thank You!

Of course, they assigned me to an upper bunk, which worried me because I'd fallen out of an upper bunk at Lehigh. But I was with my friends again: Oche, Esther, and Sylvie. Sylvie shouted with joy when she saw me. All my other friends crowded around as Sylvie

590

and I clung to each other, hugging and crying. 'Oh my baby, oh my sweetheart,' she crooned, holding me and rocking me and stroking my hair. I was sick by then, really sick. My stomach was hurting me so much, I could barely eat anymore. But it was OK. Sylvie was there. Sylvie would take care of me until the INS sent me home.

From the day I was transferred, all of my many friends tried to keep me from going back to Togo. But I was determined. I was too sick, too tired. Nobody could change my mind.

But one day I was in the bathroom standing at one of the sinks. One of my friends, who was taking a shower, called me over to her stall. She'd pulled aside the shower curtain and propped herself against the back wall of the shower stall, under the spray of water. It was so odd, so strange. Why was she showing herself to me naked? It made no sense. She was leaning against the back wall of the stall, under the shower spray, squatting slightly, braced there with legs spread apart, hands on her thighs, smiling this sad, loving, tender smile as water streamed down her body. What was she—

'Look,' she said gently.

Look? I was looking. Look where?

'Look here. I want you to see this.' She patted her thighs. My gaze moved down from her face and breasts to where she was indicating. She spread her legs wider apart. 'Here,' she said. 'Look here.'

I looked. I screamed. I covered my face with my hands and ran from the sight toward the far end of the bathroom, where I burst out sobbing.

My friend called me back, gently, lovingly, firmly. 'You have to look. You have to know. Come on. Please. You have to.'

I was crying, trembling, shaking. I hugged myself, and slowly, slowly, slowly forced myself to return. I stood in front of the shower stall again, head down, holding myself, refusing to look. I just couldn't.

'Fauziya. You have to look. Have you ever seen it? Have you ever seen what they do?'

I couldn't speak. I shook my head, tears streaming from my eyes.

'Then you have to look. Because you've been acting very stupidly lately with all this talk about going back. You don't know what you're going back to. Look. This is what you're going back to.'

There was nothing there. Nothing. She had no genitals. Just smooth flesh with a long scar running vertically between her legs where her genitals should have been. And a hole. A gaping hole where the urine and blood would pass through. She kept her legs spread apart, talked to me very calmly and soothingly, very matter-of-factly. 'You see? They cut me and then they sewed me up like this.' She looked at me with such love in her eyes. 'Fauziya,' she said. 'Do you want this to happen to you?'

I shook my head, unable to speak.

'You can't go back, Fauziya,' she said softly. 'Do you understand that now?'

I nodded, crying. 'Yes,' I said softly.

She nodded. 'Good. OK. OK, let me finish my shower now. We'll talk later.' She closed the curtain and went back to her shower.

We did talk later. She remembered everything, she told me. The whole horrible thing. She'd had children. She'd been cut and resewn before and after every birth. That's why she so desperately wanted to stay in America. If she went back to Africa, her daughters would be cut too. She wanted to protect them. 'You have to stay here too,' she said to me. 'You know that now, don't you?'

Yes. I knew. To this day, I am overwhelmed by this woman's courage, her strength. Out of respect for her, I won't reveal her name, but I will never forget what she did for me that day in the shower. It was an act of love that saved my life. She brought me back to my senses when nobody else could.

But for what purpose? To live in prison? To die in prison? To be denied asylum on appeal and be sent back to Togo anyway?

Still, there were some good moments, even in that dark period. One day I was in the small common room when a woman I knew from the Ivory Coast called me over. 'This is your sister,' she said, introducing me to a short, dark-skinned woman around my age with dark hair, a round, sweet face and big dark eyes. 'She's from your country.'

Someone from Togo? '*Efuan.*' I asked her how she was in Ewe.

'*Eh mifon,*' she answered. She spoke Ewe! That was an incredible comfort. And her name was Aicha. I screamed with excitement when I heard it. Her name sounded just like my sister's. We hugged each other for joy. She told me why she was seeking asylum. Her story was so terrible, it made me sad again. Her life was in jeopardy. She'd come to America seeking shelter, thinking America would take her in. It had, the same way it had taken me in. Into prison.

Hang in there, my many wonderful advocates kept telling me. 'Your month is running out,' I'd say. I kept reminding them. A month. I gave you a month. Time was running out. For me, too. I was having so much difficulty eating by then that I was skipping meals altogether.

February ended on a mixed note for the clinic. In the middle of the month, Karen spoke to the BIA about the hearing date. Not only did the BIA approve Karen's request for oral argument but the case would be heard 'en banc,' meaning that the entire twelve-member board (rather than the usual three board members) were going to hear arguments for my appeal. This showed that the board recognized that the issues involved with my case were important. It was also a good sign that the decision they made would be designated as precedent. What Layli had speculated about so long ago was actually coming true: my case was going to govern the decision-making in future cases like mine.

On February 28, Karen received the INS's response brief, in which General Counsel David Martin presented the arguments he would be making at my BIA hearing. The hearing was now scheduled for April 10, more than a month away. There was some hopeful stuff in the brief. Martin acknowledged up-front that FGM could qualify as a valid basis for asylum. Karen and Layli and everyone else at the clinic were very pleased about that. The INS could have disputed that point and made Karen argue it on appeal. But it didn't. As Karen put it later, David Martin had 'repudiated' half of Ferlise's ruling right there. On the negative side, Martin seized on the fact that Ferlise had found me 'not credible.' He argued that the affidavits Karen had submitted to the BIA to counter that finding – mine and Professor Posnansky's – were 'new evidence' and that it wasn't the BIA's job to consider new evidence. It was the immigration judge's job. If Karen wanted this new evidence to be factored into a credibility ruling, the only appropriate course of action was to send my case back to Ferlise and let him 'examine the evidence and determine credibility.'

Karen didn't have the final word yet, when the INS response brief arrived, on whether her efforts to arrange my release on parole were going to succeed or fail. Everything had been put on hold because Philadelphia district director J. Scott Blackman was out of the office during the week of February 19–26. But she had a feeling she knew what was coming. She gave David, Sidney, and Layli the signal: Get going full speed ahead on the writ of habeas corpus.

The next weeks were madness for everyone, including me. I continued getting sicker and sicker and still couldn't get in to see a doctor. My stomach hurt horribly. I could hardly eat at all. I was beginning to have serious dizzy spells. All my advocates knew I was sick by then. I'd complained to everyone. Karen had put Sidney to work trying to get copies of my medical records from the prison. She got the usual runaround. Sidney was talking to people at the prison about other things, too, trying to pry information out of them, memos, documents, handbooks, manuals, anything she could get in writing about prison policies, anything they could use to bolster their argument in the writ that I was being abused and mistreated, either in ways that other immigrants weren't or in ways that all immigrants were. More runaround. She finally drafted a memo describing prison policies as best she was able to understand them and sent it off to someone in authority at the prison, I'm not sure who, asking him to please review it and correct any misunderstandings on her part. She never got a response. Sidney was also working with me on another affidavit documenting my experiences in detention.

Meanwhile, Sidney stepped up her search for a

psychologist who could evaluate my emotional/ psychological state. I needed someone good, and I needed someone fast, but the first four or five people she called were all too busy. Layli turned to the Bahá'í community for help. She was referred to a Bijan Etemad, M.D., chairman and medical director of the Department of Psychiatry at Mt Sinai Hospital in Philadelphia. She called him on a Friday at the beginning of March. 'You want me to go see her?' he asked. Oh, yes, please, would he? He responded instantly: 'How's this Sunday?'

Dr Etemad came to see me on Sunday, March 3. When Layli told me he was coming, I fell apart. A psychiatrist? Why was a psychiatrist coming to talk to me? Did she think I was crazy? Was I? I cried and cried. Oh, God. Layli thought I was crazy! 'No, no, no, Fauziya,' she said. 'Nobody thinks you're crazy. But you're upset and angry and depressed because you're in prison. We need to have an expert say that. He's going to write an affidavit we can use to help get you out, that's all.' That's what she said. But I didn't believe her.

They thought I was crazy! That had to be it! People don't talk to psychiatrists and psychologists where I come from. Not unless they're seriously crazy.

When I met Dr Etemad that Sunday, I looked him straight in the eye and said, 'Please. You have to tell me. Do you think I'm crazy?' No, he said, he didn't think I was crazy. But I was upset, and I was right to be upset. He was there to talk to me, he said, so he could tell the court how much I was suffering in prison. That's all. He asked me to tell him my story, the whole thing, starting with my life in Togo. I did. I cried a lot. Cried, fell silent, talked, cried. He was so nice, so patient, so gentle. He let me cry. He listened carefully to everything I said, and asked me a lot of questions.

We talked for two hours. I asked him again at the end of our talk: Was I crazy? No, he said. But I was very sad, very angry, and very depressed. That's what he was going to say in his affidavit. And then he reached out to me personally, like a caring father. He had a daughter about my age, he said. She was in college. He said I reminded him of his daughter, and asked me if I needed anything. There was something, I told him. I had a check from Surita for $150, and I asked him if he could cash it. No he couldn't, he said, he didn't have enough cash, and since it was Sunday, the banks were closed. He gave me the money he had on him instead, $50 in cash. He just emptied his wallet and handed over everything that was in it. Before he left he also gave me his telephone number and told me to call him anytime.

David worked with him on his affidavit. It was completed within two days of Dr Etemad's visit. I wasn't crazy, but I was 'extremely depressed.' I 'portrayed a sense of hopelessness and helplessness.' I saw him and everyone else who was trying to help me as 'pretty much "impotent,"' unable to help me or do anything for me. 'She sees no hope, and wishes to be dead.' My whole sense of myself, who I was, what I could expect for myself, what I could expect from the world, my faith in fairness and justice, all this had been shattered. 'It is my recommendation that she be removed from the prison immediately before any further damage is sustained and that she be placed in a supportive, warm and loving home atmosphere either with a friend or relative, with intensive counselling and psychotherapy to see how much of the damage can be repaired,' he wrote. 'It is also my opinion that any further delay in her urgent release will increase the severity of her depression, reducing her coping ability drastically and may even lead her to attempt suicide.'

Sidney came to visit me the very next day, Monday, March 4, to work on the affidavit about the prison experiences that had reduced me to this desperate, despairing, near suicidal state. It was our first meeting in person, and her first visit to a prison. I spotted her before she spotted me. She came into the common room, a small, slender, pretty young blond woman in pink shirt and black skirt. I went over and introduced myself to her. I'd spoken to her so often by then that I didn't feel nervous about meeting her. But I felt nervous about what we had to talk about. All the worst stuff – everything I'd been through in prison. I'd have to relive it all over again. I told her at one point I didn't want to talk anymore. It was too painful. She understood, she said. We could stop if I wanted. She could come back and see me again to finish. 'No,' I said. 'Don't say that. I don't want you to come back and see me again here.' Not here! 'I want to come see you! Somewhere else. Not in prison.'

In the middle of the interview I was called away to see a doctor. Only I didn't see a doctor. I saw a nurse. I still hadn't seen a doctor. The prison would later claim that I'd missed two scheduled doctor's appointments by then, one on March 1 and another on March 2, that for some reason I hadn't shown up. Huh? You don't just go see a doctor or not go see a doctor in prison. You get called and you go. But except for that day, when I ended up seeing a nurse, who didn't do anything for me, I was never called.

Karen heard from Bo Cooper the next day, on Tuesday, March 5. Sorry, Blackman says he will not reconsider his decision. No parole. Now the push was on to get the writ done and filed as soon as humanly possible. Karen wanted me out, and she wanted no time wasted in getting me out.

Spring break was coming up at school then. Layli and Roshan had planned a week of much needed vacation around a medical conference Roshan was attending in Florida, but Layli cut it back to a few days so she could help complete the draft of the writ. There was much work to be done: reviewing and compiling the numerous attachments and drafting the writ itself. David's research on the APSO program came in handy, as did Sidney's extensive work on my prison affidavit. Karen reviewed the draft over and over, and over and over again until she was satisfied.

And in the midst of that incredible push, Karen still kept her promise to come visit me every other week. She came again, for her third visit, on Sunday, March 10. This was our last chance to review my affidavit that Sidney had prepared about the horrible conditions in detention. The writ was finally filed with the United States District Court for the Middle District of Pennsylvania three days later, on Wednesday, March 13. It was the result of weeks of marathon effort by Karen, Layli, David, Sidney, and now Richard Boswell. As Karen's closest companion and consultant, Richard had always been on the team, really. But now he'd begun taking a more active role because he had many years of expertise in federal court actions such as writs of habeas corpus. J. Scott Blackman; York Prison as well as Thomas Hogan, the warden of York; INS commissioner Doris Meissner; and Attorney General Janet Reno herself – all were named in the suit. I was being held in detention illegally, the writ said. I'd never had an APSO program screening. I qualified for parole, and Blackman abused his discretion in denying me parole. I'd been in detention for more than a year and had been abused during my time in detention, including being beaten and teargassed during a riot. See my prison affidavit. I was depressed, almost suicidal. See Dr Etemad's affidavit. The General Counsel's Office was sympathetic to our request that Fauziya be released – so sympathetic, in fact, that they agreed to ask Blackman to 'reconsider' his denial of parole. See Karen's affidavit. The prison kept changing its phone policies, making it harder and harder for my attorneys to speak with me. See Karen's affidavit. Equality Now was willing to post bond for me, give me a place to live, do whatever they needed to do to get me out of prison. See Surita Sandosham's affidavit. And so forth and so on.

Four days after the writ was filed, on Sunday, March 17, another article about me was published in *The Washington Post*, the biggest one yet. It was written by Linda Burstyn, the journalist who'd interviewed me by phone when I'd been in maximum. It was the first article to be published by a journalist who'd actually spoken with me, and she quoted me extensively. 'I keep asking the Lord, what did I do to deserve this? I can't believe this is happening.' Yes. I had said that. I did ask myself that every day. Why was this happening to me? Burstyn told my whole story, in detail, and she made no bones about being on my side. Later someone would describe this to me as 'advocacy journalism.' She ended the article with this paragraph: 'In the case of Fauzia [*sic*] Kasinga, there is no way to right what has already gone wrong. There is no way to determine the extent of the damage that has been done to her psyche and spirit, first by her own insensitive culture and then by ours. Kasinga should be released from prison, and she and other women like her – women who might become victims of what has been called the most harmful custom routinely practiced on earth – should be protected, not further brutalized, by the United States. Our government cannot protect the millions of women who are circumcised every year, but it can help this one woman. It can finally change her fate.'

The momentum of events kept escalating during those days, in good ways and bad. Calls poured into the clinic in support of me. When Equality Now got word that Karen's talks with the General Counsel's Office had failed in securing my release, they sent out a 'Women's Action' about my case, asking all their members, contacts and supporters worldwide to write letters to Attorney General Janet Reno and INS commissioner Doris Meissner calling for my release. Their letter-writing campaign got an unexpected boost from an article in the March issue of a women's magazine called *Marie Claire*, which profiled a beautiful young Somalian woman, Waris Dirie, who was a fashion model. Part of Dirie's story was about having been cut as a little girl. The article ended by asking anyone interested in 'joining the campaign to abolish FGM' to contact Equality Now. As a result, Equality Now got calls from people all over the country, each of whom was told about my case and asked to send a letter stating that the INS should free me.

Before I even knew what the word meant, I started becoming something of a celebrity. Complete strangers began writing to tell me they were rooting for me. That part I liked. I was grateful for any show of support. But that wasn't the only thing that happened. Suddenly all kinds of journalists and reporters started coming to the prison unannounced, and asking to see me. The prison had a policy that only people whose names are on an approved visiting list are allowed to visit inmates, but the rule wasn't always enforced. I got called, a lot, to see people I didn't even know, people I didn't want to talk to, people who had just taken it upon themselves to come talk to me, looking for a story, without clearing it first with Karen or Surita. I didn't like it, but it was hard for me to say no, so usually I talked to them. It was exhausting, though, especially since I was sick. And it embarrassed me because it made me a center of attention among the guards and other inmates.

The prison wasn't too keen about the publicity either. People who Karen or Surita really wanted to interview me started having trouble getting access. Denise Lang of *Day and Date*, a TV magazine show, wanted to come in with a television camera. No way, the prison said. A woman named Sheryl McCarthy from *Ms.* magazine, who I'd agreed to see, came to see me from Massachusetts, but got kicked out after thirty minutes. That was the rule – half-hour visits only, but it was haphazardly enforced. The prison started enforcing it strictly when visitors came to see me. Although I'd liked talking to Sheryl McCarthy, in general I was glad about the restriction. My advocates weren't. Sidney tried to get the prison to provide her with anything they had in writing about official policy regarding press access. Surprise, surprise: she got the runaround. She also contacted prison rights projects to get information on the range of prison policies on media access.

I finally saw a doctor on Tuesday, March 19, which was three weeks after the nurse had written on a piece of paper that I should see one. I told the doctor I had terrible heartburn, that I couldn't eat, that my belly hurt something awful. He pressed my stomach. Here. Fine. There. Fine. There. Oh, it hurt! Hmmm.

Indigestion. Acid stomach. Maybe ulcer. He prescribed some antacid medications and wrote out instructions for a blood test. A nurse called me back to the medical unit again the next day to take my blood. They didn't tell me what for.

Karen came to see me the following Sunday. She talked to me about doing more interviews. Karen felt strongly that publicity was probably our best hope, but she always made it clear that in the end I had to be the one to make the decision, and she also understood that I was very sick and under great stress. I decided that I wouldn't do any more interviews. I was too sick. I couldn't do any more. And what good did they do? Yes, people were writing to me now. I appreciated that. They were writing about me now, too. *But I was still in prison!*

After waiting almost a week to find out the results of my blood test and hearing nothing, on Wednesday, March 27, I put through another request to see the doctor because the medicine that had been prescribed wasn't helping. *I feel pain in my chest and my stomach continue to hurt me. I want to know what the result of the blood test is. Thank you very much.* I told Karen what was going on. She wrote a letter to Patricia Connally, the legal counsel for the INS on my case, expressing concern over my deteriorating health, asking for the results of my exam, and asking that I please be given another thorough exam immediately. This was one of a number of letters she wrote to Connally during that period, all of them complaining about various aspects of my incarceration.

Surita and Jessica came to visit me that Saturday, March 30. I'd never met Surita in person before. We talked on the phone all the time, but she'd never come to visit. I was so grateful that she had come all

603

that way that I tried to rouse myself, but I was so sick, I just couldn't. Jessica told me later that the whole time they were with me I sat on a metal chair in the common room doubled over, clutching my stomach, my face drawn, looking haggard and terribly, terribly depressed. She said she was really frightened for me. They stayed for a while, then told me I should go back and rest.

I headed back to my dorm to lie down. A while later when I got out of bed to go get something from my locker, I started to fall down in a faint. Thank God Officer Virginia saw what was happening and was able to catch me before I hit the floor. Oh, she was so upset for me! She helped me back to my bed and got a nurse to come check on me. The nurse took my blood pressure and said I was fine, but Virginia told me I should report what had happened to the warden. Oche wrote out a request in my name to see the warden, and two days later, on Tuesday, April 2, I was called to the counselor's office, where the deputy warden was waiting to see me. What seemed to be the problem? I was sick! I hadn't gotten the results of my blood test! I wanted to know what was wrong with me! He told me if I hadn't been given the results of the test, it meant nothing was wrong with me. That same day Karen, who'd written yet another letter to Patricia Connally when she heard what had happened to me, got a letter back from her saying that that was the day I'd be given a full physical. I wasn't.

The deputy warden told me I'd be given a full physical when an outside doctor came to the prison the following Monday, April 8. There wasn't anything I could say. I'd just have to wait until then, even though I felt that with every day things were going from bad to worse for me. On top of everything else my asthma started acting up around then and I began having trouble breathing. I spent most of my time lying on Sylvie's bunk, curled up in a ball, with Sylvie sitting next to me, holding my hand, stroking my hair, and crying.

Oh, so many things were going on then. So many things. Toward the end of March, Karen had begun talking to Celia Dugger, a reporter from *The New York Times* who was working on a story about me. Karen was talking to a lot of other people in the press, too, doing some phone interviews, fielding and sorting through requests for access to me. Besides that, she was hard at work on the oral arguments she would be presenting at my appeals hearing on April 10, and waiting for the INS to respond to the writ she'd filed. I was beginning to wonder if I was going to last long enough to make it to my hearing. My health had reached crisis state. And Sidney was still unable to get my medical records despite her best efforts. She spoke with an official at York, who assured her that he cared about his people. Assured her that there was nothing seriously wrong with me, he was confident of that.

He was wrong.

York Prison finally gave the clinic medical records on Thursday, April 4, six days before my hearing. A nurse took more blood from me that same day. I still hadn't been told the results of my first blood test. Karen, Layli, Sidney, David, everybody was very concerned about my medical condition. They passed the relevant medical records on to Roshan as soon as they got them. God had been holding Roshan in the wings. Now it was his turn to help me. Roshan is a gastro-enterologist. He looked at my records and reported symptoms. I got on the phone with him that same day. He questioned me thoroughly, had me describe my symptoms in every detail. He was the first doctor to really question me that way. He reported back to Richard that in his best professional judgment, based on what he could glean from my records and from the symptoms I described, he suspected I might be suffering from peptic ulcer disease, which, if not treated properly, could lead to serious complications such as inflammation and swelling, hemorrhaging or internal bleeding, perforation of the intestine, or gastro-intestinal obstruction. I needed to be properly diagnosed. The best way to diagnose peptic ulcer disease was through an endoscopy, which involved threading a tube with a camera down the throat and all the way down, into the intestine, where it would look for an ulcer, and a sample of the bacteria that can cause peptic ulcer disease. They had to get me diagnosed fast so I could get proper treatment. This was critical. So, on top of everything else they were dealing with, my advocates were now facing the possibility that my health might seriously deteriorate if they couldn't get me adequate medical treatment immediately.

Also around this time Celia Dugger spoke with David Martin and learned a bit of news that she thought Karen should know about, so she called Karen. You know the hearing you told me about? she asked. The one that's supposed to come up before the BIA in five days? It's been postponed due to a memorial for INS commissioner Doris Meissner's husband, who'd been in the same plane crash in Bosnia that killed Secretary of Commerce Ron Brown.

Karen was very surprised to have to learn this from Celia Dugger! Standard procedure is that if one side requests a postponement, the other side is notified of the request and allowed to voice its feelings about it before the BIA decides whether to grant it. Not only had the BIA granted the postponement without even consulting with Karen, she'd had to learn about the postponement from a reporter rather than from David Martin or the BIA. It was time for another letter – this one expressing her dismay and displeasure at how the BIA had handled things.

When I heard that my hearing had been postponed again, and no new date had been set yet, I plunged into despair. But as soon as I heard why, all my anger and anguish drained away. All I could feel was sadness for Doris Meissner. She'd lost the person she loved most in the world. I knew what that was like.

On Friday, April 5, the government's attorneys filed their response to the writ of habeas corpus. It was a long, elaborate legal document that said all kinds of things, all of which boiled down to one basic point: even if the INS and the York Prison and District Director J. Scott Blackman had done everything my attorneys were claiming they'd done, so what? My attorneys seemed to be forgetting something. I was an illegal immigrant. I was in 'exclusion proceedings.' In the eyes of the law, I'd never even entered the United States. In the eyes of the law, I basically didn't exist. The INS, Blackman, and York Prison couldn't violate my rights. I didn't have any rights to violate. That's a bit of an oversimplification. But not much of one.

And meanwhile, I was getting sicker and sicker. Two days later, on Sunday, April 7, Karen faxed another letter to Patricia Connally, telling her that on the basis of my medical records and a phone consultation with me, Dr Roshan Bashir believed I could be suffering from peptic ulcer disease and had said that in order for me to be properly diagnosed I must undergo an endoscopy. Karen wrote that my lawyers were willing to file another kind of suit if they had to, to ensure I received proper medical treatment, but she was hoping that wouldn't be necessary. It wouldn't be if the prison saw to it that I got this test.

On Monday, April 8, I was finally called to the medical unit to be examined by a visiting doctor who was a surgeon from York County Hospital. I will never, ever forget that medical examination. The doctor was gentle with me. I have no complaints about his manner toward me. But what he did! I was a nineteen-year-old Muslim virgin. I'd never ever shown the private parts of my body to any man, ever. Now, in the presence of not just one male doctor but two, because the prison doctor was there as well, I had to have a rectal examination. There are no words to explain how I felt while this was happening. And then it was over and I pulled up my pants and the doctor had me lie down on a table while he pressed down on different areas of my stomach. Here. Fine. There. Fine. There. The pain was terrible. He wrote something on a chart about acid reflux. According to Roshan, tenderness on touch is usually a sign of something more serious than mere acid reflux. The doctor prescribed more antacid medication and mentioned that I might need an 'upper GI' to determine if I might in fact have peptic ulcer. Roshan didn't feel that was the most appropriate test because an 'upper GI' might miss a peptic ulcer and would not test for the bacteria that causes ulcers. The only test that would catch that is endoscopy.

After the exam I called Karen, who was waiting to hear the results. What did the doctor say? What tests did he order? I told them. Karen got a fax that same day from Patricia Connally confirming that the doctor had ordered an 'upper GI,' and saying that the doctors who had examined me were the ones qualified to determine what care I needed and what tests should be done.

OK, time to file another suit. The Fauziya Team, which now included Dr Roshan Bashir, did another crash assignment, working on a 'temporary restraining order,' or TRO, arguing that my continued imprisonment was a serious threat to my health and possibly to my life and requesting that I be released for at least as long as it would take to be sent to a proper hospital to be properly tested and diagnosed.

Layli and Roshan tried to call me at the prison late that night to check on how I was. Horribly, horribly sick – that's how I was. But that was the day the prison decided it would no longer even take messages for me. Sorry, the guard told Layli and Roshan. No incoming calls, no messages except in emergency situations. 'Well, this is one!' Layli said. She had my 'medical expert' standing by. They needed to speak to me. Sorry. It was too late anyway. After ten P.M. It would have to wait until tomorrow. But all the pressure was apparently having some kind of effect. Sometime before the end of that same day, after the prison doctors learned of my lawyers' concerns, the doctor had changed his mind. Maybe I did need an endoscopy after all.

On Wednesday, April 10, the day my appeals hearing had originally been scheduled, syndicated newspaper columnist Ellen Goodman of *The Boston Globe* wrote a column about me. She ended the column as follows: 'This brave and traumatized young woman broke out of the prison of one culture and landed in the jails of another. It's time she got what she came for: freedom.' More calls, more letters, more support. The clinic was organizing lists of supporters. The pressure was building. I was informed the next day, Thursday, April 11, that I was scheduled for an endoscopy at York County Hospital the following Thursday, April 18. I'm not sure if Karen found out at the same time or not, but on Friday, April 12, the Fauziya Team went ahead and filed the TRO demanding that I be released from prison immediately so that I could receive necessary emergency medical care. It included an affidavit by Roshan saying that I was receiving 'incomplete' and 'substandard' and 'inadequate' therapy for my condition. Karen also argued that the prison's ever-changing phone policies were making it difficult for my lawyers and me to communicate with each other.

Friday, April 12, was also *New York Times* day. A columnist for the *Times*, none other than A. M. Rosenthal, devoted his entire column to me that day. And *Times* reporter Celia Dugger, who by then had talked to many of the people on both sides of my case, came to interview me that day. Karen had used all her powers of persuasion to get me to agree to that interview. I didn't understand the importance of the *Times*. No, I'd said when she asked initially. No more interviews. I'm too sick. I've done enough. If talking to reporters hasn't gotten me out of prison by now, then it never will. Karen told me that this was a key interview. And I'd like Celia Dugger, she said. Karen hadn't met her in person, but she'd spoken with her on the phone. She was very nice, very interested in my case, she could do me a lot of good. 'OK,' I told Karen. 'But this is the last one. The very last. No more.'

Deal.

I was so sick by then, I hardly remember the interview at all. I do remember my first impressions of Celia Dugger, though – about my height, thin, dark hair and eyes, nice-looking, very businesslike, very focused, very intelligent, very high energy, very intense. Layli, David, and Sidney all came. I made Layli sit next to me. I needed her near me for support. Celia Dugger seemed to be in a big rush. She pulled out her notepad and pen. 'OK. Fauziya.' She fired questions at me, rat-a-tat-tat, took fast notes as I answered, then cut me off when she'd heard as much as she needed for that question. She got an amazing amount of information out of me in a very short time. She knew exactly what she'd come for, she got it, and then *whoosh!* she was gone. My head spun. What a day. And it wasn't over. The next thing I knew, I was headed out to the prison yard where a *New York Times* photographer was supposed to shoot me. As soon as I went outside, I saw this guy sitting on a big motorcycle in the parking lot just outside the yard. He took my picture through the prison fence. Snap, snap, snap. And then he zoomed away. Sidney, David, and Layli sat with me for a while after that, and Layli slipped me some medicine before she left.

The weekend went by in a blur. I spent it in my bunk mainly, with Sylvie beside me, tending me. Oh, God, please, I kept begging. Please let this suffering end. I was in so much pain that I no longer cared how it ended, just that it did.

Celia Dugger's story appeared on the front page of *The New York Times* on April 15. Her article ended with these words: 'At York, the days drag on monotonously, and Ms Kasinga says she often feels despair. Sometimes, she said, she dreams she is back in Togo in her family's big house with the flowers blooming in profusion at the front porch and green fish darting in the courtyard pond. In the dream, her father is always alive. Then she wakes up on a prison pallet. "All my

611

spirit is gone," she said. "I just want to leave the prison. Why am I here?"' The story featured two photographs of me, one atop the other. There was an enlargement of just my head and shoulders, taken from my wedding photograph, which showed me all made up and decked out in my new dress and my so-called husband's jewelry, looking beautiful, looking downcast. Below that photograph was another portrait of me, taken through the chain link of the prison yard fence, hair in braids, dressed in prison-issue shirt and T-shirt, my right hand on left shoulder, prison I.D. bracelet on my left wrist, pretty much the same expression on my face.

That did it. I was famous now. Karen was right. Talking to Celia Dugger at *The New York Times* was the key. The clinic couldn't handle all the calls that came pouring in. Neither could Equality Now, which got so many they had to set up a special 800 number. Jessica told me later that 370 calls came in the first day the line was set up. People from all walks of life, all religions, all levels of society, all professions, started calling. Television producers called, newspaper and magazine writers called, radio journalists called, book publishers called, movie people called. It was incredible, everybody told me later. The calls just kept coming in. What can we do? How can we help? 'Write letters!' the Fauziya Team told everyone. Send letters, send petitions. Address them to Janet Reno and Doris Meissner. And people did. All because they were so powerfully moved by one article in one newspaper about one suffering, incarcerated female refugee. Me.

But still I remained in prison. On Tuesday, April 16, the day after Celia Dugger's article, U.S. District Judge Richard P. Conaboy issued his ruling on the TRO, the suit to have me released from prison because of my deteriorating health. Denied. The key requirement for being granted such a request, he wrote, is to present convincing evidence that 'the applicant is likely to suffer irreparable harm' before his or her case is decided if the request is not granted. I'd now been scheduled for an endoscopy at York County Hospital on Thursday, April 18. That was only two days away. Given that the test was so soon, there was insufficient proof of irreparable harm.

The same day Judge Conaboy issued his ruling, Patricia Schroeder wrote a letter to INS commissioner Doris Meissner. Let her go!

I stayed in prison, but I was a celebrity prisoner now. It seemed like there was some article about me in some newspaper almost every day after that. My friends teased me when they saw my wedding picture in *The New York Times*. Esther especially was wowed. 'This beautiful girl is you?' Letters poured in to me at prison. I couldn't believe how many letters. I'd report to Layli. 'Layli, I got three letters today. Layli, I got seven letters today. Layli, I got fifteen letters today!' Thirty letters today! Sixy-four letters today! People wrote, people sent money, T-shirts, books, treats of all kinds, photographs of their children just to cheer me. People dropped off flowers, which the guards wouldn't give to me but kept at the desk. People wrote saying they wanted to come visit me. People I didn't even know, all these good, wonderful people, wrote to me to tell me they supported me, they were rooting for me, they were outraged by the treatment I'd received, they were ashamed of their country, they wanted me freed, they wanted me to stay in America, I was the kind of person they wanted to have in this country. Such kindness, such generosity, such goodness. Mimi was right. What I'd been taught about

America, what I'd believed about the American people, the belief that had sustained me as I'd flown across the ocean more than a year ago – it was all true. The American people were good people. They believed in justice.

Yet I was still in prison!

Finally, the day I was supposed to go to the hospital, Thursday, April 18 for my endoscopy arrived. I was nervous, but Roshan had been wonderfully reassuring. There was nothing to be afraid of, he said. It wasn't going to hurt. He performed this test all the time. They'd put me to sleep and put a tube down my throat. I wouldn't feel a thing. By the time I woke up it would all be over, easy as that. I believed Roshan, but I was scared anyway. I'd never been a patient in a hospital before. The day my test was scheduled I tried to distract myself by keeping busy with my new work assignment, checking the supply room inventory. I was sick, but I still preferred working to lying on my bunk worrying about my problems. The whole time I worked I was waiting to get called. No word. When I finished in the supply room, I picked up my yarns and went to the small common room to do my crocheting. I'd done a belt and bag for Layli with some beautiful yarns her grandmother had sent me, and now I was working on a pretty lilac-colored afghan. I worked and waited, worked and waited. I was never called. A guard eventually told me that my test was canceled but she didn't know why. There was never an explanation from the prison.

Four days had now passed since Celia Dugger's article appeared. Four very busy days for the clinic. So many people were calling that my advocates had to divide up handling the calls. In addition to the average American people who called, there were calls from people who were politically influential or powerful people, people who had access to the White House, Justice Department, or Congress. Richard Boswell handled many of those calls. There were calls from the French and Swedish press. Even the BBC called. People in the entertainment world – people like Sally Field and Lauren Hutton – called the clinic, asking how they could help. People were flocking to my aid. There was talk of staging a rally at the prison.

That same day I was supposed to go to the hospital and didn't, Professor Herman Schwartz, a widely respected professor at American University who had contacts in the Justice Department, suggested that my legal team submit a renewed request, or 'petition,' for my parole directly to Attorney General Janet Reno, head of the whole Justice Department, the person who tells everyone at the INS from Doris Meissner on down what to do. Professor Schwartz was even willing to write a cover letter to someone he knew who worked in the Justice Department to make sure the request was routed directly to the attorney general.

Karen got to work on the letter immediately. It had to be perfect. It had to indicate that I would have a place to live. With Rahuf, of course. Blackman had rejected my request in part because it had included no documentation of my relationship to Rahuf. Richard called Rahuf, told him what was happening. Rahuf panicked. Of course he wanted me out. And of course he wanted to do anything he could to help me. But this – take me in to live with him, give Richard permission to include his name and details about him in the request – no, no, this he could not do. Because he had two other male roommates, you see, and there simply wasn't room and I was an innocent young Muslim woman who couldn't live in a small apartment with three men, and, and, and . . . And, well, you see, well . . .

Rahuf wasn't legal.

Layli had never really checked Rahuf's status thoroughly. Rahuf had hedged and dodged when Layli enquired about it. Now at this zero hour, the truth came out. Rahuf hadn't just spent money he didn't have to try to help me. He'd gotten involved in my immigration problems at the incredible risk of calling the INS's attention to himself. Rahuf had risked exposing himself to the INS, risked his getting found out and deported, to save me from getting deported.

My legal team had to find me another place to live. Surita had offered to take me in, but Surita was all the way up in New York City. My attorneys were all down in D.C. Then it was suggested that maybe the Bahá'ís could take me in since many of them are refugees themselves and the Bahá'ís are well known for their human rights advocacy. So while Karen wrote the petition, Layli swung into action finding me a place to live. She contacted Roshan's mother, Irma Bashir-Elahi, who chairs a Bahá'í Local Spiritual Assembly. She and her husband, Roshan's father, Dr Abbas Bashir-Elahi, decided immediately that they would take me into their home. Not only that, but Mrs Bashir-Elahi and Layli got to work immediately on getting all nine members of their Local Spiritual Assembly to agree to provide 'community support,' which is important in parole decisions, and all nine members of the National Spiritual Assembly to support such an act, which would very likely draw public attention. The decision was made overnight. Not only would I be living with the Bashir family, my parole request could also point out that I would have the support of the entire Bahá'í community.

Karen's letter to Janet Reno went in on Friday, April 19, the very day after Karen had received word that the attorney general would consider a renewed petition. Everyone waited to hear what would happen next.

I waited in prison, without knowing what was going on behind the scenes. I only knew I was still in prison, still horribly sick, that I hadn't gone to the hospital when I was supposed to, that I felt like I might die, and that I wanted to die. I talked to Karen. Hold on, Fauziya, she told me, just a little longer. Something good was going to happen very soon.

Soon. Oh, yes. That word again. Soon. But I was too sick, too weak to get angry.

On Monday, April 22, I was finally taken to the hospital – in handcuffs and chains – for my endoscopy. I was so nervous, so scared, and horribly sick by then, in pain, weak, dizzy. Once I arrived at the hospital, the chains and cuffs were taken off and I was ushered into an inner room with all kinds of strange-looking machines, handed a hospital gown, asked to change, please, lie down on the table, please. Doctors, nurses, a mask over my face . . .

I opened my eyes. David was there, standing over me, smiling. David? Oh, right. He'd said he'd be with me at the hospital. I felt so groggy and foggy and strange. Where was I? David told me that I was in the hospital, that I had finished the test and had slept for a long time afterward. The doctor came over to talk to me. They hadn't found anything, he said. Nothing was wrong with me. I was perfectly fine. What did he mean, nothing was wrong with me? I became very upset and angry. 'What are you saying? I know I'm sick. It hurts so much I can't eat! I'm sick! Tell me what's wrong!' He was cheery. 'Well, we don't see any ulcer.'

I was still too drugged, too dizzy, too confused, to argue anymore. But I knew my body. I knew he had to be wrong.

I was allowed to rest for a little while more. Then it was time to go back to prison. After David helped me up, he and the doctor left the room and a nurse helped me change back into the bright orange prison jumpsuit I'd had to put on when I went to the hospital – just in case the handcuffs and chains weren't degrading enough to have to wear in a public place. I went out into the waiting room, and the same nice male guard who had brought me there handcuffed and chained me again, apologizing as he did it. He was sorry, really, but he had to. Prison policy. I was too drugged and weak to say anything. David walked with us back down the hall, to the elevator, and when he noticed how people were staring at me, he offered me his dark sunglasses. Wonderful David.

When I got back to York I was strip-searched, which struck me as particularly absurd under the circumstances. David sat with me awhile in the common room to keep me company. Then a nice guard named Valerie helped me to my bunk, where Sylvie, Esther, Oche, and all my other dear friends gathered around me. I slept through dinner, woke up late in the afternoon. Esther and Sylvie tried to get me to eat something. They'd saved my dinner. No, I didn't want it. Esther offered me hot chocolate, she knew how much I liked it. No, I didn't want it. Sylvie insisted I at least drink some tea. She wouldn't take no for an answer. I sipped some tea, went back to sleep, and slept and slept and slept – until eleven that night, after lockdown, when somebody woke me.

Hunh? What? Officer Valerie, the same nice guard who'd helped me back to my bunk, was now standing beside it. 'Sorry, Fauziya,' she said. 'But I have to take you to B.A.U.'

What?

'Sorry. Get up. You have to go.'

B.A.U.! B.A.U. was isolation, segregation, the behavioral adjustment unit. Why? I hadn't done anything wrong! I couldn't have, I'd been sleeping all day!

Valerie reminded me that I was scheduled for another test the next morning, something called an ultrasound test. They had to make sure I didn't eat or drink any water before the test, so they were moving me to isolation.

No! I begged, I cried, I pleaded. Please! I promise I won't eat! I won't drink any water. I promise! I won't! Please! Just let me sleep here in the dorm. Don't take me to isolation! Please!

Sorry. Those were the orders.

I got up, crying. Next thing I knew I was locked up alone in a cell, a cold, barren isolation cell. Oh, God. Why were they doing this to me? I cried and cried and cried. I lay down on the thin mattress, still weak and groggy from the drugs, dizzy, hurting. I was in isolation, again.

The lights went on at seven A.M. the morning of Tuesday, April 23. Officer Geena came around and peeked into my cell. 'Good morning,' she called cheerily. 'You OK in there?' I glared at her and then I started to cry. 'No,' I said. No, I wasn't OK. Well, not to worry, she said. She'd have me out of there soon. She went away. Three hours later, she returned and unlocked the door. 'OK, let's go, let's go.' I was taken to the medical unit, told to sit on a bench. A white American inmate was already sitting there. We got to talking. She was there for a test too. The same one. But where had she spent the night? In her minimum-security dorm. She'd been told not to eat or drink any water. She'd promised she wouldn't, just like I had. But she'd been allowed to sleep in her dorm. I'd been taken to B.A.U.

When I was called in, a woman – I don't know if she was a nurse or a doctor or a technician – sat me on a table, asked me to expose my belly, rubbed jelly all over it, and then put a small hand-held metal device against my skin. She moved it around while she looked at some fuzzy images on a screen. Sound-pictures of my insides! She kept sliding the cold metal all over my belly, and asked me to tell her where it hurt. There? No. Here? No. There? Oh! Yes! There! OK. She moved it around some more. When she was finished, she told me that it would be a while before I heard anything. She didn't say how long. A guard took me back to my dorm. I went straight to my bunk, lay down on my side, curled into a ball of pain, and eventually fell asleep, with Sylvie holding my hand.

I woke up sometime late that evening, and couldn't go back to sleep. So I got up and took a shower. And then I prayed. I prayed and prayed and prayed, making up for all the prayers I'd missed in the last two days. Please, God. Please. Hear me, I beg You! Let it stop! Let it stop!

I called Karen just to let her know I was still alive. She was full of optimism. 'We're really, really close. This week. Something good is going to happen this week.'

Yeah, sure.

I couldn't sleep anymore. I went and sat in the day-room on a couch, surrounded by my friends, just being with them while they watched TV.

'What are you thinking, Fauziya?' Esther asked gently at one point. Thinking?

620

'Nothing,' I said. It was true. I hadn't been thinking. I had no thoughts, no feelings, no anything. It was like I wasn't there anymore. Didn't exist anymore. It was hard to describe, but I tried. 'I don't know,' I said. 'It's like my spirit is all gone. I feel empty.'

'Don't talk like that!' Esther said, sounding half angry, half scared.

'But it's true,' I said. 'That's how I feel.'

'You need to sleep,' Esther said.

'Yes, you need to rest,' Oche said.

'Come on, sweetie, I'm taking you back to bed,' Sylvie said. 'You shouldn't be sitting here. Let's go to bed.'

I let her lead me back to the dorm. She put me to bed. 'You sleep, now,' she said. She gave me a kiss, stroked my cheek. 'Sleep,' she said. 'You need to sleep.' She left me. Aicha came in for a while and prayed over me, reciting 'Aayatul Kursiyu,' from the last chapter of the Qur'an. Then she, too, left.

The dorm was empty and quiet. Everyone else was out watching TV. I closed my eyes. But I still couldn't sleep. I lay in my bunk, crying softly to myself, my body aching, my head hurting. So much suffering. So much loss. So much pain. I cried myself to sleep, crying and praying to God. Please, God, please. Please. Let it end. Let it end.

Let it end.

31

April 24th

When I woke up the next morning I felt much better. It was so strange – as if God had healed me overnight. Sylvie came over to check on me as I lay in bed. She bent over me, smiled tenderly, touched my cheek.

'How are you feeling?' she asked softly.

I smiled up at her, my sweet Sylvie. 'Good, Mom. I feel good.'

Grinning with relief, she helped me out of bed. 'Do you think you could eat something?'

My stomach recoiled. 'Mmmm, I don't think so, Mom.'

'Fauziya, you have to eat something. You haven't eaten for days. Come on. Just try, OK? Please? For me?'

I tried. I think I ate a piece of toast and had some tea. A mistake. As soon as the food hit my stomach, it started hurting again, same as before. I was refreshed from sleep. But I wasn't healed.

I said my prayers – the same prayer I always made now: Please, God. I beg You. Let my suffering end. Then I saw to my cleaning duties, showered, and dressed. I decided to stay in the dorm that morning, where it would be quiet. Everyone else was either outside in the yard or in the common room, so the dorm was empty. I went to my locker and got my yarns, then sat down near one of the windows that looked out over the front of the prison and the women's minimum-security yard and started to work. I liked sitting there as I crocheted, gazing out at the people and cars that passed, drinking in the green of a late April day, the green that reminded me so much of my beautiful home. My mind drifted as I crocheted. I let it float away. Fly away home.

Home. It was nothing but a memory now. A beautiful, dreamlike memory. Back in Togo, the flowers around my house would be in full bloom. I could almost smell them now. People would be returning from the pilgrimage to Mecca with gifts for their friends and families. I imagined my sisters and brothers, laughing happily together. I still hadn't heard anything from Ayisha or my mother. I'd written to them again. Nothing. Nothing. All these other wonderful people were writing to me. All these letters from strangers – and none from my family, none from home. Had they forgotten me completely? Why hadn't they written? Why?

I thought about my hearing too. It was coming up in eight days. I was so nervous, so scared. I tried not to think about it, but I couldn't help it. What if my hearing got postponed again? What if it didn't? What if I lost? What if they sent me back to Togo? All that morning after breakfast I sat by myself, crocheting, thinking, worrying, and gazing out the window. So many thoughts running through my head. I wanted it to stop! I wanted everything to stop!

Sometime just after lunch, which I skipped, as I skipped most meals those days, a Ghanaian girl named Ophelia came in to the dorm and asked me to braid her hair. 'No,' I said. 'I'm too tired. I just want to sit here and crochet.' She looked so disappointed. I had become known as the hair braider in prison. I was good at it, and it gave me pleasure to help the other women look pretty. As pretty as it's possible to look in prison.

Ophelia asked again. 'Oh, come on, Fauziya. Please? Please braid my hair? Please?'

I sighed, put down my afghan. We went into the small common room, where most of the detainees spent their time when they weren't outside. Ophelia and I settled down near the television, where I could sit on the couch and she could sit on the floor in front of me and watch a show while I worked on her hair.

At one o'clock I took a break to say my prayers again, and then went back to my braiding. The next thing I knew the loudspeaker was crackling: 'Kasinga! Come to the desk!' What was it this time? I was always being called to the front desk these days to pick up the gifts and letters that were pouring in for me from people who had read about my case in the press. 'I'll be right back,' I told Ophelia.

I went to the desk. 'You called me?'

The guard on duty was writing something on a form. Without even looking up, she lifted her pencil and pointed it somewhere over my shoulder. 'There's a gentleman here who wants to talk to you.'

A man I didn't know was standing on the visitors' side of the desk holding a small cardboard box. The guard pointed her pencil in the direction from which I'd come. 'You can talk back there.' The man nodded, walked past the desk, and accompanied me to the small common room, carrying his cardboard box. He didn't say anything to me. I didn't say anything to him. What was this about? When we entered the room, the officer on duty told everyone to leave. As soon as the room was empty, he walked over to the Ping-Pong table and put down the box. I followed, not knowing what else to do. 'I'm from the INS,' he said, very businesslike. He clicked the pen he had in his hand, as though he was about to write something. 'They sent me to talk to you. Did you have any luggage with you when you came to America?'

Luggage? This was about luggage? Maybe all of David's efforts had finally paid off. 'Yes,' I said.

'Do you remember what was in it?'

'Yes,' I said. 'I remember.'

'OK. You have to tell us so we can pay you because we can't find it. We could only find this.' He nodded toward the box.

My things? Something of mine was in the box? 'Oh, let me see!'

He opened the box.

My heart leapt. My sweater! My peach-colored sweater, the one I'd been wearing when I'd landed at Newark! The sight of it shocked me, threw me, sent me spinning back in time. It was December 17, 1994. I was standing in a huge, cold, barren room in some strange, scary, unknown place. I didn't know where I was. A big, heavy, mean-looking black woman in a uniform was standing across the room, near a heavy metal door, glaring at me.

Strip.

My sweater – the sweater Rudina had given me. 'That's my sweater,' I said.

The officer nodded. 'Good.' He pointed the click-end of his pen toward the box. 'What about the other stuff.'

I took the sweater out of the box. My jeans. I took my jeans out of the box. 'Yes, these are mine.' My socks. 'Yes.' My bra. 'Yes.' Oh. Oh, no. My throat tightened. My eyes stung with tears. My underpants. My blood-stained underpants.

Please. I'm sorry. What should I do with my pad?

Why don't you eat it!

'Yes,' I said, my voice cracking. 'Yes. This is all mine.'

'Good. OK. Wanna put it back, please?'

'But this isn't from my luggage,' I told the officer as I put everything back in the box. 'This is what I was wearing when I came.'

'OK. Then you have to tell me what was in it and give me a value so we can pay you. How much would you say in dollars?'

How much? In dollars? For what was in my luggage? Clothes, toiletries, purchasable stuff – all that was replaceable, and not worth that much. My wedding jewelry, the necklaces and bracelets, the beautiful butterfly ring – I wouldn't *want* to replace that, but it probably was worth a great deal. And the necklace and earrings my beloved grandmother Hajia Maimouna had bought for me in Mecca just before she'd died there? How much were those precious keepsakes worth in dollars? Besides the beads I was still wearing, that necklace and earring set were all I had left of her. They were worth everything to me. How could I set a price on them?

'I – I – I don't know.'

'You don't know?'

'No.'

But the officer wasn't going to give up until I gave him a dollar answer.

'Just give me an estimate,' he said. 'What. A thousand dollars?'

'I – I'm not sure.'

He seemed to think I was bargaining. 'Two thousand dollars?'

'I don't know. I'm sorry.'

The officer shifted his weight impatiently. 'Look, I need a dollar estimate. Just give me something.'

'I can't say.' Why was he pressing me so hard? 'Why do you need to know?' I asked.

'Just doing my job, ma'am.'

'But why do you have to know now?'

'Don't know, ma'am. They just told me to come and ask you.'

'I'm sorry. I can't—'

'OK, look.' He put down his pen and started closing up the box. 'When you figure it out, you let us know, OK?'

'Yes, OK. I—'

He picked up the box and left.

I stood in the empty room for a moment, trying to make sense of what had just happened. Is that what the INS always did when someone tried to track lost luggage? I'd never known that to happen before.

My friends had been waiting in the adjoining room. They came rushing back, buzzing with questions, as soon as the officer left. 'What did he want?' 'What was in the box?' 'What was that all about?'

'I'm not sure,' I said. 'He had some of my clothes in the box, what I was wearing when I came. He wanted to know what was in my luggage. He said they can't find it.'

Oche broke out in a joyous howl. 'Whaaahooo! Oh, this girl is going home!' Everyone started shouting at once. 'You're getting out, Fauziya! They're going to let you out!'

'That's it, Fauziya!' Ophelia said, grabbing my arms in excitement. She looked so funny, with her hair only half braided. 'It has to be! They looked for your luggage because they're letting you go! That's it! It is!'

Everyone was so excited. Why wasn't I excited?

Because I didn't believe it. I couldn't make myself believe I was actually going to be freed. I knew how to yearn for it, pray for it, wish for it. But believe? Truly believe I'd get out? No. I couldn't. The power to believe had wasted away during sixteen months in prison. Now, when I tried to locate it, tap it, release it, I couldn't find it. It was gone. Gone, like everything else that had been stripped from me.

'Maybe,' I said. That was the best I could do. I was so tired all of a sudden. 'Excuse me, I have to get something out of my locker,' I said, though I really didn't need anything. I just wanted to get away from all the excitement, all the excitement I didn't feel, didn't share.

Sylvie followed me out of the room to the lockers. 'See? I told you, Fauziya! I told you!' she said as we walked. Sylvie. My sweet Sylvie. She was so excited. 'Didn't I tell you you were going to get out.' Yes, she'd said it often once the cards and letters had started pouring in. I hadn't taken her seriously. 'I told you! And now you're going home.'

Going home. Prison lingo. *Going home* means being released.

I smiled. 'I hope so, Mom,' I said. 'I hope you're right.'

I distracted myself for a few minutes with something in my locker, I don't know what, and then Sylvie and I went back to the common room. Everyone had settled down again. Some women had drifted outside. Others were playing Ping-Pong, reading, talking, watching TV. I went back to braiding Ophelia's hair. Time passed. Slowly, as it does in prison. One of the women wandered over to gaze out the window that overlooks the fenced and gated parking area at the back of the prison. We did a lot of gazing out of windows in prison.

'Look at that, there's a whole bunch of people outside,' I vaguely heard her say. 'Oh, yeah?' someone else said. 'Lemme see. Oh, yeah. Hunh. Look at that.' All the women began congregating at the window, speculating among themselves about some group of people who had gathered outside. 'Who are they?' 'What do you think they want?' 'Wonder what they're doing.' 'Why're they here?' Everybody went to the window to look except Ophelia and me. I was much more interested in what I was doing than in gawking out the window, and Ophelia was perfectly content to sit there having her hair braided as she watched TV. They sounded silly, all the other women, gabbing at the window like a flock of chickens clucking over seed. So some people were standing outside. So what? Who cared? None of the women seemed to recognize anybody. Everybody looked and watched for a while. Then, when nothing seemed to be happening, one by one the women lost interest and went back to doing what they'd been doing. Me – I just kept braiding, absorbed in that.

I worked on Ophelia's hair until three o'clock, when the people who were in her Bible study class gathered. 'Can we finish later, Fauziya?' she asked. Sure, I said. It wasn't like I had anything else to do. I went back to the dorm. It was still quiet and empty. Good. I wanted quiet. I wanted to be alone, to think. I went back to my crocheting, with all kinds of thoughts racing through my head.

Could Sylvie be right? Karen had said she had a feeling that something good might be happening this week. We were really close, she'd said. Soon, she'd said. Empty words. Vague words. I'd heard them so many times before. But she hadn't just said 'close' and 'soon' this time. She'd said 'this week.' Maybe this week, she'd said. She'd sounded so sure. Oh, God. Oh, God. Now I'd gone and done it. I'd let myself think it. And as soon as I let myself think it, I felt something stir inside me, a dim, faint stirring. Hope. No. No! No, I couldn't do that to myself. Not again. It hurt too much. I tried to beat it back down. But I couldn't. I kept wondering about that officer who had come with my clothes! Why would he do that, unless, unless . . . Was it possible? Had Allah taken mercy?

I was gazing out the window, not seeing anything, still lost in thought, my afghan in my lap, when I heard someone come into the dorm maybe half an hour later. I looked up. It was Sheila, my former roommate from maximum, who'd also eventually been transferred to minimum. She was crying! Oh, no! What was wrong? And then I remembered. Today was her hearing day.

'Sheila! What happened?'

She came over and sat down on the bunk next to me, crying, covering her face with her hands. 'Oh, Fauziya,' she said. She couldn't speak. She was crying too hard. I went and sat beside her and put my arm around her. I let her cry until she was cried out. Oh, poor Sheila. She sat up finally, snuffled, wiped her red, wet, swollen eyes with the heels of her hands. 'Oh, Fauziya,' she said, her voice all wobbly. 'So bad!' Sheila was Yugoslavian, but she'd learned enough English in the past six months to be able to tell me what had happened. Everybody'd been there for the hearing, she said. Her husband, her mother, her father, her sister, the judge, the INS trial attorney. Everybody except her lawyer.

'Oh, no, Sheila!'

She nodded heavily. Yes. Just like what had

happened to Oche. But Sheila's lawyer hadn't even sent an assistant. The judge had waited. Everybody had waited. And waited. And waited. Finally the judge had said he couldn't wait any longer because he had another hearing scheduled. They'd have to reschedule. So now Sheila was back in prison.

'Oh, Sheila. I'm so sorry.' She sat slumped forward, staring at nothing. I rubbed her back. 'But no Ferlise, right?' I said, trying to cheer her. 'And you weren't denied. The judge didn't say no, right?'

She sighed. 'Yes.' No, the judge hadn't denied her. He'd simply rescheduled the hearing.

'Well, that's good, isn't it? You didn't lose. At least you didn't lose.'

She sighed again. 'Yes,' she said softly. Yes, that was good. She was silent for a while. Then she looked at me, smiled at me. 'And you, Fauziya? Better?' Sweet Sheila. How was I, she wanted to know. Did I feel better today?

Yes. 'Yes,' I said. I felt better. Today was a pretty good day for me, I told her. Something, well, interesting had happened while she'd been at court.

'Oh? What, Fauziya?'

I told her about how the officer had come with a box of my clothing, the clothes I'd been wearing when I arrived.

Sheila sat up, very interested now. 'Why, Fauziya? Why he do that?'

'I don't know,' I said. He hadn't told me.

She got excited. 'Oh, Fauziya! Maybe something good happen!'

I withdrew into caution. 'Maybe,' I said, softly, uncertainly. 'Maybe next week.' I hadn't meant to say that. It had just come out. I didn't want to let myself hope, but I couldn't help it.

We sat there together, Sheila and I, in the otherwise empty dorm. Friends. Former roommates. Just the two of us. Neither one of us was in the mood to be around other people. We just sat, being there with each other, for each other. I crocheted. Sheila gazed out the window.

And then the loudspeaker in the dormitory crackled.

'Fauziya Kasinga! Report to admissions!'

My heart stopped. My breathing stopped. Everything stopped. There was a moment of absolute stillness.

Report to admissions?

Sheila was looking at me, her eyes shining. She was smiling, grinning.

Report to admissions?

And then I exploded off the bed, screaming, 'I'm going home! I'm going home!'

I'm going home!

I flew over to Sheila, hugging her, screaming, laughing, crying. She was laughing and hugging me back. You got called to admissions only if you were being released or deported. I was getting out! I was—

No, wait. They hadn't said 'bag and baggage.' They always said 'bag and baggage' when someone was leaving. They hadn't said that! Oh, God. Maybe I wasn't getting out! Maybe it was something else.

Oh God, oh God. OK. Calm down. Get hold of yourself. Just go and see what they want.

I took a deep breath, trying to calm myself, to make myself move. I looked at Sheila. 'Well. Here I go.'

She squeezed my hand, smiling, tears in her eyes. 'Oh, I hope for you Fauziya! I hope!'

I took another deep breath, and then I walked slowly out of the dorm, through the common room, to

632

the back of the prison, toward maximum, where admissions is.

As I walked, one of the supervising officers came up to me. 'Are you going to admissions, Fauziya?' she asked.

'Yes.'

'Mind if I walk with you?'

Mind? She was asking if I minded? Excuse me? Was I dreaming here? An officer was asking an inmate if she 'minded' something? That was a first.

'Sure, you can walk with me,' I said.

We walked down the hall, casual as you please, toward the double set of locking doors that separated minimum from maximum. She didn't say anything. I didn't say anything. What was going on here? Something was going on. She was always nice. But not this nice.

We got to the metal doors.

I took a deep breath. Do it. Just do it. Get it over with.

'Excuse me,' I said nervously, 'but do you know why they called me?'

Please, God. Please, please.

She smiled just a little, like she'd been waiting for me to ask, wondering if I'd ask. 'Yeah, I think I do,' she said.

The metal door slid open. Bang! We stepped through it. It slid shut. Bang! We were locked in a metal box, one door behind us, another in front of us.

Yes? And?

The metal door in front of us slid open. Bang! We stepped through. It slid shut. Bang! We were in maximum now.

'Yeah, there's a big crowd outside, Fauziya,' she said.

Oh, please. I knew that already. I didn't care about that. Just answer the question.

She turned to me. 'There are a lot of people with cameras. I think your lawyer is out there too.'

'My lawyer!'

She smiled. 'I think you're being released, Fauziya. You're getting out.'

My knees buckled, my arms flew up. I threw my head back and cried out to heaven, loud and rejoicing.

'Allau Akbar! Allau Akbar! Allau Akbar!'

Allah is great! Allah is great! Allah is great!

Praise be to Allah. Glory be to Allah. Allah is great. Great and merciful.

God had taken mercy. God had granted my prayers. God had heard my cries.

The officer stood smiling. 'I'm happy for you, Fauziya,' she said gently. 'You take care of yourself now, OK?'

Then she walked away, leaving me to go the rest of the way to the admissions area alone, crying and thanking God with every step. Officer Virginia, the officer who'd caught me when I fainted, saw me coming down the hall and stopped me before I got to the door leading to the admissions area. 'Hey, where's your stuff?' she asked me, hands on hips, chiding like a mom, but with a smile on her face.

'My stuff?'

'Didn't they tell you to pack?'

'No.' No, they hadn't.

She turned to the guard behind the desk, spoke crossly.

'I told you to tell them "bag and baggage."'

Officer Virginia fumed a bit more at the guard, then turned back to me, her frown softening into a warm smile again. 'Go pack your stuff, silly,' she said.

'You want to stay here? Go. Go pack. You're going home.'

It was real! It was true!

I was going home!

Pack. I had to pack. I turned and began racing back toward minimum. Officer Virginia hurried after me, laughing with happiness for me. As I dashed down the hall I saw the prison counselor Amy Jefferson at the door to her office. I shouted out to her. 'Amy! Amy! I'm going home! I'm going home!'

'Yeah, I know,' she said coldly, and walked away.

That was it. No excitement, no congratulations, no nothing. She knew my story. She knew how long I'd been in prison. She knew how much I'd suffered. She was supposed to, anyway. She was the prison counselor, the person who was supposed to be there to help us. And that was her reaction. It really hurt me.

But I didn't have to care about that anymore. I was getting out! Oh, great, merciful Allah, *I was getting out!*

Next thing I knew, I was at the metal doors that separate maximum from minimum. Had I walked? Flown? Floated? I couldn't have told you. And then the doors opened and I was back in minimum. As soon as I walked into the common room I yelled, I whooped, I hollered. I shouted the news as loud as I could shout it. I wanted everyone to hear! I wanted the whole prison, the whole world to hear!

'I'm going home! I'm going home! I'm going home!'

'*Allau Akbar*,' Aicha burst out crying. Women came running toward me from everywhere. I was surrounded. Sylvie, Oche, Esther, Ophelia, Aicha, Sheila – all my friends were there, my immigrant friends, my convict friends, hugging me, kissing me, laughing, shouting, crying, whooping, hollering. Such joy! Officer Valerie was there too.

Sylvie, of course, was the most emotional of all. 'Oh, Fauziya, oh my sweetheart, oh my baby, I told you I wasn't going to cry when you got out, and now look at me! Oh, sweetie, I'm so happy for you. Oh, my baby, I'm going to miss you so much.'

Officer Valerie just stood aside while all this was going on, smiling, letting the commotion continue. Other guards would have broken it up immediately and ordered me to go directly to my locker and pack my things. But she let us all laugh and hug and shout and holler and cry for a while before putting a stop to it. And even then she was nice about it.

'You should get moving, Fauziya,' she said finally. 'You have to pack, remember?'

Pack. Oh, yes. I was leaving! I still didn't believe it. But everybody else seemed to, so it must be true.

I went to my locker, my friends with me every step of the way. In a daze, immobile, I stared at the contents of my locker. I'd told Sylvie, I'd told everyone, that if I ever got released, when that great and glorious day came, I'd run out of prison as fast as my legs could carry me. I wouldn't even pause to take a pen out of my locker. I'd just run straight for the door. But I didn't do that. I stood there staring at the contents of my locker. So much stuff! I didn't know where to begin. What should I take? What should I leave? What should I give away? And to whom? I couldn't think, couldn't make a move. I just stood there, baffled and confused.

Officer Valerie nudged me. 'Need some help?'

What? Oh. Oh, no. I'll be OK.

I took out the beautiful *mayahfi* and lovely pale-green beaded *tasbih* the men's counselor at Lehigh had given me. Aicha reached for the *mayahfi*. 'I'll take that,' she said. 'Give that to me.' Aicha. I had to laugh. She was always very direct and forceful, bossy even. Even though she is only one year older than I, that made her my big sister and the big sister gets to tell the little sister what to do. I gave it to her and my *tasbih* too. After all, she had to stay here, in this awful place. I didn't. Allah had taken mercy on me. I gave her my *tasbih* and *mayahfi* so she could pray more properly to Allah, so that He might take mercy on her too.

What else? What else?

My money, of course. I had an envelope with a lot of checks in it that people had sent me. That went in the box. I had another envelope with cash people had sent me. There was about $200 in it. I opened that envelope, took out half the money and handed it to Leah, a woman from Ghana who was the oldest of us. 'This is for all of you to share, OK?'

Leah smiled. 'OK.' She accepted it, gracefully. She did me the honor of not thanking me, our African way of saying that she knew to expect no less of me and that were our positions reversed, I could expect no less of her.

Next I reached for some photos that Frank had recently sent me from the Esmor fashion show. I'd decided to send them to my Amariya – maybe that would make her write to me, I'd thought – and had already written *Mom* on their backs. Sylvie was standing right beside me as I took out the pictures, backside up. When she saw the *Mom* written on them, she reached for them.

'Oh, sweetheart!' she said. 'For me?' I always called

her Mom. She always called me her daughter. 'Oh, my baby,' she said, crying and reaching for the photos. 'Now I'll have pictures of you. Oh, you sweetheart. Thank you, thank you.' She gave me a great big kiss and hug.

'You're welcome, Mom,' I said, hugging her back. What else could I say?

What next? My books. I had a big bag of books – books from Layli and her mother and brother, books from other members of the Fauziya Team, books from publishers and movie producers, books from people who had read about me and just wanted to send me something to show they were thinking about me. My eyes had been bothering me so much, I hadn't been able to read them, but maybe now that I was getting out of prison I could get proper medical treatment and I'd be able to read again, the way I used to. But I was getting out. I'd have so many things to do in addition to reading books. My friends here wouldn't. So I sorted through my books, taking the ones that meant the most to me, giving many others away.

I kept looking over everything in my locker and giving things away. But I hesitated over everything. I was stalling.

Officer Valerie nudged me again. 'What's the matter with you? Come on, silly. People are waiting for you. Don't you want to leave?'

'No.'

No. The truth hit me like a blow. My God, it was true! I wanted to leave this place, yes. More than anything. I wanted to leave prison. I didn't ever want to have to come back to this horrible place. But.

I looked around me, at all the wonderful women surrounding me.

Sheila.

Aicha.

Oche.

Esther.

Leah.

Sylvie.

I loved these women. I loved them with all my heart. How could I leave them? How could I leave my wonderful friends? I started to cry.

My friends. They'd supported me always. They supported me now.

Aicha took charge, spoke for all of them, 'Hurry up, Fauziya,' she ordered me sternly, tears streaming down her face. 'Go on. Get out of here.'

My friends did the rest of my packing for me. I couldn't. I just stood there, frozen, dazed, while everyone around me was in a whirl of activity.

'Ready now?' Officer Valerie asked at last.

It was time to head back to admissions and the holding area, back to maximum. Time to leave here. Leave my friends in minimum. It was time to say goodbye. How could I?

They spared me. They saved me. They helped me to do what, on my own, I couldn't bring myself to do. They helped me to leave. Go, go, go! They hustled me and Officer Valerie back down the hall to the metal doors, stood with us until the first metal door opened, hugged me, kissed me, held me, laughed and cried and congratulated me, whispered words of love in my ears. God bless you, write to me, don't forget me, pray for me, I'll be praying for you, God bless you, go now, go, go, go. And then I was being pushed through the door leading to maximum and it was banging shut behind me. Turning back to look at the window in the door, I saw all their beautiful, beaming, tear-streaked faces. And then the door to maximum banged open and Officer Valerie gently turned me around and pushed me through it before returning to minimum. It locked shut behind me. Bang!

My friends were gone.

No! Not all of them. I was in maximum. I had friends in maximum, too – Sharon and Ellen. They'd been my support system when I'd been there. How could I just leave without seeing them?

'Please,' I said to Officer Virginia, who was waiting for me when I walked into maximum. 'Please, can I say goodbye to my friends in B pod?'

'Well, it's against the rules.'

'Oh, please.'

'Well . . . OK.'

'Oh, thank you. Thank you!'

She walked me to the guard's booth and asked the guard to unlock B pod. 'She wants to say goodbye to her friends.' The guard nodded, walked me to the door, unlocked it, and waved me in. My old awful home. And then there they were, demure, gentle Ellen from Ghana, whom I had known since Esmor days, and wild, boisterous Sharon from Nigeria. I told them what was happening and hugged them both, thanking them for all they'd done for me. 'I'll pray for you,' Ellen said, still crying. 'I'll pray for your recovery, Fauziya.' She knew how sick I was. 'Pray for me, too.' I said I would. Of course I would. 'Thank you for coming to say goodbye,' she said. She hugged me again. 'Write to me, OK? Don't forget me, Fauziya.' Forget her? Never. Never. 'I won't forget you, Ellen,' I said. Never. I could sooner forget my own heart.

I said goodbye to these last two dear friends, and then Officer Virginia walked me down the hall back to admissions. As we walked a thought struck me: Oh God. 'Is anybody here to pick me up?' I asked. I knew that sometimes people got released all of a sudden, just kind of pushed out the door before they could call anyone to come get them. Oh no! What if they did that to me?

'Yes, people are here,' she said, reassuring me. 'Your lawyers are here.'

Oh, right. The other officer had told me that. I was so nervous, I'd forgotten.

She led me toward the holding room.

'You'll have to wait here for a while, OK?'

OK. Sure.

I walked in and she closed the door behind me. Another locked door. Oh, God. I was almost out!

The door opened a few minutes later and Officer Virginia came in carrying some folded clothing. 'Here you go,' she said, putting the pile down on the table. 'Try these on. See how they fit. I'll come back in a little while.' She closed the door again. I sat staring at the clothes. Clothes! I'd forgotten all about that! I was so accustomed to being put in holding rooms and then loaded into vans to be shipped off somewhere else in a prison uniform that I hadn't even thought about changing clothes. I hadn't worn real clothes in sixteen months, except for once, one day, the day of the fashion show at Esmor. I'd exchanged my prison uniform for other clothes before, but always a new prison uniform, always the same ugly prison uniform, except maybe in a different color with a slightly differently styled shirt. Now I was going to take off my prison uniform and never wear one again!

Officer Virginia had brought me a brand-new pair of black corduroy jeans and a brand-new black corduroy jeans jacket, fresh from the store. But everything was too tight, I discovered when I put them on.

Officer Virginia opened the door a crack. 'Do they fit OK?'

No, they were too small. 'Yes, they fit fine,' I said. It was this or the prison uniform, and I was never, ever going to put that on again. Ever. So help me Allah.

'Oh, good,' she said. 'I'll be back in a minute. You're going to have to wait here a little while longer, all right?'

Wait for what? Why? She'd closed the door again before I could think to ask.

I waited. I sat in my too-tight jeans and waited. Not knowing how long I was going to have to sit there.

I was right back where it had all started, back in the holding room at Newark International Airport, sitting alone, locked in a room, in jeans and jacket, not knowing why I was there, not knowing how long I'd be there, not knowing where I was going next. Where was I going now? I had no idea. People were waiting for me. But where would they take me? Where would I live? How would I live? I was heading into a complete unknown. Again. I'd done it twice already – once when I'd fled to Germany, once when I'd left Germany to come here, to the United States. Only I hadn't landed in the United States, I'd landed in prison, in 'exclusion.' Where was I heading today?

Another knock. Officer Virginia opened the door, peeked in. 'How you doing in here?'

'Please,' I said. 'Can you please tell me why I'm waiting here? Why are you keeping me here? Why can't I go?'

'We have to wait until your lawyers get here.'

'But I thought they were here!'

'No, not all of them. They're stuck in traffic or something. They called to say they're on their way.

Don't worry. They'll be here soon. Just a few more minutes. I'll come get you as soon as they're here, OK?'

I waited. I prayed.

And then the door opened again, and Officer Virginia was standing there smiling.

'Are they here?'

She grinned. 'They're here. Are you ready?'

Ready? Am I ready? I'd been waiting for this day, this glorious day, this glorious moment, for sixteen months! 'Yes, I'm ready.'

'OK, let's go then. You have to book out.' She opened the door wide and waved me through.

At the booking desk there were some further formalities – forms, questions, and so forth.

'Do you have relatives in this country?'

'Yes.'

'Who?'

I gave the man at the desk Rahuf's name, his address and telephone number.

'OK,' he said. He put a hand down on the desk, palm-up. 'May I have your wrist please?'

'My wrist?'

'Yes, your wrist. Your I.D. bracelet.'

Oh, oh, yes, of course.

My prison I.D. bracelet. My brand. The guard picked up a pair of scissors. Kim. I saw Kim with the pliers in her hand. Kim fastening my very first I.D. bracelet.

Aow! Aow! You hurt me!

That was sixteen months ago and one week tomorrow.

I held out my left wrist. He took it.

Snip!

He released my arm.

'OK, that's it,' he said. 'You're done now. You can go. You're free.'

You're free.

He didn't even look up as he spoke those words to me. This was how it ended – with a guard snipping an I.D. bracelet off my wrist and telling me I could go.

I could go. I had to go.

There was a door ahead of me, at the end of the hallway. It led outside, to the fenced-in parking area. My lawyers were out there, waiting for me.

I walked slowly. There were no chains on me, no handcuffs, no prison uniform, no prison I.D. bracelet, no INS officers or prison guards escorting me, no van waiting outside to take me to another prison. It felt so strange.

I got to the door. Walked through it. When it closed behind me, I was outside the prison but inside the fenced-in parking area.

'There she is! There she is!'

A crowd of people were gathered just outside the gates. They started clapping, whistling, cheering. 'Yaaay! Yaaay!' I could hear the clicking of cameras. Oh my goodness! What was this? Who were these people?

I felt unsure. Once again, I was going forward into an unknown future. I looked back at the minimum-security women's yard to wave goodbye to whoever was outdoors. It was empty. No-one was out there. Why not? My friends could have—

Wait a minute. How could it be that nobody was out there? Because of the cameras? Because of me?

'Fauziya! Fauziya! Fauziya!'

That was Layli's voice!

'Fauziya! Run, Fauziya! Run hard!'

And I did. I ran. Shielding my face from the cameras, I ran laughing as fast as my legs could carry me across the parking lot. I ran to Layli's voice.

I ran to freedom.

I was free!

32

Freedom

Layli was there. Karen was there. A tall, thin man –
who I soon learned was Richard Boswell – was standing close beside Karen, smiling at me like he knew me.
David was there. Sidney was there. Denise was there.
They crowded around me, and we hugged – a giant
group hug, the Fauziya Team hug.

'Can you believe that you're out?' Layli asked me.
'It's over, Fauziya. It's finally over!'

The clinic had gotten the news at one that afternoon.
Karen, Layli, and Richard were in the middle of a
lunchtime strategy session when the word came that I
would be released. After an ecstatic moment of
screaming and hugging each other, Karen got on the
phone to call Surita Sandosham, as well as Celia
Dugger and a few other key people in the media, hoping to get the information out to the press as quickly
as possible. The INS was probably hoping for the
opposite – to minimize media attention by giving so
little advance notice of my release – but word spread
fast enough that some press showed up anyway. So
from the moment I ran toward my friends on the
Fauziya Team there were cameras clicking and
reporters sticking microphones in my face, wanting to
interview me right then and there.

'What happened when you landed at Newark Airport?' they were asking, wanting to hear things from the very beginning.

'Oooh,' I said. 'It's a long story.' Talking to the press was more than I could handle at that moment.

I may not have been ready for the press, but the INS was. Even though they had released me so suddenly, they must have known that they wouldn't be able to keep the news completely quiet, because they had their version of events printed up in a press release they were handing out on the spot. They were releasing me now, it said, mainly because 'new and reliable arrangements' had been made to ensure I wouldn't skip out on my parole, meaning, I guess, that the Bahá'ís had offered to take me in. Nobody on the Fauziya Team believed that – clearly it was the media attention that had gotten me out – but the main thing for now was that I *was* out.

We started to prepare to leave, but there was one more thing I had to do. From outside the gates, I looked at York Prison one last time. I searched for the windows in the dorm that looked out onto this parking area. And there they were, all my friends with their faces pressed against the windowpanes. Their faces were just a blur from the outside, but I knew who would be there and I knew they would be waving and throwing kisses, so I did the same. I threw a special kiss to Sylvie, who had mothered me through the riot, through my sickness, through everything. 'I love you, Sylvie!' I shouted. 'I love you!' I hoped she could hear me.

The next thing I knew, I was in a car with Layli and David, in America, free – free and very, very excited, even though I was also very, very sick. Layli explained that we were going to Roshan's parents' home,

647

because they had agreed to take me in when it became clear that Rahuf was not a legal resident of the United States. That was the first I'd heard of Rahuf's legal problems. Only later would I begin to understand what a risk Rahuf must have taken in helping me, given his own situation. All the time, all I could think about was the wonder of being free, the newness of it, the surprise. Layli and I both kept looking at each other, unable to believe it, not knowing what to say to each other. But the silence didn't last long, because David immediately started to tease me and make jokes, and we all started to laugh. Layli handed me the cell phone she had in the car so I could call some of the other people who had helped. First, Equality Now. As soon as they heard my voice, everyone in the office yelled and whooped and hollered. Oh, God, I was so happy! Next I called Celia Dugger, who'd done so much for me. Many, many journalists wrote about me, but if any one journalist got me out of prison, it was Celia.

When we finally drove up to what would be my new home, it looked like a palace to my eyes. It was a big ranch house on a quiet, tree-lined street, with a wooden deck out back. Mrs Bashir met us at the door, all dressed up and looking beautiful. She's a handsome, full-figured woman, with green eyes, a lovely face, and the most loving, motherly manner. Layli told me later that from the moment she agreed to take me in, she kept asking Layli when I was coming. 'Where's my daughter?' she kept asking. 'Where's my daughter?'

Now that I had finally arrived, she made me feel instantly at home as she showed me around. Persian rugs, a whole wall of books in the living room, comfortable furniture, a fireplace, mirrors – everything was beautiful inside as well as outside. The rest of my legal team had already arrived when we got there, and the party they had planned in my honor had already begun. Mrs Bashir had cooked up a huge feast, with all kinds of wonderful Persian rice dishes and chicken and desserts. Chicken and rice – my favorites!

I got my first full-length look at myself when I walked into the Bashirs' living room and saw Layli and me reflected in a big mirror. Oh my God. That was me? It had been so long since I looked in a real glass mirror, that I didn't recognize myself. I looked horrible, horrible, even in the new outfit the prison had bought me. I had terrible pimples, which I'd never had before I was in prison. My skin was dark and blotchy. I wished I could look better, especially since a *New York Times* photographer was there to take pictures. But there was nothing I could do.

Soon after I arrived, Mrs Bashir asked me if I'd like to see my bedroom. My bedroom? My own bedroom? A whole room? Yes. And my own bathroom too. Mrs Bashir and Layli took me downstairs where there was a whole separate apartment that would be mine. I very nearly fainted for joy when I saw my bedroom. There was beautiful flowered wallpaper, a big bed with a slate blue bedspread and a pink and white and blue quilt folded up at the foot, pillows scattered on the bed, bedside tables with lamps, a blond wood dresser with a mirror above it, a rattan chair, and a big double window looking out on a green yard. On one of the bedside tables Mrs Bashir had put a beautiful little basket filled with soaps and lotions and creams that she thought I might like. All this for me. I ran and took a flying leap onto the bed and bounced up and down on it. 'Layli,' I said. 'If I'm dreaming, don't wake me up.' She and Mrs Bashir laughed.

'No, Fauziya,' Layli said. 'You're not dreaming.'

It was real. All real. I changed out of my too-tight jeans into the dress Layli had brought along for me, long and loose and flowing, with a print of tiny flowers in many different colors. I loved it. Even though it's too small for me now, I've kept it to show to the children and grandchildren I hope to have someday. When they're old enough to understand something about my life, I'll hold the dress in front of them and say, 'See this dress? Let me tell you the story of how I came to wear this dress . . .'

Rahuf arrived around ten P.M., after he got off work. Denise told me later she couldn't believe the change in me when she saw me talking to my cousin, all animated and gabbing away in our own language. She'd never seen that side of me. Rahuf told me that when he'd gotten the news, he and his roommates had stood up and danced for joy right there in their apartment – literally danced for joy. We do that where I come from. We dance our happiness. And then, like me, he had thanked Allah.

I learned an astonishing thing about Rahuf that evening. One of the reasons he'd put everything on the line to help me was that he remembered when his own sister was cut. Rahuf hadn't witnessed the procedure itself. But he'd heard his sister's screams of pain. And he'd seen her immediately afterward, walking around dazed, blood all over her. He'd been shocked, stunned. But when he asked his mother – 'What happened? What happened to her?' – she had slapped him. Every time he asked, his mother slapped him again. He was not allowed to ask questions about it or speak about it. It had been kept that secret. He hadn't really known what happened until I showed up in his life in America, this distant cousin he hadn't seen since she was a little girl. After I called him for help and told him my story, he'd called back home and talked to one of his brothers, I think, and asked about this thing I was running from. Did his brother know about it? Oh, yes. His brother filled him in. Finally he understood what had happened to his own sister. That's why he'd put himself at risk in order to help me. No. He couldn't let me get sent back to that, not if he could help it. So he'd risked everything. Even being deported himself.

I slept that night in a big, soft, comfortable bed, with big, soft, comfortable pillows. Mrs Bashir gave me a little clock and showed me how to set it so I could get up to pray at five the next morning. Of course I was going to pray the next morning. I had so many thanks to offer up to God. I didn't fall asleep until very late, though. I lay awake until around two or three A.M., thinking. About everything I'd been through. You don't just shed sixteen months in prison that easily. Do you want to know the truth? I think you never really recover from that kind of experience. I was free now. But I didn't feel free yet. And I had so many friends who weren't free, who were still in prison. I couldn't stop thinking about them, either. I remembered standing outside of the prison gates – was it just a few hours ago? – searching for the window and there they were, all my friends, their faces just a blur.

I got up to pray the next morning at five, went back to bed, and slept until ten A.M. Ten A.M.! No guards telling me when to get up, when to eat, when to do anything. I showered in the bathroom down the hall and dressed in the clothes Mrs Bashir had told me to use – her daughter Sherry's clothing. When I went upstairs, Dr Bashir was sitting at the breakfast table. Dr Bashir is a handsome, middle-aged man with black hair, bright black eyes, and a very outgoing, outspoken manner. I like that about him. I like people who just deal with you straight, tell you exactly what's on their mind. It's very un-African. But I like it. Dr Bashir loves to tease and he's very easy to be with, so he made me feel comfortable from the beginning.

Mrs Bashir had set a place for me at the table, and she was standing ready to make me any kind of breakfast I wanted that first morning. She was always pampering and spoiling me. Mrs Bashir manages her husband's medical practice. (Dr Bashir is a gastro-enterologist, like his son, Roshan.) But it was her day off so after breakfast she took me shopping. I needed everything and she bought me everything – underwear, shoes, skirts, blouses, dresses.

I spent my first weekend out of prison mainly doing what I was going to be doing for the next several weeks – answering letters, thanking people, talking to well-wishers and supporters over the phone, and dealing with the media too. I didn't want the publicity, but Karen reminded me that what had happened to me could help bring attention to the plight of many other refugees who undergo inhumane treatment at the hands of the INS. So in the days that followed I gave some interviews and I even went on a few TV shows, including *Nightline* and *CNN International*.

Rahuf took me to his house that very first Saturday and we called Togo. I spoke with Ayisha, my beloved sister, who'd risked everything to help me escape. My sister, whom I hadn't seen or spoken to in a year and eight months, ever since she'd put me on the plane to Germany in October 1994. I didn't cry on the phone, as I had feared I would. I laughed! I was so happy! But why hadn't she written to me, I wanted to know. Why hadn't she answered my last letter? Letter? What letter? Ayisha said she'd never received it. Never received it?

That's what she said. Maybe she hadn't. It's possible. But it's just as possible that she had. I'd spilled out all the horrible things I was going through in that letter. As I keep saying, people don't deal well with bad news where I come from. So I'll never really know for sure. Our mother was living in Nigeria then with one of her sisters, Ayisha said. She promised she'd get a message to her that week, telling her to come to Lomé, so that if I called again next week Amariya would be there to talk to me too. My mother! I was going to talk to my mother! I had not seen or spoken to my mother since April 1993. Oh, God, I was going to talk to my mom! I didn't know how I would be able to wait a whole week more.

After the call to Ayisha, Rahuf cooked up a lot of food. African food. Togo food. I ate and ate and ate and ate. He couldn't believe how much food I packed away! It was home food. My food. Our food. I couldn't get enough of it. I paid for it later, of course. My stomach hurt so bad! I was in such pain. But, oh, how I enjoyed that meal while it was going down.

There was a big press conference on Monday morning, April 29, the Monday after my release. It was a joint press conference, co-sponsored by Equality Now and American University's Washington College of Law. The room at the National Press Club where it was held was packed with something like 150 reporters. Surita told me later she had never, ever seen such a turn out for a human-rights press conference. Richard spoke, Layli spoke, Surita spoke, Karen spoke, David spoke, Sidney spoke. And eventually even I spoke, as clearly and calmly as I could, although I was terrified.

My BIA hearing was scheduled for Thursday, May 2. That was the day the twelve judges who make up the Board of Immigration Appeals would sit en banc and hear arguments, pro and con, as to whether I should be granted asylum and allowed to stay in America. I was out of prison now, but I was only out on parole. My fate had not yet been decided. It was up to the BIA. I was so scared, so scared. Karen reassured me that it wasn't going to be at all like my asylum hearing. I wouldn't have to talk, for one thing, because in an appeals hearing only the lawyers talk, she said. But I was still scared.

Another thing that was different was that this time I wouldn't have to go to court wearing a prison uniform and handcuffs. I could wear anything I wanted. Layli came over early the day of the hearing to help me pick out my clothes from the wardrobe Mrs Bashir had bought for me, and she watched while I did my makeup and my hair. Then it was time to go. Everyone on my legal team, as well as Celia Dugger, had gathered at the Bashirs' house, my home, to support me. So we all traveled to court together, in a caravan of cars.

When we got there, we saw that the courtroom was jammed with observers and reporters and even Congresswoman Maxine Waters, who had taken a strong interest in my case.

I sat on the left side of the courtroom, in the very front row, right behind the table where Layli, Richard, and Karen sat. I was surrounded by my supporters: Jessica, Surita, Nileema, Sidney, David, Denise. When the board members filed in in a long line wearing their black robes, we all stood up and waited for them to take their seats. They sat in two rows of big maroon leather chairs behind a long bench at the front of the room, facing us, with my legal team practically under their noses. The INS team sat at a table on the right side, separated from my team by the podium where the two opponents would stand to present their arguments.

Karen spoke first. I couldn't understand most of what she said, but I understood her tone, which was both calm and passionate at the same time. The board members listened carefully and asked a few questions, which she answered clearly and persuasively and articulately. Then it was the INS's turn to speak.

David Martin, the INS general counsel, took the position that my case should be remanded to an immigration judge, rather than being decided by the BIA. There were several pieces of evidence he thought an immigration judge should examine, he said, including the police report, which had never been translated from the French. Martin also argued that the affidavits by me and Professor Posnansky were new evidence bearing on the question of my 'credibility,' and as such should be considered by an immigration judge, not in an appeals hearing.

As with Karen, I wasn't able to understand most of what Martin said – people explained the basics to me later – but I had eyes and ears, and I could tell he wasn't doing very well that day. The board members grilled him hard, and he hesitated a lot in making his answers. And meanwhile, I could see the other lawyers at his table frowning and disagreeing among themselves, passing notes to him in the middle of his presentation. Their side seemed unhappy with the way the board members were treating them.

Martin's other arguments related to which 'circumstances' should be considered valid grounds for seeking asylum from FGM and which shouldn't. While he wasn't necessarily disputing my claim for asylum, Martin wanted the BIA to issue a ruling that other women, those who had 'consented' as babies or young girls, and those who would 'only' face ostracism if they resisted, should not be granted asylum. And he wanted the BIA to set that policy now while ruling on my case. Karen was arguing that, no, the BIA should rule on my case only, and not 'close the door' to future cases that hadn't even come before the court yet. That was the general gist of it.

There were further arguments – brief ones – from both Karen and David Martin, and then it was all over. The whole hearing had been limited to one hour. The board members thanked Karen and David Martin for their fine work. They'd let us know their decision later. Oh, God.

We held another little impromptu press conference on the plaza outside the BIA building. One lady who worked for the BIA came up and gave me a bracelet, just because she wanted to give me something, she said. I was so touched. A group of reporters stood listening as Karen spoke. Then it was David Martin's turn to speak. But as soon as my side was through and we walked away, many of the reporters started to pack up and leave. I felt sorry for him.

I had a second endoscopy test sometime shortly after my hearing. Roshan was unable to get the results of the one I'd had while in prison. Because I was still having sharp pains whenever I ate, he arranged for me to be tested again. Once I was put under, Roshan began threading the tube carefully down my throat. I was drugged, unconscious. But even under anesthesia I began fighting like crazy, trying to rip that tube out of my throat. It took four people to hold me down. And it took a lot more medication to put me deeper under so I'd stop fighting. Layli told me later that they had to give me so much to keep me down, I didn't come out of it again for more than three hours. Roshan began to wonder if the hospital the prison sent me to had been able to complete the endoscopy, because I must have fought then too. Roshan found that I did indeed have peptic ulcer disease with the bacteria present that causes the ulcers. Roshan was able to enroll me in a clinical study he was heading up to test a new treatment, which meant I could get treated for free. Half the people got the new treatment, half got a regimen of really strong antacid medication. I got the antacid medication. A second endoscopy was performed about two months later. I had the same violent reaction, more fighting, more people having to hold me down, more anesthesia. But the test results were good that time. My ulcer had healed. The problem is that the bacteria that causes peptic ulcer disease was still there. I'm still trying to get it under control. Roshan says those bacteria are endemic in my part of the world. Stress and bad nutrition and other things can cause it to flare up. After sixteen months in prison, it was no wonder I'd gotten an ulcer from it.

The weekend following my release from prison, I finally talked to my mother, to Amariya, from Rahuf's apartment. Rahuf got on the phone first. He told me my brother Babs was there too. Rahuf gave me the phone. I heard a deep voice. I asked to speak to my brother Babs. I was speaking to him, the voice said. Oh, no! His voice had changed! He'd changed too, he said. A lot. He'd just graduated from design school. Graduated! He'd only begun school when I last saw him. Yes, graduated. He was much taller now, too, he said. Taller than me now. And he had a mustache and lots of hair all over, just like Yaya. He was growing into my father's son, becoming more and more like the beloved father we'd all lost.

And then he put my mother on the phone. Amariya

tested me. Was she really speaking to her real daughter? She fell back on an old ritual of ours, the way she used to call me to come help her with something and I'd answer but not come.

'Fauziya?'

'Eh.'

'Fauziyaaa.'

'Eh.'

'Fauziya! Where are you?'

'I'm here.'

And then my mother burst out crying. 'Oh, yes, oh yes, you are really my daughter, you are really my baby, my baby girl.' And then she started apologizing to me and thanking me over and over and over. 'Oh, Fauziya, I'm sorry, I'm so sorry, I'm so sorry. Oh, my daughter, thank you, thank you, thank you.'

Sorry for what? Why was she apologizing to me? Why was she thanking me?

She was apologizing to me for all I'd been through, thanking me for staying strong, for staying in America, for not coming back, for not betraying everything my family believed in, everything my father had believed in. She was thanking me for that. I cried. No, no. No, Amariya, don't. Don't thank me. Don't apologize to me. But she did.

I asked her too. Why hadn't she written to me? Why hadn't she answered my letter! Same response. Letter? What letter? She hadn't received any letter. Maybe, and maybe not. My mother, more than anyone else I've ever known in my life, simply cannot deal with bad news. I tried to tell her just a little over the phone, just a little of what I'd been through. No! No! No, she didn't want to hear it. She didn't want to hear any of it. She'd been praying for me. I was OK now. That's all that mattered. The rest was behind me. What's past is past. She didn't want to speak of it. Ever.

I speak to my family regularly now. I've tried, often, to tell them some of what I went through during those sixteen months. They don't want to know. That hurts me sometimes. I'll find myself bursting into tears out of the blue, for no particular reason, but just because I hurt inside. Still, I understand why my family doesn't want to hear. That's our way. We don't talk about past pain and suffering. I did tell my mother all about Layli and what she'd done for me, of course. And then she sent us an audiotape of her talking to me about Layli, praising Layli, thanking Layli. Layli and I listened to it together. Layli didn't understand what my mother was saying. I translated. Layli laughed in embarrassment. But she was touched. She actually even spoke to my mother and sister on the phone after that. My Togo family and my American family finally met each other that day. Oh, it was so sweet. Layli tried so hard to learn how to say a phrase in our language, but she mangled it horribly. My mother and sister laughed and laughed.

The BIA issued its ruling on Thursday, June 13, 1996. By then I had moved into an apartment in Washington, D.C., belonging to a friend of Karen and Richard's. Karen called that day to say she'd just received the BIA's decision. I closed my eyes, sent a fervent prayer to Allah, and waited to hear the verdict.

Asylum granted. Eleven board members had ruled in my favor. One dissented, but he didn't say why.

We'd won! I'm sure Karen thought her ears would burst from the sound of my screams over the phone. On Thursday, June 13, I was truly freed. Glory be to Allah. Praise be to Allah. Allah is great.

The BIA board members had decided not to send my case back to Ferlise. They wrote in the ruling that

they'd also decided not to accept the new evidence –
my affidavit and Professor Posnansky's affidavit. They
said there was no need to, that the existing record, the
record Layli had established, was more than adequate.
They said that they'd ruled on the basis of that record
alone. Maybe they had, maybe they hadn't. Karen later
learned from a reliable source at the BIA that a three-
judge panel had drafted a decision remanding my case
to Judge Ferlise, but that decision was never issued
and my case was reassigned to the board en banc.
Karen wagers that the board was influenced by the
new evidence, which was widely reported in the
media. Either way, Layli felt incredibly affirmed by
what the board members said about the record she'd
created. Eric Bowman felt redeemed by the ruling,
too. I went to visit him later. He'd been very hurt by
Karen's attacks on his representation of me. The BIA
ruling made him feel a little better.

The board members reversed all of Ferlise's rulings.
They said he'd been wrong to find me not credible,
wrong in denying me asylum. They also rejected David
Martin's appeal for them to decide now what future
kinds of cases would or would not constitute valid
grounds for seeking asylum from FGM. They would
evaluate each future case on its own merits, they said.
God bless the BIA. Layli told me their ruling came in
for some criticism later, however. The BIA board members had ruled that I deserved asylum, and that FGM
qualified as a basis for asylum. That was precedent-
setting and binding now on all other immigration
judges, including Judge Donald V. Ferlise. But some
people felt the board members hadn't explained
clearly enough how and why they'd reached that
decision. It would have been helpful if they had, Layli
said, because then other people could have looked at

how the board members had weighed different factors and used that information to guide them in arguing future cases. There's still too much ambiguity in the law as far as she's concerned, too much leeway for denying deserving women asylum.

It's been over a year and a half now, as I write these words, since I was released from York Prison. That's not a lot of time really – little more than I spent in prison. I'm still adjusting, just starting to feel like, yes, this is my home, this is where I live. I'm in a different apartment now, nothing fancy by American standards, but fancier than anything I ever knew or saw at home. I have a computer. I even have E-mail. This is my new life.

Equality Now has helped me enormously with the adjustment. They believe in follow-through. Some human rights organizations support you until you've been freed from prison or granted asylum or whatever and then they move on to helping the next person. But Equality Now keeps on helping – helping you get settled, oriented, adjusted, helping you build some kind of life. So a couple of months after my release – on the very day I was granted asylum, as it turned out – Jessica came down to Washington from New York to take me around to visit different schools and meet with an education consultant who would help me figure out where I should study. I couldn't wait to go back to school. Jessica was the first person to focus on helping me move into this new phase of my life.

I have just finished up my first year in junior college. I've thought a lot about where I should go when I finish – what I should study, what I want to be. Right now I think I want to become a nurse. But I might change my mind again. I've changed it a few times so far. I was pretty sure for a while that I wanted to do human rights work, like all my advocates, but everyone said I'd need a law degree for that. It's so funny! I'd been taught growing up to stay away from lawyers and never to trust them. Now most of my best friends are lawyers, and I even considered becoming one myself!

A lot of things have changed for my family, too. After I was set free my mother went back to Kpalimé to my uncle's house to make peace within the family. Celia Dugger was there when she did that. My mother went to my uncle and apologized to him. I was so upset when she told me. Why was she apologizing to him? He should apologize to her! But she knew he'd never do that, and she wanted peace in the family. She said if the breach wasn't healed, it would continue from generation to generation, so she humbled herself and apologized to him. I would never have done that. But that's Amariya.

For a while after she made her apology my mother lived in my uncle's house. But now she's living in Ghana with one of her sisters. My aunt has left Kpalimé, too, and moved back north, after selling my father's house. We have no family house anymore. The house Yaya worked so hard to be able to afford to build, the house we all grew up in, now belongs to someone else. My mother said that my aunt decided to move away because she couldn't manage what was left of my father's business, and she was shamed by all the attention my case had received. The whole community knew what she had done. And a lot of white people from outside did too. Before my hearing, people from the U.S. embassy came around asking a lot of embarrassing questions, checking out my story to find out if it was true. When my case started to get a lot of attention in the press, Western reporters descended on

662

Kpalimé doing more interviews, asking more questions. I guess my aunt couldn't take the pressure.

Even though I'm back in regular contact with my family, I still miss them terribly, especially now that Rahuf is gone. My wonderful cousin went back to Togo some months ago. There was an emergency at home. He was on the plane before I even got home and heard the message he left on my machine that day. All my family, all my blood family, all the blood family I consider family, is in Africa now. And I'm in America. Alone.

I'm grateful to be in America. Very grateful. I'm grateful to the American people and government for everything they've done for me, for taking me in, giving me shelter, giving me a safe place to live. But I wish I could see my family. Although I can travel outside the United States on a refugee travel document, I cannot go back to Togo, because I'm still legally married to Ibrahim under Muslim law. Surita has offered to pay to have my mother fly to America. Bless her. But I don't want my mother to come until she has a permanent home of her own to return to. We're working on that now.

I miss my sisters and brothers too. It breaks my heart to be separated from them. I fear that by the time we do see each other again, maybe in Ghana, or Benin, or Nigeria, they won't know me anymore because I'll have changed too much. I've been through so much since I saw them, things that are part of who I am now. How will we pick up the pieces of our old way of being with each other? We talk on the phone these days. But that's not the same as being with them, teasing them, fighting with them, living with them day in and day out, morning to night, day after day. I've lost that. I've lost that forever.

And Yaya. Yaya. That hole in my heart will never heal. He still comes to me in my dreams. But that's all I have left of him now. That and the beautiful watch he gave me for my fifteenth birthday. It's still broken. I'm not going to have it fixed. I don't want to. I can't explain why. I just don't. Maybe because I don't want to part with it even for a moment. Maybe because I always think that it was what stood between the club and my wrist during the riot, and it was Yaya's way of protecting me.

My mother laughs and teases me now that she should have gone ahead and let my father paint my name on the truck he bought just after I was born, because everybody knows my name now anyway. Not everybody, of course, but a lot of people. 'You're God's chosen one,' my mother tells me. That's how she sees what happened to me. I tell her if this is what being one of God's chosen is like, I'd have been a lot happier if God hadn't chosen me, if I hadn't had to go through all that suffering, all that pain, all that loss.

Layli talks about God's purpose. And even though I think I should never have had to suffer the way I did, it does seem that some good has come of it. If the BIA decision makes it even a little easier for other women who are fleeing FGM to find asylum, I'll feel that there really was some purpose to what I went through. Not that I ever intended to become any kind of public symbol for any cause. I was just a young woman who ran away to escape two horrible fates – being cut and being sold into a forced polygamous marriage – and who then had the misfortune to land in jail in the place where she had gone to seek help. I didn't know there were people working in an active, organized way to try to end these forms of female suffering, and I didn't know they could be thought of as human rights violations. I was just trying to save myself. But my case happened to come along at exactly the right time, when it could be a symbol for what was happening to a lot of other women. Then God and Layli and Karen and Equality Now and Celia Dugger and many other people stepped in and did the rest.

Now that I know about FGM, not just as something that almost happened to me but as a worldwide problem, I know I have to speak out against it. That's why I decided to write this book. I've already seen how much publicity can do, not just for me personally but for the larger cause. I'm told that the American embassy in Togo has now decided to put more money toward helping to educate against this practice. This happened in part because of the attention focused on FGM during the women's conference in Beijing, and in part because of my case. I also heard that my tribe was going to hold a big meeting to discuss whether they should continue this practice. I haven't heard what came of that meeting, but I pray to Allah that they decided to abandon it. The people of my tribe are good people. But good people can do bad things. They need to think carefully about what they're doing and why, not just keep on doing it because that's how things have always been done in the past. Tradition doesn't make something right. That's one thing I learned from my father, who thought hard about the choices he made and left tradition behind when he thought it was bad. If the people of my tribe stood together and said, 'No, this is wrong, it has to stop,' oh, that would make me so proud. I pray to Allah that the attention my case has received will help them to do the right thing.

Another reason I decided to write this book is because the American people need to know about what happened to me right here in America. Until the publicity started, I didn't think anyone cared except the small group of people who were trying to help me. But when so many wonderful people wrote letters to tell me how angry they were about the way I was being treated I realized, yes, people do care. They care if they know. I can play a part in helping them to know that what happened to me – and worse – is still happening to countless other refugees, every single day, at prisons throughout this country. The American people are good people. I know that now. It's been proven to me over and over. The American people can stop the abuse and mistreatment of refugees like me. And they will, I think, if they know about it.

Karen, Layli, Surita, and Jessica are all still working as hard as they can to bring an end to all the kinds of suffering my story calls attention to. Surita and Jessica continue to do what Equality Now does so well – fighting to call attention to the many forms of suffering and abuse inflicted on the world's girls and women, and doing that by publicizing individual cases. Karen is back at Santa Clara University, where she founded and directs a new program called the International Human Rights and Migration Project, which includes advocacy on behalf of women refugees. In addition, along with Harvard's Deborah Anker, Karen directs a nationwide study funded by the Ford Foundation and the Joyce-Mertz Gilmore Foundation, to monitor the impact that recent changes in the immigration law has on asylum seekers. Layli graduated from law school and is practicing law at a large firm in Washington, D.C. She also started a new women's refugee center which she has named the Tahirih Justice Center: For the Promotion of Human Rights and the Protection of Immigrant Women – women like me.

Esmor has reopened. It's no longer called Esmor – it's the Elizabeth Detention Center now – but it's still Esmor. Frank is still working there, thank God. God has kept him there for a while, to help others the way he helped me. I have the Qur'an and *tasbih* Frank rescued for me. He was able to keep his promise and give them to me, in person, after I was freed.

Then there are my friends, the ones I made while I was in prison. Esther was deported back to Ghana. Oche was deported back to Nigeria. Aicha was granted aslyum and is attending college in the Philadelphia area. We see each other as much as possible. She returned my *tasbih*, kept the *mayahfi*. And Sylvie. Sylvie is still at York. Waiting.

I thank God every day, five times a day, for my own good fortune. God has blessed me. He made me suffer but He also blessed me. I'm safe and free in America, surrounded by people who love me. Others are not so fortunate. They are being held in prisons, being denied asylum, and being sent back to terrible forms of suffering. My friends, all the friends I made in prison, cried for joy for me the day I walked out into freedom. They asked only one thing. Only one thing.

'Don't forget us, Fauziya.'

I haven't forgotten them. I could never, ever forget them. This isn't just my story. It's their story too.

Epilogue

We all like stories with a happy ending, and thanks to the many people who fought on her behalf, Fauziya Kassindja's story *does* have a happy ending. On April 24, 1996, she was released from detention, and on June 13, 1996, she was granted political asylum. The happy ending to Fauziya's story has an almost fairy tale quality to it. The young woman who was treated like a criminal and suffered insults and indignities at the hands of prison guards is now sought after by journalists, celebrated by congressmembers, and embraced by notables such as Alice Walker and Gloria Steinem. In addition, the media attention devoted to her struggle for justice led to extraordinary public awareness of female genital mutilation and increased compassion for the plight of refugees.

Notwithstanding the happy ending, it is important to acknowledge the suffering Fauziya endured along the way. She suffered the pain of separation that only a refugee, forced to leave home and family behind, can know. She suffered the loneliness of exile in the strange lands of Germany and America. She suffered the humiliation of jail cells and strip searches. And she suffered the injustice and bias of an immigration judge who dismissed her reality, and refused to believe the truth she told. By telling us the details, Fauziya reminds us that her story is not the only story; she is but one of the many asylum seekers fleeing persecution who arrive on our shores.

Keeping that in mind, this story would not be complete without asking if we have learned any lessons from the mistakes we made in treating Fauziya as we did. Have we learned that asylum seekers are not criminals and should not be treated as if they were? Have we come to accept that immigration judges – like all human beings – *can* and *do* make mistakes? And knowing that immigration judges make mistakes, have we made sure that there is the opportunity to correct those mistakes? Have we come to acknowledge that women's human rights are legitimate human rights, and that women have the right to be protected as refugees even if the persecution that they fear is female genital mutilation, or some other harm unique to women which is an accepted norm in the culture in which they live?

I would like to answer each of these questions with a resounding yes. I would like to tell you that asylum seekers like Fauziya are no longer jailed, that they are assured of the right to appeal erroneous decisions of immigration judges such as Judge Ferlise, who ruled against Fauziya. I would also like to trumpet a victory for women's human rights, and women refugees, and to tell you that there is an increased acceptance that FGM, rape, domestic violence, and other violations that commonly befall women, are protected by our refugee system. It would make for a very happy ending, indeed, to be able to say that not only was Fauziya vindicated, but that her story had a larger impact on U.S. refugee law and policy. However, if I told you that, I would be engaging more in wishful thinking than in truth-telling.

There have been some encouraging developments as a result of Fauziya's struggle for justice. For example, there has been some progress in recognizing that gender-specific harms, such as FGM, should qualify a woman asylum seeker for protection. Not all judges and INS trial attorneys enthusiastically embrace the principle, but many do, and the Board of Immigration Appeals' decision established binding precedent, upon which other cases may rely.

But, for the most part, U.S. refugee policy has become harsher. A new 'expedited removal' law, enacted by Congress in September 1996, reduces procedural protections for arriving immigrants. Under this law, asylum seekers such as Fauziya, who arrive in the U.S. without legitimate travel documents, will not be permitted to apply for asylum unless they express a fear of persecution or an intent to apply for asylum to an INS officer immediately upon arriving in the U.S. This requirement may not sound unreasonable. After all, Fauziya told the INS upon her arrival that she wanted to apply for asylum. But remember that Fauziya was advised by Charlie to request asylum immediately upon arriving. Many refugees do not know that it is in their best interest to talk to the first INS officer with whom they have contact, and to ask for asylum.

Even if the asylum seeker tells the INS officer that she fears persecution or wants to apply for asylum, she will only be permitted to do so if she can convince an asylum officer of the strength of her claim in an interview, which is normally to take place within two days of arriving in the U.S. Because this interview takes place so quickly, asylum seekers may be unable to contact an attorney to assist them in presenting the important facts of their case so that they can demonstrate the strength of their claim to the asylum officer.

A committed lawyer or legal team can make all the difference in a refugee's case, as it did in Fauziya's. One of the most important roles for the lawyer at this initial stage is to reassure the asylum seeker that she can and should tell all of the reasons why she fled her home country. This reassurance is necessary not because asylum seekers want to hide the truth, but because the things that happen to refugees are often painful and humiliating – making them excruciating to recount. And yet it is often those things which are the most painful to talk about that are the most significant facts in establishing one's eligibility for political asylum.

To illustrate this point, imagine how wrenching it is for a woman to tell any stranger (especially a male) about multiple rapes and forced impregnation – a fate suffered by thousands of Bosnian Muslim refugees during the conflict in the former Yugoslavia. I have known of many asylum seekers, who only told their attorneys about rapes or other sexual violence after months of developing the trust and confidence to speak about such things. How likely is it that a woman asylum seeker will freely speak of such private things in an interview which is to take place within hours or days of arriving in the U.S.? Fauziya's case provides a good example of the way in which humiliation and a sense of personal privacy may limit the information that an asylum seeker will tell strangers. When Fauziya was questioned by an INS official at Newark Airport, she told them that her reason for seeking asylum was to flee a forced marriage. She was too embarrassed to talk about the impending genital mutilation she had fled.

Fauziya was fortunate – her failure to tell the whole story at the airport did not foreclose her from obtaining protection. She was still permitted to apply for asylum and to press her case before an immigration judge. When the immigration judge denied her claim, she had the right to appeal to the Board of Immigration Appeals. Had the board denied her claim, she would have been able to appeal her case to the U.S. federal courts. This is no longer the case for asylum seekers like Fauziya. If the asylum officer who interviews the asylum seeker is not persuaded by the strength of her claim, there is only *one* level of review of this decision. This review is done by an immigration judge, and must occur within seven days. Even if the asylum seeker has managed to obtain representation, the expedited time frame does not give the lawyer much time to gather evidence or to otherwise develop the case. If you recall, much of the key evidence in Fauziya's case – her marriage certificate, photographs of the wedding, her mother's letters, information about FGM, expert testimony regarding cultural norms in Togo – were only obtained over time.

So what would happen if Fauziya Kassindja arrived today at Newark International Airport seeking asylum? We cannot really answer this question because we don't yet know how expedited removal is working. We know that the INS officials who questioned Fauziya when she arrived at the airport in 1995 didn't believe she was from Togo. But these officers have been given additional training to carry out their new function under expedited removal, and it is possible that as a result of this training they would respond differently to Fauziya's story. We know that the immigration judge who decided Fauziya's case ruled that she was lying, and that even if she was telling the truth, fear of FGM didn't qualify her for asylum. Fauziya prevailed because she had the opportunity to appeal Judge Ferlise's decision to the Board of Immigration Appeals, which reversed the immigration judge's decision. Under expedited removal, such an appeal is no longer possible, though Fauziya would now be entitled to an interview with an asylum officer if she expressed fear of persecution. It is possible that such an interview with an asylum officer would be the measure to prevent her return to Togo. But we can only speculate about these possible results – we simply do not know what effect the elimination of procedural safeguards will have on asylum seekers like Fauziya Kassindja, who continue to arrive seeking protection.

Upon reading this, you may wonder why Congress adopted the expedited removal law, which eliminates the right to appeal and speeds up the process in a manner which appears to cut back on the safety net for asylum seekers. The proponents of expedited removal have said that it is necessary because immigrants with fraudulent claims for asylum have been taking advantage of the system. Whether or not there is merit to this concern, we must recognize that you and I – all of us who are citizens of the U.S. – are responsible for the actions of our government, and in particular for the restrictive measures against immigrants. In recent years we have expressed a fear of 'illegal immigrants,' who we imagine to be at the root of many societal problems – from unemployment, to crime, to overpopulation and environmental degradation. We fear that we are being overrun by 'aliens' and we believe that we are protecting ourselves and our families by keeping them out. Toward these ends, we have encouraged our congressional representatives to enact restrictive measures – such as expedited removal.

Yet, at the very same time that we as a nation are engaged in heated and negative anti-immigrant rhetoric, we are deeply touched by Fauziya's suffering. In April 1996 when Celia Dugger published her front page story in *The New York Times* detailing Fauziya's plight, we – her legal team – received literally hundreds of calls and letters of support for her. The callers and writers were incredulous that the U.S. would lock up a young woman such as Fauziya. They were outraged that we treated asylum seekers in this fashion. Is this a contradiction? Or is it simply the fact that when we Americans are confronted with the real story of an 'illegal immigrant' and are able to see the human face of the individual who has fled to us seeking protection, we are able to summon a noble response. We are able to put aside the rhetoric, and to replace it with concern and compassion.

America is known around the world as a defender of liberty and a haven for the oppressed. We should not pull up the drawbridge and turn a deaf ear to those who flee injustices and persecution. We should not close our eyes to suffering in the world. Instead of being motivated by our fear, we should be guided by our generosity, and remain true to Emma Lazarus's time-worn inscription on the Statue of Liberty, which stands as a welcome to all those who would arrive at our 'golden door.'

Give me your tired, your poor,
Your huddled masses yearning to breathe free,
The wretched refuse of your teeming shore.

Send these, the homeless, tempest-tost to me,
I lift my lamp beside the golden door!

—Karen Musalo

Editor's Note

In September 1996, Congress passed a law that recognizes Female Genital Mutilation as a felony and allocates money to educate immigrant populations about the practice.

Fauziya's Acknowledgments

While I was in prison, I started a journal to record some of the unbelievable things I went through. I thought that one day I might show this journal to my children and my grandchildren. I never dreamed that a book about my experiences would be published for the whole world to read. Over the past year, I've learned that putting together a book is an enormous undertaking. Luckily I had the benefit of working with really wonderful dedicated and talented individuals.

First, I am indebted to my legal team from American University's Washington College of Law who fought so hard for my asylum and who kept me from giving up hope all those months in prison. I am especially grateful to Karen Musalo, who was my tireless champion, and to Layli Miller Bashir, who told my story to whoever would listen and kept my case from falling through the cracks. Thanks also to David Shaffer, Nileema Pargaonker, Sidney Lebowitz, Denise Thomasson, and Richard Boswell for their help and moral support. Also, I am deeply grateful to Surita Sandosham and Jessica Neuwirth of Equality Now who helped see me through those darkest days in prison and, after my release, helped me establish myself in my new country. I would also like to express my deep gratitude to the Bashir family – Abbas, Irma, Roshan, and Dwight – for making me a part of their family following my release, and especially to Roshan, who provided me with badly needed medical care. I also want to thank the Miller family – Larry, Carole, Irene, Natasha, Naysan, and Langdon – for their comfort. Thanks also to Roni Dodonne, Mimi Ramsey, and the countless individuals who have reached out to a total stranger and whose visits, letters, photographs, and donations penetrated my isolation and made me feel loved and wanted. Their outpouring of affection and concern taught me that the America I longed to live in was not just a dream. Thanks, too, to my African sisters who adopted me in prison, shared my pain, and nursed me through my serious illnesses; and to Susan Toler, who helped me to recognize who I really am.

I am indebted to two remarkable women at Dell, Leslie Schnur and Cherise Davis Grant, for their dedication to telling my story, their editorial help, and their friendship. Thanks to my agent, Margaret McBride, for the tremendous work she and her staff have done and for believing in me. I am especially grateful to Jacob Cohn, my attorney and friend, who has been instrumental in guiding me through the process of writing this book. His wise guidance and support, both professionally and personally, have been invaluable. I'd also like to thank Linda Steinman of Bantam Doubleday Dell for the many laughter-filled hours we shared while going over the manuscript.

I was particularly fortunate to have Gini Kopecky as my collaborator. English is not my first language, and many of my memories were painful to recall and diffi-cult to share. Her warmth and caring during our many long talk sessions were a comfort. Working closely with me and Layli, she also helped us decide how to present my story, did the research needed to fill in parts of it, and helped us put it in writing so I could read it for the first time myself. For these and other contributions to this endeavor, I thank her. Thanks also to Marc Wallace for coming up with a great title for this book.

I was equally fortunate to have Beth Rashbaum as my manuscript editor. She condensed and shaped the manuscript into the book you see published today. She was able to shape the material in such a way as to give full voice to my feelings and my experience. I thank her for her dedication over many long months, her patience with the inevitable complications of working on such a complex project involving so many people, and most of all her unerring good judgment regarding the tone, texture, and pacing of my story.

Finally, I want to thank my family back in Africa for their support. To my sister Ayisha, you are the best sister on earth. I love you.

Laylí's Acknowledgments

First and foremost, I would like to thank God and the teachings of the Bahá'í faith for providing me with direction and inspiration. I thank my parents, Larry and Carole Miller, for their unconditional love, profound wisdom, close friendship, and shining example of service to humanity. Also, I thank the rest of my family, Natasha, Langdon, and Naysan, for their constant kindness, generosity, and positive perspective on life.

To my husband, Roshan Martin Bashir, I owe much gratitude for having patiently endured the tests and trials as well as the successes and victories associated with Fauziya's case with unconditional love and support. I must also thank him for always encouraging my ambitions, supporting my endeavors, and assisting me in navigating the choices of life.

I want to thank the other student attorneys for their long hours spent, sincere dedication exhibited, and quality work performed for Fauziya's case: Sidney Lebowitz, Nileema Pargaonker, David Shaffer, Denise Thomasson. In addition, I want to express my sincere appreciation to Michael Maggio, Jamin Raskin, Lauren Gilbert, and Bo Cooper, whose professional mentorship, personal friendship, and emotional support have meant more to me than words could ever express. I also thank Celia Dugger, Equality Now, and Karen Musalo for championing Fauziya's cause.

I want to express my appreciation to Leslie Schnur and Cherise Davis Grant, of Dell, whose endless patience in the face of many obstacles, sincere commitment to the issues of women's and immigrants' rights, and rational diligence throughout the editing process has made this book what it is. I also thank Margret McBride, of the McBride Literary Agency, without whose energy, persistence, remarkable patience, and sense of humor, this book would not have been possible. In addition, I want to express my deep appreciation to Katherine Behan, of Arnold & Porter, whose emotional and legal support through the last year and a half has been immeasurable. Her friendship, mentoring, and shining example of what a lawyer can be have meant more to me than I can convey. I must also thank Gini Kopecky for her personal friendship, persistent dedication, and untold sacrifices. Through her loving interviews and endless hours of writing, this story has been able to reflect the true spirit of its source. In addition, I want to thank Beth Rashbaum, whose editing skills have helped to develop this book into a dramatic account of Fauziya's life, and Linda Steinman of Bantam Doubleday Dell for her dedication and legal scrutiny.

Many thanks to Irma and Abbas Bashir, along with the Bahá'í community and many other individuals, for their support and dedication to Fauziya's plight.

Lastly, I would like to thank Fauziya Kassindja for her courage, endurance, and inspiration.

For more information concerning related issues, please contact the following organizations:

Táhirih Justice Center

The Táhirih Justice Center is a nonprofit organization dedicated to serving the needs of women facing international human rights abuses, with a particular emphasis on immigrant and refugee women. The center is based on the belief that the recognition of the equality of women and men is a moral imperative and a practical necessity for the advancement of society. In order to realize the equality of women and men, society must render justice to women. To this end, the Táhirih Justice Center provides legal protection for women facing human rights abuses and assists in the provision of certain social programs. The center's work revolves around a core of projects aimed at serving women's legal, health care, and social needs, each component working in unity with the others to form an organic whole, addressing the full range of women's issues.

The center was founded by Layli Miller Bashir following Fauziya Kassindja's case. The center's doors officially opened for business in September 1997. Since that time, it has developed at a rapid pace, far exceeding the expectations of its founder. At its offices in Falls Church, Virginia, the center's full-time staff provides much-needed legal representation to women facing human rights abuses and coordinates their receipt of medical services, from volunteering physicians, and other social services, from local providers.

The center is named after Táhirih (Táh-he-ray), an extraordinary nineteenth-century Persian woman, poet, and scholar who, in rejection of society's traditional subordination of women, publicly removed her veil in 1848. A member of the persecuted Bahá'í faith, Táhirih was martyred for her beliefs and actions at the age of thirty-six.

If you would like to support the Táhirih Justice Center's efforts or learn more about the center's activities, please contact us. (All donations are tax deductible.)

Táhirih Justice Center
108 N. Virginia Ave.
Suite 100
Falls Church, VA 22046
Phone: (703) 237-4554
Fax: (703) 237-4574
E-mail: justice@tahirih.org
Web site: www.tahirih.org

Equality Now

Equality Now is an international human rights organization that works for the protection and promotion of women's rights. Issues of concern to Equality Now include domestic violence, rape, female genital mutilation, reproductive rights, trafficking in women, and other forms of violence and discrimination against women that have historically been neglected by the international human rights movement. The Women's Action Network of Equality Now, which took up the case of Fauziya Kassindja in 1996, is a growing force of activists around the world campaigning for the human rights of women. We hope you will join the Women's Action Network. Write, fax, or e-mail Equality Now today for more information:

Equality Now
P.O. Box 20646
Columbus Circle Station
New York, NY 10023
Fax: (212) 586-1611
E-mail: equalitynow@igc.apc.org
Web site: www.equalitynow.org

The International Human Rights and Migration Project, Markkula Center for Applied Ethics, Santa Clara University

The International Human Rights and Migration Project (IHRMP) was founded and is directed by Karen Musalo, and is a project of Santa Clara University's Markkula Center for Applied Ethics. The International Human Rights and Migration Project engages in education, research, publication, and advocacy on human rights and immigration issues.

The IHRMP has developed the Women's Refugee Program dedicated to the enhancement of internationally protected rights for women asylum seekers. Through the Women's Refugee Program, the IHRMP provides expertise and resources to attorneys nationwide who represent women asylum seekers. The work of the Women's Refugee Program includes ongoing training and consultation with attorneys to assist them in their work on individual cases, and the writing of supporting amicus briefs in these cases. In this way the Women's Refugee Program contributes toward the protection of the individual asylum seeker as well as the development of favorable legal precedent in cases involving women's human rights violations.

The International Human Rights and Migration Project is also carrying out the Expedited Removal

Monitoring Project and Study, which is the only comprehensive nationwide study of the impact of the new immigration laws on asylum seekers. The study examines the operation of the new law to determine whether it meets its dual objectives of weeding out fraudulent asylum claims, while providing adequate protection to legitimate asylum seekers. It also examines issues of detention, including length and conditions of incarceration. The Expedited Removal Monitoring Project and Study is co-directed by Karen Musalo and Deborah Anker, at Harvard University.

If you would like more information about the International Human Rights and Migration Project, please contact us. Donations, which are tax deductible, can be earmarked for the Women's Refugee Program or the Expedited Removal Study.

International Human Rights and Migration Project
Markkula Center for Applied Ethics
Santa Clara University
500 El Camino Real
Santa Clara, CA 95053-0633
Phone: (408) 554-7890
Fax: (408) 554-2373
E-mail: kmusalo@mailer.scu.edu

PRINCESS
by Jean P Sasson

'Unforgettable . . . fascinating . . . a book to move
you to tears'
Fay Weldon

Imagine the life of a Saudi Arabian princess and what
do you see? A woman glittering with jewels, living a
life of unbelievable luxury. But in reality she lives in a
gilded cage. She has no freedom, no vote, no control
over her own life, no value but as a bearer of sons.
Hidden behind the veil she is a prisoner, her jailers
her father, her husband, her sons.

'Sultana' is a member of the Saudi Royal Family,
closely related to the King. As she tells of her life –
from her turbulent childhood to her arranged marriage – she lifts the veil and reveals a history of
appalling oppression and shocking human rights
violations such as forced marriages, sex slavery and
summary executions.

Princess is a testimony to a woman of indomitable
spirit and great courage. By speaking out, 'Sultana'
risked the wrath of the Saudi establishment. For this
reason, she has told her story anonymously.

'Anyone with the slightest interest in human
rights will find this book heart-wrenching. It is a
well-written, personal story . . . It had to come
from a native woman to be believable'
Betty Mahmoody, bestselling author of *Not
Without My Daughter*

A Bantam Paperback
0553 40570 5

RED CHINA BLUES
by Jan Wong

Jan Wong, a Canadian of Chinese descent, went to China as a starry-eyed Maoist in 1972 at the height of the Cultural Revolution. In the name of the Revolution, she renounced rock and roll, hauled pig manure in the paddy fields, and turned in a fellow student who sought her help in getting to the United States. She also met and married the only American draft dodger from the Vietnam War to seek asylum in China.

Red China Blues is Wong's startling – and ironic – memoir of her rocky six-year romance with Maoism that began to sour as she became aware of the harsh realities of Chinese communism and led to her eventual repatriation to the West. Returning to China in the late eighties as a journalist, she covered both the brutal Tiananmen Square crackdown and the tumultuous era of capitalist reforms under Deng Xiaoping. In a frank, captivating and deeply personal narrative, she relates the horrors that led to her dis-illusionment with the 'worker's paradise'. And through the stories of the people, Wong creates an extraordinary portrait of the world's most populous nation.

'With her unique perspective, Jan Wong has given us front row seats at Mao's theater of the absurd. It is hard not to laugh and cry . . . This book will become a classic, a must-read for anyone interested in China' *New York Times*

A Bantam Paperback
0 553 50554 9

A SELECTION OF NON-FICTION TITLES
AVAILABLE FROM TRANSWORLD

THE PRICES SHOWN BELOW WERE CORRECT AT THE TIME OF GOING TO PRESS. HOWEVER TRANSWORLD PUBLISHERS RESERVE THE RIGHT TO SHOW NEW RETAIL PRICES ON COVERS WHICH MAY DIFFER FROM THOSE PREVIOUSLY ADVERTISED IN THE TEXT OR ELSEWHERE.

☐ 40664 7	CHE GUEVARA	Jon Lee Anderson	£14.99
☐ 50650 1	BOUND FEET AND WESTERN DRESS	Pang-Mei Natasha Chang	£7.99
☐ 81303 X	THE RAINBOW PALACE	Tenzin Choedrak	£7.99
☐ 50582 3	BONES OF THE MASTER	George Crane	£6.99
☐ 14239 5	MY FEUDAL LORD	Tehmina Durrani	£5.99
☐ 13928 9	DAUGHTER OF PERSIA	Sattareh Farman Farmaian	£6.99
☐ 13356 6	NOT WITHOUT MY DAUGHTER	Betty Mahmoody	£6.99
☐ 14288 3	BRIDGE ACROSS MY SORROWS	Christina Noble	£6.99
☐ 14595 5	BETWEEN EXTREMES	John McCarthy and Brian Keenan	£7.99
☐ 40936 0	THE HIDDEN CHILDREN	Jane Marks	£7.99
☐ 81302 1	LA PRISONNIERE	Malika Oufkir	£6.99
☐ 81195 9	SORROW MOUNTAIN	Ani Pachen and Adelaide Donnelley	£6.99
☐ 81359 5	SIGNALS	Joel Rothschild	£6.99
☐ 40805 4	DAUGHTERS OF ARABIA	Jean P Sasson	£5.99
☐ 40570 5	PRINCESS	Jean P Sasson	£5.99
☐ 81218 1	DESERT ROYAL	Jean P Sasson	£5.99
☐ 50554 9	RED CHINA BLUES	Jan Wong	£7.99
☐ 81306 4	A LEAF IN THE BITTER WIND	Ting-Xing Ye	£8.99

All Transworld titles are available by post from:

Bookpost, P.O. Box 29, Douglas, Isle of Man IM99 1BQ

Credit cards accepted. Please telephone 01624 836000,
fax 01624 837033, Internet http://www.bookpost.co.uk or
e-mail: bookshop@enterprise.net for details.

Free postage and packing in the UK. Overseas customers allow
£1 per book (paperbacks) and £3 per book (hardbacks).